SWORDS AND SWORDSMEN

For Kim

SWORDS AND SWORDSMEN

Mike Loades

With illustrations by
Adam Des Forges

Pen & Sword
MILITARY

First published in Great Britain in 2010
and reprinted in 2012 and 2017 by
Pen & Sword Military
an imprint of
Pen & Sword Books Ltd
47 Church Street
Barnsley
South Yorkshire
S70 2AS

ISBN: 978-1-52670-646-1

Typeset in 11/13pt Ehrhardt by Concept, Huddersfield, West Yorkshire

Printed and bound in India by Replika Press Pvt. Ltd.

Pen & Sword Books Ltd incorporates the imprints of Pen & Sword Archaeology,
Atlas, Aviation, Battleground, Discovery, Family History, History, Maritime,
Military, Naval, Politics, Railways, Select, Social History, Transport, True Crime,
and Claymore Press, Frontline Books, Leo Cooper, Praetorian Press,
Remember When, Seaforth Publishing and Wharncliffe.

For a complete list of Pen & Sword titles please contact
PEN & SWORD BOOKS LIMITED
47 Church Street, Barnsley, South Yorkshire, S70 2AS, England
E-mail: enquiries@pen-and-sword.co.uk
Website: www.pen-and-sword.co.uk

Contents

Acknowledgements

My heartfelt thanks go to Dr Tobias Capwell, who has not only been generous enough to write the foreword but who also read early drafts, giving me invaluable feedback and support. In fairness to him I should point out that I didn't always act on his advice and I take full responsibility for all opinions expressed herein. My sincere gratitude also goes to Adam Des Forges, whose wonderful line drawings lifted my flagging spirits and rekindled my enthusiasm at times when the labour of this work threatened to overwhelm. Furthermore, I am truly grateful to both Toby and Adam for their warm friendship. It has endured now for many years and through many shared adventures and I am so happy that they have been able to be a part of this endeavour.

Thanks are due to Julian Alexander who first suggested to me the idea of writing this book. His guidance in the ensuing task was both insightful and invaluable.

My lifelong interest in European martial pursuits owes an immeasurable debt to John Waller. He has been my dear friend for nearly forty years now. His original thinking and unique approach to interpreting historical movement have always been a motivating force in my studies. I learned a great deal from him and thank him for his thoughtful encouragement, both in those early years and beyond.

During more than a quarter century, teaching swordfighting in London drama schools, many extremely talented students of the sword came to work and train with me. All made a contribution to my understanding of the mechanics of swordfighting and all are deserving of my gratitude. In particular I want to acknowledge the influence of Gordon Summers. Together we spent many years experimenting and shaping our ideas about historical combat and he became my teacher as much as I was his. I am indebted to him in so many ways. Tobias Capwell and Adam Des Forges also played an important part during those years of teaching and learning and others that merit special thanks incude: S.J. Vant, Tony Owen, Christine Faulconbridge, Gregory Hoffman, John Thompson, Marcello Marascalchi, Dominic Kinnaird, Ian Harvey-Stone and Natalie Dakin. Thank you all for your inspiration, for your art and especially for your friendships.

Other friends, who have been kind enough to read and critique early drafts, include Frederick Wilkinson, Frederick Chiaventone and Paul Martin. Paul, a Japanese sword specialist, was also very helpful in enabling my access to various places in Japan relevant to the production and use of the Japanese sword. Adrian Goldsworthy and

Professor Sydney Anglo were also a huge help with some translations and other invaluable insights.

A network of old friends and new acquaintances – curators, archivists and image librarians, at museums around the globe – have been extraordinarily generous with their time; answering my constant stream of questions, giving me access to objects and making photographs available. I cannot thank them all enough but the following deserve special mention: Nigel Tallis, Tony Spence and Jody Joy at the British Museum; Thom Richardson, Robert Woosnam-Savage, Michael Gilroy-Sinclair and Chris Streek at the Royal Armouries, Leeds; David Miller at the Smithsonian Institution, Washington DC; David Edge and Dr Alan Williams at The Wallace Collection, London; Christina L. Keyser and Dawn Bonner at the Mount Vernon Ladies Association, Alexandria, Virginia; Janice Mullin at the Museum of the Civil War, Harrisburg, Pennsylvania; Drury Welford at the Museum of the Confederacy, Richmond, Virginia; Tim Padley at the Tullie House Museum, Carlisle; Michael Ball and Keith Miller at the National Army Museum, London; Jane Whannel at Glasgow Museums; Giles Guthrie, Maidstone Museum; Dr Richard Mortimer and Christine Reynolds at Westminster Abbey; Ilse Jung at the Kunsthistorisches Museum, Vienna; Angela Stiffler at the William Jewell College, Liberty, Missouri; and the Queen's Armourer, Simon Metcalf, at the Royal Collection, for sharing his researches on the Edward III sword.

In addition I have had wonderfully generous assistance from individuals who have helped me both with information and photographs. I am tremendously grateful to them all for their time and their kindness: Fujishiro-sensei; Evan Lattimer; David Redden of Sothebys, New York; Claude Blair; David Oliver; Michael Gorman; Hector Cole; Annette Bächstädt, picture researcher and editor; Robert Partridge, Ancient Egypt magazine; Dave Richardson of Legio II Augusta; Mark Austin of Swordsales EU; and Sam Kennedy, Cisco Antiques.

Thanks also to Jennie Tanouye, who meticulously collated hundreds of pieces of loose paper relating to photographic permissions, that I had stuffed randomly in boxes.

To my wife, Kim, thank you for your unwavering forbearance, your ever-present sense of humour and your unflagging encouragement. Sorry it took so long and sorry for all those extended absences, cloistered away at my books and computer.

Last and, by no means least, my greatest thanks go to my editor, Phil Sidnell, without whom none of the following would have been possible.

Thank you all.

Foreword

Swordsmen have often been authors. There is something profoundly and intrinsically poetic about the use of the sword, strange as that may sound to many people. Thus it has been, since at least the fourteenth century, and possibly earlier, that swordsmen have felt a calling to write about their art. In the Middle Ages, throughout the Renaissance, and into the Enlightenment, indeed to the very end of the story of the sword's practical use, fight masters have written about their ideas in regard to how the sword is best handled in combat.

This tradition has left us with an extraordinarily rich legacy of fencing manuals, or 'fight books'. These works were written by true 'Renaissance men', people like Camillo Agrippa, mathematician, architect, engineer and friend of Michelangelo, who was also a noted fight master and author of one of the most famous fencing manuals of the sixteenth century, *Trattato di scientia d'arme* (1553), in which he argued that the fight-master should be considered the learned equal of scientists, scholars and philosophers. The Renaissance English poet and playwright John Marston may have been right when he pointed out, in *The Mountebank's Masque* (*Paradox XV*, 1617), that 'good fighting came before good writing'. But I think he was partly wrong in his assertion that 'A Master of Arms is more honourable than a Master of Arts', for it has been most often the case that the former have striven also to be the latter.

In addition to the purely practical studies, by the nineteenth century swordsmen were also writing histories of fencing. In fact all of the essential histories of swordsmanship were authored by 'men of arms', writers such as Egerton Castle, who published his famous work *Schools and Masters of Fence* in 1885. Castle was one of the first sword-fighting antiquarians to attempt to reconstruct the fighting methods of the Renaissance from the fight books of the sixteenth century; a number of charming illustrations of him exist, clad in modern sport-fencing attire and mask, swinging enthusiastically a great two-handed sword of the late sixteenth century at his opponent. One cannot help thinking that perhaps some more robust protection might have been advisable!

Castle was not alone in his passion for early sword-play. His friend Captain Alfred Hutton, an officer in the King's Dragoon Guards, was also a prolific practitioner and writer on the subject, whose works include *The Cavalry Swordsman* (1867), *Swordsmanship, for the Use of Soldiers* (1887), *Cold Steel* (1889) and *Old Swordplay: The*

Systems of Fence in Vogue During the XVIth, XVIIth, and XVIIIth Centuries (1892). Finally, even the briefest note on swordsman-authors would be sorely incomplete were it not to mention Hutton and Castle's contemporary, Sir Richard Francis Burton, the eccentric English explorer, swordsman, translator, author, soldier, ethnologist, linguist, poet, and diplomat, who wrote his famous *Book of the Sword* in 1884. Like Hutton and Castle, Burton wrote from the point of view of an experienced martial artist. At the beginning of his historic expedition into the African interior with John Hanning Speke, Burton's party were attacked by Somali warriors and Burton himself was transfixed through the head with a native spear. He still managed to fight off his attackers, with sabre and pistol, and carried the impressive scars on either side of his face for the rest of his life.

The present work can rightly be considered the most recent addition to this ancient tradition of swordsman-scholarship. In much the same way as his illustrious Victorian predecessors, Mike Loades has had many adventures across the globe, experiences that he writes about in a poetic and personal style that expresses beautifully the love he holds for his subject. This book is not merely a selection of facts and hypotheses, but is rather a personal journey through the world, made up of many exciting and unique stories, populated by flamboyant and fearsome characters from many centuries.

When I first met Mike, in London nearly twenty years ago, one of the first things we spoke of was his desire to write a book about swordsmanship. At the time he was teaching historical swordsmanship to actors and acting students at a number of London drama schools. He held passionate views about the subject, with new theories and ideas seeming to come out of him every day of the year I spent with him as his assistant. Later, Mike entered the world of film and television, as a director, presenter, historical advisor, fight choreographer and all-round action man, and what free time he had had previously only seemed to dwindle, and his book thus remained for many years an unfulfilled dream.

Although historical swordsmanship today attracts a huge following, with people in many countries reading the ancient texts and honing their personal fighting skills with the weapons of the pre-industrial past, it should be mentioned that this wider phenomenon is, for the most part, less than fifteen years old. When I met Mike in the early 1990s I had never read an historical fight book, let alone held an original in my hands. I will always remember the first such time, indeed the first time I touched a medieval manuscript of any sort, which occurred when Mike and I paid a visit to the library at the Tower of London, to examine what was then an almost-unknown early fourteenth-century text on fighting with sword and buckler. This work is now internationally famous and is usually (in the abbreviated speech of modern *amateurs d'armes*) referred to simply by its accession number: Class I, number 33, or simply 'I.33'. At the time Mike was one of only a very few people who were working with these texts and trying to incorporate their systems into modern fencing practices. Legions have since followed the example of what were once only a very small group of aficionados, of which Mike was one.

Over the past two decades I have had the very great personal pleasure of being routinely bombarded with Mike's latest ideas. In reading the manuscript of the present work, I found myself re-encountering many arguments and theories that Mike has presented to me over the years, at lunch, on the train, in the car, sitting on a horse on a freezing film set, while avoiding a sword blade aimed at my head, laying in the mud in full plate armour, on a Viking ship off the south coast of England, and in a hundred other somewhat-improbable situations. During such conversations Mike would often remark that he 'ought to write this down'.

Well, I am delighted that he finally has.

Tobias Capwell BA, MA, MA, Ph.D
Curator of Arms and Armour
The Wallace Collection
Hertford House, January 2010

Introduction

From the great deeds of mythical heroes to the gentlemanly art of duelling and the swash and swagger of the silver screen, the sword remains at the heart of our romantic imagination. It is the weapon that gives the hope that skill can triumph over brute force. It is an enchanted weapon, the one with which the hero wins out over impossible odds. Moreover it is the continuity of these thoughts in fiction that makes the sword such an enduring icon, from *Beowulf* to *The Lord of the Rings*.

Swords can also be objects of beauty. The myriad shapes of blade and hilt design, which evolved over the centuries, all have their own aesthetic. They have line and form and underpinning it all, there is the enigmatic lustre of steel. Its tones are as mutable as water, orchestrating the light spectrum with symphonic virtuosity. The finest swords are true works of art; their handsome form transcending the brutality of their intended purpose. At their best, their attractiveness derives from a purity of design that harnesses form to function. At their worst they can be either over-decorated trinkets, sacrificing clean lines to an excess of ornament or crude, poorly-made tools lacking due proportion. Refinements of design, materials and craftsmanship elevate some swords above the rest and it is an appreciation of these qualities that rewards their study and helps us distinguish the outstanding from the commonplace.

Swords have a deceptively simple form that masks a marvel of sophisticated construction. From the alchemical wonder of transforming rock (iron ore) into steel to the magic of being able to turn it into a flexible and resilient blade, to the many methods of decorative embellishment, the development of the sword-making process is a story of both manufacturing and artistic ingenuity. Swords are icons. They are symbols of rank, status and authority; the weapons upon which oaths were sworn, with which allegiances were pledged and by which honours were conferred. Swords represent cultural ideas and personal attributes. They stand for justice, courage and honour. Above all swords are personal objects. Swords tell stories.

When you hold a sword you feel its life; it is far from being an inert object. It urges your arm to swing it. Subtle nuances of weight and balance make individual swords heft differently and this gives swords, even those of the same type, a unique personality. A sword's physical characteristics inform us how it should be used. We cannot consider swords properly without considering swordsmanship. Swords were made to be wielded. Studying them without examining the way in which they were used would be like looking at musical instruments without ever having heard a tune. Styles and techniques of swordfighting changed through the centuries and it is as much a part of appreciating a sword's aesthetic character to have an image of it in action, as it is to view it as a static object. There is a tendency in the West to regard the 'martial arts' as an 'Eastern' idea but a codified, systemized 'fighting arts' tradition has long been established in Europe. It is evidenced by a huge canon of illustrated works on the subject dating from the Middle Ages onwards. Some of these 'fight books' are works of art in their own right and they depict the extraordinary beauty that is the 'art' of swordfighting.

For the majority of my adult life I have spent nearly every day with a sword in my hand, working as an historical fight arranger and teacher. It is a curious thing to have done but there it is. Movement is my passion and I especially love the dynamics of martial movement; the raw energy of exquisite lines, intent with functional purpose thrills me. It is, of course, the beauty of dance but it is no less practical or lethal for that. The swordsman seeks to achieve maximum bio-mechanical efficiency, keeping a disciplined control of all his movements; thereby creating forms, which are not only deadly in their effectiveness but also often beautiful. Fighting strains every muscle, ligament and sinew in the body; it is hard, grunting, painful, sweated labour. A swordsman must stretch and strive and strain and struggle, for that is the business of fighting but his art is in making it look effortless and graceful and in attaining perfect forms. This is only possible at the highest level but it is possible. In the heat of actual combat there would be lapses from these high ideals, moments of untidiness arising from the disorientating consequences of crunching bodily contact and injury. Nevertheless the ideals remain and there can be a great deal of 'art' in the martial arts. The idea of executing moves with beauty and grace is inherent to martial culture. Antonio Manciolino, an Italian writer on arms in the sixteenth century wrote: 'Not only should the good fencer make himself skilled at attack and defence, he should moreover give a beautiful form to his blows, mingled with sweet movements of the body'.

Nowhere was this more aspired to than in the cult of the duel, which swept across Europe as a universal and insidious craze between the sixteenth and nineteenth centuries. The probable reality of many duels was that they were short, brutal and inelegant affairs but all who carried a sword would have understood the finer points of style and expertise. 'Schools of Fence' sprang up in nearly every town and city and there was a publishing boom in 'how to fight' literature. Anyone desiring to be a gentleman undertook the exercise of arms as an integral part of his education and, for centuries, succeeding generations understood the ways of the sword.

There is no item of modern attire or use that compares to the wearing of a sword and yet, for centuries, to do so was an everyday part of life. I am frequently annoyed by actors who strut the stage grasping their hilts because they are fearful of them banging into something. To some actors swords are alien props that threaten to cause them embarrassment but to a swordsman they are simply there and he has an instinctive awareness of the space they occupy and he can move around the world freely without fussing over them. When posing for his portrait or simply standing at ease, he may rest his hand casually against the hilt but never clutch it like a child grasping its mother's hand. He may steer it effortlessly with a sweep of his palm when negotiating an obstacle. He may finger it nervously in a moment of tension but for the sword-clutching actor such subtle moments of expression are denied. He appears in a constant state of nervousness but these are the actor's nerves, not those of his character. It is in drama, of course, that we see the sword's most glamourized manifestation. From the Viking sagas to Arthurian romance to Shakespeare's plays and the modern cinema, the sword has always epitomized the ultimate in martial excellence.

However for all its romance, for all the glory of the men who bore it, the sword remains a vicious instrument of savage brutality. Killing is always a reprehensible act but there is something especially unpleasant about a weapon whose chief purpose is the hacking off of limbs or the cutting and piercing of flesh. It is often difficult to reconcile an interest and appreciation of the sword with the shocking pain and misery it is designed to inflict. Yet the lure of the sword is irresistible. There is an obvious paradox in feting an object with so grisly a purpose but paradox and contradiction are inescapable elements of the human condition. We must learn to live with them or deny the full complexity of our existence. The cultural heritage of the sword and the extraordinary characters who people its history is too rich a story to turn our back on, but it is a story that can take us to some very dark places.

There are many ways to navigate the byways of history, all provide glimpses of familiar landmarks, but the less well-trodden road can offer views we would not otherwise have seen. Whatever path we take, there will be places we miss on the way but we can take consolation in knowing that we may travel another road another day. No single book can encompass the incredibly diverse story of the sword in all its military and cultural manifestations. All I can do is lead you down a road that has fascinated me and point out some of its many vistas, in the hope that you will find hidden hamlets that bid you to return for further study.

Swords exist in all major warrior cultures. The fabulous sword of the first Qin Emperor, Qin Shi Huangdi, guarded in his afterlife by that wonderful army of terracotta warriors, was discovered still sharp and still gleaming because of its chromium coating. Swords from Arabia and Persia and India are often extremely fine weapons with exquisite forms, jewelled hilts and 'watered steel' blades. What also of the enigmatic *keris*, the wavy-bladed sword/dagger of the Malay and Indonesian archipelagos? All clamour for attention but, alas, all are beyond the scope of this present work. With two exceptions, I have concentrated on swords in the Western tradition, for theirs is a story of such complexity and diversity that I could write a dozen books and still leave much untold. The first exception is a look at the khepesh and methods of bronze sword making in Mesopotamia and Egypt. It is where the story begins. Secondly, I have chosen to write a chapter on the Japanese sword, for not only has it become as iconic in the West as any European sword but also it is always of interest to those who have a curiosity about swords and it would have been too great an omission to leave it out.

Nevertheless, the exigencies of a limited word count force hard choices to be made. For instance, I have left out the story of female fighters. From Amazons to Valkyries, ancient myths contain a rich seam of stories about women swordfighters. History too has its women warriors, though mostly they are shadowy figures. We know of Boudicca but not much about her actual life. Celtic traditions hint that women played a leading role in martial arts training. I can well believe it. Over the years I have taught many women who were every bit the equal of a man with a sword in their hand. The Vikings had 'shield-maidens' and the French had Joan of Arc. In the age of the civilian duel there were notable exceptions to it being an exclusive preserve of male ritual. Madamoiselle du Maupin, a singer at the Paris opera, once, in the guise of a man, killed three men in a single duel. However these women were the exceptions to the rule and I seek here to follow the mainstream influences that shaped the sword's developments.

Swords, the signposts for our journey, point in many directions but I have kept a bearing that essentially follows their chronological development. At times their form changes because of technology and at other times because of fashion. With the evolution of the rapier and the smallsword the sword became the instrument of the civilian duel; this is both the story of war and the story of personal quarrel. Alongside the themes of technical development and aesthetics are motifs of magic, symbol and status as well as the mastery of the sword in use. The fight masters and guilds of swordsmen who pioneered new ways of fighting with the sword are an integral part of the story of its development. So too are the customs, laws and rituals that make the sword as much a part of social history as it is of human conflict.

Above all the sword is an intensely personal object and is best understood by having some knowledge of the hand that wielded it. I have taken, as primary route markers, swords that were owned by, or at least strongly associated with, known historical figures. Real identifiable people, whose fingers once closed around the grips of these very weapons. In many cases I have visited these swords and held them. I have woven snippets of biographical detail into the relevant chapters in order to give context to the objects, now imprisoned behind glass, that were once grasped by hot and angered hands. Necessarily these are broad brushstrokes but I hope that they may help the swords live a little.

Of the thousands of swords displayed in museums, surprisingly few can be attributed to known individuals. In making the selection, I have chosen sword types that will leapfrog us across the ages, highlighting key moments in the evolution of sword design and the practice and customs of its use. The people who appear in these pages are not my heroes, all were as flawed as any human being, but they were men who represent their times and who, by chance, have left these testaments to history. Many of these swords draw us into an epoch where more than one type of sword was prevalent and while we dwell in their moment I cast around to see what other swords were present. For some of the swords, such as those of Cromwell and Henry V, cautious pedantry would urge me to say 'allegedly carried by'. However the tradition of association is strong and they are certainly the right types of swords for their respective periods.

I have written this book with the general reader in mind, covering the broad trends of an intricate pattern of development. In places I have summarized a period of time to get swiftly to where we are going and in others I have tarried to take a closer look. By its nature there will be omissions but this book was never intended to be exhaustively comprehensive; the subject is too large and I have had to make choices about what to include. I make no other claim than to offer an introduction to a subject that has captivated my imagination for more than four decades.

The next time you are in a museum that displays weapons, choose a single sword that takes your fancy and ponder on it. Don't be overwhelmed by the ranks of anonymous swords, pick just one and remember that it very likely once belonged to someone. It was chosen and purchased and cleaned and cherished. It was kept sharp and worn with pride. Look at its design and the materials it is made of. Wonder about the man who made it and the man who owned it. Consider where he might have learned to use it and what 'school of fence' he might have followed. If it is a soldier's sword, what are the battles of the period in which it may have played a part and if a civilian's weapon was it ever drawn in anger? You might even give it a name. Next time you visit you can choose another sword but the one you first chose will be there, beckoning as a familiar friend, no longer just another sword among many. You wouldn't try and meet a hundred people in a day and expect to get to know them. The same is true of beautiful objects in a museum. My advice is to examine just a few and visit often. Now, in the pages that follow, let me introduce you to some of my own favourites.

Wooden mannequin of Tutankhamun, Egyptian Museum, Cairo (© Griffith Institute, University of Oxford)

Chapter One

The Sword of Tutankhamun, Pharaoh of Egypt

The shade cast by your sword is upon your army and they go forth imbued with your power.

(Refrain to a rallying speech by Ramses III – twelfth century BC)

More than 3,300 years old, the sword of Tutankhamun resides today in the Egyptian Museum in Cairo. Looking a little neglected at the bottom of a dimly lit display case, it nonetheless retains the essence of its former splendour and remains in astonishingly good condition. The metalwork is sound and I feel sure that, if struck, it would still ring with a pure note. Dark patches mottle its surface and it no longer gleams quite as brightly but there are areas of colour, muted tones of yellow, that hint at its former, dazzling glory. Imagine it new and polished, shining brighter than the sun itself, and you will have some idea of what a fine weapon this was. Its distinctive curves are characteristic of a type of sword called a *khepesh*. Transliterated from the ancient Egyptian, '*khepesh*' is a delightfully onomatopoeic word for a sword that would swish and swoosh as it sliced through the air.

Forming part of the boy king's considerable hoard of weapons, it was among the many splendid artefacts brought to light in Howard Carter's famous excavation of Tutankhamun's tomb in late 1922 and it was found together with a second khepesh of much smaller proportions. With an overall length of 23.2 inches the larger of the two qualifies comfortably as a sword but, at just 15.8 inches in length, the shorter one may be more accurately described as a dagger or fighting knife. There is no official length at which a dagger becomes a sword but length is certainly a deciding factor and I would say the overall length should exceed around 20 inches for a weapon to be called a true sword. However, based on shape, both these weapons may be thought of as khepeshes.

Both weapons have beautiful ebony grips, the shorter one decorated with bands of gold leaf, and both are made of bronze. Bronze, that lustrous alloy of copper, which polishes to glinting gold, can be hardened by a factor of three when worked under the hammer. You can get an edge on a bronze sword that is sharp enough to shave with. It

can be cast, cut, filed and hammered into a myriad of shapes that provide both resilience and splendour. The effectiveness of a bronze sword should not be underestimated. Legions of bronze swords lie at rest in museums. They are generally in a better state of preservation than their Iron Age counterparts, though their colour has transmuted and dulled with time. In fact the soft, dusty, greyish-green appearance of so many of these weapons, caused by a coating of verdigris that forms with exposure to air, can make them appear delicate and modest, but burnish a bronze sword and you will see the fire, the toughness and a glorious, glimmering sheen that proclaims its high status and prestige. Pick one up and you will feel a weapon of weight and purpose.

Tutankhamun

Tutankhamun was a soldier pharaoh – fit, strong and adept at a range of martial skills. We call him the boy king because he came to the throne, around 1336 BC, at the tender age of 9 but he did not remain a boy for long. From the age of 15, at least, he would have been in peak physical condition and capable of leading his armies into battle. It is thought that he was at least 18 or 19 years old at the time of his death in 1327 BC – time enough to have had substantial military experience. He may have died tragically young by modern standards but it was a man who died, probably from infected wounds occasioned in a chariot accident, not a boy.

The smooth-skinned features of the fabulous golden death mask can mislead us into thinking of him as a delicate and innocent youth but the wooden mannequin found in the tomb, thought to be for putting his clothes on at night, reveals a man of powerful and athletic physique. This is the Tutankhamun who is shown, in wall paintings, galloping his chariot with the reins tied around his waist and shooting his powerful angular bow. I have done this, in a replica of his chariot and with a replica of his bow. I drove the chariot across the windswept sands at Giza, with the pyramids in the background. It is among the most thrilling experiences I have ever had and it gave me an insight into Tutankhamun's world – driving a war chariot and shooting a bow is hard, bone-shaking, physical work. Tutankhamun was far from being the milksop boy that his delicate features might suggest.

He was also a passionate hunter. There are many scenes of him hunting, both from his chariot and on foot. Two shields were

Lesser khepesh of Tutankhamun, Egyptian Museum, Cairo (© Griffith Insititute, University of Oxford)

discovered in his tomb and, on one of them, in bronze appliqué, is an image of the king despatching a lion with a khepesh. Allegorically it shows the pharaoh's dominion over the natural world but it also implies a brave and fearless hunter. Hunting, at least until the mechanized wars of the twentieth century, has always been considered to be the best training for a warrior, combining the physical rigours of the chase with a need for courage and a familiarity with the letting of blood. As far as we can tell the image of Tutankhamun as a lover of rugged, adventurous and soldierly activities was more than just propaganda – it was based on the reality of his life.

His brief nine-year reign may have been of limited political significance and he would be little more than a footnote in history if it were not for the treasures of his tomb but those treasures speak of a man of great martial spirit. Among the finds was military equipment in abundance: chariots, bows, arrows, spears, shields, axes, maces, daggers, throw-sticks, fighting-sticks and, of course, the two khepeshes.

The khepesh

Archaeologists have for many years referred to the khepesh as the 'sickle sword'. This is misleading. A lowly status is implied by suggesting that the khepesh is a derivative of the agricultural sickle. In Europe, for instance, we are used to the idea that the agricultural bill became a mainstay of medieval armies and that the threshing flail became the military flail. However, although the flail was part of pharaonic regalia, Egyptian soldiery did not go into battle with flails, sickles or any other sort of agricultural implement. Any resemblance in shape between the khepesh and the sickle is entirely superficial. On a sickle the cutting edge is on the inside of the curve, whereas on a khepesh it is on the outside. Moreover, in most examples, the shape of the curve is entirely different. That on a sickle is a steep arc, whereas on many khepeshes the curve is slight and stretched, similar in fact to the curve on the cutting edge of the epsilon axe.

So called because its three-point attachment to the haft resembled the Greek letter E, the epsilon axe was at one stage a common weapon in the Egyptian army. Introduced into Egypt from Mesopotamia at the beginning of the Middle Kingdom, epsilon axes occurred in both long and short-hafted versions. Khepeshes also evolved in Mesopotamia at around the same time, circa 2,500 BC, though it is nearly a thousand years before we have evidence of the khepesh entering Egypt. Initially only the axe migrated.

Featuring a long and narrow curving blade, the epsilon axe was not so much an axe as a sword on a stick. Unlike the many other axes in the Egyptian arsenal, wedge-shaped cleavers and hatchets, the epsilon axe cut in the same way as a sword – it sliced. Moreover it had the potential to be wielded in a very similar way to a sword. Take an epsilon axe and apply the longsword teachings of the medieval master Talhoffer to its management, for instance, and you will find that they work very well. Epsilon axes were for use with skilled and sophisticated martial art techniques. Khepesh forms owe more to the epsilon axe than they do to the sickle and the blade profile is in most cases identical.

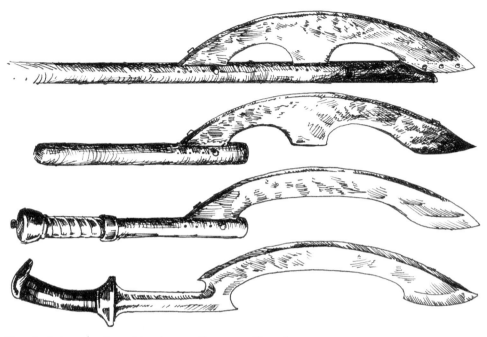

Hypothetical stages of transition from epsilon axe to khepesh

There is also an implication with the term 'sickle sword' that this is a weapon for the untutored recruit – the conscripted peasant straight from the land, utilizing whatever may come to hand as a makeshift weapon. Nothing could be further from the truth. I must confess to once subscribing to this prejudice but my eyes were opened the instant I held a replica khepesh in my hand. I was filming a television programme in Jordan, it was mainly about chariot archery but there was to be a small sequence discussing the difference between the khepesh and straight-bladed swords. Two Jordanian stuntmen were provided for me to use in the demonstration. As soon as I picked up the perfectly balanced replica khepesh, I realized that I had a superlative weapon in my hand and that every aspect of its design was there for a reason.

Curved swords give a more efficient cut, imparting a slicing motion as they strike the target. A curve also increases structural strength and enables a longer blade that is both rigid and robust. Because cast bronze can be somewhat brittle, it had been the challenge of the Bronze Age to be able to cast longer and longer swords – a feat that would be accomplished to an impressive

Egyptian with epsilon axe

degree in the late European Bronze age with straight-bladed swords – but in fourteenth-century BC Egypt it had only been possible to cast relatively short swords.

In the case of the khepesh the overall length was maximized by having, in addition to the curved section, a sturdy straight section at the hilt end – what in later swords we might call the 'forte' but which is perhaps better described on the khepesh as a shank. As well as making the sword longer than it would otherwise have been, this shank provided a dedicated section of the blade for effective defence. I tried it both against an onslaught from thrusting-spears as well as from a straight-bladed sword and it was perfect at either a straight block or at setting aside the incoming blade with a deflective beat. After all, this is the section of the blade used for this purpose on any sword and the khepesh offers all the advantages of a straight blade for these functions.

Both the khepeshes from Tutankhamun's tomb were cast with a tang – that is a continuation of the blade into the grip – making the whole a strong, single piece. With iron swords the tang became a relatively narrow, flattened rod that passed through the bored centre of a cylindrical grip. Bronze Age tangs were more often as wide as the grip itself, frequently having raised edges to create recesses for the grip plates to sit within. Many early versions of Bronze Age swords, at a time when casting technology limited the overall length of the piece, joined the grip to the blade by means of rivets. In this way the maximum length that could be cast was used entirely for the blade. Although a tanged blade is probably more robust, I think too much has been made of the likely weakness of a riveted hilt. It may be that riveted hilts did not last quite as long in heavy service but I don't doubt that they were tough enough to deliver equally strong blows and cutting blows at that.

Nineteenth-century archaeologists decided to class bronze swords with riveted hilts as rapiers, on the supposed pretext that they were suitable only for thrusting. It is an extremely misleading practice as well as being a bogus assumption. Bronze swords with riveted hilts come in all shapes and sizes, from the slenderest of stiletto blades to the broadest of cleavers. To call any of these weapons rapiers is nonsense and also misunderstands the true definition of a rapier, which is a civilian's sword. Fortunately

Great khepesh of Tutankhamun, Egyptian Museum, Cairo (courtesy of Robert Partridge, *Ancient Egypt Magazine*)

these concerns are not an issue with the tanged blade versions of Tutankhamun's specimens.

On both of Tutankhamun's khepeshes, a polished grip of the darkest ebony contrasts beautifully with the shining blade and bears all the prestigious elegance that combinations of black and gold have always conveyed. The smaller of the two has the added embellishment of gold bands around the grip. Curling slightly around the back of the hand with a spur, the khepesh grip offers security from a sword slipping from one's grasp when delivering a powerful cut and, swelling as it meets the blade, it gives a stop to the hand so that the sword may be used effectively with a thrust. An added refinement to the grip of the shorter khepesh is that it indents at the forward end.

From the evidence of art, most khepeshes were held with a regular power grip, whereby all the digits wrap around the hilt, with the thumb closing in the opposite direction to the fingers. This would work well for the thicker grip of Tutankhamun's larger khepesh. However, the more slender and indented hilt of the shorter khepesh suggests a different grasp. The shape and size of the indent mirrors the shape and size of an extended thumb, indicating that this style of khepesh was held with the thumb laid lengthwise along the grip. Consider this khepesh held with the curve of the blade facing the ground and the thumb uppermost on the hilt. If you thrust forward with your hand in this position, you will notice how the tip of your thumb ends up pointing upward. Project that angle to the upward curve of the khepesh and you will be able to visualise that a thrust delivered thus would be able to enter the soft belly of a foe and yet travel upwards behind the ribs into the vital organs. Its sleek, elegant design possessed a grim functional purpose.

Tutankhamun's larger khepesh has the point set at an angle so that when the arm is thrust forward, there is a straight line from one's shoulder to the point of the blade. With its broad, curving blade and a point of balance that gave maximum weight behind the striking point, it was also a superlative cutting weapon. Throughout the history of the sword there has been continuous debate over the relative virtues of cutting and thrusting swords. Here at the outset of that journey is a sword that combines the key elements of both designs. It is a mystery as to why it fell so completely out of use.

As with all swords, the khepesh appears in several different forms and, conveniently, the swords from the tomb represent two of the main types. As a shorthand, I propose calling the smaller one, with its simpler form, the 'lesser khepesh' and the other, with its more complex shape, the 'great khepesh'. An earlier form of khepesh, found widely in the Levant, has an especially long shank and so I call it the 'long-shanked khepesh'. Another type has only a vestigial shank and a greater curve to the blade. I call this the 'crescent khepesh'. It occurs in very early representations of the weapon and, much later, as carried by the armies of Ramses III.

Great khepeshes, long-shanked khepeshes and most crescent khepeshes possess an additional feature, not seen on any other type of sword. At the junction between the shank and the curve of the blade is a hook. On the great khepesh and the long-shanked khepesh is another hook, or barb, on the back edge of the point. The primary hook, at

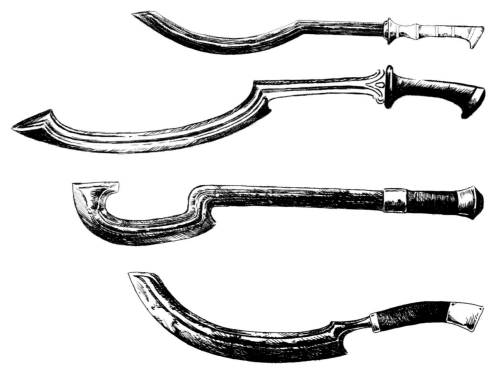

Khepesh types (top to bottom): Lesser khepesh, Great khepesh, Long-shanked khepesh and Crescent khepesh

the base of the curve, can be used to catch over the top or the side of an opponent's shield and pull it down. You can attack with a cut, and if it is parried near the edge of the shield, you can lean in a couple more inches, pushing your blade over the shield edge, hook it, draw it back or down, then in a continuous, fluid move thrust at your opponent with the point. I found these moves both natural and intuitive and working with the khepesh opened up a whole repertoire of free-flowing combination moves that transformed my opinion of this wonderful sword.

Tutoring the local stuntmen, who spoke no English, was at times challenging but it is surprising how much information one can convey with just half a dozen words of Arabic and a repertoire of mime. They were a jolly and charming pair and suitably tough. No complaint or fuss was offered when one suffered a bleeding lip as a result of a poor shield parry. Shields with only a central handgrip must either have the top edge supported, for instance by a shoulder, or the block must be made with the centre of the shield only. However, game though they were, there was no civilized way of testing my theory about a possible function for the barb behind the point. The Egyptians frequently fought foes, Nubians for example, who wore no or little body armour. One may imagine a great khepesh plunged into a bare stomach, and perhaps twisted as it was withdrawn, having an effective eviscerating capability. Whether or not this was so, the khepesh was certainly a weapon of ingenious design.

In spite of it having a clear martial application, there are a number of surviving khepeshes whose edges are conspicuously blunt. One such is the Sapara khepesh, now in the Metropolitan Museum of Art in New York. Although of substantial size, with an overall length of 21.4 inches, its form is of the lesser khepesh type. Inscribed on both sides of the blade in cuneiform script is a dedication to the Assyrian King Adadnirari. What should be the cutting edge of the blade is extremely broad and blunt, so much so that there is room enough for the inscription to be repeated here a third time. This particular khepesh is clearly not a functional weapon but a symbol of power. In addition to the inscription, the blade bears a representation of an antelope on what appears to be an altar. One can well imagine such swords being used in the ritual sacrifice of animals and that consequent associations with high priests would elevate it to a weapon of status and perhaps even magical powers.

The earliest depiction of a khepesh that I have been able to find is on the Stele of the Vultures in the Musée du Louvre in Paris. Only a few fragments remain but they clearly show the Sumerian ruler Eannatum, King of Lagash, brandishing a khepesh around 2,500 BC. In form it most closely resembles the crescent type. It was found at Tello near Basra in modern Iraq, the site of the ancient Sumerian city of Girsu. Made from carved limestone, the tele was a monument to Eannatum's victory over the land of Umma. On the stele he is depicted in two scenes with a khepesh. In one he is on foot, leading a regiment of spearmen, and in the other he holds it aloft in his war-wagon, a sort of proto-chariot. Sumerian war-wagons were heavy, lumbering vehicles drawn by onagers, bearing little relation to the light, hit-and-run, horse-drawn attack vehicles of Tutankhamun's army. The Sumerian version was most likely a mobile command post and it certainly was not a viable platform from which to use a sword. Even in Tutankhamun's day, when chariots were the principal attack platform for elite troops, they were only suitable for use with the bow and the spear. Chariots have an extremely broad wheelbase, which even the longest sword cannot reach beyond.

No other troops on the stele are shown with a khepesh. It is featured here solely as a symbol of Eannatum's royal power. Other representations of khepesh-style swords occur frequently around

Sapara khepesh, Metropolitan Museum of Art, gift of J. Pierpont Morgan, 1911 (11.166.1) (© The Metropolitan Museum of Art)

the same time in other parts of Mesopotamia (Early Dynastic III period) where they are often depicted in art being wielded by gods and kings. It is all part of a tradition of the khepesh being an emblem of high status and it would seem that this is the likely role of the khepeshes from Tutankhamun's tomb. Certainly the great khepesh is blunt and although there is a more acute edge on the lesser khepesh, it cannot be called sharp. However, unlike the Sapara khepesh, Tut's swords have normal tapers towards the cutting edge and therefore it would have been possible to hone either one to a keen edge if desired. The great khepesh (22.4 inches long) of Ramses II (1303–1213 BC), now in the Louvre, is also unsharpened, even though it too is of a fighting type that could have been given an edge.

A great many khepeshes were for ceremonial, ritual and display purposes and such swords seem always to have been left blunt or formed with edges that exaggerated bluntness. Doubtless this had meaning, perhaps to do with the relationship between power and mercy. In Egyptian tomb burials blunt khepeshes are deposited as statements of Pharaonic power. It is hardly surprising that all the khepeshes that have so far been unearthed by archaeology have come from burial chambers. Less important examples have likely been melted down. Recycling has an ancient pedigree, especially when there is profit in it. An absence of sharpened khepeshes from archaeological finds has led some to assert that the khepesh was never employed as a fighting sword at all, suggesting its role was purely symbolic. I find it impossible to believe that so perfect and ingeniously devised a sword was never used to fight with. How else could it have evolved with such superbly functional features?

Besides there are glimpses in art of the khepesh being wielded in battle. Regular Syrian troops brandish a simple khepesh in their left hand, whilst carrying a pair of javelins in their right in a scene on a painted cast from the Temple of Beit el Wali. Ramses II is depicted smiting a Libyan with a great khepesh at the same temple. Tutankhamun is shown smiting an enemy with a great khepesh in a scene embossed upon a piece of gold foil found in his tomb. One can only speculate as to whether Tutankhamun actually possessed such 'fighting' versions and, if so, the extent to which he used them.

Replica of the great khepesh from the tomb of Tutankhamun (photo courtesy of Todd Feinman; replica by Neil Burridge)

Swords, either straight-bladed or curved, do not appear in Old or Middle Kingdom Egypt. Bows, spears, maces, axes and short daggers were the traditional weapons, until around the mid-seventeenth century BC when a mysterious people invaded Egypt, bringing with them an impressive array of new military hardware. They were the Hyksos.

The Hyksos
The Hyksos (*heqa khasewet* – rulers of foreign lands) are widely believed to have introduced Egypt to the horse and the chariot, to the composite angular bow and to the khepesh – armaments that were to herald a military revolution and lay the foundation for a new age of Egyptian military might. There is some evidence – ie horse remains that slightly pre-date the Hyksos era – to suggest that this convenient marker should not be taken too literally. It is nonetheless true to say that the mainstream adoption of horses and chariots for primary use on the battlefield did not occur until after the arrival of the Hyksos. This is certainly true of the khepesh.

Historians have long debated where the Hyksos came from exactly but there is a general consensus that they came from the Levant and were most probably Canaanites. Whether they came in great multitudes, with a storm-cloud of dust hovering above their clattering and creaking chariots, crossing into Egypt via the Sinai desert on one fateful day or whether there was a gradual migration of traders settling in the region, who eventually became a significant power group that effected a palace coup is not recorded and is much debated. However, in 1648 BC the Hyksos seized power in the north and forced the ruling Egyptian dynasty to retreat to Thebes in the south. Hyksos rulers called themselves Pharaohs and governed Lower and Middle Egypt, profiting from the wealth and abundance of the Nile delta. The Theban pharaohs had to pay tribute to their foreign overlords but otherwise enjoyed a peaceful co-existence. This hiatus of Egyptian rule between the Middle and New Kingdoms is called the Second Intermediate Period.

Hyksos government centred on Memphis but their summer palace at Avaris, situated in the lush plains of the eastern delta, was an important gateway to the rest of their empire, which extended north to Syria. Avaris was a rich trading centre as well as being strategically vital. In 1997 archaeologists working at the site of Avaris (Tell el-Dab'a) unearthed a tomb in which a warrior had been buried cradling a khepesh in his arms. Dating from the Second Intermediate Period, this is the oldest specimen of a khepesh to have been found in Egypt and is of the Pi type, having a long shank and short curve. Most remarkably, and uniquely, it still retained its leather scabbard, which was a broad sheath wide enough to accommodate the curve of the sword.

Around 1552 BC, after some thirty years of armed revolt from Thebes, 108 years of Hyksos rule was brought to an abrupt end. In campaigns waged by the brilliant young Theban prince Ahmose, the Hyksos were driven from the land. Egypt was re-unified and Ahmose became the first pharaoh of the New Kingdom. It heralded a new golden age for Egypt, an age when her armies, now equipped with all the military innovations that had been introduced by the Hyksos, were to march out and expand her borders and her realm of influence. It heralded the 18th Dynasty of pharaohs, a dynasty that was to count Tutankhamun as number twelve.

Tutankhamun and the cult of the Aten

Considerable mystery surrounds Tutankhamun's ancestry. A widely accepted view is that he was the son of the Pharaoh Akhenaten and his second, minor wife, Queen Kiya. Some argue that he was the son of his immediate predecessor, the enigmatic Pharaoh Smenkhkare, but it is more likely that Smenkhkare was his sibling. According to some interpretations Smenkhkare, who ruled for less than a year, may have been a female pharaoh and so would have been Tutankhamun's sister rather than his brother, if that claim were true. Others believe that Smenkhkare was his stepmother, the legendary beauty Nefertiti, the principal wife of Akhenaten. Whatever the truth, Tutankhamun came to the throne at a turbulent time for pharaonic rule.

His father, Akhenaten, had begun his reign as Amenhotep IV. He changed his name five years later in an act of religious reformation that was to have cataclysmic impact and which rocked the foundations of the Egyptian establishment. Hitherto the Egyptians had worshipped a pantheon of gods, of which Amun was a principal, but not the sole, deity. Amenhotep, a name meaning 'Amun is satisfied', declared suddenly that Aten was the only god and changed his name to Akhenaten, meaning 'the effective spirit of Aten'. Moreover he declared himself to be the only intermediary between Aten and the people. Temples to Amun were desecrated and old practices were brutally suppressed. Akhenaten promoted his new monotheistic religion with an all-encompassing zeal. How much was motivated by genuine religious fervour and how much by political expediency, bringing an over-powerful priesthood into check, is a matter for conjecture.

Certainly, young Tut must have spent his early years in the thrall of the new religion; he may even have believed in it. When he ascended the throne, at the age of nine in 1333 BC, he did so with his birth name, Tutankhaten, which means 'the living image of Aten'. Two years later, in the most significant move of his reign, at the grand old age of eleven, he abandoned Atenism and allowed his people to return to worshipping their traditional deities. He changed his name to one that means 'The living image of Amun' – Tutankhamun. He also took a forename, Nebkheperure, meaning 'lord of the forms of Re'. It was pretty major stuff for a kid, though we may assume that the decisions were made by his regents and influenced by the disenfranchised priesthood. Akhenaten's old vizier, Ay, was his chief regent, though many believe that his stepmother, Nefertiti, may also have been a power behind the throne, along with the Chief Commander of the Army, Horemheb. Both Ay and Horemheb were to succeed Tutankhamun as Pharaoh. The young king's court was one of power-seeking and vested interests.

Records show that Nefertiti only gave birth to daughters – six of them. One of these, Ankhesenpaaten, was to become Tut's wife. She too later changed the '-aten' suffix of her name to become Ankhesenamen. Contemporary representations of her in art show her to have been a beguiling beauty and she and Tut must have made a handsome couple. Incest was of no great consequence in royal circles; the fact that she was his half-sister was of no concern. After all, previously, she was probably also married to her (and his) father, Akhenaten, and she may even have born Akhenaten children. Two still-born babies, both girls, found in the tomb are thought to have been the progeny of Tutankhamun and Ankhesamen. They had no other children.

With such a complicated family life and as an escape from the factional intrigues at court, it is little wonder that Tutankhamun devoted much of his time to hunting and martial activities. He was a virile and active young man. Together with the evidence of the quantities of military and hunting paraphernalia in his tomb, there is a great deal of art depicting Tutankhamun out hunting or fighting from his chariot. In the latter part of his reign we see him waging war against the Nubians, Egypt's powerful enemy on her southern border, and the Hittites, whose capital was at far off Hattusas, in modern day Turkey, to the north.

In the lion-slaying scene on the shield from the tomb, Tutankhamun is depicted holding the lion by the tail and raising his khepesh above his head. It is a familiar pose, mirrored in representations of other pharaoh's smiting the enemy, usually

holding them by the hair with the left hand as the right hand, armed with mace or axe, is raised aloft. Such images are clearly symbolic, pointing to the pharaoh's courage and dominion over his enemies or the natural world. A carved ivory wrist guard in the Egyptian Museum, Berlin, depicts Tuthmosis IV (1401–1390 BC) in exactly this pose with a khepesh in hand, smiting an Asiatic. Seti I (1290– 1279 BC) shown in a relief at Karnak, riding his chariot into the ranks of routed Libyans, is also wielding a khepesh, in classic smiting posture, in his right hand, whilst holding a bow in his left. As already noted, the khepesh is not a weapon that can be used effectively from a chariot, though there is the possibility that one could jump down from the platform and set about one's foe.

Shield from Tutankhamun's tomb showing the pharaoh slaying a lion with a khepesh

The extent to which Tutankhamun actually went to war is problematic because there is nothing in the written record to support the visual record. However, there is a reason for this. In a move to wipe out the heretic stain of Atenism, the reigns of the four pharaohs who had even the slightest association with the cult – Akhenaten, Smenkhkare, Tutankhamun and his successor, Ay – were expunged from the official records.

Egypt at war

Aggression towards foreigners was part of the Egyptian mindset. The faces of other races adorned the floors of royal palaces, so that they might be stepped on continuously in figurative acts of insult and subjugation. In the chaos following the re-introduction of the old religion, it seems likely that the national interest would have been well served by a focus directed at enemies beyond Egypt's borders. Whether Tutankhamun actually fought or led his armies into battle remains unproven but what is certain is that he was heir to a mighty military legacy and one that had been invigorated and empowered by all the new technologies introduced by the Hyksos some two centuries earlier. The army of New Kingdom Egypt was organized, well equipped and a professional, full time, fighting force.

Although a majority of troops were conscripted, there were also career volunteers who signed up for what was seemingly a brutal existence. 'He is hungry, his belly is in pain. He is dead whilst yet alive. He receives the corn-ration when he is released from duty, but it is not pleasant when it is ground', laments one account of the infantry-man's lot on campaign. Another report tells of daily life at the training barracks: 'He is thrashed to exhaustion. He awakens in the morning only to receive more beatings until he is split open with wounds. He is equipped with weapons upon his arm, he is standing in the drill field every day'.

Complaining about rations, punishment and drill is the universal cry of the soldier through the ages but there were also rewards. Aside from regular pay and what he could plunder when on campaign, the Egyptian soldier received gifts of land and livestock on his retirement. Advancement was possible with promotion through the ranks and there were awards in recognition of valour, though most of the public kudos for any victory was reserved for the pharaoh, not individual soldiers.

The highest military award was a golden fly, which was worn around the neck on a cord. Not a lion or any other noble and courageous animal but a common fly. This is a creature whose constant, unrelenting persistence, whose reckless determination to sit on your nose and whose ability to avoid being swatted and to return to harass and annoy time after time represents exactly the sort of fluid, hit-and-run tactics that have ever been the hallmark of

Golden fly medal – the highest military honour

warfare in the Near East and the bravado and daring required to carry them out. Choosing the fly as a badge of honour reveals a great deal about the mindset of the Egyptian army in the New Kingdom.

Buzzing flies is certainly how many might describe the chariotry of New Kingdom Egypt. Constantly on the move and harrying the enemy with stinging flights of arrows, chariot archers and their drivers were the elite. Known as the *maryannu*, the 'young heroes', they perceived the chariot as the dashing, heroic and high status way to go to war. Chariots were the main focus of Tutankhamun's military training but the khepesh was a weapon to be used on foot.

Stick-fighting

Egyptian foot-soldiers were trained in hand-to-hand combat with a variety of weapons. Images of men weightlifting with bags of sand and all manner of boxing and wrestling scenes indicate a culture that well understood the essential elements of martial training. *Sebekkah*, an ancient Egyptian style of wrestling, is still practiced today as is another ancient Egyptian martial art, *tahteeb*. *Tahteeb* is a form of stick-fighting that ranges from the punishing rigours of a true martial art, in which whirling staves lacerate and bruise the body, to a form of choreographed sword dance that is performed at festivals and marriage ceremonies and from which any martial fire has long been extinguished.

Several New Kingdom wall reliefs depict stick-fighters. It is likely that stick-fighting was practised as a sporting event, probably with an animated crowd betting on a winner and also as a martial arts display at state occasions and other festivities. Its foundation and most common use, however, must surely have been for training. Sparring with wooden weapons for sport and for training is a continuous theme throughout the history of swordfighting.

Depictions in art show that Egyptian fighting-sticks were furnished with some form of knuckle-guard, probably of hardened rawhide. They closely resemble the singlesticks of eighteenth and nineteenth century Europe. One thing that is unique about the ancient Egyptian system, however, is a specialized form of shield. From the tip of their extended fingers to the elbow on their left arm the protagonists are often shown wearing a wooden splint strapped to the forearm. I suspect that they also wore leather gloves to which the board is sewn. This might explain why their hands are open with extended fingers. These shielded left arms are held in front of the face with the forearm at right angles to the upper arm. In this guard combatants have a quick and

Fighters from a tomb at Thebes. After Gardner Wilkinson, *The Ancient Egyptians*, 1853

straightforward defence of the head, neck and shoulders and it may be that the target for this sport was restricted to these areas. Certainly some reliefs show stick-fighters with a tall conical helmet, possibly made from stiffened linen, which would offer protection to the head for training or sparring.

Stick fighting was also probably a funerary game, performed at the funerals of eminent people. To what extent Tutankhamun learned to fight with sticks is not known but there was quite a haul of fighting-sticks found in his tomb. Perhaps they were the sticks used at his own funerary games? Capped with a bronze ferrule, which seems to be on the striking end of the stave, some of them have a larger, pommel-like ferrule at the other end and all are now missing their leather hand-guards.

Fighting-sticks were not just a means of training and part of a sporting ritual; they were also used as weapons in battle. These are sturdy staves and perfectly capable of breaking bones or dashing out the brains of an unprotected skull. Certainly they were a significant element in Egyptian's martial culture and as such it seems likely that Tutankhamun would have trained in their use. Of course his experiences would have been very far from those of the common soldier but the Pharaoh was supposed to lead his armies and would therefore require an all-round military education and I suspect that stick-fighting played a part in that.

Some of the images depicting stick-fighting show fighters armed with a stick in each hand. During the European Renaissance, there were fight masters who advocated the use of a rapier in each hand, calling it a 'case of rapiers'. On the slightly crumbling stucco walls of Queen Hatshepsut's glorious temple at Deir el-Bahri, is a scene of two swordsmen wielding a khepesh in each hand. Both men look alike and are attired identically and so this is not a case of an Egyptian subjugating his enemy but rather of two Egyptians demonstrating martial skills. Whether they are engaged in a bloody form of gladiatorial contest, or displaying their art in choreographed sequences, as

Fighting sticks from the tomb of Tutankhamun, Egyptian Museum, Cairo (© Griffith Institute, University of Oxford)

Stick fighters at Medinat Habu (courtesy of Robert Partridge, *Ancient Egypt Magazine*)

the Shaolin monks might do today, or whether this was a form of mock combat with blunted weapons, is not clear. However it raises the question of how to train and spar with a khepesh. Stick-fighting is all very well to sharpen reflexes and learn basic principles of attack and defence but the khepesh is a very particular weapon and cannot be mastered just by using a stick. Although wood makes a relatively safe training weapon, it is only really useful in that role if it is the same size and shape as the weapon for which it is substituting.

Length is a crucial factor for training; one must learn to judge one's reach. Weight and balance also are important and wooden swords generally give a reasonable approximation to the parent metal sword because they are thicker in section. In the case of the khepesh, its hooking capability could not possibly be mastered with a weapon of a different shape. Wooden khepeshes have been found but it is by no means certain that this was their purpose. They could have been royal toys, votive

Fighters, each armed with a pair of khepeshes. Wall painting from Hatshepsut's mortuary temple at Deir el Bahri (courtesy of Robert Partridge, *Ancient Egypt Magazine*)

offerings or funerary gifts but the idea that they might be practice weapons remains a possibility.

Pits lined with mud-bricks are often found beneath temples and tombs containing an array of objects as talismanic wardens of the building. These offerings are known as 'foundation deposits' and a common endowment was the placing of miniature tools and weapons. In the reserve collection of the British Museum is a small wooden khepesh (17079), 9 inches long, from the 'foundation deposit' beneath the Temple of Thutmose III in Thebes. It has an incised hieroglyphic text that includes Thutmose III's *prenomen*. He ruled between 1479 and 1425 BC and the presence of this offering at his temple supports the idea that the khepesh was regarded as a weapon of royal significance at least a century before Tutankhamun.

Incidentally, miniature weapons were a feature of Late Bronze Age (1100–500 BC) urn burials in Northern Europe and Scandinavia. Miniature bronze swords, 10–15cm in length, were frequently placed in the grave alongside the urn. There is a wonderful array of these tiny masterpieces, some gold plated, in the Nationalmuseet in Copenhagen.

A fragment of a full-sized wooden sword (35902) also exists in the British Museum's Egyptian collection. It is broken at the hilt but the blade measures 15.2 inches and so it was certainly once of a size to be practical as a training sword. In this instance it is a straight bladed weapon but I am sure that, as in all other martial cultures, wooden weapons were used for practice and that this was no different for the khepesh. I can well imagine Tutankhamun learning to fight with such a weapon. Of course one other possible use for a wooden facsimile of a khepesh would be as a model from which to make the mould for casting in bronze. There were various ways of making a mould but first you had to get your bronze.

Sword manufacture in the Bronze Age

Copper-bearing rocks announce their treasure to the world by flaunting vivid hues of green that streak through the ore in broad bands and narrow stripes or gather within it in crystalline clusters like raisins in a cake. Copper advertises its presence. Egypt was blessed with abundant reserves of copper, especially around the Sinai region and production was on an industrial scale from the earliest times. An Old Kingdom smelting factory with three furnaces and large quantities of malachite ore has been discovered at the ancient fort of Buhen and an estimated 200 metric tons of slag from copper smelting has been found at the Middle Kingdom fort of Kuben. However the demand for copper was so great in the New Kingdom, feeding the cutting edge of a powerful military machine, that Egypt, at times, had to import from abroad, especially from Cyprus. Cyprus was so rich in copper that the Romans called the metal *cyprum* – this changed later to *cuprum*, giving us Cu as the chemical symbol for copper.

Copper alloyed with certain metals becomes harder and therefore better able to take an edge. Arsenic, antimony, zinc and tin all form bronze of increasing hardness. This is partly owing to different atomic sizes making slip between layers of atoms more difficult, and partly owing to the formation of inter-metallic compounds. By far the toughest and the hardest bronze was that made from an alloy of copper and tin. If the copper already contains traces of arsenic, then so much the better and Egyptian copper possessed a high percentage of arsenic, making it especially suitable for weapons manufacture.

Arsenic-copper alloys were in use for much of what we call the Bronze Age but many consider that it is not until the advent of copper-tin alloys that the true Bronze Age begins. The Early and Middle Bronze Ages are often called the Copper Ages because it is not until the Late Bronze Age, in the sixteenth century BC, that copper-tin bronzes become widespread. For Egypt that coincides with the beginning of the New Kingdom.

Tin, appearing black when found in ore deposits, was a much scarcer substance than copper. Deposits of tin have been discovered in the Alexandria region of Northern Egypt but there is no evidence that these were mined. Egypt bought her tin from Cyprus, Crete, Spain, India and also, possibly, from Cornwall in England.

Crushing the rocks and then smelting them in a furnace extracts the metal but metals do not have to be liquid in order to be separated from their parent rock. Smelting is a chemical process and not an alternative word for melting. For instance pure malachite – the most common copper-bearing ore – can be smelted at 700 degrees Celsius, whereas copper does not become fully molten, and thus suitable for casting, until it is at 1,084 degrees C. In the smelting process carbon combines under heat with the oxygen in the ore reducing the compound to its constituent elements so that, for instance, cuprite ($2CuO$), another common copper ore, combines with carbon (C) to become $2Cu + CO2$. Metals emerge as a kind of gloopy mass, not a liquid. Broken into small chunks, these metal ingots can then be heated to molten temperatures for casting. The addition of tin to copper lowers the melting temperature of the resulting bronze to around 1,000 degrees C, thus making it especially suitable for casting.

The first essential of a casting furnace is being able to get the temperature high enough to melt the metal. Instead of using open fires, where clearly all the heat escapes, the furnace is constructed like a clay oven and set in a pit. In order for the fire to burn at higher temperatures it needs to be force-fed with oxygen. There are Old Kingdom wall paintings, such as those in the Scqqara tombs of Mereruka and Ti, which show metalworkers sitting round a furnace blowing through long pipes. It is possible to create temperatures high enough to melt copper by means of the human breath, given enough people with enough puff.

By the New Kingdom though, we see the widespread use of bellows, yet another technology possibly introduced by the inventive Hyksos. Operated by hand, and

Pot bellows

Metal workers using pipe bellows, Old Kingdom. From the 'Tomb of the Two Brothers' at Saqqara (courtesy of Robert Partridge, *Ancient Egypt Magazine*)

sometimes foot, these early bellows were known as pot bellows because the air chamber was made from a clay pot. A diaphragm, made from hide, tied around a rim at the top of the pot. There was sufficient surplus leather for the diaphragm to be pumped up and down, thus forcing air into the chamber with a great whoosh. Air intake into the bellows was either by means of a hand operated valve – i.e. relaxing and pinching together a slit in the top of the skin diaphragm – or sucking air in through the same pipe that expelled it. In the latter case, using a pair of bellows circumvented the problem of drawing oxygen from the furnace. The downward push of the diaphragm forced the air out at a greater pressure than the action of drawing the air in. In order to insulate the bellows from the intense heat and to keep them securely in position whilst being used, they were set in a mound of sand a few feet away from the furnace. Pipes made from reeds carried the air from the bellows into the funnel end of pipes made from baked clay (*tuyeres*). These ensured that the forced air was carried right to the heart of the fire, fanning the charcoal embers to glow ever more intensely.

At high temperatures the slightest trace of moisture trapped in the furnace walls would transform into steam under high pressure and would risk exploding the whole thing, so precautions are taken at every stage to drive out as much moisture as possible. A fire is lit in the initial hole dug in the ground where the furnace is to be set. This pit is then lined with clay and a second fire is lit to make it as dry as possible. A third fire bakes the clay walls of the furnace that are subsequently built up over the fire pit. Broken pottery, grasses, charcoal and sand are usually added to the clay mix as a further antidote to air pockets of steam that would cause an explosion and to mitigate the effects of shrinkage caused by evaporation.

Fires are always hypnotic but sitting around the casting furnace, perhaps in the cold of a desert night, perhaps for several hours, with the insistent, unbroken rhythm of the bellows intoning like a slow steam train and one's face smarting from the searing heat, must have been a mesmerising experience. The master, judging from the colour of the fire, would know when the time was right and, jolted from their trance, the workers would then have to move with careful haste to complete the process. They probably had to bind hands and arms with wet leather before reaching into the furnace with wooden tongs to withdraw the crucible. Barely able to turn their faces towards the intense heat of the liquid bronze, they poured it gently into the mould. Great care had to be taken to prevent any of the charcoal flotsam from the furnace, now swimming atop the thick metallic soup, entering the mould and causing weaknesses in the blade. A piece of wood laid across the rim of the crucible was used to ensure that only pure liquid bronze was poured into the mould cavity.

Many moulds for bronze weapons were made from stone and it was important to warm the stone in a separate fire to ensure its passive reception of the molten bronze. Hotter than liquid fire, the golden ooze could sputter and spit back in anger from sudden contact with cold stone and there was also a risk of cracks and fractures that would ruin the casting. Carved with bronze tools, the two halves of a stone mould were sealed together with a blanket of clay and set upright in a bed of sand so that gravity could do its work in assisting the melt to find its way into every detail of the form.

On both sword examples from Tutankhamun's tomb there are deep grooves and ridges. These are arranged in such a way as to be pleasing decoratively but their principal function is to provide structural strength. One of the great things about cast weapons is that these features are created in the mould and they can therefore be very sophisticated and elaborate arrangements. It was many centuries after the introduction of iron blades, which were forged rather than cast, before an equivalent assortment of fullers and medial ridges began to mirror what had been standard practice during the Bronze Age. Fullers, that is deep grooves or fluting, are not seen on Iron Age blades much before the twelfth century AD and the medial ridge, a key strengthening factor of Late Bronze Age straight-bladed swords, is not seen before the fifteenth century AD.

It is possible that the level of detail on Tutankhamun's swords could have been achieved using stone moulds but the sort of fine detail, with delicate incised markings, to be found on many bronze swords can only be achieved from clay moulds. An advantage of a stone mould is that it has the potential to be used more than once, and there is ample evidence of this for axes, but a clay mould is what is needed when a unique piece, such as a royal sword, is to be created.

Before the mould comes the model. When carved in wood, it is pressed into clay blanks, once on each side, to create two halves of a mould that are then bound together and sealed with an outer layer of more clay. Another method, the lost wax method, is to make a model from beeswax and then completely surround it with clay to make the mould. Upon heating the wax melts and runs out of a prepared flue, leaving a hollow to be filled with the bronze. Very fine clay is required for such moulds and this has to be mixed with an amount of animal dung, so that when the mould is fired it creates a porous ceramic, making it more resilient to bursting when it encounters the extreme heat of the bronze melt. As layers of clay are built up around the wax model to give bulk to the mould, it is strengthened longitudinally by inserting splints of wood, while plant fibres wrap around it to bind it all together.

Even the finest casting needs to be cleaned and finished with a series of abrasives. Sandstone blocks make a good start but finer work is accomplished with pieces of leather that have been coated with some form of gum or adhesive and then dusted with sand. At this stage the blade would be work hardened by hammering it with a bronze hammer on a bronze anvil and then it would be put to a whetstone to give it an edge. Last of all, a charcoal dust and clay paste on a soft cloth gives a final polish, bringing to life a blade that gleamed resplendently and reflected warm golden rays as if it were the sun itself.

An army equipped fully with bronze weapons would have been a magnificent and terrifying sight. Axeheads and spearheads would play their part but the psychological intimidation created by massed ranks with sharp, glinting khepeshes must have been greater, not least because it might suggest that the soldiers were at a higher level of military training. The khepesh was a sophisticated weapon for elite troops.

Swords in the age of Ramses III

Elite troops were exactly what was needed during the reign of Ramses III (1186–1154 BC) when Egypt suffered a wave of invasions from the 'Sea Peoples'. Not since the time of the Hyksos had there been a greater outside threat to the autonomy of Egypt's ruling dynasty. On the walls of Ramses III's great mortuary temple at Medinat Habu are carved reliefs showing the Egyptian army marching out to deal with the menace. Here are regiments of soldiers brandishing khepeshes. Some carry khepesh and shield, while others bear a short axe in their right hand and a khepesh in their left. Axe and khepesh make for a very useful double weapon system. Similarly the two khepeshes of Tutankhamun would work very well together, having the great khepesh in the right hand and the lesser khepesh in the left. Fighting with a bladed weapon in each hand, commonly seen in Egyptian art, denotes an advanced and sophisticated level of martial arts technique. It is also tremendously exhilarating and I am surprised that the present day historical martial arts community do not yet give much attention to the fighting arts of ancient Egypt. There is still much to be learned from practical experimentation.

The soldiers at Medinat Habu carry the crescent khepesh. Before this we don't generally see the khepesh in the hands of the general soldiery in Egypt, though many of her enemies, such as the Hittites, appear to have used it more widely. There are daggers aplenty but swords, either curved or straight, are rarely seen in the hands of the average Egyptian soldier. There was an Egyptian form of straight sword that was contemporary with the khepesh but surviving examples are relatively short, more like a large dirk.

A painted wooden casket from Tutankhamun's tomb, now in the British Museum, shows two soldiers armed with straight swords that appear in proportion to be close to

Soldiers of Ramses III armed with khepeshes. Relief at Medinat Habu (courtesy of Robert Partridge, *Ancient Egypt Magazine*)

the size of a Roman gladius. Both soldiers have their shields slung over their back by means of a *guige* (strap) and both are slaying Nubians in the midst of a great battle. One soldier thrusts into the face of his foe, whilst the other cuts down at his man on the ground. In both instances the Egyptians are using their left hand to grab their adversary by the wrist. A third soldier on the casket performs a similar action with a dirk. Grappling is integral to swordfighting and all the great masters, throughout the ages, have taught techniques for grabbing hold of and unbalancing your enemy as you strike him. In this instance, however, there may be another significance to all these wrists being grabbed. Bureaucratically-minded Egyptian scribes demanded evidence in order to account the numbers of the slain. That evidence came mostly in the form of severed hands, which were brought before them and stacked high in grisly piles. It seems rather pointless to be so exact, given the tendency of all pharaohs to exaggerate the numbers after the fact.

The Merneptah Stele (also known as the Israel Stele), now in the Egyptian museum, Cairo, is headed with images of pharaoh receiving a khepesh as a symbol of military power from the gods. On its reverse side it recounts Merneptah's victory over the Libyans around 1207 BC. Together with shackled prisoners and piles of plundered weapons, evidence of the nine thousand Libyan slain was paraded before Merneptah in the form of grotesque heaps of severed phalluses. It may be that this appendage eliminated any risk of duplication in the counting process, as could happen with

Sea Peoples from the walls of Medinat Habu. Note the long, straight, acutely pointed swords (courtesy of Robert Partridge, *Ancient Egypt Magazine*)

hands, but it was surely an excess of bureaucratic zeal to record whether or not each individual was circumcised.

Allied to this failed Libyan invasion had been the mysterious Sea Peoples. Some thirty years later, in a second wave of attacks, the Sea Peoples returned in greater numbers and with greater force and this was the threat that Ramses III faced, in part, with his regiments of swordsmen. Theories abound as to where the Sea Peoples come from. Various parts of Greece and Anatolia have been suggested as their homeland, while others think of them as a band of international pirates. It seems likely that they were a confederation of various peoples and that at least some of them hailed from Mycenae.

Armour

At Medinat Habu we see two types of helmet, the horned and the feathered, that we also see on the celebrated 'Warrior Vase' that was found at Mycenae and which has been dated to around this time. They also appear to be wearing an early form of lino-thorax, a type of body armour made from layers of linen glued together. It is a type of armour worn famously by Alexander the Great and so is discussed in greater detail in the next chapter.

Although the Libyans to the east and Nubians to the south are represented as fighting in nothing more than a loincloth, Egypt was used to facing an armoured foe. The Hittites in particular were well armoured, favouring a knee-length hauberk of overlapping bronze scales sewn to a linen garment. An identical form of armour was found in Tutankhamun's tomb, except that instead of bronze, the scales were made of thick leather. Leather armour proved extremely effective for three thousand years and was in use by most cultures. It is an extremely practical form of protection and one that avoids the considerable heat problems that come from wearing metal armour in extreme temperatures. That Tutankhamun possessed such down-to-earth armour reinforces my opinion of him as a fighting man. However, he also possessed a most fabulous and ornate armour, constructed from interlocking gold plates and inlaid with semi-precious stones. This dazzling corselet was fit for a king and reminds us that armour, like swords, had parade and ceremonial roles as well as its more practical function.

There is always a trade-off with armour between complete protection and the ability to move, see and breathe, as well as facing the potential problem of early heat exhaustion. Ramses' khepesh-bearing troops at Medinat Habu faced no such problem, since they have been portrayed wearing nothing more than a kilt. Relying on their shields for defence against missile weapons such as spears, stones and arrows, they took their chances in hand-to-hand combat, preferring agile mobility to the smother of armour.

The long swords of the Sea Peoples

Forgoing armour was a choice they may have questioned when faced with the terrifyingly long swords of the Sea Peoples. Broad at the hilt and tapering steeply to a sharp point, these were massive weapons. If the proportions of the images at Medinat Habu are correct, then the overall length of the invaders' swords were in excess of 3 feet. This was far greater than anything that had been seen before in Egypt or its neighbouring territories. In the Aegean however, swords have been found at the Minoan palace of Mallia that are over 39 inches long. They date to the seventeenth century BC. Like the swords of the Sea Peoples they have a pronounced central rib, which gives great structural rigidity. These Minoan swords are generally thought to have been ceremonial but there is nothing about their construction that would limit them to this role and they certainly tell us that the technology for making such long-bladed

Sea Peoples warrior

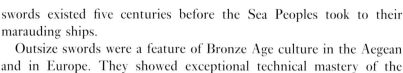

swords existed five centuries before the Sea Peoples took to their marauding ships.

Outsize swords were a feature of Bronze Age culture in the Aegean and in Europe. They showed exceptional technical mastery of the casting process. The 'Oxborough Dirk', discovered in Norfolk and now in the British Museum, weighs in at a gigantic 5lb 3oz and has a blade of 2ft 4in. Dating to around 1400 BC, it has blunt edges and possesses no means of attaching a hilt. It was clearly ceremonial, representing considerable wealth and therefore power. In Denmark's Nationalmuseet in Copenhagen, are some of the finest specimens of European Bronze Age swords, many of which are over 3 feet in length. One, from Hungary, is dated to the sixteenth century BC. Like the Minoan swords from Crete, there is no tang. Such blades were attached to the hilt by means of rivets. However there can be no doubt that the examples in the Danish museum are good, solid fighting swords.

Swords from the sixteenth and fifteenth century BC shaft graves in Mycenae are also of the riveted-hilt type but by the fourteenth century Mycenaean swords had a tang cast as one with the blade. These tangs were often 'T' shaped, allowing for the attachment of a counter-balancing pommel as well as the grip plates. From the evidence of the art, it would seem that the swords of the Sea Peoples follow this pattern. Stylistically they are consistent with the Mycenaean type.

However we should not set too much store by this. In a 2007 archaeological discovery at Amphilochia in Western Greece, a Mycenaean warrior's grave revealed a 37-inch sword. Its hilt was bound with gold wire. Austrian scientists subjected it to metallurgical analysis and found that the bronze for the twelfth-century BC blade came from Italy. Even with the copper-yielding plenty of Cyprus just a few oar-strokes away, the Mycenaeans were clearly trading for bronze objects with other civilizations around the Mediterranean.

Whether they were Mycenaeans, Anatolians, Sardinians, or Sicilians, the Sea Peoples and their long bronze swords struck terror all along the coasts of Anatolia, Syria, Palestine and Egypt during the first quarter of the twelfth century BC. It was a time of great chaos. Egypt survived the onslaught, though she was never as powerful in the world again. Mycenaean civilization collapsed and the brief flame that had been the Hittite empire was extinguished after a mere 250 years. The Sea Peoples also disappeared as enigmatically as they had arrived. There was a new world order but, more importantly, there was a new technology – iron.

Late Bronze Age leaf-bladed bronze sword found in England (photo courtesy of Culture and Sport Glasgow (Museums))

The coming of iron

In addition to the two lovely khepeshes found in the tomb of Pharaoh Nebkheperure Tutankhamun were two beautiful daggers. One, exquisite, wonderful, was made from gold but the other is even more extraordinary. It was made from meteoric iron. Not only was a meteor a gift from the gods that inspired awe, hurtling down with a great fiery tail and kicking up plumes of dust as it thudded into the ground, it was also the source of a unique material. Meteoric iron is actually a ferrous alloy containing nickel, a component that creates steel of exceptional hardness. Back on planet Earth the first nickel steel was not manufactured until 1809. It is little wonder that this extra-terrestrial bounty was turned into a weapon for the pharaoh.

Sky stones have always been regarded as omens and the bringers of either good or ill luck. In Richard II, Shakespeare tells us that 'meteors fright the fixed stars of heaven' and 'forerun the death or fall of kings'. Perhaps Tutankhamun's dagger was made from iron extracted from a meteor shower that portended his untimely death in 1327 BC. Perhaps it was simply a ceremonial totem, for certainly objects made from meteoric iron were considered to have magical powers. J.R.R. Tolkien, who was immersed in the traditions of Anglo-Saxon literature, celebrated the enduring potency of meteoric iron and magical sword myths in his fictionalized Middle-Earth sagas. He described the black sword *Anglachel* as being forged from 'iron that fell from heaven as a blazing star'. Here was a sword that would 'cleave all earth-delved iron'. Eöl, the Dark Elf, forged *Anglachel* and it was claimed that 'the dark heart of the smith' lived on in the sword.

Whether good or evil, the idea of an iron sword having magical properties remained inherent to the identity of swords long after they were made from terrestrial iron. It is an idea, I think, that first took hold with the dramatic yields of nickelliferrous iron harvested from the sky in the ancient world. Iron artefacts from meteors occur in several Bronze Age cultures but it is not until the systematic smelting of iron ores and the manufacture of everyday objects in iron that the Iron Age can be considered to have begun.

The Bronze Age did not begin everywhere at the same time and it did not transition to the Iron Age everywhere at the same time either. For instance the shift to iron in India (thirteenth century BC) occurs several centuries before it does in Central Europe (eighth century BC) and it happens there at least two centuries before it does in Northern Europe (sixth century BC). Tutankhamun just missed it. It is considered to begin in Egypt around 1200 BC, though the credit for this early start should probably go to the Hittites who are thought to be the first to bring iron weapons to the battlefield. This was the time of their empire's collapse. I am tempted to linger in the Bronze Age, to discuss so many other sword forms that were fashioned in that wonderful material, not least of all in Europe, but I know that I must quicken my step and hasten, with a great leap, to the Iron Age, for it is in the Iron Age that the sword truly became a universal weapon.

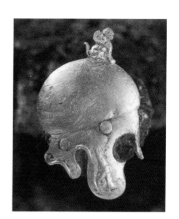

Sword from inside Tomb II, Royal Tombs at Vergina and detail of rivet washer from the pommel (image courtesy of 17th Ephorate of Prehistoric and Classical Antiquities, © Hellenic Ministry of Culture – Archaeological Receipts Fund)

Chapter 2

Swords of the Iron Age: Greek, Celtic, Roman

I will not disgrace my sacred arms nor desert my comrade, wherever I am stationed. I will fight for things sacred and things profane. And both alone and with all to help me I will transmit my fatherland not diminished but greater and better than before.

(Ephebic oath from fourth-century BC stele at Archarnae)

The Vergina swords

Burned by the fires of the funeral pyre, their hilts destroyed by the cremating flames, two iron swords from the fourth century BC lay buried amongst the charred clay-brick rubble above Tomb II at Vergina, until they were unearthed in 1977. They are examples of a type of sword known as the *xiphos*, the classic sword of the Greek and Macedonian hoplite. Hardened by the blaze, the distinctively leaf-shaped blades, with a flattened diamond cross-section, survived in surprisingly good condition; one even had the vestiges of gold hilt ornament remaining on the tang. That this had not completely liquefied suggests this sword may have been at the fringes of the blaze, perhaps shielded by other offerings. It is also possible that it was a brief cremation, more ceremonial than practical, and this may have been because cleansing flames had already stripped the body of its flesh at another location closer to the place of death. A small fire to scorch the bones and funerary goods at the site of the tomb was perhaps all that was needed to satisfy the demands of traditional ritual.

More significantly, inside the tomb itself, in the actual burial chamber, another xiphos was discovered; one that had escaped the conflagration altogether. Polished ivory, offset with subtle flourishes of gold ornament, once graced its hilt and scabbard with restrained elegance. Only traces of this luxurious opulence remain and the iron blade is now concreted within the decomposed scabbard wood and its own corrosion but there can be no doubt as to its former glory. Unlike the splodge of gold on the sword from the pyre, what remains of the tomb sword's gold embellishments is in tact. Two gold rings girdle top and bottom of the cylindrical pommel and a thin gold sheet covers the cross. From the centre of the cross, flanking the grip on either side, are delicate gold stems that terminate in intricate golden palm fronds. This fine detail is surpassed though by a miniscule decorative washer, measuring just 1.5cm across, in the form of a helmet. Also fashioned from gold, this miniature masterpiece sits on top of the pommel secured by golden nails. Close inspection reveals minute depictions of a sphinx on its crown and a lion on the cheek-piece. Here is a sword of very high status. Today it can be seen, along with the rest of the sumptuous funerary hoard and the fabulously painted tombs themselves, in the Vergina museum in Northern Greece. This underground treasure house, concealed deep beneath the great tumulus that hid these marvels from the world for over two millennia, is a secret place and full of wonder.

The tombs at Vergina, a small town sitting in the foothills of Mount Pieria, have been identified as the royal tombs of Macedon. Vergina lies on the outskirts of the ancient Macedonian capital, Aigai. For many years it was thought that Tomb II was the burial chamber of Philip II, father to Alexander III (the Great). However, recent analysis has led archaeologists to doubt this and the current theory is that it is the tomb of Alexander's half-brother Philip III Arrhidaeus, who succeeded to the throne after the untimely death of his more illustrious brother in 323 BC. Moreover current thinking suggests that the swords were part of Alexander's royal panoply and held by his brother as a sign of his royal authority.

Alexander died of a fever at the tender age of thirty three. Conspiracy theories abounded at the time and continue so to do, though genuine natural causes such as malaria remain a possibility. He died in the ancient city of Babylon, which he had intended to make the capital of his newly won empire, and he died without an heir. His son, by his wife Roxana, was as yet unborn. With Alexander on campaign was his feeble-minded half brother, for whom he had a touching affection. Philip Arrhidaeus, the progeny of a liaison between Philip II and a Thessalian dancer, was mentally unfit to be king but he became the pawn of ambitious men. Perdiccas, one of several power-hungry generals, set him upon the throne as a puppet ruler under his regency. Could it be that Perdiccas, requiring an outward show of the legitimacy of Arrhidaeus's sovereignty and links to the royal line, decided to gird him with Alexander's sword – just as Alexander had once donned what was believed to be the armour of Achilles, before leading his army into battle at the Granicus?

As far as one can tell from its damaged condition, the sword in Tomb II at Vergina appears to be very similar to the sword being worn by Alexander in the famous 'Alexander Mosaic' from Pompeii. Depicting Alexander riding hard into the thick of it during the Battle of Issus in 333 BC, the mosaic dates to around 100 BC but it is believed to be a copy of a contemporary fourth-century BC painting and so considered to represent a true likeness. Whether the sword in the tomb really was Alexander's must remain conjectural but it is certainly the same type as in the mosaic.

The xiphos

The xiphos was the archetypal sword of both Classical and Hellenistic Greece. Its 24-inch iron blade, with its distinctive waisted neck and the swelling of the blade a third of the way from the point, mirrored the leaf-shaped blades of the Greek Bronze

Age. This was an apogee of sword design that transcended the change in materials. Homer sometimes used the word *phasganon* in poetic references to swords. Scholars have traced the word back to the Linear B language of Mycenae and it may be that *phasganon* is the most appropriate word to describe the Bronze Age predecessor to the Iron Age xiphos. However, although writing of events in the thirteenth century BC, Homer lived in the eighth century BC and by that time the sword, now made of iron, was most definitely called the xiphos.

Suspended by a baldric slung over the right shoulder, the hilt of the xiphos sat high on the chest, just a few inches below the left armpit. It was sheathed in a very distinctive scabbard. At the base of the Vergina example is a large ivory roundel. Evident in art as a universal element, these chape roundels offered a smooth-edged buffer to the pointed end of the scabbard which, when worn amidst the tightly-packed rugby scrum of a pike phalanx, risked annoyance to one's comrades. For regular troops the material is more likely to have been bone. Serving the cavalryman in a similar way, its rounded edges softened any jagged abrasion against the horse's flank.

Artist's impression of how the Tomb II xiphos may have appeared when new

At the mouth of the scabbard is a broad 'T'-shaped element, reminiscent of a similar feature to be found on the scabbards of the Malaysian/Indonesian *keris*. In both cases this is to accommodate a flaring of the blade where it joins the cross. A glance at the shape of the blade on the sword from the funeral pyre confirms that this flare would necessitate the 'T' component to accommodate it. Without this the scabbard would either be so wide that the sword would be loose in it or it would not be able to sit flush with the cross.

More important is the question of why the 'cross' component developed on swords in the first place. Seemingly it offers some additional protection to the hand – it is sometimes referred to as the 'cross-guard' – but it is the back of the hand that is more vulnerable in combat and that wasn't taken care of until the closed hilts of the sixteenth century AD. The extent to which the cross defends the hand is greatly overstated, simply because it looks as if that is what it is for, but the reality is that it would be a rare occurrence for the hand to be hit on that line. Only the timid would gain reassurance from such a protective placebo. Crosses are conspicuously absent from that icon of design perfection, the Roman *gladius*, so why do they appear on the Greek xiphos?

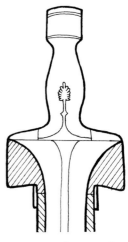

The first function of the cross is to act as a stop to the hand, preventing it from sliding forward onto the blade when thrusting against a solid object. As such it is an inferior

Cut-away diagram illustrating why xiphos blade needs T-shaped scabbard

Two *xiphoi* from the remains of a funeral pyre outside Tomb II, Royal Tombs at Vergina. Note that the one on the top retains traces of gold hilt ornament. Fire damage has distorted straightness of both blades, most noticeably on the one on the bottom (image courtesy of 17th Ephorate of Prehistoric and Classical Antiquities, © Hellenic Ministry of Culture – Archaeological Receipts Fund)

design to most Bronze Age swords, which have a rounded, inverted horseshoe shape at the junction of hilt and blade and to the ergonomically rounded shoulders of a *gladius* that sit snugly and softly into the dimple of the fist between thumb and forefinger. Thrusting against a man wearing armour with a cross-hilted sword hurts the hand. I have tried thrusting against armour (without the man in it!) for penetration tests and can confirm that it hurts a lot. Both the xiphos and the gladius are short swords with blade lengths ranging between 18 and 24 inches. We might expect them to be used in a similar way, so why this major design difference?

A possible clue lies in the shape of the proto-crosses found on some Trojan War-period (thirteenth century BC) bronze swords. One of these can be seen in the British Museum. Turn left as you go in and head for the coffee shop at the end of that first corridor (it is little used and avoids the queues and the clatter of the catering stations in the Great Court) and on the way you will pass through the Mycenaean collection. Here is a short sword (they call it a dagger), probably from Ithaca, which has project-ing lugs that curl over like half finger loops. Cross-hilts allow you, if you choose, to put a finger over the cross. This can reduce the risk of dropping the sword from a weary and probably sweaty, bloody and slippery hand in the heat of battle, as you scythe about with great slashing blows. We can see on the swords from the pyre how

Mycenaean short sword (bronze) c. 1300 BC (© The Trustees of the British Museum)

the underside of the cross and the uppermost flare of the blade combine to offer a smooth, rounded corner over which to hook a finger.

With its leaf-shaped blade, the xiphos was not only curved at its optimal striking point, it was also a 'weight-forward' weapon. Both these characteristics made it ideally suited for powerful hacking blows and its rigid, acutely pointed blade made it equally devastating as a thrusting weapon. Like the gladius, the xiphos was a dual-purpose weapon but on the battlefield it was mainly used in an entirely different context and this is the key to understanding why the hilts were different.

I shall come to the gladius more specifically in due course, but suffice to say that it was the principal weapon of the Roman legionary soldier and, when using it in tight formation, he relied more on the thrust and so the design of its hilt favoured this action. By contrast, the xiphos was a secondary weapon. The main weapons for Greek and Macedonian heavy infantry were, respectively, the long spear (*dory*) and the pike (*sarissa*). These gave reach over the locked shields of the phalanx, which was the principal method of battlefield engagement at the time. Only in the event of formations breaking up and the fight devolving to hand-to-hand combat would the sword be drawn and then it would have been a desperate business with ferocious slashing blows the order of the day. In such frantic and fatiguing circumstances, being able to grasp your weapon with greater security was essential. Hooking the finger over the cross was not a universal practice but it was an option.

Alexander the Great

Brash, vain, violent, ruthless, at times chivalrous, impossibly young, given to sulks and petulance and with the thick uncouth accent of a Greek-speaking Macedonian,

The Alexander Mosaic (detail), from the House of the Fauns, Pompeii (Museo Archeologico Nazionale, Naples)

Alexander the Great was nonetheless a dashing, charismatic and heroic leader driven by a restless spirit, indomitable determination and insatiable ambition. He was also, by his own declaration, a god.

On the battlefield he was first and foremost a cavalryman. Alexander and his elite Companion cavalry, a model of equestrian brotherhood that pre-dated by centuries the cult of the medieval knight, swept all before them. In battle he would ride at the point of the cavalry wedge formation, smashing fearlessly into the enemy. In art, where in part the legend is spun, he is usually depicted bareheaded – his leonine shock of thick hair acting both as a badge of courage and as a means of identity. Accounts suggest otherwise. Plutarch noted that at Guagamela (331 BC), Alexander wore an iron helmet that glittered like silver. According to Diodorus Siculus, the 22-year-old Alexander was also wearing a helmet at the Battle of the Granicus in 334 BC.

Describing an encounter during the battle between Alexander and Spithrobates, the satrap of Ionia, Diodorus relates how this helmet fared against a strike from a sword. It is a tale that also throws light on Alexander as a front-line warrior. At the outset of the fight they both charged at each other and Alexander was struck first by Spithrobates' well-aimed javelin. Entangled by his cloak, the missile barely grazed his cuirass and Alexander was able to riposte by driving his *xyston* into the satrap's chest. It broke against his armour.

The xyston was the principal weapon of the Macedonian Companion cavalry. It was a 12-foot lance with an iron spear point at either end. I once had to demonstrate its use and found that its being double-headed was a considerable aid to holding it in balance. This was just as well as I had been put, bareback, onto a lunatic Arab horse and we were filming in a rock strewn wadi in Tunisia – I needed every aid to balance available. Even so I was hurled to the ground three times by my bucking, rearing Bucephalus, who was frightened by his own and everyone else's shadow, before we got the sequence done. Never again! Apart from having a horse more suited to the task, the cavalryman must take care not to let the rear point of his xyston extend beyond his horse's rump, lest it endanger the companions riding hard behind, but the advantage of a double-headed lance, as Alexander was to find out, is that once the forward end has broken, you can simply lift your arm above your head and you immediately have a short stabbing spear.

In closing, Spithrobates had drawn his sword but, as he swung it, Alexander drove what remained of his xyston into Spithrobates' face, killing him outright. At that moment, Rhoesaces, the satrap's brother, 'brought his sword down on Alexander's head with such a fearful blow that it split his helmet and inflicted a slight scalp wound'. Rhoesaces drew his arm back for a second strike at the reeling king but, as he did so, Cleitus, Alexander's close friend, 'dashed up on his horse and cut off the Persian's arm'. According to Plutarch, Spithrobates was killed by Cleitus's spear and Rhoesaces cut down by Alexander's sword. Either way the sword played an important role that day and was clearly believed, by the chroniclers at least, to be a powerful weapon, capable of cleaving helms and severing limbs.

A bleak postscript to this story is that, in the aftermath of a drunken argument during a feast at Samarkand in 328 BC, Alexander killed Cleitus in a fit of uncontrolled rage. Cleitus, twenty years Alexander's senior, was mocking him about having to save his life, ridiculing that a god needed such mortal aid. Alexander seized a spear from a guard and ran him through. Hysterical with remorse, Alexander then 'snatched the spear from the body and would have plunged it into his own throat', had not his guards restrained him. Overweight, alcoholic and increasingly paranoid, Alexander had become a tragic figure. Some twelve years earlier it had been a different story.

The army of Macedon

Alexander had inherited from his father, Philip II, a superb military machine; its success founded on discipline, training and endless drilling. Philip had raised a full-time professional army, at the heart of which was the hoplite phalanx. Hoplite warfare consisted of blocks of infantry, armed with spear and shield, charging and smashing into each other with explosive energy and then slugging it out in a battle of attrition.

Hoplon is Greek for 'weapon' and so hoplite is a term meaning something like 'man-at-arms'. Philip's great revolution was to equip his hoplites, known as the Foot Companions, with enormous 18-foot sarissas (pikes). Twice the length of the Greek hoplite's dory, the sarissa was made with heavy cornelian cherry wood – a timber so dense that it doesn't float. Sarissas had a narrow iron head and a counterbalancing butt spike, nicknamed the *sauroter* (lizard killer). A phalanx of Foot Companions, perhaps sixteen rows deep, was able to project five rows of sarissa points beyond the front line, the rest remained vertical, dissipating the effect of any missiles and forming a reserve. The reach and density of a sarissa phalanx made it virtually unassailable. It was the porcupine to the Greek hoplite's hedgehog. Stepping in perfectly precise unison and chanting their signature, ululating war shout –'*alalalalai*' – this juggernauting, crunching, pile-driving mass of men struck fear into even the bravest of enemy hearts. Standing shoulder to shoulder in close-order formation, each man's shield overlapped his neighbour so that he was half defended by his own shield and half by his fellow's. Leaning their shields into the back of the man in front, the offset supporting rows gave weight to this immoveable force. Here was no room to swing a sword. Having clashed with the enemy front line, one side pushed against the other, while the long pikes jabbed and stabbed at faces, decimating the opposing force in a blood-soaked frenzy. Only when the opposing phalanx broke did the Foot Companions draw their swords and fall upon the enemy in a tidal wave of slaughter.

The business of gaining half your own protection from the shield of the man on your right meant that pike phalanxes had a habit of drifting to the right – several hundred men all inching a little bit has a magnifying effect. To help anchor the right flank and to give protection to the unshielded right side, the Macedonians used an elite light infantry corps known as *hypaspists*. Adept with every weapon, unarmoured and supremely fit, these versatile, crack troops were capable of either keeping up with the cavalry in the advance or falling back to cover the vulnerable right flank of the phalanx. In defending the phalanx they might stand with spears but when running in to exploit where the cavalry had punched through the enemy line, or in any rapid infantry manouevre, they most likely drew their swords. Prior to springing onto his horse and hunting down Darius at the Battle of Issus, Alexander had led his hypaspists on foot in an assault that punched through the Persian line. Here we may imagine him sword in hand as he cut his way to Destiny.

Hypaspisti means shield bearer and in hoplite armies the shield was a weapon of high regard. We are all familiar with various paraphrasings of Plutarch's famous quote from his *Sayings of Spartan Women*: 'Another woman handed her son his shield, and exhorted him: "Son, either[return] with this or on this".' It seems at first surprising that such an apparently humble piece of military paraphernalia should have such status. Remember though that in the culture of phalanx warfare, a shield protected not only the bearer but also his fellow in the phalanx. Shields were large and had to be carried, a doubtless onerous task, but to shirk this duty would be to imperil your comrade. Creating a tradition of stigma to the abandonment of the shield had an obvious benefit to the larger group.

All armour is a trade off between ultimate protection, mobility and temperature management. For both hoplite and hypaspist, a large shield was the answer. It allowed minimal armour whilst still protecting against push of pike and the incessant storms of javelins, arrows and stones. An ingenious addition to the shield in the previous century had been the *parablemata*, a leather apron attached to the shield's lower edge, offering added protection to the legs. Whether from missiles, spear thrusts or sword cuts, the legs are especially awkward to defend with a shield. However by the time of Alexander the parablemata had gone out of use; it must have added significant weight and slowed movement. From a swordfighting point of view it is essential to be able to move your shield rapidly.

Armour

When braced in the line, lunging forward on the left foot, the hoplite's shield covered him from knee to nose. Sculpted to fit the form of the lower leg, greaves protected the shins and a helmet covered the head. Three pairs of bronze greaves were found in Tomb II at Vergina, including one pair that had been gilded. Bronze remained the standard material for armour that required shaping, such as greaves and helmets, even though iron had been used to make swords and other weapons for several centuries.

A rare, indeed so far unique, exception to this is the iron helmet discovered at Vergina. Though now brown with corrosion, when new and polished it would have 'glittered like silver' just as Plutarch described Alexander's helm at Gaugamela. Plutarch added that it was a 'work by Theophilos', telling us that this helmet was so exceptional that it was worth recording the name of the man who made it. It is of the Phrygian style with an enormously tall iron crest curling forward from the crown. Recalling Alexander's narrow escape from the helmet-cleaving sword blow at Issus, it is easy to see the practical function of such a design.

More usually associated with Alexander and his Companion cavalry, however, is the Boeotian-style helmet. Fashioned from bronze, it has a bowl-shaped crown from which hangs a metal skirt, wrought in folds that imitate pleated fabric. Aside from being pleasing visually, these folds gave added structural strength and the flared skirt offered good defence to the ears and neck. This was a helmet designed predominantly to deflect sword cuts, suggesting that sword use was on the increase, at least by enemy cavalry.

Also found in the tomb and made of iron was an astonishingly beautiful cuirass with spectacular gold borders and decoration. It is to date the only iron cuirass to have survived from this early date and was undoubtedly a rarity in its day. Polished to bright silver it would have made a spectacular garniture with the helmet. Fifty-eight pieces of gold sheet were found at the base. Decorated with palmettes, like the ones on the sword, these oblong pieces would once have attached to leather strips that hung from the base of the cuirass. Called *pteryges*, these created a double-layered kilt that gave excellent protection to the hips and groin whilst leaving the warrior's movement entirely unimpeded.

This exceptional cuirass, known in Greek as a *thorax*, is an exact imitation, in iron, of the most common form of body defence of the day – the *linothorax*. Made by gluing together multiple layers of linen to create stiff boards, the linothorax consisted of a breastplate, a back-plate, two side-plates, shoulder-plates and *pteryges*. When laced together with thongs, it pulls into the shape of the body. This is the type of armour being worn by Alexander in the 'Alexander Mosaic' from Pompeii. In that instance, as was common, it is

Iron *thorax* and helmet from Tomb II at Vergina (courtesy of 17th Ephorate of Prehistoric and Classical Antiquities, © Hellenic Ministry of Culture-Archaeological Receipts Fund)

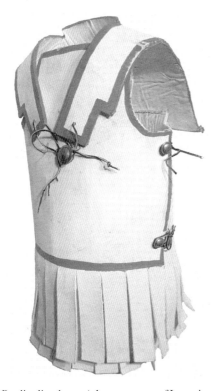

Replica linothorax (photo courtesy of Imperium Ancient Armory)

augmented with a wide band of overlapping metal scales around his midriff.

I had a 15-inch square section of linothorax made and did some rudimentary tests on it. When setting it up, I bent it to sit between pegs stuck into a straw target. Thus arched, as it would be laced around a body, it takes on the additional structural strengths of a curve and presents a glancing surface. Moreover it has a springiness that in yielding to an attack absorbs much of its energy. I threw spears, shot arrows and slung lead slingshot at it and slashed at it with a sharp sword. It stood up to a quite remarkable amount of punishment. Sword cuts that landed horizontal to the surface barely registered. Grazing cuts, drawing the sharp point across the surface, did manage to score a line through several layers, although they were not able to penetrate. Only committed thrusts with spear or sword were able to achieve significant penetration. With a sword, honed to needle-sharp, I managed only 1 inch of penetration; whereas without the linothorax and weighting my thrust as identically as possible, I was able to punch into the tightly-weft straw target to a depth of 4 inches. Although these back-garden results are only anecdotal, they indicate a surprising level of effectiveness for this type of armour.

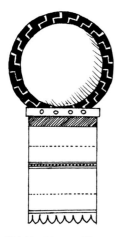

Shield with *parablemata*

Phrygian-style helmet like that at Tomb II, Vergina

Boeotian-style helmet

On crossing the Hellespont at the beginning of his expedition into Asia and making landfall at the ancient harbour at Troy, Alexander leapt from the prow of his ship in full armour, in order to be the first to wade ashore. Chest deep in the swirling brine, he was playing a part. It was a part he had been rehearsing all his life. He was Achilles.

Alexander saw himself as the living embodiment of Achilles, claiming direct descent through his mother's line. His tutor, the philosopher Aristotle, had encouraged the charade, calling his young charge Achilles by name and referring to himself as Phoenix, the tutor of Achilles. To the Greeks, the ancestors represented values and ideals that had to be lived up to and none were more potent as exemplars of conduct than the heroes of the *Iliad*. For centuries the *Iliad* had been regarded as the bible of the art of war and Alexander embraced this idea wholeheartedly. A copy of the *Iliad*, annotated by Aristotle, went with him always on campaign. He kept it in a casket under his pillow, together with his dagger.

At Troy, with all the attention to detail of a method actor preparing for a role, Alexander made a sacrifice at the temple of Athena and then exchanged his own armour for a panoply of arms that hung there, which was said to have belonged to Achilles. (Although he only wore this armour at the Battle of the Granicus, he had it carried before him in battle for the rest of his days.) He then laid a wreath at the grave of Achilles, and his lifelong companion, Hephaestion, laid a wreath at the grave of Patroclus. They ran a race, naked, in honour of their dead heroes.

In the footsteps of Achilles

It was widely accepted by Alexander's time that not only were Achilles and Patroclus real historical figures, they also were lovers. The actions of Alexander and Hephaestion at Troy are considered to be a public statement that their affections followed the same lines. Aristotle had bestowed the alter ego of Patroclus on Hephaestion as a boy and had so sown the seeds for this make-believe recreation of the heroes. In Macedonian society, as in Athens and Sparta, homosexual relationships, especially between warriors, were considered not only normal but also desirable. When Hephaestion died, Arrian reports that Alexander 'flung himself on the body of his friend and lay there nearly all day long in tears'.

When I visited the plains of Troy, modern day Hisarlik in Turkey, I kept my clothes on but I was nonetheless touched profoundly by the ghosts of the place. Galloping a chariot on the table-flat plain beneath walls of the citadel, I could see how the topography lent itself as a theatrical arena for the heroes to display their martial prowess. Here was a stage upon which their deeds could be witnessed. Of course, the way warfare was conducted in the twelfth century BC, the probable historical timeframe for the Trojan War, was entirely different to the way it was conducted at the time Homer was writing in the eighth century BC. Twelfth-century BC warfare was chariot warfare and the chariot archer reigned supreme. Anachronistically Homer has the heroes dismount from their chariots and fight with spears and swords in single combat, as they might have done in his own day.

There is no contention that Achilles was most famed for his skill with the spear, which may go some way to explain the continued pre-eminence of the spear as a weapon of status in Alexander's time. However, Homer also gives him plenty of sword action as in this edited passage from Book XX:

> Achilles drove his sword into his [Tros'] liver, and the liver came rolling out, while his bosom was all covered with the black blood that welled from the wound ... He also struck Echeclus son of Agenor on the head with his sword, which became warm with the blood ... Achilles cut his [Deucalion's] head off with a blow from his sword and flung it helmet and all away from him, and the marrow came oozing out of his backbone as he lay ... Their dying groans rose hideous as the sword smote them, and the river ran red with blood

Detail from a red figure Attic volute krater c 450 BC. Note grappling technique and sword prepared to thrust. The Metropolitan Museum of Art, Rogers fund, 1907 (07.286.84) (image © The Metropolitan Museum of Art)

This was Achilles as the quintessential warrior, mired in the midst of desperate hand-to-hand fighting and with the sword as his agent of triumph. He uses the sword again in single combat, such as when he confronts Lycaon:

> Achilles drew his keen blade, and struck him by the collar-bone on his neck;
> he plunged his two-edged sword into him to the very hilt, whereon he lay
> at full length on the ground, with the dark blood welling from him till the
> earth was soaked.

It is quite apparent from these descriptions that the xiphos is not only an extremely powerful weapon, capable of decapitation, but also that it was common practice to use it for both cut and thrust. Images of it in use are frustratingly rare. Technical manuals on the use of the sword, if they existed, have not survived. Nor has much of Greek painting, which may otherwise have given us a clearer visual picture of the ancient battlefield. What we do have though are pots. There is a wonderful pictorial resource in Attic-ware pottery.

A fifth-century BC *krater* (a bowl for mixing wine and water) in the British Museum shows Achilles in action, first against Hector and then against King Memnon of Ethiopia. In the Hector fight, both warriors are depicted using spears, even though Homer is specific that, having thrown his spear at the first moment, Hector fought this combat with a sword. On the krater both men are wearing their swords. According to the *Iliad*, Achilles triumphs with his spear and avenges the death of his beloved Patroclus.

Achilles (left) fights King Memnon, detail from red figure Attic volute krater c 480 BC (© Trustees of the British Museum)

In the funeral games held in Patroclus's honour, Achilles offers a sword as a prize for a sparring match with spears – the winner being the one who draws first blood. Homer describes it as a Thracian sword with a fine silver mounting. Achilles had taken it from Asteropaeus on the battlefield. Here is the sword as a trophy in both senses of the word.

In the *Iliad* it had taken the death of Patroclus at the hands of Hector to shift the brooding Achilles from his long sulk and move him to take to the field. The story of the *Iliad* is both paralleled and continued in the *Aethiopis* (a now lost epic, written in the following century) and here it is King Memnon of Ethiopia who provokes Achilles' vengeance by his killing of Antilochus. On the other side of the krater we see this encounter and I can't think of a more evocative, dynamic and vigorous figure in art portraying combat than the figure of Memnon, springing forward like a tiger and committing absolutely to the attack as he slashes upwards with his sword. You can almost hear his primal roar. Every sinew strains, every muscle coordinates to make the most perfect and beautiful of lines. It is a terrible beauty, revealing the bestial savagery of the human animal fighting for his life but this is not an untutored blow. Much can be made of man's fighting intuitions and instincts but there is a perfection of form that can only come from learned muscle coordinations. This is a move that could be replicated; it has martial function and therefore cannot be dismissed as an invention of the artist. I am quite sure that it comes from a culture of systemized swordfighting practice.

Achilles fights with spear and shield whilst Memnon carries two swords, one in his hand and the other still sheathed. Where Achilles holds his shield open to permit the thrust of his spear, Memnon uses a technique that we see time and again when fighting with shields. He uses it to hide the line of attack that the sword will take. From Achilles' viewpoint he will not see, until the last possible moment, whether Memnon's strike is coming in from above or below.

Single combat
Single combats such as those described in the *Iliad* should not be confused with the concept of duelling as it was to emerge later in Western Europe. *Monomachia*, as single combat was called, had a military context on the battlefield quite distinct from civilian duelling and was neither governed by the same principles of provocation nor by the same customs of practice. Most often it took place amidst the fighting of others. One is reminded of the samurai tradition of singling out a declared foe on the battlefield and announcing one's intention to fight him in particular. In either culture one is left wondering to what extent the waves parted and the named heroes were allowed to get on with it undisturbed and to what extent it was simply a literary device. Of course, in everyday life men were as likely to take slight and resort to fighting as ever they were or will be. On the expedition to India in 327 BC, Hephaestion quarrelled with Craterus, one of Alexander's most powerful and influential generals. According to Plutarch, 'they actually drew their swords and came to blows', before Alexander rode up and separated them.

Champions fighting on behalf of an army is yet another, altogether different, manifestation of single combat on the ancient battlefield. The unsettled *monomachia* between Menelaus and Paris was an attempt to resolve the Trojan War without further bloodshed among the armies but in spite of it appearing as a paradigm in the *Iliad*, Alexander never risked his fate on such a gamble.

The extent to which swordfighting technique was either valued or taught in Alexander's time is unrecorded. Plutarch tells us that Alexander endowed competitions for fighting with staves. It is perhaps most likely that these were long staves intended to substitute for spears, the weapon of first choice, but events may have also included bouts with shorter sticks as proxies for the sword. However there is no mention of a training methodology, which I find surprising. In the xiphos the sword had already evolved into an almost perfect form but one that would require good technique to fight with it effectively. Its balance and design showed an understanding of use that must surely have been accompanied with a formalized system of training both for the footsoldier and the horseman.

Makhaira/kopis/falcata

There is not enough evidence to suggest that Alexander once owned the sword from Tomb II, nor even can we be certain that it belonged to Philip Arrhidaeus. All that can be said for sure is that it is of the type used by the Macedonian army and that it resembles closely the depiction of Alexander's sword in the Alexander mosaic. He carries a similar sword in the bronze equestrian statuette of him in the Museo Nazionale in Naples and in other art works, suggesting that his weapon of choice was the xiphos but this is contrary to a commonly held view, which is that he carried into battle a type of sword called the *makhaira*. This idea is consistent with the writings of Xenophon, who was an advocate for the use of the makhaira by cavalry. Xenophon was someone who had actual cavalry experience in the field and who recorded his commentaries on horsemanship and cavalry warfare in exacting detail. Living just a generation before Alexander, his teachings remain freshly relevant to horsemen today; to Alexander they would have been the grounding gospel of his equine education. In his *On Horsemanship*, composed around 365 BC, Xenophon makes a specific recommendation:

> *I recommend the makhaira rather than the xiphos; for the rider being aloft, a cutting blow will be more in keeping than the thrust of a sword.*

Introduced around the sixth century BC, the *makhaira* has a recurved blade combining both convex and concave lines along its cutting edge. It is narrow closest to the hand with the cutting edge on the inside of the concave curve and then it swells to a broad width two thirds towards the forward end and has a cutting edge on the outside of what is now a convex curve. As it begins to sweep towards the tip, the blade re-curves again, tilting slightly upwards to orientate the point forwards in a straight line. These curves are elegant and subtle undulations. In cross section the blade is wedge shaped, having a thick back that tapers acutely towards the cutting edge. This puts a lot of weight into the blade, especially at its broader section, so that it hefts rather like an axe. An 'L'-shaped projection at the top of the hilt substituted for a pommel to prevent any risk of the makhaira slipping from the hand. A chain usually attached from the overhanging serif of the 'L' to the base of the hilt as an additional precaution. This arrangement was suited perfectly to such a blade-heavy weapon and at full swing the power was unstoppable. It was certainly a weapon to lop off the head of a Medusa but what would it do to a pig? I was once put in the position to have to answer this curious question.

We were filming a documentary on ancient surgery and my job was to create some wounds so that an expert in historical medical techniques could analyse the damage and then show how it could be remedied with contemporary techniques. The local butcher arrived with a side of pork and the hapless carcass was winched into position. With various other scenes to do that day, filming priorities meant that the pork hung there for about six hours in hot sun so that the skin hardened to a crackling crust, before I made my attempt.

I swung the sword and stepped behind the force of the blow, lending my full body weight to the momentum. The blade cut straight through the hide and bit deep into the flesh, creating a wound about 6 inches long and 4 or 5 inches deep. It didn't sever the carcass but it was enough. This was a potentially mortal wound. The makhaira is also furnished with an extremely sharp point that, because of the sophisticated re-curve of the blade, projects as a straight extension of the arm. Makhairas were cleverly designed cut-and-thrust swords. My thrust felt effortless as the blade punched straight through the carcass almost to the hilt. I then tried something else.

Many Indian swords have the cutting edge on the inside of the curve and in *shastarvidya*, the martial arts of the Sikhs, there are texts that talk about the killer blow being delivered 'when the breaths mingle'. The idea being that you manoeuvre close to your foe, lay the inwardly-curving blade on his throat and then effect the *coup de grâce* with a drawing cut as you step through. Tough, leathery pigskin, hardened by the sun, offered a significant disadvantage in attempting this move but nonetheless the makhaira did cut through, creating a wound some 4 inches deep.

Replica *makhaira/kopis* (author's collection)

I imagine that as well as using regular cutting and thrusting blows, the ancient Greeks also fought at very close quarters, with their breaths mingling, delivering the drawing cut.

Apart from affording the versatility to execute thrusts, chops and drawing cuts, the curves of the makhaira also gave it great structural strength. Multiple fullers ground along the upper edge of the blade, where it is thickest, provided additional rigidity and fine-tuned the weight and balance. It was a splendidly well-designed weapon. In many of the countries that felt the tread of Alexander's armies, it lived on in reincarnated forms such as the *kukri* and *sosun patah* in India and the *yatagan* in Turkey, but by the first century BC, swords with forward-curving blades and a cutting edge on the inside had begun to disappear from the European battlefield.

Another word linked with makhaira is *kopis* (plural *kopides*). Some argue that *kopis* (from the Greek *kopto* meaning cut) was used generically to describe any sort of curved knife, dagger or sword, whilst others state that there is a difference between the two based on alternative arrangements of curve. Weapon design was not standardized and examples could be relatively longer or shorter, broader or slimmer and with extreme or slight curves. Both words were probably interchangeable, in the same way that we can legitimately call a sabre a sword. If they were once more specific terms, their subtle differences have been lost.

What then of the *falcata* – the dread cleaving sword of Hannibal's Celtiberian troops in the third century BC – was this not of like design? The answer is yes, makhaira-type swords were not exclusive to Greece and Macedon and we see them in widespread use on the Iberian and Italian Peninsulas from the fourth to the first centuries BC, exhibiting only minor regional variations. Certainly in the case of Hannibal's Celtiberians, both infantry and cavalry, it becomes the principal weapon rather than a sidearm. However it wasn't until the nineteenth century AD that this sword type became known as the falcata – a made-up term extrapolated by Spanish scholars from a phrase in Ovid's Metamorphosis – '*ensis falcatus*'. *Ensis* is the Latin generic for sword (whereas *gladius* is a specific type of sword) and *falcatus* means 'sickle-shaped'. Clearly Ovid was referring to a kopis/makhaira-type weapon and given that the cutting edge is on the inside of the curve, it is not an unreasonable description, though we should be careful not to confuse it with the misleading 'sickle sword' cognomen of the Egyptian khepesh (see Chapter 1). 'Falcata' is used widely today as if it were a distinct type of sword but it is not a word that existed in the ancient world and nor is the sword of a different genus. Far better to use

Machiera, Villa Giulia, Rome (courtesy of Immagini della Soprintendenza per I beni archeologici dell'Etruria Meridionale)

machiera, the Latinized version of *makhaira*, when referring to the Spanish form of this sword-type.

A passage in Seneca's *De Beneficiis* uses this name – *machiera* – and alludes to the power of such weapons. He tells of an old veteran pleading his case with Julius Caesar and urging him to recall meeting him years previously after the Battle of Sucro (75 BC), where he had brought his exhausted general a drink of water in his helmet. An irritated Caesar denied that he knew the man but the plaintiff then explained the reason he did not recognize him was because he had subsequently suffered disfiguring injuries at Munda (45 BC); 'my eye was gouged out and my skull smashed in. Nor would you recognize that helmet if you saw it: it was split by a *machiera Hispania*'. The '*Hispania*' suffix may have conveyed some stylistic nicety to a contemporary but insufficient examples survive for us to classify them so precisely. They are all much the same thing.

In the Villa Giulia in Rome, a breathtaking treasure house of Etruscan and Faliscan archaeological finds, is a very good example of a *machiera Italia*. It in turn is identical to a Greek makhaira. Trade and cultural links between Etruria and Greece were strong during the classical period and there are many similarities in their art and artefacts. All we can say for sure is that these swords, with their characteristic curves, inside cutting edge and the weight-forward swell of the blade at the front third, co-existed.

It is perhaps apocryphal that the reason the Romans reinforced the edges of their shields with a metal or rawhide binding was in order to counteract the powerful blows from the machiera, with its enhanced ability to hook over the shield. It is nonetheless true that the Roman soldier had to face heavy cutting blows from the swords of his 'Celtic' enemies. However, for the most part these were not of the machiera type, rather they were the long, broad, straight-bladed weapons favoured by most 'Celtic' cultures in Iron Age Europe.

The long sword of the Celts

> *Their arms correspond in size with their physique; a long sword fastened on the right side and a long shield, and spears of like dimensions . . .*

> (Strabo, first century BC)

Our indiscriminate use of the word Celts to describe all the indigenous peoples of Iron Age Europe has been brought into question in recent years, most notably by the pioneering work of Simon James (*The Atlantic Celts*, 1999). 'Celtic' is an eighteenth-century construct and its widespread application has been somewhat romantic. Nevertheless it has entered the language so successfully that it has become difficult to avoid without seeming overly pedantic and, depending on context, there is a general understanding of what is meant by 'Celtic culture' and 'Celtic peoples'. It is important to remember, however, that the non-Roman tribes of Iron Age Europe were extremely diverse and not a single culture. Britons, Gauls, Helvetians etc were different peoples.

Gundlingen   Kammathen   Mindelheim   Muschenheim

Hallstaat C sword types

Stylistically on the other hand, and this applied especially to sword types, there were two pan-European cultural movements that dominated the Iron Age. In successive periods, objects of a common and distinct type had a universal distribution over a wide geographical area covering the bulk of central and western Europe. These material cultures transcended the ethnic, linguistic and other distinctions between different tribal identities. The first of these is known as the Hallstaat period.

Hallstaat, a small village near Salzburg in Austria, gave its name to an entire epoch and region of material cultural identity, after excavations there in the nineteenth century yielded an abundance of archaeological finds of a type that were subsequently found to be common throughout much of Europe. 'Hallstaat culture' begins in the Bronze Age around 1200 BC (Hallstaat A and B) but transforms to an Iron Age culture around 800 BC (Hallstaat C). The story of the sword in Iron Age Europe begins with Hallstaat C. Herodotus, a Greek historian writing in the fifth century BC, used the word '*keltoi*' to describe the people inhabiting an area of Austria, of which Hallstaat was a part. To that extent, at least, we may consider the homogenous artefact culture derived from Hallstaat as 'Celtic'.

Iron swords from the Hallstaat C period were typically similar to the bronze swords from previous eras, having a wide tang, a medial ridge, a sharp tapering point and leaf-shaped blades with narrow waists and broad shoulders. Mostly they were long horsemen's swords. The Iron Age didn't happen overnight and production of both bronze and iron swords continued in tandem for some considerable time. As iron manufacturing knowledge spread and improved, more swords were made, though there seems to have been a lull during the Hallstaat D period (600–450 BC). In Iron Age Celtic societies swords became an exclusively high status adjunct for the wealthy; spears remaining the most common arm for the masses.

The cultural successor to Hallstaat was La Tène. Named after its type-site on the shores of Lake Neuchatel in Switzerland, La Tène culture covered a slightly wider geographical area, including Britain, and was prolific from the mid-fifth to the first century BC. Bronze remained the metal of choice for scabbard fittings and many La Tène swords had elaborately shaped 'anthropomorphic' or 'antennae' hilts cast in bronze but blades from the La Tène period were made exclusively from iron. More exactly they were made from a low-carbon alloy of iron, a very basic form of steel. La Tène swords had straight, parallel-sided blades with narrow tangs. Towards the end of the period, La Tène swords on the continent began to favour rounded points, though many contemporary swords found in Britain remain acutely pointed.

It is my belief that rounded points developed because the metallurgy of early iron swords was not compatible with tapered points – they were too prone to bend and snap. This may seem paradoxical given the trend towards more slender tangs. However, a relatively soft metal makes for a resilient, shock-absorbing tang, whereas a point that comes into direct percussive contact with another hard surface, such as the enemy's shield, mail or bone, needs properties of hardness and toughness that only became available with the steels of later centuries. Iron Age blades were not yet tempered by quenching and had very little springiness. Once bent out of shape they could remain deformed in the same way that an iron coat hanger will hold its new shape when twisted.

Polybius, writing in the second century BC, reported that the iron swords of the Gauls bent in battle:

> from the way their swords are made, only the first cut takes effect; after this they at once assume the shape of a strigil, being so much bent both length-wise and side-wise that unless the men are given leisure to rest them on the ground and set them straight with the foot, the second blow is quite ineffectual.

I had long puzzled about this and wanted to test it. I had a replica made with about the right metallurgy. In other words it was a fairly soft wrought iron, having a low carbon content, around 0.3%, consistent with archaeological finds of the period. It was a hefty piece and I swung it with full force at a baulk of timber sunk into the ground.

The edge of the blade bit into the wood, demonstrating that the strike was effective and, sure enough, a slight bend could be perceived in the blade. This bend was along the flat of the blade rather than edgeways and so had been generated by the torque of the blow rather than the direct action of the strike but even so it showed that Polybius had a point.

It took several powerful blows before the sword was deformed to the extent that there was a need to straighten it. Any one of those blows would have killed a Roman. So if I had been a Gaul I wouldn't have been too unhappy that my sword had bent a little and if I had been a Roman I should have been wary of Polybius's confidence that the second blow would be ineffectual. I was able to straighten the blade in a matter of seconds by placing the tip on the ground and applying a sliding pressure along the blade with my foot.

The minor distortions occasioned in combat should not be confused with the quantities of Iron Age swords that have been retrieved from bogs and river beds, bent double or even folded over twice into an S shape. These swords have been ritually 'killed' and it is clear from their shape that they have been bent deliberately over a knee rather than become damaged in use. Iron Age peoples laid weapons and other precious objects in lakes and rivers and bogs as votive offerings to their gods. Sometimes they were bent before being laid in the water; sometimes they were not. Water was the divide between this life and the next. Such offerings may have been a way of giving a departed hero his sword to use in the afterlife.

Ritual offering sites may have been watched over by druidic priests or priestesses attracting centuries of tradition and mythology. It is perhaps not so very far-fetched to imagine tribal authority being bestowed upon a leader by one of these guardians presenting him with a sword dredged from one of these places. It would serve as a symbol of ancestral legitimacy and carry with it a suggestion of magical power. Could this be the origin of The Lady of the Lake? Was she an old legend who re-emerged in the Arthurian romances?

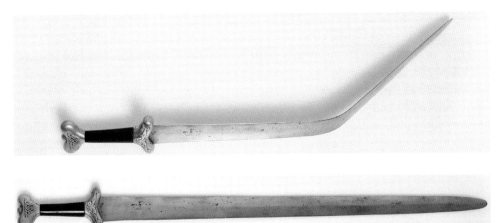

Replica Iron Age sword from author's collection, straightened by hand after bending

A current theory in circulation is that if Excalibur were bronze then it could have been made in a stone mould, hence 'the Sword in the Stone.' It's an ingenious theory but I don't see a bronze sword as having currency in the fifth century AD, which is when an Arthur figure is most likely to have existed, if he existed at all. It is perhaps easier to conceive a legend deriving from a sword that was found stuck in a crevice in a dried up riverbed; such a story could transform easily into the 'Sword in the Stone' legend.

History and legend can reverberate with a similar echo when we try to navigate in the fog of the distant past. The passage about swords that bent in battle from Polybius' *Histories* follows his account of the Battle of Telamon in 225 BC, some twenty-two years before he was born. What he says must presumably have resonated with his contemporaries but this was not eyewitness journalism.

Naked warriors

Telamon was a battle on a staggering scale between a coalition of 'Celtic' tribes, numbering some 70,000 men, and the Roman Republic mustering forces of around 75,000. Aside from the possibly exaggerated spin about the inferiority of 'Celtic' swords, Polybius' account is famous for telling us that one of the tribes fought naked:

> The Insubres and Boii wore their trousers and light cloaks, but the Gaesatae had discarded these garments owing to their proud confidence in themselves, and stood naked, with nothing but their arms, in front of the whole army, thinking that thus they would be more efficient, as some of the ground was overgrown with brambles which would catch in their clothes and impede the use of their weapons.

Brambles! A more unlikely reason for fighting naked is hard to imagine.

The Gaesatae were from Gaul and, according to Polybius, had been hired to fight alongside the Boii and Insubres. They were light front-line, skirmishing infantry and their custom of fighting naked probably had a ritual and cultish significance. Such extreme bravado and heroics might also be compared with the frenzied excesses of Viking *berserkers*. These were the men of the red mist. One may imagine a combination of alcohol and magical invocations on the morning of a battle bolstering their bellicosity and sense of invulnerability. Drink played a large part in Celtic military culture. During the Punic wars, in which the Carthaginians employed hosts of Celtic mercenaries, there is a story of one band in Sicily being so drunk that they put up virtually no resistance to their Roman foes.

At Telamon, the Gaesatae were only a very small part of the enormous Celtic army, which also included chariot squadrons and cavalry, as well as regular infantry. The Gaesatae did not fight naked because they were primitive. Good quality mail shirts, sturdy helmets, leather and woollen clothing were all available to them. The Gaesatae fought naked because, above all, it was psychologically intimidating to their enemies.

Human beings feel extremely vulnerable when naked and that is probably the point. Any warrior who can stand unbowed and naked in the middle of a battlefield would seem to have conquered fear itself and, in the words of Polybius 'the naked warriors in the front ranks made a terrifying spectacle'. He goes on to say that they 'were all men of splendid physique and in the prime of life . . . the mere sight of them was enough to arouse fear among the Romans'.

With his reference to the trousers of the other tribes, Polybius is unambiguous that in this instance he means completely naked. However, the phrase naked could equally apply to troops who were simply unarmoured or merely stripped to the waist. Baring and displaying the torso is a fundamental act of male primate aggression display – from the gorilla beating his chest to the football hooligan on a drink-fuelled night on the town with his shirt off. Military attire, from the wasp waists and puffed chests of Gothic armour to the extravagant confections of braid on a hussar's dolman, often exaggerates a proud and jutting chest. As well as the aggressive body language of taking one's shirt off, there is a consequent freedom of movement and, potentially, enhanced ability to fight. Removing all one's clothes takes these principals to the extreme.

Inextricably associated with the image of the naked or half-naked warrior, especially with regard to the Ancient Britons, is the idea that they were painted or tattooed with woad. Woad is a cabbage-like plant that produces a strong dye. Depending on how it is prepared, the dye is either black, green or blue. A blue face, seemingly drained of blood, presents a terrifying countenance. When this is combined with hair that has been spiked with lime, imitating raised hackles of anger like some proto-punk rocker, and the intimidating carelessness of nudity, a snarling Celtic warrior thus adorned would daunt even the most stoic of foes.

However, psychological warfare aside, there may have been other reasons for covering oneself with woad. In the days before the safety razor, when shaving nicks were an everyday event, a common accessory was the styptic pencil. This alum-based stick was an astringent, causing blood vessels to constrict and thus staunching the flow of blood. Woad works in exactly the same way. It is also an antiseptic, a fungicide and an insect repellent. In the interests of scientific enquiry I once tested its coagulating capability by making a cut on the back of my arm with a razor blade. Rubbing the wound with moist woad leaves had an immediate effect and the bleeding stopped. I am not suggesting that woad would have such a dramatic effect on a major sword wound like a half-severed arm, merely that it was probably used in the treatment of wounds. As such, applying it before battle may have been considered to have a magical prophylactic effect. The thinking being: if that's the stuff you need to cure wounds, then by wearing it, it will prevent you from getting them. More simply the idea of fighting naked and daubing oneself with an antiseptic paint could have derived from an observation that dirty fibres of clothing entering a wound would result in serious infection.

It would be a mistake to deduce from this, as some have, that the 'Celts' always fought completely naked. For the most part Celtic peoples were well clothed and, after around 300 BC, those that could afford them wore mail shirts in battle. Mail shirts were often handed down through the generations. Many warriors had mail, which they wore over padded linen tunics – one Irish text recommends twenty-four layers of linen for the padding. There was nonetheless a tradition of the naked warrior. In cooler climes this may only have meant stripped to the waist but the Gaesatae were not alone. A second-century BC terracotta relief from Civitalba in Italy shows near-naked warriors, wearing only cloaks and bearing shields. A completely nude warrior, armed with sword and shield, squares up to an Etruscan horseman on a fourth-century BC stone relief in Bologna.

In Rome's Villa Giulia is a set of fourteen small bronze figurines that once adorned an Etruscan cinerary urn. They date to around the time of Telamon. Standing approximately 2.5 inches high, each figure is animated differently and with a different face and body. They are an enchanting little army of toy soldiers, all of whom are naked and posed energetically in fighting postures, with a sword in one hand and some sort of cloak over their left forearm. From the scale of the figures it would seem that the cloak has been wound around the arm several times and the loose end hangs only 18 inches or so below the arm. Raising the left forearm to defend the face and other parts of the body is the most intuitive and basic form of instinctive defence for the human animal. Padding that limb with layers of textile would make even a naked warrior feel significantly less vulnerable. It would certainly be possible to step in and block sword blows with a padded arm before they reached full momentum though I doubt that wraps of textile would be sufficient to prevent the broken bones that would surely result from receiving a fully committed blow at the end of its swing.

Three figures (out of fourteen) from an Etruscan cinery urn, c 200 BC – Villa Giulia, Rome (courtesy of Immagini della Soprintendenza per I beni archeologici dell'Etruria Meridionale)

Here the hanging folds would come into play. If judged correctly it would be possible to parry a cutting blow so that the point struck just below the forearm. The loose but heavy material would absorb the energy of the blow, in the same way that loose archery backstop netting can stop an arrow, and prevent it from being able to reach the body.

Many of the figures stand with their sword-arms raised above their heads and with the blade pointing directly backwards. This suggests another application for the cloak. It could be used held in front of the sword hand to obscure that hand from an opponent's view. In this way the preparation and line of an attack is hidden until it is already underway, taking one's adversary by surprise.

Cut versus thrust

The swords of the Villa Giulia figures are large, broad-bladed weapons with rounded points in La Tene style. They are shown being wielded with cutting blows, consistent with Polybius's account: 'For as the Gallic swords were only formed to give a falling blow, a certain distance was always necessary for that purpose'. Certainly, large slashing swords have been unearthed from Iron Age sites and the larger sword is what we might expect for such elite troops in the vanguard of the assault on the enemy line, just as in later periods we expect to see the two-handed Dane axe in the hands of a Viking berserker or a great two-handed sword in the hands of a 'blood squad' Landsknecht.

Gaius Atilius Regulus, one of the two consuls commanding the Roman army at Telamon, fell victim to the scything power of a barbarian's sword. Whilst fighting valiantly in the thick of battle, he was decapitated and, according to Diodorus Siculus, 'his head was brought to the Celtic King'. Headhunting was an important armament in the Celtic arsenal of psychological warfare. Diodorus Siculus, writing in the first century BC, also reported that, 'They soak the heads of their more illustrious enemies in cedar oil and keep them carefully in a chest and show them off to strangers'.

At Telamon, hydra-like, the Roman army had another head and, under the command of the consul Lucius Aemilius Papus, Rome eventually triumphed after a day of much slaughter. It was estimated that the Celtic armies lost 40,000 men with a further 10,000 wounded. Polybius attributes this in large measure to the tactics of the legionary sword:

> The Romans, on the contrary, instead of slashing continued to thrust with their swords which did not bend, the points being very effective. Thus, striking one blow after another on the breast or face, they slew the greater part of their adversaries.

It is far too simple to say that thrust beats cut every time. Both have their different merits. However, it is probably fair to say that in a tight press of men, mass numbers thrusting with short swords create a more efficient killing machine. The immense numbers at Telamon, compressed by Roman pincer movements, meant that there was a considerable crush, thus inhibiting the Celts in their normal mode of fighting. A similar fate awaited Boudica's army in the first century AD, when they were forced back against their wagon train with no room to manoeuvre. What Polybius is really praising here is the Roman tactic of compacting the enemy and in such circumstances the Roman gladius is an ideal weapon. Longer cutting swords need a certain amount of space to be wielded effectively.

Making blades relatively thick in cross-section was a way of compensating for deficiencies in rigidity that were an inherent problem with the longer Celtic swords. This would result in quite heavy swords and heavier swords are less suitable for blocking blows; the weight of the defending sword combines with the weight of the attacking blow, making resistance more difficult. This is not too much of a problem provided that you carry a shield.

According to Polybius, the lack of shields amongst the Celts at Telamon was the reason so many perished beneath the hailstorm of *pila* (Roman javelins) hurled by the legionaries at the start of the battle. If you didn't have a shield in hand-to-hand fighting, the main defence, for swordsmen and spearmen alike, would have been dodging, sidestepping and generally avoiding blows with graceful athleticism. It was a way of fighting ideally suited for the showy prowess of a hero culture and displays of acrobatic aptitude were part of the prelude of boasts, taunts and challenges that warriors performed before a battle.

Horsemen favoured longer swords because they had the advantage of reach and, as we see with the Villa Giulia figures, some elite infantry might choose a longer sword with which to charge headlong into the enemy ranks, mowing a swathe of carnage before dying nobly. However not all Iron Age swords were of this type. On the contrary, archaeologically they are in the minority. Smaller, shorter swords have been found far more commonly, though it is difficult to tell whether this represents the actual distribution of sword types during the period or archaeological accident. Additionally there were regional preferences and fashions changed over time. Celtic armies were diverse in their troop types, giving rise to varied sword designs, but many preferred a shorter, lighter sword. They favoured speed and agility as they stepped and leapt in their nimble dance with death.

One advantage of a shorter sword, given the metallurgy of the time, is that it would be less prone to bending in battle. This meant that it was also suitable for thrusting as well as cutting and it would be a mistake to imagine that the foes of Rome never noticed how useful the thrust could be in battle. A marble statue of a fighting Gaul in the Metropolitan Museum of Art, New York, tells a different story. Although consisting only of the lower limbs, from waist to knees, and the right foot, it is enough to show that the man is stretched out, right foot forward, in an extended lunge. The most perfect example of a little Iron Age sword, suitable for both cut and thrust, is to be found in Britain. It is the sword of the Kirkburn Warrior.

The sword of the Kirkburn warrior

Then they slip between the squadrons of cavalry and leap off their chariots and fight on foot.

(Julius Caesar, *Gallic Wars* IV.3, 58–51 BC)

This exquisite specimen has been described by the British Museum, where it is now exhibited, as 'probably the finest Iron Age sword in Europe'. It is a terrific little weapon and can be dated to between 300 and 200 BC. Given its age it is in remarkable condition and was found in 1987 in a warrior's grave at Kirkburn in East Yorkshire.

The Kirkburn sword had an owner as illustrious as any to be found in other chapters of this book. We do not know his name but it is reasonable to assume that he was either a chieftain, or at the very least, a famed warrior. Aged around 30, the man with whom the sword was buried would have been an old man, given the life expectancy of the times, and he was clearly a venerated figure in his society not only to have had such a sumptuous sword but also to have been given the status of a grave burial. Three spears were driven into his chest after he was laid in the grave as part of an elaborate funeral ritual.

Grave burials were rare in the Iron Age; although in recent years there have been a number of finds of high status burials in this part of the Yorkshire Wolds. For me the most exciting of these was at Wetwang in 2001, which resulted in the BBC commissioning me to lead a team to reconstruct and field-trial an Iron Age British chariot. Driving that chariot from the British Museum to Hyde Park Corner through the London rush-hour traffic was quite an adventure and a high point in a life dabbling with things historical but that is a story for a different book. Chariots, however, are pertinent to this story. Adjacent to the grave in which the Kirkburn sword was found lay another grave in which was interred a man with a chariot. Other chariot burials in Yorkshire, nineteen to date, have been found at nearby Garton Slack, Garton Station, Ferrybridge and Wetwang. This was a chariot society and we may imagine our warrior going into battle aboard a chariot. His sword, however, is far too short to be able to be used with any effect from a chariot. It measures just over 27½ inches overall, the blade being a fraction under 22½ inches – and chariots are of necessity extremely wide-wheelbase vehicles. Even a tall man would not be able to reach beyond the wheels from the platform of a chariot with a sword of this length. In fact you would need a sword with a blade in excess of 4 feet for it to be of any use from a chariot.

A passage from Julius Caesar's Gallic Wars sheds some light on the use of chariots on the battlefield. Caesar was writing a hundred and fifty or so years later but it seems likely that the tactics he witnessed are likely to have been age-old traditions. He says:

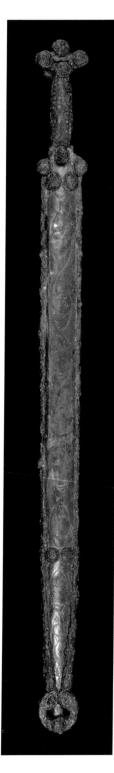

Hilt of the Kirkburn sword (© Trustees of the British Museum)

They jump down from the chariots and engage on foot. In the meantime their charioteers retire a short distance from the battle and place their chariots in such a position that their masters, if hard pressed by numbers, have an easy means of retreat to their own lines.

In other words the chariot was used as a kind of battlefield taxi and remedied the problem of enabling a warrior to catch his breath when in the thick of the fighting. Even the fittest of men will tire after several minutes of hard fighting. Delivering blows that are capable of severing limbs requires huge reserves of energy. A professional boxer today is a supremely fit athlete but needs a breather after just three minutes in the ring slugging it out with committed blows.

A sword as splendid as the Kirkburn sword may well have been exclusively for ceremonial wear but it is tempting to think of our warrior leaping from his chariot and entering the fray, sword in hand. Then, when he was tiring, the chariot would come galloping by and he would grab a handrail and leap on as it passed. I have done this and it is a very efficient way to get out of a tight spot. The trick is to pass your sword into your other hand – it is perfectly simple to grasp shield and blade in one hand – thus freeing your right hand to haul yourself aboard.

The Kirkburn sword (© Trustees of the British Museum)

Sword suspension

A possible encumbrance to jumping up smoothly would be a metal scabbard hanging from the waist-belt and an answer to this potential problem may lie with some little votive chalk figures, also found in Yorkshire and dating to the second century BC. They depict warriors with swords slung across their backs. Now exhibited in the Hull and East Riding Museum, these charmingly naïve sculptures, with their amusingly emphasized masculinity, have been found at Wetwang and at Withernsea, an outlying area of Garton Slack, both well-known sites for Yorkshire chariot burials. Wearing long, hooded cloaks and determined, grim expressions, these small figures (110mm/ 4.3in high) offer a unique view of a people barely represented in art and only glimpsed at from the writings of Roman authors. In all there are twelve figures and ten of these

Chalk figure from Withernsea, Hull and East Riding Museum (photo ©Trustees of the British Museum)

show the sword being worn on the back, attached by means of a single belt strapped around the chest. One was found with a model wooden shield. They are a rare piece of visual evidence for how the sword may have been worn by this particular warrior culture.

On the rear panel of the scabbard of the Kirkburn sword is a raised strap retainer, giving a means of attachment to a belt or baldric. This iron fixing sits at about the midway point of the sword, which would not be a good point of balance for a sword worn in a waist-belt, so it is consistent with the idea of it being slung over his back. A further corroboration is offered by the fact that the sword was found placed behind the warrior's back in the grave. Grave goods were often disassembled and laid in positions unrelated to their location in life, so they are not always a reliable indicator. Nevertheless it does seem likely that this was the fashion for this particular culture.

This is a small and lightweight sword and the strap retainer is broad and deep. I do not doubt that the sword would hold in place with a single thick strap. An advantage of this arrangement is that there would be a fair amount of pivot around this point, making it possible to change the angle of the sword as it was drawn, thus enabling it to be pulled down towards the shoulder and withdrawn almost horizontally. How wonderful our unnamed warrior must have appeared from the front with that beautiful hilt just showing itself above his shoulder. Thirty-seven pieces of iron, bronze and horn were used in the manufacture of this dazzling work of art, which was then adorned with the opulent sparkle of red glass enamel. The tarnish of time has faded much of the colour from this and other surviving Iron Age artefacts and the stereotype of a primitive people in drab rags has been the mainstay of television and cinema imagery. However, the Ancient Britons lived in a richly colourful, gaudy and beautiful visual world. Theirs was a culture steeped in craft and art; necklaces of amber beads, objects enamelled with coloured glass or studded with garnets, torques and bracelets in gold and silver, all survive to attest to a love of adornment and the sword of the Kirkburn warrior is about as pretty as it gets.

Three globular lobes function as a pommel and matching hemispherical studs are located at the top of the grip on either side, harmonizing with the lobes to make a quatrefoil arrangement. It is almost a mirror image of what is traditionally referred to as the 'cross-guard' but which I prefer to call the 'stop' on such swords. This has a trefoil arrangement of similar lobes, only set at ninety degrees to the pommel. Unusually this stop crosses the hilt in both planes. In the plane extending either side of the blade are lobes set at a downward angle. Two raised studs, placed centrally either side of the flat of the blade, complete the arrangement. Material is missing which would have filled in between the stud and the blade and only the little iron posts remain to give us evidence of how they were set. I would guess that the material might have been horn and that it would have been rounded off smoothly, making the whole configuration of the four tangential and down-turned lobes fit snugly into the dimple formed by thumb and index finger when making a fist to grasp a sword. It is a superbly ergonomic design for a thrusting sword, cushioning the impact against the hand that is otherwise so discomforted by the thrust when a cross is used as a stop.

There can be little doubt that this sword was intended for thrusting as well as cutting; it has an acutely pointed blade. Polybius has a lot to answer for. His sweeping statement that Celts used exclusively cutting blows has condemned generations of scholars into believing that this was the universal practice of all Celtic cultures throughout the entire Iron Age. The physical evidence of the Kirkburn sword and many like it found in Britain suggests a different view.

The scabbard has survived in fair condition and there are signs that it was repaired during its active lifetime, a testament to its value. Framed with an iron skeleton, it had a front panel of hammered bronze decorated with a chased La Tène-style scroll pattern. This split along one of the incised lines and it has been joined neatly with small rivets. It is brown now but imagine it pristine and gleaming golden. Traces of red glass indicate that the chape and chape-frame were coated with scarlet enamel, as were the fixing plates of the strap retainer on the reverse side. Such lavish attention to decoration in a place not seen when the sword is worn is yet further witness to its status.

Near the scabbard mouth and at the top of the chape-frame are pairs of studs with domed caps. Like the lobes on the hilt, these too were once brightly enamelled with red glass. Their function is obscure and it may be that they served only as ornament. In the next chapter we will look at 'peace strings', a custom that involved tying the sword into its scabbard. The upper studs could assist in this function but there is no record of the practice this early, neither does it explain the purpose of the lower studs. It is just possible that the studs were part of a system for wearing the sword – leather straps with keyhole slits at their ends could toggle over such an arrangement and form some sort of cross harness over the shoulders. However I think that, as on the chalk figures, a broad belt through the near-central strap retainer would be adequate.

From the evidence of the local chalk figures and from the positioning of the strap retainer near the centre of the scabbard, it seems likely that the Kirkburn warrior wore his sword across his back. Throughout the rest of the Celtic world however the normal means of sword suspension was by means of a waist belt in the form of a chain. The Celtic warrior wore his sword on his right hip, as did the Roman legionary. It is perfectly possible to draw even a moderately long sword from the right, although it

Chain sword belt

is clearly easier to negotiate longer swords with a cross draw from the left hip. To understand why both Celts and Romans wore their swords on the right, we need to look at their shields.

Celtic shields appeared in a variety of shapes and sizes but, by the late Iron Age, their larger shields were very similar to Roman shields in a number of respects. Both were large, ranging from 4ft to 4ft 10in in height, and were either oval or tall rectangles with rounded ends. Both were bound at the edges with a metal or rawhide rim. This should perhaps be more properly called a tyre because it 'tied' the boards of the shield together just as a metal tyre (tyer), contracting after being fitted red hot, 'ties' the rim of a wooden wheel together. On the Celtic shield there is a metallic axial spine, aiding structural rigidity, and a central boss. Roman shields have only the central boss. In both cases the central boss allows for and protects the fist, which carries the shield by means of a horizontal handhold. There is no other means of carrying either shield – no guige strap over the shoulder, no straps for the forearm. Celtic and Roman shields are heavy and they are carried like suitcases. Not only that but they are carried on the march. I am mystified as to why they didn't have a shoulder strap or why they didn't put their shields on a wagon for marching but they didn't, they carried them. Roman shields were often made even heavier on the march by having a thick leather cover to protect them from the elements, which could otherwise cause them to warp.

Carrying a heavy shield in the left hand for mile after mile would become excruciatingly painful if you had to hold your arm out at any sort of an angle, owing to

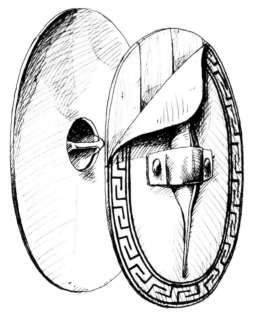

Celtic shield   Roman shield (scutum)

the bulk of a sword hilt on your left hip – try it the next time you carry a suitcase by sticking a rolled up newspaper in your belt. Some female readers may find this less difficult because in many cases there is a tendency for their arms to hyperextend at the elbow by about 10 degrees and as a consequence bags don't brush against their legs as much as they do on most men. For men, as well as affecting the angle of the arm, a sword on the left would also have a tendency to chafe when carrying a shield. Hence both Celts and Romans wore their swords on the right.

An exception to this rule was the Roman centurion. He wore his sword on his left hip but then he didn't carry a shield. It is not known whether Caius Valerius Primus was a general, a centurion or a legionary but his sword is undoubtedly a most splendid example of a *gladius.*

The sword of Caius Valerius Primus

> *Puncta duas uncias adacta mortalis est*
> *A stab wound two inches deep is fatal.*
>
> (*Vegetius – De Rei Militari*, AD 390)

Found by an amateur archaeologist on a spoil heap at Wiesbaden in Germany in 1972, this fine example of a Roman gladius is now in the Royal Armouries at Leeds. The spoil had come from an excavation of a Roman site at Mainz, the Roman *Moguntiacum,* situated on the opposite bank of the River Rhine. Dated to the second half of the first century AD, its grip and pommel have long rotted away but the blade has survived in

Gladius of Caius Valerius Primus, Royal Armouries, Leeds (© The Board of Trustees of the Armouries)

Detail of Valerius' blade, showing dot-punched inscription

good condition. Measuring 19⅛ inches, the parallel-sided blade is of flattened diamond section with a pronounced, non-flattened, diamond section point.

Both sides of the blade bear dot-punched inscriptions proclaiming the owner's name in multiple forms. On one side it is rendered as 'C. Valer Pr' and 'C. Valeri Pri' and on the other it reads 'C. Valeri P', 'C. Raniu' and 'C. Vale Primi' I'm guessing, but I suspect that C[aius] Raniu[s] was the original owner and that he either sold the sword or lost it in a game of dice to C[aius] Valeri[us] Pri[mus]. Caius Valerius the Elder, by repeating his name twice on each side, leaves us in no doubt about his superior claim to ownership. Another possibility is that Ranius may have been killed in battle. Perhaps Valerius was his friend and that is why the 'C. Raniu' has not been scratched out? Whatever the truth of this guesswork, it is none-theless thrilling to see a sword that has such a direct and personal connection to an individual Roman soldier.

Compared to swords of other periods, archaeo-logical finds of Roman swords are relatively rare and seldom in as good condition as the sword of Valerius. It is therefore difficult to determine how common it was to mark a sword with one's name. Certainly it was not a universal practice. Equally certainly, swords have always been very personal weapons – a Middle Bronze Age dagger found at Lachish, now in the Israel Museum in Jerusalem, bears an inscription in cuneiform indicating that the dagger belonged to 'R. N. S.' – and therefore seem obvious candidates for this sort of identification.

Soldiers of the early Roman Republic, a militia army recruited exclusively from landowning citizens, had good reason to mark their personal equipment and weapons – they were obliged to purchase their own! However Caius Valerius Primus was a soldier of the Roman Empire, living around 150 years after the Marian reforms. In his day weapons were provided by the state. Caius Marius, an uncle of Julius Caesar, is

The gladius of Caius Valerius with its scabbard fittings, Royal Armouries, Leeds (© The Board of Trustees of the Armouries)

often credited with introducing measures which transformed the Roman army into a full-time professional force. There were advancements in logistics, training and tactics but at the heart of these reforms had been the opportunity for Rome's poorest citizens to embark on a military career. Strictures on owning land were lifted and the *capite censi* ('the head count') flocked to the eagle standards.

If Valerius had an army-issued sword, why would he need to mark it with his name? One possibility is that men who lost army-issued equipment would likely suffer severe penalties and so the theft of other men's gear could have been a common problem. Another explanation is that this was not a regulation-issue weapon. It is undoubtedly of fine quality and therefore quite possibly the purchased sword of an officer – perhaps that of a centurion? Centurions, who on occasion rose from the ranks, were officers of considerable wealth and status. During the second half of the first century AD, a centurion, depending on his age and experience, could earn between 5,000 and 20,000 denarii per year compared to the paltry 300 denarii per year paid to a legionary.

If an officer of higher rank, such as a tribune or legate, had commissioned the sword one might expect the lettering to have been inscribed by a specialist artisan but the work is too crude for this. I suspect that Valerius did it himself, so casting him as a middle-ranking officer seems most probable. He could equally have been an *optio* (second in command to the centurion) or *tesserarius* (guard commander), but in the absence of evidence I am going to imagine him as a centurion – one who fought his way up from the lower ranks and who then proudly proclaimed his new status by inscribing this prestigious sword with his name.

Much of the prestige of this weapon also came from its fine scabbard or *vagina*. Highly decorated tinned-bronze mounts survived with the sword, though the tinning has all but worn away, and the wood and leather sheath itself has long turned into dust. Elaborate scenes depicting a winged Victory are depicted on the various fitments with cutaway and engraved motifs. This was not the sword of an ordinary soldier.

Fighting with the gladius

In its earlier incarnations the Roman army had three main types of line infantry – *hastati*, *principes* and *triarii*. They carried a sword but it was not always their primary weapon. In the hands of the *hastati* and *triari* the spear was still used to form a phalanx and was a principal weapon of hand-to-hand combat. However by the first half of the second century BC, the *hastati* had exchanged their spears for two javelins and a sword. Roman line infantry were gradually homogenized and they carved their victories with the sword. By the time of Marius all infantry troops had became the same, spears were obsolete and the sword was universal. Every legionary was armed with two *pila* (javelins) and a gladius. After the initial decimating salvo of iron-shod pila, which took place in the first few seconds of an enemy coming within 30 yards, the entire legion drew their swords and set about their bloody business.

Perhaps the most distinctive element of the sword under discussion is its reinforced diamond section point. This is clearly intended to assist in punching through armour and it is an excellent design for that purpose. The Roman gladius is frequently described as an exclusively thrusting sword but in my view that is to overstate the case. Tactics dictated that it was used in this way when employed in the tight confines of fighting in close formation, but it was equally suited for cutting and slashing moves when opportunity arose. Pick up a good replica and you will feel that you have in your hand a big slashing knife. Training and discipline can ensure that the soldier used it only for thrusts in drilled situations but once a battle became disorganized and troops spread over the field, the freedom to mix cuts with thrusts enhanced the legionary's versatility in a fight. Even the Romans could lose a lot of their formation and shape as a battle developed.

The military writer Vegetius has much to tell us about Roman fighting styles in his *De Re Militari*, though it is important to keep in mind that he was writing in AD 390 and there was a certain amount of interpretation to his accounts of past Roman practice. He was already looking back to an idealized golden era. He says:

> They were likewise taught not to cut but to thrust with their swords. For the Romans not only made a jest of those who fought with the edge of that weapon but always found them an easy conquest. A stroke with the edges, though made with ever so much force, seldom kills, as the vital parts of the body are defended both by the bones and armor. On the contrary, a stab, though it penetrates but two inches, is generally fatal.

We may quibble that a stab wound of two inches in the thigh or even the belly is unlikely to be fatal, whereas a slash across the throat is probably a mortal blow; however the essence of what he is saying is that small, economic moves were preferred to wide, swinging cuts. That is because the paramount goal of the legionary battle formation was to hold formation for as long as possible. To this end it was essential that no individual stepped out of line to engage in ad hoc combat. That meant that rigorous discipline had to be applied to which moves were permissible in line. Powerful cutting strokes could easily pull a man out of position. Short stabs were the order of the day and that also precluded the notion of the legionary thrusting his gladius into the stomach of his foe and then turning it up towards his entrails as some modern writers have suggested. Such a move, whilst viable in open combat, is too large and too time-consuming for formation fighting.

Stepping always with the left foot forward, dense and deep lines of legionaries would advance on the enemy, smashing into them with their shields as they corralled them into an ever tighter space. In striking with their shields they sought to unbalance their foe, sealing their advantage with a short, punching thrust. Moving onwards relentlessly, their arms ramming forward and drawing back like pistons, the front line attacked with an unremitting barrage of buffets and stabs. A useful tactic was to drive your shield into the man opposite you, thus neutralizing any threat from his attack, and then to thrust at the man to your right as he stumbled from the bruising impact of your neighbour's shield. As hobnailed boots trod on the freshly fallen, there were ranks of legionaries behind ready to dispatch any that moved with downward thrusts. They were also there to plug the gap, should a legionary fall. It has been said before but these coordinated and disciplined tactics turned the Roman legion into a killing machine, a meat grinder that processed enemy corpses with brutal efficiency. The realities of engagement are likely to have been a little more ragged than this ideal but the principles held broadly true.

Vegetius reminds us that many vital parts of the body were protected by armour. Bearing this in mind the optimal target for a thrusting blow is the face. It is also the most intimidating. Polybius, writing nearly 600 years earlier, tells us

> The Romans who were armed with swords that were sharpened at the point, were able to direct their thrusts against the breasts and faces of the enemy, and give wound after wound without remission.

Other clues are offered by Dionysus of Halicarnassus (63 BC–AD 14) with this description of legionaries in battle:

> Holding their sword straight out, they would strike their opponents in the groin, pierce their sides, and drive their blows through their breasts into their vitals. And if they saw any of them keeping these parts of the body protected, they would cut the tendons of their knees or ankles and topple them to the ground ...

Here we have testimony that when it was appropriate, the legionary did not disdain to use the cut. In support of this is the evidence of skeletons such as those from Maiden Castle in Dorset. This magnificent hillfort was besieged and taken by the Romans in the first century AD and the bones of the fallen, which were buried in a mass grave, show a high proportion of wounds from cutting blows. Of course any discussion about the use of the sword as a decisive weapon must be taken in the context of appreciating that the infantry legions were not the only forces on the Roman battlefield. Roman armies consisted of auxiliaries, cavalry, archers and artillery in the form of *ballistae* and *catapultae*. Missile warfare was waged on a massive scale but it is only the sword we are concerned with here and certainly it was the sword that dealt the final blows to achieve victory.

Gladius types

The term '*gladius*' derives from the phrase '*gladius hispaniensis*', used to describe a type of short sword of Spanish pedigree that was adopted by the Roman army

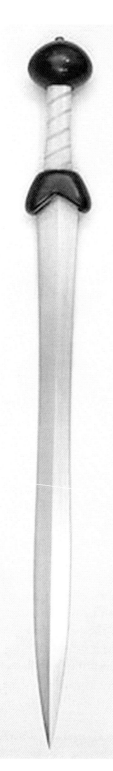

towards the end of the third century BC. Archaeological evidence is slight for early examples, the Republic-era weapons excavated at Grad near Smihel in Slovenia in the nineteenth century, dated to around 175 BC, being among the earliest found so far. From these and images in art it is generally agreed that the *gladius hispaniensis* had a leaf-shaped blade measuring around 26 inches in length. Over time the trend was for these swords to become shorter and broader.

As I have already noted the Latin word for sword is '*ensis*' and so if *gladius* is also a word for sword, the phrase *gladius hispaniensis* seems absurdly tautologous. Why would this be? Etymologists suggest that '*gladius*' was probably the native 'Celtiberian' word for sword. Certainly it is homophonic with the Gaulish '*klaydos*' and has common roots with the Gaelic *claidheamh* (as in 'claymore'), which are the words for sword in kindred languages. To any third-century BC Romans unfamiliar with the word it would need qualifying, so saying 'the *gladius hispaniensis*' would be a bit like talking about 'the *sgian dubh* Scottish dagger' or 'the *tulwar* Indian sword'; linguistically incorrect but the sort of thing that people say. However none of this tells us what was different about it. It has passed into accepted mythology that the Romans adopted a new kind of thrusting short sword that revolutionized their tactics, but the wrong importance has been attached to the length of the blade. It was the hilt that was different.

There is no trace of the hilt on the sword of Valerius but it would have conformed to the standard pattern of the day. With a greater emphasis placed on the thrust, the Roman gladius (and presumably its Spanish predecessor) favoured a domed stop rather than a cross to prevent the hand from sliding onto the blade, one that sat snugly into the dimple of the fist. Its leaf-shaped blade was a sure sign that the gladius was intended as a cut and thrust weapon and with the cross gone there was a need to find a new solution for securing the sword against slipping from a tired hand when slashing. This was achieved by providing an outsized spherical pommel to act as a backstop to the hand.

Replica gladius hispaniensis (courtesy of Nathan Bell and Morrow Blades)

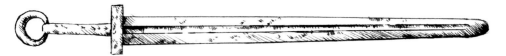

Roman ring pommel gladius

Made from light materials such as ivory, bone or wood these very large pommels had no adverse affect on the balance of the sword. Grips were ridged to further enhance the security of the grasp. Decorative variation was often achieved by selecting combinations of the various materials, so that for example you might have a pommel and stop made from maple together with a grip fashioned from either willow or bone.

During the latter part of the second century AD the Romans experimented with an entirely iron grip for the gladius. Based on swords they had encountered during their incursions into lands surrounding the Black Sea – it was a Roman characteristic to plagiarize and adapt the technologies of other cultures – these iron hilts had a narrow iron cross and an iron pommel in the shape of a ring. This cross was not wide enough to place a finger over and so served only as a harsh forward stop. Retaining a similar circumference to the old spherical pommels, the iron ring pommel continued to function as a backstop. It is also highly probable, though no evidence exists, that some form of lanyard attached to the ring to provide added insurance against a dropped sword. Ring pommels were possibly a way of retaining the external dimensions of the old spherical pommel whilst utilizing a significantly heavier material. However, by the third century AD we see a return to organic materials and spherical pommels, though in a flattened, more ovoid form.

There are two main types of gladius, identified primarily by their blade shape and known by the name of the find site where the original model was unearthed. Firstly there is the 'Mainz' gladius, which has a broad, leaf-shaped blade with lengths ranging from 16 to 22 inches. An intermediate variety, named after a specimen found at Fulham in London, has a slightly straighter blade, but it is really only a sub-type of the Mainz. Quite different was the 'Pompeii' gladius. This had straight, parallel sides, a reinforced point and ranged from 16 to 20 inches long. It began to supersede the Mainz pattern around the second half of the first century AD. Ironically, the sword of Valerius, though coming from Mainz, is actually of the Pompeii type. Although this design may suggest a greater reliance on the thrust, it had sharp edges and cutting blows remained an option.

Both legionaries (on the right) and centurions (on the left) wore the sword high on the chest so that it was kept clear of the legs. Unencumbered marching was of overriding importance. Like the Greek xiphos, the Roman gladius was suspended by means of a baldric worn over the shoulder. Although wearing the sword attached to a belt predominated after the fall of Rome, baldrics remained the system of choice in the Eastern Empire and Byzantine soldiers continued to wear even the knightly sword of the Middle Ages in this fashion.

Replica Mainz style gladius (courtesy of Legia II Augusta)

Replica Pompeii style gladius (courtesy of Legia II Augusta)

The legions of Mainz

Mainz, situated by a river in forested, iron ore-yielding country, may have been a centre for sword production. Records show that during the last quarter of the second century AD, Gaius Gentilius Victor, a veteran of Legio XXII Primigenia, spent his discharge bonus establishing a business there as a *negotiator gladiarius* – a manufacturer and dealer of arms. Like arms dealers through the ages he must have made a pretty profit and he left 8,000 *sesterces* (2,000 *denarii*) in his will for a monument to the Emperor Commodus. One of Rome's many mad emperors, Commodus actually fought in the gladiatorial arena himself and was perhaps a patron of Gentilius's wares.

Caius Valerius the Elder most likely lived during the latter part of the first century AD, so he couldn't have bought his sword from Gentilius; besides, in Gentilius's time ring pommel gladii were all the rage. Frustratingly there is nothing to tell us to which legion Valerius belonged. Legio XXII Primigenia (the 22nd 'Firstborns') was stationed at Mainz in 39 AD and remained there continuously until at least the end of the third century AD. It was the legion with the longest continuous connection to this significant frontier fortress at the very edge of the Roman Empire.

Thirty years earlier, less than a day's march away, the Roman army had suffered one of the worst defeats in its history. Three legions (XVII, XVIII and XIX) under the command of Quintilius Varus were wiped out in the Battle of the Teutobergerwald by a confederation of German tribes led by Arminius. It was a military calamity of unimaginable scale and it halted for good any aspirations of Rome to expand her influence into German lands beyond the Rhine. Mainz (Moguntiacum) guarded a tense and insecure border.

Several other legions undertook extended tours of duty at Mainz at various times including the IIII Macedonica (4th Macedonian), I Adiutrix (1st Rescuer), XXI Rapax (21st Predator) and XIIII Gemina (14th Twins). The latter also saw service in Britain and was one of the legions that defeated Boudica in 60 AD, after which they were awarded the title *Martia Vitrix* (Martial Victory). We can only guess to which legion Valerius belonged.

For a Roman, being sent to the northern borders was not always the best of postings; the climate was cold and wet and the natives hostile. Patrolling the windswept wastes of northern Britain on Hadrian's Wall, for instance, cannot have seemed an

Relief carving from the fortress at Mainz. Note these legionaries are not in armour, so this may represent a training exercise. The man in the second rank still has his pilum and shields the one in front from missiles (courtesy of Landesmuseum Mainz)

enticing prospect, even though there is evidence that they had sheepskin liners available for their boots. Mainz on the other hand offered a less harsh option. It was the base of a Roman river fleet and so, instead of footslogging marches, much of the border could be patrolled by river galley. I have bent my back to the oar on a replica of one of these craft, on the Danube at Regensburg, and have to say that it beats marching. Smaller and sleeker than their sea-going counterparts, river galleys are capable of a significant turn of speed. Standing on the forecastle at the prow and leaning against the arching neck of the figurehead as you watch water break over the ram, or contemplate gentle scenes of riparian life as they pass by, is even more pleasurable and that is where a centurion would have stood if, on occasion, he joined these patrols. Equipped with a central square sail, these galleys could also make progress along the river without any undue exertion.

Sword drill
Daily life would also have included exercise, drilling and training duties. Roman soldiers practiced their sword skills at the *pell* – a stout wooden post set into the ground and standing around 6 feet tall. Vegetius tells us that

they gave their recruits round shields woven with willows, twice as heavy as those used on real service, and wooden swords double the weight of the common ones. They exercised them with these at the post both morning and afternoon.

A clear advantage of using practice weapons that were heavier than standard is that strength and stamina could be built for the relevant muscle groups at the same time as training technique.

Vegetius explains that they sometimes aimed at 'the head or face, sometimes at the sides, at others endeavoring to strike at the thighs or legs'. In other words this wasn't just standing there and working out by striking the same spot; they mixed it up, rehearsing combinations of moves, and Vegetius goes on to say that they were 'instructed in what manner to advance and retire', letting us know that footwork was an equally important part of the pell training system. I have found that it is very effective schooling to step both clockwise and anticlockwise around the pell, changing direction at uneven intervals and to deliver a constant onslaught of thrusts and cuts as well as stepping in intermittently to smash and shoulder-check with the shield. Thrusts are perfectly possible at a round post, though, bearing in mind that it is an immoveable object, it is vital to gauge your distance accurately for fear of jamming your hand too hard against the stop. However, what such a target cries out for is cutting blows. If the Romans had intended the gladius to only be used for cutting, they would have devised a different target for training.

Training at the pell was also part of the daily regimen for gladiators but a study of their practices is beyond the scope of this present chapter. It is however worth noting that the wooden sword held a particular significance for the gladiator. Not only was it the weapon he employed to learn his trade but in the event of serving his time

and defeating all his opponents he might be awarded his freedom and the symbol of this was the presentation of a wooden sword (*rudis*).

It was the centurion's duty to keep his men fit and trained for combat. Route marches, close-order drilling and swimming were just some of the routine activities. Roman soldiers were expected not only to be able to run and jump in full kit but also to be able to swim in their armour, an especially useful ability for those stationed on the Rhine. As well as an open-faced helmet, which had a reinforced brow to protect

Practice at the pell

Wooden gladius – *rudis* – made from oak circa AD80 (Tullie House Museum and Art Gallery, Carlisle)

against downward strikes from the Celtic long sword, the legionary of the first century AD wore *lorica segmentata*. This consisted of overlapping lames of plate armour fastened together by means of leather straps and rivets. There is no evidence for anything being worn underneath other than the basic tunic. I am quite sure that there must have been some form of padded textile armour either attached as a fixture to the metal armour or worn as a separate garment. All metal armour is part of a composite defence with the metal either resisting, slowing, or deflecting the penetration potential of a strike and the padded section absorbing the shock of the blow. It makes no sense that the Romans would have disregarded this paradigm but for the moment there is a lack of evidence.

Lorica segmentata (Latin for 'segmented armour') is a modern term, coined to differentiate between various types of Roman armour. A Roman would have referred to his armour simply as *lorica*, whatever its type. Prior to the first century AD, legionaries wore a tunic of mail (*hamata*) that continued in use for auxiliary troops after the introduction of *lorica segmentata*. It is tempting to think that the Pompeii type gladius was developed to defeat the new crustacean-like plate armour but, although there was the odd revolt and discord in the Empire, Rome didn't experience civil wars in the same way that she had in the previous century. The Pompeii gladius was designed to fight Rome's enemies and they were wearing mail. Tests need to be done with replicas of the appropriate metallurgy but I suspect that a powerful man would be able to punch through mail defences with the reinforced point of a Pompeii gladius.

Replica Corbridge pattern lorica segmentata (courtesy of Imperium Ancient Armory)

For the mock battles that also formed part of a legion's regular training, sword points were covered with leather caps or wooden swords were used. Such free-style practice was essential to sharpen reflexes and responses and to familiarize the soldier with the environment of battle. Combats could be between individual pairs or with larger groups. Centurions in particular became adept martial artists capable of holding their own in the chaos and frenzy of the battlefield armed with just a sword. Grappling and unarmed techniques would have been a part of their repertoire.

On the battlefield, once the legionary lines began to unravel, and it was inevitable that they eventually did, or once the enemy began to turn, then there were opportunities for soldiers to win personal fame and glory by their martial exploits.

Discipline was of course important in holding those lines for as long as possible but battles cannot be won by discipline alone. There must be fighting spirit, martial ability and a will to win.

Screamed orders from a growling centurion, the throb of painful blows from his gnarled vine-stock (*vitis*) and the humiliation of being shamed in front of other men may keep the fearful man in the line but it will not give him victory when he comes face to face with an enemy determined to triumph. Unthinking automaton responses inculcated by endless drilling may stop the coward from running away, as did the threat of the veteran to his rear killing him before he could break rank by so much as a step, but an army of

Replica lorica hamata (Courtesy of Legio II Augusta)

drilled and disciplined men does not create a military empire of the longevity and scale of Rome if those men are too scared and frightened to fight. That was achieved by *virtus*.

Virtus was a concept that embodied ideas of manliness, honour, courage and fighting prowess. These qualities were valued highly in the Roman army as, of necessity, they are and have been in every army. Being good at fighting was something to be admired. Heroes were lauded both by the state and by their comrades. Men fight at their best when they are in pursuit of personal glory. They also fight for their comrades. Close bonds were developed within the small squad of legionaries known as a *contuburniam*. It consisted of eight men and they trained together, marched together, dined together and billeted together. In battle there was a pressure to not disgrace oneself in front of one's fellows and a desire to display bravery and skill for their admiration. In a play by Plautus (254–184 BC) the wife of a soldier sings:

> I want my man to be cried as a victor in war: that's enough for me. *Virtus* is the greatest prize. *Virtus* comes before everything, that's for sure. Liberty, safety, life, property and parents, homeland and children it guards and keeps safe. *Virtus* has everything in it: who has *virtus* has everything good.

Victory was often secured by the might of the artillery, astute tactical deployment of the legions or a timely countermove with auxiliaries but the glories attached to personal valour and great deeds of arms were largely the province of those wielding a sword.

The spatha

The gladius was not the only sword to be carried by Roman forces. Auxiliary cavalry favoured a longer-bladed weapon called the *spatha*. A magnificent example of a spatha blade, dating to between AD 80 and 100, was found at the Roman fort of Newstead (Trimontium) in the borders of Scotland. It is now in the National Museum of Scotland in Edinburgh. Including the tang, it is 30½ inches long, with a blade of 24½ inches.

An inscription on an altar-stone at the fort refers to 'Aelius Marcius, *decurion* of the Vocontian wing'. A *decurion* commanded a *turma*, which is a cavalry troop of 32 men. The wing (*ala*) comprised of either thirty-two or sixteen *turmae* and the 'Ala Augusta Vocontiorum' were an elite cavalry unit recruited from the Vocontii tribe of southern France. They shared the fort at Newstead with the XX Legion.

Cavalry swords were longer than the gladius because of the advantage in having additional reach when cutting down at men on the ground. The Roman cavalryman could lean quite a way out of his cleverly designed saddle in order to deliver these blows. Stirrups were not introduced into the West until after the incursions of the Huns in the fifth century AD. Roman cavalry used a 'horned' saddle. One of the coldest and longest nights I have ever endured was spent sitting on a Roman horned saddle. It was for television and we filmed from late afternoon until four in the morning through sleet, snow and biting winds but, in spite of the discomforts of that night, I can honestly say that there is nothing that you can do in a saddle with stirrups that you can't do in a Roman saddle, except stand up. Its only downside is that, unless you are riding in it everyday, it will fatigue you more quickly. Throughout that long, wet, shivering night there was a constant trade-off between dismounting to give one's body a rest from the pain of unsupported legs and the need to stay in the saddle in order to keep it dry. A supple young Vocontian cavalryman would not have had this problem.

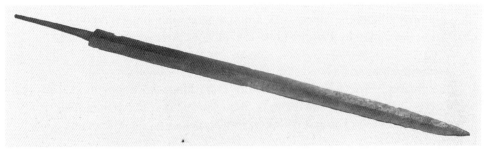

Spatha blade circa AD80–100 found at Newstead (© The Trustees of the National Museums of Scotland)

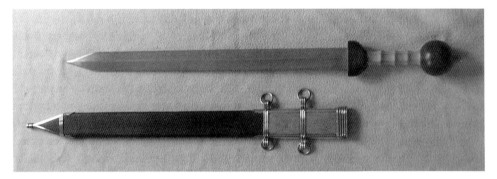

Replica spatha (courtesy of Legio II Augusta)

In terms of fighting function the Roman horned saddle works very well. Two curved horns at the front of the saddle curl over the front of the rider's thighs. By exerting pressure against these you are able to keep yourself securely seated at all paces. You are prevented from sliding back in the saddle when pushing against the forward horns because you are stopped by two upright horns at the rear. These also allow you to sit into impact, whether thrusting with spear (*contus*) or sword. When using the sword, the forward horns support you when leaning out at remarkably extreme angles and assist in levering you quickly back to an upright position. In this respect they are arguably a better aid to the swordsman than are stirrups. The spatha was a sword designed for the particular needs of the cavalryman and it was used in conjunction with a specialist saddle intended to maximize its potential.

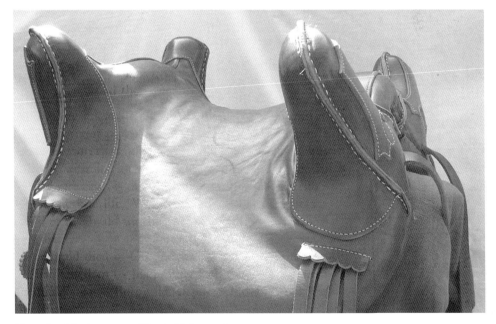

Horned saddle (courtesy of Legio II Augusta)

Blade manufacture

Whatever the type of sword, the main problem faced by Iron Age smiths was how to ensure that it had the right mix of metallurgical properties distributed throughout the blade. What we need from a sword blade is something that is both hard and tough. This means producing steel – an alloy of iron and carbon. The higher the ratio of carbon to iron, the better the quality of the steel and the greater the potential for creating a harder metal. The harder the metal, the better it can take a sharp, cutting edge. Think of a piece of tool steel, the sort that is used to make a file for instance. You can feel that it is very hard, you can see the precision of the incised lines of the file's cutting teeth and if you tap it against another piece of metal you will hear it ring in a distinctive way. This hard steel will give an excellent cutting edge but if you strike it with a hammer it will easily fracture. It is brittle and that is not a quality you want in a sword blade. Iron, on the other hand, is a soft metal. Think of a length of iron wire, such as a coat hanger. It is easy to bend but has the disadvantage that it will not take a keen cutting edge and it will bend under pressure and stay bent – not a desirable property in a sword, as Polybius was so keen to point out.

Part of the answer was to create the right sort of steel but early production methods made it difficult to ensure a consistent ratio of carbon to iron. Moreover different qualities were required for separate parts of the blade. A softer core made the blade more resilient and springy, whereas harder steels enabled the edges to be honed to a keener sharpness. It is difficult enough to produce a material that satisfies these conflicting demands with the sophisticated steels available today. In the Iron Age it was a process that was in its infancy but which produced some ingenious solutions.

In the beginning there is a lump of rock – iron ore. To extract the metal from the ore, crushed rocks are heated in a charcoal-fired furnace known as a bloomery hearth. These hearths, in effect small clay ovens, were the only method for extracting iron and they didn't reach the sorts of temperatures necessary for cast iron; this was not possible in Europe until the late 15th century. Fortunately iron can be successfully extracted from its ore without the need to liquefy it completely. At 800° Celsius the iron compounds are reduced to solid iron particles, then, at temperatures of around

A billet of low-carbon steel, Roman circa 1st century AD. Note that one end has been drawn out to show ductility and the other end has been hammered into a flare to show malleability. The shaping indicated that this was good quality workable metal. A gladius would probably require two billets (courtesy of Hector Cole)

1,200° C, the non-metallic elements in the ore, such as silicates, react to produce a liquefied, glass-like material, known as slag. This lava flow of slag runs out of the furnace, bringing with it the particles of solid iron. It cools to form a bloom – a spongy mass of iron and slag. This can be hammered out into useable ingots, although they still contain an amount of slag.

Mostly, the product that emerged from the bloomery hearth was infused with carbon derived from the charcoal in the furnace. We know it as 'wrought iron'. Insofar as it contained carbon, it was a form of steel, albeit relatively inferior by modern standards. One problem was that the carbon would not be evenly distributed throughout the bloom. Some parts might be carbon free, while others would contain a fair amount. It took a skilled ironworker to identify and separate the harder parts of the bloom from the rest. A bloom was therefore broken down, 'wrought', into smaller pieces, each with a different metallurgical profile. Swords could be made from a single piece of reasonable quality or from a composite piece of metal that was created by a method we call 'piling', which combined pieces with different levels of carbon.

Piling entailed heat forging together individual flat bars in a sandwich-like construction and then utilizing the resulting bar as the blank for the blade. So, for instance, a hard, high-carbon piece could be sandwiched between two lower-carbon bars of softer metal. More complex arrangements alternated hard and soft metals in a stack. These could be either piled up with their edges aligned and flush or with the edges offset. The resulting stock could then be worked further by re-heating and folding, which helped to homogenize the distribution of carbon. Both the Newstead spatha and the gladius of Caius Valerius were made utilizing a piled technique.

Piling was the most common method of producing Roman blades but there was another process, 'pattern welding', that had been used as early as the fourth century BC. Pattern-welding became increasingly popular in the manufacture of high-status weapons as time went on but perhaps reached its peak of prestige amongst the Germanic and Scandinavian peoples in the fifth, sixth and seventh centuries AD. In the next chapter I have chosen a sword that belonged to the leader of one of these peoples who, in the wake of Rome's abandonment of Britain in 410 AD, crossed the North Sea to create a new homeland. The people were the Angles and the sword is that of King Raedwald.

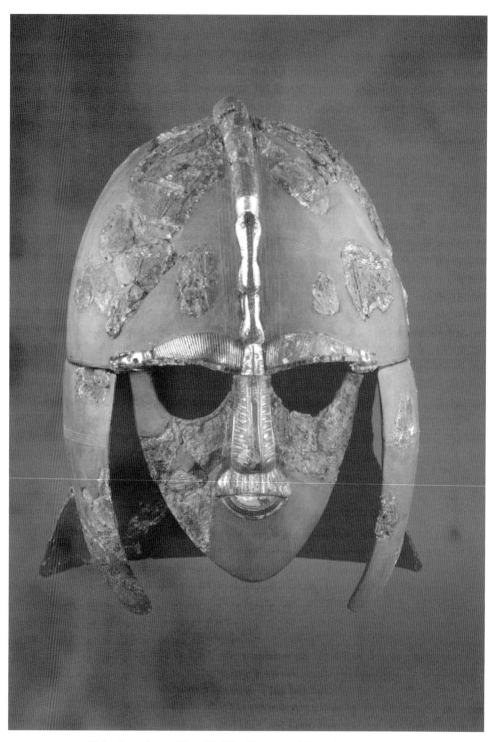

Helm from Sutton Hoo (© The Trustees of the British Museum)

Chapter 3

The Sword of King Raedwald, King of the East Angles

The sword, shining and ornamented, drove in so that the fire abated

(*Beowulf,* seventh century AD)

It lay buried for around 1,300 years. Even when found, it continued to hide its charms from the world; coyly dressed in the drab browns of corrosive rust and concreted sediment, its elegant lines bent, broken and distorted by the weight of soil and time. Imagine it, though, in its original state. Then the sword unearthed from the Sutton Hoo ship burial in 1939 would have been an object of astonishing and arresting beauty. Its broad, bright, pattern-welded blade, one of the finest examples of its type, a testament to the artistry of the man who made it; and its elegant hilt, mounted with superb gold and garnet fittings, witness to the status of the man who owned it.

That man was King Raedwald, King of the East Angles, who died around 627 AD. At least he is the most likely candidate; this burial is not without its mysteries. I've always wondered why we speak so little of the Angles, the peoples from Northern Europe in the lands between modern-day Denmark and Germany, who settled in Britain during the fifth, sixth and seventh centuries; the peoples who give us the name English. We hear of the Anglo-Saxons, we frequently hear of just the Saxons, but hardly ever do we hear of the Angles.

This seems especially strange when we consider the extraordinary splendour of the Sutton Hoo finds. The Angles weren't incidental sidekicks to the Saxons; they colonized a much wider area of Britain and theirs was an independent and vibrant cultural force all of its own. Anglian material culture was one of high artistic achievement, as the objects in the grave attest. Objects proclaiming that here was once a vibrant and energetic people ruled by a powerful and charismatic king. His sword resonates with the power of the man who bore it and his helmet, with its enigmatic, anthropomorphic face guard, stares out at us across the ages, urging us to look into the eyes of the man who wore it and to see him and his world.

Sutton Hoo lies between Ipswich and Snape on the east coast of Britain, in East Anglia. For two months in the summer of 1939, the British press buzzed with excitement as the ship burial was excavated, yielding, almost daily, some new, incomparable treasure. The grave goods were removed to the British Museum in August 1939 but when the Second World War started the precious treasure had to be entombed once more. This time, with rather less dignity, in an underground railway tunnel connecting to Aldwych station. It wasn't until 1946 that the objects were finally brought into the light. What joys they revealed!

Pattern welding

X-rays showed that the blade had been pattern-welded. A manufacturing process that produced decorative motifs, pattern-welding was achieved by heating and twisting together bundles of carbon-infused iron rods and hammering them flat into a workable bar. It was a variation on the piled method and one that enabled a visible pattern to be predetermined. These patterns were not only discernable on the surface of the metal but ran right through it in the same way that 'Blackpool' runs through a stick of rock.

As noted in the previous chapter, because of the way iron was extracted from the bloomery hearth, the rods tended to have different metallurgical compositions; some having a higher carbon content than others. Additionally, the level of impurities, known as slag and consisting largely of silicates, varied considerably. Differences in each rod's composition showed up as fine dark lines when the rods were heated and welded together under the hammer. An expert smith could control and create the pattern he wanted just by the way he set the twists in the rods. In many instances, though not all, separate steel cutting edges were then forged onto the core.

Throughout the Saxon and Viking eras, the heyday of pattern-welding, Norse poetry describes some of the patterns with phrases such as 'swathes of mown corn', 'blood eddy' and 'wavy serpent'. Clearly there was much artistry and such blades were prized as high-status objects. A great deal is talked about pattern-welded blades being of superior quality. In fact the opposite is true and they are prone to being a little brittle. Pattern-welding was used because it had aesthetic appeal and for no other reason.

Sword from Sutton Hoo (© The Trustees of the British Museum)

The swordsmith begins with iron rods that contain a chance amount of carbon from the bloomery hearth – at best, poor-quality steel. In purchasing these rods as 'trade bars', the smith would assess each individually to try to select those of the best quality. He would gauge how heavy they felt in the hand and listen to what note they sounded when rung – it wasn't science but a smith was also considered to be something of a shaman. When heated to red-hot welding heat, these rods would then absorb more carbon from the smith's forge as they were twisted and welded together.

Initially the bar of twisted rods forged by the smith is brittle and has to be tempered to reduce the risk of cracking. Tempering involves reheating the whole bar, though to a much lower temperature than for forging. Gentle reheating reduces hardness a little but reduces brittleness considerably. The length of time that the metal is held at tempering temperature is critical and a smith can just as easily ruin a blade by getting it wrong. There was skill, judgement and chance at every stage of the process. No wonder that when a sword was perfect it was revered. In spite of these improving stages, the glass-like slag inclusions could not be eliminated entirely; indeed they were fundamental to creating the pattern and it was the high incidence of these that rendered a pattern-welded sword more brittle than a steel blade forged from a single billet.

Hector Cole at his forge (author's photograph)

Whilst filming for a television series, I spent a day with blacksmith Hector Cole working on a pattern-welded sword. Hector is one of those rare individuals who inspires. The joy, the relish, the pride and the simple, infectious enthusiasm with which he goes about his work lifts the spirit. Here is a man who is so connected to what he does and who never seems to tire of its thrills. Every pull on the bellows arm and the resultant roar of flame in the furnace seems to elicit fresh delight as if he's never done it before and the excitement with which he brings a new object into the world is that of a man who knows he has just created something.

Whilst forging together bundles of rods and beating them flat, I got to work as Hector's 'striker'. The smith brings the work from the forge onto the anvil and lays on the first strike with his hammer. The striker must then follow with his strike and they continue with alternating blows until the smith indicates the return of the work to the forge by two sonorous taps on the anvil. It is essential to keep a good rhythm so that neither hammer clashes with the other and in this way a constant strike rate can be generated, maximizing the amount of work done on the piece while it is still hot. The percussive ringing of blows on the anvil was a Wagnerian moment and I was amazed at how soft the metal felt beneath the hammer.

The bundles of twisted rods were all prepared on one day and Hector set aside a separate day to forge them into a blade. That job alone is pretty much a day's work and once started cannot be interrupted. The whole piece is maintained at welding or

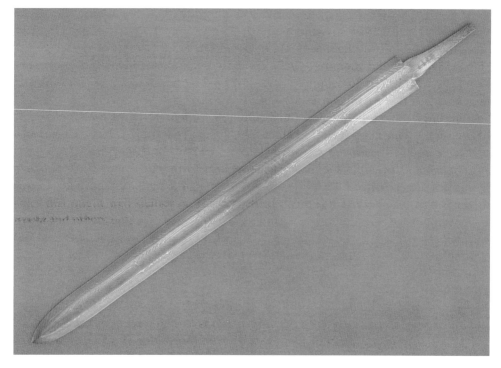

Replica of Sutton Hoo blade (© The Trustees of the British Museum)

near-welding heat until the forging is finished. Then
it is quenched; plunged sizzling and spitting into the
water tub and is reborn as a harder, tougher metal.

It is an attribute of steel that its physical properties
change when it is quenched – that is heated to red-hot
and then cooled by plunging it in a liquid. Depending on the rate of cooling, the molecules in the steel
are rearranged to create a steel of greater hardness.
Quenching hardens steel, whereas iron is unaffected
by the process. It is this unique quality that makes
steel such a perfect material for arms and armour. The
act of quenching is a moment of high drama. It is the
instant that the sword is given life. This is followed
by hours of patient grinding to smooth the surface
and sharpen the edges. Finally the hilt is fitted. Now
the sword can be held, becoming an extension of the
warrior's self.

The blade of the Sutton Hoo sword is so corroded
to the decayed wool lining and wooden boards of
its scabbard that it cannot be extricated from the
oxidized mass, but x-rays have shown the pattern to
be immensely sophisticated. On display at the British
Museum is a reconstruction of what it may have looked
like when new. Eight separate bundles, each comprising seven rods, formed the core. These bundles
were hammer-forged together, side-by-side, creating
a striped pattern down the blade and each stripe was
patterned in an alternate style. Four of the bundles
were twisted in such a way as to produce a herringbone
pattern, while the other four were left untwisted to
produce a pattern of parallel lines. These juxtaposed
patterns were framed by the plain cutting edges to
produce a blade of sophisticated beauty.

Blades can either be polished to a mirror-bright
finish or, if the pattern is to be brought out as a
feature, treated with acid. Hector uses the urine from
an in-season mare and it's pretty pungent stuff! It
was, nonetheless, a magical moment when he swabbed
it over the blade's surface. The pattern appeared in a

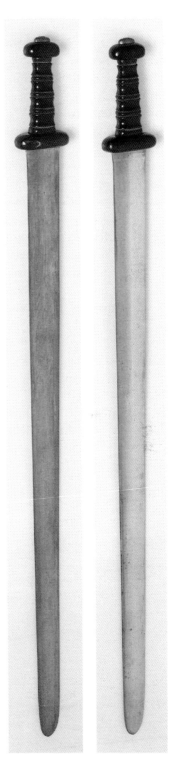

Pattern-welded sword, made by Hector Cole, from the author's
collection; one side treated with acid to show the pattern, the
other polished bright

matter of moments and it was as if the outer skin had become translucent, allowing you to see the veins and arteries. I can see how a poetic and superstitious people, with animistic beliefs, could so readily attach human character to a sword. When he judged that the acid had done sufficient work, Hector arrested the process by neutralising it with a wash of water. Not only did the blade now display its rich pattern but the acid had also induced a gentle golden patina. It was absolutely glorious. Different acids produce different tints; tannic acid, for instance, creates a bluish black. In the poetic descriptions given to swords in the Norse sagas, there are frequent hints that blades have colour as well as pattern and who can doubt that this soft gold would have been the most prized hue of all?

The pattern I had asked Hector to create was a serpent pattern, reminiscent of the markings on a snake's back. In *Beowulf* the poet describes the pattern on a blade as being 'variegated like a snake'. There is also a tale in *Kormac's Saga*, which makes reference to a snake pattern on a blade. The hero, Kormac, has to fight a duel with a famous old berserker warrior called Bersi. Kormac begs Skeggi, another famous Icelandic hero, to lend him his sword. The sword is called *Skofnung*. Skeggi tells Kormac that when he draws *Skofnung*, he should blow on the blade and he will then see a small snake slither out from under the hilt. Kormac dismisses the notion as wizardry. In the event, the story tells us, Kormac did see the snake but it was not handled as it should have been and the luck of the sword was changed.

I wanted to experiment with an idea about this snake and so I had Hector polish the blade to mirror bright. He burnished it so brightly that the markings disappeared from view altogether. Outside it was a bright, crisp, late-October morning. I took the sword into the sunlight and blew on it. As my warm breath condensed on the cold blade, the pattern appeared. Then it faded, in a shimmer of evaporation, as if slithering away. It would seem that *Skofnung* must have been polished bright; the pattern only becoming visible when breathed upon. Leaving the blade with its acid tint or polishing it bright was doubtless a choice that varied with personal preference.

Naming of swords

Skofnung's uncooperative sulk at being roughly handled highlights the fact that swords were deemed to have individual personalities, an idea that is reinforced by their having personal names. Charlemagne had *Joyeuse*, Roland had *Durandal* and

A close up of the pattern on the blade

Arthur had *Excalibur*. In *Beowulf*, the hero's sword is called *Hrunting*. Swords such as these, swords with proper names, had an additional power. Names carried a magical significance in early societies, a significance that went together with the animistic belief that objects, as well as humans and animals, had souls.

As well as having proper names, swords were also known by generic terms, many of them alluding luridly to their purpose, such as 'Bloodletter' or 'Legbiter'. Indeed the word 'sword' derives from the Norse word '*sverde*', meaning 'wounder'. Swords were referred to poetically in the sagas with phrases such as: 'Odin's Flame', 'Serpent of the Wound', 'Battle-Snake', 'The Fire of the Shields', 'The Byrnie's Fear', and 'Harmer of War-Knittings'.

All this serves to reinforce the status of the sword as an intensely personal weapon, a weapon of great value, which was imbued with its own personality and had more than a hint of magical charm about it. Pattern-welding was a highly skilled and labour-intensive process. Good swords were expensive. Swords were handed down from father to son and beautiful, pattern-welded swords were the gifts of princes and kings. Perhaps Raedwald received his sword from a fellow king on a state visit. Perhaps it was an ancestral gift handed down. Perhaps he commissioned it to be made. Certainly it was a sword of exceptionally high status. We cannot know what name he gave it but we may be certain that he gave it a name.

The hilt
Whatever the splendour of the blade, the richness and beauty of the hilt of Raedwald's sword is even more spectacular. Its 'cocked hat' pommel is faced with gorgeous garnet

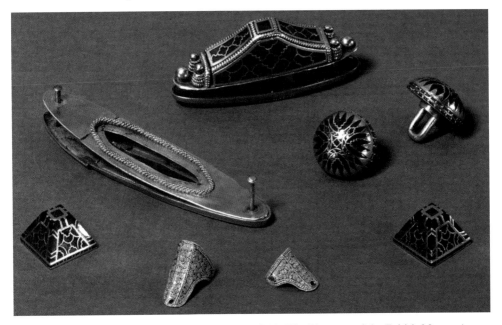

Pommel and hilt accessories from Sutton Hoo sword (© The Trustees of the British Museum)

cloisonné work. A trellis of fine gold wire has been inlaid to create an intricate pattern against the polished garnet facades and around the edges there is a heavier, beaded gold wire lending a sense of masculinity to this masterpiece of the jeweller's art. Two gold clips once adorned the grip, which was most likely made of horn. Horn grips are very elegant but can feel slippery in the hand. An antidote to this is to spit in the palm of your hand; your grip will then feel secure. I do not know why this works, just that it does. Two oval gold plates, separated either by a section of ornamental wood or horn formed the cross. Only the golden rivets that joined the two portions have survived. The length of the rivet posts suggests the infill was around a quarter of an inch. A similar arrangement existed at the pommel with an infill of wood or horn sitting between the pommel cap and a lower pommel plate. It was an elegant arrangement.

Anglo-Saxon and Viking pommels appeared in various styles but all were generally lighter than pommels of later eras. That is because they were not intended to act as a counterbalance in quite the same way as those on later swords. During the Anglo-Saxon period, whatever the shape of the upper pommel, the lower edge formed a broad T-junction with the hilt and this acted as a lever against the back of the hand. As a consequence grips were much shorter, so that the hand sat firmly against this bar. Furthermore, parallel-sided blades resulted in more mass at the point than on tapered blades and this combined with the absence of a fully counterbalancing pommel meant that such swords felt extremely blade-heavy. Swords like Raedwald's were never clumsy or awkward, they could be swung fluidly and with speed, but they did require a powerful sword arm to wield them effectively. Once launched at an adversary there is a terrifying weight and power behind the stroke.

In the heat of battle and with the hilt slick with blood, there was every possibility of these hefty swords slipping from the hand. In *Gunnlaugs Saga* there is mention of Gunnlaug carrying a second sword 'fastened by a loop to his wrist' and in *Grettis Saga*, Gretti, when out bear hunting, 'had a cord on the hilt of the sax and slipped this over his wrist'. Similarly, there is a reference in *Egils Saga* to the eponymous hero drawing his sword 'and there was a cord on the hilt'. It would seem that some form of wrist-strap offered insurance against losing one's sword.

Many swords of this style had a ring attached to the pommel, though, contrary to some opinion, this had nothing to do with the attachment of a strap. On the Sutton Hoo sword there is no evidence of one, though a ring is to be found on the accompanying shield. Ring swords, and in this case ring shields, were objects of special importance used in oath-swearing rituals. Rings, because they have no join or break, symbolize endless and unwavering loyalty and fidelity. In medieval Germany there was a custom of presenting the wedding ring to the bride on the hilt of a sword. There are examples in the old sagas of ring oaths and also of weapon oaths. The most common weapon to swear upon was the sword and a sword with a ring fixed to its hilt enabled the most powerful oath of all. In some oaths of allegiance the king or leader receiving the pledge would hold the sword with the pommel towards the person swearing his fealty. The king's hand would rest on top of the hilt and that of the man under-taking to serve him would be placed underneath, in a supplicant position.

Ring-hilted swords have been found in Scandinavia, Germany, Italy and Britain. Such weapons undoubtedly belonged to leaders, those in a position to receive oaths and pledges from others. Bonds of loyalty were further chained by gift giving. A gift-giving king was a great king and no gift was greater than that of a sword, and a ring-hilted sword the greatest gift of all. At Sutton Hoo the ring is associated with the shield; we may imagine Raedwald with his select war band sitting around the great shield and all placing their hands on the ring. It has echoes of Arthur and his round table.

Hilt of ring sword (Maidstone Museum & Bentlif Art Gallery)

The scabbard – peace strings

No less wondrous than the sword itself was the scabbard that housed it and the belt that suspended it. The scabbard was made from wooden lathes bound with leather and lined with wool, the natural oils from which would keep it from tarnishing. In the burial all this organic matter had disintegrated and fused, in a corrosive mass, to the blade. What remained intact, however, were the astonishingly ornate belt and scabbard fittings. Like the hilt, these were made from cloisonné garnets set into intricate patterns of gold latticework. There were broad rectangular plates that adorned the circumference of the belt, a fabulous, distinctively shaped buckle and, most wonderful of all, the strap distributor assembly. This consisted of three adjoining plates connected by a hinge at one junction and by a swivel arrangement, capable of 40 degrees movement from side to side, at the other. Both the hinge and the pivoting end were in perfect working order when excavated. All that was necessary to adjust the angle of suspension for riding or walking was to move a slide on one of two straps attaching the scabbard to the belt. The ingenious strap distributor device accommodated any corresponding change of angle on the companion strap.

On the outside face of the scabbard and a few inches below its mouth were found twodomed bosses. These, too, were exquisitely fashioned in garnets and gold. Different colours of garnet throw out the pattern of a cross on each one. This would imply that Raedwald acquired the sword after his conversion by St Augustine in 602. The bosses have a gold staple fixed to their back-plates so that they could attach to some part of the scabbard, probably to the broad loop of leather that secured it to its suspension straps. What was the purpose of these sparkling jewels? The answer may lie with a pair of associated objects.

Also found nearby were two little mounts in the shape of pyramids. These tiny masterpieces, faced with a mosaic of garnets and dark blue glass embedded in a gold honeycomb, exhibit the most delicate and precise craftsmanship. Garnet is a very hard stone and it is astonishing that seventh-century craftsmen were able to cut it so accurately into such small shapes. The little pyramids are hollow and have a strap

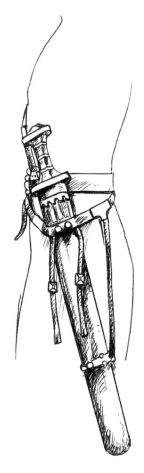

bar across the base. It is possible that these were the finials for 'peace strings' – leather thongs that attached to the back of scabbard and tied off on the ornate bosses fixed to the front, having passed over the cross of the hilt.

The sagas tell of peace strings. Their purpose was to secure the sword in the scabbard so that it couldn't be drawn too readily in hasty anger. There is a story in *Gisli Sursson's Saga* about a hot-headed youth eager to make his name by challenging the old warrior Thorkel:

> The boy said, 'The sword in your hand must be very precious; may I have a look at it?'
>
> Thorkel answered, 'This is strange but I will let you look'.
>
> The boy took the sword, turned aside and unloosed the peace-strings and drew it.
>
> Thorkel said, 'I didn't say you could draw the sword'.
>
> 'I didn't ask you', replied the boy and he swung the sword and struck at the neck of Thorkel, taking off his head.

In a society in which the quarrelsome warrior classes could walk about armed, peace strings, though easily disregarded,

Peace strings (untied)

may have had some restraining influence. When the leader of a war band went to war against his enemies, I suspect that the loosing of the peace strings was part of the ritual declaration of hostilities and that it was doubtless performed with great ceremony.

The war band

The warrior class in Anglo-Saxon societies were set apart from the rest of the population. They operated in small war bands; anything above thirty-five men was considered an army. A man's greatest desire was to win fame amongst his peers and his code was to fight to the last man standing. It was a disgrace to outlive one's lord on the battlefield. To die in battle was an honour to be sought, not a fate to be feared. The warrior code was everything. Desire to win fame and glory by heroic deeds was paramount and the virtues they cherished were bravery, fortitude and, above all, a self-sacrificing loyalty to the group. Not only did the group fight together but they also lived together. A leader would surround himself with his trusted companions and they would forge strong bonds of kinship. Feasting in the great hall, they would listen to skalds recount tales of past heroes and of mighty swords with magical properties. Such tales would inspire them, perpetuating a culture of self-sacrifice and unswerving loyalty.

The magnificence of his ship burial and the splendour of his weapons suggest that Raedwald was a leader to inspire. We may imagine him surrounded by a band of faithful retainers, sworn to defend him and his realm – drinking together, hunting together, fighting together and, if need be, dying together. A king was expected to fight with his troops. Martial ability and courage were the ultimate basis of his authority. Raedwald would have led in battle and he would have surely carried his sword – not only a magnificent symbol of his sovereignty but a versatile weapon in the cut and maul of close-quarter fighting.

In exchange for their fealty, a king or warlord would feed, clothe, arm and accommodate his warriors. These would be his household *thegns* or *gesithas* (pronounced 'yeasithas'). *Gesithas* simply means companions and they were the lord's inner circle. Some *thegns* held land independently but still owed military allegiance to their overlord. In turn these *thegns* would have *gesithas*, who would fight alongside them. *Thegns* and *gesithas* were a warrior caste. Economically they depended on the *ceorls*. *Ceorls* farmed the land and paid rent and dues to the landowning *thegns*.

Income was supplemented by war plunder. All booty was given up to the king or warlord, which he then redistributed according to his largesse. War had become an economic necessity and there was frequent raiding amongst neighbours. This, in turn, reinforced the interdependence of *thegn* and *ceorl*. To farm effectively meant having a strong military presence to defend against raiders and to have a well-equipped military force meant having a strong agricultural economy to sustain it.

Warfare was endemic amongst the German tribes in their homeland. That is to say it was frequent, though not necessarily incessant. The same applied to the Germanic settlers in Britain – the Angles, the Saxons, the Jutes, the Frisians and others. However the idea that these warlike peoples swarmed over the North Sea in the fifth century and took Britain by armed conquest is currently being reconsidered. The archaeological evidence does not support the old view that the Anglo-Saxons were conquering invaders.

The coming of the Angles

Certainly a power vacuum was created when the last of the Roman legions were recalled to defend the gates of Rome against the barbarian hordes in AD 410. Britain had no army of its own and, without Roman rule, neither did it have any coherence as a nation. Rome's retreat left the gates of Britain wide open. A combination of population expansion, climate change and rising sea levels meant that many in Northern Europe were looking for a new home. At first there may have been pockets of intolerant animosity towards the newcomers but not full-scale organized resistance. In fact the Anglo-Saxon Chronicle for the year 443 records that the the Angles were invited to Britain:

> Here the Britons sent to Rome and asked them for their help against the Picts, but they had none because they were campaigning against Attila, King of Huns; and then they sent to the Angles and made the same request to the princes of the Angle race.

Another entry for 449 says:

> Then they sent to Angeln and ordered them to send more help.

The Anglo-Saxon Chronicle was written over 400 years after these events and can hardly be considered sound contemporary evidence. It undoubtedly delved into folk-lore and myth to conjure up past history, though it may be considered a more reliable source for the events it chronicled after its inception – it was maintained until 1151.

Nevertheless, here we have the suggestion that the Angles were invited, initially at least, as allies and friends. The Picts, from north of Hadrian's Wall, were known to have launched pirate raids as far south as London, even during the Roman occupation and were clearly considered a significant menace. To what extent these first waves of Angles were welcomed by the local population is not known. We simply know that the Angles came and the Angles settled and they continued to come in the ensuing centuries. Moreover they didn't just bring their warriors, they brought their farmers too and they colonized East Anglia, Middle Anglia, Mercia, Lindsay and Northumberland – virtually the entire east coast from above Colchester to below Edinburgh and pretty much the entire Midlands. Saxons colonized Essex, Sussex and Wessex and the Jutes settled in Kent.

By the time of King Raedwald, the Anglian presence was well established. The extent to which indigenous Britons (*waeles* or foreigners in the Anglian tongue) had been forced westwards or northwards, either by economic dominance or force of arms is uncertain. Some will have integrated and some will have moved away to the edges but, by the seventh century, Anglian dominion was such that there were increasing outbreaks of resistance from those who regarded themselves as indigenous Britons.

Then, as now, the land of the East Angles was rich and fertile. In 1086, the Domesday Book recorded East Anglia as the most densely populated part of the country. Seventh-century Britain was an agrarian based economy and Raedwald ruled over one of the most desirable areas of the realm. No wonder he possessed such a fine sword.

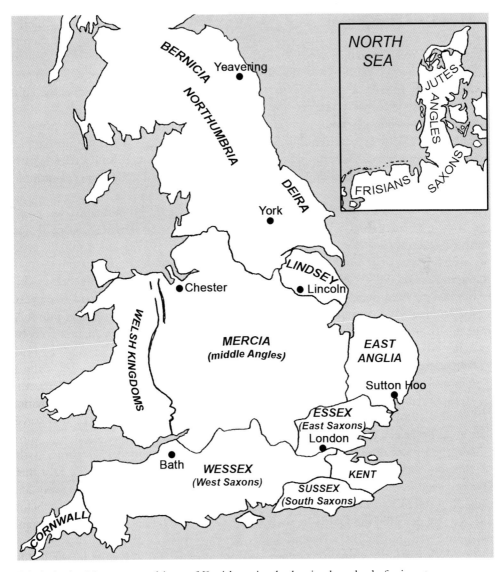

Britain in the 7th century and inset of Danish peninsula showing homeland of migrants

Raedwald's kingdom

There were no skeletal remains found in the grave. Indeed, in the absence of a body, it is not absolutely proven that Sutton Hoo is the burial chamber of King Raedwald. It is just a reasonable probability and a possible explanation for the lack of a body is that it was buried elsewhere with Christian rites. The ship burial with traditional grave goods may simply have been a form of spiritual insurance policy honouring ancestral custom. Raedwald was keen on such stratagems.

When Pope Gregory I encountered a group of young Angles for sale in one of Rome's slave markets, he was struck by their piercing blue eyes and vibrant blonde hair. He asked what race they were and was told 'Angles'. In a joke that translates well from the Latin he responded, '*Non angli, sed angeli*' – 'Not Angles, but angels . . . for they have the faces of angels'. Subsequently he sent Augustine on a mission to convert 'Angle-land' to Christianity. Raedwald was one of his early successes – well almost.

Raedwald was a Wuffinga – the Royal House of the East Angles. There are some spurious pedigrees that trace his ancestors but suffice it to say he was the king of an established dynasty, succeeding to the throne around 599. His roots were entrenched in pagan belief but, in 602, he was persuaded by Augustine and converted to Christianity. However, it is said that his wife, whose name has not come down to us, persuaded him not to forsake his old religion entirely. He famously built a temple with two altars, one to the Christian God and one to his ancestral gods. Like all sensible men, he was much influenced by his wife.

In 615, Prince Edwin of Deira sought Raedwald's protection against his rival, the Northumbrian King Aethelfrith, and took refuge in East Anglia. Raedwald was tempted to accept a bribe from Aethelfrith to have this Edwin killed but his wife persuaded him that it would be dishonourable to kill a guest. Before assuming that Raedwald always did his wife's bidding, we should consider the fate of Sigebehrt, who is thought to have been her son by a previous marriage. Raedwald had Sigebehrt exiled to Gaul. We do not know the reason for the rift with his stepson but it is probable that his actions were against his wife's wishes. On this occasion, however, he took her advice and the consequence was war with Northumbria.

Northumbria (the lands north of the Humber) was colonized by the North Angles and divided into Deira (modern-day Yorkshire) and Bernicia (modern-day Northumberland). Edwin was a prince of Deira and Aethelfrith king of Bernicia. In 604, Aethelfrith had Edwin's father killed and thus became king of Northumbria – a vast area, far larger than its present day counterpart.

Aethelfrith was an aggressive, expansionist warrior king, constantly at war with his neighbours, seeking to boost his income with tribute from newly subjugated lands. He also faced significant resistance from indigenous Britons, who rebelled against his tyrannical rule. Victorious over a massive army of Britons at the Battle of Catterick in 598, he also defeated the Dalriada Scots at Degastan in 603, his territorial ambitions extending well into southern Scotland. His was the largest of the Anglian kingdoms by far. Aethelfrith was a mighty warlord, proven in battle, but so long as Edwin lived, his power and authority over Deira were threatened. He wanted Edwin dead.

Edwin first sought protection from another Anglian king, Cearl of Mercia, but Aethelfrith ousted Cearl in 615 and installed a puppet king. Edwin was on the run. In the following year, Aethelfrith won another major victory against the Welsh at Chester and conquered the kingdom of Rheged. It was at this point that Edwin flew to shelter at the court of Raedwald. Aethelfrith was then at the height of his military power and Raedwald had to decide whether or not to side with Edwin's cause and take up arms against the mighty king of Northumberland. Was he simply persuaded by the injunctions of his wife or did Raedwald fear that Aethelfrith would eventually turn his attention to his own kingdom of East Anglia? All we know is that in 616 Raedwald summoned his army and led an expedition north to face Aethelfrith.

The fyrd and the shield wall

The Anglo-Saxon army was called the *fyrd*. The word means 'journey' in Anglo-Saxon and originally referred to a small raiding force going on a routine military expedition. In later times it came to mean the summoning of all those with an obligation to perform military service for their overlord. It is a matter of debate as to what extent the non-military classes were called up for service. Possibly, later on, in times of great national crises, such as Alfred the Great's stand against the Vikings or King Harold's defence against the Norman invasion, larger armies were sought that included the workers from the fields. In Raedwald's time it seems more likely that his *fyrd* comprised exclusively of trained and seasoned warriors – the *thegns* and *gesithas* who had sworn their oaths of allegiance.

Loyalty and kinship are, of course, essential elements in any fighting group but this was especially so for the Angles. Their style of 'shield wall' warfare hinged on the inter-dependence of the group. The front line of a mass of men would interlock their shields to withstand the attacks of the enemy and they would hold this formation, with unflinching discipline, whether advancing, retreating or standing fast. For a shield wall to be effective it must have depth. It cannot be compared to the 'thin red line' that stood against the foes of the British Empire more than a thousand years later. To demonstrate this, I once marshalled a large group of volunteers for a television programme. I had them stand, with shields, just two rows deep and strung out in a long line. I then charged them on horseback.

Don't believe all that nonsense about horses not wanting to trample people. It depends on the horse. I rode a wonderfully brave polo pony; a fiery and courageous mare who baulks at nothing. Polo ponies in general are trained to use their body mass and fearlessly barge into other ponies on the field and ride them off. Making hard contact is second nature to them. Sure enough we smashed through the line, opening up a gap and putting them into disorder. I then got everyone to form up six ranks deep. My horse snorted and stamped the ground in anticipation of another assault. We cannoned into the front rank, crashed into the second but by the third rank our momentum had slowed and we stalled. I was surrounded and ignominiously hauled from the saddle. A shield wall with depth is very hard to break.

In reality, the shield wall would not only be armed with shields but also with spears, axes and swords, making it even more hazardous to attack. If you have the larger army, you can concentrate your forces in what was known as the *svynfylking* or 'boar's snout' – This is a wedge-like formation that bulldozes its way into the centre of the enemy's line with an irresistible mass of men and muscle. The nature of forming a wedge means that you have to concentrate your forces and so adequate numbers are required if you are not to risk being outflanked. It also requires immense 'do-or-die' courage from the men at the front, but in a 'hero' culture, such men were not hard to find.

Another possibility was to try a flanking attack or, with sufficient numbers, a double flank attack in a configuration known as the 'forceps'. All these manoeuvres required slick drill discipline and the ability to deploy quickly. For the most part though, shield-wall fighting was a war of attrition. Close range missile warfare with slings, arrows, spears and throwing axes sought to weaken sections of the wall. As comrades fell, others would step into the gap created and maintain the integrity of the formation. Another tactic was for small squads of elite troops to attack the enemy line; fierce men hellbent on hacking their way through to take out the opposing leader.

Some warriors carried a fistful of *angons* (iron javelins) in their shield hand, launching them at the enemy as they closed. Alongside, *francisca* (throwing axe) men, sprinted forward, hurling a pair of somersaulting blades before drawing their swords to engage the front line. The angon and francisca were shock weapons, designed to put the enemy on the back foot at the instant of engagement. It would be conveniently neat if only the Franks used the francisca and only the Angles employed the angon but history is seldom that kind to an organizing mind. Both Angles and Franks used both weapons. Swords were especially suitable for these shock troops because they could be worn and drawn quickly from their scabbards as soon as the missile weapons had been cast. Shorter axes such as the bearded-axe, used to hook over shields, could be lodged in belts but a clear advantage of the sword was its portability.

Swordsmen were nonetheless in the minority and axemen, particularly those with great two-handed 'Dane axes', were at the forefront of these assaults, cleaving into the enemy shields with blows of terrifying power. As for the *sax*, *seax* or *scramasax*, the eponymous weapon of the Saxons, that too was carried by the Angles. Saxes ranged from 12 to 24 inches in blade length and there is debate as to whether they were really a weapon for the battlefield or just a general-purpose knife for the hunter. The sax had a single-edged blade with a cutaway section on the back edge that tapered steeply towards the point. Many were pattern-welded, high-status weapons. Most were knives for everyday use but some, especially the longer ones, *langsaxes*, were used in battle or in single combat and might be considered a form of sword. *Njals Saga*, an Icelandic tale written in the thirteenth century but harking back to events in the tenth century, recalls a fight in which Kolseggr cut off the leg of Kolr with his sax. Kolr stood looking at the stump for some time. 'You don't need to look: it's just as you think, the leg is gone', said Kolseggr. There is a strange poetry as well as a dark humour in the way the sagas state the blindingly obvious.

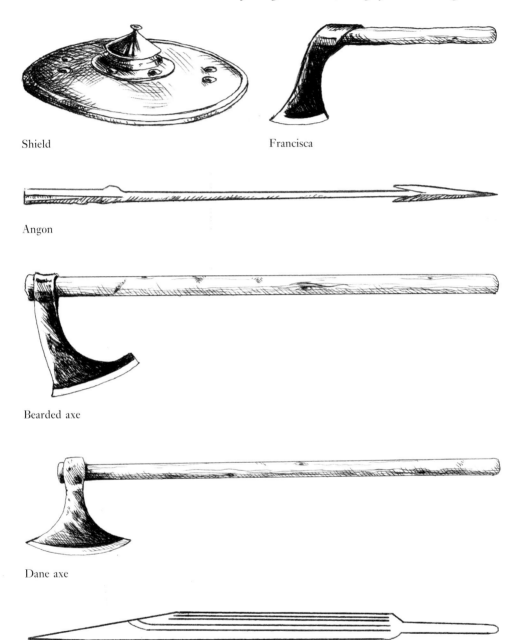

Shield

Francisca

Angon

Bearded axe

Dane axe

Sax blade from River Thames (Battersea), 28¼ inches

Anglo-Saxon weapons (not to scale)

In spite of this diverse arsenal, spears were by far the most common weapons on the battlefield at this period and the best specimens were pattern-welded. Six spears and three angons were found in Raedwald's grave. Swords may have been the more-expensive weapons but they were not yet considered intrinsically nobler. A spear, mounted on its stout ash shaft had reach, an invaluable asset for fighting over the shield–wall, whether you are attacking or defending.

The Sword in battle

Swords can be swung with ease around shields and in the deeper ranks, where an enemy may at times break through, they are better than the spear for fighting in a tight space. Besides, a thrust from a spear may lodge in a shield, causing fatal delay, whereas a sword can rain a torrent of successive blows.

When fighting in the shield wall it is slightly easier to use cutting blows. Powerful thrusts require the arm to be pulled back and that risks an elbow in the face for the man on your right – you are standing shoulder to shoulder with him in order to close the wall and receiving part of your own protection from his shield. All cuts can be hefted with the arm forward. That is not to say that swords of this period were exclusively for cutting, as is frequently suggested, just because they have rounded rather than tapered points.

Swordsmiths experimented with rounded points during the late La Tène period in an attempt to solve the problem of narrow sword tips either bending over because they were too soft or snapping because they were too brittle. In either case the properties of the metal become more critical on a slender section. As we have seen on the gladius, there were other solutions such as forging the tip in diamond section, but, until the harder and tougher quality steels of the later Middle Ages made very narrow points possible, making a resilient point was a problem. Iron Age peoples were slow to give up on tapered points but eventually the concept of a rounded point won the day.

Anglo-Saxon and Viking swords had rounded points but they were not blunt. The edges of the point were sharpened, complimenting the thrust with a cutting action that could drive through leather and textile armour, slice flesh and cut into bone. Should the thrust be parried by a shield, then an acutely tapered point would run the risk of embedding so firmly that it would be slow to withdraw; whereas a rounded point, cutting its way in, could be retracted more speedily. It would still deliver the same impact, crucially unbalancing an opponent but a redoubled attack need not be delayed because your sword was stuck in the enemy's shield.

Against mail, a tapered point would be superior, with the potential to punch through rings and split them. However a sharp-edged rounded point could still do considerable damage, cutting just enough to gain purchase and deliver the full might of the blow. Delivering the energy of the blow is the important thing, not penetration. It only requires 12 joules of energy to kill a man by means of blunt trauma, if that energy is delivered over a vital organ such as the heart. Rounded points could bite into mail ensuring the energy of the thrust was not dissipated by deflection. They could also puncture faces, not all of which were guarded by an expensive helm. There were good reasons why these swords had rounded points and I do not believe for a moment the idea that either the thrust hadn't been invented or that it was considered foul play.

Rounded point of the author's replica Saxon sword

In the brutality that is war the concept of foul play does not arise. Moreover the benefits of the thrust were well understood from fighting with spears. It is too useful a tool in the swordsman's repertoire to have been discounted.

Having said that, we should not ignore the dreadful power of the cutting blow, which was undoubtedly the principal action of these blade-heavy swords. Certainly the one that Hector Cole had made for me with its 32-inch blade was a beast – Raedwald's possessed only a 28-inch blade – and it was decided to test its cutting power. In order to evoke the spirit of Beowulf, and his fight against the sea-monster Grendel's mother, I opted to test it against a modern-day sea monster, a shark. A porbeagle shark had been caught off the Kentish coast and I hastened down to the delightful old fishing harbour at Whitstable where it had been landed. The 'monster', already dead, had been hoist on a small derrick and awaited its fate. I had the flu and was not feeling as vigorous as I might but I focussed all my energy and gave it my best shot. Sharkskin is immensely tough but the blade sliced through it without problem and cut a good 8 inches into the body, severing the spine on the way. Such a blow was certainly capable of severing a man's leg, arm or even head. It was a chilling first-hand experience of what such a weapon could do.

Archaeology also offers gruesome evidence. In 1929, twenty human skeletons were found in a mass grave just outside Chester, at Heronbridge. Most showed evidence of wounds to the head consistent with sword strikes. In 2004, a further fourteen skeletons were unearthed and the site is thought to hold many more. Radiocarbon dating confirmed the bodies were likely the victims of Aethelfrith's attack on the city in 616 – just before he had to race cross country to meet Raedwald's fyrd. Two of the skeletons in the recent find were taken for analysis. Both men were around 5ft 10in tall and both had received savage, sword-inflicted injuries. The younger man, in his early twenties, had five wounds to the head. Four of these were killing blows. One had sliced off the entire back of his skull; two others had cut into the forehead and another had cut deep into his right cheekbone. The older man, around 40, had three skull-splitting injuries and a glancing cut behind his right ear. It's not known if they were Britons or Angles but the injuries suggest that they were not wearing helms. This makes them more likely to be Britons. The Angles, full-time warriors, wore magnificent helms with elaborate faceplates.

Armour

The helm found in King Raedwald's grave was without peer. Its cap was hammered out of a single piece of iron, to which were attached separate pieces for cheek-pieces, neck-guard and faceplate, also made from iron. This functional substructure was then decorated with squares of tinned bronze foil, each stamped with a relief motif, giving the helm an opulent silver finish. Reinforcing the crown was an iron crest, inlaid with silver wire and fitted with zoomorphic gilt-bronze terminals. Adorning the faceplate, giving it its own scowling personality, were eyebrows, a moustache and a nose, all in gilt-bronze. Perhaps Raedwald sported a similar little moustache, surely the fashion of the day, and I wonder if the straight, slightly delicate nose was similar to that of Raedwald's own nose. Surely a king would not wear someone else's nose?

A coat of mail, known as a *byrnie* was the standard body armour of the time and, as might be expected, one was deposited in the grave along with the sword and the helm. Mail is an interlinked web of riveted iron rings; it is not a chain, that is a line of single links. Byrnies were artfully tailored to fit the wearer. They had a discernable waist and were fashioned to taper snugly into the armpit, enabling unimpeded movement to the sword arm. Tailoring also resulted in the warrior not having to carry any more weight than was necessary. Mail is part of a composite defence system; it doesn't work on its own. It provides a hard, metal outer skin but it is essential to have a thickly padded garment underneath to absorb the impact of blows. These quilted coats are known as 'gambesons' or 'aketons'.

The big question is: can mail withstand an attack from a sword? All armour is reasonable proof against the weapons of the day; otherwise there would be no point in having it. However, it is seldom totally proof. The extent to which mail can protect against sword blows depends on the force of the blow, the angle of strike and the level of resistance from the target; bodies move when struck and the degree of that movement will dissipate the energy delivered. A man may step back from a blow and only be caught by the tip of the sword. In such circumstances the mail is likely to work well as a deflecting surface. With swords and spears swinging in close combat, there is every likelihood of being caught by neighbouring weapons that are not directing their full force at you. Again the mail should protect you. By contrast, a full-force blow landing on top of the shoulder would meet with more resistance and thereby deliver more energy. Here there is a possibility that the mail would fail.

Not all cutting strokes would have been delivered with maximum energy. It takes time to organize the breath and centre the energy for a mighty blow. Of course, all blows would be swung with vigour, enough to do harm and destabilize an opponent, but a warrior also had to pace himself and not expend all his energy in one smite. He would only deliver fully committed attacks when he had the advantage of time and situation, such as his adversary staggering in a dazed state or stumbling. Then he could make his blow count. Certainly the sagas sing of almighty strokes that severed mail but perhaps they do so because it was a relatively rare occurrence and the telling of it imbues their hero with superhuman powers.

With all armour there is a trade-off between mobility and protection. Byrnies gave a reasonable level of insurance to the torso but they were kept short, extending to just above the knee. Sleeves were also short, coming to just above the elbow. Conical helms, padded to minimise concussion, presented glancing surfaces to turn a blade

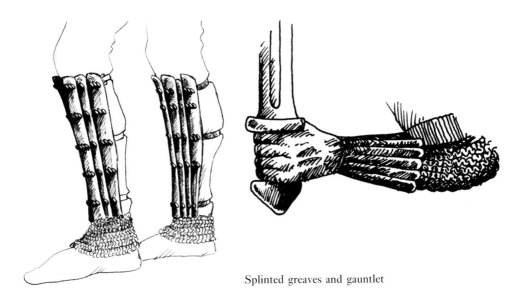

Splinted greaves and gauntlet

and faceplates offered protection from arrows and other missiles. However, the neck, throat, arms and legs of the Anglo-Saxon warrior remained vulnerable. With the exception of the head wounds at Chester, there is more evidence archaeologically for leg wounds at this period than to any other part of the body. Shields are poor at defending the lower leg.

A new form of protection for the lower leg was making an appearance at this time and Raedwald may well have been armoured with them. Known as 'splinted greaves' they consisted of staves of metal riveted to a leather backing that strapped around the calf. A box of such splints was found in a contemporary grave in Sweden. Splinted armour was certainly known to Raedwald; warriors depicted on his helm wear gauntlets on their sword hands that have splinted cuffs.

What a splendid figure Raedwald must have been in his war gear. I imagine him tall and muscular with sharp blue eyes, long blonde hair and a little blonde moustache. I see him striding with a confident gait, the jewelled hilt of his magnificent sword swinging on his hip.

The shield

Although the wooden structure of Raedwald's shield has long rotted away, its fabulously ornate shield-mounts have survived. Surrounding the huge iron boss was a frieze of animals, each with a garnet eye. As larger individual mounts, a garnet-eyed gilt-bronze dragon and a tinned-and-gilt bird of prey with gilded talons also invoke their talismanic power across the centuries. Smaller gilt-bronze bosses with tinned collars disguised the rivets securing the iron handgrip and long strips of gold foil were secured at various angles across the surface – decorative incarnations of the sort of iron braces that might have been used to strengthen and repair a cherished shield. The intricacy and fragility of this shield furniture suggests ceremonial rather than functional use and, of course, it has its ring attached, that most potent symbol of the gift-giver's claim to allegiance. Stylistically, the shield-mounts suggest Sweden as a place of manufacture. Was this shield a regular import or were there Swedish crafts-men working at the Anglian court? Or did Raedwald have political connections with Sweden? All are possibilities.

The shape of the mounts indicates that the shield board was flat – they would need to be curved to sit flush to a lens-shaped surface – which is further reason for supposing the shield was ceremonial. Images in art suggest the use of both flat and lenticular shields in battle but practical experiments persuade strongly that the lenticular shape is far superior. In tests conducted at The Royal Military College of Science I attacked various shield types with arrows, throwing axes, a great two-handed axe and a sword.

Shield types included flat wooden boards, flat boards covered in rawhide and a lenticular shield covered in rawhide. The type of timber used was lime – the 'sacred linden' of Norse mythology – which is by far the most suitable wood for shields. Firstly, it is light, which is why plasterers use it for their floats and, secondly, it has

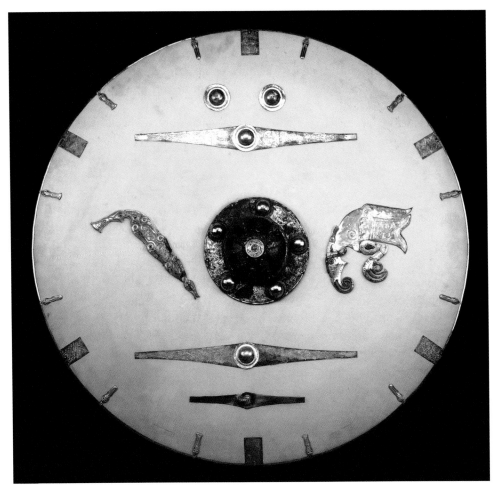

Shield fittings from Sutton Hoo (© The Trustees of the British Museum)

short, soft fibres, which is why it is the choice of artisan wood carvers. A soft wood is more absorbent to percussive blows and the short fibres mean that a fissure will not necessarily spread across the board, as it would with pine for instance.

All weapons easily defeated the plain wooden boards. A layer of rawhide was the key to the shield being at all effective. Rawhide is an immensely strong material and in some cultures shields are made from it alone. The archaeological evidence for Raedwald's period is that shields were made from wood and covered in either rawhide or cowhide leather. A tenth-century law states that no shield-maker shall cover a shield with sheepskin, which was obviously an inferior, and presumably cheaper, material. By incorporating the strength of the hide with the stiffness of the wood, a composite structure is created that maximizes the overall resilience of the shield for the minimum amount of weight. Rawhide also acts to hold the boards of the shield together. Archaeological evidence is clear that there were no transverse boards, as in later Scottish targes for instance. Shield boards were simply glued together edge on edge in the vertical plane. We used a glue recipe, made from cheese, handed down by the twelfth-century Benedictine monk Theophilus, who had recommended it for altar panels. Cheese, boiled and mixed with quicklime, makes a latex-like substance that gives remarkably good adhesion. In addition, a rawhide rim, fitted wet to the shield's perimeter, shrinks as it dries to tie everything together.

The flat shield covered with rawhide fared well against arrows and franciscas but less well against sword and axe. Slow motion camera footage revealed a large amount of distortion as the shock waves travelled through the shield and with the Dane axe the rawhide rim actually burst. The blow landed fair and square on the surface of the shield and did not cut the rim. It was the rippling distortion of the boards that caused it to break and I was reminded of a line from a tenth century poem about the Battle of Maldon: 'the rim of the shield shattered and the body armour sang one of the songs of terror'. However, the lenticular shield, also covered in rawhide, proved indestructible. Slow motion film revealed that it oscillated violently but the shape contained the deformations in a way that the flat shield could not.

In combat the shield could be used aggressively as well as defensively. Iron bosses became steel fists to punch with and a horizontal scything blow across the temples with the edge could render a man unconscious. For the swordsman, its rounded edges offered no impediment to the arcs of his cutting blows and, whether cutting or thrusting, he could often disguise the intent of his attack behind his shield. Part of the weight was supported by means of a strap, called a *guige*, that suspended the shield over the shoulder. It aided endurance in battle and it was extremely useful for carrying the shield on the march. Whether on foot or on horseback, it enabled the shield to be slung over the back.

Horses

The Anglo-Saxons typically fought on foot but they did have horses and horses were by far the quickest and least tiring way for the fyrd to travel. Adjacent to Raedwald's tomb at Sutton Hoo is another grave (Mound 17) that contained the skeleton of a horse with full trappings. On some of the plates that decorate Raedwald's helm there are images of warriors on horseback attacking infantry. The notion of mounted warfare was not at all strange to the Angles and horses were an everyday means of travel. Having made the decision to confront Aethelfrith in battle, Raedwald needed to get there quickly before Aethelfrith could summon his vast military resources from the farthest corners of his expanded kingdom. There is the implication in the chronicles that Raedwald had the advantage of numbers in the final clash and so he presumably got there very quickly indeed. Almost certainly Raedwald and his army travelled north on horseback. The place where the two forces finally met, a point on the River Idle somewhere near Doncaster, was a journey of 180 to 200 miles, perhaps three or four days' ride.

Horses in the seventh century were short by modern standards, probably no more than 12 to 14 hands. Picture Raedwald sitting tall in the saddle with his legs almost reaching the ground. If you look at medieval and earlier representations of men on horses, you will see that this was a perfectly normal image. Big men rode small horses and they did so with dignity, bearing and attitude. The type of horse was probably similar to the present day Icelandic breed. These horses are not indigenous to Iceland but have flourished there as an undiluted strain since the time of the Vikings, who took them there. Vikings briefly colonized and settled in Iceland during the Medieval Warm Period from 800 to 1200. When the temperatures dropped and the crops failed, the Vikings abandoned their farms but left their horses behind. They are shaggy-coated, hardy beasts; immensely spirited, brave and strong. They are perfect for travel and one of the few surviving breeds with a natural fifth gait, the amble. That is a gait in addition to the walk, trot, canter and gallop. Amblers were used universally for travel throughout the Middle Ages because ambling is the most comfortable, least strenuous and most efficient gait for covering long distances.

With the trot, canter and gallop there is an amount of muscular effort required on the part of the rider to synchronize with the movements of the horse. With the amble there is none, you just sit there. Horses move their legs in different sequences according to the gait. When ambling, a horse moves both right legs together and then both left legs. The effect on the rider is no more than a gentle rocking from side to side; there is no bounce. I once rode from Canterbury to London. Although it involved some hairy moments, like crossing the Medway via the M2 motorway bridge with juggernauts hurtling by a few feet away on one side and the murky waters of the river beckoning a hundred feet or so below on the other, it was an extremely congenial journey. I travelled with two close friends and for the most part we took bridle paths and ancient trackways. We alternated, four hours at a stretch, between using Icelandic ponies and modern horses. The contrast was extreme. Saddle sore and weary after walking, trotting and cantering on the modern breeds, we were refreshed and exhilarated after ambling on the Icelandics. I can only compare the experience, inadequately, to being on a super-speed moving walkway. You have the sense of doing nothing, just standing there, and yet the walls are rushing by as if you were walking extremely fast. As we ambled through the woods, at speeds between 15 and 20mph, the trees hurtled past. There was a real sense of purpose and of going somewhere and yet we weren't doing anything. Not only that but ambling horses can keep it up for hour after hour without tiring.

It would be possible to ride these horses into battle if desired; they were perfectly capable of galloping. In fact later Anglo-Saxon forces did use cavalry on occasion, notably at the second Battle of Chester in 907 and at Stamford Bridge in 1066. Cavalry were also doubtless employed in ambush and skirmish situations. What is most likely at the River Idle, however, is that Raedwald's army dismounted to draw up battle lines once the enemy were in sight. Although details are sparse about this battle, we have clues about typical practice from a wonderful, near-contemporary poem about the Battle of Maldon in 991. Here the Anglo-Saxon army rode to the site of the battle

Icelandic horses typical of the type favoured during Raedwald's reign (photo courtesy of Nick Foot, Oakfield Icelandics)

against the Danes but were then commanded to dismount and fight on foot. However their leader, Byrhtnoth, remained mounted so that he could ride quickly to different parts of the battlefield and 'rode round giving orders and instructed the warriors how they should stand and hold their positions'. We may imagine Raedwald doing this, perhaps signalling his men across the river and instructing them where to take up position. Picture him splashing into the water, his magnificent sword held high above his head, urging his faithful warriors to unleash their fury. About to face the most powerful and seasoned army in the land, his men must have been on their mettle for an uncertain outcome.

At Maldon, Byrhtnoth eventually dismounted and fought amongst his men. Initially he fought with his spear until it broke, then 'Byrhtnoth drew his sword from its sheath broad and bright of blade'. Whether Raedwald fought from horseback or on foot, there can be little doubt that he too would have been in the thick of the fray. That was a king's duty: to be conspicuous in battle. There are no eyewitness accounts but this was a pivotal power struggle and the fighting is bound to have been desperate, ferocious and savage. In the midst of it would have been Raedwald, sword in hand, mired in sweat and gore, inspiring his men to do or die.

Single combat and the origins of the duel

A full-scale battle was not inevitable, especially since the conflict was ostensibly about avenging Aethelfrith's slight on Prince Edwin. It would have been possible to challenge him to single combat. King Alfred's grandson, Athelstan, did just that before the Battle of Brunaburgh in 937. He challenged Olaf, king of Dublin, to settle the matter by means of a *holmganga* – a ritual duel in which the combatants fight within a restricted area. Olaf declined the invitation and many died securing Athelstan his victory. Famously five kings and seven earls were killed in the fighting.

'*Holmganga*' actually means 'island-going' and rowing out to a small islet, the appointed place for the duel, was the preferred option. Where this was not possible they created an 'island' by laying down a cloak, 10 feet square, and marking out an extended area with hazel wands around its perimeter. There were doubtless many variations on the rules but a common practice was for each man to have three shields and a shield bearer; there were clearly expectations about shields being destroyed in combat. Rules about stepping outside the 'hazelled field' held that one foot out meant a man had retreated; both feet out meant that he had fled. If a fighter was wounded so that blood fell upon the cloak, he could concede with honour. Such regulation required witnesses and is the foundation for the tradition of seconds that we encounter with later duelling practices. A more serious form of the duel was *einvigi*. It too was a legally sanctioned combat but fought without rules. Both systems could result in death but with *einvigi* a fatal outcome was even more probable. What little knowledge we have of these procedures comes from the later Viking sagas but it is likely that the rituals were similar amongst Anglo-Saxon peoples.

The notion of single combat as a means of settling disputes over territory or of avenging a wrong was embodied in the legal codes of the Germanic and Scandinavian peoples from at least the fifth century. It is here that we find the roots of duelling in European society. Deep roots that, as we shall see in later chapters, fed a tree with many branches. There was, above all else, a principle in law that held that a wrong-doer was not directly answerable to the law or to the state but owed recompense to the injured party. We see its legacy today in civil law, particularly in cases of libel or slander, where the state merely administers a system to determine the compensation owed to the wronged person. The state exacts no retribution or punishment on its own behalf.

Among the barbarian tribes outside the direct influence of Rome, this principle was paramount and applied to all crimes, including murder and theft as well as to civil disputes over land and property. The state assisted in the administration of this justice by providing courts to judge the case and in setting the compensation tariff. These fines, known as *wer-gild* or blood money, were not imposed as punishments but were intended to mollify the injured party so that he would not seek his right of reprisal. The interest which society felt in this process was not in the moralistic repression of crime but in the pragmatic maintenance of peace.

In cases of murder the *wer-gild* was payable to the kindred of the slain. Moreover the perpetrator of the crime was entitled to collect from his relatives a portion of the *wer-gild* he had incurred and tables were drawn up showing the amount payable by each relative according to his degree of kinship, usually extending as far as to third cousins. Even as late as the twelfth century, Icelandic law provided for a system whereby the fines exacted diminished proportionately down to relatives in the fifth degree. Each grade of the guilty party's family paid directly to the corresponding grade of the victim's family.

All of this assumed that guilt could be easily determined, which in many cases, particularly murder, it could not. In the absence of forensic science, prosecution and defence consisted mainly of swearing oaths and the veracity of these oaths was supported by other oaths from what were, in effect, character witnesses. They swore not to their knowledge of events, but that their knowledge of the man meant he was telling the truth. The number of oath-swearers depended upon the magnitude of the crime and upon a person's rank in society. For instance the word of a *thegn* was considered equal to that of seven *ceorls*. The prospect of an unjust verdict was thus highly likely, particularly since many witnesses could have a vested financial interest in the outcome and, under some laws, they may themselves be liable to pay part of the fine if the judgement went against their man.

There was one way, however, in which oaths could be rebutted. '*Ego solus jurare volo, tu, si tu audes, nega sacramentum meum et armis mecum contende*' – 'I swear alone, you, if thou darest, deny my oath and fight me' – was a principle expressed in the old Frisian code (eighth century) and the laws of most European and Scandinavian tribes allowed both plaintiff and defendant to challenge the testimony of the other side by calling for the trial by combat or wager of battle. In German law, if the relative of the slain decided to proceed by the duel, his claim of vengeance was supreme, and no other process was admissible. In primitive Icelandic law either party could at any moment interrupt the proceedings with a challenge to single combat.

A duel was not, by definition, necessarily dual, although in practice this was more often the case. The word 'duel', deriving from the Latin '*duellum*' (an alternative form of the Latin word '*bellum*') simply meant war, battle or fighting and it was not uncommon in its earliest history for there to be a number of antagonists on either side, drawn either from the principals' kinsmen or their witnesses.

As time went by, it became increasingly common for these disputes to be single combats, although justice was frequently thwarted by the use of professional fighters put in as champions. For the most part these 'duels' were a means of settling private disputes but the 'wager of battle' held such an accepted arbitrating authority that it could be invoked for settling the fate of kingdoms.

Battle at the Idle and its aftermath

Single combat probably wasn't a realistic option for Raedwald on the banks of the Idle. All we know is that he won a resounding victory after what must have been a gruelling and bloody fight. Aethelfrith was killed and his sons fled to find sanctuary in the far north. Edwin, the source of all the trouble, became king of Northumbria, reigning successfully for the next seventeen years and expanding the kingdom even further north – Edinburgh means 'Edwin's fort'.

Following his victory at the River Idle, Raedwald became *bretwalda*, overlord of all the other 'English' kingdoms (Kent, Sussex, Wessex, Essex, Northumbria and Mercia) as well as remaining king of East Anglia. Equivalent to the Irish 'high kings', he had certain land rights, obligations of allegiance and responsibilities of alliance but this elevated status fell short of being considered king of England. The country remained divided into autonomous sovereign territories ruled by their own kings.

Raedwald paid a high price for his victory. His son Raegenhere was among the fallen. Did Raedwald weep? Did he pray to his new Christian god or did it make him doubt Him more? Did Raegenhere fight valiantly and was his father proud? Did Raegenhere die by a sword hefted by a warrior of renown, or did he perish by an anonymous spear? We can only speculate but if a sword struck him down, there might, at least in theory, have been a remedy.

Swords of the third to the seventh centuries sometimes had associated crystals and semi-precious stones, known as 'life stones'. Many of these mysterious charms have been found in graves with swords, though nothing of the kind was unearthed at Sutton Hoo. Life stones are generally spherical and just a little smaller than a golf ball. They were worn as amulets, often suspended from the scabbard, and were said to be capable of healing any wound delivered by the parent sword. I don't for a moment suppose that they worked but the point about amulets is not that they work but that they inspire faith. This was a deeply superstitious age and weapons, the takers and protectors of life, were at the heart of mystic values.

A sword as splendid as that of Raedwald would have been a treasured and venerated possession. In most circumstances it would have been passed from father to son through the generations. Swords were considered to possess superior powers when inherited or gifted from a famed warrior, the implication being that the weapon was invested with its former owner's courage and valour. Only in rare cases is the sword interred for that warrior's use in the afterlife. We are fortunate indeed that the sword of Raedwald was buried and so, in time, has been passed to us.

Raedwald died in 627 and was succeeded to the East Anglian kingdom by his brother Eni, though another of Raedwald's sons, Eorpwald, deposed Eni and took the

Klein Hunungen sword with life stone

A few of the objects from the Staffordshire Hoard. Some weeks after delivering the typescript of this book to the publisher, the discovery of this remarkable treasure was made public (2009). Many of the finds were pommels (84 identified at the time of writing) and other hilt parts, as well as scabbard fittings. The style of these objects is closely similar to those from the Sutton Hoo sword (photo © Birmingham Museums & Art Gallery)

throne within a year. It was Edwin of Northumbria, however, that succeeded to the title of *bretwalda*. The English nation was still being forged, a pattern-welded structure of great resilience. There were still more ingredients to put in to the mix – the Normans, the Vikings and later waves of immigration all added to the richness and strength of an ever changing culture – but with Raedwald there was a high point in Anglian power and a moment in time that gave us both our name and the basis of our language.

The legacy of the sword lived on, doing service in battle in the hands of countless unnamed warriors. For the next few centuries it remained an exclusive weapon, not least of all because its elaborate process of manufacture meant that it was both an expensive weapon and a relatively scarce weapon. Swords were associated with wealth and power. They were the weapons of kings and princes and they carried with them that sovereign authority. Their form changed little in the ensuing centuries but there was a revolution around the corner in the way that they were made – a revolution that would see the rise of the sword as a universal weapon.

A fine Ulfberht sword (private collection; photo courtesy of Park Lane Arms Fair)

Chapter 4

The Swords of the Northmen:
Pirates to Crusaders

*Perceval de Coulanges ... struck down all he touched ... Nothing resists his
strokes; excellent, tough and very sharp his sword.*

(Guillaume de Machaut – *The Capture of Alexandria*)

On 8 June 793, a flotilla of longships with their tall, menacing prows, penetrated the
curtain of mist that shrouded the tiny island of Lindisfarne, situated just a causewayed
walk off the Northumbrian coast. Within minutes the ships crashed ashore and
disgorged their cargo of fierce warriors. Brandishing fire, axe and sword, they wrought
a terrible destruction on the monastery of St Cuthbert. The monks were cut down
and slaughtered without mercy, their holy relics defiled and their rich treasure looted.
It was the first recorded Viking raid on Britain.

'Viking' means 'pirate' and, in the last decade of the eighth century, bands of these
pagan pirates sailed from their Scandinavian homelands to raid and pillage the rich
pickings of the Christian world. In the century and a half since Raedwald, England
had become a Christian country with an opulent infrastructure of churches and
monasteries. Here was gold and silver and all manner of jewels just for the taking,
along with shiploads of captives to be sold in the lucrative slave markets of the
East. Vikings from Sweden crossed the Baltic Sea to ravage Latvia, Lithuania and
Russia; those from Norway set sail for Scotland, Ireland and the Hebrides, while
those from Denmark set their sights on England. Others even made it to America.
Every year the raiders came, seizing what they wanted and then returned home to
their farms.

In time the Vikings spent longer periods on English soil, often over-wintering in
great military camps and extorting protection money, '*Danegeld*', as a form of tribute
in return for leaving the population unharmed. By around 850 they had begun to
colonize. History remembers the Vikings as ferocious, adventuring warriors, which
indeed they were, but they were also farmers, craftsmen and traders. The fertile
lands of Britain were a magnet for an expanding population and vast tracts of the
northern and eastern seaboard came under Viking occupation. Viking artefacts show

a highly-developed culture and technology with a wide range of exquisitely crafted goods. Not least of which were their swords.

At some point in the late eighth century, it had become possible to forge blades from a single billet of wrought iron. There had been continuous refinements to the production of iron and improvements in its quality but the great breakthrough was to produce larger billets from the bloomery hearth. In essence this meant building larger hearths but the challenge had been to control the temperature. Larger hearths tended to result in much higher temperatures in the furnace, temperatures that would release pure iron in a molten form, but pure iron was not what was required. What was needed for sword blades was the bloom, that spongy mass of iron, carbon and silicates created by chemical reaction at around 1,200 degrees Celsius. It is not entirely clear how this temperature control was effected but, by the dawn of the Viking Age, larger blooms were being produced and from them larger billets of carburised iron – a form of low-grade steel.

Not only did this revolutionize production and result in swords being manufactured on a much-larger scale (because the new method was less labour intensive than the old pattern-welded way) but also the quality of the material was greatly improved. Blades forged from a single homogenous billet show a higher carbon content than those of pattern-welded swords. Pattern-welded swords continued to be produced as decorative, high-status weapons and continued to be passed through the generations but the pathways of the Viking diaspora were hewn with the keener edge of a new type of sword: one made from a single piece of homogenized steel.

A contributing factor in creating swords of a better and more consistent quality was the mass production of blades in just a few centres of manufacture; centres where the iron ore was plentiful and of superior quality and where there was an

abundant supply of timber for charcoal. One such place was Solingen in West Germany. Located on the River Wupper, it also had water power to drive trip-hammers and the wheels for grinding and polishing. Sword manufacture became a major industry here and trade secrets were passed from generation to generation of smiths. Viking traders bought blades from this region and exported them throughout the Viking world.

Smiths at work at their forge – carved wood church portal from Hylestad, Norway, 12th century (The Museum of Cultural History, University of Oslo)

Inscribed swords

Many of the finest swords were inscribed by incising letters onto the flat of a tempered blade, using either an extremely hard burin or a diamond graver. These incised letters were then inlaid either with iron, latten (a copper alloy), copper, silver or gold wire, depending on the status of the sword and the taste of the smith or his client. The wire was hammer-welded into place and the surface filed and polished until the inscription became only faintly perceptible, implanted as a ghostly image in the body of the sword. This process was only possible on a 'finished' blade, lest any extreme heating or quenching distort the lettering or melt the inlay. It was skilled work and the quality of the calligraphy is often remarkable. On swords that have come from the same workshop, a distinctive 'handwriting' style can be perceived.

Runic inscriptions were a favourite. The runic alphabet lent itself particularly well to incising because of its angular nature. Runes not only functioned as a regular alphabet, juxtaposing to form words and phrases, but they were also magical and talismanic symbols in their own right. In an age when swords were starting to be produced on a wider scale, they had lost none of their individualism or mystique. Inscriptions might be cryptic incantations to pagan gods or, more prosaically, they might simply indicate ownership, such as the runic inscription on a sword in the Oslo Museum that translates as 'Thormund possesses me'. In either case these inscriptions were a form of charm, embedded into the very heart of the weapon, appealing to the sentimental fancies of a superstitious age.

One word, in the Latin alphabet, appears more than any other inscription on swords from the eighth to tenth centuries – ULFBEHRT. It is a maker's signature. Whether the original Ulfbehrt was an individual smith or a company trade name is uncertain but the brand name continued to occur on top-quality swords for at least two centuries. Recent research has argued that the Ulfbehrt forge was located in the Solingen region and, to date, 123 swords bearing the Ulfbehrt inscription have been found throughout the Viking world from Britain to Russia. The lettering on these swords was incised in large block-capital letters, standing around 1 inch tall, along the spine of the blade. Tests on Ulfberht blades have shown many of them to be of the highest quality carbon steel, though forgeries plagiarizing the mark were common, in the same way that today prestige brands are faked for the discount market. We know of other names that competed with the Ulfberht mark – Niso,

Ulfberht blade inscription (private collection; photo courtesy of Park Lane Arms Fair)

Banto, Atabald, Leutfrit, Benno, Inno, Erholt – but only one or two examples of swords from their respective workshops have been found to date. Ulfberht was almost certainly the market leader.

Metallurgical analysis of a number of Ulfberht blades has been carried out by the archeometallurgist Dr Alan Williams and he has discovered that the best of these were made from high-carbon crucible steel. Also known as '*wootz*', this material was created by heating wrought iron with cast iron in a covered ceramic crucible. After baking in the furnace for several days, the alloy eventually absorbed enough carbon to melt and become fully liquid. This process was a considerable advance on the chemical reaction at lower temperatures that produced wrought iron blooms from the bloomery hearth. When cooled, the crucible would be broken open to release a cake of cast steel from which a blade could be forged.

Afghanistan, northern India and Persia were the exclusive centres of wootz production at this time. Crucible steels weren't manufactured in Europe until the eighteenth century. With wootz it was possible to produce blades with a delicate watered-steel appearance; one that had patterns far subtler and far more sophisticated than any pattern-welded blade. Possibly because it was a centre of trade for such blades, or because there was a tradition of manufacture there, Damascus in Syria has lent its name to this style of patterning whether it occurs in steel or silk. Lumps of wootz were traded with Northern Europe from at least the seventh century AD and the Ulfberht enterprise was most probably a chief importer.

The aesthetic attraction of 'watered steel' doesn't seem to have been the motivation for the Ulfbehrt factory; they wanted wootz because it was of superior quality. Their reputation for tough, hard, durable blades, founded on the use of wootz as a raw material, would have made Ulfberht a very prestigious brand, doubtless able to command the highest prices. However, some samples of the Ulfberht-branded blades that Dr Williams has analysed, were made from inferior bloomery metal. Without modern analytical tools, it would be impossible to tell the difference just by handling the blades. Moreover, shoddy ones could be quenched in such a way so as to make them hard enough to sharpen as keenly as wootz but with the consequence of making them brittle. These discrepancies in the quality of Ulfberht-branded swords suggests that unscrupulous smiths were passing off fake Ulfberhts as the real thing; fakes that might well shatter on the battlefield. With some swords being made with wootz and others not, with some swords well made and others not, with some swords capable of extraordinary feats of cutting and others breaking at the first contact, it is little wonder that people gave swords that were proven in battle spiritual attributions. After all, superficially they appeared to be made from the same substance, so it could only be magical powers that made one sword different from another. Another variation in Ulfberht blades is the spelling of the name. Standard spelling was not yet established at this period; moreover the word would have been inscribed by men who, at best, were probably only semi-literate. Interestingly, Dr Williams has observed that those blades that bear the ULFBERHT legend spelled incorrectly tend to be of inferior quality to those that spell it correctly.

Not everyone could afford an Ulfberht blade, or even a fake, and so had to settle for one forged from indigenous iron. An amount of iron ore was mined but a very common source of iron in the Viking age, and indeed earlier, was 'bog iron'. The peat bogs of northern Europe, especially in Scandinavia, were rich in this resource. Streams carried particles of iron in solution, leeched from nearby mountains, into the bog. A variety of reactions, both with the anaerobic environment of the bog and with certain bacteria, resulted in the formation of insoluble iron compounds about the size of a pea. These nodules, lying just a few inches below the surface, were harvested by cutting into the peat and peeling back the turves. They were then roasted to drive out moisture, possibly taking on a little carbon in the process, and then smelted in the bloomery hearth as described in the previous chapter.

Signs and symbols were frequent companions to the lettering on blades. The Ulfberht trademark, for instance, was usually rendered as +ULFBEHR+T. Sadly the meaning of the crosses is unknown but they surely meant something. On the reverse side of the blades were often patterns of other marks such as a cross within a circle, simple upright strokes, saltire crosses and interlaced bands of diagonal strokes. The swastika – an ancient symbol of creativity and the life force until the Nazis hijacked it – is another symbol occurring from time to time on swords of this period, while swirls, circles and dots were legion. No amount of modernization in the production process could release the sword from the thrall of the magical forces that empowered it.

Symbols on reverse of Ulfberht blade (private collection; photo courtesy of Park Lane Arms Fair)

Sword forms

On a more mundane level, additional strength was imparted to the sword blade by forging a groove, called a 'fuller', down the centre of the blade. Fullers were a rediscovery rather than a completely fresh invention. They are to be found on some Iron Age swords but the practice had disappeared for around four centuries. Fullers made the sword stronger and more rigid while, at the same time, making it lighter. There is a fiction, put about over the years, that the fuller is a 'blood groove', facilitating the letting of blood when the sword is thrust into an enemy's body. This has no basis in either science or fact. The fuller was there solely to create structural properties. These grooves gave a curved surface to an otherwise flattish blade and curved structures are inherently stronger, in the same way that corrugated iron is less prone to bending than a sheet of flat iron. You can test the principal of this by cutting or folding a 1 inch-wide strip of paper. Push it endwise against the wall and feel how readily it buckles. Now curl it into a 'U' shape and try again. You will encounter much greater resistance, yet the gauge, mass and nature of the materials are unchanged. A fuller introduces the reinforcing properties of this 'U' shape into the spine of a blade. Early Viking fullers were single, wide and deep extending for nearly the entire length of the blade. In later centuries, some swords carried multiple fullers, frequently three or more, which were narrower and less deeply ground, enabling the manufacture of considerably lighter blades.

Blade forms changed hardly at all from Raedwald's day, remaining lenticular in cross section and broad with rounded points. In time there was a tendency for the profile of the blade to taper more towards the point and some, not all, Viking blades began to have acutely tapered points. This last development did not signify a change in function, swords had always had a thrusting capability, but was a consequence of better-quality steel. Stronger steels allowed a tapering point that was resilient enough not to break on contact. Viking blade lengths remained in the same range as their Anglo-Saxon predecessors, with some being as short as Raedwald's 28-inch blade and others as long as 33 inches.

Similarly the form of the hilt remained much the same with a narrow cross and a short grip that set the pommel snugly against the back of the hand. With the Vikings, though, we start to see the pommel taking a more solid and weighty form. Designs of Viking pommels varied considerably, the most familiar being the tri-lobed pommel, which has been aptly described as resembling a tea cosy. Whatever its form, the important thing about Viking pommels is that they were made of solid iron and had more weight than their Anglo-Saxon forbears; thus they started to function as a counterbalance. This, combined with lighter, slightly more tapered blades meant that the sword was suited to more virtuoso management in the hand. It was a first subtle advance towards a fully counterbalanced sword.

Christian converts

By the late ninth century the Vikings, or 'Danes' as they were more commonly known in England, had established a permanent rule over the east and north of England.

Wessex, the land of the West Saxons, was a last bastion of resistance and, in May 878, King Alfred the Great faced down the threat of total Danish hegemony at the Battle of Eddington. Danes fought in an identical manner to their Anglo-Saxon cousins, using the shield-wall as their principal tactic. Though the sword was by now more common on the battlefield, it remained a high-status weapon and the spear and the axe did equal work that day. Alfred had summoned the fyrd and men from all the neighbouring shires had flocked to his cause.

There is a boulder adjacent to the ancient Ridgeway path near Uffington, which is known as the 'Alfred Stone'. Rainwater has drilled into it to create a labyrinth of internal fissures. Legend has it that when blown it produces a note that can be heard for miles around and that it was sounded by Alfred to summon the fyrd. I once visited the stone with the music historian David Edwards. He had fashioned a horn mouth-piece that fitted into the rock and I had a go at blowing it. To my astonishment I managed to produce a note – a beautiful, deep resonating note. It was a great thrill, though I don't suppose for a moment that this was how Alfred called his fyrd before that fateful encounter on the Polden Hills. For a start it is in the wrong place and I doubt that its low note would have reached the ears of more than a dozen men in the surrounding area.

Eddington was a hard, daylong, slugging match. Many blows were dealt and many warriors fell but, in the end, Alfred triumphed. It was an important victory, not just because it saw the beginning of the end of Danish oppression but because the Danish leader, Guthrum, surrendered not only his sword to Alfred but also his soul. He converted to Christianity. Only a few years earlier, Charlemagne's grandson, Louis the German (806–876), had received Viking envoys at his court. He broke their swords with his bare hands before their eyes and, by so doing, induced them also to convert to the Christian faith. The Viking Age was not entirely over but Viking was no longer synonymous with pagan.

Now we may think that Louis the German was either immensely strong or the Vikings' swords not of the highest quality, not from the Ulfbehrt factory perhaps, but even the best blade will break if bent sufficiently far. Swords also break when you don't want them to. Constant percussive striking can set up tiny hairline fractures in the blade, which can fail without warning. I remember choreographing a scene for a documentary that involved someone being decapitated by a sword against a tree. The reverse camera angle didn't require the victim in place and the swordsman simply had to strike the tree with great force. I was standing only a few yards off when the blow was struck. The sword sheared off about 6 inches from the point and this short, sharp, dagger-like shard flew at lightning speed towards my head. There was as much chance of ducking a bullet as that high-velocity missile but, fortunately for me, it whistled by safely just a few inches from my ear! Swords could, and did, break in battle. Legend has it that the sword of a young Norman knight, Tancred de Hauteville, shattered in combat but he used the jagged edge of the broken half still in his hand to thrust at his enemy's face and kill him.

Tancred lived in troubled times; petty feuds and quarrels were constantly breaking out between feudal barons and warfare was endemic. He was just seventeen years old and a troubled young man. He worried that his feudal duty was to fight as a knight and kill people and yet, as a devout Christian, his faith told him that killing was a sin. Relief for his conscience was at hand in the form of Pope Urban II. In 1095 Urban called for the first crusade to rid the Holy Land of Saracen rule. In a statement that was to change the world, the consequences of which reverberate to this day, he proclaimed:

> Whoever for devotion alone, not to gain honour or money, goes to Jerusalem to liberate the Church of God can substitute this journey for all penance.

Killing infidels, as opposed to brother Christian knights, was not only a duty, it atoned for all other sins and guaranteed a place in Paradise. Tancred's destiny was clear. He went on crusade.

The Normans were a new kind of warrior. Their name being a contraction of Norsemen (Northmen), they were the descendents of a Viking kingdom established in Northern France in the early ninth century. Norman armour and weapons had hardly changed since the time of Raedwald – a hauberk of mail, an open-faced helm, a spear and a sword – but by the dawn of the eleventh century there had evolved a new way of fighting. The Normans fought on horseback. This was the birth of the medieval knight. To support cavalry on the battlefield were combined forces of archers and men-at-arms on foot and nearly all were equipped with a sword. Swords were becoming a universal weapon.

Detailed preparations for Duke William's invasion of England are depicted in the Bayeux Tapestry. As well as horses and provisions being loaded onto the fleet of ships, we see rails of armour, racks of spears and bundles and barrels of swords, all for general issue. This wider availability of the sword and its use by troops of all ranks never detracted from its ancestral status. A knight's sword remained a prized and very personal possession; an abiding symbol of his rank.

Swords of the crusaders

Swords at this time appeared largely unchanged from the preceding generation, having broad blades with a deep central fuller and averaging 30 to 31 inches in length. The most discernable change was that the cross became significantly wider, projecting 3 to 4 inches either side of the blade. These wider crosses can be found on swords as early as the mid-tenth century, though it took some time before they became the norm. In their early forms they were simple straight bars that tapered towards their ends. The Vikings called them 'spike hilts' and one is tempted to think that they could be used offensively, by holding the blade of the sword and using the hilt in the manner of an axe, as we see in later depictions of fifteenth-century swordfighting. However there is no evidence for such a practice at this date. Irrespective of their offensive potential, these wider, and generally narrower, crosses facilitated hooking a finger over the bar and there was more chance of hanging on to one of these swords with an exhausted arm and failing fingers than there would have been to retain one such as Raedwald's with its stubby little cross.

A pommel style resembling a Brazil nut came in around 1000 AD and this was to be the most common type for the next two centuries. It could combine both the properties of counterweight and lever but, as we shall see, a trend had begun for larger, meatier pommels and longer grips, no longer sitting the pommel snugly against the back of the hand. These seemingly minute changes to the proportions of the hilt were to have a lasting impact on the development of the sword and swordfighting. The eleventh century was a transitional period and the full effect of these adjustments was still a little way in the future.

The Ulfbehrt sword-manufacturing atelier seems to have gone out of business by the time of the Norman Conquest in the mid-eleventh century, but they were succeeded in the marketplace by a new brand name: Ingelrii. The brand name was not the only inscription to change. Now we start to see, instead of pagan runes and symbols, Latin inscriptions invoking the power of the Christian God. One Ingelerii sword from Dresden bears the legend '*Homo Dei*', meaning 'Man of God', a common appellation given to Christian knights who went on crusade. Swords from the rival firm Gicelin bear the legend '*In Nomine Domini*' ('In the name of the Lord') on the reverse side. Others are inscribed with '*Sancta Maria*', '*Sanctus Petrus*' or '*Benedictus Deus*'.

Knights going to do God's work in the Holy Land first had their swords blessed by the Church, their piety and zeal matched only by their ferocity in battle. William of Malmesbury, writing of Geoffrey of Bouillon at the Battle of Antioch in 1098, tells how

> with a sword he cut asunder a Turk, so that the other half was carried off by the horse at speed. Another he clave asunder from neck to groin . . . and also cut through the saddle and backbone of the horse.

Ingelrii sword (private collection, photo courtesy of Park Lane Arms Fair)

Ingelrii hilt (private collection, photo courtesy of Park Lane Arms Fair)

This is impressive stuff, though one must always beware of a chronicler's natural tendency for exaggeration. We should also bear in mind that in 1098 the author was only eight years old and so unlikely to have been an eyewitness.

It does seem an impossible feat, however good the sword or strong the arm, but swords of this period were capable of inflicting significant damage. In most cases

good quality mail armour could turn the blade, though, as Gilbert of Bruges wrote in 1128 concerning an attack on the town, 'as to those wearing an armor, they were exempted from wounds but not from bruises'. These 'bruises', of course, could be serious contusions or hematomas. Moreover, there were many on the medieval battlefield who were unarmoured. In a test cut against a pig carcass, I used a replica of a parallel-sided twelfth-century sword made by Simon Fearnham at Raven Armouries; it had been honed to razor sharpness. To hold something that sharp with that

Detail from a 10th century mail shirt found at Gjermundbu, Norway (Museum of Cultural History, Oslo; photo: Vegard Vike)

weight was like being handed a loaded gun after only having previously handled blank-firing weapons; it felt dangerous. The carcass, a full hog, though with entrails removed, was suspended from a tree branch. As I swung the sword I brought my left hand onto the hilt, clasping it over my right, as is sometimes shown in contemporary manuscripts, in order to gain extra power. To my amazement I severed the carcass completely in half, cutting clean through the spine. That it was the size of a man, a naked pink man, tempered any sense of achievement with a feeling of absolute horror. Swords are capable of terrible things. This wasn't a new realization but it was a chilling reminder. For chivalrous knights on crusade, of course, 'terrible things' are exactly what they wanted their swords to do.

When possible, surgeons did their best to repair even extreme cases of the swordsman's butchery, as this passage from Raimon of Avignon's *Chirugia* (circa 1200) suggests:

> It often happens that a brave man is heavily struck on the neck by a sword ... If the wound is in the jugular vein ... take needle, thread and your thimble quickly and tie the vein nicely and well near its ends; but pass the thread around the back of the vein, for it must not be pierced, and draw

'*The Victory of Humility over Pride*'; Detail from the Trier *Jungfrauenspiegel*. c. 1200. Note the use of two hands for powerful blows with singlehanded sword and the effective use of the thrust with swords that still have rounded points (photo: August Kestner Museum, Hanover)

the vein out through the chest. Tie a knot over it so that it is absolutely firm. When the place is suppurating be ready for the pain you must inflict.

Medieval medicine set great store by the healing power of pus. Although some of their methods will appear primitive today, it is important to note that they did have coherent procedures and schools of medical thought that addressed remedies for some of the dreadful wounds that could be caused by the sword. In another section Raimon explains what to do 'if the skull is fractured from a powerful sword-stroke' and 'if a poorly armed knight happens to be wounded with a sword and so injured that the whole of the top of the shoulder is cut away from the neck'. Even with such terrible wounds Raimon held out hope that recovery was possible.

A classic crusading sword from the early twelfth century, now in the collection of Glasgow Museums, bears the inscription 'B O A C'. Inlaid in gold, though now only faintly discernable, the letters are repeated several times along the length of the blade, presumably to increase their talismanic power, and framed on either side with circled crosses. We can only guess the meaning of the letters but they are possibly an acronym for '*Beatus Omnipotensque Armatus Christi*' ('Blessed and Omnipotent [is] the Warrior of Christ'). If so, the owner clearly didn't feel that humility was an important knightly virtue. Slogans like this proclaimed the owner's faith, his dedication to the service of God and his belief that he had God on his side in a cause that was righteous. They were also intended to invoke heavenly protection.

On a more practical level, this sword is noteworthy because of its very large disc pommel and its extended grip. Bigger, heavier pommels and longer grips worked in conjunction with each other to the same effect – enhanced counterbalance. With the pommel sited some inches behind the hand, a sword has a different balance point and this, combined with a weighty pommel, facilitated much greater blade control and more fluid fighting techniques. Although the overall weight changed little, the sensation of weight in the hand was considerably less and the weapon could not only be wielded

BOAC sword c. 1100–1150 (courtesy of Culture and Sport Glasgow ((Museums))

Inscription from blade of BOAC sword

with greater speed, it was also significantly less tiring to do so. One consequence of being able to move a sword more quickly is that it immediately became more useful as a means of quick-response defence/attack – beating an incoming sword away and riposting in a continuous fluid move. Although little had changed to the eye of the casual observer, the sword of the early Middle Ages was a world away from its Anglo-Saxon predecessors. Heavy pommels and longer grips were here to stay and these new counterbalanced swords heralded a new age in swordfighting techniques.

From the mists of its pagan past, the sword emerged in the Middle Ages as the bright sword of chivalry. By the late twelfth century it had become the ultimate symbol of the knight and to all the ancient traditions of authority, power and status was added a final touch of Christian sanctity; its very form proclaiming the Holy Cross. In the Crusades, knights and warrior monks like the Knights Templar were exhorted by the Pope to turn their weapons on the enemies of Christ. Those who followed the cause were forgiven past sins and so it was that the chivalry of Europe took up their swords and with a clean conscience drove them into the hearts of non-believers.

In the words of a twelfth-century crusader doctrine, 'a knight should render no reason to the infidel than 6 inches of his sword into his accursed bowels'. Although slightly more tapered points were increasingly common in the twelfth century, the overriding trend was still for rounded points and yet here we have a reference that strongly infers the use of the thrust. Swords with rounded points were perfectly adequate for thrusting at mail, evidence for which is well documented in contemporary manuscripts such as the *Jungfrauenspiegel*.

In the years that followed, the tactics of warfare and many elements of military hardware changed. There were significant advances in armour as the 'age of mail' gave way to the 'age of plate'. Swords had to adapt to meet the new challenges. After centuries of only minor changes to the form of the sword, the Middle Ages saw a proliferation of design modifications and a wide variety of sword types emerge. The sword came of age and was elevated to be the most iconic weapon of the epoch; it became the weapon of everyman and yet remained the ultimate symbol of authority and status. The next sword we are going to look at, the sword of King Henry V of England, epitomizes the knightly sword of the era. It was a new type of sword for a new age and yet, imbued with ancestral majesty, it hung above the tomb of its warrior king, just as Raedwald's sword had been laid to rest with him.

Henry V (National Portrait Gallery, London)

Chapter 5

The Sword of King Henry V, King of England

Cry God for Harry, England and St George

(Shakespeare: *Henry V*)

The sword believed by many to be the battle sword of Henry V now lodges in the museum at Westminster Abbey in London. It is the sword carried before the king's standard in his funeral procession and given to the abbey in 1423. Thereafter, almost certainly, it hung over the tomb of the king until, at some unknown date, it was removed and stored in a chest with a jumble of old vestments. It was taken from that chest in 1951 and cleaned by Ewart Oakeshott. Ewart was a scholar of arms and armour, whose wonderful books inspired much of my early interest. It was my privilege to know him and to spend many hours at his house in Ely chatting about swords. His collection included a number of significant pieces, which he was pleased to show anyone who inquired. He was an enchanting and generous man and his passing is greatly mourned. In describing Henry's sword, Ewart wrote that it was 'one of the most beautiful medieval swords to handle I have ever known' and he had handled more than a few.

When I visited Henry V's sword, it was as much a pilgrimage to see the sword that my old friend had so lovingly restored to life all those years ago, as it was to view the weapon that had been held by England's most famous soldier king – perhaps the very weapon that 'did affright the air at Agincourt'. Sadly it is no longer possible to gain access to handle the sword because entombed alongside it, in a sealed glass case, is Henry's shield and this is in such a delicate state of preservation that it can no longer be exposed to the air.

Henry's sword is a classic medieval 'arming sword' with an acutely tapering blade, a wide, down-turned cross and a tremendously large pommel. In form this is a 'wheel pommel', which became the most common type during the medieval period. A central hub protrudes from the rim with a recess ground into its centre. Such recesses were often filled with enamelled roundels bearing the owner's heraldic arms. In the case of Henry's sword, the red cross of Saint George is displayed. Curiously, this has

Pommel detail of Henry V's sword, Westminster
Abbey (© Dean and Chapter of Westminster)

been painted on rather than enamelled, not what one would expect on a royal sword, and is therefore possibly a flourish that is posthumous to Henry. Perhaps it substituted for the lost enamel? Although seemingly heavy, the outer part of the massive iron pommel is in fact hollow. The proportions of the hilt, with its broad cross and large pommel, relative to the short 27-inch blade, deceive the eye into thinking that the sword is heavy and substantial; whereas, actually, it is extremely light, weighing only 2lb 3oz.

We have seen in the last chapter how the introduction of fullers during the Viking Age enabled blades to be both strengthened and lightened. An alternative method of achieving the same goal started to appear in the fourteenth century. Actually, it reappeared; many La Tène swords were made with a similar technique. This was to hollow the surface of the blade into gentle curves either side of a central rib.

On the Henry V sword, this hollowing is relatively subtle but by the end of the fifteenth century extreme hollows were ground, leaving the mid rib standing very proud. Henry's sword most likely received its shaping on the anvil, though a certain amount of hollowing could be achieved by grinding. That is not to say that such swords were 'hollow ground'; this is a specific manufacturing technique that we shall meet later, whereby the face of the blade is ground horizontally to the plane of the wheel. The arc of the hollow therefore corresponds with the arc of the grinding-wheel's circumference. For Henry's sword, and other medieval examples, the arc of the hollow would require a wheel of fairly small circumference and it is unlikely at the time that such wheels could have been turned at sufficiently high speeds to grind. A further advantage of hollowing a blade is that the hollowed curve rises towards the edge, creating a slight bevel. This can be ground at an acute angle to create a more supported and sharper cutting edge. If it had not been hollowed, Henry's blade would have appeared as a flattened diamond in cross-section, which was the most common form for all medieval swords, whether they were hollowed or not. On one side is a maker's mark stamped into the blade. Similar 'twig-like' marks have been noted on other medieval swords, though the identity of this workshop is unknown.

The sword's blade runs fairly parallel from the hilt for about two thirds of its length and then tapers steeply to an acute point. This is called the 'profile taper'. The amount that a blade tapers in thickness towards the point, that is looking at it edge on, is called the 'distal taper'. At first, both tapers on Henry's sword are gradual, they then taper acutely towards the point for the last few inches. Nuances of taper, both profile and distal, are as instrumental in creating the balance of a sword as the size of the pommel, the length of the grip, the dimensions of the blade and the depth of the fullers or hollows. Swords are sophisticated and finely tuned implements. Even the width and taper of the tang – the part of the blade that extends up through the grip to be riveted over at the top of the pommel, holding the whole assembly tightly together – can affect subtleties of balance. A sword that feels perfect to one man will not feel right to another. Balance is a very subjective and personal thing.

Henry's sword is a very light sword by the standards of the day. This does not suggest that Henry was a physically weak man; rather that he was a vigorous fighter. It hints that he would lead from the front and remain active in the fray, raining blows all about him, for as long as strength would allow. A lighter sword gave him the ability to display sustained efforts of stamina. It's an old trick for the master to have a lighter weapon than his pupils that he might dazzle them with his superior virtuosity. I think something similar was going on with Henry V and his sword. That is not to say that it was an ineffectual sword; far from it. In skilled hands it was an extremely-useful weapon.

Schools of fence

Swordfighting is an art. It has to be learnt and I would contend that it was systemized, codified and taught from the earliest times. Certainly fencing schools were a recorded feature of town and city life by the early Middle Ages. The word 'fencing' dates back to at least the thirteenth century, deriving from a contracted form of 'defence'; as in Master of (De)Fence and The Art of (De)Fence. Over time

Sword of Henry V, Westminster Abbey (©Dean and Chapter of Westminster)

A 15th century fencing school. *The Master of the Banderoles*, engraving, c. 1464 (courtesy of Prof. Sidney Anglo)

the meanings of words often change a little. Today the word 'fencing' conjures up images of the modern sport, performed exclusively with mock swords. Its tip-tap play of light, flexible blades owes a little to the techniques of eighteenth century swordfighting but nothing to the techniques of earlier eras. Modern 'fencing' certainly does not convey the broader meaning of the word in its historical sense. Originally a study of the art of (de)fence embraced a range of combat skills. 'Masters of fence' taught (de)fence not only with swords but also with other hand–held weapons such as axes, knives and staff weapons. They taught wrestling as an integral part of weapon fighting. Horsemanship and skills with cavalry weapons such as the lance were also the domain of these masters. In time some also embraced shooting and knowledge of artillery.

'Fencing' is a legitimate word for referring to medieval swordfighting, so long as we remember that in its time, and for some centuries after, it had the wider meaning of engaging in all the martial arts. Having said that, swordfighting was undoubtedly chief among the arts taught in the 'fence schools' and such establishments were often regarded as dens of thuggery and ill repute. Various laws were passed in the City of London banning the keeping of a 'sword playing house', from at least as early as 1189. In 1311 the authorities caught up with the aptly named master, Roger le Skirmisour, and sent him to prison for forty days for 'enticing thither the sons of respectable persons, so as to waste and spend the property of their fathers and mothers upon bad practices'.

The fighting arts were highly valued by the ruling class and it was not so much the martial training that was objected to, rather the environment in which it took place. What the authorities sought to clamp down on was the subculture that surrounded urban fence schools and the lower class bruisers that frequented them. In spite of such strictures in the city, the teaching of martial arts flourished, especially on the South Bank in London, alongside the taverns and brothels. A charming fifteenth-century engraving depicts a school of arms combined with a bathhouse. It is half gymnasium and half bordello. Students practice swordfighting, weight training, acrobatics, and shooting with a handgun, while naked women are on hand in an adjacent chamber to soothe them after their exertions. One couple occupy the bed in an upstairs room. The whirlpools and steam rooms of our present day gymnasia are modest recreations by comparison.

If we are to believe Shakespeare, then the young Henry V (Prince Hal in *Henry IV* pt 1) spent a wayward youth fraternizing with ne'er-do-wells in the taverns of Southwark prior to his bold encounter with Harry Percy on the battlefield at Shrewsbury. If this were so, we might imagine that he had perfected his martial skills in that vibrant medieval district. Shakespeare, however, is generally unreliable with regard to historical fact. The truth is that Henry was only sixteen years old at the time of Shrewsbury in July 1403 and his martial education had been undertaken elsewhere.

Henry's early years

Henry received the standard education of a young noble, growing up with his brothers in the household of his maternal grandmother, Joan, Countess of Hereford, in the rural backwater of Bytham in Lincolnshire. His governess, whom he remained attached to all his life, was Mary Hervy. He studied literature (historical chronicles and chivalric romances), rhetoric, theology, music (he played the harp) and became fluent in Latin and French. From the age of seven he began to learn horsemanship and how to fight with swords and other weapons. An unknown fifteenth-century chronicler wrote:

> a youth must have seen his blood flow and his teeth crack under the blow of an adversary and have been thrown to the ground twenty times ... thus will he be able to face real war with the hope of victory.

We may imagine that Henry's training was a robust and rugged experience and, since at that stage there was no prospect that he might one day be king (his father had yet to usurp the throne), it is likely that he was thrown around a little harder than he might have been otherwise. Perhaps he was tutored by the enigmatic Bertolf Vander Eme, a Flemish master of arms of whom we know nothing except that he once injured his thumb in sword practice with Henry's father, for which he was compensated with £10, a considerable sum at the time.

Henry V's father had left England to go on crusade when the boy was only three years old and his mother, Mary de Bohun, died when he was seven. Young Henry was effectively an orphan. His father, Henry Bolingbroke, Duke of Hereford, later to become King Henry IV, went on crusade not to the Holy Land but, like Chaucer's knight, to Lithuania. The 'Northern Crusades', though less well-known, were equally virulent against the pagans of Finland, Poland, Estonia, Livonia and Lithuania and against the Russian Orthodox Christians of Novgorod and Muscovy. A short trip to the Baltic was much more convenient than the long and expensive trek to the Holy Land. Once there, many English knights served under the banner of the Teutonic Knights, saving their souls on a budget. Bolingbroke was among them, crusading from 1390 to 1394, only returning after the death of his wife. The 7-year-old future Henry V, so recently bereaved of his mother, may have got to know something of his father in the immediate aftermath of his return but it was a short-lived acquaintance. Within three years Henry Bolingbroke was exiled.

Bolingbroke had been a loyal subject of Richard II, in spite of that king's autocratic and despotic rule. In fact he was his cousin, being the son of John of Gaunt and grandson of Edward III. Edward III's first son, the Black Prince, had died before he could succeed to the throne and the succession had gone to his son, Richard. Richard II remained childless and so Bolingbroke was heir to the throne, should both King Richard and Gaunt die. Bolingbroke was a powerful magnate and, since his return from the Crusades, held significant authority at the heart of royal government. It was a position of grace from which he would fall. In 1397 Bolingbroke accused Thomas Mowbray, the Duke of Norfolk, of treason. It led to the challenge of a judicial duel.

Judicial duels

By the time of the Norman Conquest the old right of trial by combat or 'wager of battle' had metamorphosed into the judicial duel. In essence the wager of battle and the judicial duel are the same insofar as they are both due processes of law. The distinction being that the wager of battle, in pre-Christian societies, was the straightforward prosecution of a secular right; whereas the judicial duel invoked the intervention of God in the same way that the trial by ordeal (holding red-hot irons etc) sought to establish guilt or innocence. It was presumed that God was the ultimate judge and that He would ensure that the innocent party triumphed. The 'justice' of this procedure was further complicated by the fact that a sideline of the fence schools was the training of professional champions, men who could be hired to fight on a plaintiff or defendant's behalf in a judicial duel. Until the introduction of grand assizes and trial by jury by Henry II in the twelfth century, a judicial duel was the only recourse to decide a matter of right in the absence of clear evidence.

Even after Henry II's reforms, it remained the ultimate legal privilege to demand to settle a case by means of the sword in a judicial duel, particularly in cases involving accusations of treason or of title and land ownership. In 1157 Robert de Montfort accused Henry of Essex of cowardice, alleging that he dropped the English standard and took flight in a campaign against the Welsh. To settle the matter, a judicial duel took place on an island in the Thames near Reading, evoking the old days of the *holmganga*. Essex was beaten and left for dead. His body was taken to the nearby Abbey, where the monks discovered he was still alive and nursed him back to health. Unfortunately for him, he was considered morally dead and so was obliged to spend the rest of his years confined at the Abbey.

Bolingbroke experienced a different banishment. Although Richard II had initially, though reluctantly, acceded to the demands for a judicial duel, he had a change of mind when his two noble lords stood before him ready to engage in combat. He stopped the proceedings and exiled both of them. Richard, always jealous of his cousin and legal heir, Bolingbroke, was much troubled by dissident nobles and no longer knew who to believe or trust. He felt safer with both men out of the way. Besides he preferred the counsel of his fawning favourites to that of the established nobility.

Knighthood

Bolingbroke went in exile to Paris and his now 10-year-old son was removed from his grandmother's care to continue his upbringing at the king's court. It is said that Richard, having no children of his own, was extremely fond of the boy, though it can hardly have escaped the young Henry's notice that he was also a hostage against his father's good conduct. King Richard knighted the young Henry personally, dubbing him with his sword in great ceremony. There were two types of ritual in which a knight could receive his appointment. One, more informal and generally used as a spontaneous moment on the battlefield, was the *colée*. For this a sponsor would punch the new knight on the chest or shoulder, this 'buffet' symbolizing the last blow a knight would take to his person without honourable retaliation. In the more formal ceremony, the laying of the sword on the shoulders carried an identical symbolic intent.

A knight's sword was sacred and in the more ritualized knighting ceremonies it would first be consecrated at the altar. At the conclusion of the elaborate ceremony the young knight was given the '*accolade*' – a tap on the shoulder with the flat of the blade. Then he was proclaimed a knight. All his accoutrements of war were given symbolic meaning. His dagger represented his trust in God; his spur, swiftness and diligence; his helm, fear of shame; his mace, courage; his saddle, duty; and his spear, truth. Most important of all was his double-edged sword; one edge represented chivalry and the other justice. All embodied ideals to which a young knight aspired.

Bolingbroke's return

Henry Bolingbroke, already feeling the smart of injustice at his banishment, had cause to be even more aggrieved in 1399. Richard II seized all of his wealth and lands on the death of John of Gaunt. Gaunt was Bolingbroke's father and also the king's uncle. It was the final straw and Bolingbroke returned to England to lead an armed rebellion against the king; one which quickly won popular support. The general feeling among the nobles was that if Bolingbroke's lands weren't safe, then whose were?

Richard was away campaigning in Ireland, quelling a rebellion led by the king of Leinster. On campaign with him was his young ward, the future Henry V – quite an experience for a 12-year-old boy. When news of Bolingbroke's landing reached Richard, he hastened back, leaving young Henry behind under guard in Trim Castle near Dublin. Richard's retinue was ambushed by Henry Percy, Duke of Northumberland, and taken to meet Bolingbroke at Flint Castle.

'I am come before my time', Bolingbroke is reported to have said in reference to his right to succession to the throne on Richard's death. He went on to say: 'Your people complain that you have ruled them badly these twenty years. Please God, I will now help you to rule them better'. King Richard II was imprisoned in the Tower of London, where he signed his abdication, and later taken to Pontefract Castle, where he died. Murder was suspected but not proven. Bolingbroke became King Henry IV on 13 October 1399. His son, Henry of Monmouth, became Duke of Cornwall, Earl of Chester, Duke of Lancaster, Duke of Aquitaine and Prince of Wales.

Glendower rebellion

Within a year there was a major uprising in Wales led by Owain Glyndŵr, a rival Prince of Wales, who had been appointed by popular acclaim. Glyndŵr, although previously loyal to Richard, now saw the time was right to strike for independent Welsh rule. It has been described as the 'War of Welsh Liberation' and it was to last, on and off, for the next ten years and have a dramatic impact on the life of Henry of Monmouth. At the outbreak of hostilities his father despatched him to Chester, where at the tender age of 13, he took up his royal duties. The military commander of the garrison was Harry 'Hotspur' Percy.

Whatever martial training the young prince had received to date, it can be assumed that it now progressed in earnest. Harry Percy was one of the most celebrated warriors of his day. Whether he had earned the soubriquet 'Hotspur' from his tendency towards hot-headed action or from his reputation for riding hard is uncertain. Either way it must have been quite thrilling for the young prince to prove his mettle under the guidance of such a battle-proven hero. In that first year, before Henry gradually assumed more responsibilities and led expeditions in his own right, they would have hunted together, patrolled together and, most probably, sparred together. Little can either of them have known that within a few years they would face each other on the battlefield as enemies. Shakespeare would have us believe that Prince Hal and Harry Percy were of a similar age. Harry Percy was actually twenty-three years older, making somewhat of a mockery of his line 'O Harry! Thou has't robbed me of my youth', when he lies dying, struck down by the prince in the play. In fact, as we shall see, Hotspur was not killed by the prince directly.

The Percys, the Earls of Northumberland, had been the chief supporters of Henry Bolingbroke when he had seized Richard's throne. They already owned vast lands in the north of England and were the chief bulwark against Scotland. As one of the most powerful families in the land, their loyalty was crucial to any king being able to govern the country. During Richard's reign they had been on the frontline against many Scottish raids, though Harry 'Hotspur' Percy, the Duke's eldest son, famously lost to the Earl of Douglas's army at Otterburn in 1388. It was an ignominious defeat following a foolhardy night attack that was instigated in a fit of rage because Douglas had unhorsed Hotspur in a joust and absconded with his pennon. Hotspur was taken prisoner and subsequently ransomed. You would think that such an incident might have dimmed his fame but it seems his reputation for daring and fighting prowess carried through even his worst reverses. He won fame, and his spurs, at twelve years old, when he led the charge through the breach at the Siege of Berwick. Now he had in his charge another young daredevil, the 13-year-old Henry of Monmouth, heir to the throne.

The campaigns against Owain Glyndŵr were brutal, with punitive raids into the heart of Wales. After the Battle of Bryn Glas in 1401, the women following Glyndŵr's victorious army killed the straggling survivors and mutilated the dead, avenging the pillage and rape the English had inflicted across the land. This was not a chivalrous war with set-piece glorious battles but a bitter conflict of raids and reprisals. Within two years the young prince was leading raids on his own account. In one expedition he burned down the homes of Owain Glyndŵr at Glyndyfrdwy and Sycharth. Henry learnt, at an impressionable age, the full extent of man's inhumanity to man.

However, such brutality was tempered by the cult of conspicuous valour that pervaded the mindset of the knight. The word 'chivalry' derives from the French '*chevalerie*' which can be loosely translated as 'horse-mastery'. The age of chivalry was the age of the mounted knight. He had codes of conduct, which he aspired to, though seldom met. Modern people often feel let down when they learn of the atrocities of medieval warfare, thinking of knights as hypocrites whilst at the same time turning a blind eye to the atrocities carried out in our own 'civilized' age. Moreover the chivalric code only applied to the nobility; it was acceptable to slaughter peasants indiscriminately. This idea, whilst it may incur allegations of moral misjudgement, at least excuses the charge of hypocrisy. People also sometimes confuse chivalry with courtesy, which was a knight's code of etiquette and behaviour towards women. War was a knight's business and chivalry his guiding values. It was tied in with an unquestioning faith in God and a commitment to piety alongside a cultural obligation to be brave, glorious and ferocious in battle. He sought honour and fame and he sought to be resplendent. Shakespeare creates a majestic and chivalrous image of the young Henry in a speech he gives to Sir Richard Vernon in *Henry IV* part 1:

> All furnished, all in arms, all plumed like ostriches that wing the wind . . . I saw young Harry with his bevor on, rise from the ground like feathered Mercury; And vaulted with such ease into his seat, As if an angel dropp'd down from the clouds to turn and wind a fiery Pegasus and witch the world with noble horsemanship.

Here we see the quintessential glamour and athletic prowess of a knight in shining armour.

Armour

By 1400 plate armour had all but fully evolved and the young Henry would have had a harness made for him that had plate coverings for his feet (sabatons), his shin and calf (greaves), his knee and upper thigh (cuisses). He would have worn a mail shirt extending down to his mid thigh, giving flexible protection over his hips and groin. His shoulders would have been protected by plates called 'spaulders'; his elbows by 'couters'; his upper and lower arms by 'cannons' and his hands by steel gauntlets. On his torso he would have worn a steel cuirass. The unique European ability to produce large plates of steel had, by around 1370, led to the production of a solid, one-piece, domed defence for the chest, which extended from the shoulders to the base of the ribcage. Attached to its lower edge was a flexible assembly of articulating plates called the 'fauld', which covered the stomach. This body armour was worn beneath a short, closely tailored 'surcoat', a textile over-garment displaying a knight's heraldic device; hence 'coat-of-arms'. Overall the lines of the armour accentuated a glamorous, puff-chested, high-waisted, hourglass figure. For extra swagger, and perhaps for some additional protection for the hip joints, Henry would have worn a low-slung broad belt studded with plates around his hips. It is what modern scholars delicately call a 'belt of plates' but which contemporary writers more robustly describe as an 'arse-girdle'.

The genius of plate armour is that it is not unduly heavy. It gains its strength as much from its shape as it does from the thickness of the metal. I have already mentioned that shape gives strength in connection with fullers and this is especially true of plate armour. It is the technology of the egg. If you hold an egg apex to base and put pressure on it, you will be amazed at how strong it is relative to the apparently insignificant thickness of the shell (note: do not hold egg over book during experiment!). So it is with armour, its domed and shaped surfaces giving the maximum resistance for the minimum gauge of metal required. Improvements in steel manufacture, making much harder metals possible, also contributed to being able to produce relatively thin plates that gave excellent protection. However, the real key to plate armour's effectiveness was padding. The gleaming exoskeleton of plate provided both a glancing surface and a defence against penetration but what it did not do was protect you from the impact of a blow. That shock was absorbed by padded garments worn beneath the armour. It is true that as the quality of plate armour improved, the padding became thinner but armour remained a composite defence of both plate and padding. Combined they created a good defence but also contributed to one of the worst aspects of wearing armour – heat.

Being a soldier then, as now, required immense fitness. The young Henry would have trained to build up his physical strength and accustom himself to the grunt and sweat of wearing armour. He would have run, lifted stone weights, ridden every day and worked out in his armour. Armour was no restriction to movement or agility,

Effigy showing armour from first decade of 15th century, St Mary's Church, Swine, East Yorkshire; possibly Sir Robert Hilton (photo courtesy of Dr Tobias Capwell)

provided that it fitted exactly. There must be no rubbing or chafing, no catching of articulated plates. All of this was possible; he would have been able to run, ride and fight in it but most of all he needed to be able to withstand the heat. I have worn full plate armour in 90-degree heat, jousting in the South of France and in the oppressive humidity of Japan. You get used to it and once you have sweated through your arming doublet and it is wringing wet, it actually starts to work to stabilize your temperature. It's thirsty work.

Weight is not a big issue for a fit man. The sort of armour that Henry might have worn at Shrewsbury weighed in around 60lbs. Bear in mind that this weight was evenly distributed over the body and that armour was of a thinner gauge on the arms and legs, where mobility was required, than it was for the helm and breastplate. A modern combat infantry soldier in the British armed forces carries a marching load of around 70lbs, most of which is on his back. The well-equipped soldier's load has remained fairly constant throughout history. A notable exception was during the Falklands War (1982) when British Royal Marines and Paratroopers marched long distances cross-country with loads far in excess of this, in some cases up to 160lbs, and then fought a battle at the end of it. Fighting in armour is, of course, gruelling work, but compared to those Marines and Paras, knights had it easy.

The French knight Jean de Mengre, called 'Boucicault', Marshal of France, who Henry was destined to face on the battlefield of Agincourt, was famed for going for a run every day in his armour. He would vault into the saddle in armour and, in full armour, would climb the underside of a ladder, hauling himself up the rungs hand over hand. These were extreme feats but it seems likely that, under the daunting aegis of Harry Hotspur, the young Prince Henry would have had many physical challenges to conquer as he prepared for war. It is not reported whether Henry, like Boucicault and as Shakespeare suggests, could vault into the saddle wearing his armour but he certainly wasn't winched up with a crane. When Laurence Olivier was making the classic 1944 film of Henry V, he consulted the then Master of the Armouries at HM Tower of London, Sir James Mann. Mann told him that it was quite wrong to suppose that medieval knights relied on such contraptions to get into the saddle. A disappointed Olivier, seeing both humour and drama in the device allegedly replied 'very well. I'll only have the French do it' – and there it is in the film, used to good comic effect. However, most young men can mount quite normally when wearing armour and those of us a little older manage perfectly well with just a leg-up.

Riding in armour

Riding a horse in armour has its own problems. Your leg is heavier as a result of wearing armour and you need to learn a lighter touch – especially with a spirited warhorse. Similarly your arms and hands are carrying additional weight, especially your bridle arm, which may bear a shield, and it is important not to let this transmit to the horse's mouth. The reason that medieval warhorses are ridden with long-shanked curb bits and long-shanked spurs is not to inflict brutality. It would be a fatal error to treat a high-mettled stallion in this way. These aids are there so as to be able to ride with a lighter touch and not wrench the animal around with large movements from a weighted body. Such riding requires tremendous finesse. Medieval stirrups are set forward of the girth, setting the riders legs at a forward angle. When leaning a little forward this sets the rider's body in a sideways V posture, enabling him to better withstand the shock of impact. You don't want to move your legs from that position to spur your horse; a slight flexion of the ankle is all that is required. Similarly, you do not want to move your shield from its position of optimum protection and so you manage the reins with subtle movements of wrist and fingers and a yielding shoulder, not by swinging your arm around.

Although very expensive, properly fitting and properly set-up armour is considerably less noisy than the loudly clattering armours worn by many of today's re-enactors, it still has an incessant noise factor. There is the heat and there is the severely restricted vision when riding with your visor down. You can see the enemy ahead of you well enough but you don't have peripheral vision of your horse and that ability to read his body language, which is so much a part of normal riding. You

must feel everything and feel it through a second skin of steel. It is the difference between driving a regular car and flying a jet plane. The fighting nobility didn't just hold their status by right of birth; they were highly and athletically skilled in the profession of war.

To swing a sword from horseback, you must first turn from the waist. It is important to not cut off the horse's ears. In turning you must minimize the amount of weight transference in your hips, lest you indicate a change of direction to your mount. Medieval warhorses were not tall, averaging 14 to 15 hands, making it possible to reach and strike at infantry with ease, even though the seat of a war saddle sits several inches higher off the horse's back than does a modern saddle. Blows must be well delivered. Learning to wield the sword fluidly through a series of patterns is one thing but being able

Cast of the effigy of Otto von Pinzenau, 1371, in the Germanisches Museum, Nuremburg. The original is in Ebersberg. Note sword attached by guard chain and the 'arse-girdle' belt (Photo courtesy of Dr Tobias Capwell)

Guard chains: German c. 1350–75, Bayerisches Armeemuseum, Ingolstadt (© Hermann Historica, Munich)

to strike with force is another. There is evidence that knights practiced against 'quintains' and pells when training with the lance and it seems probable that they used similar equipment to rehearse their mounted sword cuts. For mounted practice the *Faris* (Saracen equivalent to the knightly class) erected a long wooden stand in which they embedded reeds. They would gallop alongside with their sword outstretched, scything through the stalks. One interpretation of this is to place single reeds one inch apart along the barrier. I have tried this with fifty reeds and with a good sharp sword it is too easy, so I suspect they clumped the reeds together in tied bunches.

Swords could also be used to thrust from horseback and one imagines a stuffed target mounted atop a pell for the young prince to gallop at and drive his sword home. When riding and thrusting at a pell, it is essential to ride through the target and not let the jarring moment of impact stall the horse. It is also important to hang on to your sword.

Losing your weapons in battle was a perennial hazard. For a part of the preceding century, knights, particularly in Germany, had worn what were known as 'guard chains'. These were chains attached to the sword (and dagger, shield and helm) at one end and to the breastplate or coat-of-plates at the other. They look a little cumbersome but I have tried swinging a sword with a guard chain and, provided the chain is longer than your arm, there is no restriction to full movement whatsoever. Guard chains started to go out of fashion around the time Henry was born. I'm not sure why – they seem eminently sensible. Perhaps they added a little weight to a weary sword-arm, perhaps they were too convenient a handhold for marauding infantry, surrounding your horse and trying to haul you from the saddle. In any event they disappeared but their brief existence emphasizes the problem of being able to hang on to your sword when attempting to make powerful blows with a tired and failing arm.

Pells

Although there is no direct evidence for the pell in cavalry sword training, there are a number of manuscript illustrations that show it in use for infantry training. Essentially the medieval pell was the same as that used by the Romans – a stout wooden post set in the ground. Sometimes it is represented as a 'ragged staff' – a bough with the branches lopped off, so that the base of each fork remains proud. As a heraldic symbol the 'ragged staff' had been associated with the earls of Warwick since the thirteenth century. It was a familiar medieval image and I think it likely that it signified a pell on the earls' arms, even though, in this heraldic incarnation, it subsequently became the tethering post for the Warwick bear.

In practical terms, the spurs of timber projecting from the central post would have been extremely useful as target points and I expect that, when sharp swords were used, every effort was made to sever them. A manuscript in the British Library (Sloane 2430), from a treatise on chivalry by Jean de Meun, shows a pell with a straight trunk, clean of any branch nodules and it is clear that it has been considerably worn away from hacking blows. From this it would seem that pell practice demanded sharp swords, at least some of the time, and images in art show sharp swords being used. However, an anonymous fifteenth-century manuscript, *Knighthood and Batayle*, now in the British Library, tells us that what is required to practice at the pell is '*a fanne of doubil wight tak him his shelde, of doubil wight a mace of tre[e] to welde*'. This loosely translates as 'take a double-weight shield and a double-weight wooden baton to wield', which is more what one would expect. If sharp swords were used on occasion, I doubt they were 'good' swords; it seems like a quick way to ruin a blade. The *Faris* used conical mounds of clay for practicing their sword strokes. It was a repairable target, gave good resistance training, didn't damage the sword and allowed the master to observe and comment on the angle of strike.

Pells are invaluable for training to deliver blows with force and for rehearsing combination sequences, not least of all with the shield. In this respect they have a clear advantage over the Saracen's clay cone. Henry needed to learn to fight with sword and shield and slamming his shield into a pell, as well as delivering a full repertoire of sword strikes, was an essential part of that education. Shield slams could be executed with the shield tucked into the shoulder or it might be swung with an open arm, smashing into the target either with the flat or the edge. 'With wightynesse and weapon must he caste to fighte strong', advises the treatise, which means that a knight had to learn to wield his sword with weight behind the blows. Powerful blows were what counted on the battlefield and daily pell-bashing with double-weight weapons not only helped to build up the relevant muscles, it also accustomed the arm to the considerable shock of impact against a solid object.

Prince or not, battle-ready fitness and fighting technique could not be attained other than by hard labour and constant

Ragged staff – a possible form of medieval pell for training sword strokes

Knight training at pell. Detail from Jean de Meun's treatise on chivalry, 14th century (© The British Library Board. Licence Number: SELACA82. All Rights Reserved)

training. We may imagine the young prince, under Hostspur's watchful eye, slogging away at the pell each morning, wooden sword in hand, pounding out a relentless percussive beat as he worked up a sweat and stepped around the post with deft footwork, like a boxer at his punch-bag. Strikes at the head, face and throat, attacks to the breast and side, cuts to the hand, leg, thigh and arms – 'empeche his hed, his face, have at his gorge, bere at the breste or [strike] him on the side ... hew off his honed, his legge, his thegh, his armys' – were all practiced by schooling at the pell. As well as this target practice, the student needed to learn secure footwork that always put him 'on balance' so that he could strike from his centre with all his might and, as he moved to and fro and around the pell, to ensure that he was always at the optimum distance to launch his blow.

Walloping wood on wood accomplished many of the goals for training – power, accuracy and stamina – but in order to finesse his ability to range blows so that the right section of the blade landed with maximum force and, crucially, that the edge of the blade landed at the optimum angle, the knight had to work with a sharp sword and hew great chunks out of his pell. I suspect that both systems were used in tandem – perhaps forty-five minutes with wooden staves at one pell and then finishing off with fifteen minutes and a sharp sword at another.

Sword versus armour

In an age of plate armour, sword blows could certainly be effective on the battle-field, though they could not be expected to cut through the steel; as the author of

Knighthood and Batayle tells us, '*the smyter is deluded mony [ways], the sword may not through steel and bonys bite.*' Apart from its innate hardness, plate armour had shaped contours, which produced glancing surfaces that were designed to deflect. There was no realistic prospect of a sword shearing through a quality piece of plate armour. Manuscripts that depict this, usually whilst illustrating a biblical narrative, are almost certainly taking extreme dramatic licence. That is not to say that a sword could have no effect against armour – it could. By delivering blunt trauma to the man within, the sword remained a useful weapon in the 'age of plate' and it could deliver more energy if it bit into the metal.

In a test I tried an extremely good quality steel sword, keenly sharpened, against a superbly made replica of a thirteenth-century helm. I set the helm upon a stout wooden post and I hit it. I hit it very hard and I hit it several times, landing downward blows squarely on the crown. This helm was of superior quality and not all would have been that good but there was never a hint that it could possibly be cleaved. There was nonetheless a discernable nick. You could put your fingernail in it and feel the lip of the indent. The sword had glanced off but before doing so, it had bitten just a little into the metal and that would have imparted much of its energy to the skull within. Such a blow could have caused a range of traumas from disorientating dizziness to severe concussion, brain haemorrhaging and death. Even the least of these would be useful enough in a battle. It would have been a simple matter to set pieces of old armour upon the pell for young knights to get the feel of landing a good hit or to experience how armour could turn a blade. I don't doubt that they did it.

Swords remained effective weapons in the age of plate armour. So long as they could get bite, and therefore purchase, they could do great damage to the man within. Moreover, not everyone on the battlefield would be wearing plate armour. It was expensive. This was especially true in the case of the rebellion in Wales, which had a popular folk following. Small guerrilla bands calling themselves the *Plant Owain* (Children of Owain) flocked to Glyndŵr's banner. These were not fully armoured knights but simple peasants and against flesh the sword retained a terrible power.

Henry's sword was well suited to delivering strong cuts but that slender tapering point shouts at us to say that this was a sword primarily intended for thrusting. It has been argued that blades more suited to thrusting came into being specifically to thrust at the weak spots of plate armour – to thrust through the visor sights and to get between the joins. These options seem a little fanciful when one considers facing an upright, moving target. A more viable target perhaps was the armpit of a raised arm, though this was fairly well defended by a mail shirt worn beneath the plate. Of course, once felled and dazed, a prone knight could be vulnerable from attacks to the chinks in his armour and was – though more usually the dagger was used for this work. However, none of this was the prime function of a thrusting sword. As with cutting blows, the main objective of a thrust was to bite and gain purchase on the armour rather than be deflected. The aim was to deliver energy to the strike. What the thrust had over the cut was the 'stiletto-heel' effect. It concentrated an immense amount of energy into one tiny spot. Imagine the force of a punch from a heavyweight boxer compressed into an area the size of a sword point and you will have some idea of the power of a thrust. It could send shockwaves right through the armour to the fragile skeleton within.

Sword and shield

The earliest European treatise on swordfighting discovered to date was produced around 1300 and is today in the collection of the Royal Armouries (MS I.33). It is evidence of an established, systematic approach to the martial arts and is illustrated with drawings of a master instructing his pupil, a common device in the fencing literature of the centuries that followed. However, in this case the master is a priest! Eastern martial arts traditions, as personified by the 'Shaolin monks', offer a familiarity with the idea of monastic martial artists but there is little evidence for it being a widespread practice in medieval Europe. There are other instances of ecclesiastic 'masters of arms' later in the century – Hans Dobringer and Johannes Lekuchner were both priests but they were exceptions. Perhaps the anonymous priest who wrote MS I.33 was formerly a soldier and had taken his vows later in life? Perhaps there was a tradition of pugnacious clerics offering instruction in the fighting arts – if so it has yet to be proved. All that really matters from the point of view of the history of the sword is that here we have, for the first time, a technical manual and the establishment of the 'fight master' as a figure of influence.

Manuscript I.33 features fighting with a type of shield known as a 'buckler'. Made in steel, medieval bucklers were small with a domed boss and a solid handgrip. For the attack the buckler suited either a straightforward punch or a sideways swipe with its steel edge. In defence it was used to deflect blows by smashing them away rather than blocking them directly. Sword and buckler fighting was fast and free-flowing. Many of the figures in the manuscript show the buckler being held in front of the sword hand. This is not for shielding the hand but rather for hiding the hand; disguising the momentary preparation for a line of attack and confusing your opponent. It also meant that two hands could be used on the sword for extra-powerful blows. By far the majority of the strokes advocated in the text that accompanies each figure are thrusts. A number of basic guard positions are discussed, as are sophisticated blade techniques such as binds, whereby one sword takes control of the opposing sword, moving it out of the line of attack as the dominant sword simultaneously comes to bear in line with the opponent's body. Arm-locks and the seizing of an opponent's weapon are also shown, pre-empting techniques depicted in many fencing manuals of a later time. More than eighty years before Henry was born, this complex martial culture was fully developed.

Bucklers were light and easily portable, which made them ideal for archers and other light infantry, although knights and men-at-arms did carry them on occasion. Just to confuse us, the word 'buckler' can be used to apply to any shield but modern scholarship makes the distinction between these small 'hand shields' and the larger wooden shields with which knights were more usually equipped. Henry V's shield now hangs beside his sword in the museum at Westminster Abbey. It is a wooden shield of the sort described in the nineteenth century as 'heater'-shaped, a term deriving from the old word for a smoothing iron which was put on the stove to become hot and so was known as a 'heater'. Such shields were convex, maximizing strength through shape. Henry's shield, made for ceremonies celebrating Henry IV's engagement to Joanna of Navarre in 1403 and still preserved, was made from limewood (linden) – as we saw with Anglo-Saxon shields, this is a light timber with excellent shock-absorbing properties – and covered with four thicknesses of linen. Over these is a fabric covering of Chinese brocaded blue silk with a mulberry leaf pattern interwoven with gold fleur-de-lys. It has been embroidered with the Spanish

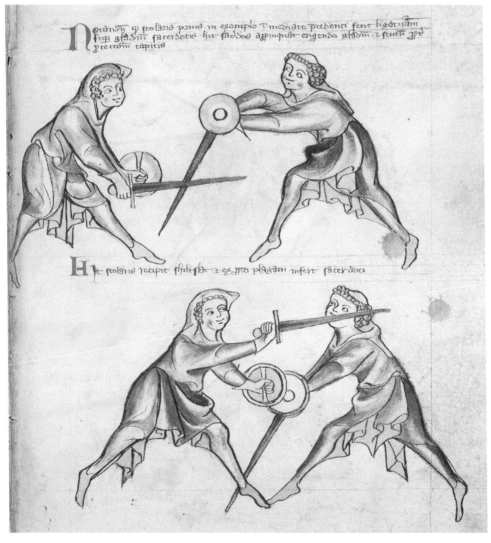

Sword and buckler fighting, 13th century, MS I.33 (© The Board of Trustees of the Armouries)

royal coat-of-arms. Apart from underlining the importance of the shield as part of a knight's accoutrements, such exotic furnishings are an interesting indicator of trade links with China.

Fighting shields, often covered in leather, bore a knight's heraldic device, so that he could be distinguished on the battlefield. A knight fighting bravely needed the world to see that it was he who was fighting bravely and commanders needed to be identifiable to their troops. Prince Henry's heraldry at the Battle of Shrewsbury would have been the arms of England – three leopards, quartered with the lilies of France – a highly symbolic heraldry, staking the English monarchy's claim to the throne of France. His shield would also have featured a 'label' – a horizontal bar with three descending verticals, like an 'E' turned on its side – that was a mark of cadence denoting him as the eldest son to the king. On the back of the shield are two straps, called 'enarmes', and a pad stuffed with horsehair felt for the forearm. A guige suspends the shield at the juncture of neck and shoulder, helping to bear some of the weight. For the cavalryman it is the first line of defence against an oncoming lance; for the man on foot it is both a means of defence and attack in hand-to-hand fighting and a shelter against a hail of arrows.

Battle of Shrewsbury, 21 July 1403, phase I

Not yet seventeen years old. His mother dead when he was seven. A father he had hardly ever known – a man he had idolized as a chivalric hero away on crusade when he was a boy but who he had seen come back and usurp the crown from the only man who had shown him any sort of fatherly love. Suddenly and unexpectedly elevated to be heir to the throne at the age of twelve, Henry's life had been full of uncertainty. Now, as he donned his arming doublet and the first uncomfortable prickles of heat crept over his body, he was preparing for his first set-piece battle. He was ready for it; he had trained for it – although he must have wondered how he would fare. How would he show himself in the eyes of his father, in the eyes of his younger brothers, both destined to become lions on the battlefield in their own right? And how would the other knights of the royal household judge him? Henry had seen war. He had seen men killed. Yet that morning he faced the prospect of having to kill, perhaps for the first time. Riding against him was Harry Percy – a man he had once called friend.

The Percys had become disillusioned with Henry IV. He rejected their counsel and Harry Percy complained constantly of a lack of resources. Furthermore, compensation for the Percy's expense in defending the Scottish border had not been forthcoming. The flashpoint came in 1402. Harry Percy was called away from his duties on the Welsh border to join with his father, Henry Percy, to retaliate against another raid by the Earl of Douglas and the Scots. They won a resounding victory at Homildon Hill and captured a vast quantity of prisoners, including the redoubtable Scottish earl. The unchallenged custom of the time was that the ransom money for prisoners belonged to the victors but Henry IV, short on funds and jealous of the prize, demanded the prisoners be turned over to the Crown. The Percys were furious. They had had enough and rose in rebellion. The Earl of Douglas rode shoulder to shoulder with them in their cause. Owain Glyndŵr, too, set aside previous enmities and rallied his army to bring support to the Percys. Men from Cheshire and Lancashire, still loyal to Richard II, also flocked to the Percy banner.

On the morning of 13 July, the army of Henry IV assembled just outside Shrewsbury. Hotspur and Douglas commanded the opposing ridge with their troops in one long battle line. Glyndŵr hadn't made it in time. Henry IV arranged his men in two divisions or 'battles', the main body, commanded by the king, and the left wing commanded by his teenage son, Henry, Prince of Wales. The battle started with an arrowstorm. Both sides had large bodies of archers and Englishman shot at English-man with a huzzing maelstrom of iron-shod shafts.

For a television sequence about riding into an arrowstorm, I once assembled twenty archers, all shooting moderately powerful bows and supplied with hard rubber-tipped arrows. I wore my armour and they shot at me. Not wishing to risk injury to a horse, I opted to use a quad bike (ATV). I revved the engine and set off at a roaring pace towards the line. They unleashed a deluge of arrows in my direction, most of which found their mark. For the last ten yards or so I could feel the sting of shafts from the more powerful bows and my armour suffered a number of dints, though it was of course all harmless. Nonetheless, it was a sobering insight into how daunting it would be to face such an onslaught, however much you trusted your armour.

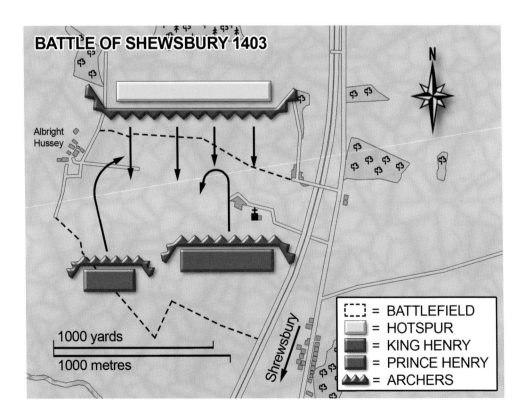

BATTLE OF SHEWSBURY 1403

N

Albright Hussey

1000 yards

1000 metres

Shrewsbury

⬚ = BATTLEFIELD
◻ = HOTSPUR
◼ = KING HENRY
◼ = PRINCE HENRY
▲▲▲ = ARCHERS

An open-faced 'bascinet' seems to have been the most popular form of helmet around the time of Shrewsbury. Characterized by a high and pointed dome, the bascinet was attached to an 'aventail' of mail. This framed the face, leaving only a small opening between the eyebrows and the top of the bottom lip unguarded (Hollywood please note that it does not sit under the chin). From the chin the aventail extended downwards, defending the throat, and then, flaring to become a mantle, it hung over the shoulders and upper chest. It was reasonable protection against sword cuts but of little use against arrows. At Shrewsbury there were arrows – thousands of them. One option the prince would have had is a type of visor designed specifically for an arrowstorm, which had acutely glancing surfaces with a set-back, conically-domed skull and a long snout. Only a dozen such helms survive in present-day collections. One is in the Wallace Collection in London and I have been lucky enough to try it on. Of all medieval helm designs, and I have tried them all, the visored bascinet offers the most restricted vision. Not only are the slits for the sights very narrow but also they sit much farther away from the eyes than on any other helmet type. You can work out the consequences with your fingers – the further away the slit is from the eyeball, the more your field of vision is limited. These sights are also split, having a central bar down the centre. Vision is perfectly adequate for perceiving your general sense of direction and advancing on the enemy – I have ridden in replicas of the type – but it is imperfect. Secondary sights, located on the underside of the snout, enable you to see down to observe the terrain you are crossing and minimize the risk of stumbling or, if mounted, to see the head and neck of your horse. It has its annoyances but it also does its job, giving very good protection against arrows. If you are a young prince, however, wishing to see all about you and direct your army in the course of battle; if you wish to shout commands, if you are hot from your exertions and fighting for breath; if you want your peripheral vision when wielding your sword; then you are very likely to throw caution to the wind and either raise your visor or dispense with it altogether.

Henry Monmouth, the Prince of Wales, was shot in the face by an arrow. He had been leading a decisive flank attack, wheeling round Hotspur's main body of men to hit them in the side and rear. The arrow entered his left cheek just above the eye-tooth and lodged, according to his surgeon, 'in the back part of the bone of the head six inches deep'. The pain is unimaginable and Henry must have felt faint and nauseous as the rusty taste of blood poured from the top of his palate into his mouth. He pulled out the shaft, leaving the arrowhead buried in his cheek. To the astonishment and admiration of all around him, Henry did not falter, remaining in the fray and urging his troops to victory. Picture his sword lifted high in the air on outstretched hand. There can be a no more defiant symbol or seductive call to arms than a raised sword, punching the air.

It is tempting to think that the sword, which hung over his tomb in Westminster Abbey, might have been the very sword that he carried into battle at Shrewsbury. With its short, light blade it would have suited the occasion well. I'm not suggesting that this was a 'boy's sword', far from it – it would have served any man at any age;

Visored bascinet c. 1400 (by kind permission of the Trustees of the Wallace Collection, London)

merely that it is an ideally sized weapon for a young prince in his first battle. To what extent he used it to strike at his foes is conjecture; certainly he was in the fighting and, just as certainly, he would have been trained to use it.

Training

As well as instructing practical techniques, the medieval masters did not neglect the mental game. *Il Fior di Battaglia* – 'The Flower of Battle' – was written by the Italian master, Fiore dei Liberi da Premariacco, around 1410, just a few years after Shrewsbury. It encapsulates much of the theory and practice with which Henry would have been familiar. Some readers will know it by its name in Latin translation – *Flos Duellatorum*. In one section there is a diagram that depicts the figure of a man crisscrossed with swords and surrounded by allegorical beasts. Known as *sette spada* – 'seven swords' – the picture shows the swords intersecting the body at angles corresponding to the principal lines of attack, although a vertical strike down to the head is conspicuous by its absence. Of particular interest are the encircling bestiary and its annotations, for here Fiore tells us what attributes and qualities a swordsman must seek to attain if he is to be victorious. In this it anticipates much of the psychological theory of eastern martial arts and in a single image declares that the martial arts of medieval Europe were every bit as sophisticated and advanced as those in the east. Fiore supplements each image with a keyword and an adage.

   Above the man's head is a lynx holding a pair of dividers, the geometrician's instrument for measuring distance:

> *Prudentia* ['Prudence' or 'Caution']
> No other creature is able to look so clearly as me, the lynx,
> and continuously by that method of the compass and measure.

Measure – timing and distance – is fundamental to all fighting technique and is constantly being calculated and adjusted by the fighter. Famed for its eyesight, the lynx represents qualities of judgement and perception with regard to measure. The word 'Prudentia' also reminds us that the brain, as well as the eyes, is located in the head and that the swordsman must not be reckless but fight wisely.

   To the left of the man is a lion, resting a paw on a heart:

> *Audatia* [Courage]
> None can bring a more daring heart than me, a lion,
> and I challenge anyone to battle.

Courage may seem a fairly obvious quality for a swordsman, but the image conveys more than just raw bravery, essential though that is; it also suggests resolution of purpose and stamina. In short, the 'heart' to carry on when all seems lost. The lion sits on the left, where the heart is.

On the man's right is a tiger, holding an arrow:

Celeritas [Speed]
I am the tiger, I am very quick to run and turn
That the arrow in the sky cannot overcome me.

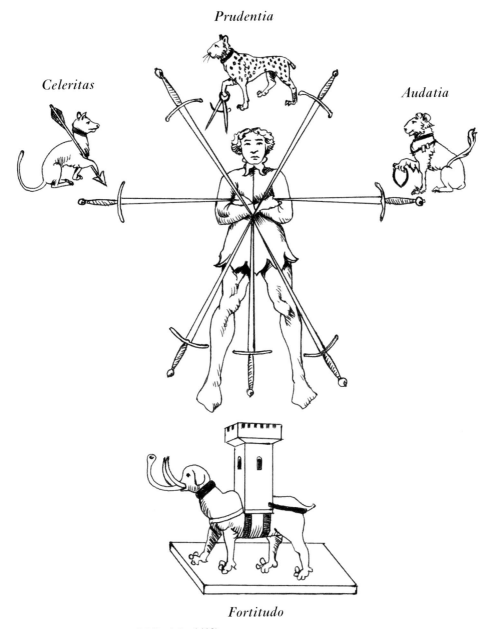

Prudentia

Celeritas

Audatia

Fortitudo

Sette Spada after Fiore dei Liberi (c. 1410)

Located by the sword-arm, the tiger, a somewhat imaginative rendering of the heraldic variety, emphasises the importance of swiftness in both striking and defending. Celerity is also vital for the swordsman's tactical brain. He must respond and react with lightning speed to a constantly changing situation. Making swift decisions as to which attacks or counters to apply is essential to his success.

The man stands upon an elephant, complete with its castellated howdah:

> *Fortitudo* [Strength]
> I am the elephant and I have a castle for a burden
> and never do I kneel down nor do I lose my true place.

Physical strength is a great advantage for the swordsman, hence all those hours spent at the pell building up the right muscles. It affects the power with which a blow can be delivered and it is decisive in many of the leverage and grappling techniques that are taught by all the masters. Visually this image also alludes to the importance of keeping a firm, balanced footing. Strong, tireless legs are the steady platform from which the swordsman launches his assaults. The value of mental strength goes without saying.

During the late fourteenth century, Fiore had trained in Germany under 'Master Johannes, the Swabian'. This is possibly Johannes Liechtenauer, an enormously influential German 'fight master', who we shall meet in the next chapter. In 1400, after many years of soldiering, Fiore was appointed fight master to the court of Niccolo III d'Este, the Marquise di Ferrara and it is to the marquise that he dedicated his treatise. Courts throughout Europe employed old soldiers and notable swordsmen as fight masters to keep the nobility in regular training for war. It was this patronage that allowed the fighting arts to develop in a systemized fashion; it gave structure to the study of arms. Prince Henry's fight master is unknown to us by name but he undoubtedly existed and was almost certainly teaching methods very similar to those advocated by Fiore.

Illustrated with 276 line drawings, *Il Fior di Battaglia* describes combat techniques on foot with various weapons; including spears, pollaxes, daggers, arming swords and longswords. Additionally there are mounted techniques with lance and sword. Wrestling techniques are taught on their own and in conjunction with weapon fights. Grappling an opponent and throwing him off balance or to the ground was an essential part of sword combat. Swords could also be used to good effect as levers in close-quarter fighting. At Shrewsbury, Henry was mounted and maestro Fiore also gives instruction on wrestling techniques from horseback. These entail several ways of grabbing your enemy round the neck and numerous locks on his sword arm. My efforts to try to understand how these moves might work in practice have usually resulted in both parties falling to the ground in an unseemly pile and with an almighty thud. Even if you win the wrestle and your opponent becomes dislodged from his saddle, all he has to do is hang onto you as he falls – you are bound to fall with him. Such techniques would be significantly more difficult carrying a shield, which is

Early 15th century fighting techniques after Fiore dei Liberi (1410)

perhaps why, apart from in one or two images of lance combat, no shields are shown in Fiore's work.

Battle of Shewsbury, phase II

A shield would have been advisable at Shrewsbury because of the arrowstorms, though it seems likely that Henry was not carrying one when he was shot in the face. Accounts of medieval battles frequently use metaphors such as arrows falling like snow and hail and the portrayal of the archer launching his arrows into the air is a familiar image. It is not, however, an image that exists in medieval art. Here archers on the battlefield are invariably shooting straight ahead – only in depictions of sieges do we see them shooting in elevation. There are instances, such as at Homildon Hill and the initial engagement at Shrewsbury, where the archers in Percy's army were atop a ridge and therefore shooting down but by the time Prince Henry swung round with his flanking manoeuvre, they had moved down onto the flat. Issues to do with arrow stocks – arrows were expensive items of ammunition – and the need for effective penetration at close range, make me believe that, for the most part, battlefield archery was conducted at relatively close range and with the archers shooting straight ahead.

Every arrow had to count and tests have shown that, to achieve effective penetration against armour, the range needs to be less than 50 yards. The annals record that the archers at Shrewsbury drew their bows with such speed that: 'the sun, which was at that time bright and clear, lost its brightness, so thick were the arrows'. Such imagery does not preclude straight on shooting – a blizzard, after all, is a horizontal experience.

A direct hit from an arrow would surely have gone straight through Henry's skull and lodged in the back of his helmet and he would have been killed outright. One plausible explanation for his miraculous survival is that it might have been an arrow that had been deflected from an adjacent knight's armour and thus lost some of its energy. Not so the arrow that struck Harry Hotspur. Moments before Henry's counter attack, Hotspur had launched a furious cavalry charge, cutting a swathe through the main body of the king's troops and making straight for the king himself. His efforts to kill the king were confounded by a subterfuge – the king had 'doubles', dressed in the royal coat of arms, around his person. The Earl of Stafford and Sir Thomas Blount were among the decoys erroneously slain. It was then that Hotspur suffered a similar fate to the Prince of Wales. An arrow pierced his eye, travelled straight to the brain and killed him.

All was lost for the Percy cause. The cry went up that he was dead and, it is said, no mercy was shown that day. Whinnying horses, their flesh lacerated by tormenting arrow-shafts, fell and staggered, crashing their riders to the ground where they were murdered by marauding dagger-men. Knights fighting on foot strained to hold their lines as blow after blow rained down on them, rendering them concussed and broken within their shells. Unarmoured archers and bill-men, their faces torn open by slashing swords, writhed screaming in the mud, holding the bloody flaps of skin in place. Others tried to staunch the flow from severed limbs, while the less fortunate looked down with glassy eyes at the disembowelled entrails hanging from their slit bellies, as their trembling lips tried to utter one last prayer. The blinded, the dazed and the simply exhausted stumbled and slipped in eddying pools of blood, making their way across the stinking corpses of the dead and dying. What friends had fallen here? The screams of men and beasts and the stench of death filled the ears and nostrils of victor and vanquished alike. Some 5,000 men lay dead. Henry, Prince of Wales had witnessed his first full-scale battle.

However, despite the horror, despite the awful tragedy of it all, despite the pity, those who survived felt a curious elation. The sheer noise and clamour of battle, the muscle-straining, heart-racing buzz of extreme exertion, the thrill of a plunging, galloping stallion, the pulsating drive of battle rage and the sheer excitement of danger had sent waves of adrenaline coursing through their bodies and they felt more alive than at any other time in their existence. They experienced a euphoria that would, again and again, lead them back to the cesspit of war, imagining it a noble adventure.

Prince Henry recovered from his wound. The royal physician, John Bradmore, designed a cunning device to extract the arrowhead – a pair of tongs that when inserted into its socket, screwed apart till they gripped its walls and it could be pulled free. Where the fleshy part of the face had closed over the entry wound, Bradmore had to widen it, over the course of several days, by inserting larger and larger 'tents of the pith of old elder, dried well and sewed well in a clean linen cloth'. These were soaked in rose honey, which contains natural antibiotics. The wound was cleansed with 'a squirtillo of white wine' and dressed with a poultice of breadcrumbs, honey, barley and turpentine. Miraculously, it healed completely within three weeks. Within a few days he was seventeen years old.

After Shrewsbury

Prior to Shrewsbury, Henry was certainly not the dissolute youth portrayed in Shakespeare; but what of his later teenage years? There is little in the record to indicate he was a hard-drinking roisterer, keeping company with the likes of Falstaff, Pistol, Nym and Bardolf but there are suggestions in later chronicles that he was fond of practical jokes. Such puerile humour is consistent with a character that, experiencing such a loss of innocence so early in his childhood, is likely to have had an arrested emotional development.

His leadership qualities, on the other hand, were fully developed to a precocious degree. From 1403 to 1409, Henry was responsible for prosecuting the war in Wales against Glyndŵr, who, in 1404, was crowned Owain IV, King of Wales. This war was a serious threat to the English crown and Glyndŵr had support from many disaffected English nobles as well as the Welsh. His was a fully-fledged force of feudal knights and their retainers and it was left solely to Prince Henry to deal with the situation. By the age of twenty he was appointed to the king's council and soon assumed the leading position in the governance of the realm. Henry IV was increasingly subject to bouts of ill health and relations between father and son became increasingly strained. Young Henry was nothing if not ambitious. One account describes how he entered the king's bedchamber and tried the crown on for size. The king awoke and caught him in the act. He was not pleased.

Henry IV died on 13 March 1413. His son, Henry of Monmouth, became King Henry V. Medieval portraits are seldom flattering but the one of King Henry V that hangs in The National Portrait Gallery is especially unfortunate. The anaemic skin colouring that looks as though it might crimson into a rage at the slightest provocation, the pursed, disapproving lips that look incapable of a smile, the bead of an eye, shielding great sadness within but not able to transmit any human warmth or outward emotion,

Owain Glyndwr, City Hall, Cardiff (courtesy of Seth Whales)

and a promontory nose conveying haughty disdain, combine with the monkish hairstyle to conjure an image of great severity (the hairstyle, incidentally, was an immensely practical 'helm cut'). Of course it is not a photograph and the artist may have done him an unkind injustice and may have been attempting to capture both the dignity of his office and a deeply devout and serious man. It is nonetheless a far cry from Laurence Olivier's romantic hero.

Henry was a pious man, spending time every day in private devotion, as well as endowing many monasteries and religious foundations. One of his first acts as king was to have the body of Richard II reburied in Westminster Abbey with full ceremony. He zealously defended the established Church and early in his reign set about putting down the Lollards, whose challenge to certain doctrines of Christian belief he regarded as heresy.

Agincourt

The Battle of Agincourt was Henry's defining moment. It is important to grasp that the English people were not at war with the French people. The Plantagenet dynasty of English kings, in the person of Henry's great grandfather Edward III, had laid claim to the French crown in 1340 and it was this claim that Henry sought to pursue. The feudal aristocracies and ruling dynasties of medieval Europe were inter-related and intermarried. They didn't rule over nation states as we understand them today but rather owned vast tracts of land by heritable right and aligned themselves with each other in ever-changing feudal hierarchies. Monarchs were sovereign over the feudal lords who owed them allegiance, while the people owed allegiance (and taxes!) to the feudal lords. Kings of England were frequently also the feudal overlords of large areas of France by virtue of marriage and inheritance. It wasn't a question of England seeking to conquer France but of individuals claiming rights of land ownership. Moreover France was not a united country; Gascony was an ally of the English crown and Burgundy was effectively an independent state, though it notionally acknowledged allegiance to the French crown. Aquitaine, considered by the Plantagenets to be their heritable right via Henry II's wife, Eleanor of Aquitaine, was always a source of contention. It was a complex situation but Henry believed passionately in his right to the French crown, almost to the point of obsession.

France, under the mad King Charles VI, was in a state of virtual civil war and Henry, with his appetite for military adventure, seized the opportunity for action. In September 1415, he set sail from Southampton with an expeditionary force. Harfleur was a crucial strategic bridgehead and it took a protracted siege to capture it. Having done so, Henry headed for Calais and home. It was then that his retreat was cut off and he found himself in the desperate situation that led to the Battle of Agincourt. Henry's army of just 6,000 (1,000 knights and men-at-arms together with 5,000 archers) faced the amassed feudal might of France numbering perhaps 20,000. The English were further disadvantaged and weakened by dysentery that had spread through the ranks. These seemed impossible odds.

In broad terms Henry had the advantage of the ground, positioned in the narrow neck of converging woods. The turf was wet and boggy, hindering the French advance. Henry's archers cut a barricade of sharpened stakes, which they drove into the ground in front of them and set at an angle so that their bristling spikes jutted forward at the height of a horse's chest. He aligned his men in three battles, commanding the centre himself. The French, under the joint field command of Constable D'Albret and Marshal Boucicaut had a plan to attack the flanks with dismounted men-at-arms and crossbowmen. They were overruled by the high command of a triumvirate of Dukes – Orleans, Alençon and Bourbon – who advocated a full frontal attack.

Thousands of armoured men were sent trudging on foot towards the English lines. They were followed by yet more thousands of mounted knights. The English archers did their work and launched squall after squall of feathered death. I have shot fifteen arrows in a minute and I know others who can shoot even faster. If we take a conservative twelve arrows per minute for 5,000 archers, that is 60,000 arrows in the air every minute. No wonder the French turned and in so doing set up another problem. The tapering woodland had already funnelled their front line into a situation of serious overcrowding. With some troops turning back only to be met by the thundering onset of the advancing cavalry, it was a crowd disaster in its own right, with men crushed and immobilized by density high spots and eddied in directions they hadn't intended by the whirlpool flows of crowd chaos.

The argument goes that the archers shot the horses and the knights fell and that once a knight in armour has fallen he is helpless, struggling like an upturned tortoise, and can't rise to his feet. This is palpable nonsense. I have ridden in full plate armour for over thirty years and have fallen, both intentionally and unintentionally, many, many times. It is perfectly possible to spring straight to your feet. Not only that but the armour itself acts as a sort of 'crash cage', protecting you from the worst of the ground impact. At Agincourt, however, there was another factor – the mud. The wet ground, now churned to a quagmire by thousands of heavily-armoured men, created freak conditions. As British soldiers were to find to their cost and discomfort in 1914, the type of loamy soil in that part of France is particularly sticky because it absorbs moisture to a remarkable degree. It would have adhered to the smooth plates of armour and created a significant suction effect.

Even so, all of this only served to even up the odds a little. Thousands of French still made it through to the front line and engaged with the English in hand-to-hand fighting. The English archers laid down their bows to take up their swords and wooden mauls, fighting stubbornly alongside the small contingent of 1,000 armoured men. Henry V was involved in the midst of the fray. Chroniclers report that he was seen mounted on a grey palfrey at the start of the battle but it is not clear whether or not he remained mounted. It is probable that he dismounted for the actual fighting – it was the 'English way' in the Hundred Years War. Besides, a 'palfrey' was not a warhorse; ideally suited for riding up and down the lines of men whilst setting positions and rousing their spirits, but not a steed for a king to fight on. My own view is that he would have dismounted to show his men that he was with them, that he

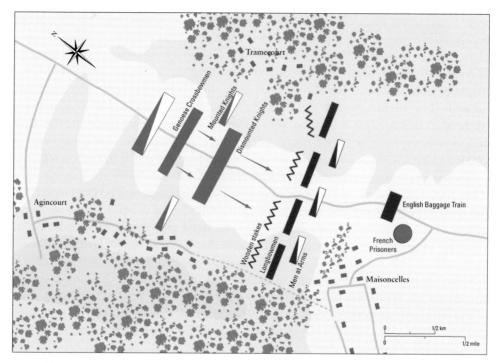

Map of Battle of Agincourt

would stand and die with them if that's what it took, rather than appear ready to flee the scene.

The sword in Westminster Abbey was ideally suited to close combat in a tight press. Manuscript art sometimes shows knights seemingly holding an opponent at arms length with their left hand, whilst striking with their sword. In a closely-packed mêlée a man could be so close to his foe that there was barely room to raise a sword. You could bludgeon his face with the pommel of the sword or you could use one of Fiore's grappling moves to off-balance him and put him at sword's length prior to driving the point into his eyes. Steel fists, armoured knees and armoured elbows were all employed in the fighting, all the time seeking that critical moment when you could land a fully committed blow with your sword. Henry wore a gold crown atop his helm and in that ferocious, bitter fight a French knight sheared off one of its fleurons. At length the day was won. It was an unbelievable feat.

Henry has often been criticized for the order to kill his prisoners at one stage in the battle, breaking the code of chivalry that said they should be held unharmed for ransom. It must be remembered, though, that the French flew their *Oriflamme* banner that day, signalling no quarter would be given and effectively lifting the chivalric injunction on the treatment of prisoners. It should also be borne in mind how desperate his situation was; with a French flanking attack approaching his rear to release the captured men, Henry had little choice. It was certainly not a choice he would have taken lightly for the potential ransom monies represented a significant and much-needed revenue.

Return

Henry returned to England where news of the victory caused an instant swelling of national pride. It soothed a troubled nation with a unifying balm. Henry was the hero of the hour. He spent the next two years at home planning to consolidate his victory. In 1417 he set sail for France once more and mounted a systematic campaign to subdue Normandy. His command of logistics and military supply are as legendary as his fighting spirit, sustaining an army in France continuously for the next three years. There was little resistance from the demoralized and still-factionalized French army but the siege of every town and castle was fought for bitterly. After the two-week siege of Caen, Henry sought to demonstrate the consequences of resistance and ordered a massacre of the townsfolk. Medieval manuscripts depicting civilian massacres usually show the sword as the weapon of choice for the perpetrators. It was not always a symbol of honour. Legend has it that Henry only ordered the slaughter halted after witnessing the headless body of a woman, with a baby in her lap still sucking at her breast. Other atrocities are alleged throughout the campaign that tarnish the reputation of this national hero. Historical figures seldom fit neatly into the roles we wish to allocate them.

Rouen held out for six long months but finally capitulated. During the siege Henry staged a 'phoney' battle outside the walls. Englishmen wearing the red cross of St George fought Englishmen wearing the white cross of St Denis. It may be history's first 're-enactment' battle. The pseudo-French forces were seen to win the day, causing rejoicing in the city as they thought that a relief force had arrived. It was a devilish stroke of psychological warfare and the citizens became despondent and defeatist when they realized that no such relief was at hand. Negotiations that started after the fall of Rouen were finally ratified at the Treaty of Troyes in 1420. Henry V was to rule as Regent of France during the lifetime of Charles VI. He was also given the hand in marriage of Charles's 19-year-old daughter, Katherine. On the death of Charles VI, Henry and Katherine's heir would succeed to the French throne.

That heir was born in 1422. At the time Henry V was laying siege to Meaux, a pocket of Dauphinist resistance. By May of that year Henry fell ill. He was only 35 but a lifetime of soldiering and living in the field had taken their toll and he is thought to have suffered severe dysentery. He hung on for a few months but died in August. Charles VI died in October and so it was that Henry's and Katherine's infant son, Henry VI, became the first and only monarch to wear both the crowns of England and France. There was jelly at his Coronation.

Legacy

Henry V's enduring legacy is as the victor of Agincourt. That the indomitable fighting spirit of Henry's army is a source of inspiration and that their triumph of the few against the many is a lasting clarion for all, individual or nation, that find themselves up against it, is indisputable. That it was a glorious moment in England's history and Henry the consummate hero is questionable. He was not a Drake or a Wellington or a Churchill, defending the country against invasion or defying a tyrant with designs on world domination. France had laid no claims to the English crown, nor did she threaten our shores. Henry was fighting a private war, for personal advancement, on borrowed money and his conduct was far from unblemished. His army followed him for employment, for adventure, for spoils and because they were there. But the how and the why of their getting there does not diminish the fact

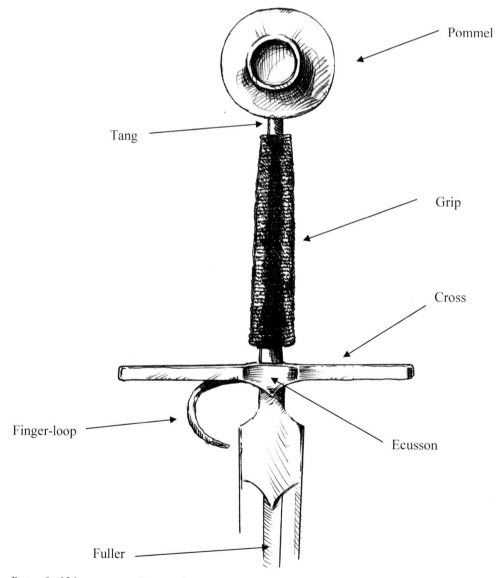

Parts of a 15th century arming sword

that, once in that situation, they exhibited a bravery, a determination and a spirit of survival against the odds that is the very essence of a nation's belief in itself.

I cannot discuss Henry V without also mentioning his reincarnations in Shakespeare and the 1944 Olivier film. They have become as much historical reality as the history itself. We should know the difference between fact and fiction but we need not dismiss one in favour of the other. We can hold a place in our heads for the one and in our hearts for the other. I first saw the Olivier film in 1960, it was shown at my school, and I read the play shortly after. Both had a profound effect on me, seducing a passion for both Shakespeare and history which I retain to this day. Shakespeare's wondrous, rousing words, William Walton's sublime music and Olivier's charismatic performance combine with vivid images, directly inspired by medieval 'Books of Hours'. It is a superbly crafted film that lifts the heart and raises the spirit. The enduring image of Olivier holding his sword in the air at the climax of his call to arms is so compelling that one cannot but believe it was so and that the sword was the one now in Westminster Abbey.

Arming swords like Henry V's were not the only sword types on the medieval battlefield. Improvements in armour had led to numerous experiments with sword design and the medieval period saw an unprecedented explosion in sword diversity. In the next chapter we look at the main types, many of which Henry, as a young prince, would almost certainly have trained with, even if he never carried them in battle.

Backsword
(R.A.M. collection)

Falchion (Thorpe)
Norwich

Two handed Scottish
(Glasgow Museums)

Type Xa
(private collection)

Type XIIIa
(Burrel collection)

Type XIIIa
(private collection)

Italian type XV
(private collection)

Dordogne, Castillion type
XVIII (R.A.M. collection)

Type XIX
(R.A.M. collection)

Type XXa
(Bayerische collection)

Chapter 6

Medieval Diversity:
Bearing Swords, Backswords,
Falchions and War Swords

I have seen the day, with my good biting falchion I would have made them skip

(Shakespeare, *King Lear*, V. III)

Developments in armour from the mid-thirteenth century had a major effect on sword design. Until then, the basic form of the sword changed very little from King Raedwald's time. There was an increase in the width of the cross, longer grips and weightier, counterbalancing pommels but the blade remained broad, parallel-sided, around 31 inches in length and with a lenticular cross-section. From 1250 onwards, however, with the introduction of plate armour, we start to see a proliferation of many different sword designs. As with Henry's funerary sword, there were changes to blade profile, cross-section and length. Some, like Henry's, were shorter. Others were longer, while others were broader and a completely different shape. Yet others were not for fighting at all; they were for ceremonial duties.

Bearing swords
Known as 'bearing swords', these symbolized the authority and legitimacy of an individual, polity or state. Many towns and cities still have a 'civic sword' that is processed before the mayor on great occasions. Almost invariably it is a sword that was previously owned by the monarch, signifying the bestowal of his authority. In Dublin there is an ornate sword made for Henry IV in 1396 by the goldsmith Herman van Cleve. It is has a long blade and a hilt of silver gilt and is of a type known as a 'war sword', complete with its 'rain-guard' (see below). Although ornate, it is stylistically like any fighting sword of its type. Henry IV presented it to the mayor of Dublin in 1403, after the Battle of Shrewsbury, granting him the right of having a sword borne before him in procession.

Just a few years earlier, at Henry IV's coronation, the Earl of Northumberland (Henry Percy) petitioned for the privilege of processing with the king's sword:

Comparative scale of Henry V's arming sword (see chapter 5) and Henry V's bearing sword

> by service of carrying on the day of the coronation of the said King and his
> heirs on the left shoulder … that naked sword which the aforesaid King
> wore called 'Lancaster's Sword' by which the aforesaid King had been
> girded when he landed at Holderness

When he had landed, Henry, the king-to-be, had immediately styled himself the
Duke of Lancaster; hence the reference to 'Lancaster's sword'. Again we may assume
that this was a proper fighting sword pressed into ceremonial service.

At The Royal Armouries in Leeds are two outsized swords, measuring some 8 feet
in overall length! Tradition has it they were carried before Henry V as he entered the
city of Harfleur at the beginning of the Agincourt campaign. These were exclusively
bearing swords, never fighting swords, and should not be confused with the true
fighting giant – the 'two-handed sword' – that we will meet in the next chapter. Some
bearing swords, like the Dublin sword, were real fighting weapons that passed into
ceremonial use. Others, like these, were made for processional and ceremonial use
only. In the museum at Westminster Abbey is a bearing sword that is said to have been
carried before Edward III. It too is enormous but it is also of very low quality. Perhaps
it was intended purely as a pageant sword, to be seen only from a distance? Another

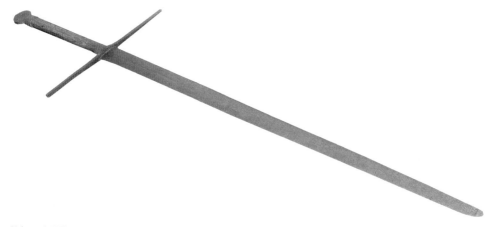

Edward III's bearing sword, Westminster Abbey (© Dean and Chapter of Westminster)

large sword, also attributed to the reign of Edward III, hangs in St George's Chapel at Windsor Castle and it is of a comparable size (6′ 8″) to the one in Westminster. However the Windsor one is of significantly greater and princely quality.

The records of the Royal Collection at Windsor contain a bill for restoration work on the sword, dated to May 8th 1387, ten years after his death:

> *Item in reparacione gladij Edwardi Fundatoris Collegij xvija*
> (for repairing the sword of Edward founder of the college 17 pence)

This was clearly a sword of importance, possibly the Sword of State or the Garter Sword (Edward founded the Order of the Garter in 1348). Although the two swords are not identical, they are similar and I think it is possible that the one now in Westminster Abbey was a rehearsal prop, intended to substitute for the one in Windsor during preparations for great state occasions. After all, rehearsal replicas of the present day 'Crown Jewels' are on display today in Westminster Abbey, whilst the genuine articles are locked safely away in H.M. Tower of London.

The present-day regalia of the British monarch, known as the Crown Jewels, includes five swords. All are carried in procession at a coronation. First in importance is The Great Sword of State, symbolizing the monarch's personal authority. The Jewelled Sword of Offering, also known as the Personal Sword, is the sword employed in knighting ceremonies. There are three swords of justice: The Sword of Spiritual Justice, The Sword of Temporal Justice and The Sword of Mercy. The point of Temporal Justice is sharp, that of Spiritual Justice blunt. The Sword of Mercy has a broken point, symbolizing that justice will be tempered with mercy. On account of the absent point this sword is often referred to as Curtana – it has been shortened, 'curtailed'.

Bearing sword of Edward III, displayed in the South Quire Aisle of St George's Chapel, Windsor Castle (© The Dean and Canons of Windsor)

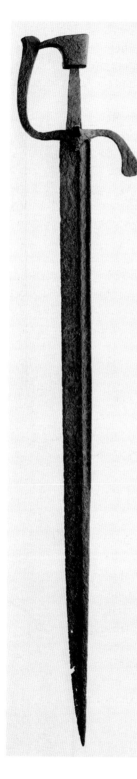

Oliver Cromwell, when he became Lord Protector in 1653, ordered the Crown Jewels to be broken down and sold as they represented the 'detestable rule of kings'. After the Restoration, new swords were produced to embody the same symbolic roles and they are what exists today. None are proper swords; all are bejewelled confections. Even so they attest to the enduring legacy and potency of the sword as a symbol.

Backsword

At the opposite end of the social scale were swords for ordinary soldiers. Mostly these were archers or spearmen and they wore a sword as a sidearm. One type of sword such troops favoured was the 'backsword'. Backswords have rarely survived but are common in art. Perhaps their failure to survive is precisely because they were the weapons of the common soldier. A knight's sword meant something and was either hung above his tomb or handed down through family generations. A soldier's sword was a commodity; one that probably ended up as scrap iron.

Backswords had a single straight edge; the back edge being flat, blunt and relatively broad. In cross-section the blade was a narrow wedge shape. This thicker back edge usually had a deep groove along its spine, giving the sword enhanced strength and rigidity. Because the strength and stiffness of the sword was assured by this design, back-swords didn't necessarily require a sophisticated level of manufacture and tempering and so could be produced as a low-budget option for the less well-off infantryman. Moreover, being sidearms and weapons of last resort, they didn't have to possess the same standards of durability as a knight's sword.

Nevertheless, this humble sidearm of the common foot-soldier was the first to exhibit a feature of sword design that would, from the sixteenth century on, become a universal element on virtually all swords. From the early fifteenth century, backswords were fitted with a 'knuckle-guard' – a curved bar extending from the cross and curling up towards the pommel – that offered protection to the back of the hand. It could also be used to punch people in

Backsword (© The Board of Trustees of the Armouries)

the face. Knuckle-guards were particularly useful for archers, who by dint of their trade, operated bare-handed. Once you have a knuckle-guard, the sword can only be used in one attitude, denying the usefulness of a double edge. It simply cannot be held the other way round and so the development of the back-edge and the knuckle-guard are synergetic.

A rare early fifteenth-century sword in the collection of The Royal Armouries in Leeds offers a different form of hand protection. It has a semi-circular loop emanating from below the cross and curling round towards the blade. Such 'finger-loops' occur occasionally in fourteenth-century art. Their purpose is to guard the index finger when hooked over the cross to give a more secure grip to a flagging grasp. As discussed in previous chapters, the risk to the forefinger is minimal; it is only really vulnerable if you are parrying a blow coming in from the high right and it quickly becomes second nature to move your finger as you move your sword to parry here. Even so, some enterprising swordsmith sought to boost his sales by coming up with the invention – offering an illusion of necessary security to the inexperienced. Although this particular sword possesses a double-edged blade, only the edge adjacent to the finger-loop can be used as the leading edge. In this respect it resembles the backsword. Also like the backsword, the finger-loop heralded a trend for developed hilts that came to fruition in the sixteenth century.

Falchion

Another weapon of the common man was the 'falchion'. A falchion was a broad-bladed, single-edged weapon with a profile taper that broadened towards the point, creating a distinctive curve to its formidable cutting edge. There were a number of variations to this basic pattern, ranging from crude machete-like cleavers to elegant weapons with fine proportions and line. Although it was favoured by light troops such as spearmen and archers, a falchion could equally well serve a knight. It probably owes its origin to Saracen scimitars encountered by crusaders and its name to the Latin '*falx*', meaning sickle. As discussed in chapter two, the term '*falcata*' is a fabrication of nineteenth-century scholars and so we cannot say the word 'falchion' derives directly from this, though clearly both words have a common root. However, if you were to take a falcata blade and bend it straight, you would have a falchion. Because of this straightening, the falchion does not have a 'sickle-like' cutting edge on the inside of a concave curve, but it nevertheless appears to derive from a transmuted form of the Greek makhaira that had a tradition of continuity in the east. Setting these semantic niggles aside, the falchion can be both a beautiful and powerful weapon.

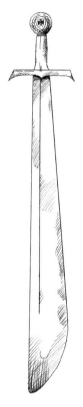

The Conyers falchion

The thirteenth-century Conyers falchion, now in Durham Cathedral is one of only a few surviving examples. On one face of the pommel are engraved the three leopards (today called lions) of England and on the other, the eagle of the Holy Roman Empire. It was made for Henry III's brother, Richard, Earl of Cornwall, who also became, at vast expense to his pocket, King of the Romans – the Holy Roman Emperor elect – although he never actually made it to the Imperial Crown. It has a broad, cleaver-shaped blade with a straight back and fullers. The blade broadens considerably towards the point with a pronounced convex curve. This is a weapon that could do a great deal of damage, whether in skilled or unskilled hands. It is a mighty sword. Owned for generations by the Conyers family it was presented by them to every new Prince Bishop when he first entered the diocese of Durham, in order to demonstrate their allegiance and right to tenure of lands in nearby Stockburn. Legend recalls that a Conyers ancestor used it to slay a dragon, the 'Stockburn Worm'. The custom of presenting it to the incoming Bishop was halted in 1860 but was reinstated in 1994. Traditionally the ceremony takes place in the mid point of the River Tees.

More typically the falchion has the back edge cut away and honed for a short section near the point creating a 'clipt' point and giving it a cusped, beak-like shape. This provided the falchion with a thrusting as well as a cutting capability. The Thorpe falchion in Norwich Castle is an elegant example of the clipt point style, as is a beautiful specimen in the Musée de l'Armée in Paris. There is another in Hamburg and a superb one tucked away in a drawer in the storerooms of the Royal Armouries in Leeds. It is from a hoard of fifteenth-century swords dredged from the preserving silts of the River Dordogne in southwest France during the mid-1970s, close to the site of the last battle of the Hundred Years War, Castillon.

By 1451, England had lost virtually all her possessions in France, Bordeaux being one of the last to fall. In 1452, Sir John Talbot was sent with an expeditionary force to recapture the town. Talbot was a veteran of campaigns in France. He had been the tactical mastermind of the fierce contest for many years, winning many victories until he was taken prisoner by Joan of Arc after the Battle of Patay in 1429. On that occasion

Falchion from Castillon (©The Board of Trustees of the Armouries)

he was ransomed, exchanged and soon back in action. Following the recapture of Falaise Castle by the French in 1450, Talbot was taken prisoner again. Once more he was ransomed but this time a condition of his release was that he had to swear never again to bear arms against France.

The citizens of Bordeaux opened their gates and their arms to the relieving English force and throughout that winter Talbot consolidated English rule. It took until July of the following year, 1453, for the French to rally and reorganize. Talbot and his 6,000 strong force met them on the approaches to Castillon, just a few miles from Bordeaux. The French had created entrenched positions, which had been carefully camouflaged. Behind their stockades lay a fearsome array of artillery and handguns. John Talbot was 69 years of age and, true to his pledge, he rode at the head of his army unarmoured and unarmed. The venerable old warrior rode into the guns on his little white horse, wearing only civilian clothes. He was caught in crossfire and shot to pieces. The war was over and so was an age.

Eighty medieval swords, of various types, were found in the river near Castillon. They were contained in two wooden casks, which presumably rolled off an over-laden barge. Some were in near-perfect condition whilst others were bent or broken. Most had signs of hard use, with many nicks on their blades. It seems likely that they had been packed up after the battle, probably scavenged from the piles of English dead before they were tumbled into their grave pits. Bordeaux subsequently returned to French hands and, just a few miles up-river, seems the most likely intended destination for this cargo. The falchion now in the Royal Armouries has a distinctive pear-shaped pommel, turned upside down from the usual orientation of this style – a feature of several of the Castillon swords. Though black with corrosion, it is still a sturdy sword and a very elegant example of the type. I have held it; it is a magnificent weapon and much lighter than it appears.

Even though falchions, like backswords, are widespread in medieval art, very few survive. This is the same for medieval armour. There is quite a lot from the late fifteenth century, when complete suits of armour became something to hand down through the generations, and a great deal of armour from the sixteenth century, but armour from the thirteenth and fourteenth centuries is exceedingly rare. A lot of armour and weapons disappear from the record because the metal is recycled for other use – a case of turning swords into ploughshares. A perfect illustration of this is a fourteenth-century helm in the British Museum. It has a chain attached because it was turned into a cooking pot! Falchions were sometimes the beneficiaries of this parsimonious salvage. In the Royal Armouries is an example, dating to the fourteenth century, of a falchion which has been made from a cut-down and re-shaped regular sword. When broken swords were the spoils of battle, resourceful men could still make use of them.

Great swords and war swords

By far the most important development in medieval sword design, emerging in response to improved armour defences, was the invention of the 'great sword' and

the war sword'. These were larger swords and capable of delivering much heavier blows. The fact that longer-bladed swords, strong enough to fight with, became possible was a testimony to continuing improvements in steel production and blade manufacture.

Medieval literature gives us the names – *grans espées* or '*grete swerdes*' (great swords) and *espées de guerre* (war swords) – but it does not supply accompanying illustrations, so we are left to interpret which tag to apply to which sword. Furthermore, at least as early as the fourteenth century we encounter the expressions '*espées a deux mains*' and '*twahandswerds*', which in this early context are merely alternative expressions for either great swords or war swords. We need to reserve the designation 'two-handed sword' for a particular sword type of that name that appears in the sixteenth century and so 'great swords' and 'war swords' are what we are left with to describe this family of bigger swords. At the time it is likely that the phrases were interchangeable but, as a modern convenience, 'great sword' is more usually applied to the larger types.

With blades ranging from 34 to 45 inches and hilts from 6 to 10 inches, great swords appeared in a wide spectrum of sizes. I have had the privilege of handling several thirteenth and fourteenth-century great swords, now in the Burrell Collection, Glasgow. As well as being in surprisingly good condition, they are light and well balanced. It is no effort to wield them with one hand. However, they were intended primarily for use with two hands and it is as a two-handed sword that they unleash their full potential as a massive shearing force. Mostly they have wheel-type pommels and all possess a simple, straight bar for a cross.

In the aftermath of the Battle of Poitiers in 1356, a young French squire, John de Hellenes, was fleeing his English pursuer when, as the chronicler Froissart reports, 'John de Hellenes turned about, put his sword under his arm in the manner of a lance and thus advanced upon his adversary'. This must surely have been a great sword and one of good length to be useful in this manner. Imagine John thundering towards his enemy, clamping the grip against his side with

Great sword/war sword, 13th century (courtesy of Sport and Culture Glasgow (Museums))

his upper arm, embedding the cross against his shoulder to deliver more force and cupping the blade in his right hand to steady and aim. In the event, he only managed to strike his man on the arm. It was enough, though, to make his opponent lose his sword. That opponent was Lord Berkeley and, as he dismounted to retrieve his weapon, John rode down upon him and 'gave him a violent thrust, which passed through both of his thighs'. The thighs seem a very curious target for a mounted man to attack and what are we to make of the implication that the sword went through plate armour – twice! Given that young John had the added impetus of a horse and that he had couched his sword like a lance, minimizing recoil on impact, it is conceivable that he might puncture leg armour. Cuisses, the armour for the front of the thighs, were of a considerably lighter gauge than armour for head or chest. Vital organs required maximum protection; limbs required optimum mobility. Moreover, cuisses do not generally extend to the back and inside of the thigh, which was usually protected by being adjacent to the saddle. It is therefore also conceivable that this notable blow only pierced one thin plate of leg armour, or even none at all. Even so, there is no doubt that the purpose of these larger swords was to hit with greater force.

A distinctive variation of the great sword type is the Scottish version. Its familiar image is with a steeply down-turned cross with quatretrefoil terminals and a disproportionately small pommel, though there were some stylistic variations to this. It is the sword so often referred to, erroneously, as the 'claymore'. Transcribed from the Gaelic '*claidheamh mor*', meaning 'big sword', the word 'claymore' should more properly be reserved for the Scottish basket-hilted sword of the seventeenth and eighteenth centuries. Here it was applied to distinguish the broad-bladed basket hilt from the *claidheamh beg* or 'smallsword'. The Scottish great sword may fit the appellation 'big sword' but it had the medieval name of *claidheamh da laidbh* (clay-da-layv), meaning 'two-handed sword'. Today it is mostly referred to, correctly, as the 'Scottish longsword' – but never claymore.

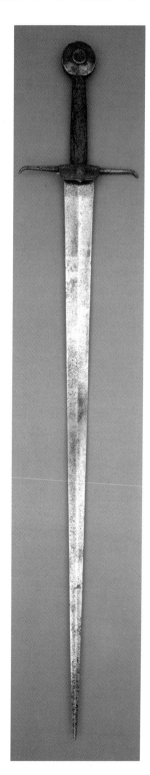

War sword, 14th century; note the rain guard (courtesy of Sport an Culture Glasgow (Museums))

Whilst on the topic of nomenclature I should clear up some other terminology. It has become increasingly common these days for people to use the term broadsword as if it were the correct term to denote a type of medieval sword. It is not. It may be true to say that virtually all medieval swords are broadswords, insofar as they are 'broad-bladed' but that does not distinguish them from the legion of other broad-bladed swords of previous or later centuries, nor is it a term that was used at the time. The term broadsword distinguishes broad-bladed swords, which may include medieval swords but also includes military swords from the seventeenth to nineteenth centuries, from other swords such as 'rapiers' and 'smallswords'. It is a term that has no meaning or usefulness until the sixteenth century when a divergent form of slender-bladed sword, in the guise of the rapier, comes into being. The correct term for the regular, single-handed sword of the Middle Ages is 'arming sword' – this is the sword that was buckled on with a knight's armour, worn in a scabbard and hung from his belt.

Literary references suggest that great swords were suspended from the saddle when carried by the mounted man, although it is not an image that has survived in art. For the foot soldier they were carried into battle resting on the shoulder. However there was a companion species of outsized sword that could be worn on the hip. This was the war sword. Bigger than the regular arming sword, the war sword still only had a blade length of between 31 and 34 inches. More significantly though, it had a longer grip. Much of the added power came not from the blade length but from the length of the grip. The wider the hands can be placed on a two-handed grip, then the greater the power advantage of them working around a fulcrum in a push/pull action.

One of the loveliest of this type is in the collection of Glasgow Museums at Kelvingrove. Rarely, it still retains, on one side, its original rain-guard. Rain-guards were common on fourteeth-century swords and consisted of a pair of thin sheets of iron that extended down on each side of the cross to seal the mouth of the scabbard, protecting the sword from rain or moisture when sheathed. They were relatively flimsy attachments and so have been lost on many swords. Engraved and fire-gilt, this is an exceptionally fine rain-guard fit for an important sword. The sword's wooden grip is also in a remarkable state of preservation and is long enough to be held with two hands, although it is equally capable of being wielded single-handedly, having a blade length of only 31 inches. It is an extremely beautiful object with the most elegant proportions and yet, to me, the most wonderful thing about it is its weight and balance. These properties are so finely tuned that the sword feels alive in the hand. I have handled dozens of original medieval swords, both in museums and private collections, but the thrill I get in holding this one is unparalleled and the presence of the rain-guard is a reminder that this was an individual's prized possession – something he took great care of and pride in. Something he would have fussed over.

Great swords were described in medieval French inventories as '*grans espées D'Allemagne*', suggesting that they were a type that may have originated in Germany.

Germany was certainly at the forefront of martial development and it is here that we find the first documented teachings on the use of the great sword in works derived from the greatest master of them all, Johannes Liechtenauer.

Johannes Liechtenauer

Liechtenauer was the master of masters and the father of a system of fighting that was reproduced, reinterpreted and illustrated by succeeding masters throughout the fifteenth and sixteenth centuries. Liechtenauer was active around the middle of the fourteenth century, somewhere in Germany. He may be the 'Johannes the Swabian' that Fiore studied under. We know virtually nothing of his life but at some stage he recorded the essence of his teachings in a few hundred lines of verse. These verses were deliberately cryptic. For the initiated they served as a mnemonic and for the tyro they conveyed just enough information to prompt him to seek further instruction from the master; for which, of course, he would have to pay. Martial training was a commercial undertaking. In 1389 a German monk, Hanko Döbringer, wrote down Liechtenauer's verse dictums with a commentary, in what is the earliest surviving manuscript of his teachings.

Liechtenauer focussed on the great sword (later to become known as the 'longsword'), though he also included tips on mounted combat, wrestling and dagger fighting. He advocated four basic 'guards', though it is important to remember that these were not exclusively defensive positions, rather they were offensive positions, which were also good places to defend from. Postures, especially those requiring precise adjustments, are cumbersome to describe in words and so it was useful shorthand to name the principal guard positions with an imagery that made them easy to remember. Liechtenauer's stances were: *Ochs* (Ox), with the hilt held above the head and the point sloping down towards the enemy's face; *Pflug* (Plough) with the hilt held at the waist and the point sloping up towards the enemy's face; *Von Dach* (From the Roof), where the sword was held high over the shoulder, with the blade angled back, ready to descend 'from the roof': *Alber* (Fool) had the sword held in front of the body with its point on the ground. This last, seemingly a defenceless invitation (hence its name), was every bit a posture of both attack and defence as the others. From the Fool position any blow, coming from any direction, could be countered simply by raising your sword swiftly and angling your wrists to left or right depending on the incoming angle. The attacking sword would be knocked and set aside. At the same time the completion of your move would automatically take you into the Ox position over either your left or right shoulder and you could follow through with your attack, performing the whole manoeuvre in one fluid movement. Similar narratives can be constructed from all Liechtenauer's stances.

I am aware that blow-by-blow, step-by-step descriptions of sword management do not transfer well to the page and seek here only to hint at the methodology. The point the lay reader should grasp from the above is that it was a scientific system; it had method and rationale. Medieval swordfighting was not about swinging your sword wildly, heedless of opening your guard. It entailed moving efficiently from one stance to another, simultaneously guarding a line from attack whilst maintaining a line from which to attack. Liechtenauer's was a graceful, athletic and tutored martial art. Footwork included the avoidance of blows by stepping forward, back, to the side and diagonally. Alternatively you could close with the enemy and grapple. At close quarters the blade of the sword could be used as a lever to unbalance an opponent and the pommel could be employed to break teeth and smash noses. It was a system of all-in fighting; crunching, bruising and rugged but nonetheless scientific.

Percussive armour-cracking weapons such as the mace, war hammer and pollaxe found increasing favour in the age of plate armour but it was the sword that lent itself to developing more sophisticated martial arts principles. Liechtenauer talks about 'fighting weakness with strength and strength with weakness', concepts that will be

1508 Liechtenauer manuscript from the Scott Library, Glasgow Museums (courtesy of Sport and Culture Glasgow (Museums)

understood by practitioners of any martial art. He refers to '*winden*', which are moves where you bind the opponent's blade, yielding and giving pressure, as you first divert the line of his attack and then push through for your own advantage. A precise understanding of time and distance was crucial. He mentions drawing cuts, where the sword is laid on windpipe or hamstring from a close-quarter position and the cut effected by slicing as you step away. Fighting with the sword in this way was a highly-trained art and very different from popular notions of indiscriminate hacking blows. Although the sword could be used to some effect by the relatively untutored hand, it required years of constant practice to attain any sort of mastery and quite possibly this daily martial arts training led, even more than its use on the battlefield, to the cult of the sword being valued above all other weapons.

Johannes Liechtenauer developed his system in the mid-fourteenth century but it was copied and freshly illustrated for many generations to come. The invention of the printing press in the mid-fifteenth century paved the way for a plethora of manuals on the subject of 'fence'; many still perpetuating the timeless wisdom of this old German master. Nevertheless the old ways of laboriously copying a manuscript continued for works of great worth and patrons of wealth. One magnificent hand-written version of Liechtenauer's teachings, produced in 1508, is illustrated with lively drawings, some of which have been delicately hand coloured. In one figure, both men are wearing doublet and hose and one, presumably the master, has the letters ABCD emblazoned down his left arm and EFGH down his left leg. It suggests a system of training where designated zones of the body would be called out to attack. We cannot see his other side but may imagine that it is similarly marked, so that the master may, for instance, call out, 'thrust left F, then strike right B' et cetera. Working with a master one-on-one was just one part of a swordsman's overall training. He also needed to work at the pell to build his stamina and learn how to deliver his blows with full force, he had to perform solo drills to perfect his form and he had to train with other students to sharpen his reactions and become accustomed to facing an aggressive opponent. Liechtenauer called lumbering maladroit swordsmen who relied purely on brute strength *Buffels* – 'buffaloes'. He had an antidote to them: 'the squinting stroke breaks whatever a buffalo strikes or thrusts'. In fact he had antidotes for most situations. The challenge was to remember under pressure and, in an illiterate age, that is where his mnemonic verses came into their own; but knowing when to deliver the 'squinting stroke' wasn't enough. It had to be rehearsed against a hulking bruiser swinging wildly for your head.

Wasters

Practice fighting in the fence schools was mainly conducted with wooden or whalebone swords, known as 'wasters'. Foiled (ie blunted) metal swords could also be used but wooden or whalebone wasters were for everyday work. The word may derive from the contemporary opinion that young men were 'wasting' their time hanging around the fence schools or from the concept of 'laying waste'. Wasters were not

simple staves but rather exact replicas, carved to look like the sword type they were substituting for and matching it for weight and balance. It is also possible that they may have been painted to look like the real thing.

Where they differed in shape from the original is they had a much thicker cross-section that allowed for broad edges. A sword's steel edges are vulnerable to constant percussion, whereas thick wooden wasters could take a great deal of punishment. Moreover they were inexpensive to replace. Wasters also allowed students to 'free play' without risk of serious injury, though heads could still be cracked quite severely. King Duarte of Portugal (1391–1438), a prolific commentator on various martial arts, recommended in his *Regimento*: 'Have spare weapons and armour at your house for anyone who comes over. Have wooden weapons to play with. When you spar use heavier weapons'.

Duarte makes a nice distinction between 'play' and 'sparring', suggesting that there are graded levels of practice. 'Play' does not mean 'childlike play' here but rather exercising with the sword against a partner as opposed to fighting him in earnest. This may take the form of pre-set sequences or a certain amount of controlled free play in which blows are only landed lightly. Such practice was essential for rehearsing muscle memory and cultivating a sense of measure. Form could be learned by performing solo sequences but 'playing' with an opponent was the only way to develop a sense of distance and timing and a feel for the pressure of blade contact. His injunction to have spares ready for visitors emphasizes how important it was to not only practice at every opportunity but also to do so with a wide range of people.

'Sparring' on the other hand implies a much more robust interchange; one that would necessitate the donning of the spare armour. It may be done with wooden weapons or with blunt iron weapons but Duarte advises that it is done with heavier weapons. One may be sure that the blows were heavier. This kind of bruising 'free play' was equally essential for sharpening up a swordsman's reactions and training him to keep a calm head in a contest that could have painful, though not fatal, consequences if either bravado or fear governed his decisions. It took a great deal of training and an

Wooden waster (author's collection)

inner stillness to be able to react according to the master's teachings in the high speed, bone-jarring ordeal of real combat.

Tests

With so much diversity in medieval sword types, the obvious question is 'how do they differ in their destructive capabilities?' In some very basic tests against a block of clay, I have compared the performance of four different types. Clay was chosen to give a consistent, measurable and visually discernable result. Raven Armouries lent me four superb, finely sharpened swords: a straight, parallel-sided one; a fifteenth-century type with an acute profile taper; a falchion and a war sword. I powered every stroke with as much force as I could muster and used both cuts and thrusts. The first three swords performed almost identically. My conclusion is that, although people were undoubtedly experimenting and looking for new designs and solutions, a sword is ultimately an iron bar with a sharpened edge and, weight for weight, any two swords are going to achieve similar results. That is not to say that there were not important differences between individual swords – there were, in the way that they handled and so how they could be fought with. However, the physics of blades of similar weight and similar sharpness striking an object with identical force remained constant despite variations in blade shape. Unsurprisingly though, the war sword fared significantly better. It cut deeper and thrust deeper, not least because it was wielded with two hands as well as having greater mass.

By the mid-fifteenth century, larger swords came to dominate the martial cultures of both the battlefield and the fence schools. At some point the war sword/great sword became the 'longsword'. Like the war sword it had a two-handed grip and it always had a long blade, in excess of 40 inches. Many, though not all, war swords/ great swords of the thirteenth and fourteenth centuries also could be accurately termed 'longswords' but I am making the very subtle distinction between these and the fifteenth-century longsword type. The subject of the next chapter is the Holy Roman Emperor, Maximilian I, and his sword of choice was the longsword.

Emperor Maximilian I by Ambrogio de'Predis. He wears the collar of the Order of the Golden Fleece (Kunsthistorisches Museum, Vienna)

Chapter 7

The Sword of Maximilian I, Holy Roman Emperor

Princes and Lords learn to survive with this art, in earnest and in play. But if you are fearful, then you should not learn to fence, because a despondent heart will always be defeated, regardless of all skill.

(Sigmund Ringeck, circa 1440)

In the old Imperial armoury that is now the Kunsthistorisches Museum in Vienna rests a classic sword of the late Middle Ages with an austere and simple beauty. It is a longsword and it was made for the Archduke Maximilian of Austria, before he became Holy Roman Emperor. Its beautiful gilded pommel and cross contrast majestically with the finely tooled black leather of the grip. Both the pommel and the cross are engraved with the emblem of the Order of the Golden Fleece. Inset on the blade is a medallion reading 'HMIADM', which stands for *'Halt Maß in Allen Dingen, Maximilian'* ('Hold steady in all things, Maximilian'), the motto of the Maßigkeitsordens, another chivalric order to which Maximilian belonged. Overall the sword is 56.2 inches and weighs 5lbs. In cross-section its 1.5 inch-wide blade is a flattened hexagon and inlaid with brass designs, showing a maker's mark in the form of a spur and the inscription *'Hi[lf] uns Ritter Sant Jorg'* ('Help us Knight St George'). A tall, scent stopper-style pommel with hexagonal facets crowns the lozenge-shaped grip, which is also hexagonal in cross-section. The lines of blade and grip, of cross and pommel, balance perfectly to the eye, just as the sword itself balances perfectly in the hand. Maximilian's longsword possesses a tasteful and restrained aesthetic, yet still boasts its princely status.

Maximilian was nothing if not princely. He was born in 1459, the son of the Holy Roman Emperor Frederick III and Eleanor of Portugal. He did not become Holy Roman Emperor until 1508, at the age of forty-nine, but his entire life was distinguished by an extravagant celebration of knightly ideals. He has been described as 'the last of the knights' and, a colossus of his age, he straddled both the medieval world he was born into and the northern Renaissance world he was instrumental in creating. Maximilian dedicated much of his life to immortalizing himself. He was obsessed with how posterity would remember him, authoring books that cast him as a chivalric hero, sponsoring aggrandizing architectural schemes and heading a glittering court at which tournaments and a celebration of the martial arts were the central focus.

Longswords

As we have seen, outsized swords began to develop in the thirteenth and fourteenth centuries as a response to improvements in armour. In their earlier incarnation they were more usually termed either 'war swords' or 'great swords', though the expression 'longsword' was equally apt for some examples. The earlier types tended to have flat blades, whereas, by the fifteenth century, hollowed blades and hexagonal blades became more common, as did the term 'longsword'. Longswords were also described variously as 'hand-and-a-half swords' or 'bastard swords'. These last two nomenclatures were intended to indicate that such swords were a hybrid, somewhere between a single-handed arming sword and the much bigger two-handed sword. Although they are clearly used with two hands, longswords are quite distinct from the two-handed sword proper, which we shall meet presently.

Longswords in the fifteenth century were a fairly homogenous type and all about the same size. On Maximilian's sword, the blade is parallel-sided for its entire length, whereas on many longswords there is quite a steep taper. Other small variations included grip design; some favoured a 'wine bottle' grip, whereby the regular broad grip for the lower hand shoulders in at the halfway point and extends into a narrower grip for the upper hand. Longswords have sleek elegant lines, augmented at most by a single side-ring, though Maximilian's remains unadorned. Although large, the longsword was a relatively lightweight and well-balanced weapon, an extremely manageable 'power sword'.

In the *Triumphzeug* ('Triumph of Maximilian'), the wonderfully-named fight master, Hans Hollywars, leads in a number of men, armed to take part in the *gefecht* – foot combats. Maximilian was at the forefront of elevating foot combat to knightly status in his glittering tournaments. It was a passion he had acquired in his youth. A woodcut showing an extremely callow Maximilian, depicts him receiving lessons in the longsword. His opponent is an especially pugnacious-looking fellow and the instructor appears to be a stern taskmaster. Learning to fight with the longsword was a tough regime of hard work and hard knocks, even for a prince. A second pair of longswords lies on the floor. It seems probable that one pair are wooden wasters and that the others are blunt steel weapons. There is also a brace of staves on the floor for quarterstaff practice and the master holds a stave to separate his young charges should they get a little over-enthusiastic.

Several texts on fighting techniques appeared in Germany around the middle of the century. Sigmund Ringeck's simply-titled *Ringeck's Fechtbuch*, basically a re-working of Liechtenauer with an additional section on Ott the Jew's wrestling techniques, was produced around 1440. Others, such as the von Danzig *fechtbuch* ('fight book'), and those of Paulus Kal and Lew the Jew, all also attribute influences to the old master,

Maximilian fighting with longswords (©The Board of Trustees of the Armouries)

Liechtenauer. However, perhaps the most prolific master, who published treatises detailing the use of the longsword and other weapons of the day, was Hans Talhoffer. His *Fechtbuch* builds on that of Liechtenauer, indeed cites it, but it also expands upon it. It appeared in six different versions, the best known of which are from 1443, 1459 and 1467. Each is superbly illustrated and it is the quality of these illustrations that make it stand out from all other works of the time. The energized, expressive figures burst from the page as if they were actually in motion. Artists of the day considered the fighting arts to be of great aesthetic value. Leonardo da Vinci, in his writings, gives favourable mention to Pietro Monte, a celebrated master of arms who published a manual in 1509. Although it remained unfinished, Albrecht Dürer began producing his own *fechtbuch* in 1512; in content it was remarkably similar to Talhoffer's, though arguably the figures have been drawn with even greater clarity and nuance. Today's refined aesthete may turn up his nose at such belligerent and sweaty exertions but to the Renaissance mind the perfection of form attainable in the martial arts held a beauty to be admired.

On a more practical note, longswords are invariably shown being used with bare hands and all the masters taught moves that required the blade to be held. These 'half-sword' techniques were fundamental to fighting with the longsword.

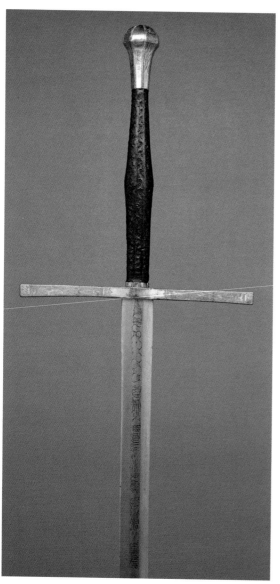

Sharpness is a relative concept. It is perfectly possible to hold fairly sharp blades with your bare hands and not draw your own blood. Even in a grapple to wrest the other man's sword from him, a firm grip and knowledge of which plane to turn it in will accomplish the manoeuvre without injury. Such plays however are only possible with a 'relatively' sharp sword. Razor sharpness would make them prohibitive but in an age of plate armour, razor sharpness was not a benefit. Brittle edges would be quickly destroyed, whereas swords of moderate sharpness stood a chance of biting into the metal and delivering the energy of the blow, as well as standing up to an amount of punishment. They could also be held by the blade.

Holding the blade shortened the sword for close-quarter work; here it could sometimes be guided to find the gaps in the armour of a standing man. It allowed the cross to be used as a hook or swung as an axe in what Talhoffer describes as the 'murder stroke', and it

The hilt of Maximilian's longsword (Kunsthistorisches Museum, Vienna)

Longsword techniques, after Talhoffer

facilitated the use of the pommel as a mace. Most importantly, though, half-sword moves enabled the longsword to be used as a lever. Longsword fighting was a lot about wrestling with an iron bar and managing that bar to use an opponent's weight and force against him. Half-sword techniques also made it possible for the fighter to dramatically change the distance at which he was fighting in an instant. Fighting with the fifteenth-century longsword may be considered a complex martial art of the highest order. Certainly training in these techniques is the greatest fun.

Fifteenth-century judicial duels

Judicial duels remained commonplace in fifteenth-century Germany and prompted a major source of employment for the fencing master. Talhoffer was master of arms to Leutold von Koningsegg, a feudatory of Count Eberhard the Bearded of Wurttenberg. His pupil triumphed in a judicial duel in 1440, thanks to Talhoffer's personal instruction.

Although the longsword and the pollaxe were the primary weapons for knightly duels, Talhoffer taught methods for other, more specialized forms of judicial duel, some of which are quite bizarre. For instance, the duel with massive 'duelling shields'. Some exmples have contours that can be used to hook an opponent. At either end

Various forms of the judicial duel in Germany, after Talhoffer

they have a sharp iron point. I had a pair of these made and experimented with their use. A continuous wooden bar runs the entire length of the back of the shield, which the hands can slide up and down, as in fighting with staffs. The face of the shield can be used to barge and destabilize an opponent, the hooks to seize neck or legs and the iron points can be used to thrust and jab. Shields such as these were used exclusively for the judicial duel and, precisely because they are not weapons in everyday use, possibly evolved from a notion of giving no favour to either party. Plaintiffs seeking to prove their case by victory in a judicial duel with such weapons would not be able to rely on superior technique and years of practice with the sword, though clearly the advantage would always reside with the more martially able. As a further leveller, to give no advantage to size and weight, grappling and wrestling were rendered impossible by the combatants donning all-in-one leather suits, which were greased with pig fat. When I experimented with duelling shields, I declined the leather and pig fat!

For all their eccentric weirdness, judicial duels with these shields were as earnest as any other. Talhoffer shows fallen victims being killed by having the iron spike driven through their ribcage. It was innate to the culture that justice could be served by arbitration in combat. Talhoffer also depicts a type of duel in which a woman could claim legal redress, in the form of a duel, against a man that had wronged her. The man is placed in a pit up to his waist and is armed with three wooden clubs. The woman moves freely on the ground above and has a grapefruit sized stone, wrapped in a cloth sling, which she wields in the manner of a flail. They are similarly attired in greased leather.

Whether these strange combats were reserved for particular crimes or for those of a lower station in society, the knightly class preferred knightly weapons – sword, lance or pollaxe – and the most illustrious of these was the longsword. It required a lifetime of constant training to master it. Martial training on a regular basis equipped a man not only for war, but for the eventuality that he might one day have to defend his rights in the judicial duel.

Guilds of Fence

The burghers of larger towns and cities formed guilds of fence, which authorized the training and licensing of masters of fence. Masters of the guilds were considered to be authorities on matters of honour and procedure. The most famous of these guilds were the Marxbruder (the Brotherhood of St Mark), more formally known as *Burgerschaft von St. Marcus von Lowenberg*. Maximilian's father, the Emperor Frederick III, granted them letters patent in 1480. Albrecht Dürer was a member. Their headquarters were in Frankfurt-am-Main and during the autumn fairs there, aspirants to join the guild were obliged to demonstrate their aptitude by fighting with the captain of the guild and as many masters as could be mustered. These 'auditions' took place on a scaffold set up in the market place and must have been a source of great entertainment to the crowds. If the candidate acquitted himself adequately, he would, on payment of the appropriate fee, be taken in for training.

Graduating masters were granted the right to bear the heraldic device of the brotherhood, a golden lion, and licensed to teach throughout Germany. Their principal rivals were the Luxbruder (Brotherhood of St Luke), but the Marxbruder did their best to maintain a monopoly. Anyone setting himself up independently was challenged by the guild and offered the alternatives of either proving themselves by fighting the captain and five masters all at once or applying to join the guild by the conventional route. Nothing is heard of the Luxbruder later than the fifteenth century, they were no match for the Marxbruder, but it is believed that a group known as the Klopffechter sprang from their ranks. From the sixteenth to the seventeenth centuries the Klopffechter travelled the country performing prizefights at fairs and festivals. *Klopf* means blow and the name 'blow-fighter' has come to mean pugilist in modern German, though originally it may have indicated a robust, knockabout form of entertainment fight.

The main business of the guilds was to teach and facilitate daily practice in the fence schools and this 'martial arts' culture is a central point in our appreciation of the sword's long history. If we only consider the horrors of the sword in war, we miss an essential element of its enduring popularity. Swordfighting was valued and practiced as a martial art in its own right and for its own sake. It was a rough, physical, often bruising experience, but within the temples of the fence schools it seldom resulted in anything worse than a cracked head. Here was none of the misery of amputated limbs or gutted bellies. Here was none of the pity of war. This was the exercise and development of skills – skills that elicited the admiration of others. It was not yet sport, though something other than art. It involved a focussed concentration to produce lightning, automatic reactions; a concentration so intense that the mind was cleared of all other thoughts. It required resolve, determination and courage. It required knowledge. Above all it was a thrilling, strenuous, exhausting exercise that necessitated physical fitness, both in terms of aerobic stamina and lithe flexibility. Work with the longsword was the highest level of martial expertise, and even more than that, it was exhilarating and fun. Fence schools were no longer the taboo haunts of urban low-life but esteemed academies for learning these noble arts; arts that were endorsed by rulers like Maximilian. Swordsmanship was at the heart of a vigorous martial culture.

The cult of Maximilian

Maximilian's passion for the arts of Mars and his militarist expansionism were part of an overall quest for immortal recognition. He wanted to be remembered for his great achievements and as the legitimate heir of great historical figures, warrior heroes who had changed the world. Court genealogists drew up spurious family trees that traced his ancestors to Charlemagne and Julius Caesar, even to King Arthur. Maximilian saw himself at the centre of an historical fantasy. He was rooted in the medieval world of noble chivalry and yet he was also the leader of a brave new Renaissance world. His court became a centre for the arts. He commissioned grand architectural schemes, promoted music, amassed a vast library and was the patron of great artists such as Albrecht Dürer and Hans Burgkmair. He was a man of letters who supported writers and the development of printing. Books on hunting and the tournament are credited to his authorship, though they were almost certainly ghost-written for him, as were a trilogy of illustrated autobiographical fantasies.

The first part of this trilogy, *Der Weisskunig*, concentrates on Maximilian's childhood; the second, *Teuerdank*, on his allegorical journey to the Netherlands to woo Mary of Burgundy; and the third, *Freydal*, celebrates his heroic deeds in jousts, tournaments and other combats. Written in verse, these books are considered the finest produced during the German Renaissance, lavishly illustrated with exquisite woodcuts and printed using an elaborately scrolled gothic font, resembling the flourishes of handwritten script. Drawing heavily from Arthurian romances and the journey quests of classical heroes, Maximilian cast himself in the role of an idealized romantic champion. His passion for the tournament verged on the obsessive. Many new forms of joust were devised for his extravagant court entertainments. No matter to what extent he embraced the new ways of waging war with artillery, harquebusiers and massed infantry, he still sought to perpetuate his chivalric pedigree with his version of a romantic Camelot. He nonetheless needed to establish a new chivalric code, where fighting on foot with the sword was considered every bit as noble as riding a foaming stallion. The future of war lay in the hands of the infantryman and so he instituted foot combats for knights as an integral part of the tournament. *Freydal* depicts him fighting on foot, in armour and with a longsword.

Freydal, unfinished at the time of Maximilian's death in 1519, shows him equipped in the style of armour that still bears his name. This new style, incorporating rippling flutes on nearly every surface, was developed under his aegis after he took the Imperial crown. It was armour for a new age but before then, in his younger years, the then Archduke Maximilian donned the fashionable armour of the late Middle Ages. His armour of around 1480 is today in the Kunsthistorisches Museum in Vienna. It is one of the finest Gothic armours ever made. The first thing one notices, not without envy, is his impressively narrow waist. He was clearly a very fit and athletic young man and he fought his first major battle on foot.

Fighting on foot in armour is extremely fatiguing. Winning a fight with a sword is about work rate; delivering blows that drain every ounce of energy, being light on your feet and moving with agility, having the stamina to beat the odds in a grapple. Even exceptionally fit young men cannot hope to sustain such activity for more than a few minutes and in armour those minutes are very few indeed. Roman legions had the second rank step forward and through the line, to relieve the men in the front rank and allow them to catch their breath. Celts sent in a chariot to retrieve a flagging warrior from the fray. Cavalry of all periods could charge, engage and then turn away to regroup and rest; but what of the knight fighting on foot? Francesco Sforza, Duke of Milan, who was fighting in the mid-fifteenth century, developed troop rotation systems, making sure he always held a reserve of fresh men. He also specified that there must be a barrel of water on the field, adjacent to their fighting station, for every eight soldiers. One advantage of armour is that it gives sufficient protection to make it possible to fight in a mêlée at a 'resting rate'. In other words to do enough to ward off the worst of the assaults, without exerting energy in full-out attacks. This could then be punctuated with short bursts of unbridled vehemence. If, in addition, a knight's squire – his right hand man, his shield bearer – was on hand to take over the larger burden of the work in this defensive phase, then it might be possible to stay in the fray for half an hour or more without retiring. A two–man 'buddy system' would not only facilitate such a rota but it would also ensure that the squire could guard his knight's back. However, until some concrete evidence comes to light, this must remain my conjecture.

The First Battle of Guinnegatte, 1479

By the fifteenth century the Duchy of Burgundy was an autonomous and powerful military force, whose territories encompassed a large part of what is modern-day France and Switzerland, as well as the Netherlands; it included the lands of Brabant, Hainault, Flanders, Holland, Artois, Zeeland, Friesland and Luxembourg. Vassalage to the kings of France had long been in contention and Burgundy saw itself as an independent state. Charles the Bold sought to expand Burgundian territories so as to create a contiguous region. The Burgundian Wars (1474–1477) saw conflict with both France and the Swiss Confederacy. However, in 1476, Charles suffered major defeats at Grandson and Morat. Then, on 5 January 1477, his army was totally vanquished at the Battle of Nancy. Charles' mutilated body was found amongst the heaps of corpses three days later. Burgundy's only heir was his daughter, a 20-year-old girl named Mary. Just a few months later, on 18 August, Mary of Burgundy was married to the 18-year-old Archduke Maximilian of Austria. They married in Ghent. It was a formidable political alliance with far-reaching implications for the history of Europe.

On hearing the news of Charles' death, the French king, Louis XI, immediately laid claim to Burgundy and sent in troops to annexe the Burgundian Netherlands. In response, Maximilian, in spite of his tender years, was swift to raise an army to defend his new domains. He had some artillery and the Imperial nobility could still muster a feudal cavalry but his was predominantly an infantry army, recruited from Flemish levies armed with pikes and English archers. Burgundy had become England's ally during the later stages of the Hundred Years War and English soldiers had sought their fortune in her armies for decades. Furthermore, Charles the Bold's widow, Margaret of York, was the sister of the reigning English king, Edward IV.

After months of skirmishing and manoeuvres, Maximilian's forces finally faced the French army in the field at Guinegatte, a small village near St Omer. According to the chronicler Jean Molinet, Maximilian created a number of new Imperial knights on the eve of the battle. Among them was the English Sir Thomas Everingham, '*expert aux armes et treas bon capitaine engleaz*'. At Guinegatte he commanded 500 English archers. An English esquire, John Hales, commanded a further 200 bowmen and there were many other Englishmen in Maximilian's army. Edward IV, embroiled in his own diplomatic negotiations with Louis XI, didn't sanction official support but it is clear where the sentiments of ordinary Englishmen lay.

However, it was the Flemish pikemen that proved to be the decisive force. In the initial stages of the battle the French cavalry routed the Imperial cavalry, but the resolute Flemish infantry slogged on for a further four hours, eventually driving the French from the field. In the midst of these big men, their powerful limbs grown in Flanders' mud, was Maximilian, his delicate features still those of a boy. He shouldered a pike and led from the front. At his side would have been a sword, almost certainly it was a longsword. When the French lines fell into disorder, he likely laid down his pike and drew that sword. The chroniclers do not tell us whether he personally took any lives at Guinegatte but he was in the thick of the fighting and so it is a fair assumption that there was blood on his blade.

Throughout the following year Maximilian consolidated his hold on the region, retaking many towns and districts, including the Duchy of Luxembourg. On 29 September 1480, at the culmination of these campaigns, he rode in triumph into the city of Luxembourg. Sitting on his hip was a beautiful sword; it was the longsword with the magnificent gilded hilt that is now in Vienna.

In the Hofkirche in Innsbruck is Maximilian's equally magnificent and grandiose memorial tomb, though his actual body is buried elsewhere, at Castle Wiener Neustadt. On the sides of the marble cenotaph are twenty-four relief carvings, each depicting key moments from his life. One of these reliefs celebrates Maximilian's victory at the First Battle of Guinegatte. It was an important moment both in his life and in the history of warfare. The nature of warfare changed during Maximilian's lifetime. He grew up during the last gasp of the medieval knight, a romantic ideal that he never shed, but he oversaw the revolution in tactics that saw the final demise of the armoured knight and a new focus on infantry warfare. Guinegatte triggered changes in the way that he would organize his future armies, which in turn led to the deployment of a very particular type of swordsman.

Landsknechts and Reisläufen

Like much change, the first rumblings had been heard for some time. The geo-political map of fifteenth-century Europe was like a board game being played out by a few overmighty princes. Towns and territories were bought and sold; duchies and regions bequeathed as dowries; and alliances forged and broken by treaty and by war. In many parts of Europe national loyalties were hard to determine. Harder still was loyalty to an amorphous Empire. In 1482, Mary of Burgundy died in a tragic accident, falling from her horse while out hawking. She was twenty-five. Maximilian inherited sole control of Burgundy and all the attendant problems of defending her borders against the encroaching French. In spite of his vast landholdings Maximilian was always short of money, forever borrowing to pay for his great schemes and for his armies.

Soldiers require pay. It was expensive to sustain a standing army and all rulers depended on recruiting mercenary troops for specific campaigns. Moreover, the technology of war had changed. Gunpowder had been increasingly present since the mid-fourteenth century but by the late fifteenth century its sulphurous bellow cracked ever louder on the battlefield. The cost of putting a feudal knight and his retinue in the field had become prohibitive to all but a wealthy few and at the same time the rise of massed ranks of pro-fessional infantry had begun to render him redundant. These infantry blocks were the spearhead of change. They were pioneered by the cantons and city-states that made up the coalition of the Helvetic Confederation (modern-day Switzerland). Theirs was a decentralized, low-income rural economy without wealthy feudal magnates to pro-vide knights and men-at-arms. When they were threatened they had to muster an army from the land. In the last quarter of the fifteenth century, they were threatened by Burgundy, a rich and powerful state with

Reislaufe banner bearer with baselard

state-of-the-art artillery and a massive feudal army. Large-limbed, strong and bored, the brawny farm boys flocked to the Confederation banner in search of adventure and employment. They were known as '*reisläufen*', which translates loosely as 'journey takers' and has a resonance with the old Anglo-Saxon fyrd.

Reisläufen were drilled and trained to operate cohesively in tight formation and armed with pikes. Early woodcuts show them marching in neat ranks and all moving forward together on the same foot. They were a type of drilled and disciplined soldier not seen since the days of Rome. The pike block was virtually impenetrable to cavalry, supported as it was by field artillery and arquebusiers. The arquebus was an early form of musket, with a simple trigger mechanism that lowered a length of burning match-cord onto the firing pan. Such troops were relatively cheap and their strength lay not only in their discipline and ability to manoeuvre en masse but also in their numbers. A block of 10,000 men was a daunting foe.

At Guinnegatte, Maximilian mustered Flemish foot soldiers and deployed them Confederation-style, to win a resounding victory over the traditional French forces of knights, men-at-arms and archers. The problem was that after the battle, they were paid off and went home. Maximilian realized that he needed a more permanent force to protect and expand his empire. He also wanted more home grown troops.

In 1486 he was elected King of The Romans, a title that meant he was Holy Roman Emperor elect and effectively the ruler of the area we now call Germany. From this position he set about recruiting a *landsknecht* army. '*Landsknecht*' means 'servant of the country'. In spite of the '*knecht*' suffix, they were in no sense 'knights'. The English word 'knight' derives from the old Anglo-Saxon (and thus German) word '*cnecht*' meaning 'servant' or 'vassal' and it is a curiosity that the English use this designation for their ennobled warriors; all other nations use the word for a horseman when referring to 'knights' (*chevalier, caballero, cavalliere, ritter* etc).

Maximilian's landsknechts were based on the model of the Confederate reisläufen. They were big, strong, sturdy men, precision drilled to fight in massive pike formations. The pike were supported by a highly trained artillery corps, arquebusiers, halberdiers and, of course, Germany's famous two-handed swordsmen. Cavalry may have been impotent against the pike block but a strike force of landsknechts with two-handed swords could get in and do some real damage, disrupting the enemy's well-formed lines. Landsknechts carried their two-handed swords over their shoulders with a raffish swagger. These extremely proportioned 'terror swords' personified both the landsknechts' brute strength and their cheerfully reckless attitude to war. The slightly more conservative reisläufen never really took to the two-handed sword, preferring the longsword for their shock troops. It could be managed with far less strain on stamina.

Landsknechts were organized along the lines of a modern professional army, ensuring an efficient infrastructure to handle the complex logistics of recruiting, feeding, billeting and paying. Wagon trains of supplies and ammunition accompanied every march, though the luxury of plentiful whores in the camp train was at the soldiers' own expense. These were uncouth, rough-hewn, hard men with a taste for beer, war and plunder. They lived life to the full, drinking, gambling and revelling. In

Landsknecht holding flamboyant-bladed, two-handed sword and wearing katzbalger. Painting on wood (author's collection; photo by Danny Brown)

battle they were ruthless, though not quite as brutal as the reisläufen, who had the unpleasant habit of removing the heart from a defeated foe as a trophy.

The nobility fought on foot alongside their comrades of lower birth, instilling a discipline and an esprit de corps borne from common experience. Maximilian himself would wear the armour of a foot soldier and take his place in the ranks and wasn't above shouldering a pike to lead his men in a triumphal parade. Landsknechts were nonetheless mercenaries, though they were not supposed to fight for enemies of the Empire. One regiment that did, the notorious Black Band, was defeated fighting for the French at Pavia in 1525. Every one of its 4,000 men was hunted down and killed. However, aside from this proviso, landsknechts fought for pay and their oath of loyalty was to their colonel. It was he who contracted with whoever was employing them and he who was responsible for their wages. Many a landsknecht colonel was forced to take out bank loans to keep his troops from deserting, while he awaited settlement from his paymaster.

Their freebooting spirit was matched by their outlandish appearance. Never had the world seen such gaudy, sumptuous and ostentatiously attired troops. Both landsknechts and reisläufen wore the most outrageous puffed and slashed clothing in the brightest of colours. Their torsos were adorned with great mutton-sleeved, striped doublets slashed in decorative designs, through which their colourful silk shirts were ruched and displayed, whilst their legs were clad in the most garish of striped hose, one leg bearing a different pattern to the other. Today's Swiss Guards at the Vatican appear restrained compared to their antecedents. Reisläufen favoured long hair and a clean-shaven look, whilst the landsknechts shaved their heads and sported extravagant beards or moustaches. Some of the old-school nobility objected to such low-born men wearing such extravagant attire, to which Maximilian replied 'leave them be; with their wretched and miserable existence you should not begrudge them a little fun'.

As time went on the landsknechts became even more 'punk' and 'grunge', adopting the fashion of wearing their leg-hose rolled down to the knee and generally cultivating a tattered, dishevelled appearance. Their trunk-hose sported garish codpieces, stuffed to ambitious proportions. These priapic aspirations were only outdone by the reisläufen's habit of wearing their short sword, the '*baselard*', slung between their legs so that the hilt thrust up from their groins. They set out to shock and they did. War was no longer the exclusive preserve of the knightly elite; it had been taken over by the bruising foot-soldier, out to fill his purse. Ostentatious display was made of portable wealth, with gold chains slung around their necks and large purses at their hips. The revolution was as much social as military.

Both landsknechts and reisläufen donned flamboyant headgear, broad-brimmed bonnets decked with feathers. The landsknechts were fairly showy with a few ostrich plumes and the odd peacock feather but the reisläufen wore such architectural displays of ostrich plumes that the landsknechts called them 'feather Johnnies'. This was the mildest of the landsknecht rebukes. When war broke out on the Confederation frontier, largely as a result of their forming an alliance with Maximilian's arch-enemy France, tensions heightened between landsknecht and reisläufe. In the early days they had often fought on the same side but now they were sworn enemies. A landsknecht would insult a reisläufe either as a '*milch-stinker*', '*chuefigger*' or '*chueschweizer*' – 'milk stinker', 'cow fucker' or 'cowherd'. In time, the abbreviated term '*schweizer*' stuck and, from that, '*Schweizerland*' – 'land of the cowherds'. Given the alternatives, they may consider themselves fortunate. Officially, Switzerland is still called Confederation Helvetica; hence the CH for vehicle licence plates and e-mail suffixes. Cuckoo clocks are the least of their embarrassments.

However, whether landsknecht or rie-slaufe, these were the men who could win battles and they ushered in a new age of warfare. To a man they were ruthless and without mercy. The letting of other men's blood was their business and they did it with zeal. Paul Dolstein, an artist and writer who was 'embedded' with a landsknecht regiment hired by the king of Denmark (and Sweden) to put down a

Landsknecht 'double-pay' man with two-handed sword and katzbalger. After Erhard Schoen

peasant uprising in 1502, wrote: 'We were 1,800 Germans and were attacked by 15,000 Swedish peasants … we struck most of them dead'. Butchery on such a scale was work for the sword, mostly I suspect for the two-handed sword.

The most feared of all landsknechts were the *doppelsoldener* ('double pay men'), the ones who fought in the front line, armed with great two-handed swords. From their ranks were drawn volunteers for the '*verlorene Haufe*', 'forlorn hope', whose function was to attack blocks of pikemen and try to punch a hole, so that the block could be disrupted. These were death-or-glory men. Aside from volunteers their small bands were made up of prisoners pressed into service and men chosen by a throw of the dice. First they would use their two-handed swords to cut off the heads of the pikes, and then, no doubt, the heads of the unfortunate pikemen.

Two-handed swords

Known also as the '*schlachtschwert*' ('slaughter sword'), the sixteenth-century two-handed sword was a real giant, measuring around 6 feet in overall length and with an extremely-broad, flat blade. Nevertheless, these colossal swords are nowhere near as heavy as they look. I have handled a number in museum collections and found them well-balanced and reasonably manageable, even with one hand. The key to their tremendous scything power was not only the mammoth blade but also the very long grip. At around 24 inches it maximized the fulcrum effect of a scissor-action strike

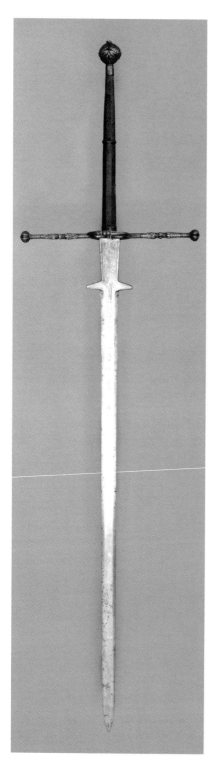

with two hands. Immense power was needed to knock aside a dense porcupine of pikes, let alone to sever their heads. The blades on some two-handed swords broaden towards the point end, giving added weight at the pendulum end of a swinging blow. Crosses were equally large, around 18 inches across, facilitating their use as a hooking, tripping and gouging device. On either side of the cross were two enormous side rings, providing enhanced protection to the hand. Some two-handed swords are less ugly than others but most lack grace in their proportions and have an ungainliness about them.

Below the hilt, the first 6 inches or so of the blade are blunt. This section, called the 'ricasso', allows one hand to be placed on the blade below the hilt to shorten the weapon for close-quarter half-sword work. Projections from the blade, known as '*parrierhaken*', offered both protection and a stop to the forward hand. Thrusts were common from the half-sword position. Ricassos on these huge swords were usually covered with a leather sleeve. This may have given a surer grip to the forward hand but it also served to protect a landsknecht's fine clothing when he shouldered his weapon for marching.

A common feature on a number of two-handed swords is what is known as a 'flamboyant' blade; one that has wavy edges. Stemming from the French for a flaming torch – *flambeau* – the expression alludes to the blade's likeness to a flickering flame. As well as being highly decorative, one probable function of flamboyant blades was to make it more difficult and hazardous for an opponent to grasp the blade – the curved edges of the serrations offering a slicing surface, which is impossible to hold. As already noted, it is perfectly possible to grip moderately sharp blades, provided that you have

Two-handed sword, 16th century (by kind permission of the Trustees of the Wallace Collection, London)

a firm grip, but as soon as the blade slips even slightly all is lost. The edges on a flamboyant blade were exceptionally sharp and there was no chance of it being grabbed and wrested from the hands of its operator. Flamboyant blades also occur on the Malayan and Indonesian keris. Here it is said to assist in cutting through bone when thrusting. Perhaps this was also true when thrusting with a flamboyant-bladed two-handed sword. A charging landsknecht, full of beer and fury, might be able to pinion more than one pikeman if he ran in bayonet style.

Another feature of many two-handed swords was a tasselled horsehair fringe around the mid-point of the grip. Fringing functions on buck-skins or on a motorcycle jacket by wicking and collecting rainwater and then guttering it away from the surface. Since two-handed swords were carried over the shoulder, it is possible that the fringes prevented rainwater amassing on the grip and running down a soldier's neck.

These giant swords were battlefield weapons and they evolved because of the new ways of waging infantry war and the need to break holes in a seemingly impenetrable wall of pikes. Giacomo de Grassi (1594) wrote of the two-handed sword:

> One may with it, as a galleon among
> many gallies, resist many swords and
> other weapons; therefore in the wars
> it is used to be placed near unto the
> Ensign ... for the defence thereof.

England's Henry VIII had an elite colour-guard who carried these immense weapons and the men who carried them were known as 'wifflers', from the whiffling sound that the blades made as they scythed through the air.

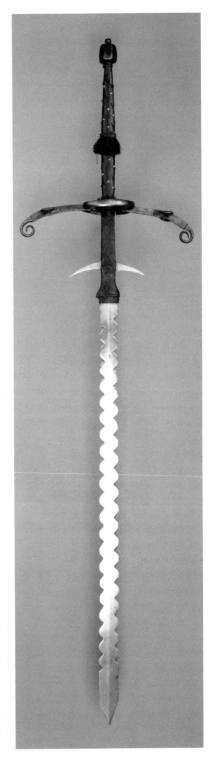

Two-handed sword with flamboyant blade, 16th century (by kind permission of the Trustees of the Wallace Collection, London)

Katzbalger and baselard

Whether his principal arm was the two-handed sword, the arquebus, the halberd or the pike, the classic sidearm of the landsknecht or reisläufe was a short, broad-bladed sword. Reisläufen favoured the '*baselard*', a sword with a distinctive T-shaped pommel, which, as previously mentioned, they often wore between their legs with a comical phallic enthusiasm. The landsknecht's sidearm was known as a '*katzbalger*' – literally 'cat scrapper'. '*Katzbalgen*' is modern German for a brawl or scuffle and the term nicely describes the context in which this weapon would be used. With a blade of around 24 inches in length, it was ideally suited to the frenzied slashing of close-quarter combat once the landsknechts had closed with the enemy and got in amongst them or, on rarer occasions, once the enemy had got in amongst the landsknechts. *Katzbalgen* have a sharpened rounded point and the hilts have a distinctive S-shaped guard, the terminals of which extend to almost touch the central scroll, thus appearing as a figure of eight. The grip flares outwards towards a wide pommel, assuring that the sword will not slip, even from a slippery, blood-drenched hand in the wild heat of a mêlée.

One magnificent example of a katzbalger, which was dredged from the River Thames, is now in the Museum of London. Its hilt is adorned with the Imperial double-headed eagle and it is believed to have been left behind

Katzbalger (courtesy of Culture and Sport Glasgow (Museums))

by someone in the retinue of the Holy Roman Emperor Charles V when he was in England to sign the Treaty of Windsor in 1522. Charles, the grandson and Imperial successor of Maximilian, sought a military alliance with Henry VIII against Francois I of France, who laid claim to the Empire. War against France was declared at Windsor on 16 June. It is most likely that this katzbalger was simply left behind but I like to think that perhaps it was a gift of exchange between a sentimental soldier of Charles's bodyguard and one of Henry's wifflers – in the same way that footballers swap shirts. That it subsequently ended up in the river suggests a careless night of revelry and catching the last barge home from Hampton Court.

Henry VIII already had strong links with the Holy Roman Empire and Maximilian had been his staunchest ally in Europe. They had fought together at the Second Battle of Guinegatte in 1513, more commonly known as the 'Battle of the Spurs' because all that could be seen were the spurs of the retreating French cavalry. Maximillian presented Henry with several gifts of armour. Indeed, arms and armour from the workshops of Maximilian's craftsmen were among the most prestigious treasures of the age.

Messer

In the Nationalmuseet in Copenhagen is an especially fabulous sword that was probably a gift from Maximilian to King Christian II of Denmark. It was made in 1496 by Maximilian's favourite swordsmith, Hans Sumersperger, and it is a '*lange messer*'. That is to say it is a '*messer*' of longsword proportions. Messer (literally 'knife'/'knives') were usually short swords with a single-edged blade, very similar to falchions. However, longer versions of these war-knives, used with a two-handed grip, can occasionally be seen in manuscript art from the thirteenth century onwards. The one in Copenhagen is a very fine example with an ornate gilded pommel and exquisitely intricate carving on the ivory hilt. Inlaid on the blade are gilt male figures and a gilt inscription calling on the aid of St Catherine and praising God – SANDT.CATRRINA HILLFV: DAS WALLTE GOT. VNS. AMIN – but the real beauty lies in the blade itself. Its entire surface has been faceted with thumbprint-sized dimples that catch the light and coruscate in a most magical way. On a practical level they serve to lighten and strengthen the blade in the same way as fullers.

This 'long knife' was in the Royal Collection in Roseberg until 1804 but it is not known how it got there. Perhaps it was a wedding present. In 1515 Christian II married one of Maximilian's four granddaughters, the fourteen-year-old Isabelle. It was an unhappy marriage. Maximilian's appetite for matchmaking and alliances stayed keen until the end but would he really have given a twenty-year-old sword as a gift, even one as magnificent as this? I think it more likely that it had been a favoured possession of Maximilian's and that it was presented to Christian by ambassadors on the occasion of his elevation to the Order of the Golden Fleece in 1520 – a year after Maximilian died. A personal memento of a dead Emperor carries rather more kudos than a second-hand gift from a living one.

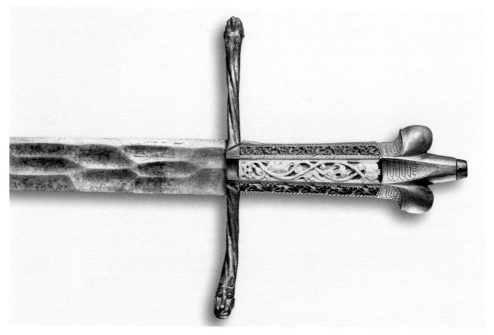

Maximilian's lange messer (Nationalmuseet, Copenhagen)

In the woodcut depicting an adolescent Maximilian at sword practice there is a pair of messer on the floor and alongside them are padded gauntlets. These are not a pair but each for the right hand and for use with the messer. In Talhoffer's representations of the messer fight, there is no grabbing of the blade. Instead there are disarms utilizing arm-locks. The defining characteristic of the messer is that it was extremely sharp – as sharp as a knife! Talhoffer shows the sword-hand of one unfortunate man being sliced off with a single blow. Clearly the hand was a principal target, which explains the need for practice gauntlets. A further characteristic of the messer fight is that the combatants are always shown with their left hand behind the back, out of harm's way. An exception to this observation is a figure in Dürer's *fechtbuch* who is shown holding a lange messer bare-handed and in the half-sword position in order to gain leverage on his opponent's longsword. His fingers rest on the blunt back edge and only the base of the thumb appears to come close to the sharp edge. Force is being applied with the flat of the hand against the flat of the blade. Given these provisos, such a move would be possible with a sharp messer, though it would be a skilled manoeuvre and is not typical of the way we see this

Dusack

Messer fighting techniques, after Talhoffer

weapon used. Aside from Maximilian's princely version, the messer was a sword for the common footsoldier – a sidearm for the pikeman or arquebusier. Certainly, amputating a hand from his enemy would ensure that he never blew a match or ported a pike again.

An alternative to wearing gauntlets for messer practice was to use a specialist type of waster known as a '*dusack*'. Known also as the 'Bohemian falchion' it was formed either from a single lathe of wood or from a single plate of steel. The dusack had an integral knuckle-guard to protect the hand; on the wooden versions this was a straightforward cut-out and on the metal variety, the steel grip turned over in a U shape to extend along the back of the hand. Curiously the messer itself was never fitted with this protection. Both varieties of dusack had blades that were more curved than the messer and, as the sixteenth century progressed, short swords with a curved blade – '*sabres*' – became increasingly common in northern Europe. These were sidearm alternatives to the falchion and the messer; they were not yet the flashing arms of the cavalryman.

Cavalry

With the new way of waging war that focussed on infantry manoeuvres, heavy cavalry had a smaller role to play on the battlefield, certainly in Maximilian's army. Light cavalry on the other hand retained a vital function as scouts and skirmishers and to harry and pursue a routed enemy. They were good at attacking supply trains and

Mounted combat techniques, after Talhoffer

marching infantry and they could ride ahead of the main army to secure local cooperation for provisions and accommodations. In particular, their job was to engage and take out enemy scouts and raiders.

Talhoffer includes instructions for the one-on-one cavalry fight. His figures are using arming swords, though the longsword was equally popular for horsemen. Here are many of the sword techniques that we see for foot combat: simultaneous defence attacks, setting the opposing blade aside as you push through on target, disarming and grappling moves. He also shows how the sword can be used to defend against the lance and how the lance may be deployed to best defend against a mounted crossbowman (slanted to shield face and body). Light cavalry were equipped with a variety of arms but all carried a sword. In spite of all the elaborate combat techniques advocated for the mounted man by most authors, the fight master Pietro Monte sounded a chilling note of pragmatism when he wrote: 'It is always easy to kill an opponent's horse ... only fools waste time trying to hit their man'.

At a time when the nobility were increasingly taking up their positions commanding infantry on the battlefield, the '*ritter*' was more likely to be a mounted man-at-arms than a feudal knight. Albrecht Dürer in one of his most famous prints, *The Knight, Death and the Devil*, gives a splendid picture of one of these horsemen. His principal weapon is a lance but slung from his waist is a magnificent longsword. It was a weapon equally suited to the cavalryman as it was to the footsoldier.

Late 15th century knight, after Dürer. Note the longsword

Boar swords

A variant of the longsword type was the 'boar sword' and Maximilian was every bit as passionate about hunting and the weapons of the chase as he was about the accoutrements of fighting. He had himself portrayed with every conceivable form of hunting weapon from crossbow to spear and from knife to sword. The eponymous hero of the second of Maximilian's fantasy autobiographies is the knight Teuerdank, which

translates as 'Sir Noble Thought'. Maximilian was not a modest man. Teuerdank encounters and overcomes countless hazards; from avalanches and storms at sea to jousting challenges and coming face to face with dangerous beasts on hunting expeditions. He fights bear with a dagger and wild boar with a sword. Hunting was a preoccupation. It not only demonstrated a ruler's dominion over the natural world, in the same way that the Romans paraded animals for slaughter in the arena, but it was a key element in a knight's training. To hunt meant long days in the saddle, riding hard. It was a communal activity that harnessed cooperative teamwork, accustomed the knight to killing and bloodletting and exposed him to danger.

The fourteenth-century Gascon knight, Gaston Phoebus, who wrote a celebrated treatise on hunting, *Le Livre De La Chasse*, said that:

> for every kind of military encounter hunting is a better training than jousting. If the tourney teaches a man to strike with a sword on a helmet, how much better he will learn by striking down on a boar, when his only chance of saving himself is by a good thrust.

Certainly to take a wild boar with the sword was considered the most dangerous and noble of hunting endeavours.

At the time of Gaston Phoebus, a regular arming sword was used for boar-hunting but by Maximilian's era a specialized form of boar sword had evolved. It could be used either on foot or on horseback. Boar swords generally have simple hilts with a straight cross and a sturdy blade, often square or triangular in cross section, which flattens and flares for the last 12 inches or so towards the point. Blades tended to be between 40 and 50 inches in length and the stout square or triangular section was necessary to be proof against buckling. These stiff-bladed swords were known as 'estocs' or 'tucks' – from the French, '*estocader*', meaning to thrust. The power of a squealing, charging tusker, weighing in at around 700lbs, was a formidable

Boar sword – note transverse bar (© The Board of Trustees of the Armouries. AL22)

force. In 1514, Charles Brandon, the Duke of Suffolk 'met the first boar and gave him the first stroke with his tokke [tuck], that he bowed it three ways to his hand, and slew him'.

The leaf-shaped, spear-like point of the boar sword had sharp cutting edges to incise the tough hide of the animal but there was an attendant risk of the onrushing boar's momentum carrying it straight up the blade and crashing into the hunter. To counter this problem, boar swords were fitted with a transverse bar, around 6 inches in width, located just above the cutting part of the blade. It supposedly acted as a stop, though Henry VIII had thought to take extra precaution by having a boar sword made with a matchlock pistol incorporated in the hilt. Transverse bars, whether of metal or horn, had the potential disadvantage of making the sword impossible to sheath. For this reason these bars were usually detachable and then slotted into place once the hunters had taken stand. One boar sword, in the Museo Dei Bargello in Florence, has spring-loaded bars that pop out when it is unsheathed.

In my more active jousting days, we used also to put on a demonstration of medieval hunting skills that included galloping down at a model of a wild boar and delivering a sword thrust to it. The skeleton of the body was constructed with cross boards of plywood and then filled in with sculpted foam. One quickly learned to one's cost that driving a sword home on a straight arm at a forty-five degree angle could be extremely painful to the hand if the sword jammed against one of the plywood cross-sections. Similarly, although not cross-sectioned with solid panels of wood, a rushing boar would feel an unstoppable force if taken head-on against the sword. Gaston Phoebus further advises that care has to be taken not to strike the mastiffs that may, at the same time, be holding the creature at bay. According to most medieval writings on the subject, the hunter has to position himself so that he can effect a downward thrust, just behind the neck, and drive the sword into the heart and lungs, in the manner of a matador. In *Teuerdank*, however, the super-hero Maximilian stands on foot, embedding his sword into the chest of the attacking boar, a hurtling mass of enraged muscle, bone and tusk.

Arms Production

Maximilian was an ardent connoisseur of arms and armour and the huge cutting-edge arms industry in Germany flourished under his patronage. The Imperial workshop was established at Innsbruck, where armour of exceptional quality was produced under the eye of Konrad Seusenhofer. Nuremberg and Augsburg were also world-famous centres for the production of plate armour and Solingen and Passau were celebrated centres of edged-weapon manufacture. Traditionally, the trademark of a running wolf was incised onto blades made in Passau but during the fifteenth century Solingen adopted the same trademark. It was a sign of quality respected the world over. German blades were imported throughout Europe and mounted onto locally-made hilts. Even Spain, which boasted a rival centre for sword production in Toledo, frequently produced swords with German blades. In the denouement to Shakespeare's Othello, the Moor brandishes 'a sword of Spain, the ice-brook's temper'. This has

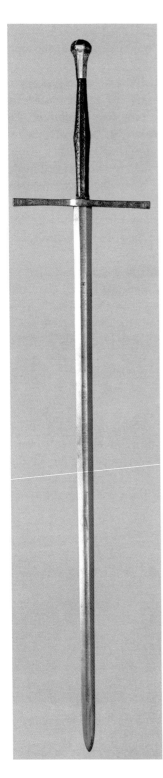

been taken to be a reference to plunging a sword into ice-cold water to temper it but, in the earlier folios of the play, the word is 'Isebrooke' and that is an anglicized version of Innsbruck. (Medieval trade inventories refer to imports of Isebruk iron). The superiority of German sword blades persisted well into the eighteenth century. I used to own a Scottish basket-hilted sword, which had a fine 'running wolf' chiselled on the blade and it is to be seen on a high proportion of blades produced over several centuries. On the best examples the chiselled lines of the running wolf are inlaid with yellow metal, creating an exquisite designer logo.

Maximilian's Empire

Maximilian's impact on the European stage was immense. The consequence of his alliances reshaped the political map. His campaigns extended to wars in Hungary and Bohemia, which he absorbed into the Empire, to war with the Turks and with the Swedes and Norwegians. In 1490 he bought Tyrol and parts of Austria from his cousin Sigismund. He joined the Holy League to fight French intervention in Italy and the Italian Wars dominated much of his reign.

In 1510 he married Bianca Sforza, the daughter of the duke of Milan. His son Philip, by his first marriage to Mary of Burgundy, predeceased him and his grandson, who became Emperor Charles V, succeeded him to the Imperial crown. By virtue of his maternal inheritance, Charles also became king of Spain, expanding the Hapsburg dynasty to the peak of its powers. Suffering from paranoia and depression, he later abdicated and retired to a monastery leaving the crown of Spain to his son Philip and the crown of the Holy Roman Empire to his brother, Maximilian's second grandson, Ferdinand.

Voltaire famously described the Holy Roman Empire as, 'neither Holy, nor Roman nor an Empire'. In his time, he was probably right but under Maximilian, the 'First Reich' was in full swing. Maximilian saw himself as the heir to Roman rule and he certainly organized his army on Roman lines. He was a devout Christian and

Maximilian's longsword (Kunsthistorisches Museum, Vienna)

saw his campaigns against the Turks as part of his religious duty. Maximilian died in 1519 at the age of sixty.

Legacy

Maximilian's martial legacy endured. He grew up during the last gasp of the medieval knight, a romantic ideal that he never shed, but he oversaw the revolution in tactics that brought the final demise of the knight and a new focus on infantry warfare. Germany remained at the forefront of arms and armour production and the monopoly of the Marxbruder stayed unchallenged until the 1570s. The contenders for this supremacy were the Freyfechter von der Feder zum Griefenfels, more familiarly known as the Federfechter, who were based at the eastern end of the Empire, in Prague. '*Feder*' – literally 'plume' or 'quill' – was colloquial German for a rapier and the Federfechter identified themselves as the leading exponents with this newly fashionable weapon. Although they also taught more traditional forms with heavier weapons such as the two-handed sword, they claimed dominance in the teaching of the rapier fight. They took every opportunity to challenge the Marxbruder to fight with rapiers but both guilds flourished, both having their captains retained at the Imperial court and both sharing the ascendancy in the teaching of the fighting arts.

The development of the rapier was the single most seminal change in the whole history of the sword. It was the instrument of an entirely new culture of civilian duelling and also an essential item of male jewellery. In the chapters on the 'Sword of Honour' and King Henri IV of France we will look at that culture as it reached its high point in the late sixteenth century but first I want to take you to the other side of the globe – to Japan.

As the polities of Europe consolidated into nation states, as the Reformation challenged old ideas and old orders, as Sir Walter Raleigh planted the first seeds of English settlement in the New World and as Shakespeare put on his wonderful plays, Japan was locked in internecine feudal warfare. It was a time when samurai warlords ruled the land and the sword rose to an exalted status.

Uesugi Kenshin (photo courtesy of Stephen Turnbull library)

Chapter 8

The Sword of Uesugi Kenshin, Samurai Warlord

As long as it is my duty towards my lord, I would like to die in battle in front of his eyes. If I die in my home, it will be a death without significance.

(Okuba Tadataka, 1622)

The Yamatorige, or Sanchomo, as the sword of Uesugi Kenshin is more popularly known, is today in the Okayama Prefecture Museum in Japan. I have never seen it other than in photographs but no matter, it is a sword of exceptional beauty. The Japanese crown jewels consist of a mirror, a jewel and a sword. They have not been seen for centuries as they are kept wrapped and locked in caskets, but their significance and prestige is undiminished. I use this slim pretext as an excuse for not having visited this particular sword. Although I have been to Japan several times, my schedules have prevented me from going to the Okayama Museum.

The Yamatorige is privately owned but on permanent loan to the museum, and has been designated officially as a Japanese National Treasure. It dates from the mid-Kamakura period – around 1250 – Japan's medieval feudal era. There is a repeating pattern of overlapping clove blossoms undulating along the *hamon*, which is that distinctive line, manifesting almost as white, that separates the ultra-hard martensitic steel of the cutting edge from the slightly softer, more resilient, pearlitic steel of the main body of a Japanese blade. A beautiful hamon is just one of many aesthetic elements that are appreciated by the connoisseur and connoisseurship of Japanese swords is in a league of its own. Kenshin's sword, though not signed by the smith, is believed to be a product of the Ichimonji school, which in turn forms part of a larger stylistic grouping of the Bizen school. Bizen is the old name for Okayama and swords from this school are considered the pinnacle of the swordsmith's art.

Uesugi Kenshin

Although his sword dates from the thirteenth century, Uesugi Kenshin was a sixteenth-century samurai. In a country where great store is placed on ancestor worship, there is tremendous status and power in an ancestral sword, although in Kenshin's case his ancestry is not what it at first may seem. Uesugi Kenshin was born in Echigo province in February 1530. Like his sword, he is known to history by more than one name. Samurai naming systems are extremely complicated and, though poetically rich, can be baffling for anyone other than the most dedicated Japanese historian. It was common practice for samurai to change their names through life. Thus Uesugi Kenshin was actually born Nagao Kagetora, the fourth son of Nagao Tamekage. As a child he was known by the nickname Torachiyo.

At the age of seven, following the death of his father in a battle against the Ikko–ikki (of whom more later) he was taken to a monastery. At the age of fourteen he left the monastery and immediately set about earning himself an impressive military reputation by leading several successful missions against his family's enemies. He had received a martial as well as a religious education from the monks. By the time he was nineteen it was evident that he was the natural leader of the family clan and his older, though weaker, brother, Nagao Harukage, was prevailed upon to step aside in favour of his precocious sibling.

Historically, the Nagao family were retainers of the more eminent Uesugi family but the Uesugi had not fared well in recent years. After a defeat by their long-term enemies, the Hojo, in 1551, the Uesugi leader, Uesugi Norimasa, was forced to seek the protection of his young-but-powerful vassal, Nagao Kagetora. As a pre-condition, Kagetora demanded that Norimasa adopt him as his heir, give him the name Uesugi and make him the Lord of Echigo. So it was that Nagao Kagetora became Uesugi Kagetora. It is believed that this is the moment that he received the ancestral Uesugi sword.

One year later he took his religious vows and, with them, the Buddhist name Kenshin. It is as Uesugi Kenshin that he is most known to history. He does have one other name though, his ancestor name. Awarded posthumously, spirit names were used in observances of ancestor worship. Uesugi Kenshin became Soshin. However, for our purposes I shall refer to him as Uesugi Kenshin or simply Kenshin.

The Japanese sword

It would be impossible to overstate the importance of the sword in Japanese culture. It is regarded as a sacred object, the embodiment of the national identity, and treated with the greatest respect and reverence. Indeed the entire culture that attends both its manufacture and use is ritualized with strictly-observed ceremony and etiquettes. Tokugawa Ieyasu, the great shogun who finally united Japan in 1600, declared that the soul of a samurai lives in his sword.

In Japanese law, traditionally-made Japanese swords are classified as art objects, not as weapons. Indeed there is a specific question on the form that one fills in when entering Japan that asks if one is bringing a sword into the country. It is illegal to import a sword into Japan without a licence. This has nothing to do with any notions of it being an offensive weapon, simply that swords not made in the traditional manner are offensive in quite a different way and they are keen to preserve the bloodstock, as it were, of pure Japanese swords.

In the hierarchy of Japanese swords, those forged between the tenth and sixteenth centuries rank the highest. These are '*koto*' ('old') swords and are generally of such a standard of workmanship that they define the art. Those of the Kamakura Period (1185–1335), the golden age of swordsmithing, are regarded as the best of all. Uesugi Kenshin's sword is a notable example.

After the mid-fourteenth century, various factors contributed to a decline in traditional skills. First there was mass production. During the Muromachi Period (1336 to 1573), more than 200,000 swords were made for export to Ming Dynasty China. Then there was a significant domestic demand to meet during a succession of civil wars. In the mid-sixteenth century a proliferation of firearms on the battlefield led to less demand for newly made swords and so smithing traditions began to decline. In other words, the smiths either had too many or too few swords to make to keep up the old traditions of high artistic standards. Swords from the late 1500's to around 1760 are known as '*shinto*' (new) swords. They are by no means shoddy; it's just that they are not quite to the standard of what went before.

However, from 1761 to 1865 there was a renaissance in traditional techniques. Suishinshi Masahide, a master swordsmith, led a movement to rediscover the old *koto* techniques and swords made during this period are referred to as '*shinshinto*' ('new-new') swords or 'revival' swords. *Shinshinto* swords rank higher than *shinto* but not quite as high as *koto*. These are the three pedigrees of the true Japanese sword.

In 1853, Commodore Matthew Perry of the US Navy sailed his ships into Tokyo harbour and forced Japan to end her self-imposed seclusion and open up to the rest of the world. A period of rapid change followed. The Haitorei Edict of 1876 virtually banned the carrying of swords and thus stifled the industry for making them. Masahide's renaissance died; the forges ran cold and the hammers fell silent.

The significance of Japan's long seclusion cannot be under-estimated. It was in 1641 that the Tokugawa Shogunate closed its doors to foreigners and foreign influences. That is not to say that Japan did not develop during this 200 years but it did so only in reference to itself. Traditional ways and traditional beliefs became deeply embedded. Of course present-day Japan is, in many ways, a

Replica of Yamatorige blade made by Ono Yoshimitsu (Photo courtesy of Okisato Fujishiro)

very modern country, leading the world in so many state-of-the-art technologies, but there remains another Japan, one that is rooted in its past. Consider the fact that it is a shorter span of time since Perry ended Japan's seclusion than the time she spent in seclusion.

There is another type of Japanese sword. It is machine-made with modern steels and often fitted with a painted metal grip. Such swords are termed as '*gunto*' (army). They came into being in the early twentieth century as Japan re-armed her forces for a series of foreign campaigns in wars against China and Russia. In 1934 the factory-produced military sword was redesigned, somewhat in the fashion of a *katana*, and re-classified as '*shingunto*'. Neither *gunto* nor *shingunto* swords are given any status as treasures in Japan. They are as worthless as any souvenir replica made in the West.

They also represent a dark chapter in the history of Japanese swords. It was such swords that were employed in the mass beheadings and massacres in Nanking and other parts of China in 1937 and it was *gunto* swords that terrorized and butchered so many in prisoner-of-war camps during the Second World War. The sensational image of the Japanese sword, as so often portrayed in Western newspapers and other media, owes much to these aberrations in the past century and little to the rich history of its more ancient past, though the samurai can hardly be said to have put the sword to gentle use.

As I write, new legislation has just passed through the British Parliament amending the existing Offensive Weapons Act. It is a government response to a recent fad by some violent criminals to use imitation Japanese swords in a range of criminal scenarios. The Home Office consultation paper that preceded the amendment order specified that it was seeking to ban the possession, import and sale of 'samurai swords'. An ill-worded effort by the British authorities attempting to define a samurai sword, reveals just how much this iconic object of classic beauty is misunderstood in the West. Describing it as 'a sword with a curved blade of 50 centimetres or over in length' hardly does justice to the serene aesthetics of Japanese steel. In practice, this rather loose definition includes a wide range of swords from a wide range of cultures but the declared intention was to criminalize only the 'samurai sword'. Subsequent appeals by affected groups have

Yamatorige replica fitted with Koshirae (Photo courtesy of Okisato Fujishiro)

produced a list of exceptions that have rendered the act virtually impotent but what interests me here is why a curved blade over 50cm was deemed to be a greater threat to society than a straight blade of similar length? The idea is nonsense of course, though I do not mean to suggest by that any support for the thugs that kill, maim and intimidate with swords or any other weapon. What concerns me are the issues surrounding the power of the Japanese sword as an icon and why the law, the popular press, and the gangster all seem to share a similar perception of it.

By the time that newspapers were reporting wars, the sword had all but passed as a mainstream battlefield weapon – not quite, but almost. Certainly by the 1930s it had ceased to be anything other than a ceremonial sidearm in the Western world. Not so in Japan. In 1937, at the height of the Sino-Japanese War, a story ran in the Tokyo newspaper *Nichi Nichi* reporting on the Japanese advance on Nanking. It carried such sensational headlines as 'A Contest to Cut Down 100 people – Both Second Lieutenants at 80 kills', 'Moving Into High Gear – Progress in the Contest to Cut Down 100 people', and 'Incredible Record In The Contest to Cut Down 100 People – Mukai 106, Noda 105 – Both Second Lieutenants Go Into Extra Innings'. The story concerns a competition between Lt Mukai and Lt Noda to see who would be the first to cut down 100 people with a sword. At the time they were hailed as war heroes, though they later divulged that the majority of the killings were beheadings of unarmed prisoners rather than the glorious hand-to-hand combat encounters that the hyped newspaper accounts had implied. In the subsequent war crimes tribunal, conducted by the Allies after the Second World War, both were convicted and hanged on 28 January 1948. A Captain Tanaka, notorious for killing '300 hateful Chinese enemies' with his sword, was also tried and hanged on the same day.

Painful memories of the Sino-Japanese war continue to strain relations between China and Japan. My purpose in recalling this story is not to rake over those coals but to highlight the significance of how newspapers characterize the Japanese sword. Atrocities are a factor of war and sadly continue to be so. In all cultures the perpetrators of atrocities have at times used swords. However, the Japanese sword is perhaps alone for being used in this context in the age of photography. It is this vivid, recorded association with barbarity and war crimes, for some still within living memory, that has contributed to the demonization of the Japanese sword by the Western press. Now combine this with the cult of Japanese martial arts films and the spread of Japanese martial arts teaching in the West since the Second World War and you have a lethal mix of associated ideas; the idea that the Japanese sword can be used to kill in cold blood and the idea that it is an arcane art and can only be used by someone of consummate skill. Thus, by bearing a Japanese-style sword a criminal sends out a twin message of terror – a message that he is prepared to use it and a message that he is adept at using it. It matters not that other swords are equally capable of butchery or that the Western martial arts tradition is equally as effective as its Eastern counterpart. These things are not understood by popular culture, which only recognizes the passing influence of a few films and sensationalized newspaper stories. Now, it could be said that this ability to create a climate of terror is a testament to the success of the Japanese sword as a weapon. Certainly a samurai would be pleased to hear that his sword inspired fear but the reasons why and the context in which it did are worlds away from present-day criminal activity.

The standing of the Japanese sword is further enhanced by a general consensus that it is perfectly designed and its age-old reputation for being especially sharp. Father Caspar Vilela, a Jesuit missionary to sixteenth-century Japan, wrote 'Their sharp swords could slice through a man in armour as easily as a butcher carves a tender rump steak'. The harmony, proportion and balance of its shape together with the aesthetic properties that are visible in the grain of the steel make the Japanese sword an art object. It has clarity of design and a complete unity of form and function. There is an expansive vocabulary of appreciation for Japanese swords that rivals the fabled hundred Inuit words for snow or the extravagent metaphors of the wine-taster's lexicon. In a chapter that can aspire to be no more than the briefest of introductions to the subject, I will avoid specialist language as far as possible, though it is inevitable that an amount of jargon will be necessary.

To appreciate fully a fine Japanese sword is an art form in itself, requiring a detailed understanding of every aspect of the sword. It is about seeing the grain of the steel, the curve and the profile of the blade and discerning the file marks on a tang in the same way that an art historian would see the brushstrokes of a painter. It is a refined connoisseurship. Happily, the recent British law yields some concessions to the connoisseur collector in permitting blades of traditional manufacture from Japan, though it discriminates against those with more modest budgets who want reasonably good examples from China or Thailand or America. There are also concessions to the bona fide martial artist. That the tacky souvenir with its wire-brushed *hamon* is less omnipresent is no great loss but this demonizing of the Japanese sword neglects to appreciate its important cultural significance.

Under the Allied occupation of Japan at the end of the Second World War, all swords and sword manufacture was banned. However, General Douglas MacArthur received a deputation led by Dr Honma Junji and was shown the splendour of traditionally made swords. To his credit, MacArthur recognized their intrinsic artistic merit and the order was amended. Only *gunto* and *shingunto* blades were destroyed, though there was considerable cultural plunder by American servicemen who, under-standably, took magnificent weapons home with them as souvenirs, along with about one million *gunto* swords.

In the years that followed, Dr Honma Junji founded Nippon Bijutsu Tôken Hozon Kyôkai, the Society for the Preservation of the Japanese Sword. Under their auspices, many swordsmiths have continued the work begun by Masahide in the eighteenth century, re-discovering the old swordmaking techniques. Present-day swords manufactured by traditional methods are known as *shinsakutô* ('newly-made swords'). They are highly valued and the methods and materials by which they are made highly regulated. Modern smiths make wonderful swords, which bear their own artistic inspiration and also facsimiles of famous swords from a previous era.

The making of a Japanese sword

Exquisite copies of Uesugi Kenshin's sword, the Yamatorige, have been made in recent years by the celebrated swordsmith Ono Yoshimitsu. I have met him and laid hand to hammer in his workshop. He is a thoughtful and gentle man with a passion for his art. At the time of my meeting him it was widely believed that he would become the next Living National Treasure. By the time you are reading this he may already have received the honour. As well as giving this honorific accolade to objects, the Japanese government awards the title of National Treasure to two living persons that embody the cultural traditions of Japan. It is a delightful idea.

In 1987 Ono Yoshimitsu was deemed *mukansa* (without judgement), which means that he no longer has to submit his work for appraisal at the annual swordsmithing exhibition. It is considered beyond competition and his swords are automatically given pride of place. His forge is a short drive from Okayama, itself a few hundred miles south of Tokyo. Of traditional design, the hearth, which is around 3 feet long and perhaps a foot wide is for forging nothing other than swords. Ono-sensei, garbed in traditional white apparel, with a white kerchief around his head, kneels at one end of the hearth, operating a trombone-like bellows with his left hand, while he holds the work in the fire with his right.

However, I get ahead of myself. Before the forging comes the steel. The steel used for traditional Japanese sword manufacture is called *tamahagane*. Only swords made from this unique material are considered 'true' swords. It arrives at the swordsmith's forge in the form of jagged rocks of metal, the size of tennis balls. As dense as meteorites, the chunks are surprisingly heavy. *Tamahagane* is silvery bright and flecked with spots of iridescent purple and orange that reveal traces of other elements in the steel. No wonder *tamahagane* means 'precious jewel' in Japanese

Steel, of course, is an alloy of iron and carbon. The carbon is infused into the iron ore in the smelting process. Iron ore is generally scarce in Japan, except for one region in the southwest of Honshu. This is the Japanese Highlands – a beautiful, remote, mountainous region. I travelled there by train, winding up the passes in precarious spirals around the high crags that were cloaked in deep powder snow. A low setting sun, causing the snow crystals to coruscate with sparkling light, made it seem a magical place where treasure was to be found. The treasure in this case was a black iron sand called *satetsu*. Possessing fewer

Tamahagane (author's collection)

Satetsu iron sand (photo by kind permission of Paul Martin)

impurities than regular iron ore, it is considered to be superior for the manufacture of steel. This iron sand, a residue washed down from the mountains, is found in the stream-beds of the region and is gathered and dried out for the annual smelting.

There are just two or three smelts each year. They take place success-ively towards the end of January. Iron sand and charcoal are smelted in a *tatara* – a large clay furnace, situated in a purpose-made build-ing. As I walked towards the barn-like edifice, enormous snowflakes fell thickly onto the already snow-covered ground, quieting every sound, except one. From quite far off I could hear the haunting groan of a giant bellows, its droning chant heralding the ancient rite that took place within.

The creation of *tamahagane* has as much to do with religion as it does technology. It is a principal of Shinto, an animistic belief, that inanimate objects, as well as natural features such as mountains, rivers and trees, have souls. Hence Tokugawa Ieyasu's famous declaration that the warrior's soul lives in his sword. The sword is the spirit of Japan and the genesis of its raw material a deeply spiritual occasion. Before entering the *tatara* building I climbed some steps to a small shrine, dedicated to the Shinto god of metal, Kanayago-kami, and made the obligatory offering of a coin, then bowed and clapped to drive the evil spirits away.

When I slid open the barn door, I was greeted with a spectacular sight and a welcome burst of warm air. The golden-yellow flames from the *tatara* soared 10 feet high above the altar-like clay hearth that sat atop an earth mound in the centre of the room, lighting the dim space with a flickering glow. It measured about 12 feet by 6 feet, with walls 8 inches thick. The top line of the long walls was dished in imitation of the boat-like crossbeam on the arch of a Shinto shrine. Many pilgrims had gathered to witness the proceedings and they stood, in reverential silence, gazing at the entrancing blaze.

Under the direction of the headman, the *murage*, a dozen workers went silently about their business. First they would approach the hearth with basketwork trays laden with charcoal, lining up uniformly on each of the long sides. At the *murage*'s behest they would feed the conflagration with more fuel, sifting it on in unison. The charcoal, of course, is also the crucial carbon that combines with the iron sand to make steel. Next they would form up with trays of iron sand. This layer-cake of charcoal and iron sand is added to every ten to fifteen minutes. The *murage* stands watchfully by the *tatara*, gauging from the colour of the flames the optimum moment to add the

Tatara (photo by kind permission of Paul Martin)

Tatara, showing the *kera* after the walls have been broken down (photo by kind permission of Paul Martin)

next layer. It is said that *murages* go blind at an early age because of all the time they spend staring into the flames.

The smelting process takes place for seventy-two hours and the attendants work in shifts, though the *murage* remains pretty much on duty the whole time. At times the space is so thronged with people that you cannot move, at others there are just a handful of watchers. Each visitor brings a bottle of sake, wrapped in white paper, to place at a shrine that lies within the building. This shrine occupies most of one wall and doubles as the repository for the black sand.

Throughout, the eerie lowing of the bellows mesmerizes with its slow, rhythmic call. It evokes an ancient and timeless atmosphere of ritual and worship. The large mound on which the *tatara* stands is in fact hollow, with underground chambers to duct away any moisture. Air from the bellows is fed into the *tatara* furnace by a series of pipes that emanate from the mound and enter at the base of the clay walls. It is the length and gauge of these pipes that causes the bellows to sound their tune with such organ-like and plangent notes. Maintaining the furnace at around 1,500 degrees Fahrenheit keeps it at the optimum temperature for the iron to absorb the carbon.

I stayed late on the first day, enthralled by the mystic ritual atmosphere and in the knowledge that the local hotel – more a bare bones youth hostel – didn't offer any enticing comforts. However, I eventually left to grab a few hours sleep and set my alarm for 3am. I was back at the *tatara* before 4am and quite a crowd was already building up. There was a definite sense of anticipation in the air and they stood, silent sentinels, their faces rapt with worship and lit by the golden glow of the flames. Just before 5am the workers ceased their labour of ferrying charcoal and iron sand and the bellows fell silent.

Iron spikes attacked the base of the walls, creating holes through which magma-like rivers of molten slag drained off into gullies in the earth. These were tamped down by great wooden mallets that resembled outsize hockey sticks. The flames died down to a flicker but bursts of searing heat gusted from the drainage holes. At length the *tatara* men began to tear down the walls from the top with hooks at the end of long poles. Now the temperature became almost unbearable and the barn doors were flung open to let some of the heat escape, illuminating the picturesque snow scene outside. Crumbled shards of broken wall were raked away with huge hoes and eventually the *kera* was revealed. Weighing in at around 2.5 tons, the *kera* is the name given to the entire semi-molten block of metal extracted from the smelt. It contains differing grades of *tamahagane*. Excess charcoal was removed from its jagged, volcanic-looking surface and there it sat – born. The heat was almost intolerable and my face felt as if it were melting.

An abrupt rattling of chains alerted me to an enormous pair of pincers that were lowered from a rafter. They were clamped to one end of the *kera* and men hauled on the chains to lift it a foot or so from the ground, so that several wooden rollers could be inserted underneath. By means of levers, the men eased the *kera* forward on the logs, scurrying to place more logs in front as the monster was eased towards the open air. It sizzled and spat and flared like an angry dragon. Once out in the snow it yielded finally and its fiery glow began to wane. There were nods of great approval all round. The beast had been tamed. Then they broke open the many bottles of sake that had been brought as offerings to the shrine. I cannot remember a better breakfast.

The cold *kera* is broken up with sledgehammers into small rocks. It is in this form that it arrives at the swordsmiths and the first task is to sort through and determine which pieces have which properties. The *kera* of *tamahagane* is rather like a fruitcake, with different clusters of ingredients in different parts of the cake. Some pieces will have an extremely-high carbon content and be very hard and brittle, whilst other pieces will be softer. It is the skill of the swordsmith both to be able to identify, by colour and feel and sound, which bits are which and to be able to blend them perfectly.

To begin forging a blade, Ono Yoshimitsu selects the best quality pieces that will make the hardest steel and hammers them into flat plates. For this, his one concession to modern technology, he uses an electrically-powered trip hammer. These small plates, in turn smashed into pieces the size of biscuits, are then placed on the working-iron for heat welding. The working-iron is a bar of iron, three feet in length, which has a 5 inch-square plate of steel welded to one end. The broken biscuits of steel are stacked 4 inches high on this plate and then wrapped in a gauze cloth to prevent them from toppling when he first introduces the work into the fire.

Red hot, the fused cube is taken out and hammered. I was his hammer man that day and once again, as at Hector Cole's, I was amazed at how soft and elastic the metal was, giving way with remarkable ease to each blow. There were numerous reheats and hammerings. Each time Ono brought the work from the fire, he coated it with a mixture of clay and singed rice straw. This was to ensure that the outside steel didn't get significantly hotter than the core. It was a sort of tandoori bake. Ono didn't speak much throughout the day. Partly, I suspect, because my rudimentary Japanese made conversation difficult but also because this was genuinely a spiritual act for him. He looked intently at the flames. At first the flames are blue but turn yellow as they reach the optimum heat. He is also listening to the steel, which makes a sound as it nears the right temperature – according to the Japanese it is the sound of the gods singing. They also say that the sparks from the forging furnace are the gods dancing. It is one of the many delights of Japan that they find such poetry in the everyday.

Once he judged the piece had been welded into a single block, he began the folding process. The trip hammer was brought into service to elongate the block a little and then a V-shaped groove was made with the use of a shaped tool. It was then onto the anvil and I swung the sledge to fold the metal over. Contrary to popular mythology, this process is only done about eight to twelve times. It is important to distinguish between the idea of folding and the idea of layers. The layers increase exponentially with each fold, they double, so that by the time you get to ten or so folds, there are a great many layers. Folding is the equivalent of kneading dough and ensures that any air pockets are removed and the molecules of iron and carbon are evenly distributed, making it a homogenous material.

Ono Yoshimitsu at his forge (photo by kind permission of Paul Martin)

This was the hard, high-carbon steel, perfect for the cutting edge but Japanese swords aren't made from one homogenous piece. They are a composite of steels. Swords need to be able to flex and be resilient against the percussive impact of deflecting blows from other weapons as well as having a hard edge. They must be able to resist breakage or permanent deformation and be able to withstand the shock of contact against hard surfaces such as armour. Samurai didn't use shields, so even greater demands were placed on their swords for defence than their European medieval counterparts. Avoidance moves played a key part in Samurai combat strategy but using the back edge and sides of the blade to set aside other swords or staff weapons was also an essential capability.

Ono forged the block of hard steel into a U-shaped sleeve into which was inserted a core of softer steel that he had prepared earlier. I like to think of this soft core as the muscles of the sword, giving it strength and stamina. Sword anatomy is inside out. Externally there is this very hard exoskeleton, with the cutting edge as its teeth but in the centre is the strong, flexible muscle. The composite ingot of steels is then re-introduced into the fire, hammered and reheated several times until the smith is content that it has become welded together as a single piece. Then the composite blank is hammered into the shape of a sword.

Ono Yoshimitsu used his trip hammer to stretch the composite billet to the right length and then worked it on the anvil by hand. After every brief period of hammering, it was put back into the forge for reheating. With artful precision he formed not only the basic shape but also calculated how it would pull into a curve after the final quenching. Most importantly however he shaped the '*niku*'. *Niku* (literally 'meat') is the amount of roundness in the cross-section of the sword. It is critical if the sword is to cut efficiently. Straight sides or a simple wedge have the effect of creating drag when cutting through anything of substantial thickness – like the human body. There is simply too much surface area in contact as it attempts to slice through the object. However, the right amount of bulge to the blade's cross-section not only reduces this drag, it cleaves the cut open, easing the sword's passage.

Test cutting

It is true that samurai tested their swords frequently on the bodies of condemned criminals or slaves. Different cuts had different names. Antique swords are often inscribed on the tang with a record of the weapon's test cutting prowess – for example '5 bodies with *Ryu Guruma* (hip cut)' or '3 bodies with *O-kesa* (diagonal cut from shoulder to opposite hip)'. A five-body blade was top of the range.

Today, *tameshigiri* (test cutting) is more likely to be carried out against *tatami* rush mats. The practice dates from at least the Edo period (seventeenth century) where they used tightly-bound bundles of straw. Now *tatami* mats are more commonly employed because they cut very consistently and because they leave decidedly less mess. The mats are rolled, usually around a length of green bamboo to simulate the human spine, to various thicknesses. Mats are soaked for many hours in water so that they gain both density and weight and then staked onto a cutting stand. When I first had a go at this, I began with a mat rolled to 4 inches in diameter. It cut with remarkable ease, even with one-handed strokes. I built up in increments from 6 to 8 to 10 inches, though the heavier gauges certainly required a two-handed grip. It was truly astonishing how clean were the cuts; every fibre was cleanly severed. There is a natural tendency when swinging a sword to draw back slightly towards the end of the cut. This is disastrous when attempting *tameshigiri*. It is essential to push forward through the cut because the part of the sword that does the work is around 8 inches below the point. A drawn cut pulls the point end over the cutting zone for the last few inches and it will fail.

Cuts are more strongly made with a diagonal stroke, albeit this means cutting through a greater surface area than a horizontal one. A good trick is to make the first cut diagonally upwards, so that the cut-off upper part of the mat sits there for a fraction of a second, allowing you to strike back and bisect it before it falls. I have tried cutting mats with swords of different specifications and there is no doubt that where a sword with the right *niku* will cut effortlessly, one with the wrong *niku* will fail. It is the skill of the swordsmith, at the forging stage, to create the *niku*. He does it by eye, shaping the hot steel with finely judged hammer strokes, each weighted and targeted to perfection. There is no grinding or filing and it is symmetrical for the whole length of the blade.

The *hamon*

It is the unique attribute of steel that it changes its properties of hardness according to the rate at which it cools upon quenching. Quenching is the process of heating the sword to red hot and then plunging it in water or other coolant. Because of this, Japanese swordsmiths are able to further sophisticate the composite characteristics of the blade by retarding cooling in specific areas. Thus a very hard band of steel, the *hamon*, is left for the cutting edge, the softer muscular core is preserved and the rest of the sword is rendered into a medium–hard pearlite steel. In this procedure the back of the sword becomes like the tough sinew of the blade and further insures it against the humiliation of breaking in battle.

Painting layers of clay upon the blade controls the cooling rate. Where the clay is thicker, the cooling will be slower and the metal softer. I sat with Ono Yoshimitsu as he painted the clay onto the sword. I knew I was in the presence of a true artist. He uses a small spatula and delicately, patiently lays the clay on the surface, starting with a thin layer for the hamon. Where the hamon line juxtaposes with the main body of the sword, a pattern is created. In this case the pattern was one of undulating peaks, evoking the distinctive horizon of Japan's mountain ranges. I was struck on the journey from Tokyo, as we passed Mount Fuji on the bullet train, how much the silhouette of the hills echoed the *hamon* pattern on so many Japanese swords. *Hamon* design is the essence of the swordsmith's personal artistic signature, though his actual signature is chiselled onto the tang. The repeating pattern of overlapping clove blossoms on the *hamon* of Uesugi Kenshin's sword is as fine as any painting with brush and canvas but remarkably, it was achieved without the use of clay layering. There is an older process and it is still not clearly understood how it was done. However, clay layering is the norm and, today, the only way that traditional swords are made.

A thicker coat of clay is applied to the back edge and then transverse lines and dots are put on at selected spots along the blade. These create failsafe soft spots, so that if the hard edge were to chip, the fracture won't run too far. When both sides are coated and dried the sword is reheated. Ono watches carefully until the colour of the flames tells him it is the right temperature and he swiftly withdraws it from the fire and plunges it hissing and spitting into the water. On cleaning, the distinctive *hamon* is apparent as a darker steel than the rest of the blade. But what really brings it out is polishing.

Polishing and sharpening

For polishing the blade goes to a *togishi*. I was once fortunate enough to be able to visit Okisato Fujishiro, one of the most highly regarded *togishi* in Tokyo today. Fujishiro-sensei is a charming man, given to laughter. He is also a man of great artistic and spiritual integrity who values swords and treats them with due reverence. All the traditional formalities were observed, such as bowing before passing a sword with the back edge towards the receiver and taking care never to speak over a blade. When taking a blade for polishing from his storage cupboard, he held the blade and bowed and then, kneeling, unwrapped it from its cloth covering with great ceremony.

On the floor of his workshop is a planked wooden trough measuring around 4 feet by 3 feet. It has a timber border of 2 inch-square batons and slopes away from where the polisher sits, allowing excess water to drain away into an outlet. At the drainage end is an oval wooden tub filled with water, in which the polishing stones are wetted. Fujishiro-sensei half sits, with his left buttock on a wooden block and with his left leg curled back. He wears traditional brown robes. Now that's just marginally uncomfortable but here's the tricky bit. There is another wooden block just in front of him, on which rests the polishing stone. This is held in place by a shaped wooden lever, which clamps on the stone at one end and is held in place by the big toe of one's right foot at the other. I tried to do it and occasioned much mirth in the old master, who sits like this with ease for hours on end. The important thing is to get your weight over the polishing work and to do this, you have to get your right knee tucked securely into your right armpit but without releasing the pressure on the stone clamp held under your right toe. To my aged body it felt like an impossible contortion. Clearly I need to take up yoga.

There are sixteen grades of stone of increasing fineness. The blade is worked rhythmically to-and-fro on the stone, polishing just one section at a time – not running the length of the blade across the stone but concentrating on one lateral section and then moving the work along the blade a few inches. Great care has to be taken to 'feel' the blade and preserve the integrity of its *niku*. Water is splashed on the stone as required. Gradually, a fine polish appears and the full beauty of the *hamon* is revealed.

After days of this painstaking work, the *togishi* moves on to 'finger stones' for finishing. These tiny, almost transparent, slivers of fine-grade stone are placed on the tip of his index finger and laboriously worked along the blade. So slight are these shards that the *togishi* can feel any slight imperfections on the surface of the blade. An amount of this polishing is necessary to ensure the flattest possible surface in order to minimize friction and drag when cutting through flesh and bone. But, for the most part, it is about art. A properly polished blade is indeed a thing of beauty. You cannot only see the *hamon* but also the grain of the steel throughout the blade. The whole, complex microcrystalline structure of the sword becomes apparent and the contrasting lustres of mirror and satin finish, of dark and light steel harmonize to perfection and give the blade life.

The blade is also given its final sharpening at the polishing stage. Japanese sword blades are exceptionally sharp. I recall filming on a bitterly cold January day on the outskirts of Washington DC. On a horse, sword in hand, attempting to explain the difference between a *tachi* and a *katana*, I looked down to see the horse splashed with blood. As is so often the case the horse had been booked by the girl in the office, a non-equestrian, and it was not accustomed to cameras or swords and, as far as I could make out, hadn't even been ridden very much. Consequently it was rebelling by giving me a rather energetic and bumpy ride. I assumed, to my horror, that it had come into contact with the razor edge of my katana during one of its more enthusiastic bucks. Upon seeing the blood I dismounted and called a halt to the proceedings. It was with some relief that I then discovered that the blood was coming from me, not the horse. I had taken a slice, the size of a dime and over a quarter inch deep, from the top of my bridle hand and was losing quite a lot of blood quite fast. Interestingly I hadn't felt a thing. The cut had also gone through my leather riding glove. First aid was at hand in the form of a wad of paper kitchen towel and a strip of black gaffer tape, which fortunately matched my glove. Although able to carry on, I did soon begin to feel faint from the loss of blood and experienced that peculiar ache that one feels after a deep cut. It is hard to imagine the pain that would accompany the sort of deep gashes delivered by swords on the battlefield.

Fittings

Once the blade is finished, other craftsmen complete its furnishings – the '*koshirae*'. The scabbard – '*saya*' – is made from wood and lacquered and provided with silken cords that are tied in a variety of formalized ways. A wooden grip, called the '*tsuka*', is fashioned to fit snugly over the tang like a sheath. It is held in place by a bamboo peg, the '*mekugi*', that passes transversally through the grip and the tang. Sometimes there are two pegs. This ingenious system allows the hilt and blade to be easily disassembled for routine polishing and maintenance. It also allows for the grip to be changed as a fashionable accessory according to the occasion. A samurai may have a different *tsuka* for battle, for everyday use and for visiting court. As with everything to do with Japanese swords, the making of the *tsuka* is an art form in its own right. The basic wooden casing is covered with manta ray skin – '*same*' – characterized by its irregular patterns of pronounced round nodules. Over this is the '*tsukaito*', an ornate binding of silk cords. Both the ray skin and the cords may be dyed in different colours and there are a number of ways in which the silk can be braided with variations on a lattice pattern that permits the ray skin to be seen underneath. Also seen underneath is a pair of '*menuki*' – hilt ornaments. Usually made of silver, these decorative pieces depicting animals or objects are bound under the silk cords to create a slightly raised section on one side of the hilt. This helps to anchor the forward hand and enhances the security of the grip.

At the junction between blade and grip is the '*tsuba*' – the guard. *Tsuba* are often highly ornamental, sometimes bearing the family crest or '*mon*'. They remain collector's items in their own right and were traditionally passed through the generations as family heirlooms. Either circular or square with rounded corners, *tsuba* were made from iron, steel,

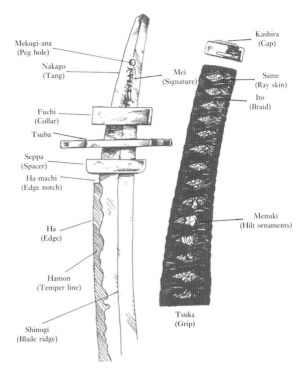

Parts of the Japanese sword

copper, brass or '*shakudo*' – an alloy of 4% gold and 96% copper, celebrated for its beautiful, dark patina of bluish-purple. Some *tsuba* are an ornate trelliswork of open design while others have a solid surface upon which decoration is laid in a different metal. That decoration may consist of *kanji* – Japanese letters – or it can be figurative, such as animals or landscape. *Tsubas*, sometimes like exquisite miniature paintings in metal, are both beautiful and functional.

Uesugi Kenshin (right) versus Takeda Shingen (left) with war fan (*tessen*)

Uesugi Kenshin's sword had no *tsuba*. He disdained its use lest it was thought he feared injury. His fighting ethos was about attack not defence. He famously attacked the curtained headquarters of his enemy, Takeda Shingen, by bursting through on his horse during the Fourth Battle of Kawanakajima. He had approached by stealth, using cloths to muffle his horse's hooves and bit. He struck down at Shingen with his sword – a blow that Shingen parried with his iron war fan (*tessen*). A savage personal duel ensued. There is a distinct nick in the blade of Kenshin's sword, though it has not been reproduced on the replica. It is at the base, near where a *tsuba* would have been. One is tempted to believe it was as a result of a parry from the war fan but of course it could have been the consequence of any one of a thousand blows dealt or received by the legendary Kenshin.

Types of Japanese sword

There are a variety of swords in the Japanese arsenal. The largest is the '*odachi*', literally 'great sword', and the blades of these monsters range from around 39 inches to a gigantic 89 ¼ inches. This, the largest of all odachi, forged in 1447 and now in the Okayama museum, has an overall length a little over 12ft 4 inches! Such outsized swords were exclusively for ceremonial purposes, often considered to be the swords of the gods and made as offerings at Shinto shrines, or they were made in order to demonstrate the swordsmith's skill. Less extravagant odachis (39–40 inches blade length), however, did have a limited presence on the battlefield. An odachi swordsman would carry his weapon in his hand, it being too large to be worn in any way, and have an aide to assist him in drawing it. After laws in the first half of the seventeenth century restricted the length of swords, many odachi were cut down or destroyed. Consequently they are extremely rare today.

Next in size is the '*nodachi*', which means 'field sword'. These are really the equivalent of the European longsword. They are traditionally worn slung over the back and are not so long that they can't be drawn from this position. Less rare than the odachi, the nodachi is still a relatively specialist sword compared to the ubiquitous '*tachi*' and '*katana*'. It is the subtle differences between these two swords that we are concerned with here.

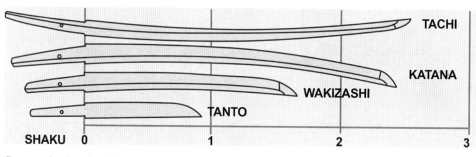

Comparative lengths of Japanese sword types. 1 shaku = 11^{15}/$_{16}$ of an inch or 30.3cm

The distinctions between the tachi and katana often blur but in essence the tachi was designed for cavalry and the katana for infantry. A tachi is worn suspended by cords from the sash belt (*obi*) with the cutting edge facing down and a katana is worn thrust through the *obi* with the cutting edge uppermost. With the katana in this attitude, the act of drawing the sword can flow seamlessly into a descending cut to the head. It is an ergonomic efficiency that declares a chillingly resolute purpose. Having said that, there remains the possibility of surprise because the swordsman can simply rotate the scabbard in his waistband with a subtle twist of his wrist and, in less than the blink of an eye, draw to unleash an attack that strikes with an upward sweep.

Swords were not always the principal weapons of the samurai – first it was the horse and the bow. Just like his European counterpart, the knight, the samurai was first and foremost a horse-borne warrior. For the samurai, though, the weapon of choice was the bow (*yumi*). Squadrons of samurai would gallop in, shooting their bows to soften up the enemy. Great kudos attached to how many of the enemy you could slay with your arrows. It was only later on in a battle that a samurai would draw his tachi.

This reverence for the bow and the days of its supremacy are echoed in the Japanese rite of *yabusame*, which continues to be practiced today. In elaborate ceremonies of Shinto ritual, horse archers run down a roped off track, called the '*baba*', and shoot three arrows at three successive targets. The Japanese bow with its eccentric limbs – the upper limb twice the length of the lower – feels initially awkward to a Western-trained archer. However I have tried it and, once you get used to a slightly different balance, it can be a joy to shoot. When I had a go at *yabusame* in Japan, I was obliged to wear the traditional garb of a novice. The clothing is comfortable to ride and shoot in, well designed for its purpose, though I have to say that I found the lack of substantial footwear and the great iron gondola stirrups difficult to negotiate. The horse I had went like a thunderbolt and it was tremendous fun as well as being quite difficult. I was lucky enough to have a respectable level of success on that occasion, which surprised my doubting hosts nearly as much as me. One can well see how this became the favoured weapon skill of the early samurai. It is exhilarating and challenging to perform, it is a conspicuous outward display of an elite skill and it requires bravery and daring to ride into the midst of battle, with no hands on the reins, shooting as you gallop. It is a sublime warrior art.

However, except when a weak enemy is put to flight, battles are seldom won by bows alone. There comes a time when you have to close with the enemy and defeat him man-to-man and that is work for a sword. As a cavalry weapon the tachi was predominantly used one handed, though its grip is long enough for two hands and there are plenty of depictions of samurai in the thick of the mêlée, using their tachi with both hands from horseback. Indeed, in that legendary surprise attack when Kenshin rode into Takeda Shingen's camp, I imagine him bearing down on his foe, with a screaming war shout to chill the blood, and using his tachi with both hands.

Well, one could say that it was a tachi that day, since Kenshin was using it from horseback. Indeed as a Kamakura Period sword it had started life as a tachi but at some point during Kenshin's lifetime, there is evidence that it was modified to become the more contemporary katana. It was common in the later half of the sixteenth century to convert tachi into katana and you can see that this has been done on Kenshin's sword by adjusting the angle of curve on the tang. The tang of a sword was not heat-treated and so remained easy to bend. It is a subtle adjustment but one that changes completely the curvature of the blade as it extends from the hilt. Every period in Japanese history saw gradual changes to the shape and design of the sword but it is generally true to say that the centre of curvature shifted from being set initially in the tang, as with the tachi in the earlier periods, to moving along the blade until, with the katana, it settled in the centre of the blade. A katana also tends to be a thicker-set sword, having greater weight in proportion to its length. It is more usually, though not exclusively, shorter than the tachi.

The need for an infantry sword (katana), rather than the traditional cavalry tachi, arose with the increased need for the samurai to fight on foot. Japan's Muromachi Period (1336–1573) was beset by civil wars. First there was the Onin War, 1467–1477. This escalated into the Sengoku or Warring States era in which virtually every *daimyo* was at war with his neighbour. '*Daimyo*' translates as 'great name' and every province had several daimyos with his own following of samurai and retainers. Uesugi Kenshin was one among many warlord daimyos living and fighting in these turbulent times. If you look at a map of Japan at this period, it resembles shattered glass, crazed with the intersecting lines of seventy-one provinces and each of these could contain several warring factions.

During these civil wars, larger armies were recruited from peasant levies. These were predominantly infantry armies, which led to the samurai fighting more and more on foot. Moreover, much of the fighting took place in mountainous or forested terrain that was not ideal for cavalry. The trend towards infantry was accelerated with the introduction of firearms. China had been supplying guns to Japan from as early as 1510 but the great revolution came in 1543, when the Portuguese introduced the arquebus. The samurai took to this new technology overnight. It is said that there were more of these firearms in Japan at the time than there were in the whole of Europe. The arquebus was an early form of the matchlock musket. A simple, lever-operated trigger lowered a length of burning matchcord into the priming pan, which set off the charge of black powder in the breech and bang! Its lead ball had a killing range of over 200 yards. Arquebuses were muzzle-loading and even a trained man would take about a minute to reload and fire. Oda Nobunaga, who we shall meet later as Kenshin's nemesis, made the process more efficient by dividing the duties of loaders and shooters and assigning three guns to each shooter.

All Japanese warlords embraced the power of the arquebus and the character of the battlefield was changed forever, as greater and greater emphasis was placed on infantry warfare. Even so, ancestrally, the samurai was a mounted warrior and Uesugi Kenshin, among others, continued to embody that ancient tradition in his personal exploits from horseback. His sword though, had been reborn into the more modern, infantry-fighting katana.

Miyamoto Musashi with *katana* and *wakizashi* thrust in belt (*obi*). Painting by Kuniyoshi (Library of Congress)

The favoured weapon of many warrior monks was not the sword, however, but the *naginata*. Similar to the European glaive, it is a staff-weapon consisting of an oval-section wooden haft, typically five feet long, mounted with a curved blade around three feet long. *Naginata* blades closely resemble katana blades, though in most cases they are a little broader, and in some instances they are actual katana blades that have been remounted as *naginata*. There is a *tsuba* between blade and haft. In skilled hands it is a terrifying weapon with a fearsome reach. Accounts tell of it being spun around like a waterwheel and the cutting power of its whirling blade is horrifying to contemplate. Against cavalry it not only had the reach to strike at the horseman's head but it was also used with brutal effectiveness to scythe at the horse's legs. Cavalry continued to play a prominent role in the warfare of the Sengoku Period, even though the battlefield was dominated by massed ranks of *ashigaru* infantry. By the late 16th century the lance (*yari*) supplanted the bow as the principal weapon of the mounted samurai. It was used with an outstretched arm, in the manner of light cavalry, rather than as the couched lance of the medieval knight. Nevertheless swords remained highly valued as secondary cavalry weapons. It was also a time, though, when increasing numbers of samurai were fighting on foot and wielding the sword as their principal weapon.

By the beginning of the seventeenth century, it became fashionable to wear two swords – the katana and the *wakizashi*. Although everything about a samurai's dress and routines is highly ordered and the katana and the wakizashi are worn in a consistent manner, there is something rakish and dashing about the way they are simply thrust into the sash belt. This seemingly casual adoption of a pair of bladed weapons was a conspicuous display of the samurai's aggressive potential – in the argot of today's underworld, everyone could see that he was 'tooled up'.

The wakizashi was simply a shorter version of the katana, typically no more than 20 inches in overall length. It could be used as a companion weapon to the katana but this style of fighting was less for the battlefield and more for the single combat duels of the *ronin* (masterless samurai) in the early seventeenth century. Miyamoto Musashi, who wrote a seminal work on Japanese swordfighting, *A Book Of Five Rings*, was legendary for his prowess with two swords. Most samurai, however, continued to use the katana with two hands.

Generally the wakizashi would be worn at all times by a samurai; from the moment he rose in the morning till the moment he placed it by his bed at night. When he entered a house, whether his own or another's, a samurai would leave his katana on a rack by the door but his wakizashi would remain firmly tucked into his belt-sash. Uesugi Kenshin owned several swords, the Yamatorige was just his most famous and most cherished. Among them was a beautiful wakizashi and like his other swords it had no *tsuba*. It also differed in having two small knives (*kogatana*) carried in the scabbard instead of the more usual arrangement of a *kogatana* and a *kogai*. These accessories were most usually a feature of the wakizashi, except for when a samurai chose to carry only a single sword. In such cases, and the Yamatorige is one of them, kogatana and kogai were sheathed into the scabbard of the katana.

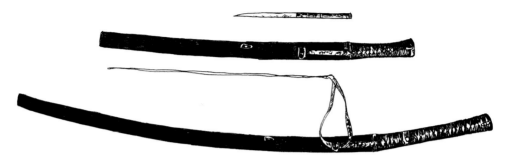

Top to bottom: Kogatana, wakizashi, katana

The kogatana was a small general-purpose knife, similar to the by-knife that was frequently found attached to medieval European scabbards. The kogai was a steel bodkin used to arrange a samurai's hair. At its top end was a little T-shaped knob with rounded terminals intended for cleaning out earwax. They were fastidious fellows these samurai!

Kogai

Warrior monks

Other than to clean his ears, Uesugi Kenshin had no need of a kogai. His hair was not coiffed with a tightly bound topknot; it was shaved. He was a Buddhist monk! A samurai daimyo, famed for his fighting prowess, who is also a Buddhist monk? Surely that is an oxymoron; surely Buddhism teaches universal peace? Well, so do Christianity and Islam – both of which have been conspicuous in their propagation of war over the centuries. Whether one chooses to describe Buddhism as a religion or as a set of teachings or philosophies, it has manifested in many divergent forms and sects. Just as there are Sunni and Shia and Sufi; just as there are Catholics and all manner of Protestants; so in Japan there are the Tendai, Jodo-Shinshu, Zen, Nichiren, Kogi Shingon and Shingi Shingon sects of Buddhism.

Buddhism had come to Japan from China, where it had already mutated from the original teachings. Even so, the core message of non-violence remained a central precept; it was preached, though it wasn't always adhered to. Buddhist teachings spread easily in Japan, partly because they found a natural resonance with the people and partly because, being non-theistic, there was no incompatibility with the beliefs of Shinto. The two co-existed and to some extent complimented each other. As the centuries passed, different schools of Buddhist thought cemented into entrenched sects with vested interests and zealous affiliations.

The most extreme were the groups of Ikko-ikki (the Single-minded League), followers of Jodo-Shinshu or 'True Pure-Land School' Buddhism, who became a significant military force in the fifteenth and sixteenth centuries. The Ikko-ikki were

Kenshin meditating (photo courtesy of Stephen Turnbull Library)

rebel peasant armies who believed that entry into Nirvana or the Pure Land – a state of grace or heaven – could be achieved by worshipping Amitabha Buddha. It was a straightforward belief that appealed to the peasantry. Peasants could understand the simple contract of being rewarded for an allegience to a higher authority. This, combined with the belief that death in battle was a guarantee of a place in heaven and the opportunity to turn against their oppressive overlords, produced fanatical warriors, fearless of death and resolute in their determination to overthrow the power of the samurai. It was the Iko-ikki who had killed Kenshin's father at the Battle of Sendanno.

At a time of constant turmoil, when every local warlord was engaged daily in a power struggle for territory and political control, the various Buddhist orders also felt the need to protect their wealth, interests and land, as well as seeking to expand their realm of influence and the propagation of their beliefs. Taking up arms and fighting for their cause were huge armies of warrior monks, *sohei*, and they became as much a part of political power play and the martial landscape as the samurai and daimyo. Some have compared them to monastic orders of knights in medieval Europe such as the Knights Templar or the Teutonic Knights but such comparisons should not be taken too literally. These were very different cultures. In Japan the association between Buddhism and martial culture endured through the centuries. The collections of The Royal Armouries at Leeds hold a nineteenth-century tachi that has the Buddhist symbols of wheels, swastikas and thunderbolts adorning its hilt.

Many daimyo and samurai became Buddhist monks, customizing their beliefs to suit their personal circumstances. Uesugi Kenshin was among them. A disciple of Shingon Buddhism, he seems to have found no inconsistency with his Buddhist beliefs and his reputation as a fierce warrior. Neither did he find any conflict with violating another basic tenet of Buddhism, revelling in the excess of his heavy drinking. However, in other ways he aspired to be a devout follower, devoting himself to meditation and the ascetic life. He was celibate and adopted two sons, Kagetora and Kagekatsu, as his heirs.

Takeda Shingen

Kenshin's arch rival, nine years his senior, was Takeda Shingen. Of noble birth, he was born Takeda Harunobu, but he also took Buddhist vows, becoming a monk and assuming the name Shingen in 1551. His first wife died at an early age and he married a second time. Renowned for his licentious lifestyle, he had three regular mistresses and countless assignations with concubines. Shingen sired seven sons and five daughters, born by various of his womenfolk. His greatest devotion, however, was to his general, Kosaka Masanobu. Homosexuality was as accepted, indeed valued, in samurai society as it had been in ancient Greece. It has a name, *shudo* – 'the way of the young men' – and it was common for a samurai to take a young man as his acolyte and lover and to train him in martial ways. Masanobu served Takeda Shingen from the age of sixteen until after his master died.

Wonderfully fierce in appearance, this squat and bellicose warlord ruled his province of Kai for the benefit of his people and their economic prosperity. He had the Fuji River dammed to provide irrigation for his farmers and he introduced an innovative tax and legal system. His thriving economy was shored up by the natural wealth of his territory – gold. Unlike other daimyo, Takeda resided in an unfortified mansion rather than a castle. He was safe among his people, a benevolent ruler and a well-read and cultivated man who delighted in the arts. Yet in war he was a ferocious, cunning and ruthless opponent.

The long-standing rivalry and conflict between Uesugi Kenshin and Takeda Shingen is legendary. They met in battle five times at the same place, Kawanakajima! On the eve of the fifth battle in 1564, Kenshin recorded what he perceived as Shingen's misdeeds, giving reasons why he must fight and defeat him. High on the list was Shingen's laxity in spiritual matters and his delegation of secular bodies to oversee ceremonies at temples and shrines in the territories he occupied. Such religious posturing had little real meaning. These were two warlords for whom waging war was a way of life and for whom having a sworn enemy formed part of their own identity. That is not to say that there is not a spiritual dimension to the warrior ideal.

Warrior training
The central aim of Buddhism is to find enlightenment and the martial arts have always been linked with certain aspects of spiritual pursuit, most particularly the Zen quest for the empty mind – *mushin*. I once visited the most beautiful dojo in Tokyo to watch around forty people engage in their early morning *kendo* session as part of their quest for *mushin*. The suffix '*do*' means 'the way of' and the prefix '*ken*' is an archaic term for sword. A *ken* was a type of double-edged, straight-bladed sword that went out of use in the ninth century when it was superseded by the tachi. The kendo sessions take place every day from 7am–9am. I spoke there to an 85-year-old man who claimed he had never missed a day in forty years. He was certainly spry for his age.

The dojo had been built in 1925, a large purpose-made, single-storey, wooden structure, with large roof windows letting in pools of softened light. One of the dojo's long side walls opened, by means of sliding screens, to a garden, admitting muted rays from the greenery. It was an architecture that orchestrated the natural light as cleverly as any church or cathedral and created an equally spiritual and dramatic effect, especially at that time of day. A shrine was set at one end, to which everyone bowed on entering, and at the other sat a huge drum. Above the screens that opened to the garden side were racks from which everyone's armour hung. This dimly lit demi-attic was a slightly mysterious place; the black armour seemed foreboding until taken down by what looked rather like a boat-hook. Kendo armour looks superb – flowing ankle length robes, wide, flaring neck guards, a lacquered breastplate and the helmet with its menacing grill, all combine to evoke a samurai spirit. Along the opposing long wall was a galleried walkway, raised some 2 feet from the dojo floor and softened with *tatami* matting. There were slim wooden pillars on the dojo side of the walkway and paper screens on the outer side, separating it from the actual entrance corridor of the building. Light filtered from the outside windows and then through these paper screens to create an ethereal light in the cloistered space. Here people would don their armour with great ceremony. It was martial arts as theatre and theatre as religion.

At the start of the proceedings the magnificent drum was sounded – solemn, primeval and wonderful. Then with great warlike shouts everyone started to belabour one another with their *shinai*. The shinai is the mock sword used in kendo and is constructed with four bamboo staves bound with leather bands. Its design, like slapsticks, deliberately exaggerates the cracking sound of a strike. In truth everyone is perfectly-well protected by his or her armour and there is no risk of pain or injury. Blows are permitted to the top of the head, the side of the head, to the sides of the torso and to the wrists. Thrusts are also allowed, though used less frequently. Kendo swordsmen (*kendoka*) are bare-footed and work on their toes, which gives a skip to their footwork. This is not to denigrate the athleticism of what they do but, in appearance, it lacks a certain martial purpose. The bamboo practice swords and padded armour (*bogu*) were introduced by Naganuma Sirozaemon Kunisato in the early eighteenth century, where lays the foundation of the modern sport. As with western fencing, as soon as rules of engagement, blunt weapons and protective equipment are employed and the objective becomes to score points, the jeopardy of injury is absent and the moves and tactics become far removed from actual fighting techniques.

In Kenshin's time samurai would spar with heavy wooden swords called '*bokuto*' (also known today as '*bokken*'). They would not wear any protective equipment and serious injuries, including broken bones, could result from training sessions. I suspect that these encounters looked very different from modern kendo. Bokuto were sometimes employed to settle private disputes in a form of duel. Before such a fight it was customary to sign a disclaimer indemnifying the opposing party in the event that a mortal wound was received. Bokuto were seemingly capable of inflicting very serious wounds indeed.

It was more common, though, for such petty duels and indeed regular practice, to call for the technique of *tsumeru*, whereby the swordsman pulls his blow. Tremendous prestige was attached to a swordsman's ability to execute precise control with his *tsumeru*. With this technique, the concept of free-play training could be extended to sparring with sharp swords, although one would clearly need to

Bokken (author's collection)

trust in one's opponent's ability. The legendary Miyamoto Musashi is said to have been able to bisect a grain of rice placed on a man's forehead without leaving so much as a scratch.

Nonetheless, with or without protective equipment or technique, some form of free-play sparring is an essential element in the training of a swordsman and kendo continues that tradition for the modern martial artist. Kendo is said to mould the mind and body and to cultivate a vigorous spirit. The *kiai* – the shout – that accompanies attacking moves not only harnesses the breath but also inculcates sustained aggression. Rage tends to be a short-lived emotion and is all but useless to the warrior, since it also blinds his judgement, but habitual training with a focused bellicosity is a vital tool in the swordsman's armoury. Most importantly, activities such as kendo nurture stamina and sharpen reaction speeds. The concept of *mushin*, 'empty mind', is key to attaining the most rapid and instinctive responses and it is sought after by all *kendoka*. It is a focus understood by people who perform highly-skilled and sometimes dangerous feats at high speed. Many sportsmen at the highest level understand it.

However, speed is nothing without form and it is here that the greatest emphasis is placed in Japanese martial training. At Hayashi-sensei's dojo in the outskirts of Tokyo, I witnessed and took part in an *iai battojutso* training session. Here *kata* – choreographed patterns – are practised both as solo exercises, in pairs and with multiple opponents. I was taught some sequences in which I was attacked by two assailants. These *kata* were performed with sharp swords, adding a little adrenalin and focus to the undertaking. It was both exhilarating and great fun. I did not achieve 'empty mindedness' or any other enlightened state but I did experience a heightened state of concentration. When done at speed, there is no time for thought and you have to surrender yourself to trusting that you will instinctively produce the correct learned responses. I imagine that, at a higher level, the effect on the mind may be similar to that which some people experience in car accidents and other traumatic situations. They have a perception that time has slowed. Now clearly, if you could induce such a state at will, you would have the power to deal with an onslaught of blows, however thick and fast they came. More pragmatically, however, samurai took the precaution of wearing armour on the battlefield.

Armour

Evidence from surviving portraits and statues suggests that both Uesugi Kenshin and Takeda Shingen struck imposing figures. Kenshin characteristically wore a cowl, an outward sign of his Buddhist faith, instead of a helmet, but was otherwise decked in the most resplendent armour. Shingen also wore magnificent armour and a helmet famous for its dense and extravagant mane of white horsehair, lending him a surreal leonine ferocity. His Buddhist affiliation was gestured with a saffron scarf, the *kesa*, which he wore over his breastplate.

Japanese armour consists of multiple steel plates that are laced together by silk cords. Japan has a damp climate and so each plate is lacquered black in order to protect

Uesugi Kenshin in armour (photo courtesy of Stephen Turnbull Library)

it from rust. There are instances of red armour and blue armour and gold armour but it is mostly black, apart from the kaleidoscope of brilliant hues created by the vibrant lacing. In 1995 I was invited to join a team from the Royal Armouries, Leeds in a visit to the Nikko Toshugo Shrine in Japan. It was to celebrate the twinning arrangement with the museum there and we were to display some European martial skills and armour at their annual yabusame festival. As a mark of honour I was fortunate enough to be picked as one of three Brits to ride in a parade around the town precincts and I was to don full Japanese armour. The armour fitted well and was, if anything, slightly more comfortable and a fraction lighter than my full European harness. It was also similar in that there was an elaborate procedure to put it on; one that cannot be achieved without assistance.

The horses provided for the parade were tall (17 hands) English hunter types. It was quite a haul to get up there, especially as the Japanese ride with short stirrups and I am not blessed with much in the way of leg length. Our peregrination was halted frequently in order to dismount and make observances at one of the multitude of Shinto shrines. Each time it became more and more laborious to remount. It was raining. Eventually I resorted to scaling a wall – a wet, slippery, stone wall, in order to gain some height advantage. It was only after I had clambered atop the rough-hewn rocks that I was informed that the Emperor's personal dresser had dressed me and that I was wearing original seventeenth-century armour!

As previously observed, all armour is more or less proof against the weapons of the day; otherwise there is little point in having it. It's just not 100% proof. However, Uesugi Kenshin's armour served him well the day he rode into Takeda Shingen's camp and engaged in perhaps the most famous single combat in samurai history. Kenshin's legendary heroics took place in 1561 during the fourth battle of Kawanakajima but before that great, dramatic moment, the Uesugi and Takeda armies had been rehearsing their feud for many years on the Kawanakajima plains.

The Battles of Kawanakajima

Lying between the Uesugi territory of Echigo and the Takeda lands of Kai, was the mountainous province of Shinano. In 1542 Takeda Shingen began a series of campaigns that were to see him, twelve years later, in overall military command of Shinano. He was in no mood to stop there and Uesugi Kenshin's Echigo homeland was in his sights. Kawanakajima, a vast flat plain on the Echigo/Shinano border surrounded by high mountains and divided by mighty rivers, was the perfect stage for these two master tacticians to stalk each other in a series of elaborate military manoeuvres. It was a contest that was to last, on and off, for eleven years. More analogous to the Battle of the Somme than regular place-name battles, Kawanakajima was an area of land fought for over a period of time, rather than a single encounter at a single place on a single day. In fact the 'First Battle of Kawanakajima' in 1553 was more of a rolling campaign, involving various castle sieges and minor skirmishes as opposed to a set-piece battle.

The second battle, in 1555, was a stand off, with each army arrayed on opposite banks of the Sai River for four months. Both commanders made an impressive show of strength with troop numbers in excess of 3,000 but, other than night raids and small skirmishing forays, there was little action. Eventually the call of the harvest became more pressing than the need for military resolution and the *ashigaru* returned to their fields. Recruited from the peasant farmer classes, the *ashigaru* formed an increasingly large part of samurai armies from the mid-sixteenth century onwards. They were expendable, available in large numbers and could be trained quickly in the use of firearms, which now began to proliferate.

Takeda forces came again to Kawanakajima in March 1557 for what is known as the Third Battle and they came in even greater force. Shingen's general Babu Nobuharu besieged the castle of Katsurayama with 6,000 men. In the bitter snows of a late winter, the castle fell to the Takeda and they went on to capture the border fortress of Nagahama before moving on to lay siege to another border castle at Liyama. They were at Echigo's front door. Uesugi Kenshin responded with a series of troop manoeuvres designed to lure Takeda Shingen into a set-piece pitched battle. Countless ruses were thwarted and the two main armies avoided each other until September. Finally the Takeda made a dawn raid on the Uesugi camp at Uenohara, just as the Uesugi men were having breakfast. In the battle that followed each side lost around 1,000 men and then withdrew, with no settled conclusion.

As with the preceding three 'battles', the Fourth Battle of Kawanakajima started with a series of troop movements, raids and counter-raids but it culminated, on 18 October 1561, in one of the most celebrated pitched battles in samurai history. On the night of 17 October, both armies deployed under the cover of darkness and took up positions by the Chikuma River at a place called Hachimanbara. Shingen's troops had crossed the river to get there and Kenshin's forces had crept down from secret passes in the mountains, muffling the sound of their horses by binding their hooves with soft cloths. So practiced and disciplined were they at these night manoeuvres that neither side realized that the other was there. Records suggest that Shingen had at least 8,000 men and that Kenshin may have had as many as 13,000. It was quite an achievement to move them with such stealth.

At dawn, a watery sun appeared as a faint yellow glow through the heavy mists that curled off the river, and out of the gloom could be heard the clatter and rumble of cavalry, growing ever louder and more terrifying as it drew nearer the Takeda camp. Uesugi Kenshin had launched a massive mounted charge with over a thousand horsemen bearing down on the Takeda lines in a daring surprise dawn offensive. The poet Rai San'yo described it as 'a whip crack across the river'. Somewhere at the head of the charge, a ghostly figure in the dense mists, was Uesugi Kenshin, screaming his war-shout of 'Ei! Ei!' as he spurred on his foam-flecked steed and brandished his precious sword, the Yamatorige, high above his cowled head. 'O! O!', cried his loyal followers in refrain. There was fierce fighting as Kenshin's vanguard, under Kakizaki Kageie, crashed into the central divisions of the Takeda army. Caught unawares they were put into disarray and Shingen's brother was among the first casualties. Wave after wave of Uesugi horsemen rolled onto the Takeda shore. Takeda Shingen himself sat on his stool at his curtained command post, receiving reports from the field and despatching his messengers urgently with fresh orders.

Suddenly Uesugi Kenshin burst through the curtained enclosure on his horse, riding down the bodyguards who tried to block his way. So swift and decisive was his attack that Takeda Shingen didn't have time to draw his sword. Barely with time to rise from his stool, he only just managed to parry the blow from Kenshin's sword with his war fan. War fans (*tessen*) were iron versions of civilian fans that were used by commanders as signalling devices. Kenshin managed to deliver three cuts to Shingen, each deflected with the fan, before Shingen's shocked and startled guards sprang into action. Hara Osumi-no-kami used Shingen's own mother-of-pearl inlaid spear to thrust at the fearless Kenshin. Its blade glanced harmlessly off Kenshin's *watagami* (shoulder defences), proving the worth of his armour. However Kenshin's horse is said to have reared at this attack and then bolted with him back to his own lines. It is remarkable that he escaped alive.

There are alternative accounts that claim that it was not Kenshin but one of his samurai, Arakawa, who made it through to Shingen's inner sanctum. However, as is so often the case with great military deeds, the legend is too powerful to be eclipsed by

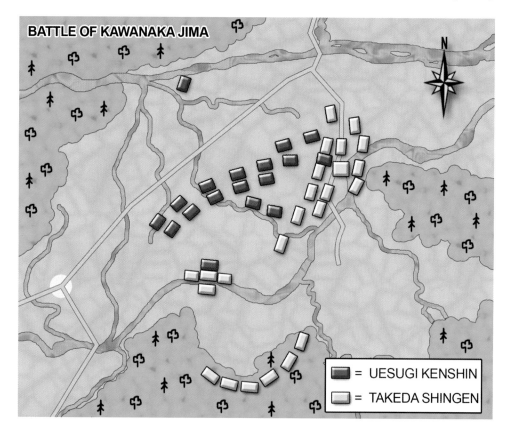

BATTLE OF KAWANAKA JIMA

■ = UESUGI KENSHIN
□ = TAKEDA SHINGEN

Kawanakajima, by Utagawa Yoshikazu, 1857 (Library of Congress)

Kenshin at Kawanakajima (photo courtesy of Stephen Turnbull Library)

such theories. Uesugi Kenshin's actions that day, heedless of all dangers in order to face his enemy man to man in glorious hand-to-hand combat, personify the abiding spirit of the samurai as a courageous warrior and adherent of *bushido*.

Bushido

Bushido is the warrior code of the samurai. It is akin to Western concepts of chivalry insofar as it encompasses similar ideals. However there are many situations where a samurai's actions would differ from those of a medieval knight, so we cannot say that they are the same. First among the tenets of bushido is the overriding obligation of duty to one's overlord. Hierarchical structures were strictly adhered to in Japanese society and the concept of loyal and faithful service was a keystone. Clearly there was a breakdown of this principle during the Warring States Period or else all the individual daimyo would have been loyally obedient to the central will of the Shogun. On a more local level though, samurai did remain fiercely loyal to their daimyo. The concept of service was innate, more as it had been in the pre-chivalric 'heroic age' of Raedwald's time, when there was no greater honour than to die in battle in the service of one's lord.

Valour and bravery were key to the bushido code and a samurai must show no fear in the face of danger. Indeed he must generally show no emotion at all. Japanese concepts of losing face remain occasionally bewildering to western eyes but they are deeply rooted in the samurai code. The way that a samurai conducted himself both on and off the battlefield was of crucial importance. Bushido guided the samurai in rituals of grooming and appearance. Correct behaviour in everyday things, what we might call decorum, was central to his reputation and reputation was everything.

Respect and even generosity towards one's sworn enemy was typical of the honourable conduct between samurai. In 1568, the immensely powerful Hojo clan, who sought to bring Takeda Shingen into line, imposed sanctions on his landlocked provinces, prohibiting trade in rice and salt. On hearing of the embargo, Uesugi Kenshin despatched a substantial consignment of salt to his lifelong foe, with the message 'our conflict is one of bows and arrows, not of rice and salt'.

Kamiizumi Hidetsuna, an ally and vassal of the Uesugi clan, had received a similarly magnanimous gesture from Takeda Shingen after the fall of Minowa castle in 1567. Hidetsuna, who had seen his daimyo killed in a heroic assault on Shingen's men, now found himself without an immediate overlord. Out of respect for Hidetsuna's martial prowess – he was a swordsman of legendary ability – Shingen offered him a place at court as his personal fencing master. Mastery of the martial arts was a key tenet of bushido and those who practiced them at the highest level were deemed worthy of high regard from friend or foe. On this occasion Shingen's benevolent offer was declined and Hidetsuna instead set out on a *musha shugyo*, which is roughly equivalent to a knight errant journeying on his 'quest'. Hidetsuna hoped that his wanderings would bring him enlightenment and prepare him for death. And that was what the code was all about – a constant preparation for a noble and honourable death.

Seppuku is ritual suicide and considered an honourable course of action for a samurai who failed to uphold the ideals of bushido or who had been disgraced or defeated. It was a redeeming act of great bravery. In *hara-kiri*, one of several forms of *seppuku*, the protagonist disembowels himself with his *tanto* (dagger). A second, *kaishaku*, usually stands by to decapitate him after he has done the deed. Yamamoto Tsunetomo, writing of instances in the past when the head travelled further than intended, had good advice for the second: 'it was best to leave a little skin remaining so that it [the head] did not fly off in the direction of the verifying officials'.

Seppuku was often prompted by defeat in battle. Takeda Shingen's one-legged general Yamamoto Kansuke, who had masterminded the Takeda tactics at the Fourth Battle of Kawanakajima, perceived, in the aftermath of Kenshin's personal attack on Shingen and the continuous pulverising assaults by Uesugi forces, that his plans were leading to a Takeda defeat. Armed only with a long spear, he waded unaccompanied into the midst of the Uesugi forces where he fought valiantly, taking several lives. He suffered no less than eighty wounds to his body and, weak and exhausted, he then crawled to a nearby mound where he committed *hara kiri*. If only he had persevered a little longer. The forces that he had sent to cut off the Uesugi army in the mountains realized that they had been outwitted and now came streaming down into the valley to trap the Uesugi forces in a pincer movement. Kansuke's suicide had been premature. In the event the Takeda forces prevailed at Fourth Kawanakajima.

Perhaps the most famous incident of committing suicide in the face of defeat is that of Nitta Yoshisada. In an attack on the monks of Fujishima in 1338, Yoshisada's horse was felled by an arrow, trapping its rider's leg under its dead weight. A sitting duck, Yoshisada was then struck by an arrow that penetrated his helmet and entered his forehead. Nitta Yoshisada then drew his sword and with one blow decapitated himself. If there is any truth to this legend at all, it is an unrivalled testimony to the sharpness of the Japanese sword.

Decapitation was an integral part of samurai warfare with the custom of taking heads as war trophies. In a practice known as '*buntori*' a samurai would decapitate his enemy with his katana and present the head to his daimyo as proof of his abilities as a warrior. It is a custom that resonates with the ancient Egyptian procedure of severing hands in order to count the fallen. Of course the heads had to be those of other samurai, not ordinary men, but even so several hundred heads might be paraded after a battle in what became an elaborate ritual. Done correctly, the heads would be washed, hair combed and mortician's cosmetics applied by women followers. Such formality was not always possible or practical in the midst of a campaign and heads could be brought before the daimyo straight from the battlefield, sometimes skewered upon the point of a katana. Head-taking generally took place at the end of a battle, although this ran the risk of rivals stealing heads that did not rightfully belong to them. On the other hand taking heads during the course of battle could be considered a dereliction of duty and would also expose the head-taker to additional danger.

During the grim cranial harvest that followed the fourth encounter at Kawanakajima, trophy hunters roamed the battlefield in search of the heads of high-ranking samurai.

Takeda Shingen (photo courtesy of Stephen Turnbull Library)

Post-battle skirmishes broke out to recover the heads of distinguished warriors. A man named Yamadera slew the man who had taken the head of Takeda Tenkyu Nobushige, Shingen's brother. It meant that he not only denied that prize to the Uesugi but that he also added one more head to the Takeda count. The head of Shingen's uncle, Morozumi Masakiyo, was retrieved in similar fashion and it was brought back to Shingen's camp along with several more heads lopped from Uesugi shoulders. In the head-viewing ceremony that followed, Takeda Shingen was able to count 3,117 heads. There is no record of the Uesugi count but it is likely to have been similar. The Fourth Battle of Kawanakajima was a draw – an indecisive encounter that had resulted in a terrible loss of life.

Three years later, the two tenacious warlords came with their armies to the plain of Kawanakajima once again. Uesugi Kenshin, responding to forays on his borders by Shingen's forces, took to the field in September 1564 and threw down a challenge for decisive resolution between them. To his great annoyance, Takeda Shingen didn't pick up the gauntlet for nearly a month. When he did so, finally, he outmanoeuvred Kenshin by bringing his troops through passes that allowed him to command the higher ground. Uesugi found himself in a tactically impossible position and withdrew. This bloodless encounter is known as the Fifth Battle of Kawanakajima.

Oda Nobunaga

Elsewhere in Japan another warlord was beginning to make a name for himself. His name was Oda Nobunaga and his campaigns were to have an impact on the lives of both Uesugi Kenshin and Takeda Shingen. He was to have an even greater impact on the fate of Japan. In 1567 Oda Nobunaga had the words '*Tenka Fubu*' set into his seal. Sometimes translated as 'one realm under one sword', it was a declaration of his intent to unify Japan, to wipe out the power of the monks and to put a stop to the internecine warring between daimyo. The following year he marched his army into the capital Kyoto and set up a puppet shogunate under Ashikaga Yoshiaki. The long process of unification had begun.

The third day of August 1568 saw Uesugi Kenshin and Takeda Shingen square up to one another one more time. In fact there was nearly a sixth battle of Kawanakajima. In the event they just drew up their forces on their respective borders and growled at each other. Both were secure with the territories they had and both were aware that, following Nobunaga's move on Kyoto, the balance of power in Japan had shifted. Their disputes were no longer of any significance.

Takeda Shingen turned his attention to a new rival, Tokugawa Ieyasu. The 25-year-old Ieyasu was an ally of Oda Nobunaga and controlled territories to the south of Kai. It was whilst besieging Ieyasu's castle at Noda in 1573 that the head of the mighty Takeda clan was struck down by a drunken sniper. Legend has it that Shingen's army had won the day and that the defenders of the castle were preparing to surrender honourably the following morning. That evening, however, they broke out their reserves of sake and all got roaring drunk. Lured by a haunting melody that one of the revellers was playing on his flute, Takeda Shingen approached the ramparts to hear it better. It was then that the sniper struck.

Uesugi Kenshin died five years later on 13 April 1578. There is a persistent, and rather gruesome, legend that he died at the hands of a diminutive ninja, sent by Oda Nobunaga. The ninja, Ukifune Jinnai, was allegedly less than 3 feet tall and, the story goes, he lay in ambush, concealing himself in Kenshin's lavatory overnight. The lavatory was set over a large hole in the ground and Ukifune is said to have used some kind of snorkel in order to breathe in the foul pit.

I once had to pass myself off as a ninja for a television programme. It was the most unlikely casting imaginable. Aside from the fact that I was already in my late fifties and long past the willowy athleticism usually associated with these supple soldiers of stealth, I was at the time suffering from a severe bout of bronchitis. I was running a high temperature, I could hardly breathe and I had what seemed like a consumptive cough. The weather was below freezing and I was bundled up with multiple layers of clothing. Fortunately, the production company had hired me a large-sized ninja suit that I was able to put on over my many layers of warm clothes, though, it must be confessed, the resulting silhouette was more rounded than the usual image. I dive-rolled and jumped off sea containers and generally stalked and clambered in a ninja fashion through an industrial landscape before producing my '*fukiya*'. The programme was about blowpipes and this scenario introduced the blowpipe of the ninjas – the *fukiya*. I remember it as being a miserable experience.

My misery that day cannot compare to the misery of Ukifune hiding in the cesspit below Uesugi Kenshin's lavatory. It may be that his snorkelling apparatus was a blowpipe, a simple bamboo tube. Certainly the account of the raid on Kenshin's headquarters tells of a group of ninjas, armed with blowpipes, killing Kenshin's own ninja guards with their poison darts (*fukibari*). However, one of Kenshin's guards, a ninja by the name of Kasumi Danjo, survived the attack and, so he thought, defeated all the would-be assassins by breaking their necks. What Danjo hadn't realized, of course, was that all this was merely a distraction so that Ukifune could lay his grim ambush. In the morning, Uesugi Kenshin had a spear thrust up his rectum as he sat on the toilet. He died four days later. Some modern scholars dismiss the story as a fable, but it is too good a story not to tell. Current thinking is that he did have a fit whilst visiting the lavatory but that his death was caused by stomach cancer or some other intestinal problems brought on by a lifetime of heavy drinking.

Four years later, in 1582, Oda Nobunaga was betrayed by one of his generals, Akechi Mitsuhide, and he committed *seppuku* as the Honnoji Temple in Kyoto burned around him. Mitsuhide's victory was short lived and he was defeated at the Battle of Yamazaki thirteen days later by Nobunaga's most loyal and gifted general – Toyotomi Hideyoshi. At the time of his death Nobunaga controlled most of central Japan and he had effectively destroyed the power of the Buddhist warrior monks. Shingen was dead, Kenshin was dead and the stronghold of the fanatical Ikko–ikki had been wiped out.

The Tokugawa Shogunate

Hideyoshi, a military genius of humble birth, known as the Napoleon of Japan, became shogun and, in a series of brilliant campaigns, extended central control to an even wider area, including the islands. He even embarked on expeditions for the Japanese conquest of China, channelling the belligerance of the warring samurai against a foreign foe. His legacy at home included the rigid categorization of the Japanese class system by which the peasantry were disarmed and it became law that only the samurai could bear arms. By this act he ensured the enduring prestige and significance of the sword in Japanese culture.

His death in 1598 triggered a power struggle that was only settled two years later at the Battle of Sekigahara, the most important battle in Japanese history. It marked the end of the Warring States period and the victor, Tokugawa Ieyasu, became the most significant shogun to ever rule Japan. Under the Tokugawa Shogunate, a now-fully united Japan closed her doors to the world. It was a period of unprecedented peace and a period in which the samurai flourished and nurtured their martial traditions. It was the age of the sword. An age in which disbanded samurai, *ronin*, roamed the land looking for fights and duels.

In 1600, the same year as the Battle of Sekigahara, but on the other side of the world in Paris, another veteran of domestic religious wars, Henri IV of France, married Catherine de Medici. Among his wedding presents was a matching rapier and dagger. These were the weapons of the civilian duel in Europe and they are the subjects of my next study but first we must look at how the European civilian duel came about.

Rapier, Victoria and Albert Museum, London (© V&A Images)

Chapter 9

The Sword of Honour and the Rise of the Civilian Duel

I believe his first duty is to know how to handle expertly every kind of weapon, either on foot or mounted, to understand all their finer points, and to be especially well informed about all those weapons commonly used among gentlemen ... Often differences arise between one gentleman and another and lead to duels and very often the weapons used are those that come immediately to hand.

(Baldesar Castiglione, *El Libro del Cortegiano*, 1528)

The duel

In his seminal book of the age, *The Book of the Courtier*, Baldesar Castiglione defined what was expected of a Renaissance gentleman. Skill at arms and a readiness to defend one's honour in a duel were central tenets and these ideals were aspired to throughout sixteenth-century Europe, giving much employment to the masters of fence. However, fine points of etiquette and the precise observance of formalities – *punctilio* – became easy mechanisms for picking a fight and the duelling codes of the nobility were often hijacked by thugs and psychopathic bullies on a spree of violence. By the latter part of the century duelling had become all the rage for both the upper and the middle classes.

'Why, thou wilt quarrel with a man that hath a hair more or a hair less, in his beard than thou hast ...' says Mercutio in his satirical tirade against the craze for civilian duelling in Shakespeare's play *Romeo and Juliet*. A friend of Romeo's, this sharp-witted joker goes on to say, 'thou wilt quarrel with a man for cracking nuts, having no reason but because thou hast hazel eyes'. Though both funny and ridiculous, the tragedy is that such preposterous pretexts were not that far removed from what young men chose to quarrel over; fabricated displeasures that led to thousands of duels and much employment for gravediggers. By the 1570s duelling had reached epidemic proportions amongst belligerent young men looking for any excuse to prove their skill with the sword. 'Thou hast quarrelled with a man for coughing in the street, because he hath wakened thy dog that hath lain asleep in the sun', chides Mercutio, striving to point out the stupidity of it all. Yet this same Mercutio is the first to scorn Romeo's conciliatory embassies towards Tybalt. This same Mercutio, who scoffed 'Didst thou not fall out with a tailor for wearing his new doublet before Easter?', reached for his own sword without hesitation when he thought that his friend was letting the side down and, with an unceremonious 'I am for you', launched into an attack that would, a few blows later, lead to his death. Young men are rash and proud and quick to anger and they have a highly developed sense of honour and sensitivity to grievance. It is to be seen in the gang cultures of both the past and the present day. The cult of duelling fanned these flames. Mercutio was a fictional character but Shakespeare gave him the voice of a generation. His head knew to condemn the extreme excesses of senseless violence but his heart was unable to bear a perceived slight to his friend without retaliation.

Gurus of Renaissance manners created codes of honour categorizing looks, gestures and terms of defamation into degrees of insult that warranted satisfaction on the duelling ground. Books and pamphlets set out the conditions and causes that obliged a gentleman to defend his honour in the fighting of a duel. Dressed up in cod legal language that sought to legitimize this resort to violence in the face of the slightest slight, these 'codes of the duel' reduced honour to a set of absurd rules. Absurd or not, the consequences of failing to adhere to these principles of honour meant being ostracized and suffering a loss of reputation. Honourable reputation was essential for economic survival in a society that placed great store by such things and was not something to be disregarded lightly. A fall from good standing and loss of trade or employment had no safety net and so it really wasn't an option for a courtier or a professional man or a merchant to risk the stain of dishonour by not issuing or accepting a challenge as circumstances dictated. It was even less of an option for a military man. Numerous edicts both in England and in France outlawed duelling but the fashion for it was unstoppable. Duelling became endemic in society and everyone

Rapier practice at the target after the German school of Meyer

who aspired to be a gentleman laid claim to the right to duel as a means of settling private quarrels.

At the roots of this claim were the ancient rights of the 'wager of battle' and the judicial duel which embodied the principle in law that an injured party could seek recompense and atonement directly from the person who had wronged him. At some point early in the sixteenth century these rights diluted and transferred to become a non-regulated civilian custom. A duel no longer had to be decreed by the authorities; it was simply consented to by both parties. Usually, an appointment was made for the encounter, though on occasion the duellists might set to on the spot. The principal difference between a duel and a fight or a brawl is that it is entered into by agreement by both sides, that it addressed retribution for some perceived imputation of honour and that they choose to call it a duel. It was a contract to fight. In essence duellists were exercising the ancestral rights of the privileged classes to settle their private disputes by means of an archaic combat ritual. It was a statement of privilege. In turn, as the practice grew, even the lower classes sometimes aped their 'betters' and the custom spread like a contagion.

The social changes that led to this state of affairs were the same ones that had set the scene for the new fashion for civilians to wear swords. Throughout the medieval period the sword was not generally worn with civilian dress. It was buckled on with a knight's war gear or carried by travellers but not worn in everyday life. During the Renaissance, a gentleman would wear his sword in public at all times. This had to do both with the status of the sword and with the status of a new class of aspiring gentleman.

Initially the feudal system meant that knights owed military service in exchange for land and privilege. Accordingly those who owned the land, and therefore had power, were the military classes and the symbol of their ruling status was the sword. It defended a knight's honour and slew the enemies of Christ. The sword was an ancestral badge of rank. Lines became blurred during the twelfth and thirteenth centuries with the introduction of *scutage*, which meant that a landowner could buy out of his military obligations; the money was then used to hire professional mercenaries. Nobles were no longer exclusively military men and, from the mid-thirteenth century, the power base of military aristocracy was increasingly blended with the merchant and professional classes. These men made money by other means than war and thus they could buy land and thereby power. The tax-yielding wealth of trade funded the new mass armies and an ever more complex society required literate administration. Society saw the gradual ascendency of the bourgeoisie.

The last two decades of the fifteenth century were a time of great social mobility and an outward show of status became ever more important. It is then that we start to see men wearing swords with civilian dress. Established nobility adopted the fashion to assert their old authority; the new bourgeois gentleman class did it to establish equal claim to that authority. Both did it to proclaim that they were 'men of honour' and therefore prepared to defend that honour in a duel. Moreover, population growth in the towns and cities led to an increase in violent crime and a gentlemen also felt the need to carry a sword for self-defence. Spanish inventories of the time identify such a sword as an *espada ropera* – a 'robing sword'. In other words a sword to be worn with civilian dress; as opposed to a soldier's sword that was worn with military attire. '*Espada ropera*' was rendered in French as '*epée de la rapière*' and from that derives the English word 'rapier'.

The rapier

As soon as the sword was worn with civilian dress it became a fashion statement. Rapiers became lighter and finer and, to give some protection to the civilian's un-armoured hand, there were major changes to the hilt. The cross began to be called the 'quillons' (respectively the forward quillon and the rear quillon) and these were augmented with rings in both planes below and with multiple knuckle guards above.

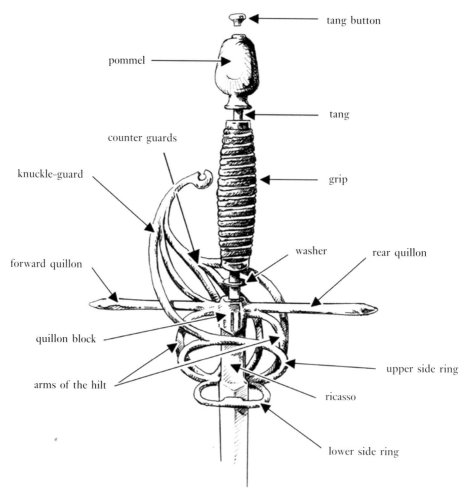

The parts of a rapier

These additions happened gradually over several decades until the arrival mid-century of the fully developed 'swept hilt', with its energetic array of bars, guarding the hand in sinuous, sweeping curves. It was a very good sword hilt and a fabulous piece of costume jewellery. Swept hilts were often gilded, silvered, blued, blacked, counterfeit-damascened, set with precious stones or etched, chiselled or pierced with all manner of decoration. Rapiers became synonymous with elaborate developed hilts. However the more significant change was in the form of the blade.

In cross-section, rapier blades were usually either ovoid, flattened-diamond or hexagonal. Initially they were slightly more slender and slightly longer than the blades of a typical arming sword but in the second half of the century the trend for longer blades took over. A longer blade had an advantage of reach, something that could be exploited in a one-on-one duel far more than it could in the tight press of a battlefield. Long-bladed swords had an obvious phallic swagger for fashion-conscious young men out to impress with boastful virility. Moreover, to possess a rapier that was both extremely long and extremely narrow was to own something at the peak of techno-logical achievement. Such blades were very difficult to make because, in order to maintain rigidity without mass, they had to be very hard and thus expertly tempered. Tolerances were critical. If hardened too much, the blade would break too easily and if too soft, it would be too pliant. If you wanted to stab someone with spaghetti, you would neither want it fully cooked and limp nor fully dry and brittle.

Sir John Smythe, in his *Instructions, Observations and Orders Militarie* (1591), complained that, 'rapier blades being so narrow and so small substance and made of very hard temper to fight in privat fraies, in lighting with any blow upon armour, do presently breake'. These same blades were very well suited to piercing unprotected flesh but were useless on the battlefield. Nevertheless the rapier had become so firmly entrenched as a status symbol that gentlemen soldiers felt obliged to carry it into battle to display their rank. It was clearly unsuited to the task. A later remedy was for military gentlemen to have rapier-style developed hilts mounted onto broader, sturdier blades. This has been annoying for subsequent generations of students of the sword because it confounds an easy definition of what a rapier is. Is it defined by its hilt or by its blade? Rapiers were designed to be worn primarily with civilian

A 'hanger' for wearing a rapier

dress and in this context the developed hilt evolved, but their defining characteristic is that they have long and narrow blades. Thus, in a military context, a broad-bladed weapon is a sword, not a rapier, even if it possesses a developed hilt in the civilian style.

The considerable length of some rapiers necessitated a special type of suspension system called a 'hanger'. This consisted of a triangular panel that retained the sword by means of loops and slides along its bottom edge. A hook attached the apex of the triangle to the belt and the front corner of the bottom edge also connected to the belt by means of an adjustable strap. Hangers enabled rapiers to be carried at a diagonal angle across the back of the left hip, thus accommodating very long blades indeed. It was an angle of carriage that also made possible the drawing of such lengthy weapons. I have drawn a rapier with a blade length of over five feet from a hanger, which would not have been doable with a conventional belt-slung scabbard. Most hangers were made of leather, often finely tooled, though it was also the vogue to have them covered in silk, often embroidered, or other fabrics to coordinate with the wearer's clothes.

An entry in John Stowe's *Annales* for 1570 reports that around this date it became fashionable not only to sport extravagantly broad ruffs but also to wear

> long tucks and long rapiers ... The offence to the eye of the one and the hurt that came by the other caused Her Majesty to make proclamation against them both and to place selected grave citizens at every gate, to cut the ruffs and break the rapier points of all passengers that exceeded a yard in length of their rapiers and a nail of a yard in depth of their ruffs.

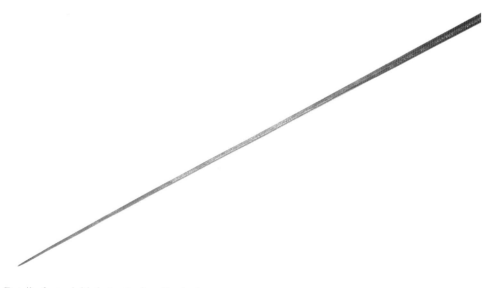

Detail of a tuck blade (author's collection)

Stowe was at least a decade late with his account. Queen Elizabeth had in fact issued a statute as early as 1562 prohibiting rapiers beyond 'one yard and one halfe quarter'. This was reiteration of an order proclaimed five years earlier by Queen Mary. She had set the limit at the same length, which was around 40½ inches. However, fashion is a stronger power than the law of the land and Elizabeth's petty officials must have had a busy time of it putting travellers' ruffs to the shears and their swords to the stone – 'cutting them down to size'. Many swords of the period sported blades of 48 to 50 inches.

William Bullein in his 1562 book on medicine states, 'There are a new kind of instrument to let blood withal . . . called the ruffians tucke and long foining [thrusting] rapier'. The term 'tuck' derives from the French '*estocade*', meaning thrust. Tucks were long bodkin-style blades with no cutting edges. These were what George Silver, master of fence, scathingly referred to as 'bird spits'. Most rapier blades were typically 1 inch in width but tuck blades could be half this. The technical challenges of making a blade longer were amplified considerably when having to produce something this slender. I own one, made by Hans Ollich around 1610. It is a superb piece of dense, hard steel and still feels tough and strong. Many didn't match this quality. Like long skewers, the tuck's capacity to pierce flesh was undoubtedly its primary purpose but that is not to say that cutting-style blows need be ruled out of its fighting repertoire. The edges on my sword are not sharp but they are nonetheless acute; moreover the blade has considerable weight and is perfectly capable of cracking an unprotected skull.

A refinement to the standard tuck blade was to produce it so that it flared into a cutting blade a few inches from the tip. Such a design lent itself to the execution of the *stramazone*, a cutting-stroke with a flicking action, delivered from the wrist,

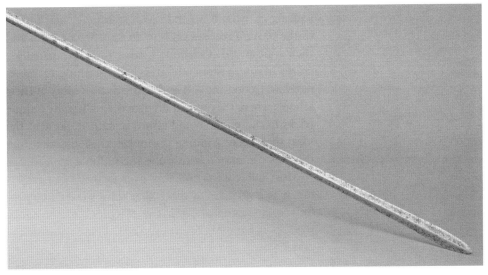

Detail of a stramazone blade (by kind permission of the Trustees of the Wallace Collection, London)

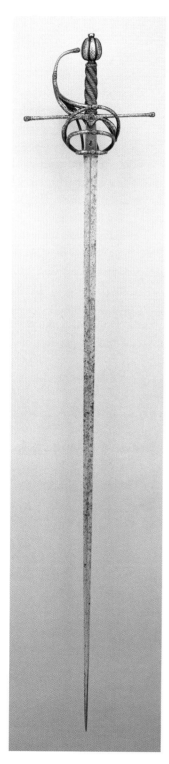

that was especially popular in the Italian rapier fight. Mercutio alludes to it in his death speech when he says of Tybalt's fighting style 'a scratch, a scratch; marry 'tis enough ... zounds a cat, a dog to scratch a man to death'. A 'scratching' cut may sound less than decisive but it can be delivered very speedily without preparation at certain distances. If it succeeds, the drawing of blood is always a good psychological advantage and if it is parried it offers the opportunity of an instant follow-through in a compound attack. At the windpipe it could be instantly fatal. Vincentio Saviolo, a renowned Elizabethan master of fence wrote that, 'Every little hit in the face stayeth the fury of a man [more] than any other place in his body', and the face was a prime target for the *stramazone* cut.

The masters of the noble science of defence

The development of the rapier as a dedicated weapon for the civilian led to a shift in emphasis for the syllabus at fence schools. Less attention was given to techniques that would serve on the battlefield or in the judicial duel, though they were still taught, and more attention was given to self-defence and duelling techniques. There was also an enormous proliferation of 'how to' manuals. Europe's new printing presses groaned as their massive wooden screws, creaking and squeaking, wound up and down stamping their blocks to the page. Treatises on how to fight were legion and their widespread availability further fuelled the duelling craze. Many masters advertised the teaching of '*bottes secrettes*' (secret moves) and had private rooms in their schools where they would divulge their allegedly unique tricks to those who could afford it. Others derided the idea that such winning formulae existed, regarding them as phony ploys to dupe the gullible.

Most duels were probably over in just a few moves but it is a mistake to think that they were all clumsy brawls far removed from the teachings of the fence schools, as has often been suggested. Those who duelled

Swept hilt rapier, Spanish, circa 1620 (by kind permission of the Trustees of the Wallace Collection, London)

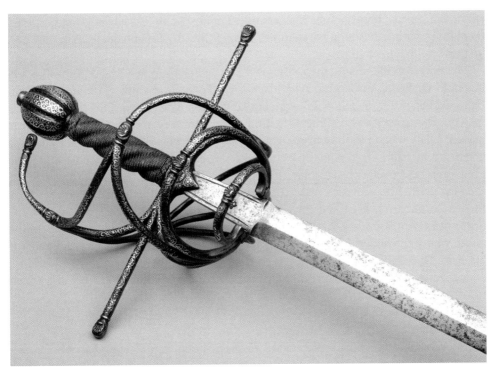

Hilt of rapier, Spanish, circa 1620 (by kind permission of the Trustees of the Wallace Collection, London)

took their martial practice seriously. This is what they trained for. Castiglione wrote, 'I am not one of those who assert that all skill is forgotten in a fight; because anyone who loses his skill at such a time shows that he has allowed his fear to rob him of his courage and his wits'. There was obviously divided opinion at the time on the subject but the point Castiglione is making is that it wasn't always so and he further implies that maintaining good technical form was a requirement for a gentleman. The fencing master Saviolo also had views on the subject. He said that there were some who 'suffer themselves to be overcome with fury and so never remember their art and some being so timorous ... that they seem amazed and void of fence', but he also added that 'I have seen many that being fearful by nature, through daily practice have become courageous'.

Henry VIII, an aficionado of all the martial arts, sought to regulate the teaching of fence and to get rid of the bad teachers that had brought the science into such ill repute. In 1540 he granted letters patent to 'The London Company of Maisters', effectively giving them a monopoly on the teaching of arms. A principle obligation placed on members of the company was to seek out unlicensed masters and bring them to the attention of the authorities. They could be prosecuted under the 'Statute of Rogues' on the basis that they were not licensed to teach fence and so therefore had no legal occupation and could be considered vagabonds punishable by being sent to jail or the stocks. The London Masters operated a strictly 'closed shop' and ordered themselves with an elaborate system of rules, enforced with an equally elaborate and lucrative schedule of fines.

The lowest grade of student was known as a 'scholar'. When he felt himself ready he could challenge to become a 'free scholar'. To achieve this degree he must win fights against six of his fellow scholars in two weapon disciplines. This test, known as 'playing the prize', was conducted within the confines of the school. If the scholar passed, a date was set for him to challenge in public. Two weeks notice of the trial was given and he had to face as many free scholars as chose to come up against him. The event was held over two days, one for each weapon. Before he could challenge for the next grade, the provost's prize, a free scholar had to study under his master for a further seven years. With the consent of his master he could then apply to play his next prize. Permission for this was granted, or not, by the four senior members of the guild, who went under the grandiose title of The Four Ancient Masters. To play for his prize, the free scholar had to issue a challenge to every provost living within a twenty-mile radius of London and he paid a fine of five shillings for every accredited provost that he omitted from his challenge. Any provost who failed to appear was liable to a fine of six shillings and eight pence. Three weeks notice was required before the challenge.

If successful, a provost was licensed to teach but was still bound to his master, who took a share of his takings. A provost might open his own school or might teach within the environs of his master's establishment. A further seven years had to elapse before the provost could play for the prize of becoming a master. He then had to gain permission from The Four Ancient Masters, give four weeks notice of challenge to any master living within a sixty-mile radius of London and was responsible for paying their travelling expenses. Playing the master's prize happened just once or twice a year and proficiency had to be shown with at least four different weapons. It was a major event and crowds from all stations of society flocked to see it. The venue was usually the courtyard of an inn and the crowds were lured there by the proceeding pomp of a grand parade.

Ears pricked at the distant sound of the marching drums. A brisk, rousing military beat. Apprentices looked hopefully to their masters, shopkeepers looked to their shutters and delivery boys hurried to offload their wares. As the pulsing beat drew closer, the insistent rhythms set every heart racing. The excited crowds swelled and jostled in the busy Elizabethan street for a view of the procession. In front of the drummers was born the great red banner of the Company, emblazoned with a silver sword. Behind them paraded the masters, their faces well known and the favoured celebrities among them raising a shout from the onlookers. Following the masters were the hopeful 'prizors' and behind them the provosts, free scholars and scholars.

Having played the prize, being elevated to the next degree was by no means a foregone conclusion. In 1582 John Dewell was 'not admitted Provost for his disorder'. Ten years earlier, John Blinkinsop, playing his scholar's prize, 'was not admitted by cause of misdemeanour committed by him and for want of his games which were not in place'. Perhaps the misdemeanour was a foul stroke and 'the games' were the stake he was required to put up to pay for the attendance expenses of the free scholars. Eighteen of them turned up to challenge him at sword and buckler so he would have had to dig deep into his pockets that day. Blenkinsop tried again and eventually made it to his master's prize in 1583. He was subsequently immortalized in Ben Johnson's *The New Inn* as '*Blenkinsopps the bold*'.

It is hard to know to what extent these prize contests represented fighting in earnest. In adjudicating, the Four Ancient Masters opined on technique and style and the idea was clearly to demonstrate proficiency with a variety of weapons rather than to inflict serious harm. However 'playing the prize' was a robust affair – it was said that a master who had more than one eye was a lucky man. One rule stated that anyone who challenged a *prizor* and 'doth strike his blow and close withal so that the prizor cannot strike his blow after again, shall win no game … although it should break the prizor's head'. This suggests that a cracked skull was an entirely likely outcome and that we may therefore assume no head protection was worn.

Almost certainly the weapons were blunt but it is not specifically recorded. Whether wood or steel, they were perfectly capable of splitting skulls or breaking bones. However 'playing the prize' was a commercial undertaking, not an affair of

Engraving of a fencing school at the University of Leyden, Swaneburgh, late 16th century (courtesy of Prof Sydney Anglo)

honour. The Company sought to earn money from the entertainment and to promote the celebrity and talents of its members in order to attract fee-paying students to its schools. Injury was an occupational hazard but not something a well-established master would want to expose himself to lightly, just to help some young provost rise to equal rank. It is probable that stoutly-padded doublets were worn and thrusts were prohibited in all weapons, save for the rapier. A further safety measure for the ingénue was 'scholar's privilege', which forbade all strikes to the face for those playing to be a free scholar.

Supervising the strict adherence to the rules were the 'sticklers'. Two sticklers occupied the platform with the combatants, ready to rush in and separate them or beat down their weapons with their staves at the first sign of any infringement. Osric, in Hamlet, was a stickler. It was the stickler's job to act as umpire and to call out when a man had been fairly struck – 'a hit, a palpable hit'.

A master could set up his own school of fence and Roger Ascham, who taught Queen Elizabeth I both archery and Latin, tells us that there were schools of fence 'almost in every town'. However, under Elizabeth the vagrancy laws were extended to specifically include 'fencers', at least those not accredited to the Company of Masters. The Punishment of Vagabonds Act (1572) ruled that 'jugglers, tinkers, chapmen, pedlars, fencers, bearwards and common players' were to be considered 'sturdy beggars' – that is able-bodied unemployed – who could be sent back to their parish of permanent residence, where they must seek employment or face a prison sentence. An exception to this was if they were licensed by two justices of the peace or were the accredited employees of a peer of the realm. So it was that both professional swordsmen and actors shared a common destiny, both dependent on licence and patronage. Moreover they frequented the same haunts. *The Theatre* and *The Curtain*, the first public theatres, which opened in London in the 1570s, became popular venues for the playing of a prize, rivalling the courtyard inns for their capacity to accommodate a crowd and give a view of the proceedings.

One celebrated Elizabethan straddled both camps. He was the great comic actor Richard Tarlton. This 'fellow of infinite jest' is thought to have been the model for the description of Yorick in *Hamlet* and he was a great favourite of the Queen. His celebrity extended well beyond his own lifetime and his image adorned inn signs for more than a century after his death. Tarlton was a member of The Queen's Men, a licensed troupe to which a young William Shakespeare belonged while he was learning his trade as an actor, but he also held another license. Richard Tarlton was a master of the London Masters of Defence. In spite of belonging to two authorised bodies, the Queen's Men and the London Masters, Tarlton also had a job as 'groom in ordinary' to Her Majesty's Chamber and so was quite immune from any vagrancy prosecutions. Many masters took the expedient of having another occupation, like Richard Best who was one of the Four Ancient Masters but also a gunner at the Tower of London. Though expertise in martial skill was highly valued, respectability for professional practitioners remained elusive.

Richard Tarlton was most famous for his jigs and his comedy improvisations and his *Book of Jests* was a best seller. In *Hamlet*, Shakespeare gives him an affectionate obituary when Hamlet soliloquises to a skull he has found in the graveyard, referring to it as that of 'Yorick', which is an amalgamation of 'yore', meaning old, and 'Ric' – '*alas, poor old Ric*'. Shakespeare packed his plays with fights, brawls and battles. Having a martial artist of Ric Tarlton's calibre in the company, an Elizabethan Jackie Chan, must have spiced up their execution no end. Elizabethan audiences knew a thing or two about swordfighting and would have jeered any sub-standard offerings. How thrilling and spectacular these early performances must have been. Physical, energetic, stylish and with an edge of danger, they would have heightened the atmosphere and underpinned dramatic conflict in a way so sadly lacking in many of today's pedestrian theatrical presentations.

George Silver and the Italian Masters

Ric Tarlton was originally a swineherd from Shropshire. At the opposite end of the social scale was George Silver. Silver was a master of defence who sprang from the minor gentry and he and his brother Toby established themselves as private tutors to other gentlemen, rather than as masters in the common fence schools. Unfortunately the modish young bucks of Elizabethan London preferred to bestow their patronage on a coterie of Italian fencing masters who had set up shop around the Blackfriars. Silver's treatise *Paradoxes of Defence*, published in 1599, begins with a diatribe against these Italian teachers, who were poaching his clientele, and continues in much the same vein. It is unfortunate that he is best remembered for these jingoistic railings, scorning their 'tempestuous terms' and describing their fight as 'false ... weak ...

fantastical ... most devilish and imperfect', because it has sometimes detracted from the fact that his own practical teachings are perfectly sound. As might be expected, Silver's xenophobic rants found a ready audience with the average Englishman, something that Shakespeare was not slow to exploit – Mercutio again: 'Ah the immortal passado! The punto reverso, the hai! ... the pox of such antic, lisping, affecting fantasticoes, these new tuners of accents'. Nevertheless, while the lower classes enjoyed laughing at foreigners, especially Catholic ones, the nobility flocked to the exclusive halls of the fashionable Italian masters.

George Silver

In essence, Silver was a cut-and-thrust man who favoured swords of moderate length and reasonable width. They were civilian swords intended for the civilian duel and he advocated using them in conjunction with a companion dagger. He has often been painted as very 'old school' but this is a relative perception; he was a man of his times, teaching the contemporary style of fighting, just not the hyper-modish Italian fight with long and slender tucks. Silver decried the over-reliance on the thrust that characterized the Italian method and lamented that, 'there are now in these days no gripes, closes, wrestlings, striking with the hilts, daggers or bucklers used in Fence schooles'. His was a pragmatic, straightforward approach to surviving a fight, prioritizing sound defence before reckless attack. As with the masters of old, he incorporated hand-to-hand techniques alongside his sword stratagems and one of his favoured recommendations was the 'kicke to ye coddes'.

Although Silver was the first Englishman to write a treatise, his was not the first in the English language. That laurel went to Giacomo Di Grassi whose *True Arte of Defence* was 'Englished' in 1594 by 'I.G., gentleman', a quarter of a century after it had first appeared in Italian. Di Grassi placed great emphasis on using the sword for defensive moves at a time when such measures were being increasingly delegated to the dagger. He did not neglect the dagger, though, and among his tricks is a disarm whereby the opponent's sword is engaged by the sword and then rapped sharply with the dagger to induce the opponent to let go.

Case of rapiers and sword and buckler after Di Grassi

Rocco Bonetti, a former captain in the Venetian army and probable spy, didn't leave us a manual of his teachings but is considered to be the first of the Italian masters to establish a fence school in London. Most of what we know about him comes from the writings of George Silver who tells us that Bonetti rather self-importantly referred to his school as a 'colledge'. This college was located in a fine house in Warwick Lane and there were benches and stools at one end of the main teaching area so that his patrons could sit and watch others practice their skills; something that he obliged them to do in lead-weighted shoes, 'the better to bring them of nimbleness of feet'. Additionally he provided an elegant square table, covered with a cloth in crimson velvet and complete with 'inke, pens, pin dust, and sealing waxe and quiers of verie excellent fine paper gilded'. Signor Bonetti's clientele were exclusively 'Noblemen and gentlemen of the Court' requiring such facilities to conduct court business at all times of the day. A great clock in the corner of the room established his upmarket credentials beyond doubt. To cap it all he had a private room for the teaching of his 'secret fight'. The London Masters were peeved that he operated outside their control and offered to bring him into their fold by waiving all qualifying stipulations, saying that he could fight the master's prize without preliminaries. Bonetti snubbed them on grounds of class.

Someone we know only as 'Jeronimo' took over Bonetti's college after his death in 1587. In 1590 Jeronimo went into business with Vincentio Saviolo, an Italian master from Padua who had taught extensively in Europe before coming to England under the patronage of Elizabeth's favourite, the Earl of Essex. Saviolo has the distinction of

Rapier fighting after Saviolo

being the first to write a fight treatise in English and *His Practice in two Bookes* was published in 1595, just a year after the translation of Di Grassi appeared. Book one was about rapier fighting and book two dealt with matters of honour. Saviolo concentrated on the use of the single rapier, though rapier and dagger are given some attention. His work embodied principles of a most vibrant athleticism; necessitating a caving and arching of the body to avoid thrusts and swirling, circular patterns of footwork, creating attacks from all angles:

> make a stoccata to his bellye ... and then you must play with your body toward your left side, and bearing the thrust on your right side, passe a little on his right side and make a riversa above his sword ... or else make a passata resolutlie, wheeling half about.

He was ill-served by his illustrator; the few woodcuts that accompany his work are of stilted, awkward figures conveying nothing of the dynamism of his system.

While he concedes that using the sword may be necessary to parry or, to use his term 'break', cuts, he disallows its use to parry a thrust, saying 'I wish you not to defend any thrust with the sword, because in doing so you lose the point'. He adds that the left hand should be used either to beat aside the rapier 'not at the point but at the strength and middle of the weapon' or 'to catch his sword fast and so command him at your pleasure'. Saviolo stresses that the rapier should be used in conjunction with a mail gauntlet on the left hand and 'if a man be without a glove, it were better to hazard a little hurt of the hand, thereby to become master of his enemy's sword, than to break [parry] with the sword and so give his enemy advantage over him'.

George Silver tells us that the Italians seldom fought without a pair of duel-

ling gauntlets. These consisted of sections of fine mail sewn onto linen gloves. Surviving examples show the mail to be closely meshed. On the right hand there was mail only on the back, the thumb and on the deep cuff protecting both the inside and outside of the wrist. Fingers and palm were left clear to close round the sword grip. Left-handed gauntlets had mail on the back, fingers and palm. I have experimented with a replica *duelling gauntlet* and can vouch that one

16th century Italian duelling gauntlets (©The Board of Trustees of the Armouries. III.144-1)

can take a direct thrust to the palm with a sharp point without fear of puncture. Well, that's not strictly true – I had the fear of puncture but happily the mail did its work and rendered my fears unfounded. The disadvantage to the duelling gauntlet is that the density of mail can inhibit closing the hand fully and I think it would be difficult to seize the opposing blade if it were a narrow tuck.

Silver avowed to bring them 'out of their fence tricks' but the Italians offered much more than tricks. Theirs was a sophisticated and complicated system requiring great nerve and an extremely highly developed level of skill; but if you had these it could be deadly effective. Saviolo's fight was challenging and interesting to study for athletic young men and also offered a higher level of aesthetic form. It was the tango to George Silver's waltz but he was right that it was dangerous and the average swordsman would have been better off sticking to his less demanding methods.

Both Saviolo and Jeronimo were assailed at various times by English ruffians out to best them. Saviolo showed great restraint when Bartholomew Bramble called him a coward and poured beer over his head in a Somerset pub, declining the invitation to fight. On another occasion a street brawl, involving a gang of London Masters against Saviolo and Jeronimo, was broken up when a 'wench' in the Italians' company ran for help. Jeronimo, again in female company, finally met his end when a man called Cheese stopped their coach. A fight ensued and Jeronimo was run through. George Silver and his brother Toby were rather more honourable, though no less disdainful, in their dealings. They issued a challenge to Saviolo and Jeronimo to play a prize with them at an inn called *The Bell Savage*. The aloof Italians didn't deign to give a reply. A gentleman was only required to answer a challenge from his social equal and the Italian pair, like Bonetti before them, took a rather elevated view of their station.

By the last decades of the century, the rapier was established as the principal weapon taught at the fence schools. Other weapons applicable for military use, such as the messer and falchion (dusack play), the halberd, the half pike and the two-handed sword, remained on the curriculum and all featured prominently in the treatises produced by the masters, but it was the rapier fight that most people wanted to learn.

Estocs

Though related etymologically, the 'estoc' is quite different from the tuck-style rapier. Long-bladed, dedicated thrusting weapons of this name had been known as early as the fourteenth century. Characterized by extremely rigid square, hexagonal or triangular-section blades, these were either a two-handed weapon of longsword proportions or, for the cavalryman, fitted with a short grip. They had sturdy bodkin points and no cutting edges. Clearly they were of great use against armour and two-handed tucks were especially popular for use in fifteenth-century judicial duels. They were also one of a number of weapons used for combats at the 'barriers'. Fighting 'at the barriers' became increasingly common at tournaments in the sixteenth century, an era in which this arena for tough martial display was diluted with ever more safety measures. At the barriers, the combatants were separated by a waist-high fence,

sometimes two parallel fences, intended to prevent them from grappling and to make the target area equivalent to that for mounted combat.

Most masters continued to teach the fight with the two-handed sword and some favoured the two-handed estoc. Given that the use of the sword as a lever was an essential component of any fight with two-handed weapons, the estoc with its exceptionally strong, stiff blade was by no means limited to thrusting. Moreover, the lack of a cutting edge does not necessarily exclude the use of blows. The wide spacing of the hands, afforded by the very long grips of these swords, enabled great acceleration and huge momentum to be imparted to the stroke. It is of little comfort, after receiving a powerful whack around the head with an iron bar, to learn that it does not have a cutting edge. Though considerably smaller and lighter than the two-handed swords of the landsknechts, the estoc was hardly a weapon to carry about the streets and a principal reason for its continued instruction in the fence schools was that it could still be designated for use in a judicial duel. There were occasions though when even a sword of this size could be used in self-defence.

George Silver tells the story of one Austin Bagger, 'who being merrie amongst his friends' decided to pick a fight with 'Signior Rocco' and called on him at his house in Blackfriars. He was referring, of course, to Rocco Bonetti. Shouting from the street, Bagger mocked the Italian's claims of superior swordsmanship; in particular, Rocco's assertion that he 'could hit anie Englishman with a thrust upon anie button'. This was the Italian master's advertising slogan, famously lampooned by Shakespeare in Romeo and Juliet when he has Mercutio refer to Tybalt as 'the very butcher of a silk button'. However, when faced with the drunken bruiser Bagger, armed with sword and buckler, Bonetti elected to come out of his house armed not with his precision rapier but with his 'two-hand sword'. It is my guess that this was of the estoc variety. Against the odds, Baggar won the fight and with

Two-handed estoc (by kind permission of the Trustees of the Wallace Collection, London)

hooligan charm 'cut him over the breech and trode upon him and most grievously hurt him'. It should be added that Silver was writing more than a decade after the alleged event and his agenda was to discredit the Italian masters, so we might take this triumph of xenophobic English thuggery with a pinch of salt.

Wasters and foils

The fencing manuals of the period depict combatants with sharp weapons, often skewering vital organs with a consequent issue of blood. These illustrations are intended to show the worth of the master's moves in actual combat but clearly he would not wish to lose the custom of his well-heeled clients at such an alarming rate. Weapons used on a daily basis in the schools were blunt. As discussed in previous chapters, wooden weapons called wasters had been the principal tools of practice during the medieval period and John Stowe in his 1598 *Survey of London* refers to the youths of the city exercising with 'their wasters and bucklers', confirming their continued use in the sixteenth century. Wooden substitutes were all very well for swords with a broad blade but new solutions had to be found to rehearse the rapier fight. The answer was steel 'foils' with large padded ends. Blunted weapons, of any type, are known as foils – 'as blunt as the fencer's foils, which hit, but hurt not', as Shakespeare puts it in *Much Ado About Nothing*. It simply means that the point and edges have been 'foiled' or rebated so that they are blunt. Blunt they may be but these were not the flimsy weapons of the modern sport fencer. They were weapons of weight and rigidity.

Such practice weapons are rare but in the Victoria and Albert Museum in London there is a foiled sixteenth-century rapier and dagger set.

Practice Rapier and dagger (© V&A Images/Victoria and Albert museum, London)

The square-sectioned blades are blunt and there are small flat discs at the points like the head of a nail and about the size of a twopence piece. They look heavy and cumbersome but I have handled these weapons and they balance perfectly and are as light in the hand as equivalently sized rapiers with sharpened edges and needle points. The function of the disc on each point is for the attachment of a pad. The padding material, probably felt, is held in place by a circle of parchment, which is then tied onto the sword behind the button, its skirts flaring behind the tie to give the appearance of a shuttlecock. Over time these pads grew larger. Joseph Swetnum, an English fencing master writing in 1617, recommended a pad the size of a tennis ball, which meant, in theory, that you could receive a thump in the eye without losing your sight – the size of the pad being larger than the eye socket – but what a thump that must have been! A straight-arm thrust, carrying the weight of a 2.5lb rapier and driven home at full velocity with a surface area one third of the size of a boxing glove, could deliver a very concentrated force. When one considers the damage that is possible from a boxer's punch, a strike in the face from a padded rapier must also have carried the risk of incurring brain damage, concussion, whiplash, a broken nose, jaw or teeth.

Practice rapiers from *Ein Neu Kunstliches Fechtbuch im Rappier*, Michael Hundt, 1611 (German National Museum)

Such large pads were not always used. Lord Sanquhar, lost an eye while 'playing at foils' with his master, John Turner, in 1607. Convinced that this was no accident, he hired assassins to murder his unfortunate tutor. Sanquhar was tried for the crime and sent to the gallows, where, as a peer of the realm, he was hung with a silken cord. It seems that Sanquhar may have had a point though, for Joseph Swetnum tells us that Turner 'by his unlucky hand thrust out two or three eyes and was praised by the public for his skill'. In particular he makes reference to an incident at the *Swan* theatre where Turner 'thrust Dunne into the eye and he was killed speedily'.

Some masters suggested that it was essential for a student to have some experience of facing sharps. An author known to us only as GH wrote in 1614 'at blunt a man may come boldly on and is not troubled with any such consideration, as at sharp must of necessity disorder his remembrance and put him out of fight'. Whatever the truth of this, and it seems self-evident, practice with sharps was problematic and could only be done with extremely proficient and trusted opponents. For the most part any freeplay had to be conducted with foils or wasters.

As well as fighting with the sword alone, most masters also taught fighting with a companion dagger and also dagger fighting as a skill in its own right. An excellent solution to the problem of making a practice dagger is to be found in one of Rabelais' satirical novels. These were written during the reign of Henri IV of France, a contemporary of Elizabeth I and subject of the next chapter. In them we read how the hero, Gargantua, had a 'dagger of boiled leather'. Boiled leather or '*cuir bouilli*' was widely used for armour in the early Middle Ages and is extremely tough and rigid. Rolled in the manner of a rawhide dog-chew, it is easy to imagine it being ideally suited to the manufacture of practice weapons.

Sword and dagger

The dagger as a companion weapon to the sword is first encountered in the works of the father of civilian fighting styles, Achille Marozzo. Marozzo ran a celebrated *sala d'arme* in Bologna and, at the age of 51, he published his *Opera Nova dell'Arte delle Armi* (*New Work For The Art of Arms*) in 1536. This work was a distillation of decades of teaching and new thinking. *Opera Nova*, alongside works by other Italian writers such as Antonio Manciolino, was in the vanguard of literature dealing with a new style of fighting for the new age of the civilian duel. However Marozzo offered by far the most comprehensive and practical system, illustrating his work with eighty-two stunningly beautiful and informative woodcuts. Many of these show the index finger hooked over the cross of the sword. As well as giving security to the grip, this also shifts the balance of the sword and affords greater control of the point, setting a trend that subsequent masters would elaborate upon. Although he wrote at a time before the introduction of long tucks and used swords that George Silver would have approved of, Marozzo's work remained the classic foundation for the rapier fight. His work was reprinted many times over a period of fifty years.

Marozzo devoted a chapter to the subject of honour, as did most masters. Masters of fence became arbiters on the nuances of when and how to deliver a challenge and it

Fighting systems after Marozzo, 1536. Note finger over the cross

was, of course, in their commercial interests to maintain a heightened atmosphere around these matters. As well as laying the foundations for fighting with a sword in the right hand and a dagger in the left, a style that characterized an epoch, Marozzo also instructed in the use of various other companion weapons.

Bucklers and targets

The buckler remained a popular companion to the rapier for much of the sixteenth century and all the masters write of its use. So popular was it in Elizabethan England that the London apprentices would gather every Sunday morning for sword and buckler practice. This was a roughhouse sort of gathering and the swaggering youths wore their bucklers slung over their sword hilts, so that they would 'swash' and clatter as they strutted to their school of hard knocks. Hence the term 'swashbuckler' was coined; meaning, originally, loutish afficianados of the sword.

Marozzo also shows the fight with rapier and 'target', the latter being a round convex shield about two feet in diameter. Such shields were extremely popular in the late sixteenth century and followed the fashion for evoking antiquity in arms and armour. Some, astonishingly beautiful art objects, were made from thick *cuir bouilli* that was elaborately embossed and tooled. Others, equally beautiful, had etched or embossed steel surfaces depicting classical scenes or were made of wood covered with leather and painted exquisitely.

In addition to their uses for parade and display and in rapier combat, large round shields also saw use on the Renaissance battlefield. The Scottish 'targe', its surface decorated with elaborate nail-work, was in common use from the sixteenth to the eighteenth centuries and steel targets of a similar size, also known as 'bucklers', were favoured by the Spanish during the early years of the sixteenth century. At the height of the Conquistadors' expansion into the New World, around twenty per cent of the Spanish infantry were sword-and-buckler men. They were particularly good at engaging blocks of musketeers. A sword alone is a poor defensive tool when warding off blows from a heavy musket used as a club but with a shield to deflect such onslaughts, the sword-and-bucklermen were able to capitalize on their superior agility and cut the gunmen down.

However, it is the use of the target in the civilian rapier fight that concerns us here and the first question is to what extent targets were carried in everyday life. The answer is that they weren't. Nevertheless the evidence of the manuals for their use in the civilian fight is overwhelming and so I can only conclude that they were taken to the duelling ground by pre-arrangement. Of more practical use on an ad hoc basis was the smaller steel buckler. These were still worn by 'swashbuckling' young men as they swaggered through the streets.

The terms 'target', 'rondache' and 'buckler' are to some extent interchangeable. 'Buckler' is a catch-all generic that can be applied to any shield and 'rondache' is just an alternative name for the larger circular target. More specifically though, the buckler remained a particular type of shield in its own right – much smaller, usually made of steel and held in the fist. Renaissance bucklers tended to be slightly

larger than their medieval forbears and appeared in a number of shapes. Some had a long spike projecting from the centre of the boss, with an obvious offensive potential; others had a hook in the centre so that it could hook onto one's belt. One such buckler, in the Wallace Collection, still retains its original lining of striped silk. It probably once matched some gentleman's hanger and sword-belt from which it was hung with the fancy lining on display to the world.

Concentric rings of raised bars on the surface of some bucklers were intended to entrap a sword blade, which on striking could slide along the surface of the buckler and lodge, albeit momentarily, beneath the bar. This gave the defender a significant advantage of time. In swordfighting

Buckler. Note hook for belt suspension and concentric rings for catching a blade (by kind permission of the Trustees of the Wallace Collection, London)

timing is everything. A man whose sword is fouled, even for a fraction of a second, is extremely vulnerable to a well-timed counter attack.

What advantage is offered by a rectangular over a circular buckler is less clear. Giacomo Di Grassi gives us a clue when he says,

> with the square Target, better than with any other, he may warde edge-blowes, because it is of square forme: and the edge of the sword may easely be retained with the streight side thereof.

If used injudiciously there is a risk with a buckler that a blow may glance from its surface to land upon one's person. Indeed Di Grassi goes on to advise that the best way to attack a buckler man is to launch attacks 'athwarte', in other words both thrusts and cuts should be angled to approach him on his right hand side. In this way the sword 'maie easelie slippe and strike either the heade or thighs'. I can see that in parrying across to one's right against an incoming blow, there may be slightly more security with a square shield but one wonders why in previous ages, when more 'edge-blows' could be expected, bucklers were universally round. Besides, when dressing to leave the house in the morning, how do you decide whether you are more likely to encounter a ruffian who favours edge over point or one who relies solely on the thrust?

Rapier and cloak

Many masters advocated the use of the cloak as a companion to the rapier. As part of everyday fashionable attire, it was a convenient accessory. A cloak could be wrapped over the arm and used to parry; it could be swirled to distract the eye and gain advantage of time and distance; it could be flicked to catch the wrist of an opponent's sword-arm and deflect the line of a thrust. In fortunate circumstances, such a move might even disarm. It could be trailed in retreat, with the hope of enticing an adversary to step on it, resulting in being able to pull it away and trip him. It could be thrown at his face, momentarily blinding him to the attack.

I once fought against an opponent armed with sword and cloak for a documentary. The fight took place on steps. They were attractive Palladian steps. We had counselled the director that no self-respecting swordsman, outside Hollywood, would fight on steps but he insisted and we demurred. I was armed with sword and dagger. He thrust at my face and my move, previously rehearsed on flat ground, was to duck slightly, parrying and lifting his sword with my dagger as I closed for a shoulder check, stepping forward onto my left foot. As you may imagine the move had to be executed with some urgency. I sprang forward with my full weight and my right foot lodged against a step, which prevented it from being able to pivot. All the strain went to my knee and it ripped my cruciate ligaments. The pain was intense. With the assistance of whisky and painkillers I managed to stumble through a few more isolated moves to complete the sequence but that night in hospital I contemplated the importance of

Detail of rapier hilt, Victoria and Albert Museum (© V&A Images)

fighting on suitable ground. The controlled environment of the fence schools was all very well but the swordsman needed also to train on uneven ground, cobbled streets, mud and slippery grass.

Case of rapiers

Another system, though not one advocated by Marozzo, was to fight with a rapier in each hand. It was called the 'case of rapiers'. I know of no instances where a 'case of rapiers' has been reported being used in an actual duel, though there are examples of swords being manufactured in pairs so that they fit into a single scabbard; hence the expression 'case'. Their hilts have been flattened on one side in order to fit together in the scabbard and appear to the eye as one sword. Being able to produce two swords from a single scabbard had elements of surprise and intimidation. Di Grassi was a great fan of fighting

Case of rapiers, after Agrippa

with two swords, suggesting that one can be used to feint, while the other is used to strike. However he tells the fencer that he should not continually 'strike his enemy with one and defend his person with the other'. For there to be an advantage, attacks should be equally strong and varied from either sword.

Using the rapier primarily for attack and the left-hand weapon primarily for defence was better done with a dagger as the companion arm. From the mid-sixteenth century to the first quarter of the seventeeth, 'rapier and dagger' was by far the most common system of civilian sword combat. In the next chapter we look at the lovely matched rapier and dagger belonging to King Henry IV of France and consider a country in which the duelling craze received extreme popularity.

Anonymous 17th century portait of Henri IV, Musée Des Beaux-Arts, Grenoble (Photo © Josse/Leemage)

Chapter 10

The Sword of Henri IV, King of France

Henri III of Navarre, who became King Henri IV of France on 2 August 1589, has often been lionized as the greatest and most respected monarch in that nation's history. His reign was opposed by the Catholic League and he had to fight for his kingdom. Ultimately Henri united the country after years of rancorous religious strife, restored it to prosperity and returned it to European political and cultural dominance. He was also a strong but benevolent ruler. On accession to the throne he declared, 'If God allows me to live, I will see that there is not a single labourer in my kingdom who does not have a chicken in his pot every Sunday'. Henri IV was a great king and such was the iconic potency of his sword that Napoleon carried it with him in his carriage when on campaign. He thought it would bring good luck. That sword now rests in the Musée de l'Armée in Paris. It is a rapier.

The base colour of the hilt and most of the blade is a seductive shade of blue, contrasting beautifully with dense swirls of gold ornament. 'Bluing', a common treatment for weapons and armour of the period, is created by a combination of chemical and heat treatments that produce a layer of oxidisation on the steel's surface. It gave objects a decorative splendour that was the height of fashion. Depending on the actual chemicals and oils used, each having different refractive properties, various shades of blue or black were possible. Henri's rapier has lost a little of its original colour over time but it would once have flashed with the brightest iridescent blue. A gorgeous, dazzling blue that would have made the metal seem almost liquid, appearing to have layer upon layer of graded light with seemingly infinite depths and, thrown into relief by these brilliant hues of blue, was a trellis of 'counterfeit-damascened' gold. Counterfeit-damascening was a popular decorative technique whereby an intricate interlace of lines was hatched onto the surface of the metal and then filled with fine gold wire. As a final flourish the artist swordsmith has dappled one side of the blade with pools of light, in the form of twelve mother-of-pearl plaques, each with an intaglio engraving of a sign of the zodiac. Other medallions, some plain, some carved with symbols, decorate key points of the hilt. Henri IV's rapier was an ornate item of costume jewellery, a fashionable accessory but also a serviceable weapon of self-defence.

When Henri married his second wife, Marie de Medici, in Paris on 13 December 1600, this exquisite weapon was presented to him by the city authorities. It came complete with an *en suite* companion dagger. A cynic might find amusement in the choice of such a gift, given that the occasion of Henri's first marriage, to Marguerite de Valois on 24 August 1572, was the flashpoint for the infamous St Bartholomew's Day Massacre, when the streets of Paris ran with Protestant blood. Thousands were slaughtered in an orgy of religious hatred. Perhaps the burghers of Paris wished Henri to have the means to defend himself this time around.

At the time of his first marriage, he was plain Henri of Navarre, leader of the French Protestants or 'Huguenots' as they were more commonly known. France had been torn apart by religious conflict for years and marriage to the Catholic Marguerite de Valois, known as La Reine Margot, was intended as an act of reconciliation. Loyal to his Protestant convictions, Henri spent most of the service standing outside the church. When asked to pledge her vows, the nineteen-year-old 'Margot' remained silent and King Charles IX placed his hand on her head, obliging her to nod acceptance.

By the time of Henri's marriage to Marie de Medici, he had become King Henri IV of France and converted publicly to Catholicism. In due course he became one of France's best loved kings and, for a time at least, quelled the wars of religion with The Treaty of Nantes in 1598, assuring tolerance for both Protestant and Catholic beliefs. He was responsible for the regeneration of Paris and much of the architecture still stands today, including his wonderful Pont Neuf, at one end of which is his proud equestrian statue. As with all other statues of French monarchs, it was torn down during the Revolution but it was the first to be put back, following the restoration of the monarchy in 1814. The gigantic bronze horse was originally sculpted and cast by a pupil of Michelangelo and intended for the monument of Ferdinand, Duke of Tuscany. The duke died before it was completed and his successor gave the horse to Marie de Medici, who had it shipped to France. The vessel carrying it was shipwrecked off the coast of Normandy and the statue remained at the bottom of the English Channel for over a year. Recovered at great expense, it finally arrived in Paris and was set upon its plinth in 1614, remaining without a rider until finally mounted with the superb bronze figure of Henri IV in 1635 – twenty-five years after his death. His fame and his popularity endured.

A large painting by Ingres, first shown in 1814, and now in a private collection, titled *Don Pedro of Toledo Kissing the Sword of Henri IV*, is based on the story that Don Pedro, ambassador of France's long-standing enemy, Philip II of Spain, encountered a page carrying the sword of Henri IV in the Louvre palace. He dropped to his knees and kissed the sword saying: 'I render honour to the most glorious sword in

Christendom'. It highlights the great esteem in which this monarch was held and also the lasting significance of the sword as a symbol of royal power. On the pommel of Henri's sword, an inlaid French inscription reads:

A CET HENRY VAINQUEUR	TO THIS HENRY THE CONQUEROR,
LES ASTRES PLUS FIDELL	[MAY] THE MOST FAITHFUL STARS
DEPARTENT LE BONHEUR	BESTOW HAPPINESS,
ORDINAIRE AUX MERVEILE	FROM THE ORDINARY TO THE MARVELLOUS

On the bars of the hilt is another inscription in French, which may be rendered (loosely) as:

LE FER FLAMBOYANT	THE FLAMING BLADE
A CET VAINQUEUR [GIFT]	TO THIS CONQUEROR
LES ASTRES PLUS FIDELLES	[FROM] THE MOST FAITHFUL STARS
VA L'AER ASTONNANT	CLEAVES THE AIR TO THE ASTONISHMENT
DE CEUS QUIL ATTERRE	OF THOSE WHOM HE OVERTHROWS
PAR MER ET PAR TERRE	BY SEA AND BY LAND

Also one in Latin:

PROTECTOR PIORUM TERROR	PROTECTOR OF THE GODLY. TERROR
IMPIORUM CREDENTIUM CUSTOS	OF THE UNGODLY. GUARDIAN OF THE
	FAITHFUL.
IMPIORUM TERROR	TERROR OF THE UNGODLY.

The intaglio medallions on the hilt display the arms of France and of the Medici, the fleur de lys surmounted with the royal crown and the insignia of The Order of the Holy Spirit, a chivalric order founded by Henri III in 1578, to which Henri IV belonged. Set between the zodiac plaques on the front of the blade are commemorations of his military victories and other key moments in his life, including the Battle of Ivry, his reconciliation with Henri III and the recovery of Paris. The reverse of the blade carries a dedication to the occasion of the king's marriage:

LE ROI HENRI DE BOURBON IIII DE CE NOM PAR LA GRACE DE DIEU ROY DE FRANCE ET DE NAVARRE ET DE MONTMELIANT ET MAITRE DE SALUCE LE 13 DE DESCEMBRE EPOUSA MARIE DE MEDICI

KING HENRY OF BOURBON, FOURTH OF THIS NAME, BY THE GRACE OF GOD KING OF FRANCE AND NAVARRE AND MONTMELIANT AND MASTER OF SALUCE, MARRIED MARIE DE MEDICI THIS 13TH OF DECEMBER

In 1600 Henri was at the height of his powers but it had been a long journey and he had been an unlikely candidate to wear the French crown. When King Henri II was killed in a jousting accident in 1559, a series of misfortunes quickly extinguished his direct descendents. His first son, Francois II, husband of Mary Queen of Scots, died within a year of ascending the throne. Charles IX, his second son, died of tuberculosis in 1574 and was succeeded by his brother, Henri III. In 1589, Henri III was assassinated

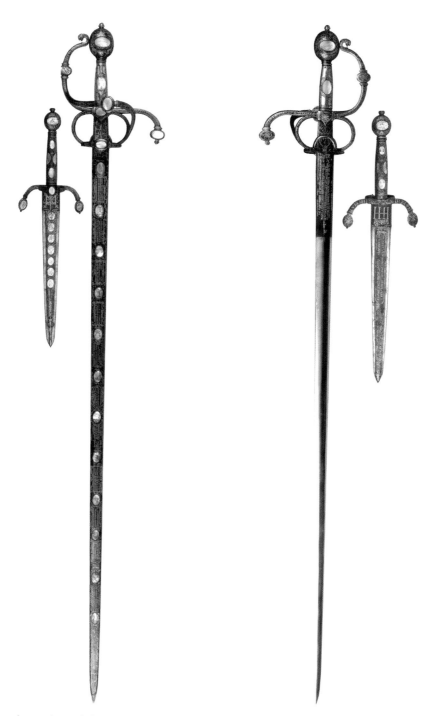

Front and rear views of the rapier and matching dagger of Henri IV (rapier: Musee de l'armee Paris, Dist. RMN © Pascal Segrett; dagger: by kind permission of the Trustees of the Wallace Collection, London)

by a Dominican friar, Jacques Clémant, who stabbed him in the stomach with a concealed knife. The king pulled the knife out and struck the friar in the face, before falling. He had no natural heirs and on his deathbed he named Henri of Navarre as his successor. This Henri, our Henri, could claim a direct line of descent back to Philippe VI, king of France in the fourteenth century. Furthermore, his wife was Henri II's daughter, Marguerite de Valois. He was of royal blood and married to royal blood and so, at the age of thirty-six, Henri of Navarre became Henri IV of France, founding the Bourbon dynasty. He ruled at a period not only of religious conflict but also when the cult of duelling had reached its zenith in France. It has been calculated from legal records that over 4,000 gentlemen were killed in duels during the last two decades of Henri's reign and that he granted 7,000 pardons for duelling in a period of nineteen years – averaging more than one a day! His chief minister, the Duc de Sully, complained, 'that the facility with which the King forgave duels tended to multiply them'.

The duel of Seigneur de la Chastaigneraye and le comte de Jarnac

Historians of the duel often cite an encounter between François de Vivonne, Seigneur de la Chastaigneraye and Guy Chabot, le comte de Jarnac as a point of transition between the medieval judicial duel and the renaissance duel of honour. It occurred in 1547, just six years before Henri was born. By the time he was a young man, duelling in France had reached epidemic proportions.

Chastaigneraye, at the Dauphin's bidding, had accused Jarnac of being a kept man and having a sexual relationship with his stepmother, the Duchesse d'Etampes. Jarnac had countered that Chastaigneraye was lying. 'Giving the lie' was grounds for a duel and Chastaigneraye, who had the reputation of being the greatest swordsman and wrestler in France, requested the field. At first this was refused by the then king, François I, but when Henri II came to the throne in 1547, the application was granted. In cause, it was in the spirit of the duel of honour but in custom, having been sanctioned by royal decree, it followed the practices of the judicial duel.

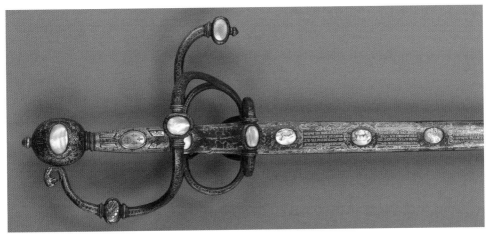

Detail of the hilt of Henry IV's rapier (Musee de l'armee Paris, Dist. RMN ©Pascal Segret)

Jarnac was given the choice of arms, though by right this belonged to Chastaigneraye, and he stipulated thirty different kinds of armament for foot and mounted combat. Chastaigneraye complained, 'Jarnac means to challenge my wits and my purse'. It was the custom in duels for both protagonists to be armed alike. Fearing Chastaigneraye's famed superiority at close quarters, Jarnac specified a special type of defence for the left arm, which prevented it from moving at the elbow, thus inhibiting any grappling. Chastaigneraye's right arm was already weakened from a previous injury. There was to be one long dagger worn on a waist-belt and one short dagger stuck into the boot as a further precaution against Chastaigneraye's wrestling tricks. Four swords were brought into the arena (two as reserves) with the provision that whatever happened, neither party was to have any more. In addition to these and other detailed specifications, both duellists were searched before the encounter to ensure that they had neither magical charms, 'wicked words', mottoes nor prayers concealed about them. In a superstitious age such supernatural assistance was commonly sought.

Eventually, after much stalling and preparation, the two men took to the field. King Henri II presided over the proceedings and all the court factions took sides. Antoine de Bourbon, father of the future Henri IV, was there, a supporter of de Jarnac; the king and his followers were for Chastaigneraye. There were grandstands and attendants and heralds; there was pageantry and fanfare and ceremony. It was said that Chastaigneraye, arrogantly confident of victory, made no effort to prepare, other than to arrange a great banquet for his anticipated triumphal celebrations. In contrast, Jarnac trained assiduously with his fencing master. Jarnac's diligence paid off and France's most celebrated swordsman was cut, in two successive blows, on each of his hamstrings. Even so, the valiant Chastaigneraye, whilst losing a great deal of blood, still made two attempts to spring at his adversary before the king signalled the combat to stop. When his wounds were dressed, Chastaigneraye tore off his bandages repeatedly, crying out, 'kill me, kill me', but no further action was required; he died of his wounds and the court servants consumed his banquet.

The greatest significance of the Chastaigneraye/Jarnac duel was that it was famous. Reports of it spread throughout Europe and it became a template for honourable conduct. La Chastaigneraye and de Jarnac became role-models for others to follow. This was how high-ranking nobles addressed insults and slights of honour and aspiring gentlemen everywhere sought to emulate them. Not everyone could expect to have their grievances arbitrated in official duels authorised by the monarch but they could still fight, making the arrangements themselves, whether legal or not. By his victory, Jarnac may have, to some extent, expunged the slur on his reputation but much more importantly his fame was enhanced. He became a celebrity, immortalized as the originator of the '*coup de Jarnac*' and vanquisher of a superior foe. For his part, Chastaigneraye was not disgraced. His bravery in fighting on when all was lost and his willingness to die was what was remembered. The original cause of the duel was forgotten. Embracing death transforms a loser into a hero. In the halls of duelling posterity there are no losers, save those who lose their nerve and display cowardice. For many the challenge to a duel was a welcome opportunity to prove their courage and achieve fame. The social conditions of the time were fallow ground for such exploits and the Chastaigneraye/Jarnac duel grabbed the popular imagination. It was not a single event that changed everything but it was arguably an accelerant. Not only did it help to glamorize duelling, it also marked the end of the old legal procedures.

In the decades that followed, duels were seldom either official or public; increasingly they were private, often secret affairs. By the time Henri IV took the throne, private duelling had become all the rage. Like his contemporary, Elizabeth I of England, he attempted to ban it, issuing the Edict of Blois in 1602 and the Edict of Trent in1608. Yet his ready inclination to grant pardons rather undermined these efforts. Duelling was endemic and increasingly casual. There were those who sought out duels just for the sport of it. One such enthusiast was the Chevalier D'Andrieux. On one occasion his opponent boasted, 'Chevalier, you will be the tenth man I have killed in a duel', to which D'Andrieux replied, 'and you will be my seventy-second!' He was as good as his word. D'Andrieux was reputed to offer to spare the life of a defeated opponent on condition that they deny God. When they complied, he cut their throats, delighting at killing their body and their soul with a single stroke. In an atmosphere of religious hatred, such depraved thinking was quick to take root.

Benefit of Clergy
Duelling was also illegal in England and, if a man killed another in a duel, the deed was considered murder and punishable by death. However there was a legal loophole, much used, known as 'Benefit of Clergy'. If an accused duellist could prove that he was a lay preacher or cleric of the Church, then he had the right to be tried by canon (Church) law rather than by the secular courts. Church courts tended to take rather a lenient view of first-time offenders and generally let the accused off with a hefty fine; a policy that had the added benefit of boosting the Church's coffers. Proposed limitations to the exercise of this right were one of the aggravating causes that led to Henry VIII's split with Rome.

Proof of cleric status hinged on the ability of the defendant to read a religious text in Latin. The first verse of Psalm 51 became the standard – '*Miserere mei, Deus, secundum misericordiam tuam*' (Have mercy upon me, O God, according to thine heartfelt mercifulness) – so that even the illiterate were able to claim 'Benefit' by simply committing 'The Miserere' to memory. Ben Johnson, the renowned Elizabethan dramatist, was involved in a number duels and had cause to seek the protection offered by this expedient. His thumb was branded with a black spot, signifying conviction by this process. For most duellists this supposed stigma was a mark they bore with pride.

Seconds
According to secular law, those who accompanied the principles in a fatal duel and facilitated arrangements, the 'seconds', could be charged as accessories to murder.

In the old judicial duel, court heralds ensured that certain formalities were adhered to and the king had the ultimate authority of being able to halt the fighting by throwing down his baton. However, when gentlemen took it into their heads to venture to the duelling ground of their own accord, the need arose to regulate the affair with some semblance of ordered procedure. This gave rise to the introduction of seconds; assistants who were on hand to see fair play, to negotiate terms and, in the unhappy event that their champion should lose, to get him medical attention. In spite of his edicts against duels, Henri IV favoured them in private. When the Marquis de Crequi asked leave to fight Philip of Savoy, he is reported to have said 'Go, and if I were not a king I would be your second'.

As Henri of Navarre, attending the court of Henri III of France, the future Henri IV was exposed to the new duelling culture in full flood. On one famous occasion in 1578, known as the '*Duel des Mignons*', the seconds played a notable role. '*Mignon*' can be loosely translated as 'cutie' and the word had disparaging connotations, denoting a type of courtier who was both effeminate and shallow. Henri III, renowned for his homosexual preferences, in addition to his appetite for mistresses, had many *mignons* at his court. Two of these gentlemen, Jacques de Quelus and Charles de Balzac, Baron d'Etrangues, quarrelled over some ladies, for whose attentions they were vying. A possible, deeper motive behind the quarrel was the factionalism at court. D'Etrangues was a supporter of the king's bitter rival, the Duc de Guise. Quelus was a supporter and favourite of the king. Henri III may have been put out a little by the inconstancy of his pet's affections but was even more distressed at the outcome of the quarrel. Quelus and d'Etrangues fought a duel near the Porte Saint-Antoine and each brought along two seconds – Mangiron and Livarot for Quelus, Riberac and Schomberg for d'Etrangues. No sooner had the principals begun their combat, than Mangiron picked a quarrel with Riberac and Liverot challenged Schomberg. The fight was furious with all parties receiving serious wounds. Mangiron died on the spot and Riberac the following day. Schomberg was killed by a thrust but Liverot survived, only to be killed in another duel two years later. D'Etrangues, though wounded, survived and Quelus, who received no less than nineteen cuts, expired within the month. On his deathbed Quelus was still protesting that the combat was unfair because D'Etrangues had been additionally armed with a dagger. He complained that when he had pointed this out to his foe, D'Etrangues had scoffed 'So much the worse for you. You should not have been such a fool as to have left it at home'.

Companion dagger

As noted in the preceding chapter it became increasingly common in the sixteenth century for the rapier to be used in conjunction with a 'companion dagger'. Rapiers were long weapons and when extended at full thrust there was a perceptible time delay before the weapon could be brought back to a close guard. A dagger afforded the opportunity to maintain constant and instant protection, whilst at the same time exploring long-range probing attacks with the sword. Where chance permitted, a dagger could be used to attack in its own right and employed to engage and occupy the enemy's weapon during a counterattack.

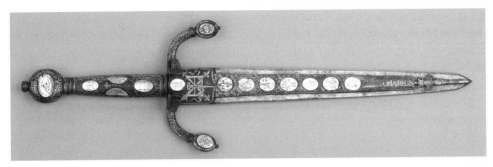

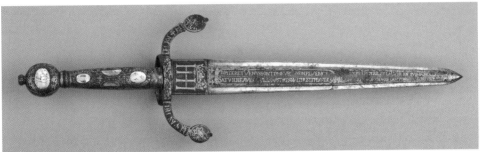

Henry IV's dagger – front and rear (by kind permission of the Trustees of the Wallace Collection, London)

The companion dagger to the rapier presented to Henri IV by the city of Paris on the occasion of his marriage to Marie de Medici is now in The Wallace Collection in London. I have held it and it is remarkably light, though by no means flimsy. You could trust your life to making a parry with it. It was made *en suite* with the sword; blued, counterfeit-damascened in gold and inlaid with mother-of-pearl medallions. The bluing has survived less well than on the sword, and now appears as a russet brown, though this colour is still very pleasing against the gold. Gold monograms of the king, a crowned 'H', and his bride, 'MM', adorn the hilt and inlaid on the quillons is the same verse about 'Henri the conqueror' that adorns the pommel of the sword.

Superimposed onto the surface of both faces of the plain steel blade is a decorative central rib in blued steel that has been cut with ornate terminals. Seven mother-of pearl medallions have been inset into this rib on the back of the blade, each bearing emblems such as the fleur-de-lys and other heraldic foliage. Inlaid into the rib on the front side of the blade is an astrological prophecy that reads:

> *JUPITER ET VENUS SONT DHEUREUSE INFLUENCE*
> *STURN AVEC QUES MARS TRES MALIGNS ET PERVERS*
> *MERCUR ET SOLEIL ET LA LUNE EN PUISSANCE*
> *MEDIOCRES TOUSIOURS GOVERNENT L'UNIVERS*

Perilously close to the 'wicked words' proscribed for the Chastaigneraye/Jarnac duel, such astrological incantations were taken extremely seriously in sixteenth-century France. This was the world of Nostradamus. He had died only thirty-four years earlier, having served both Catherine de Medici and her son Charles IX. On seeing the infant Henri of Navarre, he had predicted that he would become king of France. It is possibly a record of the astrological configurations for the day but I had struggled with the meaning of the last line. Surely it could not mean, 'the mediocre will always govern the world' – though we may all hold views in that vein from time to time. '*Mediocris*' in Latin means 'middle, moderate, tolerable' suggesting a translation along the lines of:

> JUPITER AND VENUS ARE OF GOOD ASPECT,
> SATURN WITH MARS MALIGN AND MOST PERVERSE
> SUN, MOON AND MERCURY WITH POWER ARE DECKED.
> AND MODERATES EVER RULE THE UNIVERSE.

This would, at least, acknowledge Henri's moderating and middle path policies of religious toleration. '*Mediocres*' also has echoes of Aristotle's 'Golden Mien', by which he held that all excess was wrong and only a delicate middle path would hold the world in balance. This was the French Renaissance; classical authorities were held in high esteem.

Monograms, foliage and the royal standard of Navarre adorn the mother-of-pearl medallions on the grip. On one side of the pommel is a medallion carved with a hand grasping a quill pen and the legend: '*JE RE[SIST]E.A.LA.FORCE*' (I stand firm against force). On the other side of the pommel is a medallion with the words: '*PRUDENCE MESURE LA. [FI]N DE TOUTE CHOSE*' (Prudence measures the end of everything) and the ancient sign of the 'eye-in-the-hand', a symbol associated with the Order of the Holy Spirit. This pan-cultural icon is thought to have originated in the Middle East but is to be found in most parts of the world, including in the art of native North and Central Americans, throughout Africa, India and Asia. The eye represents both sensing and observation, while the hand signifies doing and acting. Together these two abilities represent omniscience and omnipotence. It is a talisman offering magical protection.

Offering a rather more mundane form of protection is a side-ring extending from the junction of the grip and the quillons. Side-rings were depicted as early as 1536 on the daggers in Marozzo's treatise. Marozzo, a founding father of the Bolognese school, also shows the quillons turning downwards and away from the plane of the blade. Accordingly, such daggers are often referred to as the 'Bolognese type'. These angulated quillons, a feature also found on the Henri IV dagger, had the potential to catch a sword, trapping it between quillon and blade. Such a move requires impeccable timing and is not easily achieved but, with a sharp twist, you can get some purchase on the attacking blade. It is extremely unlikely that you will be able to break the opponent's blade but, by putting it under resistance, you can at least break your opponent's timing and thereby gain an advantage.

A specialized form of parrying dagger, purposely designed to catch and hinder an adversary's blade, was an ingenious spring-loaded version. Operated by a sliding stud on the ricasso of the blade, the two sides of the blade shot open by means of the spring mechanism. These were hinged at the ricasso, either side of a stiletto-like

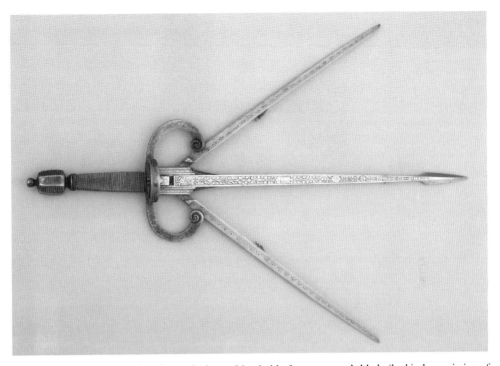

Spring-operated dagger designed to assist in catching hold of an opponent's blade (by kind permission of the Trustees of the Wallace Collection, London)

central section, producing a three-bladed weapon. I have set off a magnificent example of this type housed in the Wallace Collection and it is astonishing how smoothly and powerfully the mechanism still works today. I also had a replica of one and it was an irresistible toy to play with. In fighting with the replica I found it extremely easy to catch and delay the opposing sword. The popular idea that daggers of this type could be used to 'break' a sword is however nonsense. It would require wrists of unimaginable power and the unlikely co-operation of the opposition. It was a notion that probably came about in the nineteenth century from a misreading of Saviolo, who uses the word 'break' to mean parry.

Another type of dagger erroneously described as a 'sword-breaker', has one edge of the blade deeply incised, producing a series of jagged teeth. The theory being that a parried sword can catch in these and then be twisted to break it. I find the idea implausible. Such blades are more correctly described as 'sword-catchers' and the function of the teeth was to ensnare and impede the opponent's blade. They had the added advantage of making it impossible to grab the blade and wrest it from an opponent's hand.

One extreme measure to prevent the left hand being used to grab weapons was employed by the Vicomte d'Allemagne and the Sieur de la Rocque. They fought a duel in which they held each other by the left hand, whilst endeavouring to strike each other with daggers in their right hands. This bizarre combat took place during the

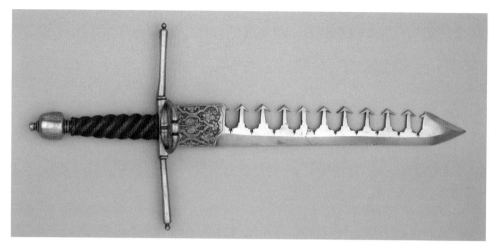

Another dagger designed to catch opponent's blade (by kind permission of the Trustees of the Wallace Collection, London)

reign of Louis XIII, Henri IV's son, but before we look beyond Henri's reign, we need to track back a little and consider his life before he became the king of France.

Henri of Navarre

Navarre, a small independent kingdom that straddled the Pyrenees, sat uneasily between its ally France and her Hapsburg enemy Spain. It was the Basque lands. Since 1513 the southern end of the country had been annexed by Spain. For France, what remained was a vital buffer zone guarding the mountain passes; the Kingdom of Navarre had power at the French court. Henri was born in 1553, in Pau, on the French side of the mountains. As an infant he was given to a noble family in the locality with instructions that he should be brought up as a country boy, not '*mignardé délicatement*' (nancy-fancy). He ate plain food and was encouraged to associate with the local peasant boys, who gave no deference to his rank. It was an experience that made him tough, practical and self-reliant. In later life, snooty Parisian courtiers sneered at some of his uncouth country ways.

Henri's mother, Jeanne d'Albret was a zealous Calvinist convert. His father, Antoine de Bourbon, had for several years attended both Mass and Protestant services, seeing which way the wind blew until, for political expediency, he finally came down on the Catholic side in 1561. Within a year he had sent Henri's mother away– they were never to meet again – and France had plunged into a horrific civil war of religion. It was then that an 8-year-old Henri came to stay with his father. Jeanne had made him promise to never attend Mass, threatening that she would disown and disinherit him if he did. Antoine, on the other hand, compelled the boy to do so by means of flogging. Perhaps a psychologist might say that Henri's determination to heal the religious wounds of the nation after becoming king was the cry of a child still trying to reconcile his parents. France may be grateful for his family's dysfunction.

Kings of Navarre spent their time not in their own small kingdom but at the French court in Paris and that is where the young Henri came to continue his education. He had private tutors and also attended a college. Among his classmates were the 12-year-old King Charles IX and his younger brother, the future Henri III of France, the man who would one day bequeath Henri his throne. Their mother, Catherine de Medici, governed France as regent. Also at the college was the future Duc de Guise, nearly three years Henri's senior. As the founder of the Catholic League, de Guise was destined to become Henri's sworn enemy. In fact signs of the enmity between them were apparent in their schooldays. An English diplomat reported an argument between the two boys that 'progressed from words to deeds', for which, we are told, 'they were chastised'. Whether these 'deeds' were any more than wrestling or fisticuffs is unrecorded. Whatever the nature of the altercation, all the young princes and gentlemen would have received regular fencing lessons and it is probable that they received this martial education together. Italian influences dominated court behaviour and practices and it was Italian masters of fence who led the way in arms. Frenchmen went to Italy to study fencing and Italian masters came to France to ply their trade. As an adult, Henri practiced regularly with a French master, Pierre Duportal, but as a boy he was instructed in the Italian school.

An account by Pierre de Bourdeille, the Seigneur de Brantome, a contemporary chronicler of duelling and Chastaigneraye's nephew, reports seeing Charles IX

> with a very finely wrought sword and dagger, which seemed to have cutting edges, though in fact they did not. Against him with the same arms came the Milanese, Pompée, who had taught him to dance and use arms.

It is a point worth noting that many fencing masters also taught their charges to dance, both disciplines requiring muscular strength, coordinated grace and a fine sense of timing. Charles was only fifteen at the time but Brantome goes on to tell us that 'the king showing such skill with the arms, and such assurance in combat, . . . knocked the said Pompée to the ground and pretended to kill him'.

Afterwards, Charles' brother Henri, a year younger, tried his hand 'against Sylvie his fencing master and did the same to him'. Spelling, and especially the rendition of proper names, was highly eccentric at this period. 'Sylvie' was often also rendered as 'Salvio' and it is just possible, though by no means certain, that this Sylvie/Salvio was none other than Vincentio Saviolo. The celebrated master did not travel to England until 1590, twenty-five years later, and we know that before that he was teaching in Europe. It is therefore a possibility that it was a young Saviolo who first taught the future Henri IV how to fight. Writing of Saviolo in 1591, John Florio commented 'hee hath good skill in every kinde of weapon . . . hee is a good dancer, hee dances verie well'. Such a man would certainly seem a likely associate of the terpsichorean Pompée. If the young Henri was indeed taught by these two masters, their deference in allowing themselves to be beaten by adolescent boys must have been quite a shock to him and very different to the 'no quarter' rough and tumble of his childhood in Navarre.

The 'Science of Arms'

An important work published in 1553, the year of Henri's birth, was the '*Trattato di Scientia d'Arme*' by Camillo Agrippa. It marked a shift from the art to the science of arms. Agrippa was a mathematician, architect and engineer. Renaissance man strove for ideas of classical beauty, where balance, symmetry and harmony governed all the arts, including the fighting arts. However there was also a quest for scientific rationalism and Agrippa was among the first to apply intricate geometric matrices to the swordsman's art, a practice taken to extremes by the Spanish school a decade or so later. He was not a professional fencing master but, like all his contemporaries, spent much of his time in the *sala d'arma*. What is important about his treatise is not that it shows us innovative moves, though he places a new emphasis on the thrust, but that he seeks to analyse them according to scientific principles. This was the spirit of the age and both the method and procedure of duelling were still being governed by the Italian masters.

In 1567, the seventeen-year-old Charles IX ratified the Statutes for the Parisian *Maistres jouers et escrimeurs d'espee*, an equivalent institution to the London Masters of Defence, with admission along similar lines. It was the beginning of a French assault on Italian supremacy. The first treatise by a known French author to deal with the 'new style' of rapier combat was that of Henri de Saint Didier in 1573. Saint Didier's '*Traite*' was dedicated to Charles IX. Like Agrippa's work he advocated having a more or less straight sword-arm, whether guarding or attacking and, like Saviolo, he championed combat with the sword alone. His publication coincided with Henri being kept a virtual prisoner at court by the mercurial Charles IX, following the 'St Bartholomew Day Massacre'. Perhaps Henri, feeling caged and bored, spent time taking instruction from M. Saint Didier, gentleman of Provence? Had he usurped Pompée and Salvio as the court *maitres d'armes*? Intriguingly, the artistic style of the figures that illustrate Saint Didier's work are virtually identical to those in Saviolo's work twenty years later. Saint Didier is more copiously illustrated and he shows many

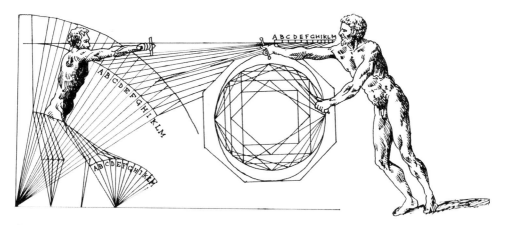

Geometric studies of the swordsman's guards and attacks according to Agrippa 1553

The rapier fight after Saint Didier 1573 – note sword grabbing

blade-grabbing disarms but the main difference is that Saviolo depicts his fighters on a grid, whereas Saint Didiers' are on uneven ground in a natural landscape.

I have no doubt that the esoteric methods of these masters could, in the right hands, be effective and deadly in a duel with rapiers but they were of very little use on the battlefield. Whether Henri learned his military skills from Pompeio, Salvio, Saint Didier or from another, he certainly learned them well. He was a formidable soldier – and he needed to be.

Wars of Religion

The French Wars of Religion (1562–1598) are far too complex to go into here in any detail. They involve too many characters and too many shifting alliances but they are nonetheless an important thread through Henri's life, so I shall endeavour to summarize. The Catholic faction was championed by the Dukes of Guise, while the Protestants, known as Huguenots, were led by Louis de Bourbon, Prince de Condé, Henri's uncle. An adolescent Louis IX, under the control of his Catholic mother, Catherine de Medici, nominally supported the Catholic cause but royal power was not quite absolute in these uncertain times and some leading Protestant nobles held immense power both in the country and at court. Moreover, France's finances were in a very poor state and seeking peace between the warring factions was the economic expedient. Appeasement, intrigue and clandestine politics were the order of the day. Henri's mother was of royal blood (descended from Francois I) and so, although a Protestant, held high rank at court. Henri enjoyed the same status and privileges.

At the outset of the wars, Condé, supported by English finance and German troops, had a certain amount of military success until he was killed at the Battle of Jarnac in 1569. His heir apparent was the 16-year-old Henri. The austere Gaspard de Coligny, Henri's regent since the death of his father at the siege of Rouen in 1562, assumed control of the Huguenot forces. In 1572, after reaching his majority, Henri was crowned King Henri III of Navarre. He was nineteen-years-old. Later that year he was married to Maguerite de Valois, a Catholic of the royal blood. It was intended that the union should seal an uneasy truce and bring peace but tragically, on the day of the wedding, what became known as the 'St Bartholomew's Day Massacre' erupted. Fearing a Huguenot coup, the Duke of Guise sent agents to kill Coligny at his Paris lodgings. His body was thrown from the window into the street where it was mutilated, castrated, dragged through the mud, hung up on a gallows and finally burned. Nothing in the human experience can compare to the violent depravities awakened in a mob fired with religious zeal. During the following five days mob violence took over completely and over 2,000 Huguenots were slaughtered in Paris. Their murderous frenzy spread to the provinces, where it is estimated that a further 8,000 Huguenots were slaughtered in their homes. Henri and his cousin, Henri de Bourbon the second Prince of Condé, were only spared the sword by agreeing to convert to Catholicism. Both were kept in Paris, effectively under house arrest, for the next two years; though they retained their status and privilege within the confines of the court. It was a period when Henri likely spent much of his day practising his martial skills.

Two years later Charles IX died and his younger brother Henri succeeded to the throne. He was his mother's favourite, known to her as '*chers yeux*' ('precious eyes'). Both Henri of Navarre and the Prince of Condé left Paris and recanted their previously enforced Catholic conversion. Henri III of France sought reconciliation with the Huguenots and sued for peace. In response the Duke de Guise formed the

'Catholic League', an extremist fundamentalist movement sworn to eradicate Protestantism from the country. It was backed both by Spain and the Pope. Sporadic military action and pockets of civilian uprising flared in various parts of the country over the next decade. Henri of Navarre proved himself an able soldier. In 1580 he took Cahors, street by street. It was hard won and Henri fought at the head of his men over the course of five days. Cahors established his reputation for courage and honour, as his wife Marguerite wrote, 'not of a prince but of a bold captain'. Both sides saw victories and

Marguerite de Valois –'La Reine Margot' (Museé Condé, Chantilly)

reverses but nothing much changed, other than the desperate plight of the people, which continued to worsen.

Matters finally came to a head when King Henri III's younger brother, the duc d'Alencon, died of malaria in 1584. The king had no children, which meant that the Protestant Henri of Navarre became the rightful heir to the throne. De Guise's agenda was now to depose Henri III as well as to wipe out the Huguenots. So began a tripartite struggle between Henri III of France, Henri I of Guise and Henri III of Navarre – 'The War of the Three Henrys'. At first, Henri III was inclined to be against the Huguenots in an attempt to appease the De Guise faction, though he also wavered with periodic attempts to protect his childhood friend and now heir, Henri of Navarre. As before, military action was intermittent and intrigue constant. Only on one occasion did Henri, reluctantly, engage with royalist forces. It was at Coutras in 1587 and he was victorious. However on 12 May 1588, the Paris mob once again changed the course of events. Known as 'The Day of the Barricades' , they chained carts together on the streets, took control of the city, overthrew the government and caused Henri III to flee Paris. He set up court at Blois and, the following year, he lured de Guise into a trap there and had him murdered.

The Catholic League had other leaders and continued its campaigns with renewed vigour and with renewed resources from Philip II of Spain. To counter them, Henri of Navarre raised a sizeable Huguenot army, supplemented with thousands of Swiss and German mercenaries. In 1589 he joined forces with Henri III against the League. The two Henris met on 30 April and embraced each other as the childhood friends they had once been. They had not met since Navarre had left Paris in 1574. By the end of July 1589 their combined forces, around 30,000 men, were laying siege to the League stronghold of Paris. On 1 August, Henri III of France was assassinated.

Henri of Navarre became Henri IV of France and was, in his own words 'a king without a kingdom, a warrior without money, and a husband without a wife'. This last remark was a reference to his now-estranged relationship with Marguerite. He borrowed more money from England and set about winning his kingdom. He began with Normandy where, apart from Paris, the League was at its strongest. He defeated their forces in a major victory at Arques in September and continued to make small gains over the winter. On 14 March 1590, Henri, with vastly inferior forces, faced the Catholic League at the Battle of Ivry. At a key point in the battle, when his troops, thinking Henri killed, had turned to flee, he made his way to the front telling them, '*Tournez visage, afin que si vous ne voulez combattre, vous me voyiez du moins mourir*' ('Turn your faces, so that even if you don't fight you can at least see me dying'). His charismatic leadership and personal heroism inspired his army to a famous victory. A painting of the battle by Rubens celebrates Henri's courageous flair and depicts him dressed as a classical hero, as was the iconographic fashion of the time. Afterwards, Henri moved methodically towards Paris, taking towns and cutting off the city's supply routes as he went. By July he was encamped at Montmartre, just outside the city walls. However, after months of laying siege, his army was driven off by League forces in September. It was a bitter setback.

More years of fighting followed but in July 1593 he abjured Protestantism and became a Catholic. This time it was of his own volition. Finally, in the following year, he entered Paris, his capital city, when he is alleged to have said, '*Paris vaut bien une messe*' (Paris is worth a mass). It wasn't the end of the fighting entirely; he declared war on Spain in 1595 to demonstrate that support for the League was support for a foreign enemy. Military action was mainly in the north – the Spanish captured Calais in 1596 – but peace was finally achieved with the Treaty of Nantes in 1598. Healing took a little longer.

Le Vert Gallant

Henri was known affectionately as '*le vert gallant*' (green gallant); an expression that indicated a man full of youthful vigour, in spite of advancing years, and with the connotation that he had a wandering eye. This aspect of his character was celebrated in a royalist anthem popular before and after the French Revolution.

Vive Henri quatre	*Long live Henry Four*
Vive ce Roi valiant	*Long live this valiant king*
Ce diable à quatre	*This fourfold devil*
A le triple talent	*With the three talents*
De boire de battre	*Drinking, fighting*
Et d'être un vert galant	*And womanizing*

The song is intended to humanize rather than trivialize a great man. Henri IV's contribution to the welfare of France was immense. He was a serious, thoughtful and brave leader. It is true, though, that he did have a number of women in his life. He was a compulsive playboy.

On seeing Henri's first wife, Marguerite de Valois, Brantome wrote, 'One had never seen anything lovelier in the world'. However the marriage was childless and, though for quite a while warm and supportive, ultimately unhappy. Both were unfaithful to each other on an epic scale. As well as being a regular *habitué* of Paris brothels, Henri had many mistresses, often several at a time, by which he had several children. During the early years his favourite was Charlotte de Sauve. In 1575 Marguerite wrote, 'I could not endure the pain that I felt and I stopped sleeping with the King my husband'. She found consolation with a series of lovers. The once cordial relations between Henri and Marguerite became increasingly strained and on separate occasions she tried both to poison him and shoot him with a pistol.

It is generally believed that the true love of his life was Gabrielle d'Estrées, who became his mistress in 1591. She was twenty, he thirty-eight. She was a Catholic and it was she who persuaded him to convert for the sake of the peace of the nation. Henri, with his usual no-nonsense approach, appointed her 'Titulary Mistress of His Majesty, the King of France' and made it compulsory for all ambassadors to his court to have an audience with her. She was a powerful and conciliatory negotiator. When Henri converted, the Pope had refused to acknowledge it, believing it insincere, and had continued to support Philip II of Spain's frequent raids in the south. However, Gabrielle interceded with the Pope with the result that he issued an instruction for all religious houses in France to pray for the health of the king. It was the beginning of a dialogue with Catholic interests that finally led to peace and the Treaty of Nantes. Henri had three children by Gabrielle.

In 1599, after having his marriage to Marguerite annulled by the now-friendly Pope, Henri presented Gabrielle d'Estrées, with his coronation ring as a sign of betrothal. Gabrielle was overjoyed at the prospect of marriage to the king, whose fourth child she was carrying. The famously naughty portrait of her, nude with her sister tweaking her nipple (a sign of pregnancy), shows her holding the coronation ring. Tragically, within days of the proposal Gabrielle fell ill and gave birth to a stillborn son before herself dying. Henri was grief-stricken. He went into mourning, wore black and gave her the funeral of a queen. She is remembered in France as La Belle Gabrielle.

Overcoming his sorrow by his usual means of consolation, Henri was quick to find a replacement for his affections, elevating Henriette d'Entragues to chief mistress in the same year. At the same time, political expediency and the lack of a legitimate heir forced him to agree to marriage with Marie de Medici. On news of the engagement,

Anonymous painting (c. 1595) of Gabrielle d'Estrées favourite mistress of Henri IV (right, holding coronation ring), and her sister, the Duchess of Villars. The Duchess' gesture indicates that Gabrielle is pregnant (Musée du Louvre, Paris)

Medallion showing Henri IV and Maria de Medici
(by kind permission of the Trustees of the Wallace
Collection, London)

the Pope sent Henri a sword as a wedding gift – it was a rapier, the hilt fabulously chiseled with scenes from the life of Christ (now in the Musée de l'Armée, Paris). Henri and Marie were married on 13 December 1600. He was in Paris and Marie took her vows by proxy in Florence. The burghers of Paris, so long his sworn enemies, also presented him with a magnificent wedding gift – the thoughtfully designed *en suite* rapier and dagger, celebrating his achievements, that is the subject of this chapter. It is one of the many paradoxes of the sword that it can, on occasion, be a symbol of peace and reconciliation.

The long climb to restore peace and prosperity to a war-torn nation had begun. Henri's chief minister, the Duc de Sully, was the architect of a phenomenal economic recovery and instigated substantial investment in public works. These created employment and brought people together with a sense of national pride. Sully had also been the one to suggest the marriage alliance with Marie de Medici. She bore Henri six children, securing a stable succession, but the marriage was not idyllic. Henri was unfaithful to her from the outset and insisted that she raise his illegitimate children along with her own. Intrigues continued at court but now they were more to do with plots by the queen against the king's mistresses than with affairs of state. The first decade of the seventeenth century was generally a time of healing and growth for France.

Only one blight remained. After so many years of endemic violence, nurtured in an atmosphere of suspicion and hatred, in an era of debased values and disregard for human life, the cult of the duel flourished as never before. Moreover, the nobility had convinced themselves that, despite its worst excesses, dueling was an essential and beneficial safety valve for society. Brantome argued that a few deaths in regulated fights did no harm compared to the conflicts that might otherwise occur if powerful men took up arms against each other with troops of retainers. Superficially he appears to have a point but the reality was that most duels were very silly affairs. One, occurring in the same year that Henri married Marie, typified the senseless violence of the era.

Duel of the Hat

The 'Duel of the Hat' was fought between M. Lagarde and M. Bazanez, both celebrated and quarrelsome duellists of the time. Bazanez decided to provoke Lagarde into a duel by sending him an ostentatiously feathered hat, accompanied by a note declaring that he would wear the hat in public at his peril. The dare was irresistible to Lagarde and, donning the provocative millinery, he promptly set forth.

Within moments of meeting, Lagarde struck the first blow. It snapped down upon Bazanez's head. We are told that the blow was sufficiently hard to both bend the sword and to deflect it. Reportedly Lagarde followed with three thrusts, each of which found their mark, declaring 'this is for the hat', 'this is for the feathers' and 'this is for the tassel'. Though losing blood rapidly and becoming faint, Bazanez managed to wrestle Lagarde to the ground, where, in a frenzied onslaught, he stabbed him fourteen times with his dagger between his neck and his navel, spluttering, 'I am giving you a scarf to wear with the hat'. Before both parties lost consciousness from loss of blood, Lagarde managed to reply by biting off a portion of his assailant's chin and dishing his skull with the pommel of his sword.

Remarkably, both survived the ordeal. Bazanez was to perish in an ambush a few years later. The belligerent Lagarde sustained a long career as a duellist, notorious for his customary challenge: 'I have reduced your house to ashes, ravished your wife, and hanged your children, and I now have the honour to be your mortal enemy'. The sociopathic thuggery of such men was the scourge of the age.

Secrets and privy coats

That first blow to Bazanez's head, reported to be so hard that the sword was both bent and deflected raises the question of whether Bazanez was wearing a 'secret'. Secrets were little iron skullcaps, worn beneath soft headgear. A Soldier, wishing to cut a dash on the battlefield with a *chapeau* might wear one but a secret could also be employed as added security in a duel.

After the St Bartholomew's Day Massacre, Henri was kept a virtual prisoner at court. It was a tense and dangerous environment. In 1575 he wrote in a letter: 'We are nearly always ready to cut each other's throats. We carry daggers and wear mail shirts under our cloaks.' These mail shirts, typically sleeveless, were known as 'privy coats'. They were made of very fine, densely linked mail, tailored precisely to the body and worn 'privately' beneath civilian dress. They were the bulletproof vests of the day, as essential for the young Henri then as to a high-profile politician today. The pugnacious atmosphere of the French court at that time was reminiscent of the English court some twenty years earlier under the reign of Mary I. Her Spanish and English courtiers were constantly at daggers-

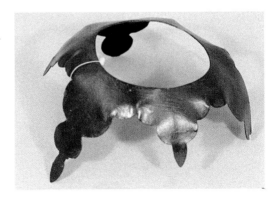

Secret (© The Board of Trustees of the Armouries)

drawn. One anonymous Spaniard in Mary's entourage wrote home in 1554 that 'The English hate us Spaniards, which comes out in violent quarrels between them and us, and not a day passes without some knife-work in the palace between the two nations'. Writing of the Italians, George Silver, stated that they 'seldom fight in their own country unarmed ... a pair of gauntlets upon their hands, and a good shirt of mail upon their bodies'. He intended both to imply an unworthiness to their 'honourable' conduct and to make the case that their long, thrusting rapiers were extremely perilous. In the same way as the bodkin arrowhead was developed in an attempt to defeat armour, perhaps the tuck blade evolved to defeat the privy coat?

Although usually of mail, privy coats were sometimes of brigandine construction, whereby small plates of iron, usually tinned to prevent rust, were riveted onto a fabric foundation. Others were a combination of a brigandine style torso with mail for the skirt, neck and shoulders. Privy coats could be worn covertly for a duel, as well as for everyday protection such as Henri required at court. Another form of armour for the duel was the 'doublet of defence', which was an ordinary doublet that had been especially thickly quilted. Amongst gentlemen of honour, however, the wearing of such defences was frowned upon. In 1600 Jean de La Taille wrote that, 'In shirt-sleeves and on foot is the form that is considered the most generous'. Not only did this disdain for armour endow the participants with a certain reckless heroism but it also aimed to make duels more speedily decisive.

Pierre de Bourdeille, the Seigneur of Brantome was a leading figure of the age. His memoirs, fifteen volumes chronicling his life and times, with one devoted entirely

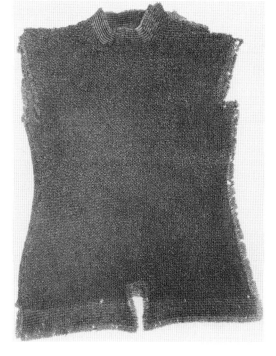

to *Anecdotes of Duelling*, were published after his death in 1614. He had willed it that the first edition to be printed should be bound in velvet and presented to Marguerite de Valois. In telling the story of a duel between the Baron de Vitaux and a gentleman known only as Millaud, Brantome raises an accusation against Millaud that was a cause for speculation at the time. It had been agreed between the two that they should fight in their shirts alone. When Vitaux's representatives had come to inspect Milaud, he threw open his shirt and declared, 'Nothing there, you see'. The suggestion that was made by

Privy coat (© The Board of Trustees of the Armouries)

Vitaux supporters afterwards (Vitaux was killed in the duel) was that Milaud was wearing a very fine steel cuirass, which had been painted to look like real flesh. Suspicions were raised because Vitaux's sword was discovered to have been blunted at the tip. Brantome was equivocal on the issue, wondering if the opinion of a first-rate artist would confirm whether a cuirass could be so painted.

Brantome had got the story from his own personal fencing master, Jacques Ferron, who claimed to have witnessed the duel from the branches of a nearby nut tree. According to Ferron, Vitaux made a brave show of it. Starting some fifty paces from his opponent, he strode towards him fiercely twirling his moustache with one hand; then, at twenty paces off, he put his right hand to his sword, which he carried in his left. As he came forward he gave it a shake, which sent the sheath flying through the air. Brantome tells us that this was 'the thing to do', showing the proper sort of coolness and confidence and he disparaged those who drew their swords too early. Demeanour, style and bravado were essential qualities for a duellist and the wearing of privy coats, though a wise precaution for daily life at a factionalized and literally backstabbing court, was 'not done' in a duel of honour.

Jacques Ferron is an interesting name for a master of fence. *Le fer* (iron) is the usual slang term for a sword in French and so a free translation of his name could give us 'Jack Blades.' It has echoes of Roger Le Skirmisour, who we met in Chapter 5, and I'm sure such names were made up for the benefits of commercial branding. This must surely have been the case with Ridolfo Capoferro – 'Rudy Ironhead' – who published his *Gran Simulacro dell'arte e dell'uso della Scherma* in 1610.

Capoferro

Although the word 'simulacrum' (likeness) has certain abstruse meanings in the context of Platonic art theory, in this context '*Gran Simulacro*' was probably intended to mean simply, 'a great array of images' and that without doubt is what Capoferro has given us. The illustrations to his treatise are arguably the most beautiful ever drawn, exceeding even those in the works of Talhoffer in the fifteenth and Angelo in the eighteenth century. There is such muscular grace in his figures that they bid you to believe that the rapier fight is the most sublimely aesthetic of all the fighting arts. Printed from copper plates, the images were originally produced by the artist Raffaello Schiamminossi and are among the most convincing, dynamic and forceful representations of the human form in action. They have grace, poise, function and balance. Each plate is an art treasure in its own right. Few other images can so vividly convey the importance that beauty of form played in the martial consciousness of this violent age.

Capoferro's techniques are no less beautiful – the one supports the other – and he has wise, practical observations to make about the business of killing. He covers the single sword, sword and cloak, and sword and target but he is the strongest advocate for, and the master of, the sword used in conjunction with a companion dagger. His swords are elegant, long-bladed swept-hilt rapiers and his daggers identical to that of Henri IV.

Discussing the dagger, Capoferro comments that,

> it, as in everything, brings opportunity and brings some hindrance ...
> one can not employ it without uncovering somewhat more of the vita and
> shortening the line to strike a little.

This means that, although it is very useful to have a dagger for parrying, using it
affects your stance and that has consequences. A dagger is useless held behind your
back, which it would be, for instance, in the sideways stance of a modern fencer. The
'rapier-and-dagger man' has to stand more square-on to bring his dagger into play.
What Capoferro calls the 'vita' is the area between the naval and the pubic bone – the
'vitals' – and so he is suggesting that by standing more square-on this area is slightly
less well guarded. Also by maintaining this stance, the length of one's lunge may be
shorter. All in all, though, he finds the benefits greater than the disadvantages.

Nerves of steel, as well as an iron head, were required to execute Capoferro's style
of fight. He commands that a fencer must never parry without responding with a
strike and instructs that, 'when the dagger departs to parry, the sword must depart to
strike'. In other words, defence and attack are simultaneous. He says that feints are not
good because they lose *tempo* and *misura* – time and distance. These two fundamental
concepts are what he refers to again and again. Capoferro's fight is a difficult,
challenging and interesting style to accomplish. In a duel I'd probably feel safer
following the precepts of George Silver but to train in, as a martial art, Capoferro has
the edge – and the point. No wonder the Italian style was so popular among the elite
martial arts enthusiasts of the day.

Being able acquit oneself in a duel was obviously the principle reason for diligent
study with a master but swordfighting was also a respected art form in its own right,
one at which a gentleman was expected to excel. However appalled we may be by
senseless killing, we must remind ourselves that training in arms is exciting and fun and

The rapier fight, after Capoferro

studying these arts for their own sake had a significant recreational benefit. Moreover, there was one other reason to keep brushed up with one's martial skills – self-defence.

Assassination

There were many assassination attempts during Henri's reign. The father of the real D'Artagnan (Alexander Dumas based his fictional character on a real person) was a member of Henri's personal bodyguard, who died fighting off an attack on the king. It was one of several attempts. Henri was finally assassinated by François Ravaillac on 14 May 1610. Ravaillac was a religious fanatic beset with a vision telling him to convince Henri to convert the Huguenots.

Henri was planning to invade the Netherlands in a campaign against the Pope. Determined to stop him, Ravaillac ambushed the king's carriage, which had come to a standstill in traffic on the Rue de la Ferronnerie in Paris, and stabbed him three times with a dagger. Henri Quartre, who was not wearing his privy coat that day, died from his wounds.

Legacy

At eight years old, Henri's son, Louis XIII, was too young to rule at the time of his father's death. His mother, Marie de Medici, ruled as Regent, reversing many of her dead husband's policies. Louis eventually wrested power from his mother and banished her. Although from then on he ruled autonomously, he was greatly influenced by his chief minister, Cardinal Richelieu.

Henri and Marie's daughter, Henrietta-Maria, married Charles I of England. Their two sons, Charles and James, became Charles II and James II of England. Henri IV of France was therefore the grandfather of two kings of England as well as of Louis XIV of France. His daughter Elizabeth, as wife to Philip IV, was queen of Spain. There was a time when Henri might even have been king of England himself. Prior to his marriage to 'La Reine Margot', the English ambassador, Sir Francis Walsingham, was concerned that the union might strengthen the French Crown more than England wished and he offered the 18-year-old Henri the prospect of marrying the 36-year-old Queen Elizabeth. Henri's mother opposed the match, but what a glittering pair they might have made.

Henri IV died when Henrietta-Maria was still a child and so it was her brother, Louis XIII, who arranged her marriage to Charles I, forming finally that brief alliance of the French and British royal families – a marriage that was opposed by the English Parliament because Henrietta-Maria was a Catholic. Charles was only 5 feet 4 inches tall and so underdeveloped that he couldn't walk until he was four years old and then only with the aid of reinforced boots. The Puritanical nemesis of this frail and diminutive man, Oliver Cromwell, is the subject of the next chapter. Before we move on, however, it is worth considering the man who, but for fate, might otherwise have been king at the time of the English Civil War. Charles had an elder brother, Prince Henry, who, in 1612, died of typhoid at the age of eighteen. He was everything that Charles was not – strong, vigorous, charismatic and popular.

When the boys' father, James VI of Scotland, became James I of England in 1603, following the death of Elizabeth I, Henri IV of France sent an embassy to the new court. With it he sent a gift of fine weapons for the young Prince Henry and a French master-of-arms to instruct him in their use. That master was Pierre Bourdin de Saint Anthime, who in turn brought with him his nephew, Julian Bourdin, as an assistant. The Bourdins continued as his tutors in the fighting arts until Prince Henry's untimely death. In 1606, the French Ambassador was specifically charged with checking on the young prince's progress. He attended one of the prince's daily lessons and was able to report to Henri IV that the boy was acquitting himself manfully. It is a testament to how important these matters were to Henri. In addition to the Bourdin's, another French master was engaged for a while, a Monsieur Gherhot, and most famously an English master of fence by the name of Joseph Swetnum. King James had decreed from the outset that his eldest son should be equipped with 'the rapier sword and the dagger' and at this Swetnum was a specialist. In his treatise *School of Defence*', Swetnum asserts that a rapier blade should be at least 4 feet in length and that the companion dagger should have a blade of 2 feet. Swetnum was a chauvinistic and reactionary character, who also wrote an intemperate tract entitled *The Arraignment of Women*, vilifying the fairer sex. A contemporary play by an anonymous author, *Swetnum the Woman Hater, Arraigned by Women*, was a satirical riposte to his extreme views that has him bested by various women in a number of swordfights.

We can only speculate how history would have turned if the martial Prince Henry had become king instead of his less fortunate brother Charles. Henri IV's interest in the prince's education suggests that he had originally hoped for this more valiant scion of the House of Stuart to become his daughter's consort but fate decreed it otherwise. She was married, by proxy, to Charles I in 1625, two months after he acceded to the throne. When she arrived at court, a pie was brought before the queen at a banquet. From it emerged Jeffery Hudson. He was a dwarf. Henrietta Maria was delighted. Hudson became a firm court favourite and was knighted. He allegedly had a full set of armour made for his perfectly proportioned body and commanded a troop of horse during the Civil War. At the war's end he fled to France with the queen. There he was mocked by William Crofts, a member of the Royal Household. Lord Minimus, as he was affectionately known, challenged Crofts to a duel. Crofts didn't take the challenge seriously and arrived at the appointed place with a water-squirt. However Hudson was in earnest and insisted on fighting with pistols on horseback. He shot Crofts through the heart and killed him.

Pistols were not yet a weapon of choice for the duel. Swords still reigned supreme, though clearly Hudson would have been disadvantaged by his height from gaining victory with a blade. On the battlefield, however, the pistol was in favour and as we shall see in the next chapter, its invention revolutionized cavalry warfare. Once fired, it could not be easily reloaded and defence once again fell to the sword. Cavalry swords in the seventeenth century assumed a new form and there is no more splendid example of the type than the sword of Oliver Cromwell.

Oliver Cromwell by Robert Walker, 1649 (National Portrait Gallery, London)

Chapter 11

The Sword of Oliver Cromwell, Lord Protector of England

They stood at the sword's point a pretty while, hacking one another

(Leonard Watson, scoutmaster-general of the
Parliamentary army, writing of Marston Moor 1644)

Just around the corner from where he lost his real head, the bronze head of Henri IV's son-in-law, Charles I, nestles in a gothic tracery niche on the west face of St Margaret's Church, Westminster. The pinched and dapper face of this pious and anguished man, who famously asked for a second shirt to wear at his execution lest his shivering be misconstrued for fear, stares across to the Houses of Parliament and holds in its reproving gaze the statue of a man who signed his death warrant. The imposing, full-size statue of Oliver Cromwell, erected in 1899 at the behest of the Liberal prime-minister Lord Rosebery, stands with head bowed immediately opposite the deposed king's forlorn stare. It is a whimsical, if cruel, historical joke.

Cromwell's bronze stands leaning on his drawn sword. It is what collectors today call a 'mortuary sword'. The fencing historian Egerton Castle attempted to explain the term in 1885, saying, 'swords of this type are often called "mortuary" as a number of them were made in memory of Charles I and bear his likeness upon the hilt'. It is not a good theory. Hundreds of similar swords survive or are represented in art. There are but two or three that bear likenesses of the king and the vast majority do not. Most also predate his death and were in common use during the Civil War. Of the few that do portray the king's head, they also display the features of his queen, Henrietta Maria, who survived him. That a unique sword type evolved to commemorate a dead king is a romantic idea but it doesn't bear scrutiny.

Housed in the collections of the Royal Armouries in Leeds is a sword that is thought to have belonged to Oliver Cromwell. It is of this 'mortuary' sword type but the catalogue entry simply states 'military backsword, British c 1640' and this is a better description.

I have handled it and it is a splendid fighting sword. Like any good quality sword, it is well balanced and just blade-heavy enough for purpose. It weighs 2lb 6oz, has a

The statue of Oliver Cromwell outside the Houses of Parliament and the head of Charles I on the opposite bank of the Thames on St. Margaret's Church (photos: Chris Hawkins)

broad single-edged blade of 31.9 inches with a single fuller adjacent to the spine and measures 38.2 inches overall. A 'dish-guard', which rises to halfway up the length of the grip like the prow of a boat, and then adjoins a central knuckle-guard that fixes to the pommel by means of a screw, has a scroll to the rear and two 'langets' (one broken) that extend down either side of the blade. Langets are small tongues of metal that sit outside the scabbard, so acting in a similar manner to a rainguard. Moreover, if the fit is right, they can help to snap the sword securely into the scabbard. Most importantly, langets act as a buffer zone for any parries taken at the junction of the blade and the hilt, the weakest part of any sword. Each side of the hilt has a side knuckle-guard and these are joined to the one in the centre by means of scroll-guards, creating an early form of basket hilt. Although affording ample room for a gloved hand, the basket on Cromwell's sword is narrower than usual, lending an uncharacteristic elegance to what is often a rather ungainly type. This specimen, however, is a jewel!

The guard-plate, knuckle-guards and bud-shaped pommel have all been black 'japanned' and decorated with foliage and trophies of arms painted in gold. Japanning is a process in which a thick coloured lacquer, similar to enamel paint, is painted onto an object as a decorative and protective coating. It is applied in heat-dried layers that are then polished to a high finish. Originating in the East, lacquered goods were originally referred to as 'Indiaware' but Japan soon established a reputation for the best examples. Japanning became widely popular in Europe in the mid-seventeenth century, just as Japan herself was closing her doors to the world. On Cromwell's sword the japanning is exquisite and appears freshly done, glistening as if it were wet paint.

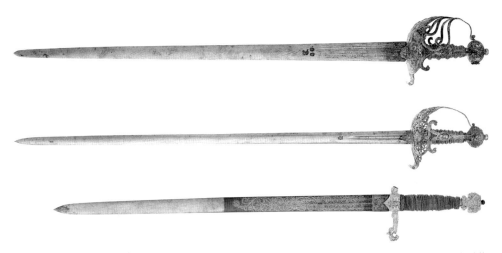

The Huntingdon swords: (top) Basket-hilted sword with Cromwell's arms and crest chiselled on the hilt. Though not apparent in this photograph, it still retains its sword-knot of green braid, the earliest surviving example of a sword-knot; (centre) basket-hilted sword bearing the stamp OC; (bottom) Cromwell's Sword of State (Cromwell Museum, Huntingdon)

The guard-plate has been pierced with irregular geometric patterns, accentuating the play of light and giving a rich surface texture. Complimenting these perforations is the black fishskin-covered grip with its nodular surface. Top and bottom of the grip are finished with Turk's-head bands in copper wire. Cromwell's sword combines a restrained opulence with a self-regarding grandeur.

I say 'Cromwell's sword' but it is by no means certain that this sword belonged to him, although the tradition that it did is very strong. It is also one of at least nine contenders and three of these have even greater claims to authentic provenance. These three swords are now in the Cromwell Museum in Huntingdon. Two are superb basket-hilted backswords; one bearing Cromwell's heraldic arms. The second bears the incised initials 'OC' on the blade but, though having Cromwell connections, it probably wasn't a sword he carried personally. There is a tradition that Cromwell commissioned swords with this mark as gifts for his personal friends. Both swords, although exceedingly fine, are duplicates of the type and space does not allow their detailed examination here. The third sword in the Cromwell Museum is believed to have been his Sword of State – his bearing sword – and it is a straightforward cross-hilted sword in faux-medieval style and has no relevance to this present chapter. My rationale in spotlighting the one in the collection of the Royal Armouries is purely personal fancy. It is a sword that I especially like.

Oliver Cromwell excites polarized opinions. Some laud him as the father of parliamentary democracy; others damn him as a regicidal tyrant. Some think of him as a humble Christian who believed in justice and equality; others only see a Puritanical zealot who repressed his own people and inflicted atrocities abroad. Even outside the role-playing world of Civil War reenactment, the people of Great Britain can readily identify themselves as either cavaliers or roundheads; enduring stereotypes that typify

The hilt of Cromwell's sword (© The Board of Trustees of the Armouries – RA IX 1096)

two main branches of the national character. Cromwell is a paradox: as is his sword. Its rich beauty lives hand-in-hand with its dread capacity as an instrument of butchery and that sword, now sitting quietly in the Royal Armouries Museum, is thought to be the very sword that Oliver Cromwell raised in fury at the siege of Drogheda.

Drogheda

In 1649 Cromwell besieged and took the city of Drogheda in southern Ireland. It was the scene of an in-famous massacre. It is alleged that over 3,500 people, civilians, priests and friars as well as soldiers, were put to the sword in the aftermath. The royalist governor Sir Arthur Aston, who had boasted 'he who could take Drogheda could take Hell', had his brains dashed out with his own wooden leg! Most of the survivors were trans-ported to Barbados for a life of slavery. Cromwell's losses numbered just 150.

The conventions of seventeenth-century warfare dictated that a town or city that had turned down the chance to surrender and had declared that it would hold out against a siege could expect no mercy if it was subsequently taken. Such brutal acts were not viewed as atrocities at the time but merely the natural course of war. Moreover, Cromwell argued that the bloodshed was a just penalty for those Catholics who had slaughtered the Protestant settlers in the 'Irish Uprising' of 1641. It is with such thoughts of rightous justification that men forever perpetuate their wars. The Drogheda massacre seared lasting resentment in the Irish collective conscience and to this day, in Ireland, Cromwell remains a name of darkest infamy.

Cromwell and the Civil Wars

Cromwell's campaigns in Ireland were the culmination of a virtually continuous conflict that had raged in Britain for over ten years known as the Civil Wars. There was not one war but several. In 1625, Charles I succeeded to the three thrones of England, Scotland and Ireland. Each was a separate kingdom, not part of a unified state, and each nurtured its own grievances with Charles's rule. He believed in the

'Divine Right' of kings, overtaxed his subjects and disdained the will of parliament. Protestants distrusted him because he had a Catholic for a wife and Catholics feared the imposition of Protestant hegemony. The precise reasons and chain of events that led up to each of the civil wars were exceedingly complex and can only adequately be dealt with in more extensive works on the subject. Here are just a few headlines to give context to our subject. The wars began in Scotland with the First Bishop's War in 1638 and the Second Bishop's War in 1640. Then there was the so-called Irish Rebellion of 1641. In 1642 the First English Civil War broke out, concluding in 1646 with final victory for the Parliamentary forces. Though held a prisoner, Charles was allowed to keep his throne. In 1648 hostilities recommenced with the Second English Civil War, leading to Charles's execution in 1649. Later that year a Third English Civil War erupted with attempts by Charles's son, Charles II, to take back the throne and with renewed conflicts in Scotland and Ireland that continued until 1651.

Oliver Cromwell first comes to our attention during the First English Civil War. For four long years Englishman slaughtered Englishman in a series of pitched battles, skirmishes and sieges. Many fought for a belief in their cause but many more fought for pay. Harangued by preachers whipping up fear and hatred, men were pulled from mundane existences to experience the charged atmosphere of life on campaign. The insistent roll of the drums that never fails to get the heart racing, the intoxicating smell of gunpowder forever in the air, the roar and boom of the guns, the tramp of thousands of feet and the cameraderie of other men; all combined to seduce ordinary folk to become soldiers and to belong to one or other of the warring tribes. Into this theatre stepped Oliver Cromwell. He wasn't the instigator of the drama but he was a natural leader of men and he made his presence felt on its stage.

Cromwell, born in 1599, was a minor country squire from Huntingdon in the flat fenlands of Cambridgeshire. He once said of himself, 'I was by birth a gentleman, living neither in considerable height, nor yet in obscurity'. He attended Cambridge University, though never completed his studies, leaving to care for his mother and six sisters on the death of his father. A contemporary biographer, James Heath, suggested that Cromwell was not a very diligent student but was, 'one of the chief matchmakers and players of football, cudgels, or any other boysterous sport or game'. 'Cudgels' was a form of stick-fighting with what became known later as 'single-sticks'. If Cambridge taught the young Oliver nothing else it taught him to fight.

Cromwell was politically minded from an early stage, becoming Member of Parliament for Huntingdon in 1628. In the same year he sought treatment for melancholia from a doctor in London. Failing fortunes forced him to move to a small farmstead in St Ives, Cambridgeshire and it seems to have been at some point towards the end of the 1630s that he became a radical Puritan, believing the entire nation was living in sin and that the last vestiges of Catholic ceremony, such as music, must be expunged from the English Church. He embraced these puritanical creeds with a chilling zeal but didn't affiliate himself with any religious body, preferring an 'independent' relationship with his God. When, in 1640, Charles had to summon Parliament once more in order to raise taxes to fund his army in Scotland, Cromwell returned as the MP for Cambridge. By that time his personal fortunes had changed; he had inherited several properties in Ely from his uncle. Though still a minor player in the great movements afoot, he was becoming increasingly vociferous.

When the opposing commanders, Prince Rupert and the Earl of Essex, set their battle lines for the first major engagement of the English Civil War (Edgehill, 1642), Oliver Cromwell was not there. Accounts differ, some maintaining that he was not there at all and others that the 43-year-old Captain Cromwell, commanding a small troop of horse, arrived midway through the battle. Edgehill was an indecisive victory for the Parliamentary army and everyone went away to regroup. For his part Cromwell resolved to raise and train a cavalry regiment that would sweep all before them. At Edgehill he had a troop of sixty men; two years later, Cromwell's 'double' regiment was eleven hundred strong! He was elevated to colonel in 1643. Cromwell recruited men with religious conviction, ready to lay down their lives for a cause and drilled them with rigid discipline; he wrote: 'No man swears but he pays his twelve pence; if he is in drink he is set in the stocks or worse'. Moral discipline was instilled with equal measure to military discipline and he created cavalry capable of holding their formations and of regrouping quickly after either charge or chase. This contrasted with the 'cavalier' flourish of the Royalist cavalry, who at Edgehill had made only one glorious charge. Swords drawn, they had burst through the Parliamentary ranks and then continued in a stampeding herd, unable to stop and wheel about, for miles. They never rejoined the battle.

Cromwell was a harsh martinet, with public floggings a regular occurrence, but he also took care of his men, taking pains to ensure that they were fed and paid, albeit sometimes in arrears. He made sure that they were well horsed and well armoured. Cromwell's troopers became known as 'Ironsides' and he 'Old Ironsides'. It was likely a reference to the sturdy 'back and breast' armour that they wore.

Armour

Damage on the blade of the sword in Leeds is indicative that it may have been struck by two musket balls, about 6 and 8 inches from the hilt. It is crazed around the crater of the strikes and a small rise can be detected on the surface of the other side, more by feel than sight. Certainly it is likely that Cromwell was in the thick of the fighting at Drogheda, clambering through the breach in the walls, and surely, if his blade was hit, then he too must have been caught in the vollies of musket fire. Muskets of the period were not particularly effective, except at relatively close range, and even then his fighting apparel would have been reasonable protection. In 1650, as depicted in the wonderful Robert Walker painting of him, now in the National Portrait Gallery, Cromwell possessed an extremely fine cuirassier's three-quarter armour, as sleekly tailored as a second skin, which would have been proof against musket shot.

Quality armours of the period were proofed by shooting at them at close range, thus proving that they were capable of resisting musket fire; the resulting indentation became the proof mark. It was a system open to abuse because armourers could cheat by using a smaller than usual charge of powder for the test, thereby creating the distinctive hollow on the armour without risk of penetration. Such fraudulent measures were unlikely with a very expensive armour such as Oliver Cromwell's. However, full armours like this were becoming increasingly scarce on the battlefield, the popular view being that they were overly heavy and cumbersome.

In 1639, Sir Edmund Verney, in a letter to his eldest son during the civil war in Scotland, reflected contemporary opinion when he wrote:

> I believe there is never a long gauntlett sent, lett Hill [his armourer] make one with all speede he can possibly; for it will kill a man to serve in a whole cuirass. I am resolved to use nothing but back, brest and gauntlet; if I had a Pott for the Head that were pistoll proofe it may be that I would use it if it were light ... say nothing of this gauntlett to yor mother, it may cause her careless fears.

It is telling that he prioritized an armoured gauntlet above a pot-helm. Cavalrymen wore steel 'bridle gauntlets' to protect the left hand and arm up to the elbow and Verney clearly considered this to be the most vulnerable part of his person; a primary target for a mounted foe with a sword.

In spite of these protestations there is a superb Van Dyck portrait of Sir Edmund, painted in about 1640, wearing full armour, which, like Cromwell's, has been 'blacked' as was the fashion of the day. 'Blacking' like 'bluing' was created by a combination of chemical and heat treatments, resulting in a surface coating that was not only very attractive but also rust resistant. Notwithstanding the preferences of portrait painters, the preference of those in the field was to wear a back and breast, a bridle gauntlet, a 'buff coat' and a pot helmet. Verney was in two minds over the pot-helmet, considering its principal worth to be protection against pistol shots. The alternative was to wear a soft hat, with a secret underneath, which would give some defence against vertical sword blows. Pot helmets had the added security of a three-bar guard that shielded against cuts across the face but many, like Verney, preferred comfort and lightness to complete safety.

Three years after Verney wrote to his son about the gauntlet, and with such touching concern for his wife, father and son found themselves on opposite sides. At the outbreak of the English Civil War, Ralph Verney joined the Parliamentary forces. Such is the particular and terrible tragedy of civil war. At the Battle of Edgehill, Sir Edmund Verney rode into the fray as the king's official standard bearer. After the battle, his dead and mutilated body was only identified by his severed hand, still holding onto the royal standard. If only he had bid Hill make a long gauntlet for his right as well as his left arm! Still, no armour in the world can be protection enough for men that brave and that stubborn.

The other items of armour championed by Verney were the 'back and breast' – a steel backplate and breastplate. These safeguarded the vital organs against musket and pistol shot. Prior to the invention of the wheel-lock mechanism in the mid-sixteenth century, firearms had required two hands to operate them. With the wheel-lock it became possible to load and prime a gun and stand it by, ready to shoot just by pulling the trigger, thus enabling single-handed operation. This led to the development of the pistol, which in turn re-invigorated the role of cavalry on the battlefield. Ready primed and charged, multiple wheel-lock pistols could be carried in holsters slung over the saddle or even stuffed into the tops of a horseman's thigh-length boots. They were one-shot weapons.

Prior to the Civil Wars the tactic had been for formations of cavalry to ride up to a wall of pike or block of musketeers, discharge their pieces and retire. Musketeers still used the old, slow-loading, match-lock mechanism. Wheel-locks were relatively expensive and largely restricted to the cavalry, who were also accustomed to shoot their pre-loaded pistols in cavalry-on-cavalry engagements, usually at extremely close range; hence Verney's consideration of a pot, if it 'were pistoll proofe'. However, inspired by the success of aggressive shock-action tactics by the Swedish general,

Gustavus Adolphus, Civil War cavalry commanders from Prince Rupert to Cromwell advised their troopers to reserve their pistols for the 'execution', as the rout was then called. That meant starting out with swords drawn, riding headlong at the enemy and hurtling into him at speed.

The main protection against the sword, for those who could afford it, was the 'buff coat'. This was a three-quarter length coat made from thick 'buff' leather and lined with either linen or silk. It was worn under the back and breast. I have worn a buff coat, riding hard on a hot day; it feels heavy and is insufferably hot and stuffy. Plate armour in the seventeenth century was generally heavier than its medieval counterpart, because proofing against shot was partly achieved by increasing the gauge of the metal. By contrast, buff coats were certainly a lighter alternative, just not as light and airy as they might appear. Buff, an undyed, oil-tanned leather is a remarkably strong

Buff coat, pot helmet, bridle gauntlet, back and breast (courtesy of Culture and Sport Glasgow (Museums))

material affording not only a reasonable level of protection against sword cuts but also to 'soft hits' from musket balls ricocheting or decelerating at the end of their trajectory. A buff coat in the collection of Glasgow Museums has a discernable dent in it where it has stopped a musket ball. Another, in the same collection, is scored by deep sword cuts to the bridle arm. The gashes are concentrated around the inside of the elbow and just above where a bridle gauntlet would terminate. Although these were clearly very deliberate strikes, they have not fully penetrated the tough leather. It would seem, from the angle of the cuts, that the attacking horseman had got behind and to the left hand side of his man, who was presumably making to gallop off, and had slashed repeatedly at his bridle arm.

Writing some years after the Civil Wars, Sir James Turner (in *Pallas Armata*, 1683) complained,

> It were to be wish'd that if Horsemen be obliged by their capitulation to furnish themselves with swords, that their Officers would see them provided of better than ordinarily most of them carry, which are such as may be well enough resisted by either a good Felt, or a Buff-coat.

It is a clear testimony to the effectiveness of a buff coat, though it calls into question standards of sword manufacture. As the size of professional armies grew ever larger, so too did the need for swords to be produced in quantity and the more that swords were mass produced, the more quality became an issue.

Hounslow swords

By the beginning of the sixteenth century the main centres of sword production in England were Birmingham and London, the latter controlled by the restrictive guild practices of the London Cutlers Company. This guild, known originally as The Mystery of Cutlers, first received its royal charter in 1416, the year after Agincourt, possibly as part payment for arms supplied to that campaign. The charter granted them a monopoly controlling the trade in and around London, which they did with rigorous protectionist policies. There was some blade production but many cutlers simply made hilts and mounted them on blades that had been purchased in bulk from overseas, either from Toledo, Venice or Solingen. Solingen, in Germany, had the reputation of producing the best quality steel and of having the best sword craftsmen in the world. Each concentrated on a particular aspect of the trade. Swordsmiths forged the basic blades and then had specialists to temper and harden them; grinders gave them a fell edge and polishers buffed them bright. It was mass production and the sword-makers of Solingen were able to turn out quality blades in their thousands.

A bitter conflict between Europe's Protestants and Catholics, known as the Thirty Years War, had been raging in Germany since 1618 and many of Solingen's Protestant sword-makers had fled to Holland to escape the persecution and carnage. In 1629, agents of Charles I recruited a number of these sword-makers to come to England and work under royal patronage. They set up their houses and factories on Hounslow

Heath alongside the New Cutt, a man-made canal joining the Colne and Isleworth rivers. It flowed fast enough to turn the waterwheels that drove the bellows, the trip hammers and the grinding and polishing wheels. There was quite a din. In 1630, Benjamin Stone, cutler, signed a lease for a sword-mill that was 'lately erected upon a parcel of waste ground called Hounslow Heath'. Today, Hounslow Heath is a different sort of waste-ground; concrete criss-crossed with the ribbons of runways and roads that is the sprawl of Heathrow Airport. Stone was a colourful, if unscrupulous, character who had had a number of run-ins with the London Cutlers Company. He was fined and arrested for offences such as striking other cutlers, putting unauthorized marks on his blades, buying knives made outside London, swearing at officers and keeping unregistered apprentices. Hounslow Heath sat outside the jurisdiction of the London Cutlers Company and so was an ideal spot for his new business. Stone now bought his blades directly from the Solingen immigrants. They imported their steel from Germany and produced a superior product. Stone claimed,

> I have perfected the art of blade making and my factory at Hounslow Heath could produce blades as good and cheap as any to be found in the Christian world. The price being fortified by the long experience and quality on the part of my German blade makers.

This advertising was somewhat disingenuous, insofar as his mill did no more than grind, polish and mount the blades he had bought from the Germans. Nevertheless in 1631 Stone delivered 4,356 swords to the Office of Ordnance. All were basket hilts (known then as 'Irish' hilts) and cost six shillings each. In all probability, at such a bargain price, the hilts had been cast in brass. Stone was a pioneer of brass hilts.

The London Cutlers Company considered brass too soft a metal to be used in any aspect of sword production and prohibited its use. Subsequent arsenals of brass-hilted weapons have proved that they were wrong and from this time on we begin to see more and more military swords with perfectly serviceable brass hilts. Brass could be cast in moulds, whereas steel hilts had to be built by hand. A single mould could produce a great many hilts with consequent economies of scale. By 1636, Stone was producing 500 swords a week. A trade war raged between Stone and the London Cutlers and a wily Office of Ordnance was happy to benefit from the competitive bids tendered by both suppliers. In 1640, 3,000 swords were produced by the London Cutlers for delivery to the Office of Ordnance.

At the outset of the English Civil War in 1642, the parliamentary forces seized all sword-making facilities at Hounslow, including Stone's mill. He and a number of the Solingen sword-makers fled to the Royalist stronghold of Oxford, where he set up a Royalist sword-mill just outside

The running wolf mark of the Solingen blade-makers

the city at Wolvergate. Initially Birmingham had been the principal supplier of swords to the Royalist army. Prince Rupert ordered 15,000 blades from Robert Porter of Birmingham in 1643 but Porter's factory was destroyed by Parliamentary forces, almost before the ink was dry on the contract. After that the Oxford mills became more important. Some of the Solingen men, who after all were Protestants, remained and produced swords for the Parliamentary cause but output was not on the same scale as it had been before the war and many of the mills were converted for gunpowder production. London was the bigger centre for Parliamentarian supply. General Fairfax's New Model Army received more than 2,000 swords from the London Cutlers Company in 1645. After the Civil Wars, the fortunes of the Hounslow industry picked up. New entrepreneurs opened up the mills, doing a thriving trade until the first decade of the Restoration, when activity seems to have tailed off.

During its heyday, both before and after the Civil Wars, Hounslow sword makers produced a variety of swords, including basket-hilted backswords and rapiers. These were not all cheap brass-hilted 'munition' arms ; many were exquisite custom-made pieces. Hounslow swords were much sought after. The German bladesmiths punched the fuller of their blades with the word 'Hounslow', albeit rendered in a variety of imaginative spellings. Perhaps tests might show that, like Ulfbehrt swords in the tenth century, those with less orthodox spellings were fakes and of inferior quality? Certainly 'Hounslow' was considered to be a stamp of quality equal to the 'running wolf' mark that hailed the superior quality of the blades produced in their home towns of Passau and Solingen. There was one particular type of sword, however, that was associated with Hounslow more than any other. It was the Hounslow 'hanger'.

Hangers

In this context, 'hanger' describes a type of sword, not, as in the previous century, a contraption for wearing the sword. By the second decade of the seventeenth century, the waist-belt style of sword suspension with its hanger had gone out of fashion in favour of the baldric, a type of shoulder-belt that hung the sword at the hip. As a sword type, hangers can be detected as early as the fourteenth century, where we see the word 'hyngler' used to describe a smallish sword used for hunting deer, the etymology – 'hyn' (hind) – giving a clue to its function. In 1587 John Selwyn was hunting deer in Oatlands Park. Queen Elizabeth I witnessed the scene. Selwyn leapt from his horse onto a stag's back, steered it towards the Queen and then slaughtered it before her eyes by plunging his hanger into its neck. Aside from this unique instance of ostentatious brutality, early hunting hangers were more usually used from horseback. By the seventeenth century hunting practices had changed and the sword was no longer employed directly in the chase, though it continued to be used in macabre rituals of butchery after the quarry had been killed. It also remained an essential accoutrement to hunting attire, retaining a symbolic function that signified the wearer was a gentleman. It was around this time that the use of the word 'hanger'

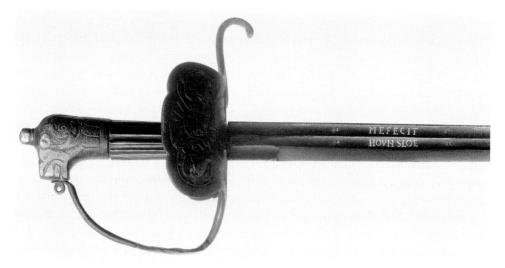

Hounslow hanger, circa 1640. Note the lion's head pommel, typical of Hounslow swords (© Museum of London)

broadened to describe a range of sword types, characteristically short, employed for hunting, travelling and war.

Military hangers were often entirely different stylistically from those carried in the hunting field. Hounslow swordsmiths manufactured both fine hunting hangers for gentlemen and military hangers for soldiers. Hanger became a loosely applied designation, mainly denoting that the sword was a sidearm, rather than of a particular style. Pikemen, musketeers and artillerymen were among those for whom the sword remained an indispensable weapon of last resort but the nature of their primary roles meant that it was inconvenient to wear swords of any length. Short-bladed hangers were the answer, especially ones of quality from the Hounslow mills.

Hangers also maintained a parallel development as sidearms for cavalry gentlemen but the cavalry hanger was more a feature of the following century. During the Civil Wars, the cavalry soldier favoured either the rapier or, more usually, the basket-hilted backsword. Hounslow excelled at the manufacture of both. Whatever type of sword the cavalryman chose it should, as John Cruso put it, 'be a good sword which was to be very stiffe, cutting and sharp pointed'.

The cavalry sword in action
John Cruso published *Militarie Instructions to the Cavalry* in 1632. Among his tips for using the sword he says, 'The best manner of using is to place the pummell of it upon his right thigh, and so with his right hand to direct or raise the point to his mark, higher or lower as occasion serveth'. In other words he is advising the cavalryman to brace and lock the pommel of the sword against his thigh and angle the aim, according to preference, for the enemy's stomach, armpit or throat. He suggests that a blow to the throat delivered in this way to an armoured opponent will at least unhorse the

man, even if it doesn't pierce his armour. In the event of missing the target altogether Cruso enjoins his students, 'Being past his enemie, he is to make a back blow at him, aiming to cut the buckle of his poldron, whereby he disarmeth one of his arms'. In both scenarios Cruso envisaged an opponent in full armour as did another well-known military instructor of the time, George Basta, who produced *The Government of the Light Horse* in 1631. He commended 'aiming at the enemies sight and so by raising the vizures of his casque with the point of the sword, to run him into the head. But this seemeth not so likely to take effect as that of aiming at the throat'. No wonder the gorget became such a signature item of seventeenth-century armour.

Basta also encapsulated the basic tactics of mounted swordfighting that were as true in his own time as they were throughout the ages from Alexander to Wellington. The first pre-requisite was to get on your enemy's left side, where it is much harder for him to reach over and parry. Secondly, the horseman must try to stay slightly to the rear of his opponent. It is virtually impossible for a rider to land any sort of a blow on either man or horse when they are tailing him a few feet to his rear on the left-hand side. Consequently a great deal of cavalry fighting involves jockeying for position. Moreover Basta counsels that a collected canter is the best pace, arguing that it is difficult to manage a sword well at a flat-out gallop. Along with other contemporary writers on the subject, he also advised that the best course of action was to strike the horse, not the man. He elaborated that he considered it important to inflict 'a wound so deep that the blood cannot issue forth', rendering the horse immobile. I am uncertain as to the veterinary realism of this but perhaps what is meant is that pin-prick thrusts, causing the superficial muscle to bleed, are of small consequence to the mass of a horse. What is needed is deep thrusts, penetrating into the vital organs; the wound, being plugged by the entering blade, will not 'issue' blood until it is withdrawn and the poor animal should drop dead before that happens.

This gruesome advice would have been of benefit to Captain Richard Atkyns, Royalist, who had a prolonged encounter with Sir Arthur Haselrigge, Parliamentarian, at the Battle of Roundway Down in 1643.

Before the Enclosure Acts of the eighteenth century parcelled England up with a spider's web of hedges and fences, it was good riding country and there was many a chase in the Civil War that went pell mell for miles. Atkyns versus Haselrigge was one such running battle. Haselrigge was colonel of a regiment of cuirassiers, known as 'Haselrigge's Lobsters' because of the crustacean-like plates of their armour. Cuirassiers in heavy armour were a dying

A cuirassier, after Cruso

breed by the time of the English Civil War but Sir Arthur and his men were a notable exception. Atkyns describes how Haselrigge discharged both his carbine and his pistol at him as he rode towards him, missing on both counts. Not wishing to risk a similar error, Atkins tells us that he 'touched him before I discharged mine'. It is a testament to Haselrigge's armourer that the ball did no apparent damage but now a chase was on. Atkyns took over a hundred yards to catch up with his prize again and this time, firing his second pistol, he claimed 'I'm sure I hit his head, for I touched it before I gave fire'. Again, to Atkyns' amazement, the armour did its work. Both men galloped another hundred yards or so until Atkyns drew level once more, and with his sword

> tried him from head to the saddle, and could not penetrate him, nor do him any hurt; but in this attempt he cut my horse's nose, that you might put a finger in the wound, and gave me such a blow on the inside of my arm amongst the veins that I could hardly hold my sword.

After another frantic pursuit, the men engaged again and this time Haselrigge employed his sword, cutting at the head of Atkyns' horse and severing the headstall (part of the bridle, not essential for control). Atkyns responded with a thrust into the flank of Haselrigge's horse. Next Atkyns was joined by his friend Mr Holmes who also shot at the old lobster at point blank range. Atkins reported 'twas but a flea-biting to him'. Then, whilst Holmes set about Haselrigge with his sword, Atkyns set about killing his horse, thrusting at it in several places including the neck. He laments that he would have 'run him through the head', if it weren't for his own horse stumbling. Atkyns and Holmes were then joined by a Captain Buck, who also tried his hand at shooting the redoubtable curassier. Buck too failed with his firearm and joined in with his sword. Haselrigge remained unscathed, though doubtless exhausted, within his steel carapace, but his horse, suffering great loss of blood began finally to falter. Reluctantly, Haselrigge surrendered to his resolute pursuers and Atkins bade him to 'deliver his sword, which he was loathe to do; and being tied twice about his wrist, he was fumbling a great while before he would part with it'. But before he had parted

The cavalry fight, after General Albrecht von Wallenstein

with it, a small troop of Parliamentrians galloped up and rescued him, giving Atkyns a pistol shot that just skinned his shoulder.

That Atkyns, early in the fight, received a deep cut on his sword arm but did not relinquish his sword probably suggests that it was secured by a 'sword-knot', looping around his wrist from the grip of his sword. Even if momentarily dropped it could be quickly recovered. An author known only as JB, writing of cavalry during the Civil War, noted that their swords were hanging at their wrists by a string and clearly Sir Arthur Haselrigge was more than a little fastidious about securing his. Sword-knots were most often leather straps but could also be tasselled cords or even brightly coloured, thick ribbons.

Basta had advice for wearing the sword on horseback. He recommended tying the scabbard to the thigh with a strap, so that it didn't dance about at the gallop, with the attendant risk of it jumping out of its scabbard. Certainly 'dancing' swords can be a great annoyance when riding. However, strapping the scabbard to your thigh in the manner of a gunslinger's holster could cause greater inconvenience in the event of being unseated or your horse being shot. Better, I should have thought, to ensure your sword is suspended at a good angle by the baldric and that this is kept firmly in place by the sash. These devices were adequately designed for purpose; it was simply a matter of knowing how to set them up correctly.

Atkyns tells us that Haselrigge's sword was 'two edged and [had] a ridge in the middle'. It is quite possible that it was a Hounslow sword for only a few months earlier, Haselrigge had ordered 'two hundred swords of Kennet's making at Hounslow'. When he arrived from Solingen, Johann Kindt had anglicised his name to Kennet and was one of the most regarded of the Hounslow swordsmiths. Although it was more common, and sensible, for mounted troops to carry a broad-bladed weapon, there were those who opted to carry rapier-type swords onto the battlefield as an indicator of status. Atkyns' account reports that his own weapon was 'a strong tucke'. I dare say Captain Atkyns was a showy young man. However, at least his tuck was a strong one, though with such a spike he should perhaps have been better able to deliver the deep thrusts counselled by Basta.

Cup-hilts

Rapiers and tucks were the choice of gentleman infantry officers as well as cavalry dandies and the fashionable style at this time, for both military and civilian wear, was the cup- hilt. Three main types were in use – the Spanish, the Italian and the English/German. In form, the Spanish cup-hilt had a hemispherical cup with a turned over rim called the '*rompepuntas*'. Although I doubt the ability of the rompepuntas (literally 'point-breaker') to actually break any but the most inferior of blades, it nonetheless had the potential to stop any thrust grazing the top half of the cup from glancing onto the arm. Italian cup-hilts differed from their Spanish counterparts in that the cup was significantly deeper and had no rompepuntas. In other respects the types were similar, having very broad quillons, a knuckle-guard, arms of the hilt and a '*guardapolvo*'. The guardapolvo was a metal disc that sat inside

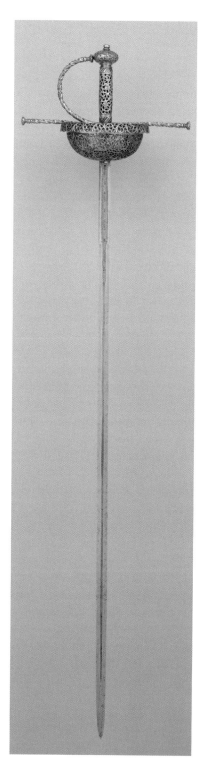

the cup and through which the blade passed. One might suppose from its literal meaning, 'dust guard', that it was intended to protect the blade from dust and moisture, collected by the funnel-like properties of the cup, but in practice the guardapolvo served no such discernable function, since, almost invariably, they were decoratively pierced or cut into foliate shapes. English/German cup-hilts had a much shallower cup, barely a saucer in fact, which was often also asymmetrical and with scalloped edges. Irrespective of the country of manufacture, all three styles were commonly seen at the sides of English gentlemen during and after the Civil Wars.

Whether of English, German, Spanish or Italian style, the expansive surfaces of cup guards lent themselves to elaborate decoration with the most ornate and wonderful piercing, chiselling or *repoussé* work. Artistically, the cups on some swords are masterpieces in their own right. Blades on civilian cup-hilts were generally long tuck blades and, as was the case with Captain Atkyns, this type was also found on swords in military use. More usually though, military cup-hilts had slightly broader blades.

Daggers were still used in the left hand as companion weapons for civilian duelling. The type of dagger used with cup-hilt rapiers characteristically had a guard for the hand, similar in shape to a billowing spinnaker and was usually pierced or chiselled in the same elaborate style as its companion rapier. In addition to offering unrivalled protection to the hand, these guards also presented the opportunity for offensive use, capable of being used to punch in the same way that one does with a buckler. The blades on these daggers are especially distinctive. In their most usual form they can be divided into four parts. At the top of the blade is a rectangular,

Spanish cup-hilt rapier (by kind permission of the Trustees of the Wallace Collection, London)

square-section ricasso with a dimple on the reverse side to accommodate the thumb. Below this are two pierced circles, which give structural strength to the potentially weak junction of narrow blade and wide ricasso. Typically, the upper blade is triangular in section and incised with notches. These notches serve no practical function and the irregular patterns vary considerably between individual daggers. With a parrying dagger it is the upper portion of the back edge that receives all the parries and consequently a dagger that had seen much service in combat would bear the scars of multiple notches on this section of the blade. This would doubtless have a considerable cachet to a boastful duellist and it is easy to see how this 'used' look became fashionable and is perhaps why bladesmiths incorporated these stylized simulations of blade damage in their designs. One is reminded of Falstaff's braggadocio in Shakespeare's *Henry IV Part 1*, where he claims to have won a fight against ruffians. His cowardly pleas for mercy were witnessed by Prince Hal, who reproved him saying, 'What a slave thou art, to hack thy sword as thou hast done and then say it was in a fight!' It suggests that the idea of notching a blade to imply heroic conduct was well established.

Nineteenth-century antiquarians referred to this type of dagger as a '*main gauche*', literally 'left hand', dagger. It is an expression that still lingers and is useful only to distinguish between this seventeenth-century type of parrying dagger and its sixteenth-century predecessor, the Bolognese type, even though that too was used in the left hand. Of course all companion or parrying daggers are used in the left hand – except when employed by a left-handed person. I find the term '*main gauche*' tautologous and annoying and I generally try to avoid it.

Fighting with the rapier and dagger remained popular for duels in England during the earlier part of the seventeenth-century, though by the time of the Civil Wars it was more usual for gentlemen to fight with the sword alone. Certainly, the

Spanish companion dagger (by kind permission of the Trustees of the Wallace Collection, London)

practice of duelling continued to flourish throughout the century and in 1654, Cromwell, as Lord Protector, issued a proclamation against it. It had been rife during the Civil Wars, which was perhaps to be expected amongst the fashionable gentlemen of the Royalist camp but it was also prevalent amongst Parliamentary troops. The Articles of War of the Parliamentary army stipulated that, 'No Corporal, or other officer commanding the Watch, shall willingly suffer a Souldier to go forth to a Duel, or private Fight, upon pain of death'. By its very existence, such a regulation is a sure sign that the practice was common.

The New Model Army

Cromwell was a harsh disciplinarian who punished the misdemeanours of his men in strict accordance with regulations; a trait that also ensured a tight discipline on the battlefield, something that was to be a decisive factor at Marston Moor in 1644. Although at a numerical disadvantage, the Royalist cavalry under Prince Rupert tasted first blood, putting to flight all the cavalry regiments on the Parliamentary right wing. However, where Fairfax failed, Cromwell, on the left wing, held steady and Leonard Watson, the Parliamentary scoutmaster-general, later wrote that the discipline of Cromwell's troopers was 'the bravest sight in all the world'. During these initial engagements, Cromwell was wounded in the neck, possibly from a sword cut. He retired briefly to have it dressed but he swiftly returned and for the rest of the tense two-hour battle held his regiments in place until they prevailed. According to Leonard Watson,

> Cromwell's own division had a hard pull of it; for they were charged by Rupert's bravest men both in front and flank; they stood at the sword's point a pretty while, hacking one another; but at last (it so pleased God) he [Cromwell] brake through them, scattering them before him like a little dust

Having repelled the Royalist horse and driven them from the field, Cromwell's cavalry turned their attention to the enemy infantry. He later wrote, 'God made them as stubble to our swords. We charged their regiments of foot with our horse and routed all we charged'. As a newly risen full moon lit this bloodied Yorkshire moor with an eerie light, Cromwell and his God-fearing troopers rode after the scattered hordes and, with aching arms limp from exhaustion, brought down the keen edges of their swords upon the backs of their defeated foes. At Marston Moor, the Parliamentary army fought in alliance with an army of psalm-singing Scots Covenanters. In seeking to emphasize the importance of Cromwell's impact, I don't wish to neglect the significant assistance he received from Sir David Leslie's Scots cavalry, who were drawn up behind him. However, Cromwell was the man of the hour. Cromwell did not start the Civil War nor did he have overall command of the Parliamentary forces during it but at Marston Moor he was the agent of victory; a victory that was a crucial turning point in the war. It was also a victory for iron discipline.

In December 1644 Oliver Cromwell made a speech to Parliament proposing an idea originated by Sir William Waller. It concerned a 'new model' for the Parliamentary army. Hitherto the army had consisted of regional associations and men could be reluctant to campaign out of their immediate area. This made strategic operations difficult and the plan was for a national army without regional affiliations. The New Model Army Ordnance was passed on 19 February 1645. Sir Thomas Fairfax was appointed captain-general and commander-in-chief. Philip Skippon commanded the infantry and Cromwell was made lieutenant general of horse and second-in-command of the army.

Now all regiments of Parliamentary horse were subjected to the same discipline as the Ironsides. In the pursuit after a battle, they would never dismount to secure personal booty, as was the custom, but rather hunt down and kill every last man without mercy. On the battlefield they would not break for the final rout until ordered. They would charge, break up the enemy, then regroup ready to charge again at a different target, always holding the battlefield. This was the key to their success. At Naseby, a few months later, the New Model Army swept all before it, with Cromwell and his old Ironsides playing a leading role. It was effectively the end for the king's cause. Some Royalist hope lingered, mainly in the southwest, but Naseby was the last major battle. Parliament ruled and the king was king only in name.

Having won the war, the soldiers in the army soon became unhappy with Parliament. There were arrears of pay and they wanted immunity from prosecution for 'crimes' committed during the wars. For instance Cromwell secured many of the hundreds of horses needed for his regiments by ordering his men to steal them. After the war some of these men were hung for these thefts. The New Model was an army unlike any other. Its men were not only professional soldiers, well trained, well drilled and well disciplined but they also carried the fervour of belief in their hearts; belief that they fought for a just cause. They received good rates of pay – eight pence a day for infantry and two shillings a day for cavalry – and they had an unprecedented political voice. Two representatives from each regiment called 'agitators' were appointed to speak for soldier's rights, including financial relief for widows and for the wounded. One agitator declared in 1647

> We were not a mere mercenary army, hired to serve any arbitrary power of a state, but called forth and conjured by the several declarations of Parliament to the defence of our own and the People's just Rights and Liberties.

Above all the army felt that they had been 'conjured' by Parliament to rid the nation of a corrupt king – a cause so many had died for – and in the aftermath of the fighting, they perceived that Parliament wasn't doing enough to curb royal power. The army marched on London. In the strained atmosphere that followed, some regiments mutinied but Cromwell quashed all dissent with an iron fist.

Meanwhile, plotting between the king and his allies north of the border led to the outbreak of the Second English Civil War. Armies from Scotland, led by the

Duke of Hamilton, crossed into England, where English royalists flocked to their banner. There were a number of small fights and uprisings but the decisive blow to the Royalist cause came when Cromwell and the New Model Army crushed a massive Royalist army of 18,000 men at the Battle of Preston in 1648. Now the cries were heard for the king's head and Cromwell was among the chief callers, declaring impatiently to the judges at the king's trial, 'I tell you we will cut off his head with the crown upon it'. By 'we' he meant 'his' army and they were now the real power in the land. Charles I was executed on 30 January 1649. After his beheading, spectators were permitted, for a fee, to dip their handkerchiefs in his blood, believing that it would have magical curative properties. Shortly afterwards, Cromwell and the New Model Army were sent to Ireland.

Ireland

Ireland was considered to be a threat to the new Commonwealth and a place where Royalist sympathizers could muster and plan an invasion. The main rallying figure was the Duke of Ormonde. He commanded a confederation of resident Anglo-Irish Protestants and English Royalists who had fled to his banner from across the water. It was a sizeable army. Moreover by mounting an Irish expedition, Parliament hoped to dampen a growing restlessness in the New Model Army. Without a campaign to occupy them, frustrations amongst the men, mainly because of the amount of back pay they were owed, threatened to destabilize the country. Ireland offered a new enemy to focus on and the prospect of compensating the men with land grants. However, many refused to go and regiments had to draw lots to select who would serve. When they landed at Dublin in August 1649, the infantry that disembarked were wearing coats of Venetian red with white facings – it was the first 'redcoat' army on its first overseas campaign.

It is impossible in a work of this nature to go into adequate detail about the sensitive and complicated history of the English in Ireland; a history of conquest and settlement that began in the twelfth century. The Ireland in which Cromwell went to war was already a divided country. Most of the west was governed by native Irish chieftains, a great deal of the south was controlled by Anglo-Irish lords and a substantial portion of the east of the country, including Drogheda and Dublin, was under direct English rule. This area was known as the Pale (boundary) from the Latin '*palus*' meaning stake. In fact the boundaried area was surrounded by a ditch rather than a palisade. Successive military campaigns under Henry VIII and Elizabeth I in the sixteenth century had seen extensive land confiscation from those that resisted them. Under James I these lands, mostly in the north of the country, were settled by English and Scottish 'planters'; thus extending English rule beyond the Pale. That the settlers were Protestants grafted onto the existing Catholic population simply made an unjust situation even more volatile. This situation exploded in 1641 with the 'Irish Rebellion', in which Irish Catholics turned on the planters, killing thousands and driving many thousands more from their land. Vengeance for this was one of Cromwell's declared reasons for his campaign.

Drogheda was in the Pale, part of the old English colony, and was a highly-successful trading port. Its English governor, the one-legged Sir Arthur Aston, veteran of the English Civil Wars, commanded a substantial Royalist garrison. He was both a Catholic and a loyal supporter of the king and he refused to surrender. In September Cromwell breached the walls with heavy artillery bombardment. Legend has it that after being repulsed twice, he personally led his men into the town, climbing and stumbling over the rubbled ruins of the walls. It was probably then that his sword was struck by musket balls. Once through the walls, he and his men set about hunting down every last man that had held out against them. He later wrote, with apparent pride, 'The enemy were about 3,000 strong in the town. I believe we put to the sword the whole number of the defendants. I do not think thirty of the whole number escaped with their lives.'

The extent to which civilians were part of the massacre is debated, though it must be obvious that there were some 'collateral' civilian casualties in such a bloodbath. After the slaughter Cromwell said, 'This is a righteous judgement of God upon these barbarous wretches, who have imbrued their hands in so much innocent blood'. He had in mind the massacres of the 1641 rebellion. A dark spirit of retribution pervaded his psyche. Some eighty English Royalists in the town sought refuge in St Peter's Church. Cromwell recorded, as if pleased by it, 'I ordered the church steeple to be fired, when one of them was heard to say "God damn me, God confound me, I burn, I burn"'. It is this apparently callous and casual attitude to what was done that has made him such a enduring object of Irish loathing.

His defenders argue that though Cromwell and his soldiers perpetrated terrible acts at Drogheda, these were within the established customs of warfare at the time – no quarter to a garrison that does not surrender – and that is undoubtedly true. It is a case that is harder to make for Wexford, which fell to his sword in the following month. Negotiations were under way for an orderly surrender, when Cromwell's New Model Army took matters into their own hands and stormed the town. Accounts suggest that 2–3,000 were put to the sword, including a number

Cromwell's sword (© The Board of Trustees of the Armouries – RA IX 1096)

of women and children. Cromwell's report echoed the sentiments of vengeance he had displayed at Drogheda. He wrote, 'They were made with their blood to answer for the cruelties they had exercised upon diverse poor Protestants'. In wishing that, 'an honest people would come and plant here; where are very good houses and other accommodations', he declared the town virtually empty, saying with chilling understatement, that 'Most of them are run away and many of them were killed in the service'.

Cromwell was in Ireland for just nine months. After Drogheda and Wexford his army had a harder time of it, facing fierce fighting from Ormonde's Confederate forces, dysentery and, at Clonmel, a defeat.

After Ireland

By the time Cromwell returned to England, the future Charles II had raised an army in Scotland and was marching south, beginning the Third English Civil War (1650–1651). Cromwell, as commander-in-chief, led his New Model Army to notable victories at Dunbar and Worcester. In a final bloody rampage that saw his soldiers cut down fugitives as they ran through the streets of Worcester, the tragic wars that had set brother against brother for so long finally came to an end. If it is true that the sword now in Leeds is the one Cromwell bore at Drogheda, then it is almost certainly also the one he carried at Wexford and Dunbar and Worcester. He may even have had it as early as Marston Moor and Naseby. That it is a handsome sword there can be no doubt; one might even say that it was a sword fit for a king.

Oliver Cromwell became Lord Protector in 1653, signing himself 'Oliver P' (Oliver Protector) in a grandiose parody of kings – eg 'Charles R' (Charles Rex). He was appointed to the position for life and he had absolute autonomy, including the power to summon and dismiss Parliament. The Protectorate ushered in a period of puritanical repression at home and surprising adventures abroad, beginning in the middle of a naval war with the Protestant Dutch. In the Anglo-Spanish War, the New Model Army, as well as making assaults on the Spanish mainland, seized Jamaica from Spain in 1655. Cromwell also made an unlikely alliance with the Catholic Louis XIV of France to chase the Spanish out of the Netherlands. In 1658 the New Model Army drove the Spanish out of Dunkirk and in the treaty that followed France ceded the town to England. Louis XIV handed the keys over in person to Cromwell's commander, Sir William Lockhart.

Throughout his rule as Lord Protector, Cromwell suffered from bouts of malaria, which he had contracted during his Irish campaigns. He died, at the age of 59, in 1658 from a combination of malaria and an infection caused by a kidney stone. He was given a full state funeral and buried with due pomp at Westminster Abbey. At the restoration of Charles II two years later, his body was disinterred and taken to Tyburn where it was hung upon the gibbet for public display before being taken down and decapitated. The beheading, a macabre retribution for Cromwell's order to behead Charles I, took three blows. Both Charles I and Cromwell were beheaded with an axe but the sword also held a long tradition for this grim task.

Execution swords

Skeletal remains found at Stonehenge indicate marks consistent with a ritual behead-ing by sword some 2,000 years ago. In Medieval and Renaissance Europe beheading with the sword was considered the more noble option – after all a knight might expect to die by the sword on the battlefield. It was also thought to be the more humane option compared to the heavier but duller and slower axe; an instrument that cleaved rather than cut. Poor Mary Queen of Scots suffered three blows of the axe before her slender neck succumbed in 1587. It was for these reasons that Henry VIII agreed to Anne Boleyn's request for a French swordsman when her time came. Fortunately for her, the deed was swiftly accomplished in one blow.

Execution swords were typically around 4 feet in length, had a two-handed hilt and a very broad blade. This exaggerated width was partly for weight, partly to allow a gradual taper to the keenest of edges and partly to provide plenty of material for constant re-sharpening. Their superfluous points were rounded and blunt. The steel had to be of exceptional quality to take a keen edge and the executioner had to be highly accomplished at his work. It was the best headsman in France who was sent for to despatch Anne Boleyn. When beheadings were carried out with the axe, the head was placed upon a block. It could be awkward to bring the blade down at the correct angle and thus multiple blows resulted. Victims would customarily tip the headsman to encourage him to do the job cleanly. With the sword, the condemned prisoner had their hands tied, was set in a kneeling position and blindfolded, to ensure that they didn't move out of position involuntarily. Anne Boleyn's executioner considerately kept his sword hidden beneath the straw on the scaffold until her blindfold was in place.

Dr Guillotin's mechanical device was developed in 1792, in Revolutionary France, as a swift and humane alternative to the random abilities of a headsman and in response to the predicament of the state executioner, Charles-Henri Sanson, who was faced with increasing demands on his trade. Sanson neatly summed up the associated problems:

> After each execution the sword is unfit to perform another. It is essential that the sword, which is liable to damage, be sharpened and reset if there are several condemned persons to be executed at the same time. The Paris executioner has only two swords.

He also said, one assumes with unintentional humour: 'The executioner must be very skilful and the condemned very composed, otherwise it may be impossible to complete the execution by the sword without the risk of dangerous incidents occurring'. That an executioner should consider a sword fit only for a single use before being put to the whetstone raises an interesting point about battlefield swords. Clearly the sort of brittle edges necessary to achieve the razor-blade sharpness that M. Sanson required would not be practical for battle. Sharpness is a relative concept and, as has been stated many times in previous chapters, a battle sword need only be sharp enough to bite into an enemy's armour, be it steel carapace or buff coat.

Execution sword

Though the axe and the rope were the principal means of execution in England and Germany (one sixteenth-century executioner in Nuremberg made an exception for women, who, out of compassion, he seated in a chair and beheaded from behind with his sword), the sword was favoured in France, China, Japan and throughout the Arab world. Today, decapitation with the sword is only carried out in certain Arab countries adhering to Sharia law. In 2005 there were 88 men and 2 women executed with the sword in Saudi Arabia. The executioner swings his sword around his head several times to limber up and then jabs the blindfolded victim in the back, triggering a reflex that raises their head. He severs it in a single blow. If you kneel, with your hands together as if tied, and get someone to give you a push on the back, you will find it an instinctive reaction to maintain your balance by throwing your shoulders back and lifting your head, thus presenting the perfect target for the headsman.

Oliver Cromwell's cadaver needed no prompting for its butchery by the axe. His head was set upon a pole and displayed on the roof of Westminster Hall as a deterrent to any future regicides. It blew down during a gale in 1684 and was retrieved by a sentry, who kept it hidden for many years. It changed hands many times for large sums of cash and was exhibited in museums of curiosities. It was finally bought by Josiah Wilkinson in 1814 and remained in the family for generations. Its last owner, Canon Wilkinson, kept it in a wooden box and delighted to show it to local school-children. On his death it was donated to Cromwell's old university college, Sidney Sussex, Cambridge, where it was duly buried in an unmarked spot in the college chapel in February 1960.

Writing of Cromwell, Voltaire said that he had

> the Bible in one hand and a sword in the other, wearing the mask of religion on his face and disguising in his government the crimes of a usurper under the qualities of a great king.

It is an opinion shared by many, although the renowned American statesmen, and later President, John Adams, took a different view. When he and Thomas Jefferson visited the site of the Battle of Worcester in 1778, they were shocked at how little local people knew about their history. Adams wrote,

> The people in the neighborhood appeared so ignorant and careless at Worcester that I was provoked and asked 'And do Englishmen so soon

forget the ground where liberty was fought for? Tell your neighbors and your children that this is holy ground, much holier than that on which your churches stand. All England should come in pilgrimage to this hill, once a year'.

Oliver Cromwell is destined to forever provoke such controversy.

Restoration

Oliver Cromwell was succeeded as Lord Protector by his son, Richard Cromwell. It was an ill-starred elevation, having awkward parallels with royal inheritance. It was also a disaster politically and within a year the army council seized power. The country became increasingly ungovernable and in the following year, 1660, Parliament restored the House of Stuart to the British Crown in the person of Charles II.

Since Worcester, Charles had been living in exile at the French court of Louis XIV and from the moment of his accession he popularized French customs: full-bottomed wigs, red heels to shoes, mistresses and the smallsword. The smallsword was the successor to the rapier. As the name implies it was a far smaller weapon and it became the essential accessory to fashionable dress for all gentlemen. It wasn't unknown in England before the Restoration – a few well-travelled folk had already taken to wearing them – but it was only after 1660 that smallswords were adopted universally. We will follow the trail of the smallsword more closely in the chapters that follow but we will also see other ways in which the Restoration had a dramatic impact on swordfighting in popular culture.

Smallsword, circa 1760 (author's collection)

Chapter 12

The Gentleman's Companion: The Age of the Smallsword

Knowledge of the Small-Sword ... [is] an Art so necessary to be known, and so proper a Qualification for the constituting of a Man a Gentleman, that I had almost said, he can be none that is not skill'd therein.

(Henry Blackwell, *The English Fencing Master*, 1705)

Swords and gentlemen

Puritans had regarded swords as the necessary adjunct of the army but frowned upon the martial arts as an integrated part of a gentleman's cultural education. Indeed under the Commonwealth the habit of wearing a sword with everyday dress had subsided among the civilian population. However, with the death of Oliver Cromwell in 1658, there were inklings of the old ways returning and, in a letter of that year, Lord Windsor wrote to his friend Christopher Hatton in London: 'I observe that all gentlemen wear swords and that I may not look more like a bumpkin than the rest, I desire you would buy me a little riding sword and belt. I would not exceed five pounds price'. Fashion is an unstoppable tyrant that cannot be turned with either reason or stricture, though in Lord Windsor's case it did have a price limit.

Aspiring young gentlemen went to France for their 'finishing'. Here they would study all the martial and physical accomplishments befitting their station such as equitation, dancing, gymnastics and, of course, the art of fence. Among the English establishment, the notion persisted that equal emphasis be placed on these endeavours as on more scholarly pursuits. To cater for the latter, students were accompanied by private tutors to instruct them in Greek, Latin, Literature, Philosophy, Law and Mathematics. It was a distant homage to Castiglione's ideal of 'Renaissance man'. One suspects that the poor tutors may have had rather a hard time of it, endeavouring to press their wards to diligence in cerebral studies, whilst the worldly diversions of Paris beckoned them away from their books.

Of equal concern was that instruction, in still largely Catholic France, be given by men of Protestant conviction. An admirable solution arrived in the form of Monsieur Solomon Faubert. He was a Huguenot and, in 1679, fell foul of Louis XIV's new law that forbade Protestant masters of academies in France. Huguenot persecution was once again on the rise. His school in Paris was closed and he fled the country. Despite his secret Catholic sympathies, Charles II was well aware that he ruled a Protestant nation and in the same year approved an order allowing Huguenot immigration and naturalization. They came in their thousands and yet another strain of energetic, enterprising blood was introduced to the mongrel peoples of the British Isles. Among them was Solomon Faubert, who not only secured royal favour, becoming an equerry at court, but he also established an 'Academy of Arms' in the Soho area of London. Soho in the 1680s was a rather genteel suburb. Following the construction of Regent Street and the development of the West End in the eighteenth century, the site of Monsieur Faubert's academy has now disappeared. The only clue to its former existence being the little alleyway behind Regent Street now called Foubert's Place. This passage once led to the renowned establishment where M. Faubert inculcated the sons of illustrious men in 'riding, fencing, dancing, handling arms, and mathematics'. It set the tone of the age and a gracious skill with the new 'smallsword' became an accomplishment of paramount importance.

The Smallsword

The smallsword is really a species of rapier, in the sense that it originated as a civilian's weapon. Other countries, perhaps more aptly, have called it the 'town sword' or the 'walking sword' but to the English-speaking world it is known simply as the smallsword. It is a weapon of simple elegance and, no matter that it required athleticism and practised skill to manage it effectively, it nonetheless became the essential everyday dress accessory for urban fop and portly squire alike, whether he knew how to use it or not. To this day Members of the British Parliament have a little velvet ribbon suspended from their coat hook in the cloakrooms of the Palace of Westminster, so that they may hang up their smallsword before entering the chamber.

One early antecedent of the smallsword was sometimes known as the 'pillow sword', on the basis that it was considered a convenient size to hang at the bed-head in readiness to defend against nocturnal assaults. Modern scholarship scoffs at the term, preferring to call it the 'scarf sword', a phrase in contemporary use, and because it is the sort of sword you also see worn in the waist sash, so common a feature of seventeenth-century dress. Scarf swords had short quillons and a side-ring but with no other guards for the hand. In length they were somewhere between a rapier and a smallsword. This struggle for nomenclature highlights the problem of establishing exactly when a sword is a smallsword. Smaller, lighter civilian swords were already making an appearance by the third decade of the seventeenth century, manifesting in what are often described as 'transitional rapiers'. By the last quarter of the century it becomes quite easy to identify when a sword may be properly called a smallsword – there is a unity of basic design that continues unchanged into the nineteenth century, but the transitional period (circa 1620–1660) presents us with so many examples that are not easily pigeonholed. It is frustrating to the student of arms that so many swords, in an age of sword proliferation, defy an easy categorization but there it is.

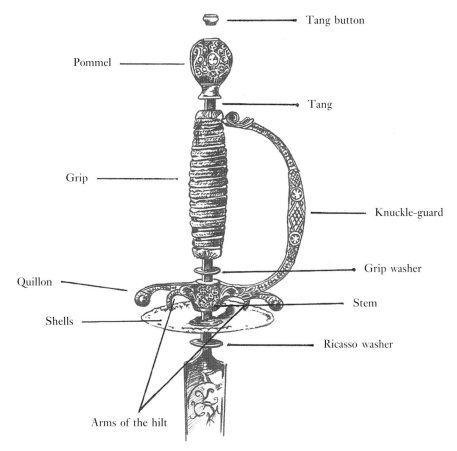

Tang button

Pommel

Tang

Grip

Knuckle-guard

Grip washer

Quillon

Stem

Shells

Ricasso washer

Arms of the hilt

The parts of a smallsword

Of course every variant sweep of a knuckle-guard, every angled slope of a side-ring or perforation of a guard-plate and every nuance of pommel design has been painstakingly recorded and grouped into catalogue pairings of style and date by knowledgeable curators and scholarly art historians but such erudition doesn't help us when we want to give the thing a simple everyday name. We are stuck with the inadequate and imprecise term, 'transitional rapier'. I'm afraid it is beyond the scope of this present work to attempt a remedy and so I shall hasten to 1660, when the smallsword has arrived on the scene in recognizable form.

   Stylistically, the smallsword owes much to the influences of Dutch town swords in the earlier part of the century and we can only speculate whether the smallsword was developed first in Holland or in France. Certainly the latter had the greater influence on its manner of use. It is possible that smaller swords developed because they were more convenient to wear in the increasingly crowded cities. Samual Pepys recorded in his diary for 10 January 1660: 'So to Westminster, overtaking Capt. Okeshott in his silk cloak, whose sword got hold of many people in walking'.

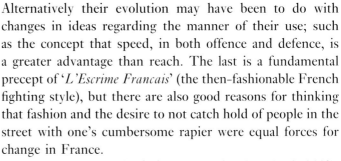

Alternatively their evolution may have been to do with changes in ideas regarding the manner of their use; such as the concept that speed, in both offence and defence, is a greater advantage than reach. The last is a fundamental precept of '*L'Escrime Francais*' (the then-fashionable French fighting style), but there are also good reasons for thinking that fashion and the desire to not catch hold of people in the street with one's cumbersome rapier were equal forces for change in France.

During the second half of Louis XIII's reign (1610–1643), Cardinal Richelieu promoted a movement of cultural chauvinism, seeking to eclipse the domination of the Italian Renaissance and re-establish France as the cultural heartbeat of Europe. He enacted various sumptuary laws banning, for instance, the wearing of velvet and brocade imported from Italy and Spain. His bid to purge France of foreign influence and create a particular French style probably also played its part in catalysing the development of a sword type that was distinctively French. French fashion became more restrained, having a minimalist simplicity, against which the extravagant proportions of an Italian or Spanish swept-hilt rapier would look out of place. Moreover the long blades of these rapiers necessitated them being worn in the hanger, suspending them at an angle across the back of the wearer's legs. The new fashion for outdoor wear at Louis XIII's court was for long capes (*manteaux*) and for three-quarter length coats (*cassoques*). In order for these to hang elegantly, they had to be worn with a shorter sword, which would suspend at a steeper angle, and one with a smaller hilt, which would sit more snugly at the waist. Whether the new dress fashion created the need for the smaller sword or whether the existence of a smaller sword allowed the development of the new fashion is difficult to say but, either way, the smallsword was born and with it a new 'French' system of fighting, which eventually came to dominate; just as France's cultural influence again held sway in Europe.

Smallswords were of a fairly universal design, having slender blades ranging between 30 and 32 inches. Guards consisted of a pair of joined oval plates, usually pierced or chiselled with ornate decoration and a knuckle-bow that

Hilt and forte of Colichmarde sword (author's collection)

emerged on the opposite side of the hilt to become a small, down-turned rear quillon. A pair of three-quarter circle bars, the 'arms of the hilt', supported the space between the knuckle-bow and the guard plates. Hilts were made in a variety of materials, most commonly steel, brass or silver, and were decorated in a variety of ways according to taste and fashion.

A distinctive variation to the standard smallsword type was the 'colichmarde'. The term referred to a style of blade that was broad at the hilt end for about one third of the distance down the blade, where it then shouldered in steeply, continuing at a regular slender width to the point. Its advantages are clear – more weight and rigidity at the point of parry, without sacrificing the lightness and finesse with which the point could be deployed. For a gentleman-officer carrying his smallsword on the battlefield, it was just that little bit more rugged and was therefore popular on military smallswords, though the style also found favour in civilian fashion. 'Colichmarde' – supposedly the French rendering of 'Köningsmark' – is said to derive from the blade's eponymous inventor and mercenary soldier, Philippe Christoph, Count of Köningsmark, a former pupil of Monsieur Faubert's academy in London. Unfortunately for this theory, the Count was not born until 1665, and blades of this type exist prior to that. However it is quite probable that the colichmarde was a favoured weapon for this Swedish soldier of fortune. It would certainly be a favoured weapon of mine.

Standard blades were most usually triangular in section and hollow ground, meaning that each of the three faces was worked at 90° to a small-circumference grind wheel, so that it was given a deep concave arch. Hollow grinding required a geared system of wheels powered by a water-mill, each having a leather belt to turn the adjacent, smaller wheel at an ever faster rate. It was an industrial process. Hollow-ground blades were the ultimate in combining extreme lightness with extreme rigidity and some of the best examples were made in the north of England by The Hollow Sword Blade Company.

The sign of the crossed swords

The fast-flowing River Derwent had the power to drive mill wheels at great speed. Millstone grit gleaned from its riverbed was a perfect material for sharpening blades, forests of woodland for making charcoal abounded in the area and there was plentiful local iron ore to be mined. Straddling its banks, with Northumberland on one side and County Durham on the other, was the small village of Shotley Bridge. It was here that an enclave of Solingen sword-makers set up shop in 1688. Located just a few miles from Newcastle-upon-Tyne, which was at the time Britain's second largest port after London, the Solingen men were able to bring supplies in and send merchandise out by barge. The Derwent flowed into the Tyne. Shotley Bridge is now a suburb of Consett, which until the works closed in 1980, was the largest steel-producing town in Britain.

Four Englishmen, John Sanford, John Bell, Peter Justice and John Parsons leased land in Shotley Bridge in 1688, the year that William of Orange was set upon the

British throne. It was they who invited the German workers to emigrate. They came, just like the Hounslow men a generation before them, partly to escape the fear of religious persecution – Louis XIV had revoked the Edict of Nantes and had declared that he would invade Northern Germany to re-establish Catholicism – and partly for commercial reasons. The very strict craft guilds in Solingen didn't favour independent enterprise and, by moving to England, the émigrés may have thought that they would corner the market because they would be able to undercut Solingen imports that were taxed with heavy duties. This was almost certainly the motive for their English bosses.

According to a summons issued by the Solingen court on 26 September 1688, Clemens Hohemann was the ringleader of the German men. Apparently

> Clemens Hohemann enticed away several craftsmen who have long been established and connected with this area to the Kingdom of England . . . Clemens Hohemann is accused of being a seducer deserving the severest punishment, along with all the other people involved.

The summons goes on to list twenty other names. Curiously there is no record of Herr Hohemann ever reaching Shotley Bridge; perhaps he received 'the severest punishment' or perhaps he changed his name. Many others on the list, however, are known to have settled at Shotley, among them being Hermann Mohl and Adam Ohlig, who became the leaders of the Shotley Bridge swordmaking community. I own a rapier blade, dateable to around 1610, that was made by Hans Ohlig and an extremely fine blade it is. The Ohligs were an old Solingen family and their craft secrets were passed through the generations. It was these secrets that the court and guilds of Solingen were so keen to protect from going overseas.

However, business was established quickly at Shotley Bridge and an issue of the London Gazette in 1690 carried an advertisement for swords made 'in Newcastle' by German workers. In September 1691 a royal charter was granted to 'The Governor and Company for making Hollow Sword Blades in England'. The preamble to the charter refers to the risk taken by the

> divers persons, who have exercised in their own country the said art of making hollow sword blades by use of certain newly invented instruments, engines and mills . . . and have prevailed upon them to expose themselves, to the hazard of their lives to impart to our said subjects their art and mystery.

It would seem from this that the death penalty was a possible risk for those taking Solingen's secrets to a foreign land. Fortunately, for them, The Company of Hollow Sword Blades did a brisk trade, selling not only smallswords but also military swords and tools. Blades from the Shotley mills were stamped with the word 'SHOTLEY' on one side and 'BRIDG' on the other. In addition the 'BRIDG' side of the blade was sometimes inscribed with the famous Solingen running wolf mark. More usually though it bore a new mark – the sign of the crossed swords. When, over 200 years later in 1920, Hermann Mohl's descendent, Robert Mole, joined his sword-making business with that of Henry Wilkinson, the 'crossed swords' mark was taken up by the new company. Shotley Bridge blades were of very high quality and the company's English directors exploited every opportunity to market them. In July 1699, the *London Gazette* announced that a consignment of their blades for auction could be viewed at the company's London warehouse in New Street. They were to be sold by 'candle sale'. Candle sales, in some ways the precursor of the 'e-Bay' concept, were a type of auction with a time limit. A candle was lit and bids were permitted until it went out.

The street of houses where the sword-makers lived remained standing until it was demolished in the 1960's. Stone lintels carried inscriptions in German. Many were quotations from the psalms, though the only complete one to survive translates as a eulogy to the puritan work ethic: 'The Lord's blessing will make you rich and free from all worry as long as you work hard at your job and do what is demanded of you'. Hard work and skill undoubtedly contributed to the community's success but so too did the quality of the steel they used. This was manufactured in smelting-mills and forges just a few miles downstream from the sword-mills and, though using local iron ore, borrowed trade secrets from Solingen methods. Bars of wrought iron were stacked between layers of charcoal and packed into sealed clay pots. These were then placed in a kiln, which was fired for several days. Gradually, carbon from the charcoal diffused into the iron. The bars were then forged together and, together with more charcoal, reheated in the kiln. Gases generated during the reheating process caused blisters to appear on the surface of the steel, giving it the name 'blister steel'. This blister steel was then heated to red hot and forged and folded by hammer several times in order to produce a homogenous material. It was known as 'shear steel' and it made excellent sword blades; in particular superior-quality smallsword blades.

L'Escrime Francais
Smallswords required a different system of management to fight with them effectively – a system that capitalized on their lightness and consequent speed. Throughout the rapier's history there were those that inclined towards its use as a single weapon, not paired with a companion weapon like the dagger. In such circumstances there was a natural tendency to adjust the posture by bringing the left foot in line behind the right, compared to the more open stance required for fighting with a double weapon system. With the introduction of the smallsword this became an imperative. The feet were set at right angles with the left heel exactly in line with the right heel, resulting in the sword having to travel a shorter distance to close off the line on either side. This in turn made the response time from parry to riposte much faster. Speed became everything and consequently the demand for lighter, faster swords increased. Swords

soon reached a stage where there was not enough weight in the blade to deliver an effective cut and so all pretence of retaining this dual ability was abandoned in favour of hollow ground, triangular section blades designed purely for thrusting.

The point ruled and swordfighting now relied entirely on an exchange of thrusts and, as a result, greater emphasis was placed on the lunge. Combatants, striking like cobras, extended their arms and advanced with the right leg, stretching every sinew to snapping point in an effort to gain more reach, and then with lightning alacrity recovered to their first position in the blink of an eye. None of this was entirely new. The extended lunge formed an integral part of the repertoire for fighting with the rapier in the Renaissance but it was exactly that, part of a repertoire. Now it became the soloist. In order to accommodate the requirements for the lunge and the heel-aligned body posture, a new mode of locomotion was developed. Previously all systems employed a 'passing step', in which one leg passed the other as in walking. The new 'fencing step' meant that virtually all movement forward and back was effected by maintaining the relative position of the feet, with the right foot forward. It is the same step that you see modern sport fencers doing. There were exceptions, for instance the 'passing lunge', where the left leg shoots forward from behind, extending the right leg into a full lunge and carrying a tactical element of surprise. There was the 'demi-volt' with which an attack was launched by the left leg snapping forward behind the right leg, so that the toes came into alignment. Counter-intuitively this move advanced the sword-point towards an opponent for a distance nearly equivalent to a full lunge and was delivered with driving momentum by bringing the left hand down sharply behind the back. Demi-volts had the extra advantage of rotating the attacker's torso out of line with the opponent's blade whilst at the same time launching the strike.

The carriage of the upper body was elegant. Although it is true to say that the placing of the left heel in line with that of the right reduces the area the sword has to guard, it is not to say that the body should be twisted sideways to make a smaller target. Many modern fencers do this, which not only spoils the line of their body but also can put undue strain on the cruciate ligaments in the forward knee. The eighteenth century way was to maintain a forward-facing posture with the hips and chest. In this way there was less strain on the joints and the ribcage was enabled to maximize its protective function – a ribcage is skeletal armour protecting the vital organs of heart and lungs. In a side-on stance the swordsman exposes far too much of the vulnerable area beneath the arm. A ribcage is not impenetrable but it's a sight more difficult to puncture than an armpit.

Complimenting the actions of sword-arm and legs was the left arm. It is a counterbalance and the lighter the sword, the higher the left arm is carried. When mimicked in parody it can seem effete but actually the left arm is a vigorous powerhouse that puts real force behind a thrust, striving to drive it deep into an antagonist's body. It also assists in recovering quickly from an extended lunge; by throwing it forcefully in the air it accelerates bringing your front foot back. Modern sport fencers seem to dangle the hand over their heads with an arm that's bent

A fencing exercise machine from a 1796 manual by a Swiss master, Balthazar Ficher, who had a school in St Petersburg. As the left hand is brought down in the action of lunging, it releases a cord, allowing a wooden heart to fall by gravity. The object is to pin the target before it reaches the base of the machine (photo courtesy of the National Fencing Museum)

forward. In my view, it is not a good look. In the eighteenth century the arm, only slightly crooked, was carried behind the head and the fingers extended in a pleasing line. The balance and poise of this posture facilitated a very subtle management of the blade. Concepts of taking control of the opponent's blade were as old as Liechtenauer but, with the smallsword, dramatic effects could be achieved with the slightest movements of wrist and arm. In practiced hands the 'bind', where your blade is wrapped in a corkscrew around that of your adversary, or the *glissade*, where it slides briskly down the length of his blade, are both moves that can send the sword flying from his hand. Disarming techniques epitomize the sword's ability to be an equalizer. Skill triumphs over brute force. No matter how big he is, if I can whip my opponent's sword from his hand with just a flick of the wrist, he is rendered instantly helpless.

As the seventeenth century gave way to the eighteenth, the smallsword continued to increase in popular esteem. However, there was a parallel trend, mainly amongst the poorer classes, for fighting with cudgels and staves and the broad-bladed, basket-hilted backsword. These were the weapons of choice for the professional gladiators, men who fought in swordfighting displays. Public 'combat performances' began during the Restoration and remained popular throughout the eighteenth and into the early nineteenth century. They were the forerunners of today's martial arts and swashbuckling movies. It is an old appetite.

The new gladiators

After the dour days of the Commonwealth, during which the Puritan regime had banned public entertainments, there was rejoicing in the streets. With the restoration of Charles II in 1660, the theatres were reopened and an enterprising group set themselves up as The Masters of Defence. They evoked the nostalgia of the lost tradition of the old Corporation of Masters of the Noble Science of Defence but, in practice, paid no heed to the spirit of 'playing the prize' as it had been conducted in Elizabethan times. These new masters were self-appointed, holding no charter or authority, and their pugnacious displays were purely for commercial benefit. 'Playing the prize' evolved into the 'prizefight', a gladiatorial contest intended only to entertain the crowds and performed not for the advancement of professional status but for money. Antagonists would stake their own purse and receive a share of the takings, as well as gathering all the money that was flung at the stage during the contest by a crowd urging them to greater violence.

Samuel Pepys attended such a prizefight in 1663:

> It was between Matthews and one Westwicke, who was soundly cut several times in the head and the legs that he was all over blood … it was very well worth seeing, because I did to this day think it was a cheat … but they did it in good earnest; and I felt one of their swords and found it little, if at all, blunter than common swords are.

An account by a French visitor to this peculiarly English form of entertainment gives us even greater insights into the conduct of these affairs. Monsieur de Rochfort tells us of a match he saw in which one man was struck on the wrist so that it was almost cut off. The wound was dressed, alcohol was imbibed and the fight continued. The man with the wounded wrist gained revenge by delivering a stroke to his opponent, 'which took off a slice of his head and almost all his ear'. Once again wounds were dressed and the combat rejoined. Another blow to the already cut wrist 'divided the sinews' and, at last, victory was conceded.

Fatalities were rare and it seems that the old rules with regard to thrusting were still adhered to. What the paying audience wanted, of course, was blood and that they got aplenty. A correspondent to *The Spectator* magazine (5 August 1712) reported on a conversation he had overhead between two would-be combatants agreeing to a challenge:

> One asked the other 'Will you give cuts or receive?' The other answered, 'Receive'. It was replied 'Are you a passionate man?' – 'No provided you cut no more nor no deeper than we agree'.

So it seems that, rather like professional wrestling today, there was at least some tacit agreement about injury and stunts to titillate the crowd, and surely, in many instances, actually fixing the outcome of the affray. Prizefighting was show business.

Nonetheless it was a very rugged and dangerous form of entertainment for the participants. In the same issue of *The Spectator*, another correspondent wrote about a fight between Buck and Miller, two celebrity champions of the day. Buck struck Miller across the forehead and 'much effusion of blood covered his eyes in a moment'. The wound was dressed and the combatants set to again. This time Miller received a cut to the left leg and 'the wound was exposed to the view of all who could delight in it and sewed up on the stage'. One can hear the bloodthirsty crowd sucking in their breath across the centuries with delighted horror.

Although the smallsword was worn by many officers on the battlefield and by all gentlemen in the street, it was hardly used at all in the prizefight arena; it was too dangerous. An odd exception to this was the sword and 'gafflet'. Gafflets were steel spurs that fitted to the heels of fighting cocks but, in this context, the word referred to a projection of the sword blade beyond the pad. In other words it was a small barb, just enough to prick, draw blood and visually register a hit but short enough that it would do no real damage. A substantial pad still offered protection against the consequences of a thrust penetrating to any depth. I know of no reference to an Elizabethan equivalent but such a device would explain an apparent conundrum in the fight between Hamlet and Laertes. It is set up in the image of a 'prize playing', with a set number of passes and with rebated weapons – 'These foils have all a length?', asks Hamlet. The problem arises that if the weapons were blunt, how could Laertes produce a poisoned sharp without it being noticed, particularly given that Elizabthan foils had large pads tied to the buttoned end? Something like the gafflet offers a plausible solution. However the mainstays of the prizefight arena were backswords and cudgels and perhaps the greatest eighteenth-century exponent of such contests was James Figg.

James Figg

Immortalized by his image on a handbill that advertised his services and which was drawn by William Hogarth, Figg appears the archetypal bruiser; tall, muscular and rough-hewn. His shaven, angular skull framed an equally angular face with deep-set eyes, a long nose and a small, expressionless mouth. He is depicted on the leaflet, backsword in hand, standing defiantly on a raised stage, similar in size and design to a modern boxing ring. He describes himself as a 'Master of the Noble Science of Defence' and advertises that he 'teaches gentlemen y use of small [and] backsword & quarterstaff at home & abroad'.

Figg was an entrepreneur, having his own amphitheatre in which public combats were staged. It was situated just off Oxford Street in the area where Berners Street runs today. Here he set up business, offering tuition to gentlemen in the weapons listed on his broadsheet. In that insightful series of paintings (and subsequent engravings) satirising the profligacy of the age – *The Rake's Progress* – Hogarth indicates the fashionable popularity of martial training to aspiring young gentleman by depicting his subject negotiating the services of no less than a trio of 'Figgs'. They attend his morning levee alongside other professionals seeking to relieve the young man of his recent inheritance. One is a fencing master with his buttoned foil, a second stands by with a pair of staves and the third is a disreputable, dissolute and overweight old soldier, hand on hilt in the action of drawing his sword, and catching the ear of his prospective patron as if to say 'A quiet word, guv'nor. I've been around a little and I

Figg's handbill, drawn by William Hogarth

can show you a few things that'll keep you safe down a dark alley of a night time. Tricks you won't learn at no gen'leman's school.' As in previous ages, whilst martial skill was considered an essential gentlemanly accomplishment, those who taught the art were very often scurrilous rogues.

In addition to teaching young gentlemen and putting on performances at his amphitheatre, Figg regularly staged prizefights at which he was himself a frequent contender. In fact the redoubtable Figg fought no less than 271 contests during his career, which spanned some twenty years until his death in 1734 at the age of fifty. Some of these matches were with fisticuffs, a newly fashionable sport, and Figg was acclaimed the very first British Boxing Champion. However, it was for the back-sword that he was most renowned. One of his students, a Captain Godfrey, wrote, 'I purchased my knowledge of the backsword with many a broken head and bruise in every part of me'. Although Figg appreciated the value of hard knocks and rough and tumble for the delectation of the crowds and the education of military men, he was shrewd enough to realize that it was education in the arts of the smallsword that would solicit the custom of young bucks, who may have need of it on the duelling ground.

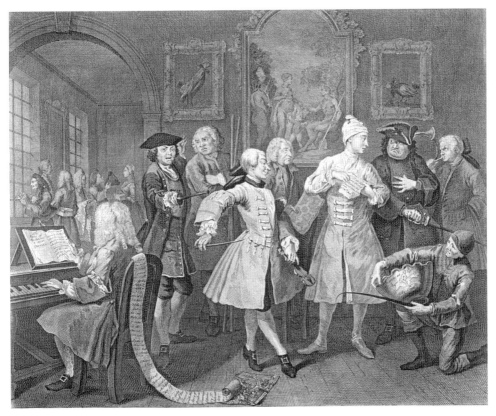

A Rake's Progress, plate II, William Hogarth. Note the three masters of arms – with foil, staves and smallsword – all soliciting for business (© Museum of London)

Masters of the smallsword

Across the Irish Sea, in Dublin, the English fencing master, Andrew Mahon, published a treatise in 1734, the year of Figg's death. It was called *The Art of Fencing* and in his introduction he asserts: 'A man who wears a Sword without knowing how to use it is full as ridiculous as a man who carries Books about him without knowing how to read'. It is an injunction that suggests there were many who wore a sword that had neither the patience nor the aptitude to study its proper use.

Mahon's treatise was actually a translation of the work of a French master, Labat, which had been published some forty years earlier. I love the illustrations in Labat's original work. They are full of energy and character and depict all the beauty of the smallsword fight. Here are passing steps onto the left foot delivered with exquisite grace and poise, perfectly timed demi-volts performed with matadorial élan and magnificently elastic lunges. There are moves which demonstrate the courage and confidence of a truly practiced master; one who drops his body in the lunge, lowering it just enough for the opposing thrust to pass inches over his head, as he sends his own point home on the opponent's chest. It is skilful and daring and sublime. There are neat seizures of the adversary's sword, timing a side-step just so to wrest it from his grasp with scientific leverage and, above all, there is a deportment which is as pleasing to the eye as it is effective in the balanced management of the body.

A distinctive feature of Labat's work is that the figures in his illustrations are using a new type of foil. It is pliable. We have looked at foils in the sixteenth century, when the word simply meant a blunt weapon, but they were still rigid. Now we see a thin piece of spring steel, pre-curved to dictate the direction of the bend on contact,

Smallsword techniques after Labat

exactly the same as on modern fencing equipment. Yet again improvements in steel manufacture had enabled a step forward in weapon design and gentlemen could now 'play at foils' with relative impunity. Fencing masks had yet to be invented in Labat's time and there was still hazard to the face but, with their buttoned ends, these little foils had taken much of the thump out of sparring.

All this refinement and gentility did not detract from the deadliness of the smallsword when used in earnest. It could find its mark and penetrate with alarming alacrity. As the Scottish fencing master Donald McBane put it 'the Small Sword hath great odds of the Broad, for the Small-Sword kills and you may receive forty cuts and not be disabled'. McBane enjoyed a colourful life, serving in various armies. He fought in many battles and, at Ramillies in 1706, he suffered a head wound that necessitated the insertion of a silver plate. One can only assume that this unorthodox cranial armour was an asset to a man who still took part in prizefights at the age of sixty-three, claiming, on that occasion, that he gave his young opponent seven wounds and a broken arm. Throughout his career he engaged in numerous private quarrels and supplemented his income between campaigns by teaching swordfighting. Mrs McBane also assisted in augmenting the family income by providing other services to an army on the move. She ran a mobile bordello! McBane relates that, in 1704, at Marlborough's campaign headquarters at Friedberg, he set up tents for gaming and had sixty 'campaign ladies' on standby for other amusements. Seeking to boost his provision of whores, he and fifteen companions raided a similar institution operating in the camp of Marlborough's ally, the cross-dressing military genius Prince Eugene.

> We got fourteen brave Dutch Lasses as a reinforcement. Next day came twenty-four swordsmen and demanded the ladies again. We had a drink, fought two and two, eleven Dutch killed and seven of our men. I fought eight running, we buried the dead and parted.

McBane was a practical fighter and his *Expert Swordsman's Companion*, published in 1728, contains not only his adventurous recollections but also many sound tips. He warns that coats should be removed before a duel, lest the opponent is concealing dirt or snuff in his pockets to throw in your face. He advocates reversing the sword and using the hilt to punch an adversary in the face and to manoeuvre so that the sun is in his eyes. His advice for fighting on wet or slippery ground is to turn the left foot so that foot is edgeways and not flat. Until reading McBane, I had for years berated students for this sloppy habit, which can delay the speed of a recovery and risk injury to ankle and knee joints as well as mar the elegance of line. I would still regard it as bad form on flat and dry ground but the expediency of a specific situation must always be taken into account. I had also thought it to be a small fault in the teaching of Labat, whose beautiful illustrations also show this rolled over foot, but McBane has made sense of it all and any swordsman facing an opponent in earnest would have benefited much from his pragmatic teachings.

No less effective but superficially more graceful were the teachings of Domenico Angelo Tremamondo, who came to prominence in the second half of the eighteenth century. Originally from Livorno in Italy, this most celebrated and remembered of all the smallsword masters established not just a school of fence in London but a dynasty. With a talent for self-promotion, his business card read simply 'Angelo'; thus joining that unique cadre of celebrities through the ages who have been known by a single name. Angelo had studied fencing in France under the tutelage of the legendary Teillagory. He also studied high school equitation under the even-more-legendary La Guernière. It was during a dalliance with an Irish actress, whom he followed from Paris to Dublin, that Angelo met a young English girl, Elizabeth Johnson. She was seventeen, he thirty-eight. They married in 1755 and moved to London, where they remained together happily for the rest of their lives. Signor Tremamondo senior, however, dismayed at what he perceived to be his son's dissolute life, finally cut him off from all funds. During a brief spell of employment as riding master to the Earl of Pembroke, Angelo's horsemanship was witnessed by George II, who declared 'Mr Angelo is the most elegant rider in Europe'. 'Mr Angelo' subsequently secured the position of riding and fencing master to George, Prince of Wales (later George III), and Edward, Duke of York.

Having accepted this elevated post, Angelo became the victim of the same sort of xenophobic bad temper that had beset Saviolo and Bonetti in Elizabethan London. In this case, Angelo's would-be nemesis came in the burly form of an Irish doctor by the name of Keyes. Unaware of the doctor's hostile opinion of him, Angelo was persuaded by friends to accept a challenge to a match at the *Thatched House Tavern* in St James's Street. By this time, 1760, a match meant a 'fencing' match in more or less the terms we would understand it today, in other words regulation had reduced it to a sort of sporting game. These fencing exhibitions were quite different from the robust entertainments staged by Figg and his ilk. The use of pliable foils and a convention to only make thrusts against the chest meant that such encounters risked little hurt, apart from accidents to the face. At some point during the 1750's a French master, La Boëssiere *père*, had invented a wire mesh mask to protect the face but it was considered effeminate and, initially, not used for public matches. Angelo disliked masks intently and always banned them in his school. It was also thought cowardly to evade a hit by retreating and fencers were expected to more or less stand their ground with the left foot, venturing forward and back only with the lunging right foot. Foils had buttoned tips that were furnished with parchment-covered pads. These were dipped in wet pigment, either black or vermilion, so that any hits would register visually on the opponent's body.

Dr Keyes, with his sleeves rolled up and himself rolling from the effects of the large brandies he had ostentatiously downed in front of the crowd, was a large man, having the appearance more of a navvy than a doctor. He attacked with wild fury and without etiquette. Angelo dealt with every assault masterfully, with minimum movements and graceful ease. At one point he disarmed the truculent doctor, flicking his sword from his hand with a bind. Puce with indignation, Keyes snatched back his sword, which

Smallsword techniques after Angelo, *Ecole des Armes*, 1763

Angelo had graciously proffered, and attempted a sneaky lunge. Angelo dealt with it deftly; then proceeded to decorate the Irishman's chest with an elaborate pattern of vermilion roundels. In order to complete the furious doctor's humiliation, Angelo concluded by disarming him again, this time by a different method. Angelo was famed for his numerous disarming techniques; my favourite being 'Angelo's deception' whereby the left foot passes forward and to the side, whilst at the same time grabbing your opponent's wrist with your left hand and bringing your own sword behind your back to menace at his.

As a result of this stylish victory, Angelo received not only plaudits but also clamours from influential quarters for him to open his own school. This he did, acquiring Carlisle House in Soho Square as his premises. Angelo's 'school of arms', which had a riding ménage as well as a *salle d'armes* was successful from the start and frequented by the most illustrious names of the age. In 1763 his treatise, *Ecole des Armes*, was first published and it is still regarded as the definitive work on fighting with the smallsword. Much of its fame resided in the fine quality of the illustrations, which were drawn by the artist John Gwynn. Angelo himself posed as one of the figures in each drawing and it is thought that his opponent may have been modeled by his brother and assistant, John Xavier Tremamondo.

Publication of *Ecole des Armes* coincided with the period when Denis Diderot was compiling his great encyclopaedia in Paris. He selected Angelo's text and pictures for the entry under 'Fencing', causing a tremendous jealous furore amongst the ranks of the Compagnie des Maitres en fait d'Armes des Academies du Roy en la Ville et les Fauxbourgs de Paris. Not only was Angelo not French, he was neither an accredited *maitre d'armes*, approved by the academy's examinations. Guillaume Danet, the head of the academy, was the most vociferous in his condemnations. Danet published

Smallsword techniques after Danet, *Art des Armes*, 1766

his own work, *Art des Armes*, in 1766, which contained snide comments about 'the author from London' and denouncements of Angelo's favoured techniques, such as disarms, voltes and passes. Mindful of previous slights, Angelo wrote in the London newspapers that M. Danet's forthcoming work had plagiarized his own. It was an ill-founded charge and Danet responded, abandoning any pretence of professional courtesy, with

> I should indeed have to be pitied if I had been obliged to copy the drawings and the theories in M. Angelo's treatise ... As to my plates ... it may be that they are not so beautifully engraved as those of Mr Angelo ... but my drawings are far more correct if regarded as accurate illustrations of the true principles of my art.

Angelo's accusation, at least with regard to theory, was unfounded, but vituperative rhetoric has ever been a characteristic of exchanges between rivals in the profession of arms (viz: George Silver); indeed it surfaces from time to time among practicing masters of historical fencing and dramatic combat to this day! Angelo, incidentally, taught many actors at his school, including his close friend and the greatest theatrical celebrity of the day, David Garrick.

By the second half of the eighteenth century, duelling with the sword had begun to be eclipsed by the pistol. In order to attract sufficient clientele to provide him with the income he desired, Angelo thought to promote the benefits of a martial education in ways other than equipping a gentleman with the necessary skills to survive in a duel. Self-defence remained an important reason and Angelo also taught how to defend against sword and dagger, and sword and lantern – the fighting systems of continental footpads likely to waylay a gentleman on the 'grand tour'. In such circumstances, he advocated pressing the cloak or coat into service as an additional means of defence. However, it was the development of 'fencing with foils' as a genteel and gentlemanly recreation with strict limitations on target and freedom of movement that was the greatest departure from the past. The emphasis of his teaching was on beautiful movements, poise and carriage; he was known as 'Monsieur Perpendicular'. Geometrically speaking, this was a misnomer since he actually advocated a stance in which much of the weight was on the left foot with the body leaning back a little. It was intended to keep the face as far away as possible from chance hits. Angelo was both the last of the old masters and the first of the new. He taught practical skills with the smallsword that were intended to kill an opponent as efficiently as possible but it is also from his salon that we can date the emergence of 'sport fencing' in a form that we would recognize. Domenico Angelo was still giving lessons with foils, to the pupils of Eton College, up to the time of his death, at the age of 86, in 1802.

Seventeen years earlier, at the age of 69, Angelo had made over the main business to his son, Henry (Harry) Angelo. Harry, who had studied in Paris and qualified as a *maitre d'armes*, was for ten years, usher, that is assistant master, to his father at Carlisle House from 1775. The younger Angelo's skills as an equestrian however were indifferent and shortly after taking over at Carlisle House, he abandoned the premises, with its ménage, for rooms at The Royal Opera House. In those days this was not at its present location in Bow Street but rather in the Haymarket at the heart of theatre-land. Harry Angelo not only sought out the company of actors and taught actors swordfighting skills for the stage, he was an actor himself, known to have a talent for broad comedy. It wasn't just the theatrical set who attended his academy however; the Angelo name continued to carry prestige and the best blades in town furthered their education under Harry's tutelage. I have choreographed fights for dozens of productions and taught several courses at the present Royal Opera House and am always aware of both the privilege and the continuity of teaching at an institution once frequented by an Angelo. In 1789 fire gutted the Opera House and Harry's rooms there. He relocated to Bond Street, where he remained until 1820. Forced to retire after tearing the tendons in his left thigh during a fight rehearsal with the leading actor of the day, Edmund Kean, Harry handed over the Angelo School of Arms to his son, Henry. This Angelo, Angelo III, continued to run the school but also, in 1833, became 'Superintendant of Sword Exercise' in the army, a post that was also held by his son Henry Angelo IV. Though to some extent diluted with 'fencing' as a recreational pastime and with fighting for the stage, the Angelo dynasty remained firmly connected with real fighting arts.

Military swords in the eighteenth century

Even in this age of cannon and muskets and pistols, the sword continued to see service on the battlefield, particularly in cavalry regiments. During the War of Austrian Succession, Private Thomas Brown of the 3rd Hussars received rather more than his fair share of French steel at the Battle of Dettingen in 1743. Having already had two horses killed under him and two fingers severed from his bridle hand during the early stages of the battle, he gallantly charged into the thick of the fighting to recover the regimental standard, which he did successfully. For his trouble he was rewarded with eight sabre cuts to his head, face and neck, two bullets in his back and a cut across his forehead that went down to his right eyebrow. He also had his nose cut off. The Battle of Dettingen was the last battle in which a British monarch, in this case George II, led his troops into battle and Thomas Brown was the last man to be knighted on the battlefield. He died at home in England three years later and was buried in an unmarked pauper's grave. Brown's sword of course was a cavalry sabre, not a smallsword.

Whatever the style of sword borne by either a soldier or a gentleman, it represented his personal honour and there was no greater shame or disgrace than having one's sword broken. It sometimes happened that a sword was ritually broken after a Court Martial that concluded with an officer being dishonourably discharged. This famously happened in the Dreyfus Affair in France in 1894, when an artillery officer, Alfred Dreyfus, was convicted, wrongly, for treason. Another famous instance of a gentleman having his sword broken occurred in the first of two duels between Angelo's close friend and pupil, the hot-tempered Irish playwright Richard Brinsley Sheridan and Captain Matthews. Besting the captain with one of Angelo's proprietary disarms, Sheridan then broke his sword over his knee. The second duel between the two, in which Sheridan came off the worst with multiple perforations, was a consequence of this humiliation being made public.

In 1760, Lord George Sackville was cashiered for cowardice after refusing orders to lead a charge at the Battle of Minden in 1759. The court ruled that he was 'unfit to serve His Majesty in any military capacity whatsoever'. There is no record of what happened to his sword; it may have been broken or it may have been ritually surrendered. Sackville's father was Lord Lieutenant of Ireland, then still a British colony. At the age of twenty-one, Lord George, while studying at Trinity College, Dublin, had been a student of the celebrated fencing master Andrew Mahon and so we can assume that he had some ability with the blade, if lacking a little steel in his heart. Yet, before his funk at Minden, he had had a relatively distinguished military career, leading a charge of the Duke of Cumberland's infantry at Fontenoy in 1745, where he was wounded and captured. The following year he was colonel of the 20th Foot Regiment who fought for Cumberland's army, butchering Bonnie Prince Charlie's Highlanders at Culloden Moor. After that he commanded the 7th Irish Horse on campaign in Holland. Throughout his career he was known for his homosexual promiscuity and so had no cause to visit the ladies that the Mrs McBanes of this world provided for a soldier's comfort. He fought for Marlborough in the Seven Years War and after Marlborough's death became commander of the British Forces. It was in that capacity that he ignored the call from his ally, Duke Ferdinand of Brunswick, to launch a decisive cavalry attack at Minden.

In an effort to blot out the stain to his reputation, he changed his name to Lord Germain, in 1770, following a benefit he received in a will. Five years later, Lord North appointed him Secretary of State for the American Department. Prime responsibility for suppressing the American revolt fell to him. With customary arrogance, he said at the time: 'these country clowns cannot whip us'. One 'country clown' possessed with altogether more dignity, honour and valour was to prove him wrong. His name was George Washington and he was a man for whom the sword was both an abiding symbol and an essential tool of war.

George Washington by Charles Willson Peale (© The Metropolitan Museum of Art)

Chapter 13

The Many Swords of George Washington: Swords in the American Revolutionary War

As the sword was the last resort for the preservation of our liberties, so it ought to be the first to be laid aside when those liberties are firmly established.

(George Washington, 1776)

At Mount Vernon, George Washington's beloved country estate, with its peerless panoramas of the Potomac and the pastoral splendour of rolling green Virginia countryside, four of his several swords are laid to rest in their glass sepulchres. The first of these, a gem among gems, is a 1753 silver-hilted English smallsword.

The Braddock Sword

Its hilt is beautifully decorated with chase and chisel work. Chasing is a method of embellishing the plain surface or refining the patterned surface of a cast, working the metal with a hard stylus by pushing the material rather than removing it. Chiselling removes material from the work. In this case the processes are used to achieve a writhen effect in places so that the pommel, parts of the knuckle guard and rear quillon knop appear as if the metal has been twisted like a stick of barley sugar. It has a strikingly energetic effect without seeming too fussy. The wooden grip is almost certainly a replacement. Originally it would most likely have been wrapped with a braid of silver wires.

It is a very handsome sword and mounted on a very serviceable blade, one that is stoutly broad at its base but which tapers to a needle point. The sword's overall length is 36½ inches with a blade of 30 inches that has the classic smallsword cross-section of a hollow triangle with a prominent ridge on the top edge, lending it rigidity. I own a smallsword with an almost identical blade and have always found it to be the ideal embodiment of the form. Its balance assists the arm intuitively into a neat parade of parries and it seems to accelerate the thrust. It feels comfortably light in the hand and yet never flimsy.

It is known as the 'Braddock Sword' because this is the sword that George Washington carried on the Braddock campaign, an ill-feted expedition, which culminated in a disastrous defeat at the fight at Monongahela River in 1755. General Edward Braddock was commander-in-chief of the British forces during the early years of the French and Indian War, the North American component of the wider conflict known as the Seven Years War. The French, with their Native American allies, were fighting against the British and their American colonists for dominion of much of the North American continent. Braddock's campaign centred on the struggle for control of the Hudson River. As a loyal British subject, the 23-year-old Washington had volunteered as Braddock's aide-de-camp. A tradition grew up that the Braddock Sword was the general's own, handed to Washington as he lay dying on the battlefield. However there is no evidence to support such a theory. It is a romantic idea that was first suggested by popular art. The image became common in depictions of the battle by post-Revolutionary War artists. They found symbolism in a British commander yielding power to the young Washington (and thus to America). They were in the business of mythologizing the recent past and Washington's role in it. Of more substance is the tradition that Washington subsequently owned Braddock's bloodstained sash and pistol. Both of these are also exhibited at Mount Vernon. The sword, in all probability, was Washington's own.

On this occasion George Washington was of civilian rank, but he had already been blooded in the service of king and country and was a commissioned officer. Major Washington fought for the British cause from the very outset of the conflict when, as a raw 21-year-old in 1753, the same year that the Braddock Sword was made, he was sent with a letter to the commander of the French troops occupying land to the west of the Blue Ridge Mountains. The letter registered objections from the Governor of Virginia to the French presence in the area which was 'so notoriously known to be the property of the Crown of Great Britain, that it is a matter of equal concern and surprise to hear that a body French forces are erecting Fortresses and making settlements ... within his Majesty's Dominion'.

Close up of the hilt of the Braddock sword (Courtesy of the Mount Vernon Ladies' Association)

In the following year Lieutenant Colonel Washington of the British Army led a force of 160 men on a mission to secure a strategic point on the perimeter of the territory. He built a makeshift fort, which he named Fort Necessity, and allied with the local Indian tribe under Chief Tanarcharison. With his Indian allies he attacked a French patrol and killed ten men. Whether any of these kills were by his own hand is not recorded. The French commander, M. de Jumonville, was wounded and taken prisoner. As Jumonville attempted to explain that he was actually on a peace mission to negotiate terms, Chief Tanarcharison, who spoke French, pre-empted Washington's response to the translation by splitting open Jumonville's skull with his tomahawk, pulling out his brain and washing his hands in the blood. His warriors at once slaughtered all the remaining prisoners and scalped them. Washington played the incident down, reporting only that Jumonville had been killed in the action but the repercussions of the massacre led directly to a full-scale outbreak of hostilities and were a dark chapter in Washington's early career.

The Braddock campaign of 1755 was a major offensive to capture the French stronghold at Fort Duquesne in Pennsylvania. Braddock set out from Maryland, with an army of around 2,000, for the 110-mile march. Benjamin Franklin procured an extensive wagon train and supplies for the journey. Among the British officers were Thomas Gage, destined to become commander of the British forces at the outset of the Revolutionary War, Charles Lee and Horatio Gates who were both to take prominent roles in Washington's Continental army. What tricks destiny was to play on them.

Captain Lienard De Beaujeu, the commander of the French garrison, was greatly outnumbered, having only a force of around 900, of which 640 were his native allies. Knowing that he could not withstand an artillery attack on the fort, he dressed himself in tribal war gear, streaked his face with war paint and heroically led his men to intercept Braddock's army as they crossed the Monongahela River. Arriving too late for an ambush, he nonetheless engaged the British column with great success. Lieutenant Dunbar wrote: 'We had not marched 800 yards from the river when we were alarmed by the Indian Hollow [yell] and in an instant found ourselves attacked on all sides'. De Beaujeu was killed early in the battle but his men fought on undaunted. Braddock was also mortally wounded, dying the following day.

Colonel George Washington, as he now was, though suffering from both dysentery and piles, fought with distinction. He eased his discomfort by placing a cushion on his saddle and rode into the fray. Two horses were shot from under him and four musket balls holed his coat. Miraculously he survived unhurt. With uncharacteristic braggadocio, the youthful Washington wrote afterwards to his brother Lawrence: 'I heard the bullets whistle and believe me, there is something charming in the sound'. Upon reading this extract from the letter, which was published subsequently in a London newspaper, George II is said to have observed: 'He would not say so had he heard many'.

Be that as it may, as the hapless and mortally wounded Braddock was stretchered from the field, Washington formed a rearguard that brought some order to the chaotic British troops and allowed them to disengage.

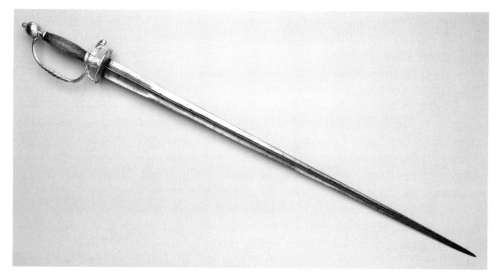

The Braddock sword (Courtesy of the Mount Vernon Ladies' Association)

The Indian tactic of sniping from behind trees occasioned much of the British disarray. Dunbar again: 'Our men, unaccustomed to that way of fighting, were quite confounded and behaved like poltroons'. Braddock's contingent of British and Americans suffered 877 casualties, whereas the French and Indian force acknowledged only 23 killed and 16 wounded. It was a painful object lesson in the efficacy of guerrilla tactics that would serve Washington so well in the latter years of the Revolutionary War.

At Monongahela, Washington would probably have carried a pair of pistols slung across his saddle but these were one-shot weapons and, having been discharged, were too time-consuming to reload in the midst of a mêlée. The only recourse would have been to draw his sword and lay about him. Writing of the panic and confusion among the British troops, Lieutenant Dunbar goes on to say, 'We begged of them [the common soldiers] not to throw away their fire but to follow us [the officers] with fixed bayonets, to drive them from the hill and trees'. It is precisely in such circumstances that an officer would draw his sword. The smallsword, in skilled hands, was an admirable weapon of self-defence for the officer class. It could perforate a soldier's coat with ease and precision and find his eye with surgical accuracy. The Braddock Sword has a sturdy, soldierly blade and one may well imagine Washington fighting with it for his life. He was a man of conspicuous bravery and a warrior of the front line.

In later years he presented the Braddock Sword to his favourite nephew, George Lewis. George Lewis was the fourth of Washington's sister Betty's nine sons. It is not clear when the gift was made. It may have been when Lieutenant Lewis was serving as second-in-command of the Life Guards, a corps of hand-picked men detailed as couriers and the personal guard of the commander-in-chief and Mrs Washington during the Revolutionary War. He also fought bravely at Trenton and Princeton. He rose to the rank of captain during the war and afterwards, at the time of the Whiskey Rebellion (1794), to major. At that time it was reported that Washington said to him: 'George you are the eldest of five nephews that I have in the Army. Let your conduct be an example to them, and do not turn your back until you are ordered.' It was as Major Lewis that President Washington dispatched him on a secret and dangerous mission to the French and Indians in Canada. Perhaps this was the occasion of the gift. It would certainly have had a resonance with the sword's earlier association during the French and Indian War.

The John Augustine Sword

The sword that Washington carried during most of the French and Indian War was of a different type altogether. It was a 'cutto'. The word 'cutto' stemmed from the French '*couteau de chasse*' (hunting sword) and so derived in exactly the same way as the word 'hanger' (described in Chapter 11). There was, however, a distinction between them. 'Hanger' was used more freely to describe various styles of short swords, whereas 'cutto' referred to a particular style of hunting sword – a style that was, in the eighteenth century, also adopted for military wear. Thus one may say that not all hangers were cuttos but all cuttos were hangers.

Typically, eighteenth-century military cuttos had irregularly-shaped grips, often either made from or imitative of stag antler, curving and flaring towards the pommel,

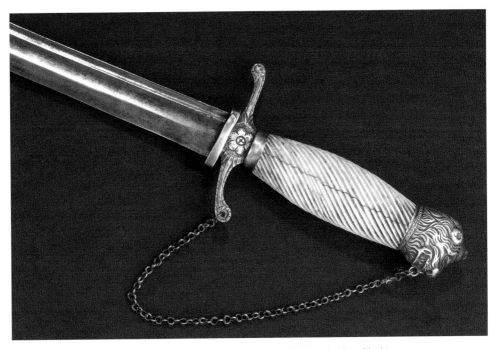

Hilt detail of the the John Augustine Sword (Courtesy of Sotheby's New York)

no knuckle-guard and only the most vestigial of quillons. They were the mirror of their hunting counterparts. In some examples, they possessed a chain as a sort of proto-knuckle-guard, offering some security from being dropped but none against a strike. When carried by officers in the field, this lack of obvious hand protection gave them a certain devil-may-care dash. Compared to a cavalry sabre, a cutto was a much shorter and lightweight alternative, but one that could sever the sinews of a man's arm or gash his face equally well. In Washington's case, his giant frame and long arms more than compensated for any deficiency in length. He stood an imposing 6 feet 2 inches. A cutto advertised an officer's credentials as a gentleman every bit as much as did the military smallsword, but it did so with a little more swagger, bringing with it the cachet of the hard-riding huntsman. Washington was a passionate foxhunter and a very aspirational gentleman. It should be no surprise that he favoured such swords.

This particular cutto was an especially good-looking specimen, having a silver lion's head pommel, silver S-curved quillons, a single silver chain in place of a knuckle-guard and a short 29½-inch blade. Its ivory grip, writhen with deeply cut spirals, was typical of both English and German manufacture during the 1750s. At the time of writing it was still privately owned by the Lattimer Family Collection, though, following the death of Dr John K Lattimer in 2007, it was destined for public auction. Until recently it was displayed at The National Portrait Gallery in Washington DC but returned to the family in 1999. I was just in time, and fortunate indeed, to be able to visit the beautiful family home in New Jersey and meet Evan Lattimer, the late doctor's daughter, herself immensely knowledgeable about the swords in the collection. She kindly allowed me to pore over dusty documents relating to the sword's history.

As with the Braddock Sword, it all boils down to word-of-mouth family tradition. I cannot say whether all the stories are true, merely that these are the stories. In the case of the 'John Augustine Sword', the most compelling information comes from William Lanier Washington. He became the proud inheritor of the sword and sought con-firmation of the family stories from Lawrence Washington, the last descendent to live

One of 58 fine examples of lion-headed hangers in the Lattimer Family Collection (Courtesy of Sotheby's, New York)

at Mount Vernon. In 1933 he signed a sworn statement reporting his interview with Lawrence. He also sent the sword to noted arms historians of the day for appraisal. The 'Lanier papers' are the basis of this sword's provenance. As such they are certainly not proof of the fact and Lanier was sometimes thought to gild the lily when it came to the provenance of Washington memorabilia, which he traded to a hungry market. However, this sword was not something he was seeking to trade and I am inclined to believe its reported history.

The story goes that Washington carried this sword during the French and Indian War and the early years of the Revolutionary War, until he gave it to his brother John Augustine Washington. It was to John Augustine, known to Washington as 'Jack', that he wrote phlegmatically a few days after the Braddock defeat:

> As I have heard since my arriv'l at this place, a circumstantial acct. of my death and dying speech, I take this early oppertunity of contradicting both, and of assuring you that I now exist and appear in the land of the living.

John Augustine is said to have received the sword when he became a county lieutenant in the Virginia Militia. Records show that, although he was made a colonel in the Virginia Militia in 1775, he did not become county lieutenant (of Westmoreland County) until 1779/80.

Now, the acceptance of this sword as one George Washington used in the French and India War doesn't necessarily contradict the provenance of the Braddock Sword. He could have had both simultaneously or not acquired the Lattimer specimen until '56 or '57, after the Braddock campaign. Moreover, at the time of the Braddock campaign, he was serving as a gentleman volunteer and so might have adopted a more civilian type sword on that occasion.

Intriguingly, there is a silver belt clasp, engraved 'GW 1757', which was on a sword belt that has previously been associated with the famous Washington 'Battle Sword' that is now in the Smithsonian Institution. That association is certainly erroneous since, as you will read presently, the maker of the Battle Sword, John Bailey, could not have produced this sword prior to 1778. The clasp is, however, for a sword belt and it is possible that it relates to the John Augustine Sword – certainly the date would fit.

The legend that the clasp and buckskin belt were associated with the Battle Sword derives from when the latter was presented to Congress in 1843 by one of George Washington's great-nephews, Samuel T. Washington. Clasp and belt were said to 'accompany' the sword. Together with the sword, the clasp was transferred to the Smithsonian in 1922. What became of it is a mystery, for it can no longer be traced.

Whether the GW 1757 clasp is associated with the John Augustine Sword or not, it seems probable that this is the sword he was carrying at a famous incident in 1758. In November of that year Washington, as a serving British officer, was leading his Virginia Regiment towards Fort Duquesne, that fateful objective of the Braddock campaign three years earlier, when they encountered a reconnaissance unit. In the

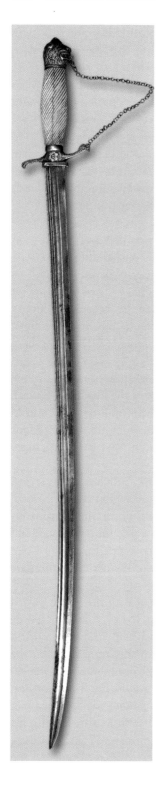

ensuing firefight there was considerable confusion and his men were falling from 'friendly fire'. Black powder muskets are deployed at relatively short range and give off a great deal of thick smoke. Vision can quickly become obscured. It is one of the reasons why eighteenth-century armies favoured such brightly coloured uniforms, to distinguish friend from foe in the dense fog of battle. Washington rode, with the utmost bravery, through the opposing lines of his own men, knocking up their muskets with his sword. It was an act of considerable courage. He confessed in his later years that his life was in greater peril at that moment than at any other. The sword he may have been using in that moment was the John Augustine cutto.

This style of hanger/cutto, with its chain and lion-head pommel, seems to have been especially popular in eighteenth-century America. There are fifty-eight fine examples in the Lattimer Family Collection alone. Pommels representing the British lion appear to have been by far the most popular, though there are also examples of dog heads and horse heads. Eagle heads are also found from the mid-eighteenth century, even though the bald eagle did not become the American national symbol until 1782. Thereafter, of course, eagle heads become almost ubiquitous on American swords. Swords from different sword-makers appear with identical lion-head pommels, so we must assume that rough casts were widely available from the same supplier and that these were then chased and finished by individual silversmiths.

It has been suggested that the reason George Washington decided to present this sword to his brother was that he considered it inappropriate, as commander-in-chief of the Continental Army, to be carrying a sword bearing the emblem of the enemy.

If I am correct in deducing that this didn't happen until 1779, then it wasn't an instant or pressing concern to him and it means that the John Augustine Sword is the one he carried at Long Island in August 1776, when he effected the miraculous withdrawal of what remained of the Continental Army after its crushing defeat under

The John Augustine Sword (Courtesy of Sotheby's New York)

the generalship, or rather mis-generalship, of that colourful adventurer Major-General Charles Lee. Washington, seeing the battle lost, took command in the field personally and organized the complete evacuation of his 10,000-strong force under cover of darkness. It required consummate leadership to maintain order, calm and quiet in such circumstances and if he hadn't succeeded it is most likely that his army and the cause for American independence would have been lost. The winning of wars is often as much about the careful management of defeats as it is about the prosecution of victories.

On paper, the Continental army could just about claim 20,000 men, including State militias. Most were ill-trained and at least half, stricken with smallpox, were too ill to fight. Thus there were around 10,000 at Long Island. It is astonishing that so great a fate depended on so small an army. Long Island, 27–30 August 1776, was the first major engagement to be fought by the newly-declared United States of America. Arrayed against them was Lord Howe's British expeditionary force. Thirty warships and 500 troop carriers had sailed into New York harbour that summer. It was the largest military force to assemble in one place during the entire war, with an estimated 32,000 soldiers and 10,000 sailors.

The odds against Washington's army were overwhelming; intriguingly, though, if one is to believe the precise detail of accounts of what befell a New York landmark a few weeks earlier, it had been provided with sufficient munitions to annihilate every one of Howe's men. A gilded lead equestrian statue of George III, which had been set up at the Bowling Green end of Broadway in 1770, was, on 9 July 1776, assailed by a jubilant mob. They lassoed it with ropes and brought it tumbling to the ground in a scene reminiscent of the toppling of another statue some centuries later (Baghdad, 9 April 2004). King George's dismembered head was carried off to a nearby tavern but the rest of the statue was melted down to produce 42,000 musket balls, a number that curiously corresponds to Howe's combined land and sea forces. The occasion of the statue's demise was the announcement to Washington's troops of The Declaration of Independence.

Various dates compete in significance for recognizing the moment of American independence and 4 July is one of the least convincing contenders. It is not just that a state of war had existed between Britain and its colonies since April 1775 or that a peace treaty recognizing American independence was not signed until 1783 but that there are earlier claims to the moment of political declaration, albeit by a matter of days. On 1 June 1776, Richard Henry Lee, a delegate from Virginia to the second Continental Congress, proposed a resolution for independence, known as The Lee Resolution. Congress passed it on 2 July 1776 and it stated:

> Resolved, that these United Colonies are, and of right ought to be, free and independent States, that they are absolved from all allegiance to the British Crown, and that all political connection between them and the State of Great Britain is, and ought to be, totally dissolved.

Thomas Jefferson's Declaration of Independence, with its embodiment of ideals and itemization of perceived wrongs justifying the claim to independence, was an augmentation to Lee's basic political act. Congress also passed Jefferson's declaration – two days later on 4 July. There is no dispute that it is an inspirational document and worthy of celebration but its anniversary, celebrated as Independence Day, is not strictly speaking the anniversary of American Independence; it is simply the anniversary of Jefferson's document. Independence had been asserted quite un-ambiguously by the passing of Lee's Resolution two days earlier on 2 July. John Adams was in no doubt. On 3 July he wrote to his wife Abigail:

> The second day of July, 1776, will be the most memorable epoch in the history of America. I am apt to believe that it will be celebrated by succeeding generations as the great anniversary festival. It ought to be commemorated as the day of deliverance, by solemn acts of devotion to God Almighty. It ought to be solemnized with pomp and parade, with shows, games, sports, guns, bells, bonfires, and illuminations, from one end of this continent to the other, from this time forward forever more.

There is a further complication. Of the thirteen colonies represented at the Continental Congress, only twelve passed either Lee's Resolution or Jefferson's Declaration. New York abstained from both votes. Washington, marshalling his beleaguered troops in New York, was a signatory to neither document. In fact it wasn't until 2 August that a fair printing of Jefferson's Declaration received multiple signatures. The original copies, rushed from the presses for immediate distribution, bore only the signature of John Hancock, president of the Congress, and its secretary, Charles Thomson.

On 9 July copies of the Declaration of Independence reached New York. On that date New York finally voted for independence, making it a unanimous resolution of the former colonies. Also on 9 July, George Washington gave orders that copies of the Declaration were to be collected from the Adjutant General's Office and distributed to the colonels of every regiment. His orders of the day went on to state:

> The Hon. The Continental Congress, impelled by the dictates of duty, policy and necessity, having been pleased to dissolve the Connection which subsisted between this Country, and Great Britain, and to declare the United Colonies of North America, free and independent States: The several brigades are to be drawn up this evening on their respective Parades, at Six O'Clock, when the declaration of Congress, shewing the grounds and reasons of this measure, is to be read with an audible voice.

Who can doubt that Washington himself was on parade at six o'clock that evening and who can doubt that he was wearing a sword? Moreover it is more than a little probable that that sword was the John Augustine cutto. At the moment the leaden statue of George III came crashing down on Broadway and at the moment his hard-pressed men threw their hats in the air at the historic news from Congress, George Washington must have reflected on the fight ahead and perhaps placed one of those giant hands on the lion pommel of the silver-hilted John Augustine Sword as he inwardly resolved to make that independence a reality.

However, whether you argue for 2 July or 9 July as the more significant date, George Washington was in no doubt that it should be 4 July. In 1778 he marked that day with a double ration of rum for his soldiers and an artillery salute to commemorate the anniversary of American independence. The John Augustine would doubtless have sat on his hip that day also, as it must have done earlier at the battles of Trenton and Princeton, where he was so famously victorious following the near disaster at Long Island.

Emmanuel Leutze's painting of Washington crossing the Delaware on the eve of Trenton, as heroically iconic as any of David's paintings of Napoleon, shows him wearing the Battle Sword – the one that is in the Smithsonian Institution. Painted some seventy-five years after the event, it is not, of course, an eyewitness record of the undertaking but a romanticized portrayal. In it, the curve of the sword has been exaggerated to accentuate the sweep of forceful energy that the picture so encapsulates. It captures the essential dash and flair of a charismatic leader; a spirit emphasized by his dashing and stylish sword.

We are so used to the rather dour and morose image of Washington on the dollar bill, taken from the Stuart portrait of his careworn later years, that it is easy to forget the vigour of the man who defied the odds to found a nation. The sword in the Leutze painting is a potent symbol of that endeavour and it matters not whether it was the Battle Sword or the John Augustine Sword on that occasion – both have equally swash-buckling élan.

It was the evening of Christmas Day 1776 when Washington, in one of the boldest moves of the war, began to lead his troops across the frozen waters of the Delaware River for a surprise attack on the British and Hessian troops at Trenton the following day. There was a blizzard, many of his men were without shoes and their endurance is almost beyond

George Washington receiving a salute at Trenton. Engraving by Holl after painting by John Faed (Image: Library of Congress)

Crossing the Delaware, engraved by Paul Girardet after Leutze (Courtesy of the Mount Vernon Ladies' Association)

imagination. What is certain is that Trenton and the nearby Battle of Princeton, fought just a week later, were decisive turning points in the Revolutionary War and that these victories secured Washington's reputation as a general more than any other.

He would have worn the John Augustine Sword at his defeats at Brandywine and Germantown in 1777 and it is the John Augustine Sword that he most likely wore during that terrible winter of '77/'78 at Valley Forge, where his demoralized, bare-footed, barely-clad, starving and diseased army spent a cruel winter. The strength of character and fortitude of Washington and these men, holding out against insuperable odds is the stuff of legend. But Valley Forge wasn't the coldest winter they endured. That was at Morristown a year later. Morristown was the coldest winter of the century – the Hudson River froze to a depth of fifteen feet. And Morristown is home to yet another of Washington's swords.

The Darke Sword

Washington received this sword from his lifelong friend, Colonel William Darke, an officer in the Revolutionary War and a comrade on the Braddock campaign. It belongs to the Washington Association of New Jersey who are custodians of the Morristown Washington Headquarters Museum. I was frustrated on my trip there to find the collections museum closed for renovation and subsequently discovered the sword temporarily on loan to an exhibit at Washington's birthplace in Virginia.

It is a classic silver-hilted smallsword, bearing the London mark for 1770, and stamped with what appears to be 'J.P.' on the hilt, indicating the maker to be James Perry of 10, Crown Court, Fleet Street, London. There is gadrooned decoration on the hilt, almost identical to the Braddock Sword. The guard plate is quite different however, looking similar to the top plan of a little boat. Overall the sword measures 34¾ inches and it has a colichmarde blade, ornamented with etched, blued and gilded designs.

Shortly before he died, Washington gave the 'Darke Sword' to his nephew, Lawrence Augustine Washington, son of his eldest full brother, Samuel. Lawrence, who was twenty-two when Washington died, also received the suit of clothes that Washington wore at his Presidential inauguration in 1789. There is debate, largely

The Darke Sword (Courtesy of Morristown National Historical Park)

based on the association of the clothes, as to whether the sword he wore at his inauguration was this one or the one commonly referred to as the 'State Sword', which is at Mount Vernon.

In 1976 the US Bicentennial Society favoured the claim of the 'Darke Sword' and commissioned 1,000 replicas from Wilkinson Sword in London. A correspondent to the Smithsonian magazine at the time lamented that one of the selling points of the replicas was that they had 'been quenched in whale oil'. He opined that it 'is immoral to kill an intelligent being in order to make a trivial memento'. Wilkinson's responded that they had last bought a consignment in the 1950's and that, at the time of writing, they had enough to last a further ten years. Certainly, the quenching of a smallsword blade is critical in order to make one of the right temper. Though of necessity they must be slender and rigid, they also need great pliability and springiness. Domenico Angelo, that doyen of eighteenth-century fencing lore, advising on the purchase of a sword, suggests:

> The temper of the blade is to be tried by bending it against anything, and it is a bad sign when the bending begins at the point; a good blade will generally form half a circle to within a foot of the shell and spring back again. If it should remain in any degree bent it is a sign that the temper is too soft – but though it is a fault, these blades seldom break. Those which are stubborn in the bending are badly tempered, often break, and very easily.

It was common to buy blades and hilts separately. One might either replace a damaged or worn-out blade in a favourite hilt or one might select a more-fashionable new hilt for an old and trusted blade. Equally, one might select the two together anew and have them mounted at the fourbisseurs. The tang of the sword passes through the hilt and is then peened over with a hammer until all is tight. In order to compress the parts securely together, a leather washer sits between the hilt and the forte of the blade. This washer is very evident on the Darke sword because it is a more recent replacement for the original.

George Washington married Martha Dandridge Custis in 1759. He married 'up' and her considerable fortune secured him the lifestyle of the landowning squire that he so aspired to. He turned his Mount Vernon plantation into a highly profitable business, growing tobacco, wheat and marijuana – the latter for the hemp fibres that were used in rope-making. Agriculture was his passion and he was a great innovator of new farming practices. Soldiering and statesmanship were duties.

After the French and Indian War, Great Britain sought to recoup some of the vast finances it had spent on protecting its colonists from the territorial ambitions of the French. That was Parliament's rationale in seeking a range of taxation measures on its American subjects. However those subjects were opposed to taxation without representation. Moreover there was a mood amongst America's intellectual elite that favoured ideas of liberty and equality put forward by radical thinkers like Thomas Payne, author of *Common Sense*. George Washington was sympathetic to many of the ideas of the Enlightenment and to Payne's inspirational notion that 'We have it in our power to begin our world over again'. The rest, as they say, is history.

George and Martha remained devoted until his death in 1799, although his letters suggest that he never lost his yearning for his unrequited true love, Sally, the wife of his friend William Fairfax. In any event there were no offspring to the Washington marriage. Martha, who had been widowed, already had two children, which he treated as his own. They both died tragically at a young age and Washington reached out his paternal embrace to his twenty-three nieces and nephews. For a man who had no children of his own, his extended family, by means of the offspring of his half-brother, three full brothers and sister, was vast. Five of these, one son for each sibling, were singled out in his will for the special honour of receiving one of his swords. The will reads:

> To each of my Nephews, William Augustine Washington, George Lewis, George Steptoe Washington, Bushrod Washington and Samuel Washington, I give one of the Swords or Cutteaux of which I may die possessed; and they are to chuse in the order they are named. These Swords are accompanied with an injunction not to unsheath them for the purpose of shedding blood, except it be for self defence, or in defence of their Country and its rights; and in the latter case, to keep them unsheathed, and prefer falling with them in their hands, to the relinquishment thereof.

The Battle Sword

The first to choose, by the terms of the will, William Augustine Washington, was ill at the time and unable to attend the selection. By common accord, the others agreed that though last in the list, Samuel Washington, son of George's brother Charles, should receive the general's 'Battle Sword' on the grounds that he was still a serving officer in the army.

What a prize! This glorious sword, with its set-back, green-stained, ivory grip wound with two thicknesses of silver ribbands, moulded silver S-curved quillons and curved blade is now in the Smithsonian Institution in Washington DC and has traditionally been hailed as the one he carried throughout the Revolutionary War.

That claim may have to be modified a little in light of the probability that it was the John Augustine Sword that he wore until late 1778, but it does not diminish the splendour of this highly significant sword that he undoubtedly carried thereafter. I went to visit it and was permitted to remove it from its display case. It is as light as air; I have held heavier feathers. Yet, because the distinctive shape of the grip so perfectly nestles in the hand, it feels substantial and secure to wield. Its gently curved, short blade, a mere 30 inches, scythes through the air as quick as a whip, and, despite the curve, comes to point in a perfect straight line from the shoulder when held in

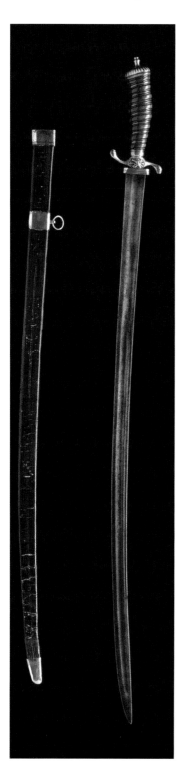

pronation. Its sinewy lines are rakish and cavalier. For an otherwise very conventional man, this was the equivalent of a bright tie worn with a conservative business suit. It is a cutto.

I got a real thrill from holding this sword. It was an immense privilege – the undisputed highlight of my day, though it was run a close second by the museum dog. When I went subsequently to the storeroom, I encountered a black Labrador belonging to one of the staff. I had been away from home and living in Washington for many months and was missing my own dog, of the same ilk, greatly.

Intriguingly, there are small nicks on the blade consistent with it having had blade-to-blade contact. These cluster around the area of the optimal striking point and there are a few others nearer the hilt where it may have been used to parry. More prosaically, it is entirely possible that such damage was caused when some of the nephews, as children, played with uncle's sword on a visit to Mount Vernon.

As noted in the paragraphs concerning the John Augustine Sword, there is, or at least was, a silver clasp on a sword belt, engraved with the initials G.W. and the date 1757, which has traditionally been associated with the Battle Sword but such an association is highly improbable. On the silver locket that sits at the throat of the scabbard of the Battle Sword is its maker's name and location: 'J. Bailey of Fishkill, New York'. John Bailey did not move to Fishkill until 1778, so the belt clasp and the associated scabbard cannot be contemporary.

It is remotely possible that the scabbard is a later replacement or that the sword was re-mounted. It was common to have new blades fitted to hilts or new hilts fitted to blades. Indeed there is a letter from Tench Tilghman, Washington's loyal aide and confidential secretary, to the quartermaster, Colonel Hughes, who was based at Fishkill, saying: 'If you have occasion to pass your neighbour, Bailey, be

The Battle Sword (National Museum of American History, Smithsonian Institution)

good enough to remind him he has a Cutteau of mine to new mount. You know he wants jogging.'

In just a few words, Tilghman paints a wonderful picture of everyday life during the Revolutionary War. It flags up the importance of little things, even in momentous times, and which of us does not know a tradesman who needs jogging? Hughes replied: 'Your Cutteau is not quite finished. The scabbard is finished but there are some small matters to do yet. Bailey says he has not the ingredients to stain the handle. He promises to complete the rest in two or three days, but you are no stranger to the man.'

John Bailey tanned the leather for his scabbards himself, though it was his wife who stitched them, which explains why that item, at least, was ready. He was famous for his beautiful jade-green stained grips and 'waiting for materials' is a stock response for the procrastinating tradesman. Bailey was well known to officers of the Continental Army. Indeed, according to his daughter Charlotte, both George Washington and the Marquis De Lafayette visited him personally at Fishkill.

Another letter to Hughes, this time from Washington himself, reads,

> General Washington presents his compliments to Col. Hughes and begs the favour of him to request Mr. Bailey to put a blade into the enclosed handle of a knife – and soon – the general would be glad of Col. Hughes' company to dine with him the first time he crosses the river.

On this occasion the 'and soon' was adhered to. Hughes wrote back to Washington just two weeks later, enclosing the newly bladed knife.

Thomas Anbury, a British officer who was taken there as a prisoner after Saratoga, described Fishkill, which is about 5 miles east of the Hudson River near New York, as having around fifty homes and as being, 'the principal depot of Washington's army, where there are magazines, hospitals, workshops etc which form a town of themselves … and some well constructed barracks, with a prison'.

Bailey set up shop there in 1778, as recorded in *The New York Packet and American Advertiser* (14 May), which carried the following advertisement:

> John Bailey, cutler from New York, is removed from Fredericksburgh to Fishkill, where he intends to carry on his business extensively in its several branches. Workmen are much needed, such as Cutlers, who are capable of making surgeons instruments, who can file well, Silver Smiths, White and Black-smiths who will meet with the best encouragement.

He purchased a 200-acre farm just west of the village and worked it along with his cutlery business. His daughter claims he produced two-dozen swords a week, which suggests he managed to recruit at least some of the staff he was looking for.

John Bailey had come to America in 1755, at the age of nineteen. With him was his brother William, older by a year. Born in Yorkshire in 1736, John apprenticed his

366   *Swords and Swordsmen*

trade in Sheffield, then at the cutting edge of the cutlery industry. He settled in New York City where he doubtless prospered. Certainly, by 1771 he was in a position to set up his own business, which he did with another Yorkshireman, James Youle. *The New York Gazette and Weekly Mercury* (4 March) announces 'Bailey and Youle, Cutlers from Sheffield at their shop near the Merchant's Coffee House makes ...'; it goes on to list more than fifty products from surgical instruments, to irons for lame legs, to scissors, knives, cleavers and other tools. It mentions that they fix new blades into any kind of haft but, other than sword-canes, there is no mention of sword production. There are, however, several swords in existence that bear the legend 'J. Bailey N. York'. The business was located at the southeast corner of Wall Street and John Bailey lived above the shop. He married Anne Brickstock the following year.

He dissolved his partnership with Youle in 1772 and continued trading as sole proprietor. His advertisement for October of that year reads, 'J. Bailey, Cutler from Sheffield at the sign of the Cross Swords'. Such signage may be an indication that he was now making swords in greater quantity. Many of the surviving Bailey swords from this period are hunting swords, presaging his reputation for specializing in these stylish arms.

While Bailey prospered, America was moving irrevocably into conflict. The Boston Tea Party took place in 1773 and the Battle of Lexington/Concord in 1775. In August 1775, the 64-gun British warship *Asia* opened fire from New York harbour. At 3 o'clock in the morning she fired a 32-gun broadside, lighting up the night sky. Anne Bailey was on her porch, overlooking the East River, with an infant in her arms. A cannonball flew within inches of her head. Terrified, she retreated to the cellar for two days, surviving on the oysters that were stored there.

On 4 February 1776, the British general Sir Henry Clinton sailed into New York harbour with a fresh supply of British troops. The war was on. Along with thousands of other evacuees, John Bailey, his family and two servants loaded what they could onto a wagon and drove out of the city. They moved first to Peekskill in Westchester County where they sought refuge with his brother William. When Bailey returned to New York to finalize his affairs and collect the remainder of his goods, he discovered that his clerk had sold the entire contents of his shop and run off with the proceeds!

It is the greatest tragedy of civil wars, and in many ways the Revolutionary War was just that, that father is set against son and brother is pitted against brother. Benjamin Franklin's son, William, sided with the British. John Bailey supported the patriot cause; his brother William was a loyalist, who eventually enlisted in the Loyal American Regiment, fighting for the British. John Bailey moved to Fredericksburg, New York, where he began making swords under contract for the Continental Army. He is listed as a 'Separate Exempt', indicating that he was excused military service on the grounds that he was employed in supplying vital services. Those services were best supplied with his subsequent move to Fishkill, a thriving, bustling centre of arms procurement for the Continental Army.

After the war, John Bailey returned to New York, selling his farm in 1784. He was granted American citizenship and set up his cutlery business at 22, Little Dock Street.

Whether he reconciled with his brother is not known. In later years he became established as a minter of coins but it is as the maker of George Washington's Battle Sword that he will always be remembered.

The first engagement at which it would be possible for Washington to have carried the John Bailey sword was the battle of Monmouth Court House in June 1778. It is possible that he was still using the John Augustine Sword at this date, but equally possible that he laid it aside, acquiring the fabulous green-hilted cutto soon after Bailey set up shop in Fishkill and only thinking to send his old sword to his brother a year later to mark his promotion to county lieutenant. There is no record of Washington, as commander-in-chief, having ever used his sword in anger during the Revolutionary War, though LaFayette remembers him in action at Monmouth Court House: 'General Washington was never greater in battle than in this action. His presence stopped the retreat ... His stately appearance on horseback, his calm, dignified courage'. We may imagine him, sword in hand, directing the turnaround. We cannot know if he came to blows with an enemy but he was certainly in the thick of the fray and, perhaps, brandishing his stylish new cutto.

After the war, Washington sheathed his sword, relinquished his command and returned to Mount Vernon to pursue life as a country gentleman. Destiny had other ideas and he was persuaded to take the Presidency of the new nation six years later, for fear that all he had fought for would unravel in what was rapidly becoming a disunited States.

That beautiful green and silver hilt and sweeping blade were called into service to sit on his hip on one other occasion. The Whiskey Rebellion began in 1791 as a protest against federal taxes on distilled spirits. Washington's federal government, under Alexander Hamilton's stewardship of the Treasury, had assumed the debt that all thirteen states had incurred during the Revolutionary War and money was needed to pay for it. Western settlers depended on distilling their grain into spirits in order to get it to distant markets at a time of poor or non-existent roads. They thought the tax unfair and their already perilous livelihoods were threatened

'Whiskey Boys' began violent protests in Pennsylvania, Maryland, Virginia, North and South Carolina, and Georgia. By the summer of 1794, tensions had escalated to the point that the civil protests became an armed rebellion. The first shots were fired ten miles south of Pittsburgh. It now became a matter of establishing federal authority. Washington declared Martial Law and summoned the militias.

This federal army assembled in Harrisburg, Pennsylvania in October 1794. It numbered some 13,000 men, almost the size of the entire Continental Army in the Revolutionary War. Washington resumed the role of commander-in-chief, strapped on his famous 'Battle Sword' and addressed the troops. It was not a random choice to wear the John Bailey sword, Washington was well aware of the significance and power of symbols. In the event, this show of force calmed things down, a few rebels were arrested, the rebellion petered out and federal authority was established. The sword was put away again for the last time.

The Frederick Sword

In William Augustine Washington's absence, Judge Bushrod Washington then selected for him the 'Frederick Sword'. William Augustine was the son of Washington's half-brother Augustine. The 'Frederick Sword' is so called because family tradition has it that it was presented to Washington by Frederick the Great of Prussia, who conveyed with it the sentiment 'from the oldest general in the world to the greatest'. Sadly there is no evidence whatsoever to support this claim.

Certainly, Washington was an admirer of Frederick both as a pioneering military mind and as ruler who dabbled, albeit with hypocrisy and contradiction, in ideas of the Enlightenment. He ordered a bust of him for Mount Vernon and his library contained thirteen volumes of his translated works. One wonders, though, whether he was aware of Frederick's less attractive foibles, such as his habit of striking people across the face with his cane or kicking women in the street; acts that he excused on the grounds of religious zeal.

Frederick, on the other hand, is not recorded as having anything other than a passing interest in George Washington. In response to an enquiry as to his thoughts on the outcome of the Revolutionary War, Frederick wrote cautiously:

> I should perhaps venture an opinion that the colonies will become indepen-
> dent, because they certainly will not be crushed in this campaign, and the
> government of the God-dammes [popular European slang for the English]
> will find it difficult to dip in the purses of the people.

In spite of his accurate prophesy, Frederick refused to receive America's envoy, Arthur Lee, or to recognize American independence until France had done so – hardly the stance of a committed admirer.

There is then nothing, other than popular mythology, to suggest that the sword came from Frederick. It is not even typical of German workmanship. In fact, such faceted steel hilts were known as an English speciality and most particularly a speciality of the Birmingham firm of Mathew Boulton and James Watt – yes that James Watt. Their pattern book, now in the Birmingham Public Library, is full of such designs. Cut-steel jewellery was as much a part of their industrial catalogue as were their improvements to the Newcomen steam engine. However, this sword can be no more surely linked to their manufacture than it can be to Frederick's gift.

As a popular myth the 'Frederick Sword' is a powerful one, symbolizing the passing of the sword from the old world to the new but it is no more than that – a fable. There is a parallel story, printed in *The New Jersey Journal* of 9 August 1780, which claims that Frederick sent Washington a portrait of himself bearing the famous inscription. Again there is no evidence that such a picture ever existed.

Washington wore this sword on numerous State occasions, such as in 1791 when he received the Senate at his private residence in Philadelphia, and it features in the retro-spective 1834 portrait by Vanderlyn, which hangs in the House of Representatives. Ella Basset, the widow of Colonel Lewis Washington, sold the Frederick Sword in

The Frederick Sword (Courtesy of the New York State Library, manuscripts and special collections)

1873 to the New York State Library in Albany, where it remains to this day. It became slightly damaged in the fire that ravaged the State Capitol in 1911 but is now fully restored.

The hilt is finely made but exhibits, to my mind, an excess of fussy ornament. It is a smallsword and the steel hilt is all black with a multi-faceted grip and adorned with bijou encrustations of black pearls. In the latter half of the nineteenth century, the curator of the State Library, Mr Howell said 'The impression that the sight of it made on me – with its steel beads instead of jewels – was that it was a very niggardly present for a monarch to make to a man like Washington'.

After William Augustine's death, the sword passed through the generations until, when in the possession of Colonel Lewis W. Washington, it was seized in the prelude to John Brown's daring raid on Harper's Ferry on 16 October 1859. Washington's great-grandnephew was among the first captured as a hostage and with him the Frederick Sword, which was prized by Brown as a talismanic trophy. After years of leading anti-slavery campaigns, John Brown had come to raise an armed rebellion that he intended would ensure abolition.

George Washington owned slaves all his life; it was the world he was born into. On his father's death, when George was eleven, he inherited ten slaves. At the time of his own death he owned 124 slaves in his own right. His will ponders the dilemma of giving these slaves their freedom before the decease of his wife, Martha, since many of her personally-owned slaves were married to his and it was not in his gift to set them free also. He concluded that to

Hilt detail of The Frederick sword (Courtesy of the New York State Library, manuscripts and special collections)

emancipate his own slaves during her lifetime 'would be attended with such insuperable difficulties on account of their intermixture by Marriages with the dower Negroes, as to excite the most painful sensations, if not disagreeable consequences'. He certainly espoused the cause of emancipation, writing enthusiastically to his friend and surrogate son, Lafayette, to applaud him on his scheme to establish a colony in the Caribbean for freed slaves. Yet he wavered from any direct action during the time of his Presidency for fear of fracturing the consensus of the new Union. It is also widely believed that his dentures, today displayed at Mount Vernon, contained the teeth of deceased slaves. Certainly Washington's attitude to slavery changed over his lifetime but he was, at best, a lukewarm abolitionist.

Harper's Ferry, along with Springfield, had been established by George Washington as one of the national arsenals and was stockpiled with weapons. John Brown's aim in capturing it was to arm a full-scale slave rebellion. His small raiding party consisted of just twenty-one followers, comprising five black men and fourteen white sympathizers, including two of his own sons. One of his sons died fighting with the Frederick Sword in his hand. The insurgents held out for two days against the local militia, though they suffered a number of casualties. On 18 October, the arrival of Federal forces under the command of Colonel Robert E. Lee, forced them to take refuge in what has become known as John Brown's fort. This was actually the small fire engine house of the armoury.

With only fourteen of his men still alive, Brown remained defiant against the superior force, perhaps thinking that his several hostages would buy him more time. However, when he refused the ultimatum to surrender, a squad of marines, led by Lieutenant Israel Green, were ordered to storm his impromptu fort.

In his account of the assault, which appeared in *The North American Review* in December 1885, Green described how his men used a ladder as a battering ram to smash through the door and that he was the first to climb through the splintered aperture into a scene of smoke-filled confusion. He recounts that the marine who followed him in was shot in the abdomen by a Sharpe's cavalry carbine and that the men, who came in quickly after that, immediately killed two of Brown's followers with their bayonets.

The first person that Green encountered was Colonel Lewis Washington, who was standing near the hose cart and who greeted him calmly with 'Hello, Green'. A few feet to his left knelt a man with a Sharpe's cavalry carbine in his hand. He was pulling the lever to reload. 'This is Ossawatomie', said Colonel Washington, referring to Brown by the nickname he had acquired during his abolitionist campaigns in Kansas. As he spoke, John Brown turned his head to look up. Green described what happened next:

> Quicker than thought I brought my saber down with all my strength upon his head. He was moving as the blow fell, and I suppose I did not strike him where I intended, for he received a deep saber cut in the back of the neck. He fell senseless on his side, then rolled over on his back. Instinctively as

> Brown fell I gave him a saber thrust in the left breast. The sword I carried was a light uniform weapon, and, either not having a point or striking something hard in Brown's accoutrements, did not penetrate. The blade bent double.

Well, I very much doubt that it bent quite double but it is not unheard of for an object in the breast pocket to frustrate the intentions of either a sword blade or a bullet. Bibles and whisky flasks are the most common guardians, though it is not recorded whether either played a part in this scenario. Certainly the ineffectiveness of both blows is a poor reflection on either Lieutenant Green's aptitude with a sword or the quality of the sword itself.

John Brown was captured, tried and sentenced to hang for treason but the idea that all men are born free could not be dispatched so lightly. Within two years America had plunged into a rancorous civil war.

For safekeeping during the American Civil War, Lewis Washington gave the Frederick Sword, along with other family treasures, to his poor neighbour, a Mr Odin, who kept it undisturbed in his humble cabin. Well it just gets stranger, doesn't it? This fabled sword, with its accumulated associations, now comes into the care of a namesake of a Norse God, who himself has strong associations with mythical swords. On the one hand the Frederick Sword is, according to one's taste, a rather over-decorated gentleman's dress sword and on the other a veritable Excalibur.

The State Sword

George Lewis, already the proud possessor of the Braddock Sword, was the first to make his own choice. He selected the 'State Sword' – the sword that Washington wore when he resigned his commission as commander-in-chief to Congress in 1783 and on the occasion of his inauguration as the first President of the United States in 1789. Those who propose the Darke Sword for that honour, of course, dispute the latter claim, but this is the one that has always been known as the 'State Sword' and it is considered that George Lewis believed it to be so. Washington was elected twice to the presidency, in 1789 and 1793, so it may be that both swords have a rightful claim to have been worn at one or other of the inaugurations.

It is an English-made smallsword, bearing the London date mark for 1767, with an etched, three-edged colichmarde blade. The hilt is of silver gilt, fashionably displaying both white and yellow gold, which juxtaposes to make the light sparkle as vibrantly as from any jewel. Its pommel and nearly circular guard plate are pierced with filigree work and the knuckle guard is faceted with sharp geometric designs. An associated cloth-covered, vellum scabbard bears the words 'FESEY – Cutler to His Majesty'. Matthew Fesey, who had an establishment in London's fashionable Pall Mall, was a well-known supplier of fine swords.

Washington seems to have found no political inconsistency in displaying British-manufactured items both during and after the war. Their cachet was undiminished by

George Washington delivering his inaugural address, April 1879, in the old city hall New York. Engraving by H. S. Sadd after painting by T.H. Matteson (Image: Library of Congress)

national animosities. He presumably bought the sword shortly after it was produced in 1767 – he was forever sending to London for fine goods at that time. It was a high-status dress sword that he had acquired for himself as a gentleman long before he imagined the elevated status he would attain as 'His Excellency George Washington, President of the United States' – a modest title compared to some that were mooted by the first Congress, which included 'His Exalted Mightiness, George Washington'. He was ever a modest man and it is telling that when inaugurated he chose to wear a sword already in his possession, albeit a very splendid one, rather than have new trappings of State commissioned.

He is wearing this sword in the 1780 Peale portrait. Charles Peale depicts him at Trenton, a colossus of a man, ruddy-cheeked and physically powerful, smiling and with an enormous hand resting on a cannon. Those huge hands would suggest the need for a larger hilt and in the State Sword this is evident. The overall length of the sword is 44 inches and the blade, itself long compared to most, is 33½ inches. The hilt is 10½ inches long! The hilts on Washington's other swords seem large by comparison to the majority of smallswords but this one is genuinely outsized. Washington was known to have large and powerful hands and was able to crack walnuts barehanded for the amusement of his friends.

One of the things one immediately notices about the State Sword is that the arms of the hilt are very small. On the Braddock Sword and the 'Mourning Sword' (see below), for instance, you will notice that they are much larger. Certainly, with the standard smallsword grip, the index finger passes partially through the one on the

Hilt detail of the State Sword (Courtesy of the Mount Vernon Ladies' Association)

knuckle guard side but it is erroneous to believe that two fingers are passed through these loops.

This common misunderstanding arises from the fact that there is an Italian style of fencing épée, popular in the nineteenth century, which features two finger loops, through which both the index finger and the middle finger are passed. However this is an adaptation for a sport fencing style where the sword is held in 'supination' – palm up. Smallswords were held in pronation, rather like holding a pen, for the default guard of tierce, defending the outside right. Yes, the hand does roll into semi-supination when defending on the left, such as in quarte, and some attacks are delivered in supination but the basic stance requires that the knuckle guard is on the outside of the hand, where it has a function of defence, and this is only achieved in pronation on the right hand side. Arms of the hilt were a feature derived from rapiers and there is a certain amount of additional security of grip achieved by locking a finger through one of the rings but never both. Part of the thumb pad intrudes through the other ring but it is not passed through – this would result in a very awkward grip. With the lighter play of the smallsword these rings became increasingly redundant and so by the mid-seventeenth century we see them, as with this sword, becoming vestigial.

In the portrait, Washington is wearing the sword suspended from a broad blue sash. This was a common alternative to the sword belt for grand formal occasions. It was also quite usual on

The State Sword (Courtesy of the Mount Vernon Ladies' Association)

the battlefield, where, in an emergency, the sash could be used either as a tourniquet or as an aid to carrying a wounded man from the field.

Imported blades

Although many swords in America were imported from England, France and, to a lesser extent, Germany, there was a well-established indigenous sword manufacturing industry. American swordsmiths, cutlers and silversmiths did mount their own blades in many instances but it was more common, especially before the Revolutionary War, for them to use imported blades.

There is a John Bailey sword, exhibited in the Metropolitan Museum of Art in New York (though belonging to the Lattimer Family Collection), which has a silver lion-head pommel, knuckle chain and S-shaped quillons – very similar to the John Augustine Sword. Its ivory grip is stained a vivid green and wound with filigree silver bands – similar to the Battle Sword. It is splendid. Upon the broad blade is stamped, on the one side, 'AN + DR + EA' and, on the other, 'FA + RA + RA'.

Andrea Ferara, as the name is most usually rendered, was one of the most famous names of blade-makers for three centuries. The original, and genuine, Andrea Ferara, 1530–1583, lived and worked in a small village called Belluno near Venice. His blades were of legendary quality and held a certain snob appeal. So much so that the name was plagiarized for centuries as a stamp of excellence, just like 'Ulfbehrt' and 'Hounslow' and in the same way that forgeries of famous brand names and logos are produced today in foreign markets. Eighteenth-century Scottish basket-hilted swords, in particular, are well known for having Ferara stamped blades and such swords were legion amongst British regiments fighting in the Revolutionary War.

Andrea Ferara trademarks appearing after his death-date are of spurious provenance, though many bearing the mark are exceedingly good blades. In contrast the 'running wolf' mark of the Solingen and Passau blade-smiths represented production not from a single factory but from the authorized guild members of a region. Consequently, genuine examples span the centuries. A John Bailey sword in the museum at Fort Ticonderoga bears a 'running wolf' on its blade. It belonged to William Wikoff and dates to Bailey's early years in New York. As discussed in past chapters, Solingen blades had long been considered the best in the world. However, its 'running wolf' mark was not immune from imitations – I have to confess to plagiarizing it myself, when I named my video company Running Wolf Productions in the early nineties – but it did generally have a legitimacy that the Andrea Ferara mark sometimes did not. Whilst not bearing the actual running wolf mark there is a notable sword, now at Mount Vernon and once belonging to George Washington, which was made by a Solingen sword-maker.

The Alte Sword

This sword was selected by George Steptoe Washington, the third to choose under the terms of the will and the son of Washington's brother Samuel. Known as the

'Alte Sword' because it was a gift to Washington from a Solingen sword-maker by the name of Theophilus Alte. It has a most curious story and indeed, is a most curious sword.

It is a stirrup-hilted cavalry sword. The hilt was once all gilt but much has worn away, revealing the brass beneath. At the base of the black leather grip is a copper band and the grip is spiralled with a twist of copper wire. There is such visual disharmony between the gilt, brass and copper that one wonders why it has so often been described as an elegant sword. It is probable that the grip, with its copper wire, is a replacement and in its original state the hilt would have been all gilt. Even so it appears a rather ungainly weapon to my eye.

Detail of the Alte Sword depicting Washington as the slayer of the British lion (Courtesy of the Mount Vernon Ladies' Association)

It has a broad, heavy blade, measuring 33¾ inches, which is blued for half its length and elaborately decorated with gold inlay and cut steel. Looking at it from the hilt on one side, one sees portrayed, in gold inlay, an image of a general, complete with field marshal's baton and sword on hip, standing victoriously astride a slain lion and unicorn – the symbols of the British Crown. Above him, revealed in incised lines of bright steel, is an image of celestial blessing with a fan of rays emanating from clouds. If there were any doubt that this figure is supposed to be George Washington, then it is dispelled by the banner strip above, crowned with drums and standards, all inlaid in gold, and within the strip the legend 'GEORGE WASHINGTON'. More abstract decorations in cut steel complete the design of the blued section.

Inscription on the Alte Sword (Courtesy of the Mount Vernon Ladies' Association)

Similar decorations appear on the reverse side except that at the hilt end is a gold inlaid inscription set within a scrolled cartouche. It reads:

VERTILGER DES DESPOTISM
BESCHUTZER DER FREIHEIT
BEHARRLICHER MANN
NIMM, VON MEINES SOHNES HAND DIES SCHWERD
ICH BITTE DICH

Theophilus Alte, Solingen

For a translation, I can do no better than use Washington's own words, for he offered one in a letter he sent in 1796 to his ambassador at The Hague, John Quincy Adams. Here is the letter and, as you can see, it sets up one devil of a mystery.

Dear Sir,

To open a correspondence with you on so trifling a subject, as that which gives birth to this letter, would hardly be justified, were it not for the singularity of the case. This singularity will, I hope, apologize for the act.

Some time ago, perhaps two or three months, I read in some gazette ... that a celebrated artist had presented or was about to present to the President of the United States a sword of masterly workmanship as an evidence of his veneration &c.

I thought no more of the matter afterwards, until a gentleman with whom I have no acquaintance, coming from and going to I know not where, at a tavern I never could get information of, came across this sword (for it is presumed to be the same) pawned for thirty dollars, which he paid, left it in Alexandria, nine miles from my house in Virginia, with a person who refunded him the money, and sent the sword to me.

This is all I have been able to learn of this curious affair. The blade is highly wrought and decorated with many military emblems. It has my name engraved thereon and the following inscription, translated from the Dutch 'Condemner of despotism, preserver of Liberty,

The Alte sword (Courtesy of the Mount Vernon Ladies' Association)

glorious Man, take from my son's hands this sword, I beg you. A. Solingen.'
The hilt is either gold, or richly plated in that metal and the whole carries
with it the form of a horseman's sword or long sabre.

The matter as far as it appears at present, is a perfect enigma. How
should it have come into this country without a letter or an accompanying
message, how afterwards it should have got into such loose hands, and
whither the person having it in possession was steering his course, remain as
yet to be explained. Some of these points, probably, can only be explained
by the maker, and the maker is no otherwise to be discovered than by the
inscription and name, A Solingen, who from the impression that dwells on
my mind, is of Amsterdam.

If sir, with this clew you can develop the history of this sword, the value
of it, the character of the maker, and his probable object in sending it, you
wuld oblige me; and by relating these facts to him, might obviate doubts,
which otherwise might be entertained by him of its fate or its reception.

With great esteem and regard, I am dear sir &c George Washington.

One might wish that so illustrious a President of The United States of America had a
better grasp of geography or, at least, the use of an atlas but he was obviously misled
on the matter. He presumably had someone translate the inscription for him and was
told that it was Dutch and therefore made the assumption about Amsterdam. Now it
is true that the New York Dutch were from Holland, but the Pennsylvania Dutch
were from Germany. It all rests on the colloquial distortion of the word *Deutch*, which
is German for 'German'. Solingen, of course, is in Germany.

Confusion may also have arisen because it appears, from their names, that the
agents in getting the sword to Washington were both of Dutch extraction. In
September 1796, he received a letter from a Joseph Vanmeter – the gentleman with
whom he had no acquaintance – saying:

I am happy to hear that the sword I left with Mr Lawrence Hooff pleases
you, I ought to have wrote respecting the manner in which I came by it, but
being an indifferent penman and much hurried with business, as also
stating the matter to Mr Hooff in full, whom I knew was a gentleman you
had an acquaintance with. These are the reasons I omitted giving you a
written detail of this matter.

He goes on to say that he paid $35 for it and that it was thought to be worth perhaps
$200 'and I shall cheerfully take any sum you may think the sword worth'. Mr
Vanmeter, it would seem, was on the make. From Washington's letter to John Quincy
Adams, it would appear that Mr Hooff – presumably the person in Alexandria
who refunded him the money – had driven him a hard bargain. Vanmeter sheds no
further light on the sword's origins, other than the fact that he bought it from a

'Bremener' in a tavern and had got the landlord to bargain for it, as he spoke the man's tongue.

In January of the following year, Washington received a letter from Theophilus Alte, which went some way to explaining the mystery. It appears that Alte had sent his son, Daniel, to America to make his way 'in a country of liberty' and had sent with him the sword, as a gift to Washington. Alte had heard rumours – 'malicious informations' – about the non-delivery of the sword and, in his imperfect English, excused his son's neglect, 'as an unexperimented traveller [he] has either been intimidated or frightened'.

Despite his father's loyal faith, it appears that young Daniel was hawking the sword for sale soon after he arrived in Philadelphia, probably to settle the debts of youthful excess or to pay his tavern account. We may fill in the gaps. Vanmeter recognized it for what it was – there had been reports of it, as witnessed in the newspaper article Washington had read – bought it and took it to Alexandria, where he had hoped to turn a handsome profit. So much is clear.

Theophilus Alte's motive for his gift is less clear. He writes in his effusive letter:

> I took the liberty to send by him a sword mounted which has been made in our fabrick [workshop], destined it to you, as the only man I know in this world who acted in an uninterested manner for the happiness of his country.

Few could argue the veracity of his tribute to Washington but, reading between the lines, might he also be saying 'because you and I are alike, George. Men like us are not motivated by personal gain'. Indeed he goes on to protest, perhaps a little too much, that

> I assure you on my honesty Reverend President that I took the liberty of sending the sword to you in no criticized manner, I only sent it to you as to whom who delivered a country as yours from all esclavage.

A second letter, written in November 1797, stresses the point 'I charged him to present to you in an uninterested manner, a mounted sword'. Although Alte's English spelling had improved by the time of the second letter, his insistence that he was not acting out of self interest remained as firm as ever, though, in the second letter, he can't help mentioning that he had despatched his son to Philadelphia 'with different sorts of iron wares of our manufacture'.

Until the Revolutionary War, American gentlemen of European taste, especially Washington, had favoured London as the place to send to for fine swords and other goods. In the post-war years, now that its colonial overlords no longer controlled the terms of trade, the United States could be considered a rich new market, ripe for exploitation. Was Alte simply trying to win orders for his company?

A report, in the aftermath of the 'Bread Riots' that erupted in parts of Germany in 1795 states:

> The participants could not be discovered by the most severe examination for some have died and others have left the country – these include among them the extremely suspected Theophilus Alte who now lives in the French Republic and endeavours to transplant there the Solingen industries.

So it would seem that the Alte family had fallen on hard times and what a coincidence that, in the very same year he is reported as trying to set up Solingen-style industries in France, he sends his son to America with samples of his wares and a gift for the President.

Until the elimination of the artisan's monopoly privileges in 1809, the only people permitted to make sword blades in Solingen were the guild-recognized swordsmiths. It was a strictly controlled closed shop. Their books and trademark rolls do not include the name Alte, so he must have been something other than a blade maker. Around the first quarter of the eighteenth century, Solingen craftsmen began to decorate their swords artistically, with etched and inlaid designs and that is what Theophilus Alte was – a *Gelbgiesser* – a hilt maker and engraver. By the 1770s these fancified swords were highly sought after but the artisans, like Alte, who created them had their rates of pay and conditions controlled by the ancient guilds who commissioned their work. The manufacture of blades by non-guild swordsmiths was forbidden, so Alte was entirely dependent on them to provide his steel canvases. That is until he set up shop in France.

Feeling exploited and stifled by antiquated customs, Alte doubtless longed for the opportunities and freedoms he had read about across the Atlantic and genuinely espoused the American cause of liberty. But I doubt his gift to Washington was pure Alte-ruism – he also wanted a slice of the action.

The Mourning Sword

The White House was in flames. A small woman looked back on the terrifying scene, clutching a blanket in which was rolled a large painting that she had stripped from its frame. The year was 1814, the penultimate year of the 'War of 1812' – a war between the United States and Great Britain. War had been declared by America because of objections to Britain's blockade and capture of American ships trading with Napoleon's France and British support for Native American tribes resisting American expansion westwards. The British were in Washington in force and they had fired the White House.

The woman was Dolly Madison, wife of the then-President James Madison, and the painting she had saved from the conflagration was one of several full-length portraits of George Washington painted by Gilbert Stuart. They are known as the Landsdowne Portraits because they were commissioned by Mrs. William Bingham as

The hilt of the Mourning Sword (Courtesy of the Mount Vernon Ladies' Association)

a gift for the first Marquis of Lansdowne, a British supporter of the American cause during the Revolutionary War. In these portraits Washington wears a sword.

It is a smallsword with a gilt pommel and guard of fairly plain moulded decoration. The grip is of ridged black leather. This is the sword chosen by Judge Bushrod Washington and it too survives in the collections at Mount Vernon. Bushrod was the son of John Augustine Washington, George's second brother.

When I visited Mount Vernon to look over records and archives, I was most graciously received and seated at a large writing table under the watchful gaze of Bushrod; his portrait hung on the wall above my desk. He seemed a serious and austere gentleman and it little surprises me that he opted for this relatively modest sword, which is remarkable only in that, like the State Sword, it has an unusually long blade for a smallsword, measuring some 35 inches. Though now obliterated by rust, it is recorded that it was inscribed on one side with the motto '*recti fece ice*' ('do what is right'), and upon the other with '*nemine timeus*' ('fear no man'). Perhaps it was these noble injunctions that inspired his choice or perhaps he simply thought it proper and fitting, following the death of his uncle, to choose what is known as the Mourning Sword. From his portrait, Bushrod seemed to me a very proper sort of gentleman.

This is the sword that George Washington commonly wore at funerals, though he was also known to have worn it at presidential levees and, indeed, in his most famous of portraits. In the summer of

The Mourning Sword (Courtesy of the Mount Vernon Ladies' Association)

1773, following the death of Martha's daughter Patsy, Washington received from London materials for mourning including 'a genteel mourning sword with belt swivels'. It is likely that this is that sword. In the nineteenth century, mourning swords were universally black in all parts of the hilt, but, in the eighteenth century, silver hilts were still *de rigueur* on such occasions.

In the Stuart portrait, the sword is swathed with an elaborate sword-knot, a length of gold cloth that is wound around the top couple of inches of the grip and then wrapped spirally around the knuckle guard; its loose end hangs below the guard plate and is finished with a gold tassel. One may imagine it being substituted at funerals and during periods of mourning with an equivalent arrangement in black silk.

During the Civil War, the Mourning Sword was hidden for safekeeping in a pigeon house belonging to Edward Turner of Farquar, Virginia – a neighbour to the Washington descendent who owned it. It is here that it was so attacked by rust that the inscriptions on the blade became obscured. These corrosive conditions also caused it to break, some 8½ inches from the point; a misadventure that was rectified by joining the two parts by means of a gold band.

Although the damage is regrettable, the caution that occasioned it to be hidden is understandable; for the person who had inherited the Mourning Sword was none other than Colonel Lewis Washington – the same Colonel Washington who had also inherited the 'Frederick Sword', so nearly lost at the hands of John Brown.

However, it wasn't he that hid the Mourning Sword; it was his cousin John Augustine Washington. The fact was, Colonel Lewis Washington didn't much care for the Mourning Sword and had swapped it with his cousin for the John Augustine Sword – the one with the lion's head pommel. This John Augustine, of course, was a descendent of Washington's brother of the same name and he was never to retrieve his treasured heirloom. He joined the Confederate army, serving as an aide-de-camp on the staff of Robert E Lee, and was shot by a bushwhacker whilst reconnoitring in the Cheat Mountains of West Virginia in the autumn of 1861.

The other swords

In an inventory that was taken in 1800, shortly after Washington's death in December 1799, there is a listing in his study for seven swords and one blade. Frustratingly there is no description of the swords – just an overall value of $120. At this point I have discussed eight of Washington's swords but three of them – the Braddock Sword, the John Augustine Sword and the Darke Sword – were gifted long before his death and so are unlikely to have been in the house at this time. The other five swords that we have looked at may or may not have been among the inventoried seven but what are we to make of the other two swords and the unmounted blade?

The inventory of 1802, after Martha's death, makes no mention of swords. Martha had died of a fever on 22 May. Before she died she protected the privacy of her relationship with George from the probing eyes of history by burning all their letters to each other, but everything else has been carefully preserved. Whilst at Mount

Vernon I was able to see an account book that detailed the proceeds from a private sale of Washington's effects held by the legatees on 22 July 1802. It contains the following entries:

> Mr Carter – sword blade to be charged to T Peter – $2
> A Park: for a sword – $2.50
> Gen'l Spotswood – a saw sword – $4
> Mr Law 2 canes and a sword – $6.20
> B Washington – one sword – $1

Now we have an embarrassment of swords. I was looking for two and a blade and found four and a blade! The inventories are meticulous, itemizing such things as a 'pea strainer' valued at 50 cents, 'a machine to scrape shoes on' at $2 and 'a box of military figures' at $2 (it is fun to imagine George setting out these tin soldiers to plan his campaigns). The point is that it is extremely unlikely that a sword would be missed in these comprehensive listings. It is probable, therefore, that the four swords and a blade mentioned in the sale counted among the seven swords and a blade reckoned in the inventory. This now leaves three swords to be accounted for in the inventory.

If we allow say $1 each for Mr Law's purchase of canes, then the total value of swords in the sale is $13.70, quite a way short of the $120 valuation for the swords in the inventory. So the other three must each have been of a greater value. Let us suppose that the favoured nephews had met and decided upon their bequeathed swords before the inventory was taken. Some will have been removed at that time but others may have been left. For instance William Augustine Washington was ill, so the Frederick Sword chosen for him may still have been awaiting his collection. Judge Bushrod Washington had been left the bulk of the Mount Vernon estate and so he may not have deemed it necessary to have taken his sword – the Mourning Sword – from the house. Pure speculation, of course, but if it were so then there is only one more sword to be identified.

Washington was an inveterate shopper, forever sending to London for fine goods in the pre-Revolutionary War years. Shortly after he was made a colonel in the Virginia Militia in 1756, he wrote to his London agent to buy for him 'a small sword of 8 to 10 guineas in price'. None of the surviving swords fit this description or date. Could it have been the seventh sword in the inventory?

The Saw Sword
The only sword in the sale lists that receives any description is the 'Saw Sword'. Purchased by General Spotswood, who was married to Elizabeth Washington, daughter of George's half-brother Augustine, it remained in the family. A number of military swords are furnished with a saw-tooth back to the blade, so that they can double in the field both as regular defence weapons and to saw wood or meat carcasses. They were usually issued to pioneer units, working on reconnaissance and

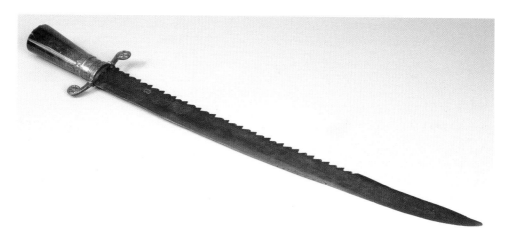

The saw sword (Courtesy of Morristown National Historical Park)

engineering duties such as bridge building. Saw backed swords were also given to bandsmen, who often worked as medical orderlies in time of war – the saw blade here having more grisly work to perform.

The use of the plural 'cutteaux' in Washington's will indicates there was more than one of these weapons at Mount Vernon at the time of his death. There is, of course, that most famous cutto, the Battle Sword, but there is also another. Like the Darke Sword, it belongs to the Washington Association of New Jersey and it is not only a cutto, it is saw-backed. This must surely be the 'Saw Sword" referred to in the sale accounts. It is a beautiful hunting sword with an agate grip and inscribed on the blade is the monogram GW. As we have seen, the cutto style was fashionable as a military sidearm but this one was for the hunting field. It was common for such swords to have the saw-tooth back, invaluable for clearing obstructions in a dense thicket or for removing a fox's head as a trophy.

The Lafayette Sword

I was fortunate, when I first visited Mount Vernon, to coincide with an exhibit on Gilbert Du Motier, Marquis De Lafayette. It focused on the extraordinarily close, filial relationship between Washington and the dashing young French aristocrat, twenty-five years his junior. LaFayette, the idealistic young man who had fled France under pain of arrest to join the American Revolution; Lafayette the hero of many of its battles; Lafayette the statesman, who more than any other, cajoled crucial French support for the Revolution; Lafayette the architect of the French Revolution, liberator of the Bastille (its key, sent to Washington, still hangs at Mount Vernon) and Lafayette the tragic figure who became a victim of its darker forces.

One of his swords was there on display; a 32½-inch triangular-bladed smallsword with a gilded hilt. It has a pierced boat-shaped guard, typical of many military small-swords and hangers, and a pommel in the form of a Phrygian cap – the cap of Liberty.

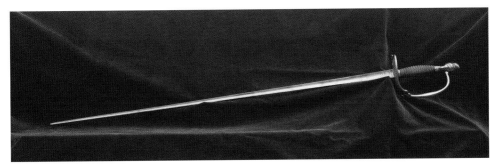

Smallsword belonging to the Marquis de Lafayette (Courtesy of Lafayette College, Pennsylvania)

Dating to after the Revolutionary War, legend has it that the hilt was fashioned with iron from the bars of the Bastille – I think it unlikely, as the hilt appears to be gilt over copper. Its blade was made in Germany, bearing, on one side, the inscription '*De La Marque Des Mouchettes a Solingen*'. On the other there is a somewhat enigmatic and worn inscription referring, in French, to the 'Sign of the Grand Monarch in Paris'. This is the sword that was taken from him by Austrian forces in 1792. Lafayette, now out of favour with the Jacobin forces that had hijacked the Revolution, was attempting to flee France and make his way to America. However, he was captured by the Austrian troops who were fighting to restore the French monarchy. Together with their Prussian allies they decided that Lafayette was ideologically too dangerous to the old regimes of Europe to be set free. So began his five years of incarceration in

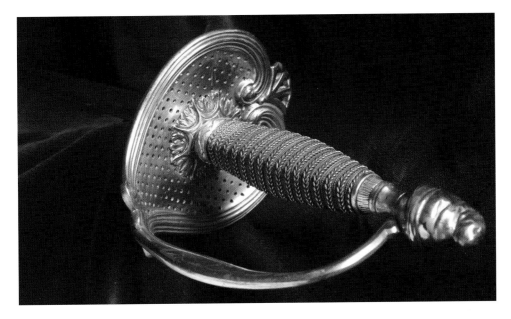

Pommel of Lafayette's sword in the form of 'phrygian cap' or 'cap of liberty' (Courtesy of Lafayette College, Pennsylvania)

Detail of inscription on Lafayette's sword (Courtesy of Lafayette College, Pennsylvania)

the dank dungeons of Olmutz Prison. When he was finally freed, all of his other confiscated belongings, including another sword, were returned to him in good order. A French revolutionary banner and the smallsword with the Phrygian-cap pommel were not. They had been sold to the Prussian minister for war, General Count Schulenburg. It was perhaps believed that such emblems of liberty and revolution did not warrant the respect normally granted to the effects of an officer prisoner-of-war.

It was believed, though it is likely apocryphal, that the Phrygian cap, a soft bonnet rather like a nightcap with its crown hanging limply forward, was worn by liberated slaves in Ancient Rome. Phrygia was a region in Asia Minor from where many slaves were taken and the thought was that, on being liberated, they would once again don their traditional caps. Whatever the truth of the legend, the Phrygian cap became a symbol of liberty and freedom during the Enlightenment and manifested in many guises during the Revolutionary War. Within a few years it became the universal emblem of the French Revolution.

Lafayette wrote to Schulenburg on his release to ask for the return of the sword. There was every indication that the count was disposed to grant the marquis his wish but the deed was never done. The sword passed through generations of Schulenburg heirs until it was donated by one of his descendents to Lafayette College, Pennsylvania in 1932.

More pertinent to this present chapter, however, is a sword that was a gift from the Marquis De Lafayette to his adored George Washington. This lovely object is now kept in a sealed glass cabinet, in a locked chest in the Gano chapel at the William Jewell College, Liberty, Missouri. It is a silver-hilted cutto with a lion-head pommel, an ivory grip decorated with silver wire and a curved blade stamped with the ANDREA FERARA mark. Punctuating every two letters of ANDREA on one side

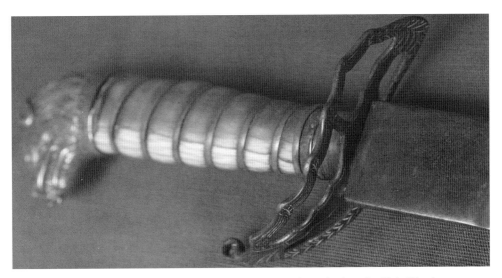

Hilt of the Gano sword (William Jewell College, Liberty, Missouri; photo by Kyle Rivas)

and FERRARA on the other is a stamped impression of a head with a conspicuously bulbous nose. Very similar head marks appear on the many Andrea Ferara blades mounted in Scottish basket hilts and is an indication that the blade was made in Germany.

Considerable evidence of damage appears on the cutting edge of the blade in the form of several deep nicks. Was this damage caused by blade-on-blade contact in battle or was it a consequence of later abuse, either in play or misuse, such as chopping wood? We will probably never know.

In 1996, the college received the sword from the great-great-great-great-grand-daughter of The Reverend John Gano, a Baptist minister who was Washington's chaplain throughout the Revolutionary War. He was known as 'The Fighting Chaplain'. According to Gano family tradition, Washington presented the sword, given to him by his dear Marquis, to Gano in gratitude for his loyal service.

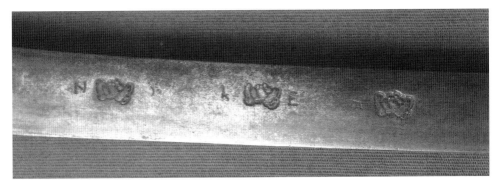

Maker's stamp on the blade of the Gano sword (William Jewell College, Liberty, Missouri; photo by Kyle Rivas)

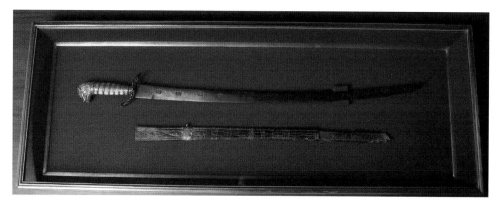

The Gano sword and associated scabbard (William Jewell College, Liberty, Missouri; photo by Kyle Rivas)

There is an associated scabbard in the case with the sword. It is damaged and in poor repair, yet retains a silver mount inscribed with the date 1776. However, it is by no means certain that the scabbard is correctly associated with the sword. Owing to the extent of damage it is hard to tell but it doesn't exhibit the degree of curve one would expect of a sheath for this blade.

Washington would appear to have been highly aware of the symbolic importance of swords as gifts, yet almost casual when it came to passing such gifts on to others. One wonders, did Lafayette mind that his hero gave the sword he gave him to someone else?

In his turn, Lafayette was also presented with a sword, not personally by Washington, but by Congress. Though now lost, it was described at the time as having, on one side of the blade, an engraving depicting Lafayette slaying the British lion and upon the other, America, released from her chains, handing him an olive branch. So began a tradition of special presentation 'Congressional Swords'.

Congressional swords

Benjamin Franklin became the United States ambassador in Paris in 1776, its first ambassador anywhere. Among his papers for August 1779 is a receipted bill for 4,800 livres, payment for a sword ornamented with gold relief work, presented, by order of the Continental Congress to the Marquis de la Fayette. The Congressional order reads: 'By resolution of Congress, 28th Oct 1778, an elegant sword with proper devices, for his zeal, courage and abilities on many signal occasions in the service of the United States to be presented to Major General the Marquis de LaFayette'.

The bill is from C. Liger of Paris, a celebrated fourbisseur, that is a sword merchant. There is a splendid picture in Diderot's *Encyclopaedia* (1751) of a fourbisseur's shop where you can see that hilts and blades were displayed separately, then assembled to order by the retailer. Some surviving hilts can still be found in the velvet-lined boxes that they were sold in. Such containers were typically shaped in the form of the hilt. You might, for instance, buy a hilt at a jeweler or silversmith and then take it to a

Fourbisseur's shop, Diderot's *Encyclopaedia of Trades and Industry*, 1751

fourbisseur to select a blade and have it fitted. He would also 'refurbish' old swords, cleaning them and replacing parts as necessary. A fourbisseur would also have swords custom made to individual design.

Liger was one of Paris' finest fourbisseurs and it was to him that Congress went for its 'presentation swords'. During the Revolutionary War it authorized fifteen 'elegant swords' to be awarded to those who had given conspicuous service. The Marquis De Lafayette was fortunate indeed in receiving his within a year of its award. Colonel Marinus Willet, among others, had to wait eleven years for his!

It wasn't until 1786, three years after the war, and in many cases more than a decade after being awarded, that ten, of the total of fifteen, were finally purchased from France. They bear the coat of arms of the United States on one side of the grip and a dedication inscribed on the other such as: 'Congress to Col. Willett, Oct. 11, 1777'. As well as having an elaborately decorative hilt, this sword has a blued blade, blued to the brightest iridescence, save for the last 3 inches which are left as bright steel, and adorned with gilt scrollwork. It is a pretty jewel, a bauble. Willet's Congressional sword is in the Metropolitan Museum of Art in New York where it sits beneath his portrait by Ralph Earl. He is wearing the sword in the painting. He is also wearing the insignia of The Order of the Cincinnati.

At Andersen House, the headquarters and museum of the Order in Washington DC, there are another two Congressional swords, awarded to Samuel Smith and Tench Tilghman. Anderson House is a mansion in Washington's Embassy Row and has been decorated in the most ostentatious French style – all gilt and grandeur. When I visited (they have an excellent library) I was introduced to a direct descendant of Alexander Hamilton who just happened to be there! The Order is the only hereditary institution in the United States, open only to descendants of officers, both American and French, who fought for the revolutionary cause, though some Presidents of the United States and others have been made honorary members. The society was inaugurated in Fishkill, the military town where John Bailey had plied his trade, in 1783.

The order is named after Lucius Quinctius Cincinnatus, a fifth-century BC Roman, who reluctantly left his farm to answer the call of public duty. He became *magister populi* (Master of the People), effectively a dictator, at a time of national emergency when hostile indigenous tribes threatened the overthrow of Rome. When the crisis was over, he returned power to the Senate and went back to ploughing his fields. The parallels with Washington are clear.

Washington, however, along with Franklin and Jefferson, was among those who criticized the creation of such a hereditary order on the grounds that it smacked too much of old European aristocracy. He was instrumental in several changes to its constitution and finally overcame his objections out of loyalty to the men who had fought with him, and became the society's first President-General. The city of Cincinnati was founded in homage to the society.

I wonder how many of the Order's founders were aware that, in the original Latin, Cincinnatus is a *cognomen* (nickname) for 'curly-hair'. Perhaps the irony of calling themselves the 'Order of the Curly-Hair' escaped them when they chose the bald eagle as their emblem, which they did less than a year after it appeared as the national symbol on the Great Seal, and this too was found objectionable by Franklin: 'I wish the Bald Eagle had not been chosen as the Representative of our Country. He is a bird of bad moral character. He does not get his living honestly'. Franklin advocated the turkey. If he had had his way, we should now have swords with turkey-head pommels!

Franklin's reservations about select societies did not extend to the Freemasons. He was an extremely active Mason, as was Washington, many of the founding fathers and the great majority of his officers. Swords frequently comprise part of a Mason's regalia, though they are purely ceremonial and often fashioned in a cod-medieval style, rather like the cheapest of Toledo souvenirs. They barely qualify for the description 'sword'. Whether or not Washington possessed a Masonic sword is not recorded. Masonic affiliations were sometimes advertised on an officer's service sword. There is a silver-hilted John Bailey sword – with a lion-head pommel, green-stained ivory grip and S-curved quillons – in the collections of the Ohio Historical Society, which has a Masonic emblem inscribed on its scabbard mount beneath the owner's name, H.M. Cannol.

It was only because LaFayette was a Mason that he was able to obtain a commission at a time when the mood had turned against accepting foreign officers into the Continental Army. The Marquis de Lafayette, along with Baron de Kalb (he wasn't really a baron but that's another story), met with Franklin in Paris and argued their case as fellow Masons. Franklin, who had raised an enormous sum for the revolutionary coffers from French Masons, was well-disposed.

When de Kalb died, after receiving eleven wounds at the Battle of Camden in 1780, the commander of the victorious British forces, Lord Charles Cornwallis, also a Mason, ordered that he be given a full Masonic military funeral.

On 19th October 1781, it was Brigadier-General Charles O'Hara who offered the sword of Earl Cornwallis, the commander of the defeated Government forces at Yorktown, in a ritual act of surrender. Cornwallis pleaded sickness and remained in his quarters. O'Hara first proffered it to the French commander, the Comte de Rochambeau, who declined, saying that General Washington should receive the surrender. Washington also declined and waved O'Hara towards his second-in-command, Major-General Benjamin Lincoln. Protocol was preserved and the second-in-command surrendered his sword to the second-in-command. After so much bloodshed, so much suffering, at the end of a long war and at the very moment a nation was born, such niceties were observed and, at the heart of it, the sword remained the potent symbol it had always been. The British forces laid down their arms at Yorktown and among them were 2,000 swords.

Cornwallis's sword, as seen represented in art, was a smallsword. It is not known what happened to it. Could it have been one of the swords kept in the corner of Washington's study, its provenance unremembered? Could it account for one of the swords sold in the sale of Washington's effects in 1802? We may never know. Most

British surrender at Yorktown, French engraving by Francois Godefroy (Image: Library of Congress)

probably it was returned to Cornwallis after it had served its official function as an instrument of surrender.

The sword of the man who first received it, Benjamin Lincoln, was a small, light-bladed cutto with a pierced silver guard and a green-stained ivory hilt. It is now in the collections of the Smithsonian Institute. Also there is an exceptionally beautiful smallsword that George Washington presented to Major General Lincoln some time after Yorktown for his services during the war. Its silver scabbard mount is engraved 'Presented By Gen. Washington to Gen. Benj. Lincoln'. Benjamin Lincoln was among that coterie of young officers that Washington considered his surrogate sons. The pierced and chiselled hilt is gilt brass and the colichmarde blade has been etched and gilt with elaborate designs, including a highly stylised 'L' close to the hilt on either side. It's a stunning sword and handles as well as any I have held.

American silver hilts

Like Washington's own swords, the sword he chose for his friend Lincoln was ornate and sumptuous, most likely of French origin. Washington was a man of European tastes and his choice in swords was quite contrary to the prevailing American fashion. As one might expect, in a country steeped in puritan belief, plain hilts were preferred; their surfaces unfussed by surface decoration. There was a strong artistic tradition, centred around New York, Boston and New England (c 1700–1815) for American swordsmiths to produce silver-hilted smallswords that relied on purity of line and form for aesthetic impact rather than the fol-de-rols of ornament. Paul Revere, famous for that ride, was a silversmith and hilt-maker in Boston. He was just one of many producing handsome plain hilts with a smooth silver surface. Records indicate over fifty silversmiths working in America at the time who specialized in the manufacture of plain silver hilts. So far as we can tell, Washington never possessed one of these quintessentially American swords, though they were produced in considerable numbers.

Doubtless there are swords with Washington connections that have, so far, failed to come to my attention. Swords played an important role in his life – as symbols of authority, as practical weapons, as items of fashionable dress and as gifts, totems of esteem, both received and bestowed.

Swords, duels and pistols

Inherent to the custom of a gentleman wearing a sword is the tacit declaration that he is a man of honour and ready to defend that honour in a duel. George Washington never fought a duel; perhaps he had witnessed enough real bloodshed not to be moved by such posturing gestures. But then, even before he had been in the cauldron of the Revolutionary War, there were signs that he could command reason over emotion. In 1755, he was involved in an argument over an election dispute. The young Washington was struck and knocked to the ground. Everyone expected a duel between Washington and his attacker the following day but Washington demurred and conceded that he had been in the wrong. There was no duel.

Perhaps the most notable American duel took place in 1804, fought between Jefferson's vice-president, Aaron Burr, and Alexander Hamilton, who had been Secretary of the Treasury under George Washington and whose own son had been tragically killed in a duel just three years earlier. It was with pistols, not swords. Some reports opine that Hamilton 'deloped' (shot into the air intentionally), others suggest that the hair trigger on his pistol caused him to fire prematurely and others say that he simply never fired. Whatever the truth of this detail, it seems clear that Burr chose to take his shot after Hamilton's pistol had discharged. Hamilton died from his wounds the following day. Burr was acquitted of manslaughter, but his political career was effectively over.

Hamilton had been Washington's aide-de-camp and a trusted personal friend; one of the surrogate sons, like Lafayette and Lincoln, that he fostered during the war.

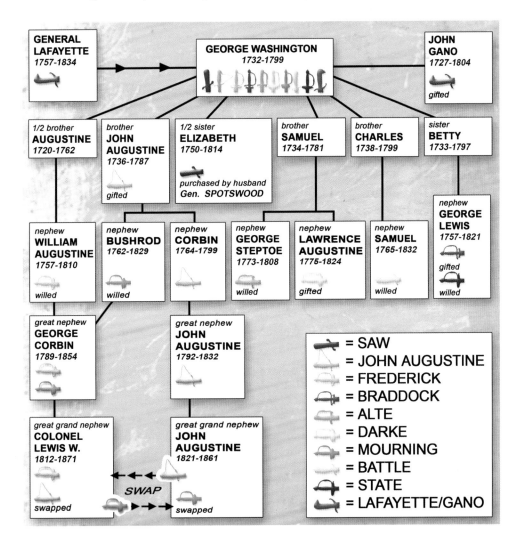

Burr also had a distinguished career as a soldier in the Revolutionary War and earned a place on Washington's staff. Washington respected his valour but didn't trust him.

The Burr/Hamilton duel was a sensational event because of the protagonists' standing in society but duelling itself was not generally something to raise an eyebrow. It remained an accepted practice both in Europe and America, though by this time it had become rare for duels to be fought with swords. John McArthur who published *The Army and Navy Gentleman's Companion* in 1780 wrote with some regret: 'Few who devote themselves to duelling understand fencing. Pistols are the weapons now generally made of use.'

Although basic forms of hand-held firearm had existed from as early as the late fourteenth century and pistols with a wheel-lock mechanism, adequately suitable for duelling, had existed since the sixteenth, it wasn't until after the mid-eighteenth century that it became at all common to duel with pistols.

In part this was owing to improvements in pistol design. Early pistols were unreliable, inaccurate and large but the relatively-late adoption of the pistol for duelling also owes much to the cultural perceptions of the duel. In a ritual that invoked ancestral links of class and privilege, the sword – that defining emblem of a gentleman – was considered the more honourable weapon and the sword prevailed as the weapon of choice long after firearms could have superseded it. In many ways it is remarkable that the sword lasted so long, since it required, at the very least, a modicum of training, practice and physical fitness to manage it well, whereas any presumptuous parvenu, however plump and untutored, could fire a pistol. On the other hand there was a great deal of chance with early firearms; if you only have one shot, then you want to know that there is at least a reasonable possibility of the mechanism firing.

By the mid-eighteenth century however, not only were firearms more reliable, they had also become indispensable on the battlefield. In particular, the pistol had become a standard sidearm for an officer and an essential weapon for the cavalryman – a weapon with which he won honour and glory in war. The stigma had begun to fade. Coupled with this was the fact that, in Britain at least, the sword started to go out of fashion as part of a gentleman's everyday dress. That effete guru of eighteenth-century fashion, Beau Nash, had extinguished the practice in Bath by 1775 and the Baroness d'Oberkirch, writing in 1784, cited the influence of English fashion to account for the fact that the sword was no longer worn in France. The America of George Washington lagged a little behind these trends and swords remained an essential part of formal dress in the United States. There is barely a portrait of the first President without one.

Pistols, on the other hand, had become all the rage. A young man making his way in society or a young officer seeking the approval of his fellows held a certain standing if it became known that he had 'blazed'. His reputation was enhanced as a man of courage and of honour. A new era for the duel had begun. With it emerged the specially designed duelling pistol with its fine balance, elegant lines and hair trigger. The hair trigger was quite unsuitable to the jolting environment of a battlefield but on the duelling ground it allowed firing with just the slightest finger pressure and so aided accuracy. It was a technology that usurped the supremacy of the sword – on the duelling ground at least.

George Washington's swords were as individual as the man himself but many of the swords in the Revolutionary War were of a standard-issue regulation pattern, especially the British ones. In the year of Washington's celebrated Farewell Address to the nation, the British Army introduced its 1796 regulation-pattern light cavalry sabre. It is arguably the finest pattern sword ever designed and it is the subject of the next chapter. As our guide is a sword that belonged not to a king or a war-leader, but to an ordinary man, Lieutenant Henry Lane.

An Officer of the 15th, King's Own, Hussars. Taken from life. Probably by Denis Dighton, c. 1806 (National Portrait Gallery, London)

Chapter 14

The Sword of Lieutenant Henry Lane, Hussar at Waterloo

The French certainly are fine and brave soldiers, but the superiority of our English horses, and more particularly the superiority of swordsmanship our fellows showed, decided every contest in our favour

(Officer of 13th Light Dragoons, Campo Mayor, 1811)

Henry Lane was a lieutenant in the 15th (King's) Hussars at the Battle of Waterloo and the sword he carried that day is now preserved in the collections of the National Army Museum in Chelsea, London. At first glance it appears to be a regulation-pattern M1796 Light Cavalry Sword. The M1796 was standard for all British light cavalry regiments and its flashing broad blade was the pride of gallant hussars and light dragoons alike. However, Henry Lane's sword doesn't quite fit the bill. Its hilt, though having langets with an unusual scalloped edge, is otherwise right enough, but the blade has been replaced. Not only that, but the work has been poorly done. Offset slightly from centre, the blade is now loose in its fitting, a possible consequence of age but equally possibly shoddy workmanship. More damningly, it is a cheap blade, typical of the sort imported from Germany at the time, and not strictly of the 1796 pattern. It is uniformly narrow, less than an inch wide for the whole of its 33¾ inches length and it weighs a measly 1lb 5oz compared to the more usual 2lb 2oz for the M1796. I have handled Lane's sword and it is hard to believe that it would do any great damage other than to unprotected flesh.

There is nothing to tell us when the re-blading was carried out and it may be that it was later in Lane's life – perchance as an elderly gentleman he wished for something lighter for dress occasions? This re-blading may also have been a consequence of significant damage to the original blade, whether in service or from neglect, or it may have been a question of buying the least expensive sword he could find when he first joined the regiment as an impecunious young man, still in his early teens.

Henry Lane bought his commission, as a cornet, into the 15th Hussars on 10 December 1811. I have not been able to find his birth record but he states in the 1841 census that he is forty-five years old, which gives a date of birth of 1796, making

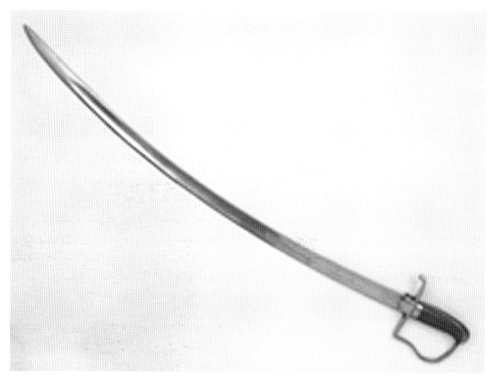

Lieutenant Henry Lane's sword in the National Army Museum (Courtesy of the Council of the National Army Museum, London)

him a mere sprat of fifteen when he joined the regiment. The purchase of such an inexpensive sword therefore seems consistent with his young age. Cornet was the lowest commissioned rank in the cavalry (equivalent today to a second lieutenant) but, even so, Lane would have been obliged to buy his own sword, along with other items of personal equipment, uniform and his horse. If he purchased his sword in its current form, he is likely to have paid no more than two or three guineas for it, whereas a decent-quality sword would have cost around five guineas. Now as a cornet he would have earned 8 shillings per day, out of which he would have to find subsistence for his horse at around 9 pence per day. A guinea was worth 21 shillings (20 shillings to the pound). A quality sword would therefore represent over two weeks pay, whereas a two-guinea sword could be paid for in less than a week. Henry Lane eventually achieved the rank of colonel, when he would certainly have been able to afford a sword of far better quality and a fine and fancy one at that. Indeed, it may be that he did purchase a better sword later in his career, though if I'd carried a sword at Waterloo, however cheap and shoddy, all the money in the world wouldn't be able to buy me one of greater value.

Lane's Waterloo sword was carried in a regular metal scabbard with two suspension rings, so that when worn sheathed it would have been indistinguishable from the regulation pattern. It was a feature of both the 1796 light and heavy cavalry patterns that swords were worn suspended from the waistbelt rather than from a shoulder belt as before. Hussar regiments in India favoured leather scabbards with brass fittings but the heavy, clanking metal sheaths of the regulation pattern were considered more serviceable for regiments fighting in Europe. There are several nicks on the blade but there is no way of telling whether these were received in combat or larking about or, in later years, gardening. There are some faintly-etched cartouches of floral design and a parade of arms on each side of the blade and the faded evidence of gilding, so, although cheap and nasty, the blade pretended to be a sword of quality. My guess is that, at fifteen, Henry Lane thought it would do. He may even have been persuaded by the seller that he was getting the proper regulation weapon.

The M1796 Light Cavalry Sword

The M1796 Light Cavalry Sword was the most enduring, and in my view, the most pleasing of all the regulation pattern swords issued to the British army. It wasn't superseded officially until 1821, and it remained in use by its aficionados long after that. Quite simply, it was a very well designed and effective weapon. Until the late eighteenth century regimental swords conformed to a general style but each was an individual bespoke piece. In March 1788 a Board of General Officers was set up to lay down official specifications for both light and heavy cavalry swords. Hitherto it had been the colonel of the regiment who determined the style of arms borne by his men. Now the idea was to have uniformity and a set standard of performance. That first pattern in 1788 was determined as being 36 inches long, 1½ inches wide and having a blade curvature of 1¾ inches – taken from a straight line running from the point to the back of the blade at the guard. The hilt was more loosely defined as being 'the same form as that now used by light dragoons'. With this rather loose definition, sword design entered a new age and within a dozen years, for the cavalry sword at least, it reached its apogee with the M1796 Light Cavalry Sword.

The terms 'sword' for a straight-bladed weapon and 'sabre' for a curve-bladed weapon were common parlance at the time but were not reflected in the language of the regulations. In spite of its distinctively curved blade the Model 1796 Light Cavalry pattern is referred to officially as a sword. I own one and to hold it gives a chilling sense of its dreadful power. It is a sword with splendid and complex shapes. From hilt to point it measures 33 inches and, for most of its length, the blade is 1⅜ inches wide but then it broadens to a flare of 1⅝ inches, giving maximum weight behind the optimal striking point. It also swells to 1⅝ inches at its junction with the hilt, perfecting the point of balance and urging the arm to strike. The back of the blade tapers from a chunky ⅜ inch at the hilt to where it narrows to become an effective back edge that can be honed to razor sharpness. A blend of strength and lightness is created by the robust back of the blade and a single broad fuller that travels from the hilt to within 8 inches of the point.

The point itself is 'hatchet' shaped, a style designed to favour the cut and the M1796 is above all else a cutting weapon; that said, when held with the knuckle-guard

uppermost, the point comes in line with the shoulder and it is perfectly possible to thrust effectively with it. It has a well-designed grip of ridged wood covered with leather that sits snugly and ergonomically in the hand and a distinctive stirrup hilt with a single rear quillon. The single knuckle-bow has been criticized as giving poor protection to the hand but frankly I think it is adequate and it certainly makes a damned good knuckle-duster as well as keeping the overall weight down. Its complex bend, rather than a simple curve, gives it additional strength through shape. In a cavalry mêlée it is easy to get wedged in a press of men with limited room or time to deliver a sweeping blow. In such circumstances a straight punch with the hilt is a good option and an M1796 hilt would be unlikely to buckle even if you struck a cuirassier's helmet with full force.

Attached to the hilt are two 'U'-shaped langets. Many surviving swords of this pattern show that it was common for them to be removed by troops in the field; clearly they were thought to be of little use. Nevertheless the British M1796 Light Cavalry Sword was a masterpiece of design; when you pick one up you can feel that you have a weapon in your hand capable of the most appalling savagery and yet its sweeping lines are all dash and elegance. Officers' swords were usually finished with blue and gilt decoration, creating a vivid splash of colour on the broad blade. Further customized with brass or gilded hilts, officer's swords sported either black leather grips wound with ornamental wire or grips made of ivory.

The one I own is a plain trooper's sword and it sits beside me on the desk as I write. From time to time I pick it up and it is so

M1796 Light Cavalry Sword (author's collection)

perfectly weighted and balanced that it feels immediately like a natural extension of one's own arm. Refusing to stay still, at ease only when in motion, it somehow coaxes the arm to wield it with a flourish. It is a sword to give even a humble trooper swagger. On the spine of the blade, near the hilt, can be made out worn lettering, which tells it was made by Woolley, Deakin & Co. Sword cutlers James Woolley and Thomas Deakin set up business at 74 Edmund Street, Camberwell in 1798. Now a residential area of London, Camberwell was then just emerging from being a small agricultural village a couple of miles south of London Bridge. In 1806 Woolley and Deakin expanded the business and took on John and Joseph Dutton and Richard Johnston as partners. The maker's mark changed with each change of association. In fact the legend Woolley, Deakin and Co only appeared on swords manufactured between 1805 and 1806, which gives a very narrow date margin for when my sword was produced. As a trooper's sword it would have been bought by the regiment and given out as standard issue.

It wasn't until 1865 that regulations for all regiments stipulated that swords should be marked fully with identity marks, though the practice had been adopted gradually by some regiments since the beginning of the century. In particular, hussar regiments

Detail of the author's M1796 Light Cavalry Sword. Note the maker's name on the back of the blade and '6C' stamped on the langet

had their swords stamped with troop letters and trooper numbers from an early stage, as a deterrent against troopers purloining each other's weapons. Even in a regiment of gallant hussars, the ranks were drawn from the seedier echelons of society. It was not thought necessary to specify the regiment, since troopers' swords were bought en masse by the regiment from a sole supplier and so the maker's name signified enough. In 1812 an order was made to mark all government-owned accoutrements with a letter signifying the regiment.

On the sword in my possession that letter is an 'H', indicating that it belonged to a hussar regiment. Below the 'H', stamped on the knuckle-guard, is a 'B' and below that the number 38. So the sword was carried by Trooper 38 of B Troop in a regiment of hussars. The question is which regiment? On one of the langets is another marking – 6C. Now this can't mean the 6th Cavalry Regiment, as that was a heavy cavalry unit at the time, and this is clearly a light cavalry sword. Most probably it suggests that this sword belonged to a hussar regiment under the 6th Cavalry Brigade. At the time of Waterloo the two British hussar regiments in the 6th Cavalry Brigade were the 10th (Prince of Wales Own) and the 18th (King's Irish). The 10th Hussars distinguished their swords with distinctive diamond-shaped langets and so, by elimination, the sword on my desk once belonged to Trooper 38 of B troop of the King's Irish Hussars and had been purchased by the regiment just a few years before Waterloo.

So much is reasoned fact. I cannot know whether or not this particular sword was carried into battle at Waterloo but its dates are consistent with the possibility and I

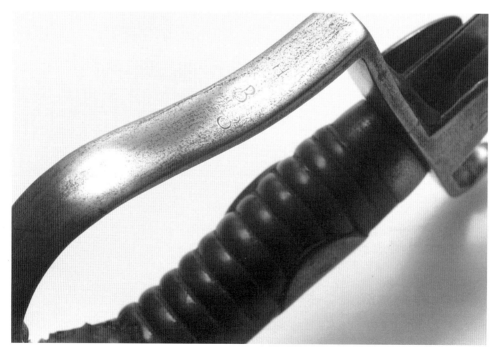

Knuckle bow stamped 'H' for Hussar regiment, 'B' for B Troop and 38 for trooper's number

like to think that it probably was. There are four small notches on the blade around the optimal striking point that may have come from its use in action. At the very least it is a sword that saw service during the Napoleonic Wars. If at Waterloo then it is likely to have been used in the final rout. The 18th (King's Irish) Hussars were deployed at the eastern end of the British line for most of the day and saw no action, indeed owing to the dense pall of gun smoke over the field, they saw nothing at all. However, in the late afternoon Major-General Sir Hussey Vivian, commander of the 6th Cavalry Brigade, ordered the 18th to move with the rest of the brigade behind the centre. From here they formed part of the spearhead of the general advance, which began around 8.30 in the evening. It being mid-June, there was still natural light until after 10pm.

Harrying the French from the field was a brutal business. In military terms it was a necessary action but for the soldier it meant seeking out defeated men and then cutting them down. Stumbling in the mire of their comrades' blood and the churned mud, men appeared in small groups, their silhouettes coming into view gradually like dim spectres in the drifting clouds of thick smoke. It was butcher's work and it was dangerous work. The army that stood with Napoleon that day was one of the finest and proudest armies the world has known. They quit the field reluctantly and with fight still in their hearts. The 18th Hussars paid for their grim efforts with 104 casualties, nearly a quarter of the regiment. We do not know the number of casualties they inflicted but may surmise that they were of a far greater number, as their dread blades slashed down, slicing through woollen coats, filleting the flesh beneath and biting into the bone of their retreating quarry.

After Waterloo, with Napoleon out of harm's way on St. Helena, the threat from the Continent subsided and the British army was scaled down with a drastic cut in numbers. One consequence of this troop reduction was a surplus in government swords that could now be sold off and the M1796 Light Cavalry Sword was especially suitable for arming yeomanry regiments of cavalry. These were volunteer regiments, raised initially as a sort of Home Guard against the threat of invasion from Napoleon, but in the years following Waterloo they were increasingly employed as a police force to quell growing civil unrest. Mass unemployment, widespread famine, the Corn Laws and a corrupt electoral system combined to create a climate of discontent and rebellion.

Four years after Waterloo, the 15th Hussars, the Manchester Yeomanry Cavalry and the Cheshire Yeomanry Cavalry drew their M1796 Light Cavalry Swords and charged at an altogether different foe than the one encountered on the fields outside Brussels. On 16 August 1819, a crowd of some 80,000 citizens gathered at St Peter's Field in Manchester to demand fair representation in Parliament. The 15th Hussars charged from the eastern end of the field at the same time that the Cheshire Yeomanry Cavalry charged from the southern end. The Manchester Yeomanry were already in amongst the demonstrators. Fifteen people were killed and some 600 were injured, either trampled or sabred. Many of the victims were women. While some accounts accuse the cavalry of cutting at every one they could reach, others claim that they showed restraint by using the flat of the blade. Local infirmaries saw plenty of evidence that night to confirm the former, though there may have been a greater casualty list if there were not also some truth in the latter. The official historical record of the 15th Hussars states, rather ambiguously, that they dispersed the crowd 'in as gentle a manner as possible'. Nevertheless, one officer of the 15th is reported elsewhere as crying out, 'For shame! For shame! Gentlemen: forbear, forbear! The people cannot get away!'

In an ironic parody of the nation's pride in its victory at Waterloo, this moment of national shame became known as the Peterloo Massacre. It is just possible that the sword on the desk before me was used in both encounters. G 32 CYC has been stamped on the underside of its cross-guard indicating that, subsequent to its being sold off by the 18th Hussars at the end of the Napoleonic wars, it went into service with the Cheshire Yeomanry Cavalry and that it was born by Trooper 32 of G Troop. Whether he was a green young man, panicked and frightened by the angry crowd, who lashed out indiscriminately with his sword, or whether he was a steady old soldier who tried to restrain his comrades from their worst excesses, I cannot know. Nor can I be certain that this sword was there, any more than I can be certain it was at Waterloo, but it is possible.

Stamped over the G, with bolder indentation and a much larger letter, is a D. It is a decommissioning stamp, signifying the end of the sword's official Army life. It has survived the intervening years in remarkably good condition; arguably in as good temper now as when it was first inspected. On the blade is a Board of Ordnance view mark, consisting of a crown over the figure 8, as proof of that first inspection. Such

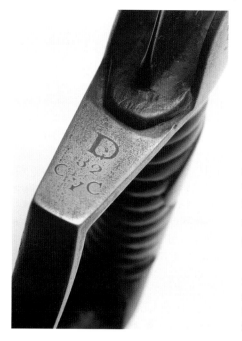

marks were introduced in 1788, when 'viewing houses' were set up at HM Tower of London and in Birmingham to essay the quality of blades purchased by the government. A light cavalry blade was expected to be shortened by 5½ inches on bending without signs of failure and to spring back to the straight. I set up a measure on the wall and, with my heart in my mouth, slowly bent my 1796 until the hilt had travelled 5½ inches. It is a very significant bend of the blade and yet when I released the pressure it sprang back with an elastic alacrity that defied the years.

Underside of cross-guard showing later stamp 'G 32 CYC' indicating issue to Trooper 32 of G Troop, Cheshire Yeomanry Cavalry and 'D' decommissioning stamp

A numeral below the crown stamp designated the manufacturer of the sword, for instance a 9 was for Thomas Gill. In this case it is an 8, signifying Woolley, Deakin & Co. James Woolley was a well-established figure in the sword-manufacturing trade, having first set up shop in Birmingham in 1779. Even after moving to Camberwell in 1790 and going into partnership with Thomas Deakin in 1798, he retained ownership of his own blade-grinding mill near Birmingham and he went on, with various partnerships, mass-manufacturing swords until after Waterloo. James Woolley was one of a triumvirate of leading sword makers of the time who were instrumental in establishing the proving tests. Along

Detail of the blade showing Board of Ordnance viewing mark

with Thomas Gill and Samuel Harvey, Woolley gave evidence to the first meeting of the Board of Ordnance in May 1788. Thomas Gill, a Birmingham manufacturer famous for marking all his blades with the claim 'Warranted Never To Fail', advocated that in addition to bending tests, swords should be struck on the edge on an iron bar. Samuel Harvey thought it better to strike on a flat surface. Woolley argued that the bending test was sufficient and that striking tests risked setting up hairline fractures in the steel.

Woolley, Gill and Harvey were joined at their second meeting, a month later, by John Justus Runkel, the leading supplier of Solingen blades. These German imports accounted for a very high percentage of the swords in the British Army at the time and their worth was challenged by the British manufacturers. However, tests carried out on the spot by the Board of Ordnance demonstrated that Runkel's blades were generally of a higher quality than their British counterparts. They were also less expensive. This reputation for superior blades at reasonable prices may have persuaded the fifteen-year-old Cornet Lane that he was buying a decent sword at a bargain price when he forked out for his cheap German import. Of course not all German blades were of the Solingen standard. As a consequence of their findings the Board recommended that the government levy an import duty on blades of foreign manufacture, thus levelling the playing field and making British manufacturers competitive with Runkel on price. As for quality, they decided that all regulation swords be subjected to both a striking and a bending test.

When young and full of wine, friends and I would take my M1796 Light Cavalry Sword and conduct a different kind of test. We would test our nerve and control by slicing apples, held on upturned bare palms, completely in half. I am happy to report there were no mishaps. It is an exercise known as the 'Napier Feat', because it was first performed on Sir Charles Napier's hand by a Sikh swordsman when he was in India in the 1840s. The recipient keeps his fingers together and flexes them downwards to raise the palm of the hand. The swordsman has to take care to avoid any drawing action to the cut and to judge the force precisely. My favourite trick with my M1796 sword, though, was an emulation of a feat regularly performed by Frederick the Great's cavalry general, Friedrich, Baron von Seidlitz. He would gallop in front of his men and have an apple thrown in the air, which he would duly slice in half.

Le Marchant and sword exercise for the cavalry

The 1796 Light Cavalry Sword, though based heavily on an Austrian pattern, was officially designed by General John Gaspard Le Marchant, a military reformer who also wrote an instruction manual, *Rules and Regulations for the Sword Exercise of the Cavalry*. He campaigned for better officer training, at a time when gentlemen simply bought their commissions, and was largely responsible for the creation of the military academy at Sandhurst. He saw active service in the Peninsular War and was killed at Salamanca in 1812, while pursuing fleeing French infantry. Le Marchant is said to have cut down six of them with his sword before he fell.

When Henry Lane was commissioned into the regiment, he would have begun his training following Le Marchant's drills and exercises. At the time there was a raging

Sword drills after Le Marchant

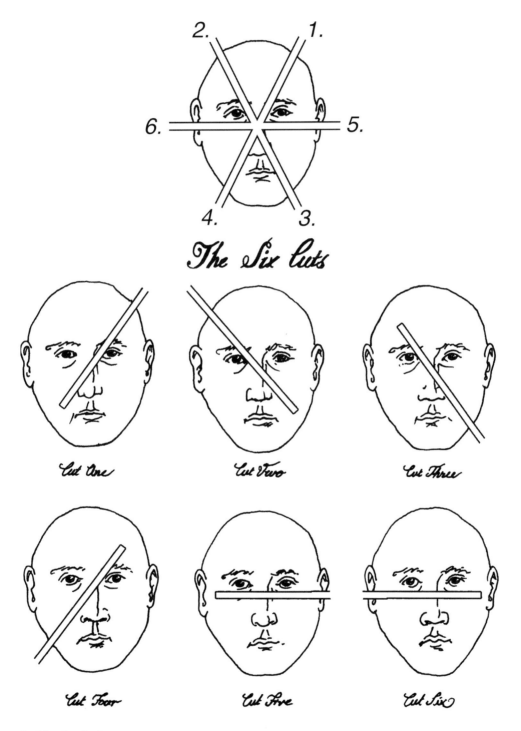

Le Marchant's six cuts

debate over the supremacy of either the cut or the thrust. Maurice de Saxe, a French general, was an ardent proponent of the thrust to the extent that he urged the edges of French blades to be blunted in order to compel its use, 'that the soldier may be effectually prevented cutting with it in action, which method of using the sword never does execution'. Captain Charles Parquin of the French Chasseurs à Cheval reported:

> We always thrust with the point of our sabres, whereas they [the British] always cut with their blade which was three inches wide. Consequently out of every twenty blows aimed by them, nineteen missed. If, however, the edge of the blade found its mark only once, it was a terrible blow, and it was not unusual to see an arm cut clean from the body.

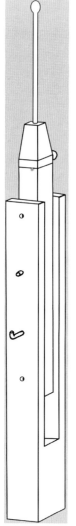

British cavalrymen missing nineteen out of twenty blows because they favoured the cut seems a farcical assertion, confirming only that proponents of either the thrust or the cut were prone to making up bogus statistics to prove their point. However, his exaggeration of the sword's width suggests that a broad blade had an intimidating psychological effect.

General le Marchant favoured a combination of both cut and thrust. Raw recruits were initially drilled on foot, standing 6 feet from a wall upon which a circle, 2 feet in diameter, had been drawn at head height. This was bisected with lines representing the six basic cuts and the recruits had to perform them in sequence with precise discipline. Le Marchant insisted that a sword-knot be worn at all times, preventing 'accidents that are liable to occur by the sword escaping from the hand, when not restrained'. Yet more drills on foot instilled the recruit with reflex responses to the correct parry positions. These were linked to different attacking moves, so that having delivered a cut, the trooper would follow through by coming to the relevant guard because, as Le Marchant explained,

> In an attack of cavalry, no movement can be made without being in consequence of retort. It therefore must be an invaluable rule after making an offensive movement, to come to the protection of the part exposed thereby

Cutting practice was at willow wands, secured in specially designed posts. These were placed at several stations around the training arena and at various heights. Swords for this training were only sharpened for a distance of six inches from the point, in order to ensure that the right part of the blade was used. According to the *Rules and Regulations*,

Le Marchant's sword-cut post

It should be remembered that little force is requisite to produce effect from the application of the edge, if conducted with skill, and that, whether with a straight sword or a scymitar blade, no cut can be made with effect or security, where the weapon does not at once free itself from the object to which it is applied, otherwise it must turn in the hand and give contusion rather than a cut, for which reason those wounds are most severe, which are made nearest to the point.

Cutting the willows cleanly was also only possible by presenting the edge at the correct angle.

Despite the contemporary commentaries implying that the 1796 Light Cavalry Sword was only suitable as a cutting weapon, it could also be used to thrust perfectly well and Le Marchant devised an elaborate apparatus to train for this action. An adjustable post, from which a metal ring was suspended at a height equivalent to an enemy cavalryman's head, was set up and troopers had to take the ring on the end of their swords and carry it. This had to be done at the gallop or, as Le Marchant puts it, 'with considerable rapidity'. Tyros could start with a 4-inch diameter ring but they were soon required to progress to smaller rings 'till they are enabled to give point with tolerable degree of certainty, within the diameter of a crown piece'. Thrusting down at enemy infantry was practiced by lowering the post to the height of a standing man and substituting the ring with a canvas ball stuffed with hay.

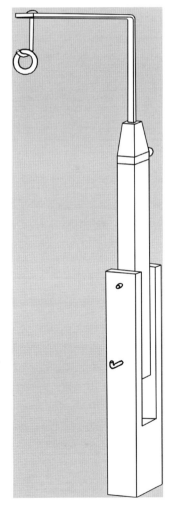

Freestyle practice and sparring were as important in training for the mounted fight as they had always been for fighting on foot. As well as sword strokes it was essential to practice the manoeuvring of one's horse in relation to the enemy's. Le Marchant counselled 'never to allow your horse to be in a line parallel with his at the instant of attack'. This was because it would put your horse's head in the front line of a counterattack from your foe. He recommended that in the last couple of yards of your approach, you turn your horse's head away, thus swinging yourself a few feet closer and the horse's head just out of reach of the enemy's sword. Squads were formed in two ranks and front and rear rank attacked each other alternately. Acknowledging

Le Marchant's ring post

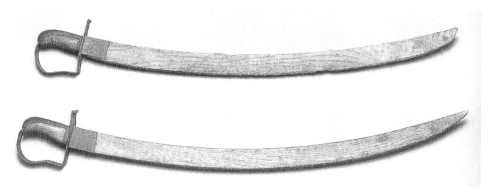

Wooden practice sabres of the Percy Tenantry Volunteer Cavalry; formerly in a private collection, now in the Royal Armouries, Leeds (photo courtesy of Park Lane Arms Fair)

that practice between opposing troopers would result in blades clashing and mindful that the replacement of damaged blades was an unwelcome regimental expense, Le Marchant advised that, 'all practice in the modes of defence and attack may be executed with the flat and back of the blade in place of the edge'. He adds the caveat that this exercise can only be undertaken once the recruits have it fully ingrained in their muscle memory how to lay on the edge when necessary. An alternative was to use wooden weapons. Examples exist of wooden swords in the shape of the M1796 Light Cavalry Sword, although, as often as not, squads probably used the common singlestick, which would have done the job equally well.

Singlesticks and lead cutters

For sparring practice on foot, soldiers used 'singlesticks'. Singlesticks (or cudgels) were ash staves, about an inch in diameter and 3 feet in length, with a globular guard, made either of wicker or boiled hide. These were the primary training weapons for backswording and became so popular in their own right that contests with singlesticks became increasingly common attractions. Victory was usually agreed at first blood, defined as the skin being sufficiently broken that an inch of blood flowed. A curious practice arising in the nineteenth century was for the left hand to be hooked into a sling that passed between the legs, so that the elbow could be raised as high as the head, but no higher. Constrained in this way, the left arm could be used to parry blows aimed at the head. There is a good account of a singlestick encounter in the novel *Tom Brown's Schooldays* by Thomas Hughes – 'a very slight blow with a stick will fetch blood, so that it is by no means a punishing pastime, if the men don't play on purpose and savagely at the body and arms of their adversaries'. Hughes is recalling the time when singlestick tournaments were a regular feature at country fairs and stout-hearted men stood up to take a few knocks and compete for a prize. However, he was writing at a time, around 1850, when these contests were beginning to go out of fashion. Nevertheless, singlesticks remained in use as sporting weapons – in the

Singlesticks (author's collection)

Army, the Navy and the Boy Scouts – well into the first half of the twentieth century, though it became increasingly common to seek more protection in the form of pads and helmets.

Along with jujitsu, wrestling and boxing, the irrepressible Theodore Roosevelt was an afficionado of singlestick play. A 1905 edition of *Harper's Weekly* reported that the pugnacious President arrived at a White House reception with his arm bandaged, as a result of a singlestick bout with his close friend, General Leonard Wood. In the same year he was blinded in one eye during a boxing bout, though it was ten years before he admitted this misadventure to the world.

The National Army Museum houses a number of specialist training swords that were developed for specific exercises. Gymnasium swords, used with masks for free-play practice, were heavyweight versions of the regular fencing sabre, having a blade width of ⅝ inch. Consequently they were also much stiffer than today's equivalent. Another type of heavyweight sword was the 'lead cutter'. This was used to cut through blocks of lead, developing the strength of the sword arm, accustoming it to meeting resistance and, most importantly, learning to lay a blow with the correct angle of edge. Cutting bars of lead with a sword is thought to date back to the Crusades. In fact the feat is known as the 'Coeur de Lion' in reference to King Richard I, who allegedly demonstrated his skill at it in front of Saladin. During the eighteenth and nineteenth centuries, the bars used were triangular in section and around 12 inches long. Depending on the skill and strength of the striker, the faces of these lead '*Toblerones*' varied between 1 and 2 inches. The bar could either be suspended from the rafters, set upright upon a table or thrown in the air. It was struck with a horizontal cut. J.M. Waite, who published *Lessons in Sabre, Singlestick, Sabre and Bayonet, and Sword Feats* in 1880, advises smearing tallow on the blade so that you can see what part of the blade you have cut with. Judging to strike at the 'point of percussion' – that part of the blade which causes the least vibrations on impact, equivalent to the

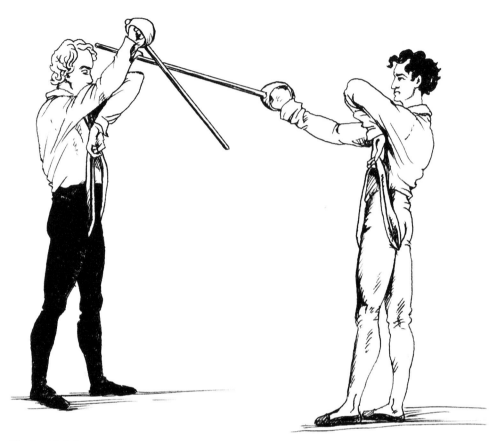

Singlestick fighters

'sweet spot' on a tennis racquet or baseball bat – was a chief aim of the exercise. He adds that the tallow will 'also slightly assist the cut'. Lead-cutting swords have very broad blades, some in excess of 2 inches, and hilts in the style of a naval cutlass. Wilkinson's of Pall Mall manufactured them in a variety of weights and sizes from No. 1 to No. 4 and a mould for the lead bar was included with the purchase. I have handled a No. 4 and it is very heavy indeed, weighing in at around 4lbs. It has a 33¼ inch blade and feels quite unwieldy. Waite advises that 'a weak man would cut better with a smaller weapon and a very powerful man would find a larger one more suitable'. I suspect that I would need a No. 1. However a man who could have wielded a No. 4 with great ease was Ensign Charles Ewart.

Leadcutter

The M1796 Heavy Cavalry Sword

Ensign Charles Ewart of the Scots Greys has left us a gripping account of what it was like to fight with a sword from horseback in the thick of battle. He was 6 feet 4 inches tall and immensely powerful. In the encounter he described, he fought his way through to capture the Eagle of the French 45th Regiment ('The Invincibles') at the Battle of Waterloo. He wrote:

> One made a thrust at my groin; I parried him off and cut him down through the head. A lancer came at me – I threw the lance off by my right side and cut him through the chin and upwards through the teeth. Next, a foot soldier fired at me and then charged me with his bayonet, which I also had the good luck to parry, and then I cut him down through the head.

This hapless French infantryman was born a few decades too early to receive the advice of Henry Angelo IV, who published his *Bayonet Exercise* in 1857. In it he instructs a man on the ground how to proceed against a mounted attacker. He tells him to 'endeavour to keep on his [the horseman's] left side, where he has less power of defending himself or his horse and cannot reach so far in attacking as on his right'.

Ewart was armed with the M1796 Heavy Cavalry Sword. Two inches longer than the light cavalry pattern, the heavy weighed in around the same, at 2lb 2oz. It had a straight, single-edged blade and a hatchet point. After the action at Villagarcia in 1812, Captain Bragge of the British 3rd Dragoons wrote that,

> It is worthy of remark that scarcely one Frenchman died of his wounds although dreadfully chopped, whereas 12 English

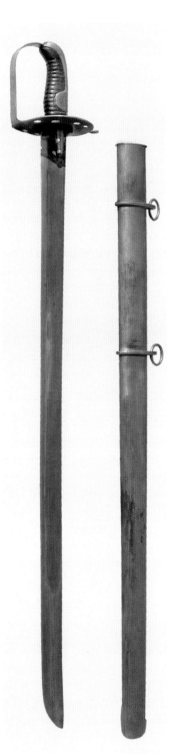

M1796 Heavy Cavalry Sword (photo courtesy of Sword Sales EU)

Swordpoint profiles: (top) spear point (bottom) hatchet point

Dragoons were killed on the spot and others dangerously wounded by thrusts. If our men had used their swords so, three times the number of French would have been killed.

A hatchet point on a straight blade was certainly of no use for thrusting and before the Battle of Waterloo an order was given to the British Heavy Brigade to customize their swords by grinding them to a spear point, so that they would bite into the French cuirassiers' armour.

Where possible, of course, thrusts were directed, not at the cuirass, but at the face or throat. An attack by two French cuirassiers against a British Life Guard at Waterloo was witnessed by Sergeant Thomas Morris of the 73rd Foot who later wrote,

> He bravely maintained the unequal combat for a minute or two, then he disposed of one them by a deadly thrust to the throat. His combat with the other one lasted about five minutes, when the Guardsman struck his opponent a slashing backhand stroke, and sent his helmet some distance with his head still in it. The horse galloped away, the headless rider sitting erect in the saddle, the blood spurting out of the arteries like so many fountains.

This un-named Life Guard, as well as having remarkable stamina, ably demonstrated the worth of Le Marchant's cut and thrust principles. As for the headless rider, he would have done well to adhere to Cruso's injunction to keep on a horseman's left hand side.

Like its light cavalry counterpart, the M1796 Heavy Cavalry Sword was well designed and well made, though in the case of Corporal John Shaw, of the 2nd Life Guards, it wasn't quite robust enough for his beserker rage. It is alleged that at Waterloo Shaw got very drunk on gin before the battle and set to with an energetic fury, cutting down at least ten men before his sword broke. Hurling the hilt at one man, he then grabbed his helmet by its strap, removed it, and used it as a club before finally succumbing to a cuirassier's thrust.

Uniform

Cuirassiers wore steel breastplates and Life Guards had metal helmets but armour was otherwise absent from the Napoleonic battlefield. However, it would be a mistake to suppose that soldiers' attire did not offer some protection against the sword. Note that Ewart cut up, under the chin of his lancer foe. The hard leather lancer's cap – the *czapka* – had a square top, like a mortar-board, designed to take the force out of a downward blow from a sword. Similarly, a tall bearskin makes it extremely difficult for the swordsman to raise his arm high enough above his opponent in order to bring it down with any force. At Fuentes d'Onoro in 1811, Cornet Francis Hall of the 14th Light Dragoons reported that,

> Their broadswords, ably wielded, flashed over the Frenchmen's heads and obliged them to cower in their saddlebows. The alarm was indeed greater than the hurt, for their cloaks were so well rolled across their left shoulders that it was no easy matter to give a mortal blow with the broad edge of a sabre whereas their swords, which were straight and pointed, though their effect on the eyes was les formidable, were capable of inflicting a much severer wound.

Cornet Hall and his fellows would have carried the M1796 light cavalry sword and here he vents his frustration that cutting blows with this weapon were foiled by a rolled-up cloak.

The soldiers' uniforms for both Wellington's and Napoleon's army were, with the possible exception of Maximilian's landsknechts, the most ostentatiously extravagant blaze of colour and ornament that the world had ever seen and there was none prettier nor more glamorous than a hussar. Hussar regiments in the British army were essentially light dragoons with moustaches and dressed in the most exotic of military couture. Between 1806 and 1807, four regiments of light dragoons – 7th, 10th, 15th and 18th – were reincarnated as hussar regiments. Additionally, the King's German Legion had three regiments of hussars, making seven regiments in all serving during the Napoleonic period. Their peacock pageantry was in stark contrast to the realities of war at the time. Warfare is always horrific but the Napoleonic period saw battlefield carnage on a new level. Cannon balls, both round shot and canister, scythed through ranks of infantry, creating wounds and amputations on a massive scale. Muskets spat their lead balls deep into unprotected flesh. Bayonets disembowelled with surgical efficiency and, despite occasional obstructions from furled cloaks and the like, the sword came into its own. Men, no longer armoured in steel, were cut down with deep gashing wounds and their limbs could be severed at a stroke. Having said that, there was generally more chance of survival from a sword cut than from a musket ball wound. Lead shot driven deep into the body, taking fibres of filthy clothing with it, was likely to kill you by infection if it didn't do so outright by striking a vital organ; whereas sword wounds could be treated by cauterization, making it less probable that the victim would get gangrene. Many soldiers survived the most dreadful, often multiple, sword wounds.

Resplendent uniforms created a culture of pride and bravado that was essential to urge men to venture forth into the slaughterhouse of Napoleonic battle. Henry Lane's regiment, the 15th Hussar's, wore a tight-fitting, blue dolmen (jacket) with red facings and a spaghetti scramble of silver braids. Slung from the shoulder, with a studied air of casualness, was a second, fur-lined over-jacket, the pelisse, that also functioned as a shield for the bridle arm. Breeches were of white buckskin. From 1809, the regiment switched from busbies (fur caps) to bright red shakos (tall, cylindrical caps, made from pasteboard and leather) with a white-over-red cock-feather plume. A belt of whitened buff leather suspended a carbine, a cartridge pouch and a leaky wooden canteen over the shoulder and another hung the sword from the waist. Also affixed to an officer's sword belt was the sabretache (literally – 'sabre bag'), a flat leather satchel with a stiffened front that could act as a writing desk when mounted. Reconnaissance was a key role for the cavalry and the sabretache always contained maps, paper and a pencil, as well as other essentials such as tobacco and a pipe.

In the soldier's slang of the day a sword was known as a 'tail'. A trooper's 'tail' was attached to two low-slung straps, suspending the sword from the belt at a convenient angle when mounted. When dismounted, it had to be hooked up to the belt, lest it dragged along the ground. Of great annoyance for the trooper, slogging in the saddle for hours over the dry terrain of the Iberian Peninsula, was the incessant noise of his sabre rattling in its metal scabbard. Many surviving scabbards exhibit vice marks near the throat, where they have been clamped to ensure the sword stayed in place quietly. This modification needed to be done adroitly for fear of serious embarrassment at the command to draw sabres! With regulation-pattern swords of the eighteenth and nineteenth centuries, the scabbards were not lined as they had been in previous eras. British soldiers often complained that their swords too-quickly lost their edge and it wasn't until the 1864-pattern cavalry sword that wood linings were introduced. The rediscovery of this essential means of sword care was prompted by the British experience in India, where it was observed that native blades were sharper; they had wood linings to their scabbards.

The road to Waterloo

Henry Lane's regiment, the 15th Hussars, was commanded by Lieutenant Colonel Sir Colquhoun Grant. His dictum, 'a hussar does not fall from his horse, he falls with it', succinctly encapsulates the high standard of horsemanship expected of his men. Battlefield riding skills and horses had been through a major change in the preceding century, a revolution pioneered by Baron von Seidlitz, Frederick the Great's cavalry general. For the massed charge he wanted horses and riders that would simply go forward with dash and speed. Medieval and Renaissance warhorses were ridden in 'collection', where the action of the horse is 'collected' beneath the rider, so that he can affect its motions by subtle changes of balance as if he were standing on a giant ball. There is not the space in a work of this nature to go into the arcane details but the point to take is that horses ridden in collection were highly trained and expensive and it took highly trained and expensive riders to ride them.

With the onset of the indiscriminate carnage wrought by improved mobile field artillery, modern armies needed horses and riders that were quicker to train and cheaper to replace. General Seidlitz advocated riding in 'extension', where the horse stretches out in the manner of a modern racehorse. Requiring less skill from the rider, the only things that mattered were staying on and going forward at speed and Seidlitz's system was soon adopted by cavalry regiments throughout Europe. Indeed, the Duke of Wellington once famously complained during the Peninsular War that the British cavalry were guilty of 'galloping at everything'. The idea of horses galloping into a barrage of artillery fire may seem like a difficult mission to accomplish but the horse, we may presume, has no foresight of the possible consequences of the hurtling missiles, clouds of smoke or the flash and bang of the guns. These are stimuli to which it reacts only on a superficial level. For the purposes of recreating battle scenes of the period for television, I have often ridden horses through a field of laid explosions. Pots of black powder are embedded beneath the turf and packed with peat, which is first sifted to ensure there are no stones in it. The pots are detonated electronically as one gallops through them. They make a tremendous din, create smoke and flash and throw up plumes of dirt to simulate the fall of cannon ball all around. Certainly horses jink and baulk (especially when you ride over a pot as it is exploding!) and it is a fairly hairy experience, but the horses get used to doing it and react with less alarm each time you do it. More significantly they are prepared to do it again and again. When Henry Lane joined the regiment (December 1811), he would first have undergone rigorous training from the regimental riding master.

Lane's first experience of action with the regiment was not a death-or-glory charge on the battlefield but the rather unpleasant business of quelling civil unrest. The 15th Hussars were sent to assist the civil authorities during the Luddite riots that began in 1811. Fighting to protect their jobs in the face of advancements in machinery, the Luddites were textile workers who resorted to violent protest, smashing up the new machines. They were dealt with harshly. A civilian police force had yet to be established and matters of civil order were entrusted to the Army. In 1816, the 15th were again involved in suppressing riots, this time in Birmingham, where Major Joseph Thackwell was struck on the head by a stone and lay unconscious for several hours. They put down the Jeremiah Brandreth Riots in Nottingham in 1817 and, of course, were at 'Peterloo' in

Officer's pattern 1796 Light Cavalry Sword with blue gilt blade (courtesy of the Council of the National Army Museum, London)

1819. It was not the sort of work that a gallant hussar joined up to do. He craved adventure against a foreign foe.

That adventure arrived for the men of the 15th Hussars in February 1813, when six troops embarked at Portsmouth for Lisbon to join Sir Thomas Graham's force on the Peninsula. After enduring the bitter cold and surmounting the difficulties of crossing the high passes of the Tras-os-Montes with their horses, they swept down onto the plain in time to prevent the French from crossing the River Douro. On the 31st May, the 15th Hussars, under Captain Thackwell's command, forded the river with the 51st (King's Own Yorkshire) Light Infantry clinging to their stirrups. It was a bold and dangerous gambit and many men were swept away by the fast flowing torrent. However, on gaining the opposite bank, Captain Thackwell spurred his horse forward as he led two squadrons in pursuit of French heavy dragoons, who had turned tail. In a chase of over two miles, the 15th managed to close with the enemy on a number of occasions, and, their sabres flashing, killed and wounded several and took many more prisoners. The 15th sustained only the loss of one horse killed, with five men and three horses wounded.

Subsequently, the regiment saw action at Morales (2 June), Burgos (12 June), Osma (18 June) and Vittoria (21 June). Henry Lane is not listed in the regiment's records as serving in any of these battles. He, to his undoubted chagrin, was left to moulder back in England as part of the depot squadron. While his fellows found fame and glory on the Peninsula, he was engaged in drills and civic duties and the frustrating boredom of life in barracks. Hussars were known, above all, for their devil-may-care spirit. The contemporary saying that 'a hussar not dead at 30 is a scoundrel' was not for nothing and the necessity of leaving reserve troops behind must have been especially irksome to men of such character. However, the exploits of those in the field are no less a part of Lane's story. He and the others left behind would have eagerly awaited despatches from the front line and tracked their every move with fanatical interest and pride. Following the fate and fortune of the fighting troops is likely to have been an integral part of Lane's daily life in England, connecting him to the regimental collective memory. Cornet Lane was advanced in rank on 3 September 1812 and it was as Lieutenant Lane that he finally joined his regiment overseas, arriving in Pamplona on 28 October. Four days later the regiment, along with the rest of Wellington's army, started the long march over the Pyrenees, pushing Napoleon back into France. By early 1814, Napoleon's forces were fighting defensive actions on their own soil. Lieutenant Lane is listed as receiving the medal and clasps for battles at both Orthes and Toulouse.

Orthez (as it is spelled today) is a beautiful medieval town in southwestern France. I visited there in the late seventies, in my jousting days, and rode across its magnificent 14th-century bridge wearing full armour. It is extraordinary and fortunate that the bridge was not destroyed in the intense fighting for the town that took place on 27 February 1814. At Orthez Wellington brought 31,000 men to bear on Marshal Soult's defending army of 36,000. It was a very tough fight, the sabres of the 15th Hussars playing a crucial part, but Wellington prevailed, sustaining just over

2,000 casualties to Soult's loss of 4,000. Toulouse was the end of the line for Soult, the 15th and other cavalry regiments having harried his army there all the way from Orthez, with many minor engagements on the way. At Toulouse the 15th were stationed to defend the infantry from a French cavalry counterattack and to cut off the retreat of any fleeing the town. In this position they suffered a number of casualties from the enemy's artillery. Wellington was victorious, though he gained Soult's surrender at a high cost of lives, only discovering later that Napoleon had abdicated four days previously.

After Toulouse, the 15th were sent to Ireland. Whilst the infantry were embarked home from nearby Bordeaux, Wellington's entire cavalry had to march to Calais in order to take ship. Setting off from Toulouse on 1 June, they finally arrived in Dover on 17 July. There were parades and reviews and the cheers of the crowd to be acknowledged and there was extended leave, at least for the officers. It wasn't until 22 December 1814 that the 15th finally arrived in Dublin. They had been in Ireland for less than three months when Bonaparte reappeared on the European stage, the Grand Army flocking to his call. The 15th Hussars embarked from Cork on 12 May 1815, setting sail for Ostend.

Life on campaign was not always arduous for officers, as this extract from the journal of Major Edwin Griffiths relates, recalling an evening he and his friends spent at an Inn near Ghent; 'We . . . got an excellent dinner, plenty of wine, beer &c &c, and the amount of the bill was only 25 francs. Less than two shillings and fourpence a head!' Griffiths was much enamoured of both the architecture and the people he encountered, although he bemoaned the fact that Flanders 'generally speaking has not much female beauty to boast' – doubtless he had a hussar's eye for the ladies! What seemed like a summer holiday for the regiment came to an abrupt halt on 16 June, when they were ordered to the front. They covered the fifty miles from Oudenarde to Quatre Bras in a single day, arriving around midnight.

In a bloody prelude to the major battle ahead, the Battle of Quatre Bras, a fight for the strategically crucial Quatre Bras crossroads, took place on 16 June. The 15th Hussars remained in reserve but around 4,000 Frenchmen and 5,000 Englishmen either lost their lives or were severely wounded in the encounter. Although a tactical draw, the French succeeded in preventing the British from joining up with the Prussians who were fighting their own action against the French at Ligny, less than ten miles away.

As the British, Prussian and French armies manoeuvred towards the final show-down, the entire area was chaotic with troop movements and minor skirmishes. On the day after Quatre Bras, 17 June, a troop of the 15th Hussars, under Captain Wodehouse, saw action against some French squadrons, which had intercepted some wagons carrying wounded soldiers along the Nivelles Road. Captain Wodehouse's troop charged them and took prisoners. Though there is no actual record of which troop Henry Lane was attached to, Edwin Griffith's journal entry, which mentions Lane's arrival in Spain, does so in a context of discussing Captain Wodehouse's command. So there is a reasonable possibility that Lane was serving in Wodehouse's troop on this occasion and that his humble little sword was among a select few to taste French blood on the eve of Waterloo.

Waterloo, 18 June 1815

There is nothing quite like the misery of minor discomforts to unsettle the nerves and Lieutenant Henry Lane, not yet twenty years old, had more than his fair share of discomfort on the morning of the Battle of Waterloo. The 15th had bivouacked in a rye field, near to the Mont St Jean farm, and it had rained hard all night. It was bitterly cold and it was wet and the ground was a complete quagmire, with horses sinking up to their knees in places. Shivering from the cold and with their stomachs churning from a mixture of hunger, fear and excitement, the men of the 15th Hussars rose before daylight, saw to their horses and applied a whetstone to their blades one last time. Unlike many less-fortunate regiments, their supply wagon had found them and there were victuals for the men and fodder for the horses. At 4am the regiment marched to take up position, in the first line, on a ridge to the rear of Hougoumont chateau and farm.

Waterloo is one of the most complex and fascinating battles in British history. Oceans of ink have been expended on recording every detail of every hour of this long day and here is not the place to relive the glories of the staunch British squares, the fight for the Le Hay Sainte farmhouse or the glorious charge of the Heavy Brigade, though I have already found it irresistible to recount Ensign Charles Ewart's celebrated escapade in capturing the eagle of the 'Invincibles' and the feats of an anonymous Life Guard. Now, however, I must concentrate solely on how the day passed for Lieutenant Henry Lane and the rest of the 15th Hussars.

The first cannon shots rang out around 11.30am and the Hougoument compound, held by British Guards, was the first section of Wellington's line to come under attack. Remaining on station until the early afternoon, the 15th were initially mere spectators, though they took some casualties from cannonades that had overshot. Around 2pm however, Napoleon's heavy cavalry began their thundering charges against the British infantry squares and the 15th were moved forward to defend them. In a letter, written later in his life, Henry Lane recalled: 'We were no sooner on our ground than we advanced in line, and charged the Grenadiers à Cheval, who fled from us.' Well, to have the Grenadiers à Cheval de la Garde Imperiale flee from you is quite a thing. They were the elite cavalry regiment in the French army, the bravest of the brave. In order to join this regiment it was necessary to be recommended by a superior officer as someone who had already demonstrated bravery and had served with distinction elsewhere. Their nickname was 'Gros-Bottes' ('Big Boots'), a reference that alluded both to their high status and to their physical size. The minimum height requirement was 5 feet 9 inches (176cm), though mounted on their great black chargers and wearing their very tall bearskins they must have assumed the terrifying presence of giant centaurs. These were the men whom Henry Lane and his comrades chased from the field in their first dash at Waterloo. What a thrill it must have been.

The 15th Hussars, in red shakos, in action at Waterloo. Painting by Denis Dighton (1792–1827) (The Bridgeman Art Library/Getty Images)

Lane's letter continues:

> Our next attack (in line without reserve) was [on] a square of French
> Infantry, and our horses were within a few feet of the square. We did not
> succeed in breaking it, and, of course, suffered most severely. In short,
> during the day we were constantly on the move, attacking and retreating
> to our lines, so that, at the close of the battle, the two squadrons were
> dreadfully cut up.

It was in the attacks against the French infantry squares that several of Henry Lane's
fellows lost their lives. Having ridden their horses to a lather, defending their own
squares against wave after wave of French cavalry, four troops of the 15th Hussars
(approximately 240 officers and men) crested the hill and bore down upon the enemy
infantry. Colonel Dalrymple was struck at the outset of the first charge; a cannon
ball shattering his left leg, so that it hung by its tendons, and killing his horse. The ball
passed through Dalrymple's poor steed and hit Colonel Grant's mount, who galloped
beside him. It was one of five horses he lost that day. Major Edwin Griffith took
command and led the charge home. Sharpshooters in the French squares singled out
the officers. Major Griffith and his horse, Forrester, were shot to pieces.

Command of the regiment then passed to Captain Joseph Thackwell who led
further charges against the infantry. His horse was killed under him in his first charge
but he was provided with a remount and rode out again. This time he was shot in the
left forearm but, according to the official historical record of the regiment,

> he instantly seized the bridle with his right hand, in which was his sword,
> and still dashed on at the head of his regiment, the command of which
> had devolved upon him. Another shot took effect on the same arm but he
> immediately seized the bridle with his teeth.

At the close of the day his left arm was amputated close to the shoulder. This is
the man who, the following year, was stoned by a Birmingham mob. After Captain
Thackwell had been obliged to retire from the field, Captain Hancox took command.
He led yet more charges, before retiring the regiment behind the lines. They then
took no further part in the battle until the general advance that began around 8.30pm.
Along with all the other cavalry regiments the 15th took part in the pursuit, in
particular chasing down French infantry as they fled the field. However, after chasing
their quarry for around three miles, men and horses were utterly exhausted and had to
pull to a halt. For the 15th Hussars the Battle of Waterloo ended at about 9.30 in the
evening.

Thoughts of Waterloo always bring to my mind the words of the Duke of
Wellington, as he surveyed the heaps of dead and wounded: 'Believe me, nothing
except a battle lost can be half so melancholy as a battle won'. However, I shall close
this episode with a verse written in memoriam of Major Edwin Griffith, by his sisters:

Weep not; he died as heroes die
The death permitted to the brave
Mourn not; he lies where soldiers lie
And valour envies such a grave.

The occupation

After Waterloo the 15th were stationed at Cambrai, Wellington's headquarters for the occupation. Both Lord Liverpool's government and Wellington took the view that victory had been won over Napoleon, not all of France. Besides they had restored the Bourbon monarchy. Troops were instructed to behave in a civil manner to the populace and, in today's parlance, 'win the peace'. Many normal reparations were waived and the plan was generally to get France back on her feet again. Nevertheless, there were frictions between former foes and Napoleon's erstwhile officers, who now faced boredom and unemployment as well as the shame of defeat, harboured a simmering resentment. Not only that but men on all sides, though mostly grateful for the peace, missed the adrenaline rush of war. As a consequence it became common for French officers to challenge British, Austrian and Prussian officers to private duels; known as the 'Waterloo Duels'. British officers had a reputation for a particular tactic in these encounters. As soon as the formalities on the duelling ground were concluded they would run at their opponent full pelt, arm outstretched as if in a cavalry charge. Apparently it was a ruse that met with some success, although I should have thought it a simple matter for any half-decent swordsman to sidestep their rush and hamstring them for good measure.

The 15th Hussars were one of the first regiments ordered back to England in May 1816, where they were needed to police the spate of riots that were breaking out. Henry Lane was promoted to captain in 1818, major in 1824 and lieutenant-colonel (half-pay, unattached) in 1825. In December 1825 he married Harriet Frances, daughter of Lord Dundas. He became a colonel in 1838 and left the Army in 1840 to live in retirement at his home in Wetherby. I imagine the sights and sounds of Waterloo played in his head until the day he died, at the age of 76, in 1871. Moreover I suspect that the inexpensive, poorly-mounted sword he had bought as a green lad of fifteen forever had pride of place in his study.

Regulation military-pattern swords continued to develop throughout the nineteenth century, both in Europe and the United States, producing literally dozens of different designs, though to my mind, there was never an improvement on the Model 1796 Light Cavalry Pattern. Aside from its powerful elegance, it did what a sword should – it assisted the arm to strike. You didn't have to override its inertia; it became an integral part of the skeletal system from the moment you took it up and from that instant it was alive, an animated object that you simply had to steady or guide to unleash its savage potential. Many argue that the 1908 Pattern Cavalry Sword was the ultimate in sword design, with its thumb-dimpled grip and angled tang, setting it in the hand for the perfect thrust. In my view it is little more than a short lance. Give me an M1796 any day.

A curious coda to the M1796 story is that, after the Napoleonic Wars, surplus stocks found great trading value among the tribes of the North American Indians. There is no record of their specific use in battle but there are many drawings and photographs of Indians with these swords and they were probably highly regarded

The Peterloo Massacre (courtesy of Fotosearch)

as regalia. Many were traded at the Bordeaux Trading Post in Nebraska, where Jim Bordeaux supplied weapons to the tribes that wiped out General George Custer at the Battle of the Little Big Horn in 1876. But as we shall see in the next chapter, George Custer earned a celebrity long before that fateful encounter. Famed as the boy general of the Union army in the American Civil War, he won many an engagement with sword in hand. The American Civil War is often described as the first 'modern' war, fought at the outset of the industrial age. With its long-range rifles and artillery, it heralded a new era of fighting a distant foe. Nevertheless there were still occasions where fighting man to man with cold steel was the only option, especially for the cavalry, and the great exponents of cavalry warfare were G.A. Custer and his swash-buckling counterpart in the Confederate army, J.E.B. Stewart.

J.E.B. Stuart (courtesy of Museum of the Confederacy, Richmond, Virginia)

Albumen photograph of Brigadier General George A. Custer taken on or about January 25, 1864 by William Frank Browne (courtesy of John Peter Beckendorf)

Chapter 15

The Swords of J.E.B. Stuart and G.A. Custer: Cavalry Generals in the American Civil War

It is well that war is so terrible – lest we should grow too fond of it

(Robert E. Lee)

As he lay dying after being shot at the Battle of Yellow Tavern on 11 May 1864, General James Ewell Brown Stuart, known affectionately as 'Jeb' or 'Beauty', arguably the most dashing cavalry commander of the Confederate Army, gave instructions for the dispersal of his personal effects. *Harpers Weekly*, 6 August 1864, recorded the event:

> To Mrs. Lee, the wife of General Lee, he directed that his golden spurs be given, as a dying memento of his love and esteem for her husband. To his staff officers he gave his horses. So particular was he in small things, even in the dying hour, that he said to one of his staff, who was a heavy-built man, 'You had better take the larger horse; he will carry you better.' To his young son he left his glorious sword.

That 'glorious' sword was a Model 1860 US Officer's Cavalry Sabre (modern US spelling = *saber*) and was used by Stuart throughout his career with the Confederacy. It passed down through the Stuart generations and is now displayed at the Museum of the Confederacy in Richmond, Virginia, whose current president, J.E.B. Stuart IV, is a direct descendent.

Two other swords once owned by Stuart are today in the National Civil War Museum in Harrisburg, Pennsylvania. One of these is also an M1860 US Cavalry Sabre but the other is a Model 1840 US cavalry sabre. The M1840 was known at the time as 'ol' wristbreaker'.

Ol' Wristbreaker

'Old Wristbreaker' got its name because it was an especially heavy sword, weighing in at a massive 4lbs 8oz and with a scabbard that weighed an additional 2lbs 2oz. This was extremely heavy for a sword and recruits often complained about the effort required to heft it. More seasoned warriors, on the other hand, praised its devastating shearing power. Based on the French M1822 light cavalry sabre, it had a 35-inch single-edged blade and a brass three-bar hilt.

The M1840 cavalry sabre saw widespread service during the Mexican War (1846–1848) and on the western frontier. It also continued to be used by many throughout the American Civil War, even though by then it had been superseded by the lighter M1860. During the early years of the war, Old Wristbreaker remained standard issue to the Union cavalry. Supply problems were one reason for this and the other was that some men simply preferred it. Major General George B. McClellan of the Union army carried one and southern cavalry general Nathan Bedford Forrest sharpened both edges of his. Both the M1840 and M1860 had blades of very high-quality steel.

In 1840, the United States Ordnance Department sent a fact-finding mission to Europe to gather information about various arms manufacturing techniques carried out there. The sword factory at Chatellerault in France, established by the French government in 1819, was of particular interest and a report was sent back of the techniques employed there:

> The blades of swords are formed of steel fagotted. Eighteen layers of steel plates, each 3 inches wide by 0.25, are laid up in one pile, heated in a hollow fire and welded up under the trip hammer. This bar is afterwards cut, and piled one piece on the other and the two are welded and drawn again. This process is sometimes repeated, making three welding heats and 72 layers of steel in a bar of about 1¼ by ¾ inches.

It was a process that produced steel bars of the very highest quality and toughness, which could then be forged by hand with the use of pattern swages and then ground into excellent blades. Blades were tempered by heating to cherry red and then

> run into a heap of moistened iron scales that are collected from about the anvils and which serves to cool the edges, and prevent their cracking when suddenly immersed. The blade is then plunged into cold water, from which it comes very hard and brittle, and sometimes considerably warped. It is then drawn through the blaze of a charcoal fire, until it assumes a blue color, when it is straightened on the anvil by the hammer and again plunged into water, which gives it its proper elastic temper.

According to the report, one man at a trip-hammer could draw out 250 blades per day. By the mid-nineteenth century sword production was being carried out on this scale both in Europe and in the United States. Between 1840 and 1858, an estimated 23,000 M1840 'Old Wristbreaker' US cavalry sabres were manufactured both at home and abroad. One of these belonged to Jeb Stuart.

Stuart on the frontier

J.E.B. Stuart graduated from West Point in October 1854. He was twenty-one years old. On gaining his commission he was sent to fight against Apache and Commanche Indians in Texas. In the three months he was there, he never actually caught sight of a hostile Indian, though he did have his horse stolen from outside his tent one night. By the summer of 1855, he was stationed with the 1st Cavalry at Fort Leavenworth in the Kansas territory, which is where he met his soon-to-be bride. On the pommel of Stuart's M1840 sword is the inscription: 'J.E.B. Stuart U.S.A. from A.S. Brown'. Archibald Stuart Brown was Jeb's cousin and the occasion of the gift was Jeb's wedding to Miss Flora Cooke on 14 November 1855. She was the daughter of Colonel Philip St. George Cooke, commander of the 2nd Dragoons. Jeb and Flora set up home at Fort Leavenworth. Jeb was both a romantic and a great nature lover and it was during their time in Kansas that he kept a scrapbook both of his poetry and of his botanical findings. His military duties were mostly related to protecting settlers against Indian attacks but in 1855 there was another source of tension in Kansas.

'Bleeding Kansas' was a term coined by Horace Greeley of the *New York Tribune* to describe the troubles that beset the territory from 1854–1858. In what was part of

Stuart's M1840 US cavalry sabre, inscribed on the pommel with the words: 'J.E.B. Stuart U.S.A. from A.S.' It was given to him on the occasion of his marriage to Flora Cooke in November 1855 (photo courtesy of The National Civil War Museum, Harrisburg, Pennsylvania)

a long prelude to the Civil War, there were murders, atrocities and small skirmishes. The issue was slavery and whether or not Kansas would join the Union as a 'slave-free' or 'pro-slavery' state. John Brown, the great abolitionist, had been active for some years, initiating outbreaks of violence in a bid to prick the conscience of a nation, and he arrived in Kansas in 1855 to continue his campaigns. The Army's job was to impose order and although Stuart once had occasion to negotiate with Brown over some hostages, he never fought with him.

In July 1857 Lieutenant J.E.B. Stuart took part in an expedition against Cheyenne Indians who had been raiding settlers in the west. It culminated in his first cavalry charge. At Solomon's Fork on the Smokey Hill River, six companies of US cavalry (the paper strength being sixty men per company), under the command of Colonel Edwin Sumner, encountered a massive war party of 300 Cheyenne warriors. Expecting to engage with pistols and carbines, Stuart and his fellows were both surprised and elated when Sumner gave the commands, 'Draw sabres! Charge!' There was a deafening screech as over 300 glinting blades were ripped from their steel scabbards and a great bloodcurdling cry went up as they hurtled towards the enemy. Brandishing M1840 sabres, the one carried by Stuart most probably being the one given to him by his cousin Archibald, the thundering dust cloud of 'long-knives' fell upon the Cheyenne, scattering them in all directions. During the pursuit, Stuart came to the rescue of three of his men held at gunpoint by a Cheyenne brave. Without delay Stuart spurred his horse forward and charged. His sabre bit into the Indian's flesh but, as it did so, a bullet from the Indian's revolver struck him in the chest. Surviving to be carried to a doctor three miles away, he was fortunate not to have been killed on the spot by such a close-range shot. Miraculously he was back in the saddle after just ten days rest and heading for Fort Phil Kearny, some 120 miles away. The Indian brave survived Stuart's sabre stroke but was then cut down by the three men whose lives Stuart had saved.

Towards the end of the year he was transferred further west to Fort Riley, Kansas. It was here that he invented a device for the sword belt, consisting of a stout brass hook that allowed the sabre and scabbard to be removed quickly from the belt and transferred, equally swiftly, to the saddle and vice versa. Cavalry frequently carried their swords on the saddle for long marches but needed them at their side in a hurry if they had to dismount and fight on foot, which was often the case in frontier warfare. Two years later the War Department gave him six months leave to travel to Washington in order to secure a patent and sell his 'hook'. He sold the patent to the government for $5,000 and, in addition, he negotiated to receive $1 royalty for every one sold.

Harper's Ferry

While Stuart was in Washington, news arrived of John Brown's raid on Harper's Ferry, the national armoury. President James Buchanan dispatched Colonel Robert E. Lee, who Stuart had studied under at West Point, to secure the armoury and quell the anticipated rebellion. Lee was later to become a general, in command of the

Confederate army. On 18 October 1859 Stuart volunteered to be his aide and the two men hastened by train to Harper's Ferry, where, arriving around 10 o'clock in the evening, they met with a detachment of marines and the Maryland militia. I have recounted a little of what went on at Harper's Ferry in Chapter 13, in relation to John Brown's capture of the 'Frederick Sword' from a descendent of George Washington who was involved in the incident. What I didn't mention was that it was Lieutenant J.E.B. Stuart who called out the ultimatum for Brown to surrender and gave the order to storm 'John Brown's fort'. Stuart, of course, had already encountered John Brown in Kansas, so when he called out it was a voice that would have been familiar. No matter, Brown did not heed the command. Again it was Stuart who ordered the snatch squad led by Lieutenant Green to storm the 'fort'. Green's bungled efforts with his sword against Brown, also reported in Chapter 13, culminated in Brown's arrest and subsequent trial. Among his last words, spoken as he approached the scaffold, John Brown declared prophetically, 'I, John Brown, am now quite certain that the crimes of this guilty land will never be purged away but with blood'.

Taking sides

The Civil War started in earnest less than two years later on 10 April 1861, when Brigadier General Beauregard ordered the opening salvos of his attack on Fort Sumter. After Abraham Lincoln's election in 1860, the pro-slavery states of the South seceded from the Union. In their eyes it was a conflict not only about the future of slavery but also about the sovereignty of the Federal Union. Fort Sumter at Charleston, South Carolina, was a Union stronghold in the heart of Confederate territory. It fell without casualties, save for two Union artillerymen who died as a result of a cannon exploding during the evacuation salute. Nonetheless the American Civil War had begun and men had to decide on which side they would fight. For many the decision was not about their personal beliefs with regard to slavery but based on their loyalty to their home state, their neighbours and their kin. The commander-in-chief of the Confederate army, General Robert E. Lee, said when the war was over,

> So far from engaging in a war to perpetuate slavery, I am rejoiced that slavery is abolished. I believe it will be greatly for the interest of the South. So fully am I satisfied of this that I would have cheerfully lost all that I have lost by the war, and have suffered all that I have suffered to have this object attained.

There were others though who held white-supremacist views about slavery. The point is that not all Confederate sympathizers were pro-slavery supporters; many simply believed in the sovereignty of their state. The Union was still very young and a fragile concept. Stuart's views on slavery are not clear, though when they were in Kansas he and Flora did refuse the gift of a slave offered by her mother. His outpourings prior to the Civil War were concerned with his loyalty to his home state of Virginia, rather than about the slavery issue.

The politics of secession were extremely complex and far beyond the scope of this present work. Moreover the motivations of individuals, in opting to join one side or the other, were rarely the result of a cerebral examination of the issues. Most often, a man's allegiance was determined by geography, not politics. Certainly when you look at photographs of the time and see the callow and innocent faces of the thousands of mere boys who joined up on both sides, it is hard to imagine they gave the matter any considered thought at all.

J.E.B. Stuart, however, already a serving officer in the Union army, had to make an altogether more deliberate decision. In January 1861 he wrote concerning the possibility that Virginia may secede, 'For my part I have no hesitancy from the first that right or wrong, alone or otherwise, I go with Virginia'. Robert E. Lee, who had taught Stuart at West Point, declared in the following month:

> My loyalty to Virginia ought to take precedence over that which is due the federal government. If Virginia stands by the old Union, so will I. But if she secedes then I will still follow my native state with my sword, and if need be with my life.

These were hard choices for men who had sworn an oath of loyalty to the Union. Virginia did secede and Stuart resigned his commission in early May. His decision, 'from a sense of duty to my native Virginia', was to fight for the Confederacy. It was a choice that would not only lead to fighting against former comrades but also against kin. A hand-tinted photograph of his wife, Flora, now in the Museum of the Confederacy, shows a prim, neat little woman in a plaid dress with lace collar. Her eyes are full of anguish, revealing the pain of divided loyalties. Her father, General Philip St. George Cooke, and her brother, John, were in the Union army. In a letter to his wife, Stuart writes,

> I am extremely anxious about Pa and John R. Cooke. I do hope they resign at once. How can they serve Lincoln's diabolical government? . . . Principal, interest and affection demand his immediate resignation and return to his native state.

John Cooke did resign and rose to the rank of Brigadier General in the Confederate army but General Cooke remained loyal to the Union, stating, 'I owe Virginia little, my country much'. His son-in-law was unequivocal in his condemnation of what he saw as a betrayal of Virgina, proclaiming that Cooke would, 'regret it but once, and that will be continually'. So embittered were Stuart's feelings towards his father-in-law that he cajoled Flora into changing the name of their one-year-old son. He had been christened Phillip St. George Cooke Stuart, in honour of his grandfather, but

Sword of Brigadier General Philip St George Cooke (photo courtesy of The Museum of the Confederacy, Richmond, Virginia; photography by Alan Thompson)

Flora acquiesced to her husband's rage and the boy's name was changed to James Ewell Brown Stuart junior; he was known as Jimmy. Such is the particular tragedy of civil war.

General Philip St. George Cooke's M1860 Field Officer's Sword, now on display at the Museum of the Confederacy, has a slender, flattened-diamond-section blade and a brass hilt with magnificent relief casting. The guard has a hinged side-plate, allowing it to sit neatly against the hip.' It is a pretty thing but swords like this were worn as designations of rank rather than as fighting weapons. During his early career, General Cooke had been a cavalryman and an advocate of the sabre. During the Crimean War (1853–1856) he was sent by the US War Department to observe European cavalry in action. Following this survey, he drew up a manual of cavalry tactics for the US army, which was first published in 1860. A revised second edition, approved by President Lincoln, came out in 1862.

Sword drills

Cooke's manual, *Regulations for the Instruction, Formations and Movements of the Cavalry*, is a comprehensive work dealing with the basic training of both riders and horses, as well as giving drills and a large repertoire of commands for a range of formations and intricate manoeuvres. It also deals with the use of arms. For the sabre, which he spelled in its old European form, he advocated two basic guard positions, quarte on the left and tierce on the right, with the addition of a sloping parry for the head. In order to 'render the joints of the arm and wrist supple', he recommended that troopers be exercised with the 'moulinet' – a circular cut, prepared with a wrist-twirling flourish. A continuous and fluid succession of moulinets in a figure-of-eight pattern built strength and dexterity. Cooke warned that the motions of the blade 'shall not fall too near the body, for fear of wounding the horse' and that men shouldn't employ too much force, 'which not only is less necessary than skill and suppleness, but which is even prejudicial'.

Of particular concern was that the rider didn't lean too much into the cut. Cooke counseled that great attention be paid to 'maintaining the proper position and balance of the body; as by too great an exertion in delivering a cut or point a horseman may be thrown'. Similarly, he stated that the trooper 'should have confidence in his parries, and not trust to his avoiding the attack of his opponent by turning or drawing back the body'. It would seem that General Cooke had a fairly low estimation of the average trooper's riding skills and likely that his son-in-law Jeb would have scoffed at such timid caution.

When the manual was first prepared, conflict with Native American tribes was more anticipated than war with other states and in this context he discusses the best tactics against both the lancer and the mounted archer. He agrees with earlier writers, such as Cruso, who advised that the safest position against a mounted swordsman was to be on his left rear flank. However Cooke points out that the right rear is the best position to occupy against an opponent armed with either a lance or bow and arrow. It is extremely awkward for a horseman to use these weapons on this angle.

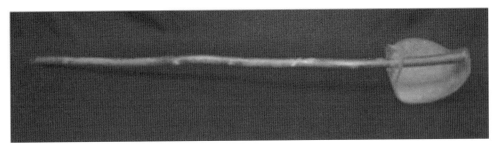

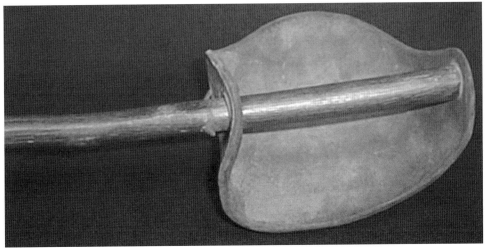

US army singlestick (36½ inches, c 1860 (photo courtesy of Steve Heller, Civil War Antique Shop)

Although he prescribed several cutting exercises, Cooke favoured thrusts, which he said, 'should always be used in preference, as they require less force, and their result is more prompt, sure, and decisive'. He argued that, 'cuts very often fail from the sabre turning enough to make the blow one with the flat; at best the wound is generally trifling compared to those made by thrusts'.

Cooke's cavalry manual reflected the tactics adhered to by Union and Confederate armies alike. At the outset of the Civil War there were five cavalry regiments in the US Army, commanded by a total of 176 officers. 104 of these officers joined the Confederate cause, giving the Confederate cavalry initial battlefield dominance.

Stuart's M1860 US Cavalry Sabres

While 'Old Wristbreaker' remained in general use, a new, much-lighter model sword had become available for the cavalryman. It was the M1860 US Cavalry Sabre. Although similar in appearance, the M1860 was more than a pound lighter than the M1840, weighing just 3lb 7oz and with a scabbard of 1lb 4oz. Stuart immediately took to the new model. He nevertheless retained a sentimental attachment to the wedding gift from his cousin and he can be seen wearing it in a photograph from the winter of 1863–64. However it was the M1860 that he carried into battle. He had two. One

is in the National Civil War Museum in Harrisburg and the other in the Museum of the Confederacy, in Richmond. Scratched onto the pommel of the Harrisburg sword are some cavalry guidons (pennons). I wonder if these guidons represent captured enemy flags, though there is no actual evidence to suggest they do. It is likely that this was Stuart's sword but its only provenance is that it was found in the same Florida attic as, and bundled together with, the A.S. Brown wedding gift sword. Supposedly, a relative of Stuart's once lived in the house. It is a plain-hilted trooper's version, whereas the one in the Museum of the Confederacy not only has a stronger provenance, coming directly from the family, but it is also the slightly grander officer's type. This is the sword that I most associate with Stuart's civil war exploits but there is no reason to doubt that the plainer version also saw a share of the action.

Setting off, with unintentional irony, from the grandly magnificent Union station in Washington DC, I took the train to Richmond to view Stuart's M1860 sword there. As I passed through mile after mile of woodland and through the heart of Civil War country, I was prompted to think what perfect terrain this was for the use of cavalry in war. The woods are dense insofar as there is limited depth of vision – ideal for covert reconnaissance – and yet the straight and narrow trunks of, mainly, birch are sufficiently spaced to allow a bold cavalryman to jink his horse through the timber at full pelt.

The Museum of The Confederacy is a concrete building situated alongside Jefferson Davis' White House, which is actually painted a light green. This seems from the outside to be a modestly-sized, though very elegant, Georgian town house. Inside, the 'Davis White House' seems much larger and its chintzy rooms, evoking the tastes of the times, have an incongruously homely air. Here was the beating pulse of Johnny Reb's heartbeat. Next door, in the museum, are all manner of artifacts that once belonged to the men who fought in that war. There is Jeb Stuart's famous hat, buff-coloured, with its brim turned up on the right-hand side and cockaded with a peacock feather that winds around the dome, from just left of centre, to spill over the brim behind his

Stuart's M1860 US cavalry sabre, standard version (photo courtesy of The National Civil War Museum, Harrisburg, Pennsylvania)

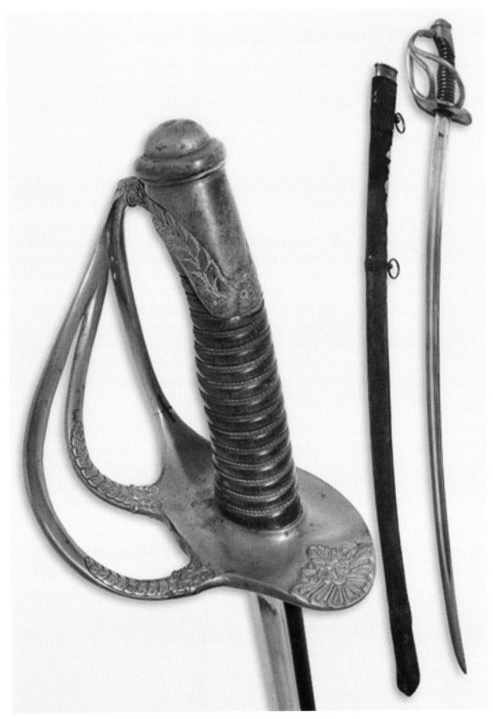

Stuart's M1860 officer's cavalry sabre (photo courtesy of The Museum of the Confederacy, Richmond, Virginia; photography by Alan Thompson)

right ear. His yellow deerskin gauntlets with their broad cuffs and his swashbuckling, black leather thigh boots are yet more clues to the sartorial flair of this warrior dandy who sported a red-lined cape and a red rose in his lapel, ensembled with his gold spurs and yellow sash. It was the outward display of a charismatic and dashing leader, who went into the stench of battle perfumed with cologne and frequently accompanied by his mounted banjo player, Sam Sweeney, strumming out cheerful songs to the counterpoint of the enemy's guns. Alongside his items of clothing are his Calisher and Terry carbine and his LeMat revolver. There is also his saddle and there is his M1860 officer's pattern sabre.

Stuart's sabre was manufactured by the highly fashionable firm of F.P. Devisme of Paris, France, makers of prestige swords and firearms. In business between 1815 and 1867, Devisme had a reputation for work of the highest quality, supplying weapons to European royalty as well as to luminaries in the Confederate cause; Robert E. Lee owned a Devisme sword and Jefferson Davis had one of their rifles. The excellence of their manufacture was acknowledged with gold medals at both the 1851 London Exhibition and the 1867 Paris Exhibition. The sword they made for J.E.B. Stuart accorded with the standard pattern for an M1860 US Officer's Cavalry Sabre and is conspicuously long, 41 inches overall with the blade measuring 35 inches. Leaning out at a great angle from the secure, deep seat of a McClellan saddle, it would have an extreme reach. It is a characteristic of French and French-influenced cavalry sabres that they are very long and these extra inches had a gruesome purpose; they enabled the cavalryman to strike at men lying prone on the ground. These might be wounded men or they might be those shamming death.

The three-bar hilt is sturdily cast in brass, with just a discreet hint of officer-status decoration, having raised foliage patterns on the inside of the bars, the guard-plate and the pommel. Its grip, ridged and bound in brown leather, is set at an obtuse angle, allowing the point of its curved blade to be presented for a thrust from a straight arm.

There is a great deal of scratching and abrasion on the blade, owing not to over-zealous cleaning but rather to the action of repeatedly drawing it from its scabbard. The scabbard is fitted with a spring clip just inside the throat to prevent it from falling out when riding hard. It was an ingenious, and generally satisfactory, solution to an old problem, although it was not infallible. Lieutenant Theodore S. Garnett, Stuart's aide de camp, recalls in his memoirs an occasion where he was riding furiously to try and make his escape from a woodland fire:

> I came to a steep rocky mound, some twenty feet high, and determined to scale it, if possible, and from its top take a view of the surrounding country. In my effort to ride up its steep sides, my sabre was jerked entirely out of its scabbard and left hanging on a bush behind me. I had to dismount to retrieve it.

Garnett was in no doubt as to the importance of the sabre on the civil war battlefield, despite all the military advancements of the industrial age. He wrote: 'for fields on which thousands of cavalry strive for mastery in the shock of great battle, may the sabers of Stuart, of Forrest and of Hampton ever lead the charging squadrons to victory or death'. Of these there is little doubt that Stuart was the epitome of an old school 'beau sabreur' and the most glamourous leader of them all.

Stuart in the Civil War

At Chancellorsville, 1–5 May 1863, J.E.B. Stuart took command of Stonewall Jackson's brigade, after the dying general, shot by friendly fire, had cried out 'send for Stuart'. Although an admirer of Stuart, Jackson was not an aficionado of the sword. He said that the only use for a sabre was roasting meat and his own, retained solely as a badge of rank, remained firmly sheathed until Cedar Mountain in August 1862. Hard-pressed he sought to rally his men by riding into the thick of the fray and drawing his sword but it had rusted into its scabbard! Undeterred, he brandished it anyway, scabbard and all, and turned the tide in the Confederacy's favour.

Stuart's sword, however, was ever quick to flash. Chancellorsville was perhaps the greatest victory of the war for the Confederate army and Stuart played a significant role after taking Jackson's command on the third day of the fighting. He launched audacious frontal assaults on the enemy line, demonstrating his tactical grasp of the use of artillery and infantry as well as his own beloved cavalry. These had the effect of pushing the enemy back and in spite of being outnumbered by more than two to one, the Confederate forces were able to win a resounding victory; one that many thought heralded their ultimate victory in the war. Jeb Stuart was certainly the hero of the hour.

He also led major cavalry engagements at the battles of The Seven Days, 2nd Bull Run, Antietam, Fredericksburg, Gettysburg, the Wilderness and, fatally, Yellow Tavern. Famed also as a bold and cunning raider, Stuart delighted in wreaking havoc behind enemy lines, sabotaging communications and looting supply wagons and depots. Twice he led his command around McClellan's army, causing damaging disruption, once in the Peninsula Campaign and once after the Battle of Antietam, where he inflicted some 230 casualties while losing only 27 of his own men. During the 2nd Manassas Campaign, he lost his famed plumed hat and cloak to pursuing Union troopers. In a later raid, Stuart managed to overrun Union army commander General John Pope's headquarters and capture his full uniform and orders, providing Lee with much valuable intelligence and himself with reparations for his captured attire.

George Armstrong Custer

If J.E.B. Stuart was a peacock, then his nemesis, George Armstrong Custer, was a bird-of-paradise. At West Point he had been nicknamed 'Fanny' because of his slightly effeminate looks. Even more self-consciously aware of his appearance than 'Old Beauty', 'Fanny' slept with his legendary golden locks entwined around candles to give them their famous curl and scented his hair with cinnamon oil. Nothing about his dress was regulation. He wore broad brimmed hats at rakish angles – that is when they weren't swept from his head by the wind of a charge, leaving his tresses alone to signal his heroic panache. His jackets were of black velveteen, bedecked with gold adornment of his own design. After he became a general, he sported a sailor collar, worn outside his coat, with gold stars on its lapel points. Most characteristically, as if he weren't already identifiable enough, he always wore an extravagant red cravat. Before long his loyal troops of the Michigan cavalry, the 'Wolverines', also took to wearing red cravats. Later in the war, when he became commander of the 3rd Cavalry Division, the entire division adopted this sartorial tribute, becoming known as the 'Red Tie Boys'. Men were proud to be under Custer's command and he inspired their devotion and loyalty. Whether he was on patrol with a small squadron or leading an entire brigade in battle, George Armstrong Custer always led by example and he always led from the front. Captain S. Ballard of the 6th Michigan Cavalry wrote, 'when Custer made a charge he was always the first sabre that struck, for he was always ahead'.

As a cadet at West Point he had proved himself a first-class horseman and held the record for jumping the highest hurdle, whilst at the same time cutting at a dummy with his sabre. His academic record was less distinguished and Custer was constantly on the verge of being dismissed on account of his bad behaviour. He led late-night sorties to Benny Haven's Tavern at Buttermilk Falls, an out-of-bounds drinking hole, and, as a fun-loving prankster, was extremely popular with his fellow cadets. Tragically, a majority of his closest associates were from the South. Indeed his best

General Custer saluting his former best friend from West Point, the Confederate General Tom Rosser, before fighting him at the Battle of Tom's Brook, 9 October 1864, sketched by Alfred R. Waud dated the same day (Library of Congress)

friend, Tom Rosser, became a Confederate general who Custer later faced on the battlefield at Tom's Brook and Trevilian Station. His minor misdemeanours, such as gazing about the ranks, talking and laughing in class and throwing bread in the mess hall, were indicators of a lively mind in need of proper stimulation and of a restless spirit in need of adventure. His many demerits for being unshaven and having long hair were indicators of the individual approach he took to his appearance. He later wrote of his time at West Point, 'My offences against law and order were not great in enormity, but what they lacked in magnitude they made up in number'. In spite of his constant brushes with authority, Custer did graduate, bottom of his class, in June 1861. He was commissioned as a second lieutenant.

Whilst on leave towards the end of the following year, he met the love of his life, Elizabeth 'Libby' Bacon, in his hometown of Monroe, Michigan. He proposed to her there after attending a masquerade that had been held in his honour; he had gone as Louis XVI and she as a gypsy girl, complete with tambourine. However, her father was an eminent judge and hostile to the idea of his only daughter marrying a social inferior such as Custer. Only after he had been promoted to the rank of Brigadier General on 29 June 1863 (at the age of 24!) was Custer able to gain Judge Bacon's approval. The wedding took place on 9 February 1864. They were a devoted couple and some years after the Civil War, General Custer was court-martialed and suspended from duty for a year because he had absconded from his post on the western frontier to go home and visit his wife.

General George Armstrong Custer was known as 'Autie', short for Armstrong, to his wife, close friends and family, as the 'Boy General' to the press and public and 'Old Curley' to his men of the Michigan Cavalry Brigade. They idolized him. Private Victor E. Comte, a Frenchman in Company C of the 5th Michigan Cavalry, rode at Custer's side at Falling Waters in July 1863. He wrote afterwards to his wife, telling her that Custer, 'commanded in person and I saw him plunge his saber into the belly of a rebel who was trying to kill him. You can guess how bravely soldiers fight for such a general'. In spite of the horrors they witnessed, Custer's Michigan boys held romantic notions of glory and nothing quickened their pulses to greater heights of exhilaration than the command 'Draw sabres!'

Custer's missing swords

Shortly after graduating from West Point, Second Lieutenant Custer visited the New York emporium of Horstmann Bros and Allien in order to equip himself with a uniform, Colt revolver, sabre and sundry other accoutrements. From there he went by train to Washington to receive his orders. Horstmann were one of the larger suppliers of swords to the Union army during the Civil War, selling more than 25,000 to the government in addition to private sales to officers. Their founder, a German immigrant named William H. Horstmann, first set up a military goods business in Philadelphia in the 1820's. Initially swords were imported from Germany but, as the business prospered, Horstmann supplemented these imports by contracting American manufacturers, such as The Ames Sword Company, to supply them with blades. Local foundries produced the brass hilts and Horstmann then assembled the swords at their Philadelphia works. There were several corporate name changes as the Horstmann generations styled themselves either as Horstmann & Sons or Horstmann Bros. At the time of Custer's patronage, the Philadelphia branch of the business was Horstmann Bros. & Co. It was only the New York outlet that was in partnership with Henry V. Allien and this business dealt exclusively with imports. What Custer paid for his sword is not known but it is likely that he was being economically prudent in purchasing from the New York store. Government contracts at the same period show that cavalry sabres from Horstmann Bros. & Co in Philadelphia were priced at $6.87½, whereas those from Horstmann Bros. and Allien in New York were only $6.75.

No record exists of what type of sword Custer purchased but by far the most plentiful of Horstmann's stock at this date was the M1840 Cavalry Sabre (Old Wristbreaker) and it is likely that this is the sword that Custer bought. There is no longer any trace of the sword itself but it was first drawn in battle on 21 July 1861. The first pitched battle of the war took place at Manassas Junction, some 30 miles from Washington DC. This battle is known in the north as 'First Bull Run' and in the south as 'First Manassas'. Second Lieutenant George Armstrong Custer was there. Arrayed on the crest of a hill, his company tried to steady their nerves as they awaited the expected order to charge. Outranking Custer by a matter of days was Second Lieutenant Leicester Walker. However, Lieutenant Walker had been commissioned as a civilian volunteer and knew nothing of military thinking. Trying not to lose face, he casually asked the West Point-trained Custer what weapon he was going to choose for the eagerly anticipated charge. Custer drew his sabre; Walker followed suite. However, having thus acted with impetuous flourish, Custer pondered the question and, sheathing his sword, drew his revolver. Walker did the same. It is quite possible that Custer was simply being mischievous and showing the men who was really in charge but the incident highlights an important debate. A revolver had the potential to cause a rapid succession of serious wounds and with less physical exertion than did a sword. Nevertheless it could only really be used effectively from horseback at very close range. Before it could be useful against other cavalry, both sides would be intermingled in a mêlée. In such circumstances the risks of casualties from friendly fire were considerable. Moreover, once the chamber was emptied there was a moment of vulnerability before the sabre could be drawn. Custer holstered his revolver and drew his sabre again. He doubtless chuckled to himself as Lieutenant Walker was once again obliged to follow his action. That particular charge never happened and the Union forces were routed. Custer's company nonetheless won their share of the glory by acting as the rearguard to the Union retreat. They were one of the last units to leave the field.

Another sword that Custer is believed to have possessed was one he captured whilst on a reconnaissance mission behind southern lines in August 1862. It was loaned to the Smithsonian Institution by Libby Custer in 1912 but returned to the executors of her estate in 1943. I have not been able to establish its current whereabouts. A museum bulletin in 1932 described the sword as a Spanish sabre, having an exceptionally long 38-inch double-edged Toledo blade with three narrow fullers on each side. It was broad, the blade being 1½ inches wide, and said to be extremely heavy with a brass three-bar hilt. The blade bore the inscription '*No mi saques sin raizon; No mi enbaines sin honor*' – 'Do not draw me without reason, do not sheathe me without honour'. Tradition has it that Custer favoured this sword for much of the rest of the war, though there are other swords with equal claim.

His fondness for heavy blades was also catered for with another captured treasure, one that he took from one of Major General Wade Hampton's officers at the Battle of Trevilian Station in June 1864. Hampton had purchased a number of especially large swords for himself and his officers. They were produced by Kraft, Goldsmith and Kraft of Columbia, South Carolina, and fitted with broad double-edged blades. These also were a massive 38 inches in length and had been manufactured by Schimmelbusch and Joest of Solingen, Germany, during the first half of the nineteenth century. Custer's delight at seizing such a splendid trophy was somewhat dampened by the fact that his own personal baggage was snatched by Confederate raiders during the same engagement. Among the many effects seized was Custer's boxed Tiffany sword.

Custer's Tiffany sword

A plaque on the scabbard of this fine presentation sword reads: 'Presented to Gen'l G.A. Custer by Commissioned Officers of the Staff, June 29, 1863', the date he was made a Brigadier General. Above it, in raised letters, is the legend Tiffany & Co. Then, as today, Tiffany had a certain style appeal and it well suited Custer's cavalier ostentation. Based on a standard M1860 cavalry sabre, the gilded hilt was cast in silver. Its surface features decorative foliage and the pommel is in the form of an American eagle with outstretched wings. It has a standard blade with etched designs and the words 'Tiffany and Co., New York' on one side and the designation 'U.S.' on the other. The silver-plated scabbard is even more ornate with highly ornamental gilt ring mounts and drag. Below the brand name on the scabbard is a raised letter 'M'. This stood for Edward C. Moore, who was the manager of silver products and design director at Tiffany & Co at the time. As well as the sword and scabbard he would also have designed the elegant rosewood box, lined with dark green velvet. On its lid the box carried a silver medallion engraved with Custer's name.

The sword, in its box, was taken from Custer's wagon train during the punishing six-hour fight at Trevilian Station by Lieutenant Frank Blair, along with Custer's dress uniform, boots, document case, field desk, haversack and a lock of hair intended for his wife. Eliza Brown, Custer's African-American personal cook, was also captured. Eliza was a former slave who had run away to join the Union army. As she later told Libby Custer, 'everybody was a standin' up for liberty, and I wasent goin' to stay home when everybody else was a goin' … I didn't set down to wait to have 'em all free me. I helped to free myself.' Lieutenant Blair sent his prizes, excluding Eliza, home to Texas for safekeeping. Eliza Brown subsequently escaped. Blair sold his 'Custer collection' in 1897, since when it has passed, intact, through the hands of four

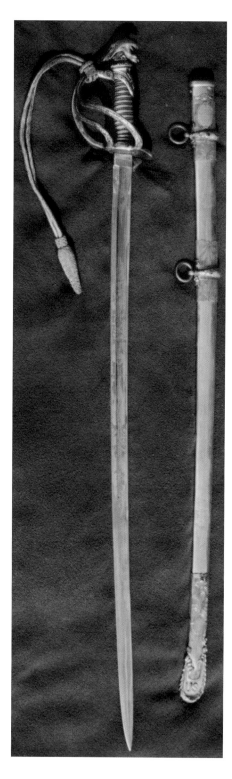

private collectors until purchased in 2000 by Sam Kennedy of Cisco Antiques, Couer D'Alene, Idaho. At the time of writing it remains in Mr. Kennedy's care.

Charles Lewis Tiffany began his jewelry and silverware business in 1837 with premises at 550 Broadway, New York. The business diversified and by the time of the Civil War they were selling firearms, uniforms, luggage and flags, as well as luxury goods and swords. As silversmiths, Tiffany & Co. produced numerous high-quality presentation swords but they also won contracts for regular supplies. In 1861 they contracted with the Federal Government to supply 1,516 non-commissioned officers' swords, 59 foot-artillery swords and 7,526 cavalry sabres. By 1863 they had sold over 19,000 swords to the Ordnance Department.

Like Horstmann, Tiffany & Co were assemblers and retailers, importing both finished swords and parts for assembly. A high proportion of their blades came from Solingen in Germany but they also purchased from English manufacturers. Profiting from both sides during the war was Robert Mole and Son of 171–172 Broad Street, Islington, London. They sold M1853 cavalry sabres, with brass hilts, to the Confederacy, and iron-hilted M1821 cavalry sabres to Tiffanys, who sold on around 6,000 of these to the US government.

The colossal demand for swords during the American Civil War could only be met by contracting from multiple suppliers. By far the biggest supplier in the north was The Ames Sword Company , established in 1791 by Nathan P. Ames who set up shop in Chelmsford, Massachusetts. His sons

Custer's presentation sword by Tiffany &Co (courtesy of Sam Kennedy of Cisco's, Coeur D'Alene, Idaho)

Custer's Tiffany sword in presentation box (courtesy of Sam Kennedy)

expanded the business, moving production to Chicopee, Massachusetts in 1829. During the Civil War, Ames supplied more than 100,000 swords to the Union army. Another major supplier, producing over 48,000 swords, was also based in Chelmsford, Massachusetts; this was The Christopher Roby Company and George Armstrong Custer owned one of their M1860 cavalry sabres.

Inscription on the scabbard of Custer's Tiffany sword (courtesy of Sam Kennedy)

Pommel of the Tiffany sword in the form of an American Eagle (courtesy of Sam Kennedy)

Custer's M1860 Cavalry Sabre

This sword, now in private hands, was a plain enlisted man's version of this classic model, of which J.E.B. Stuart had the officer's type. I own one identical to that owned by Custer. It is a magnificent sword, big and powerful with a long reach and yet well balanced and extremely manageable. It was markedly different from 'Old Wristbreaker'.

Before the Civil War, Christopher Roby and Company produced agricultural blades, such as scythes, and hunting knives. At the outset of the war they geared up for sword production, specializing, almost exclusively, in the M1860 Cavalry Sabre. They produced officer-pattern swords for private sale but the one Custer owned was purchased by the government. Both Custer's sword and the one in my collection carry a 'U.S. 1864' acquisition date stamp on the blade and below this are the initials 'A.G.M.', for the government quality inspector Alfred G. Manning. That it was an enlisted man's sword is intriguing. Custer, after all, was known for extravagant outward display and might have been expected to have the most elaborate model available. However, he was also a leader who took pains to share the same conditions and dangers as those of his men. If a consignment of government-purchased swords arrived for his beloved Michiganders, it is in keeping with his character to have taken one for himself, saying something along the lines of 'I'll fight with the same as you boys.'

Roby swords, even those for enlisted men, were of the highest quality and had certain unique Roby features. They had a slightly slimmer grip that had a flat-sided profile with shallower grooves. Combined with the standard centre swell of an M1860 grip, this made for a secure and ergonomic grasp in a gloved hand. Small details, such as the wire on the grip taking a few extra turns so that it terminated under the pommel cap – instead of at the top of the exposed portion of the grip where it could unravel – made the difference between a Roby sword and inferior models. Roby blades were also superior to most and only equalled by those of The Ames Sword Company.

This is Custer's actual M1860 enlisted man's sabre. This is the only available photograph of this sword, which is now in a private collection (Photo courtesy of James D. Julia Auctions, Fairfield, Maine)

The American Civil War ended on 9 April 1865 and so Custer's Roby sword, dated 1864, can only have been pressed into service during the final year. For Custer it was a year of glorious victories, culminating in his distinguished contribution to the Appomattox campaign with triumphal successes at Waynesboro, Dinwiddie Court House and Five Forks. General Custer received the first flag of surrender from the Confederate army and he was present at the signing of the surrender at Appomattox Court House on 12 April 1865. In acknowledgement of his contribution and gallantry, he was given the table on which the surrender document was signed. It seems likely that he wore his Roby sword that day.

US 1864 on Custer's sword is the date stamp of acquisition by the Union army. A.G.M. are the initials of the sword quality inspector Alfred G. Manning

It is also possible that he carried his Roby sabre to the fight at Yellow Tavern on 11 May 1864. The tide of the war had turned and the Union army had launched a major offensive south into Virginia. As they approached Richmond, Jeb Stuart was sent to intercept them and prevent an attack on the Confederate capital. Yellow

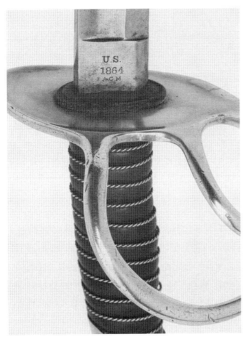

Markings on the blade of a regulation pattern M1860 enlisted man's cavalry sabre in the author's collection. This sword is identical in every respect to the one owned by Custer. On one side it has the same 1864 acquisition stamp and inspector's initials. On the other is the maker's stamp: Christopher Roby of West Chelmsford, Massachusetts (photography by Marty Kelly)

Tavern was just six miles north of Richmond and Stuart arrayed his troops there in a bid to halt the Yankee advance. Custer and his Michigan Brigade played a significant role throughout the day and, around 4 o'clock, launched a heroic sabre charge against the enemy gun emplacements, located behind a screen of trees on the ridge of a hill.

One eyewitness, Lieutenant Asa B. Isham, reported that the 1st Michigan Cavalry had just returned from furlough and that its ranks were freshly recruited to 1,000 men. He added:

> In squadron front it covered over two hundred and fifty feet by one hundred and twenty in depth and it formed a weight of six hundred tons that was about to be hurled across the fields and ravines upon that battery and its supports. It was a magnificent engine of warfare.

An officer on General Wesley Merritt's staff also witnessed the scene as General Custer led his men in the gallant charge, he later wrote:

> His headquarters flag ... was flying in advance of the moving mass of glittering blades. The shrill blast of one hundred bugles and the familiar air of Yankee Doodle rang out upon the battlefield while ... brave men of the Michigan brigade rode boot to boot into what seemed the very jaws of death.

Miraculously the 1st Michigan got among the guns with minimal casualties and set about the crews with their long sabres.

General J.E.B. Stuart rallied to the threat on his line and rushed to its defence. In the confusion that followed he was shot in the stomach by one of Custer's men. More than one claimed the shot. Stuart was taken from the field and hurried to Richmond in an ambulance. He refused the offer of whisky to dull the pain, recalling a vow of abstinence that he had made to his mother at the age of twelve. James Ewell Brown Stuart died the following day. On hearing of his death, Lee declared 'I can hardly think of him without weeping'.

As for Custer, he still had many more battles to fight before the war was over but at Yellow Tavern his long-running rivalry with Jeb Stuart had finally come to an end. It had been a clash of two men cast from the same mould. Both were brave beyond the ordinary run of men, both were flamboyant dressers, almost to the point of foppishness, and both were charismatic leaders of men. What is more, in an age of trains for troop transport, carbines, revolvers and rifled cannon, in an age of industrial warfare, both men believed in the supremacy of the horse and in the superiority of the sword. J.E.B. Stuart and G.A. Custer were first and foremost cavalrymen who led daring and dashing cavalry charges and they led them sword in hand. Eleven months earlier, those swords were drawn to telling effect in the largest cavalry engagement ever fought on American soil.

Brandy Station, 9 June 1863

General J.E.B. Stuart commanded the Southern horse and among the Union officers against him was Captain G.A. Custer. It wasn't the first time they had ridden on the same battlefield but Brandy Station was a significant turning point in their respective fortunes.

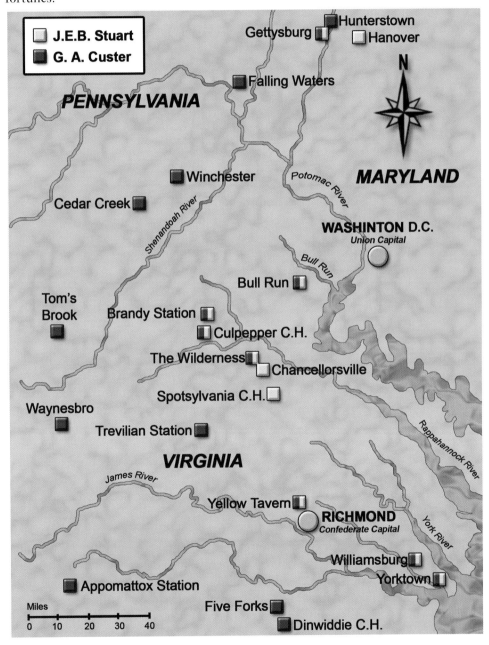

Selected Civil War battles of Generals Stuart and Custer

Following their victory at Chancellorsville in May, the Confederate army mustered in Culpeper County, Virginia, preparing to launch a major offensive north into Pennsylvania. Stuart's cavalry divisions were camped around Brandy Station. Several days before the battle Stuart led a review of his troops. Special trains were laid on to ferry in spectators from nearby Richmond and Charlottesville. It was a gala occasion and the townsfolk and ladies flocked to see the South's debonair hero at the head of his army. He paraded 9,000 mounted troopers and 4 batteries of horse artillery. Guns were fired, bugles were sounded and cavalry, sabres drawn, charged back and forth to the delight of the adoring crowds. The band played, striking up Jeb Stuart's favourite song·

> If you want to have a good time, jine the cavalry
> Jine the cavalry! Jine the cavalry!
> If you want to catch the Devil, if you want to have fun,
> If you want to smell Hell, jine the cavalry!

Critics complained that Stuart was simply feeding his ego and exhausting the horses. After the parade there was a grand ball held outside and illuminated by lanterns and bonfires. At this stage in the war, the Confederate army had reason to believe that they might prevail. Stuart mustered all his troops for review yet again on the day before the battle. This time General Lee attended and all was much as before, except that the powder was saved for what was to come. Lee wrote to his wife that 'It was a splendid sight'.

Camped on the opposite bank of the Rappahannock River was a cavalry strike force of 11,000 men under the command of Major General Alfred Pleasonton, who had been sent to disperse and destroy the Confederate forces. Captain Custer was his aide-de-camp. There were two places, about 7 miles apart, where the Rappahannock could be easily crossed, Kelly's Ford and Beverly Ford. Pleasonton had planned a dawn raid for 4am, using both crossings, which meant that preparations in the Union camp were underway at 2am. Custer was sent, as an observer, to accompany 8th New York Cavalry under the command of Colonel Benjamin Davis. With his usual enthusiasm, Custer rode at the head of the column as they splashed across Beverly Ford to ransack the enemy encampment.

The scene was one of utter chaos as men, startled from their sleep, scrambled from their tents to find their boots, only to be cut down by a swinging sabre or trampled by galloping hooves. The fight was not all one way. Revolvers and carbines cracked, the flames from their muzzles blazing bright in the dim early-morning light. Panic set in along the Confederate horse lines as men hastened to mount their tethered steeds. Here the Union troopers could wreak terrible havoc, slashing the rope lines and causing the terrified steeds to bolt. Piercing whinnies mixed with the screams of wounded men, bugle calls and the frantic shouts of officers trying to command their scattered men. From his vantage point on Fleetwood Hill, overlooking the scene, General Stuart heard the furore and acted quickly to dispatch reinforcements both to the camp at Beverly Ford and to Kelly's Ford, where he correctly guessed the Federals would also be coming from. Meanwhile Davis and Custer led their men, whooping and hollering, into the woods, where they chased and sabred fleeing Confederates until they came to a clearing by St James Church. At the other end of this long stretch of clear ground was a Confederate artillery battery.

Davis ordered the charge. As they drew near the guns, a flanking countercharge of 150 horse burst from the woods under the command of Major Cabell E. Flourney. Many of the Union cavalry were turned, though Colonel Davis resolutely galloped forward. He was shot in the forehead. Although there are no official reports to corroborate it, some accounts say that Captain Custer assumed command not only of the 8th New York but also of two other regiments who had collected at the tree line. Time and again, he led brave charges against the enemy, having two horses shot from under him. In his despatches, General Pleasonton praised his aide for 'gallantry throughout the fight'. The Custer legend had begun to take root. Stuart, on the other hand, was furious that he had been caught napping. Hitherto, he had always held the upper hand in cavalry warfare. His men were known as 'The Invincibles' – that was now in question.

Although the battle at Brandy Station was inconclusive, most commentators were agreed about one thing, perhaps best expressed in the words of Stuart's adjutant, Major Henry B. McClellan:

> It made the Federal cavalry. Up to that time confessedly inferior to the Southern horsemen, they gained on this day that confidence in themselves and in their commanders which enabled them to contest so fiercely the subsequent battle-fields.

And the most significant of those subsequent battlefields was Gettysburg.

Gettysburg, 1–3 July 1863
Following Brandy Station, Custer was promoted to Brigadier General and given his own command – the Michigan Cavalry Brigade. Within a week of that promotion he was leading them in decisive actions in the most pivotal battle of the war. The fighting at Gettysburg lasted for three days but factors that decided its outcome were in play for several days before the first shots were fired.

Robert E. Lee had marched his army north into Pennsylvania. Confederate forces had won a string of victories and he felt he had the Union army on the back foot. He thought that a major offensive could bring the war to an end and sunk all his resources into the push north. Meanwhile, General J.E.B. Stuart was fighting his own war. He was having a fine time around the outskirts of Washington, cutting telegraph wires, tearing up railway tracks and capturing supply wagons. What he was not doing was maintaining contact with Lee and not fulfilling his principal role – to be Lee's eyes and ears. Lee was marching deep into enemy territory without adequate cavalry reconnaissance. He knew neither the strength nor the whereabouts of the Union army.

General George Meade, appointed by Lincoln to command the Union army only weeks previously, was very well informed of Lee's movements – he had the benefit of local intelligence – and he brought him to battle at Gettysburg on 1 July. The first day saw heavy fighting in which the Confederates came close to victory. Some consider that Meade was only saved by the fall of darkness. Custer and his cavalry had waited impatiently in the wings but were never called to action. Stuart was on his way north but had run into trouble with Union cavalry (not Custer's) at Hanover, and was further delayed by having to circumnavigate enemy forces. On the day the battle started he was laying siege to the garrison at Carlisle, 25 miles north of Gettysburg, in order to get provisions for his men and animals.

J.E.B. Stuart's men and horses were weary to the point of exhaustion, having been marching for days in search of Lee's army. Stuart himself reported that, 'Whole regiments slept in the saddle, their faithful animals keeping the road unguided. In some instances they fell from their horses, overcome with physical fatigue'. Such a resolute effort was of little use to General Lee who complained to Major-General Richard Anderson:

> I cannot think what has become of Stuart. I ought to have heard from him long before now. He may have met with disaster, but I hope not. In the absence of reports from him, I am ignorant of what we have in front of us here. It may be the whole federal army or it may only be a detachment'.

When Stuart was eventually found by one of Lee's messengers in the early hours of 2 July, he was ordered to report to Lee at Gettysburg without delay. Again Stuart and his men slept in their saddles as they trudged wearily towards the great battle.

On the second day, the attritional conflict waged ever more ferociously. In different parts of the battlefield, artillery and infantry worked tirelessly to slaughter each other on an unprecedented scale. Cemetery Ridge, Cemetery Hill, Culp's Hill, Little Round Top, Big Round Top, the Peach Orchard and the Wheatfield are the names of topographical features that became, like so many fortresses, the objects of conquest and battles within a battle. Their soil became drenched in the blood of both sides. As on the first day, the cavalry had not been involved but patrolled and reconnoitred the surrounding area. Stuart finally arrived and reported to Lee in the late afternoon. Around the same time, Custer led his first charge as a general. It did not go well. Poor reconnaissance had him believing there were no more than 200 dismounted troopers from Wade Hampton's brigade, hidden behind rail fences in fields of tall grass, with rifles. In fact there were nearer 600 and Custer's charge with Company A of the 6th Michigan Cavalry was a disaster. His horse was shot from under him and he escaped certain death only because one of his troopers went back for him and hauled him onto the back of his mount. Company A were routed.

Having snatched a few hours sleep, Jeb Stuart and 6,000 of his cavalry were on the move before dawn on 3 July, the third day of the battle. Lee was planning a frontal assault on the centre of the Union line with eleven infantry brigades under the command of Major General George E. Pickett. Stuart's job was to get round behind the right of the line and at the opportune moment attack the Union troops in the rear, catching them in a pincer movement. Somewhat later in the day, around 8am, General Custer joined forces with General David Gregg at Rummel's Farm, about three miles east of the main battlefield. They were charged with defending Meade's right flank. Around 10am, Jeb Stuart wheeled his 6,000 men off the road and into position on some high ground known as Cress Ridge. It was little more than a mile away from where Custer and Gregg were stationed. Custer's patrols had already detected the Confederate presence but Stuart confirmed it by ordering an artillery battery to fire four shots shortly after midday. It has been reasonably argued that these four shots were the signal to Lee that Stuart was in position and that Lee could now order Pickett's charge at any time.

The battle between General Stuart and Generals Custer and Gregg began with artillery fire and dismounted skirmishers sniping at long-range – it was a mirror of the larger battle down the road. At around 1pm the ground shook and the air reverberated with the thunder of the biggest artillery bombardment of the war. The roar came first from Lee's main batteries. It was answered by Meade's. The noise was deafening and it signalled to Stuart that Lee was attempting to soften up the Union line before launching Pickett's brigades. He realized that he had little time and immediately increased the frequency and vehemence of his attacks on Gregg and Custer, using both artillery and mainly dismounted skirmishers. The 5th Michigan, also fighting on foot, were in danger of being routed when General George Armstrong Custer came to their rescue. In the words of one eyewitness, 'Squadron succeeded squadron until an entire regiment came into view, with sabres gleaming and colors gaily fluttering in the breeze'. With the shout 'Come on you

The author's M1860 sabre, identical to one owned by Custer (photography by Marty Kelly)

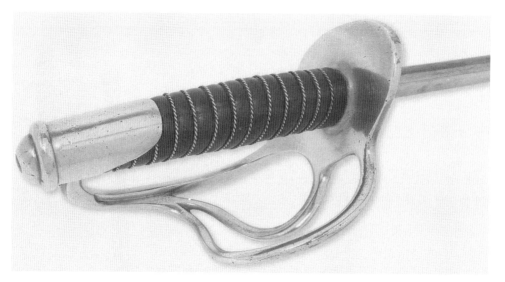

Hilt detail of the author's M1860 sabre (photography by Marty Kelly)

Wolverines!', Custer led the 7th Michigan Cavalry in a heroic charge, complete with bloodcurdling whoops. They scattered and turned Stuart's men, in spite of being heavily outnumbered. Suddenly, disaster struck. Obscured from view and on the other side of a rise was a stone wall surmounted by a rail fence. Riding hell-for-leather the 7th Michigan slammed into the wall like waves upon a rocky shore. Horses and men were a mass of broken and tangled limbs. Custer himself had somehow managed to pull up before the rise and he quickly ordered his men to tear down a section of the rail. This they did, then jumped the wall and continued their pursuit. However the fight eventually became too much for them and they were forced to retreat back over the wall.

Time was running out for Jeb Stuart. If he was to support Pickett's charge, he must act without delay. He called forward eight regiments of cavalry to attack the centre of Gregg's line. Captain William Miller of the 3rd Pennsylvania recalled later that, 'A grander spectacle than their advance has rarely been beheld. They marched with well-aligned fronts and steady reins. Their polished saber-blades dazzled in the sun'. The vast grey cloud descended towards the blue line first at a trot, then a canter and then, with a shrieking rebel yell, at an all-out gallop. Custer rode over to the 1st Michigan Cavalry (the 5th and 7th were still regrouping) and ordered them to follow him in a countercharge. He punched his sabre high in the air and again cried 'Come on you Wolverines!' His yellow hair streaming in the wind, Custer led them in a head-on course towards the enemy. Captain Miller described what followed:

> A crash, like the falling of timber, betokened the crisis. So sudden and violent was the collision that many of the horses were turned end over end and crushed the riders beneath them. The clashing of sabers, the demands

for surrender, the firing of pistols and cries of the combatants now filled the air.

It was a desperate, bitter, savage fight. After the battle, it is said, some of the slain were found 'pinned to each other by tightly-clenched sabers driven through their bodies'. Custer, with a characteristic lack of modesty, declared 'I challenge the annals of warfare to produce a more brilliant or successful charge of cavalry'. Captain Miller, who had been ordered to hold his position, saw that Custer was on the verge of turning Stuart's grey storm and, risking a court martial, disobeyed his orders by ordering a charge of the 3rd Pennsylvania Cavalry in support of Custer. At about the same time the 5th and 7th Michigan had rallied and they too smashed into the Confederate flanks, cutting all about them. All the while, Custer fought valiantly in the thick of the struggle. It won the admiration of his men; this was not what generals generally did. He supposedly had seven horses shot from under him during the two days he was engaged at Gettysburg. Out-maneuvered and out-sabred, Stuart's cavalry retreated to the safety of Cress Ridge. Remarkably, Custer only reported 29 of his Michiganders killed, with 123 wounded.

Unsupported by Stuart, Pickett's charge failed. It is remembered as being one of the most terrible military disasters of all time with over 7,000 Confederate casualties, over 2,000 of which were killed. If it hadn't been for George Armstrong Custer and the sabres of his Michigan boys, it might have been a different story – one that could have determined a different outcome to the war.

The Wolverines

Custer's famous battle cry, 'Come on you Wolverines!', was first heard at Gettysburg. In the months that followed, Custer and his 'Wolverines' were engaged in numerous operations and skirmishes as the Yankees probed south in a bid to bring Lee and his Confederate forces to a final and decisive battle. However Lee was masterful in defence and remained elusive. On 13 September 1863, Custer's cavalry won a notable victory against Jeb Stuart's forces at Culpepper Court House. In a charge against a gun battery, a bursting shell killed Custer's white stallion and ripped through his boot, grazing his calf. Undeterred, he leapt upon a remount and led his hellions in furious charges through the streets of Culpepper. General Stuart was forced to abandon his headquarters, his uneaten dinner remaining on the table.

Stuart, however, remained a force to be reckoned with and his well-organized cavalry screen held the Yankees at bay and frustrated their efforts to gain intelligence. Moreover, he initiated constant skirmish attacks on Custer's patrols. In late October, Custer and the 5th Michigan found themselves cut off behind enemy lines in the vicinity of Brandy Station, near the site of the earlier battle; in fact they were surrounded by enemy cavalry. Custer had the solution; he rallied his men, 'Boys of Michigan, there are some people between us and home; I'm going home, who else goes? All we have to do is open the way with our sabres'. He then signaled his bandmaster to strike up *Yankee Doodle*.

Charge of the 6th Michigan cavalry over rebel earthworks near Falling Waters, Alfred R. Waud, 14 July 1863 (Library of Congress)

The Michigan Cavalry Brigade were famous for their band who, as reported by the artist James E. Taylor, 'were not much of players, perhaps, but what is better, capable of sticking to their posts under fire and playing enlivening pieces to the shrill accompaniment of whistling lead'. In an obituary notice for Custer, posted in the *Grand Rapids Eagle* in 1876, a veteran of the 6th Michigan recalled 'Our old brigade band was always on the skirmish line, and at *Yankee Doodle* every man's hand went to his sabre. It was always the signal for a charge'. So it was at this fight. Custer later wrote 'I gave the word Charge! – and away we went, whooping and yelling like so many demons'. This was the essence of the Custer spirit and nothing thrilled him more than leading a sabre charge. He said, 'I never expect to see a prettier sight. I frequently turned in my saddle to see the glittering sabres advance in the sunlight'.

However the mad dash was brought to an abrupt halt when faced with a ditch, too broad to jump. On the other side Jeb Stuart's men opened fire with their carbines. Custer had two horses shot from beneath him before finding a way around the ditch and, pushing on, he and his Michiganders drove the Confederates from their position. There was intermittent skirmishing for another eight hours before Custer finally crossed the Rappahannock around 10pm. He wrote afterwards to his future-wife's friend, Annette Humphrey, who acted as a go-between during his protracted court-ship; the words, of course were intended for Libby: 'Oh, could you have seen some of the charges that were made! While thinking of them I cannot but exclaim "Glorious War!"'

For men like Custer and Stuart war was glorious; to them it was a great adventure and they relished the thrill of battle, with its opportunities to prove skill, initiative and courage. Their war was not immune from the horrors of mass slaughter suffered by the infantry, nor from the lottery of death dealt by long-range firepower, but they were to some extent removed from it. The cavalry war was a separate experience.

In total, some 360,000 Union and 260,000 Confederate soldiers died in the American Civil War. Less than a third of these died as a result of wounds received in battle. Most were killed by typhoid fever or dysentery caused by insanitary camp conditions, while others fell to epidemics of measles, whooping cough and chickenpox. Sword wounds accounted for less than two per cent of battlefield casualties and, although gangrene was an ever-present threat and amputation an ever-present remedy, a man suffering a sabre blow, provided that the bleeding could be staunched, stood a good chance of survival.

That is not to say that Stuart and Custer were somehow being deliberately humane in choosing to fight with sabres so as not to hurt the other chap too badly. Far from it; they were ruthless men, capable of looking a man in the eye and bringing their sword down upon his body with such force that they intended to kill him. It is merely to suggest that in the midst of the first 'modern' war, the cavalry fought an older style of conflict. Custer and Stuart may sometimes be perceived as archaic romantics but behind the manufactured glamour of their persona were intelligent military minds. They were equally at home directing artillery fire or using carbines and revolvers, as the situation demanded. However, when they used the sabre, it was not as an outmoded affectation but because it was still the right tool for the job. Stuart died sword in hand. Custer's death was in altogether different circumstances.

Little Big Horn

In popular culture Custer is most often associated with the day he died, 26 June 1876, at The Battle of the Little Big Horn, known to the Sioux as 'Greasy Grass'. He has been judged harshly for his actions that day and made a scapegoat for the policies of government. The suppression of the Native American peoples in order to accommodate the white man's drive west, and the manner in which it was done, is indeed a matter for blame but that blame lies more with the men in Washington than with those sent to carry out their orders. From the point of view of this study, Little Big Horn is only significant as being the occasion of Custer's death and for the fact that there were NO swords. Only one of Custer's men on the expedition, the eccentric Lieutenant Charles DeRudio, insisted on carrying his sword. He claimed it was a necessary precaution against rattlesnakes! Custer had otherwise ordered that all swords be boxed up and left at base camp. The great cavalier, the beau sabreur of the Union army, had realized that the days of the sword were over.

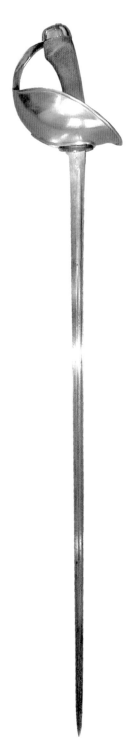

British 1908 pattern cavalry sword (photo courtesy of Swordsales EU)

Chapter 16

Epilogue

It is too bad that death often results from duelling, for duels otherwise help keep up politeness in society.

(Napoleon I, 1816)

The decline of the duel

Duelling came in with the military caste and went out with the military caste, even though at its faddish peak it was essentially a civilian affair. By the mid-nineteenth century, by far the greatest incidence of duels in Britain was among officers in the army. Although strictly speaking it was banned, The Rules and Articles of War contained a clause that positively promoted the practice. It stated that: 'An officer who submitted to insults was guilty of scandalous and infamous behaviour unbecoming to a gentleman'. Since a breach of these rules could result in a court martial, carrying with it the consequence of being cashiered, an officer had little choice but to issue a challenge in such circumstances. Captain Griffin was charged and court martialed in 1808 because he had 'suffered abusive language to be applied to him by Lieutenant Dove, viz poltroon and scoundrel, without taking measures appropriate to the vindication of his honour'. Lord William Pitt Lennox, who was commissioned into the Horse Guards in 1813, recalled, 'So strict was the code that none could refuse a challenge. In the army an officer would be tried by court-martial, or be compelled to leave his regiment, albeit an order existed against duelling.'

In civilian life duelling had long been illegal, although, as the anonymous author of *The British Code of the Duel* points out, there was no actual law against duelling as such, rather that indirectly it was prohibited by the laws of murder and breach of the peace. The *Code*, published in 1824, helpfully goes on to advise would-be duellists that the old dodge of crossing the channel to conduct a duel outside British jurisdiction was a loophole that had been closed. It wasn't that duelling wasn't permitted in France, Englishmen domiciled there were permitted to duel, but that France would 'not permit its territory to be made an object of mere convenience, and parties attempting it have been arrested or have had very narrow escapes'.

Such ruses were a last gasp of what was rapidly becoming an anachronistic ritual. In 1843 the Anti-Duelling Association was formed and in March 1844 Queen Victoria's private diary records a conversation she had with her Prime Minister, Sir Robert Peel, in which they discussed restricting, as far as possible, duels in the army. The first measure was to repeal the article that cashiered officers who declined to redeem their honour in a duel. Later that year the War Office took matters a stage further, ordering that any officer who issued a challenge, took part in a duel or knew of a duel and did nothing to stop it, would be court-martialled and, if found guilty, be cashiered. Indeed, any officer who participated as a second was liable to be punished in the same way. Accepting an apology, rather than declaring or accepting a challenge was deemed officially as the honourable course of action.

The duel in the USA

In the United States the notion of the duel hung on a little longer, particularly in the Southern States. In 1838 John Lyde Wilson, a former governor of South Carolina published *The Code of Honor or Rules For The Government of Principals and Seconds in Duelling*. It was re-published, after the author's death, as late as 1858. These rules are concerned principally with pistol duelling though it does also cover the use of swords: 'If swords are used, the parties engage until one is well blooded, disabled or disarmed; or until, after receiving a wound, and blood being drawn, the aggressor begs pardon'. Governor Wilson goes on to rule that a disarm is considered the same as a disable and that the disarmer is permitted to break his adversary's sword, unless it is the challenger who is disarmed, in which case it is considered ungenerous to do so.

Already one can see a custom in decline; the duel had become moribund. With its made up rules, full of puff and faux antiquity, had lost much of its visceral character. In addition to its elaborate rules, duelling in the mid-nineteenth century was already less dangerous than previously, owing to the fact that the majority of duels were conducted with the pistol. James Purdy, the renowned gunsmith, writing in 1836 under the pseudonym 'A. Traveller', calculated that the chances of being killed in a pistol duel were 14 to 1 and of being hit 6 to 1. At least you may be sure that in a duel with swords, someone is going to get hurt.

Wilson was seeking to hold onto a sense of time-honoured ritual as a way of proclaiming gentility, privilege and a link with the Old World. In practice he simply reduced the duel to melodramatic nonsense, with fatuous invented regulations worthy only of the schoolyard: 'In case the challenged be disarmed and refuses to ask pardon or atone, he must not be killed as formerly; but the challenger may lay his sword on the aggressor's shoulder, then break the aggressor's sword, and say "I spare your life!"'. Spare us Governor Wilson – really!

In the years that followed the Civil War a more vigorous and deadly form of duel manifested for a brief spell in America with the Western gunfight but both there and in Europe the idea of duelling with swords had become as antiquated and unthinkable as the notion of wearing a sword with one's everyday dress.

The duel for women

In 1890, the Paris League for the Emancipation of Women ruled that a woman permitting a man to defend her honour was guilty of a 'deed of inferiority'. Duels between women resulting from this declaration were usually conducted with pistols. One notable exception was a duel fought in Vaduz, Liechtenstein, in 1892 between Princess Pauline Metternich, Honorary President of the Vienna Musical and Theatrical Exhibition, and Baroness Kilmannsegg, President of the Ladies' Committee of the said exhibition. They had fallen out about arrangements for the event. As well as another princess and a countess attending as seconds, the affair was presided over by Baroness Lubinska of Poland. She held a degree in medicine and, knowing that most deaths resulted from infections caused by fragments of clothing driven into the wound, insisted that both women fought stripped naked to the waist. Their weapons were '*epées de combat*' – almost identical to sport epées but with slightly stiffer blades and sharp points – doused in disinfectant. Honour was satisfied with minor wounds, Princess Pauline receiving a scratch on the nose and the Baroness a gash on the arm. The person who fared worse in the proceedings was the coachman. Though bidden to stay some way off, curiosity had lured him to spy on the scene, where of course he discovered the noble ladies in their scandalous state of undress. The formidable Baroness Lubinska was unsparing as she belaboured him about the head with her rolled umbrella.

This was not the first occasion that ladies stripped to the waist in order to duel. It had been established a few years earlier by the Parisian *demimonde*, who had taken to duelling in this manner in the Bois du Boulogne, and immortalized in the 1884 painting *Une affaire d'honneur* by Emile Bayard,. The work was exhibited in various parts of the world and a reporter for *The New York Times* (18 May, 1884) wrote, 'It represents a duel between two women nude to the waist. They are not ethereal types by any means: they rather incline to be vigorously developed specimens. The idea is a queer one but it is full of interest'. So full of interest that Bayard made a fortune from the sale of numerous prints of the original and 'obtained a world-wide celebrity by the

reproductions that figure on the lids of matchboxes'. This last quote, also from the *New York Times* but four years later (2 November 1888), is from a report of another topless duel between 'cocottes' in the Bois de Boulogne. The author speculates that aside from the declared motive of a romantic

Une affaire d'honneur, by Emile Bayard, 1884 (print, author's collection)

grievance, the women fought in order to court celebrity: 'according to modern Parisian theories, a duel gives a man position. Why should it not do the same for a woman? The first thing a young man does who makes his debut in the Paris press is to seek a quarrel and a noisy duel'.

The mensur

Duelling began as a means of defending one's reputation but from quite early on it became a vehicle for making one's reputation and perhaps the most extreme example of this was the '*Mensur*'. This was a distinctive form of duelling ritual engaged in by student fraternities at certain German and Austrian Universities. They fought with a type of sword called a '*schläger*'. Like the singlestick, the schläger evolved as a practice weapon for the backsword. Unlike the singlestick, the schläger had a steel blade – a flat, relatively light blade of around ¾ inch in width and 3 feet in length. Schläger blades have extremely sharp edges but blunt, rounded points. Extremely large steel baskets enclose the hilt, giving complete protection to the hand, whilst at the same time allowing the weapon to be manipulated freely with tight, flipping wrist movements. The basket itself has a steel liner which is covered inside and out with felt. The exterior side is banded with felt in three different colours denoting the livery of the different student corps.

The mensur is commonly referred to as the 'German student duel' but it isn't really a duel at all, rather a bizarre ritual which has as its principal objective the gaining of a scar – a *schmiss* – which the recipient bears with consummate pride. Mark Twain, who witnessed several bouts in Heidelberg during his 1879 European tour, wrote, 'these face wounds are so prized that youths have even been known to pull

Mensur

Schläger

them apart from time to time and put red wine in them to make them heal badly and leave as ugly a scar as possible'. Some fraternities require a large disc of scalp to be sliced off in order for a hit to be registered. These pieces of flesh, hair, and sometimes bone, are then nailed to the walls!

Combatants are protected by padded jackets with an extra-heavily padded right arm and exceptionally high collar giving complete protection to the neck and throat. The eyes are protected by a pair of steel goggles – *paukbrille* – that have a steel projection to give partial cover to the nose and wide leather straps to give some protection to the ears. A variety of materials have been used for padding and wrapping, including layers of silk scarves for the neck, leather and mail for the body and, in popular use today, Kevlar. Only the face and the scalp remain entirely unprotected.

These mummified statues can hardly move, which is just as well since the rules require them to stand stock still, their feet parallel with their toes against a line. Rules and customs vary slightly from city to city but the essentials are that the fighters stand in this fixed position, a blade's length apart and try to strike each other's faces or skulls. A mensur lasts, on average, for thirty or forty rounds and each round requires around six cuts from each fencer. The left arm is held behind the back and the schlager is held, point down, at the end of an extended and elevated right arm. They work with a very fluid moulinet action from the wrist, seeking to parry the blows of their opponent simultaneously as they themselves attack. Parries may be taken with the sword or the heavily padded arm. Purely defensive moves, however, are unacceptable. This is not the spirit of the mensur. In fact they have to control any tendency to move or wince, even when hit. There are no winners or losers, it doesn't matter who hits whom the most. All that matters is that courage, grace and good fighting morale are displayed. If a contender should move, he is immediately taken out of the match. That is the simple ordeal of the mensur, to prove that you can face pain and danger without flinching.

It wasn't always so. Otto von Bismarck, who fought twenty-five *mensuren* when he was a student in the early 1830's, remarked some forty years later to a heavily-scarred young man that, in his day, blades were parried with steel not with one's face. In its present form the mensur has little to do with the art of swordfighting, which is all about being able to move the body efficiently and displaying both the art and the science of defence. With the essential concepts of defence removed the mensur became no more than a rite of passage, a test of character. It was nonetheless a powerful cultural concept that defined the Prussian fighting spirit for generations and it is curious to note that it was undertaken by as diverse a bunch as Kaiser Willhelm, the composer Robert Schumann and Karl Marx. Hitler made it illegal, as did the allies after the Second World War. Mensuren were carried on in secret throughout the 1940s, adding to their slightly seedy but romantic cachet, until the German Supreme Court lifted the ban in the 1950s. Today there are around 1,500 to 2,000 Mensuren fought each year.

The universities at Leipzig and Jena had traditionally a high proportion of Divinity and Theology students for whom it would have been unseemly to bear a facial scar. Their remedy was in the combat with dish-hilt rapiers. These weapons, used exclusively for this ritualized encounter, had long bodkin like blades of over 5 feet and a dish guard the size of a dinner plate. The objective was to fight to first blood and the principal target was a puncture wound on the arm. Accounts recall that four wounds were sometimes achieved with a single thrust to a bent arm, comprising entry and exit wounds on both the lower and upper sections. Students were renowned for parading in public with rolled up sleeves to display their piercings as a testament to their courage. Less fortunate were those who received a '*lungenfuscher*', a fatal wound that entered the chest cavity and perforated their lungs.

The last charge

We have seen in the last chapter that the sword survived the onset of modern, industrial warfare and that, in the hands of cavalry at least, it remained an effective primary arm. However unless there was a Stuart or a Custer in command, cunning men who knew when the cut of cold steel would count, rash gestures of cavalry bravado could cost many lives for no military advantage. One such act was the futile charge of the Light Brigade at the Battle of Balaclava in 1854. Misdirected to the wrong objective by confused orders, the gallant Light Brigade drew their sabres and rode towards the angry mouths of the Russian guns, only to die a pointless, albeit heroic, death.

The sword used by most cavalry regiments in the Crimea was the M1853 pattern, which had a three-bar, wrought-iron hilt and a 35½-inch back-edged blade with a spear point. Following the Battle of Balaclava, Lieutenant-Colonel Henry Griffith, commander of the Royal Scots Greys, wrote to the War Office, complaining that

> Our swords were very defective – as in our engagement, when our men made a thrust with the sword they all bent and would not go into a man's body and many of our poor fellows got sadly wounded and some lost their lives entirely from the unserviceable state of their arms.

Sir Evelyn Wood, who was present at the battle, was less harsh about the general performance of these swords, describing the wounds inflicted on Russian heads as appalling, 'in some cases the head-dress and skull being divided down to the chin'. He continued, thereby endorsing Lieutenant-Colonel Griffith's frustration, by stating that 'the edge of the sword was used, for the greatcoats worn by the Russians were difficult to pierce with the point'. Slow motion film of swords cutting through objects, even low-resistance objects like melons, demonstrates the remarkable amount of wave-action bend that is imparted to a blade when its meets resistance. In order to be durable, good cutting swords therefore had to have reasonable pliability. When made too pliable, however, as was the case with the M1853 sword, they lacked the necessary stiffness to execute an effective thrust against thick, pliant targets and a Russian greatcoat was very thick and very pliant. New technologies in steel manufacture and the economies of mass production were no substitute for the centuries-old knowledge of how a sword should be made. British lives were lost because of poor equipment; though it may be argued that Russian lives were saved for the same reason.

The charge of the Light Brigade was immortalized by Tennyson in his poem of that name; it includes the evocative line, 'Flash'd all their sabres bare, flash'd as they turn'd in air'. However, Tennyson also wrote a companion poem, *The Charge of The Heavy Brigade*, chronicling the bravery of the Scots Greys and and a couple of squadrons of Inniskillens in their famous charge against the Russian cavalry. It too is full of romantic references to swords, with lines such as: 'Sway'd his sabre, and held his own ... rode flashing blow upon blow' and 'whirling their sabres in circles of light!' Firepower was undoubtedly winning the uneven contest for battlefield supremacy but so long as poets write lines like this, the sword will remain the champion of our imaginations.

The M1853 cavalry sword was superseded in Britain by a new model in 1864. However, two years later, and in spite of the bad press it had received in the Crimea, the M1853 had a surprising re-incarnation on the other side of the world. Between 1863 and 1868 there was a civil war in Japan. It was the struggle between the modernizing Emperor Meiji and the Tokugawa Bakufu, the last of the samurai warlords. In 1866, Wilkinson supplied two-dozen M1853 swords to the Yokohama Mounted Volunteers. It was a period during which European weapons were favoured in Japan, including British-made swords, although the katana was still worn as a dress sword by most troops. Subsequent

British 1853 pattern cavalry sword. This example made by Wilkinsons for the Yokohama Mounted Volunteers (photo courtesy of Swordsales EU)

British 1888 pattern sword (author's collection)

anti-foreign sentiment saw the re-establishment of the katana as the sword of choice for combat as well as ceremony.

Increasingly, as the nineteenth century edged towards the twentieth, swords in both Europe and America became almost exclusively for ceremonial wear. There were occasions when the sword was still used in battle such as at the Battle of Omdurman in the Sudan in 1898. A young Lieutenant Winston Churchill, on attachment from the 4th Hussars, led a charge by a troop of the 21st Lancers. Swords were used by both sides. Churchill reported: 'The Dervishes fought manfully. They tried to hamstring the horses ... They cut reins and stirrup leathers ... and besides they swung sharp, heavy swords, which bit deep'. Many Sudanese swords were mounted with broad European blades, some dating to the fifteenth or sixteenth centuries, which had been acquired cheaply as surplus stocks. Even today, fine medieval blades can still sometimes be found in the salerooms mounted on Sudanese kaskara hilts.

Cavalry swords continued to play a role in various wars around the globe right up to The First World War. At the Battle of Beersheba (1917) in Palestine, the Australian cavalry charged with cold steel against Turkish machine guns and artillery. It was valiant and heroic and successful. That it was in the spirit of a death or glory, sabres drawn, old-fashioned cavalry charge, is without question. However the Australian light cavalry didn't have sabres – they charged with their bayonets! In reality the days of the sword as a weapon of war were over. Not only had the gun finally supplanted the 'white arm' but mechanization was rapidly making the horse redundant.

The last regulation-pattern sword designed to be used in warfare was the US M1913 cavalry sword. Based, almost to the point of plagiarism, on the British M1908 pattern cavalry sabre, the US version was designed by Lieutenant George Patton, later to become General Patton, famed for his flamboyant and eccentric leadership in the Second World War and known as 'Old Blood and Guts'. As a pentathlete in the 1912 Olympics, Patton had come third in the fencing event and when he returned to active service at Fort Riley he was appointed the first 'Master of the Sword' at the Mounted Service School there. He immediately designed his new sword. Like the British M1908, Patton's sword had a thumb dimple on the top-side of the grip and the tang was angled so as to make the sword a straight extension of the arm. Patton believed wholeheartedly in the absolute supremacy of the thrust. His sword had a fully sharp front edge and half the back edge was also sharpened, ' so that it may more easily be withdrawn from the body'. He advocated the use of cavalry as shock troops, instilling in his men what he called 'offensive cavalry spirit'. In 1914 he published a

Sword exercises devised by Second Lieutenant George S. Patton, Jr., 15th Cavalry, Master of the Sword at the Mounted Service School, 1914

US 1913 pattern sword, designed by George Patton

small, illustrated book entitled simply *Saber Exercise*. Its philosophy is summed up in a single paragraph:

> The saber is soley a weapon of offense and is used in conjunction with the other offensive weapon, the horse. In all training the idea of speed must be conserved. No direct parries are taught, because at the completion of a parry the enemy is already beyond the reach of attack. The surest parry is a disabled opponent.

The illustrations of Patton's various athletic attack postures have all the beauty and dynamism of the old masters and yet, with dismissive bombast, he waived aside millennia of received wisdom and sought to reduce the sword to a mere poking stick. However, he was too late, the sword was never again to be a mainstream weapon of war.

Historical fencing

Modern 'sport fencers' exhibit great athleticism and continue a tradition of playing with foils that the great Angelo and his contemporaries would recognize, though they would likely raise their eyebrows at some aspects of the modern style. Devoid of any threat of physical harm, modern fencing has strayed a long way from the essential principles of swordfighting. Fiore's '*Prudentia*' is a quality not seen often on the modern piste and the concept of 'right of way' would have been regarded as ludicrous on either the battlefield or the duelling ground. It may make for exciting sport but when electronic equipment is required to establish who hit who first, and therefore who gets the point, then clearly sound principles of defence are not being applied. This is swordplay, not swordfighting. It is no less skilful for that but we must not confuse it with the genuine martial arts.

In Japan, the essence of samurai swordfighting was ostensibly preserved in an unbroken and cherished martial arts tradition, although even here the great masters, like Musashi, would be shocked at how much the art had mutated. Nevertheless, there is a widespread acknowledgement that most of the Japanese fighting arts embody an authentic martial application; whereas until very recently, the heritage of the great European masters had been entirely lost. However, in both Europe and America, recent decades have seen the growth of a movement of 'historical fencers', who have set out to rediscover these Western martial arts traditions. Research and practical experiment by knowledgeable enthusiasts into the teachings of the great masters has built up a tremendous database of understanding. Even so, our knowledge of the old techniques and systems remains incomplete; there is still much to find out, which makes it an exciting time to be a 'historical fencer'. There has never been such a wealth of resources available to the student of arms. When I was starting out, you had to book an appointment at a museum library in order to study an old fight manual. Now many of them are published and freely available. In addition there are now many flourishing associations and societies that practice and teach old historical fighting systems. The 'historical fencing' movement has been an extraordinary success, with thousands of people worldwide now interested in the subject. By the beginning of the twentieth century, swordfighting according to the historical model was a completely lost art. Now it is living again and thriving amongst communities of people who share a passion for the sword. Once again there is 'art' in the fighting arts, as opponents thrust, parry, grapple and cut in ever-changing, and often beautiful, shapes; appearing at times to have stepped directly from the pages of Talhoffer or Marozzo or Labat. It is in the daily exertions of these historical fencers that the true legacy of the sword lives on, still carrying with it the promise that skill can triumph over brute force.

Glossary

Aketon	A padded coat worn beneath armour. From the Arabic *al-qutun* meaning cotton. The word was adopted into English following the Crusades but is now applied retrospectively to garments dating prior to this period.
Angon	An Anglo-Saxon type of barbed throwing spear.
Arming sword	The standard medieval sword that a knight strapped on with his armour. It is a term that distinguishes it from other types of sword of the period, such as those used for ceremonial or hunting and from larger versions of fighting sword, such as great swords, war swords and longswords.
Arms of the hilt	The pair of semi-circular bars that extend below the quillons on a rapier or smallsword.
Arse-girdle	A fourteenth-century term for the belt-of-plates; a wide belt, affixed with rectangular armour plates, that was worn low around the hips as part of a knight's armour.
Ashigaru	Japanese lightly-armed foot soldiers, usually conscripted from the peasant classes.
Back and breast	A backplate and breastplate ensemble that was popular during the seventeenth century.
Backsword	A type of broad-bladed, single-edged sword with some form of knuckle-guard; fifteenth to nineteenth centuries.
Baldric	A shoulder strap for carrying the sword, worn diagonally across the torso
Barriers	A low wooden fence, standing approximately at waist height, that separated combatants during foot combats at a tournament.
Bascinet	A type of medieval helm, often with a conical crown. Frequently augmented with a moveable visor.
Baselard	A type of short sword or dagger, characterized by an I–shaped hilt, used widely by Swiss footsoldiers between the fourteenth and sixteenth centuries.
Bastard sword	A contemporary alternative name for the hand-and-a-half sword or longsword.
Bearing sword	A sword intended for bearing in ceremonial procession.
Belt of plates	See **arse-girdle**

Bill	A pole weapon derived from an agricultural tool of the same name. Typically it possessed a blade that curled over in the manner of a hook. In addition it was often augmented with a spike at the fore-end and sharp lugs at the base and back of the blade.
Bind	To take control of and move an opponent's blade by means of leverage and pressure.
Bloom	A porous block of slag and iron that is produced by smelting iron ore in a bloomery hearth.
Bloomery hearth	A type of charcoal fired furnace that extracts iron from the ore by smelting. It never reaches temperatures to liquefy it completely.
Boar sword	A sword specially designed for hunting wild boar. It is characterized by having a transverse bar some inches from the point. This is intended to act as a stop to prevent the boar running too far onto the sword.
Bog iron	Deposits of iron ore occurring on the surface of bogs and swamps.
Bohemian falchion	An alternative term for the dusack.
Bokken/bokuto	Japanese wooden practice sword, most usually substituting for the katana.
Bottes secretes	Literally 'secret moves'. The promise of such knowledge was a mainstay in many a fight master's advertising.
Bridle gauntlet	A plate armour gauntlet (seventeenth century) with extended cuff for the left hand. It defended the arm that held the reins when riding.
Buckler	This can be used as a generic word for all shields. More specifically it refers to a type of small shield that was worn on the belt and was popular from the early middle ages to the end of the sixteenth century. Typically made of steel, with a prominent central boss, bucklers were used offensively to punch as well as to defend against blows.
Buff coat	A type of thick leather coat, resistant to sword strokes, used as armour during the seventeenth century.
Buntori	The Japanese practice of gathering enemy heads as trophies.
Bushido	The warrior code of the samurai.
Button	Blunt point of a practice sword, in the form of a small disc, which can be augmented by having a pad tied to it.
Byrnie	A three-quarter length, short-sleeved mail coat, as worn by Anglo-Saxons and Vikings.
Cannons	Components of plate armour that protect the upper and lower arm.
Chape	A metal mount at the bottom end of a scabbard to protect it from wear.
Claidheamh mor (modern rendering = claymore)	Literally 'great sword' in Gaelic. The term came into use to describe Scottish basket-hilted swords from the sixteenth century onwards.
Claidheamh beg	Gaelic for small sword.
Claidheamh da laidbh	Gaelic for two-handed sword.

Clipt point	On a sword or knife, where the back edge curves concavely to create a long and narrow point, supported by that curve, such as on a Bowie knife.
Coat of plates	This poncho-style garment consisted of large armour plates enclosed by and riveted to a fabric coat. An earlier form was known as a 'pair of plates'. Both were worn beneath the surcoat; twelfth to fourteenth century.
Colichmarde	A type of smallsword that had an extra-wide forte (top third of the blade), which then shouldered steeply into a blade of usual smallsword proportions.
Companion dagger	A dagger that is used in conjunction with the sword both for attack and defence, especially with a rapier.
Counterfeit damascening	A method of decorating a metal surface in imitation of true damascening. True damascening requires cutting a groove into the metal surface and then inlaying it with gold or silver wire. With counterfeit (or false) damascening, the decorative metal is applied as a thin sheet of foil and hammered onto a scored (scratched) surface. It is then heat treated to fuse the metals together. Both methods are used to produce highly intricate designs.
Couters	Components of plate armour that protect the elbows
Cross	A transverse bar at the base of the hilt, acting primarily as a stop to prevent the hand from sliding onto the blade when thrusting.
Cuir Bouilli	Literally 'boiled leather', it was most likely prepared in hot oil. Used extensively for body armour during the thirteenth century.
Cuirass	Deriving from leather (*cuir*) breastplates, it became generic for all forms of breastplate and back-and-breast assembly.
Cuisses	Armour for the thighs.
Cup hilt	Type of hilt most common on rapiers during the seventeenth century and characterized by having a hemispherical cup to guard the hand.
Cutler	A manufacturer, assembler or trader of swords or knives.
Cutto	From the French '*couteau de chasse*'; a cutto was a type of hunting sword, which also became fashionable with military dress.
Dane axe	A large two-handed axe, the signature weapon of the Vikings.
Demi volt	A defensive and offensive move in smallsword fencing in which the body is taken away from the line of attack by swinging the left foot forward and behind the right knee. This action also advances the right shoulder forward so that an attack with the sword may be made simultaneously. The left arm drops down and forward behind the back with considerable vigour in order to impart momentum to the move.
Dish guard	A type of hilt that has a shallow dish to protect the hand, as opposed to a hemispherical cup.
Distal taper	This refers to how the cross-section of the blade, its depth, tapers from hilt to point.
Dory	Thrusting spear used by Greek hoplites, averaging 8 feet in length.

Duelling shields	A special type of shield used exclusively for the judicial duel in German lands. Standing as tall as a man, they were held by a vertical central bar. Iron spikes at the top and bottom could be used to kill an opponent and many such shields had cut out sides that assisted in hooking an opponent.
Dusack	A blunt sword with a short, curved, broad blade and an integral hilt. Fashioned from either wood or steel, dusacks were used exclusively for either training or sparring.
Einvigi	An unregulated form of Viking single combat duel
Enarmes	The straps on the inside of a shield. The arm passes through one and the hand grips the other.
Épée	(From the French *épée* = sword) A type of very narrow and extremely pliable sword used in modern sport fencing, having an offset cup hilt. Of similar proportions but with a stiffer blade and sharp point was the 'épée de combat', which saw some use as a dueling weapon during the nineteenth century.
Epsilon axe	An Egyptian battle axe, so called because its curved blade attached to the haft by means of three sockets, making it resemble the Greek letter E.
Estoc	A rigid thrusting sword, often having a triangular or square cross-section.
Falcata	A nineteenth-century term for the Celtiberian version of the kopis/makhaira
Falchion	A heavy, single-edged sword with a blade that broadened towards the point. Popular throughout the middle ages.
Fauld	A skirt of articulated plates of armour that extends from below the sternum to below the groin.
Fechtbuch	(German, literally 'fight book'). A manual, often illustrated, showing methods of fighting.
Fighting-sticks	Wooden sticks fitted with leather hand guards used in Ancient Egypt for practice and sparring. Analogous to singlesticks.
Finger-loop	A semi-circular bar adjacent to the blade below the cross, offering protection to a finger that is hooked over the cross.
Flamboyant blade	A blade with wavy edges, resembling a flame (French *flambe*).
Foible/Forte	The foible is the weak part of the blade from the mid section to the point. The forte is the strong part of the blade from the mid section to the hilt. These properties relate to the blade's ability to act as a lever. Parrying with the strong part of the blade against an opponent's weak section gives a leverage advantage, enabling the defender to move the opponent's blade into a different line. A counter to this, used extensively in longsword fighting, is to close rapidly and slide the blade in, meeting forte to forte.
Foil	Any sword that has been blunted for use as a practice weapon. A sharp blade may be 'foiled' either by filing or by covering point and/or edges, with leather for instance.

Fourbisseur	A merchant or artisan specializing in the mounting of hilts onto blades. Also a blade polisher.
Francisca	Short-handled throwing axe, favoured by Anglo-Saxons as well as Franks.
Fuller	A groove in the blade, intended to both lighten and strengthen it. Fullers can run virtually the whole length of the blade or only part of it. They can be single or multiple.
Gafflet	A short spur or barb attached to the pad of an eighteenth-century foil. In the prize-fighting arena it allowed a hit to be registered by pricking the opponent enough to draw blood but offered no significant hazard.
Gambeson	A heavily padded coat. It can be worn either under armour or independently.
Gladius	The Roman legionary sword. Also referred to as '*gladius hispaniensis*'.
Greaves	Armour for the lower leg.
Splinted greaves	made with vertical strips of steel, attached to a fabric backing.
Great Sword	An early term (fourteenth century) for a larger than average sword. See also 'war sword'.
Guardapolvo	Literally 'dust protector'. A disc that sat inside the cup of a cup-hilt rapier, below the arms of the hilt. Usually elaborately pierced for decorative purposes.
Guard chains	Chains that attached the sword, also the helm and the dagger, to the body armour; fourteenth century
Guige	A strap for a shield that helps to support its weight on the neck and shoulder
Gunto	Munition-grade Japanese swords, machine-made with modern steels; also known as 'army' swords.
Hamata	Latin for mail. A Roman mail tunic
Hamon	A band of extra-hard steel creating the cutting edge of a Japanese sword. It is visually distinguishable from the softer steel of the main body and back of the sword by being of a different colour. The union between the hamon and the rest of the sword is a highly decorative and irregular line, which is considered to have artistic merit. The swordsmith creates its pattern with this aesthetic in mind.
Hand-and-a-half sword	An alternative fifteenth-century name for the longsword. Also known as a bastard sword.
Hanger (1)	A short-bladed hunting sword.
Hanger (2)	A sword, of generally shorter blade length, carried as a sidearm, especially during seventeenth and eighteenth centuries. Hangers appeared in various forms.
Hanger (3)	A device for suspending the rapier from a waist belt.
Hara-kiri	Literally 'belly cutting'; Japanese ritual suicide by disembowelment.
Hilt	The assembly of cross, grip and pommel that attaches to the sword by means of the tang.

Anthropomorphic	A Celtic style of hilt consisting of a stylized human figure whose outstretched arms and head formed the pommel and whose outstretched legs formed the cross.
Antennae	A Celtic style of hilt, which possessed long projecting bars, resembling antennae, extending from the grip and acting as a pommel.
Spike	A Viking type of hilt, possessing a cross that tapered acutely into a spike at both ends.
Holmganga	Literally 'island going', this was a highly regulated form of Viking duel that frequently took place on small islands.
Hollow grinding	A method of lightening and strengthening a blade by grinding it at a 90 degree angle to the wheel. Thus the arc of the wheel creates a hollow along the length of the blade. Each face of the blade is given two symmetrical hollow arcs; where they meet in the centre they create a ridge and where they rise up towards the edge, they formed a supported angle for grinding the cutting edge.
Hoplite	Greek heavy infantry soldier.
Hypaspists	Meaning 'shield bearers', these were an elite Macedonian infantry guard.
Katana	Japanese sword that is worn thrust through the sash-belt (*obi*) with the cutting edge uppermost. It is mostly used as an infantry sword and there are subtle differences of blade curvature between it and the horseman's tachi.
Katzbalger	Literally 'cat-scrapper'; a short, broad-bladed sword carried as a sidearm by Landsknechts.
Keris	The short sword or dagger of the Malay peninsular and Indonesia. It has a distinctive wavy blade.
Khepesh	A type of sword that has a curved blade with the cutting edge on the inside of the curve. It was common from Egypt to Anatolia during the Bronze Age.
Knuckle-bow, knuckle-guard	The bar extending from the pommel to the cross of a sword, offering protection to the back of the hand.
Kogai (head-pin)	A skewer used primarily for arranging a samurai's hair. It was carried in a sheath attached to the scabbard of a Japanese sword.
Kogatana	A small general-purpose knife, carried in a sheath attached to the scabbard of a Japanese sword
Kopis	A Greek sword, having a curved blade with the cutting edge on the inside of the curve. Some more complex versions combined both convex and concave lines along the cutting edge. (see also **falcata** and **makhaira**)
Koshirae	All the various hilt furniture used to dress a Japanese blade, making it ready for use or display.
Koto	The oldest pedigree of Japanese swords referring to those manufactured between the tenth and early sixteenth centuries.
Landsknecht	Mercenary soldier from the German lands; fifteenth to sixteenth century.

Langets	Metal projections, usually around 1 inch in length, that extend from the base of the hilt and sit parallel to the flat of the blade and on either side of it. When the sword is sheathed, they are located outside the scabbard.
Lead cutter	A nineteenth-century heavy-bladed weapon used as an exercise sword to build up the strength of the sword arm by cutting through lead bars.
Longsword	Medieval term for a sword which was longer than the standard length and had a hilt long enough to be used with two hands. Great sword ('grete swerde') and war sword were other contemporary terms for outsized swords.
Lorica	The Roman word for armour, applied to leather, mail or plate armour
Lorica Segmentata	Specifically Roman segmented plate armour. This is a later term, not contemporary with the Roman period.
Makhaira	An alternative word for the kopis. It is rendered in Latin as machiera.
Mekugi	Bamboo pegs that plug transversally through the tang to affix the hilt to the blade of a Japanese sword.
Mensur	A ritualized combat practiced by German student fraternities.
Menuki	Hilt ornaments that are bound beneath the silk wrapping and which assist in providing a secure grip.
Messer, lange messer	Literally knife and long knife respectively; a falchion-like single-edged sword with especially sharp edges.
Molinello (Italian), moulinet (French)	Literally 'little windmill'; a move whereby the sword is rotated rapidly in the wrist, either as a preparation for a blow or repetitively as a form of flourish or exercise.
Mortuary sword	A name given to a type of mid-seventeenth century English basket-hilted sword. So called because of an erroneous mythology that such swords bore an image of the executed Charles I.
Munition, munition grade	Low grade of arms or armour that is for general issue and has been produced in volume
Naginata	A Japanese polearm consisting of a wooden haft and a long single-edged blade.
Niku	Literally 'meat', niku refers to the amount of roundness, or bulge, that a Japanese sword has in cross-section.
Nodachi	Japanese sword of larger size, equivalent to the European longsword.
Odachi	Outsized Japanese sword. Those of extreme length – 11 feet – were purely for ceremonial purposes. However, more modest versions, around 6 feet, could be used on the battlefield by special troops.
Parablemata	A leather apron attached to the lower edge of a Greek hoplite's shield to protect the lower legs.
Parrierhaken	Lugs that extend from the blade of a sixteenth-century two-handed sword below the 8 to 10-inch long ricasso. They offered

	some protection to the forward hand when it was placed on the ricasso in order to foreshorten the weapon for bayonet-style jabs.
Passing lunge	A lunge whereby the left leg lunges forward, passing the right leg, at the same time as the right arm and sword are extended.
Pattern welding	A blade-manufacturing process, whereby metal rods, having different metallurgical properties ranging from soft iron to various grades of steel, are twisted and hammer-forged together to create a pre-determined pattern in the blade.
Peace strings	Cords, attached to the scabbard, which pass over the cross of the hilt, securing it in place.
Pell	A wooden post set into the ground to act as a target for the purposes of training with a sword.
Piling	A method of blade construction, whereby layers of steel/iron of varying metallurgical properties are piled one atop the other in a layered, sandwich-like construction. They are then heat-welded together under the hammer.
Pilum, (pl. pila)	Javelin of the Roman legionary. He carried two, of different weights. One was for throwing at medium range and the other for close range. It consisted of an iron fore-shaft mounted on a wooden haft. On striking and penetrating a shield, the soft iron fore-shaft was intended to bend and thus render both the pilum and the shield no longer useable. Its conical steel head assisted with penetration but made withdrawal difficult.
Pommel	An attachment at the top of the hilt, above the grip, that prevented the hand from sliding off the sword when wielding it with force. It was also sometimes a counter-balance.
Privy coat	A fine mail coat or brigandine, usually sleeveless, worn beneath civilian clothing.
Profile taper	The taper of a sword blade as seen from observing the flat of the blade from hilt to point.
Pteryges	A skirt of leather or reinforced linen flaps worn by Greek and Roman soldiers.
Quarte	The fourth guard position in fencing, defending the upper-left line.
Quenching	Cooling a pre-heated blade by plunging it in cold water or other liquid. It is the unique property of steel to change its micro-structure as a result of quenching, producing a steel of the required hardness.
Quillons	The name given to the bars of the cross from the sixteenth century onwards.
Quintain	A piece of training equipment consisting of a stout post in the ground and having a wooden bar mounted transversally on top, which has the ability to rotate. A shield or other target was usually affixed to one end of the bar. Quintains were principally used for mounted drills with the lance but could also be used for sword practice.

Rain-guard	A metal flange that attached to the cross, turning down towards the blade of the sword. It fitted over the outside of the scabbard when the sword was sheathed, thus protecting the blade from the elements.
Rapier	A civilian sword of the sixteenth and seventeenth centuries, usually having a long and narrow blade and an elaborate set of guards for the hilt.
Case of rapiers	A form of fight that employed a rapier in each hand. A pair of rapiers were sometimes manufactured in such a way that they both fitted into a single scabbard (case).
Reisläufen	Mercenary infantry recruited from the Swiss cantons; fifteenth to sixteenth centuries.
Ricasso	A short portion of the blade immediately below the cross. This was usually blunt to allow a finger to be hooked over the cross and lay adjacent to the blade.
Rompepuntas	Literally 'point-breaker'; the turned over rim of the Spanish cup-hilted rapier, intended to stop an opponent's blade from glancing off the cup and on to the defender's arm. Italian cup-hilted rapiers did not have this feature.
Ronin	A samurai with no master, usually owing either to his lord's death or displeasure.
Rudis	A wooden version of the gladius, often given as a prize in gladiatorial contests.
Sabatons	Plate armour for the feet.
Sabre	A single-edged sword with a curved blade, intended principally for use on horseback.
Sarissa	The Macedonian pike. Significantly longer than the Greek hoplite's dory, it ranged between 13 and 21 feet in length.
Satetsu	Black iron sand, used in the traditional manufacture of **tamahagane** the steel for Japanese swords.
Saya	Japanese scabbard
Sax, seax or scamasax	A long all-purpose knife used by Anglo-Saxons and Vikings.
Schlachtschwert	Literally 'slaughter sword', a nickname for the large two-handed swords of the sixteenth century.
Schläger	Type of sword used in the **Mensur**.
Secret	Steel skull cap worn beneath soft headgear; sixteenth to seventeenth centuries.
Seppuku	Ritual suicide for a samurai
Shinai	A training sword made from split bamboo and used in kendo
Shingunto	Gunto swords made after 1934.
Shinsakuto	Traditionally-made Japanese sword made since WWII.
Shinshinto	Literally 'new, new'. Japanese swords made between 1760 and 1865.
Shinto	Literally 'new'. Japanese swords made between the late sixteenth century and 1760.
Sgian dubh	Meaning 'black knife' in Gaelic, this is the small knife that Scots tuck into their stocking top when wearing traditional dress.

Side ring   A ring guard that was positioned at the centre of the cross and at right angles to it. It could be a stand-alone feature, especially on companion daggers, but was also part of a series of additional guards on a developed swept hilt.

Singlestick   A wooden sword for training, sparring or playing at 'cudgels', consisting of a round wooden blade and a basket-shaped hand guard, made either from wicker or leather.

Spatha   A straight-bladed sword, longer than the gladius, used by Roman cavalry.

Stop   A swelling at the base of the hilt intended to prevent the hand from slipping forward onto the blade when thrusting against a resistant target. This term describes this feature as it appears on swords such as the gladius, before it can be properly called a cross, which is the more common later term.

Smallsword   A species of rapier popular for civilian wear after the mid-seventeenth century. It had a stiff, medium-length, slender blade. The hilt typically had a pair of solid plates, known as shells, in lieu of a cross. Most also had a knuckle-bow.

Swept-hilt   A type of rapier hilt that has several bars, augmenting the main knuckle guard, all 'sweeping' in an elegant curve.

Stramazone   A move in Italian rapier fighting in which a cut is delivered with a flicking wrist action and with the point of the sword, as opposed to the edge.

Surcoat   A fabric coat that is worn over the top of armour, often emblazoned with heraldic display.

Spaulders   An early form of plate armour shoulder defence.

Svynfylking   The 'boar snout' formation of an Anglo-Saxon or Viking shield wall, in which it concentrates its forces in a wedge to ram through an opposing shield wall.

Sword-knot   A leather or fabric loop that attaches to the sword hilt and secures the sword in the hand by wrapping around the wrist.

Tachi   A Japanese sword that is worn suspended by cords from the sash-belt (*obi*), with the cutting edge facing down. It is mostly used as a cavalry sword and there are subtle differences of blade curvature between it and the katana.

Tamahagane   The steel used to make a traditional Japanese sword.

Tameshigiri   The art of cutting with the Japanese sword, usually practiced by striking at rolled up tatami mats.

Tang   A tongue of metal that extends from the blade to form a foundation for the grip. Grips either slot over the tang or are riveted to it. The tang passes through the pommel, which is secured either by riveting over or by a nut that screws to the top of the tang. The tang is not hardened, retaining softer metal properties in order to absorb the shock of concussion. Many tangs are set at an angle to the blade, creating an alignment of the point with an extended arm.

Tanto	Japanese dagger
Target	A round shield between 18 and 24 inches in diameter popular during the Renaissance. In Scotland it survived for longer as the targe.
Tartara	Japanese smelting furnace.
Tempering	The act of gently reheating a quenched sword to make the steel springier and less brittle.
Tessen	Japanese war-fan, usually made of iron.
Tierce	The third guard position in fencing, defending the upper-right line.
Tsuba	The guard-plate on a Japanese sword.
Tsuka	The grip of the Japanese sword.
Tsukaito	The binding for the grip of the Japanese sword.
Throw-sticks	Curved sticks, resembling non-returning boomerangs, that were used by the ancient Egyptians for hunting birds and small mammals.
Tuck	A type of rapier blade that is characterized by being especially narrow, almost needle-like.
Tulwar	An Indian sword with a curved blade and a distinctive disc hilt.
Two-handed sword	Although the term can be applied to any large sword capable of being wielded with two hands, it more specifically refers to a type of outsized sword popular in the sixteenth century. These swords were often up to six feet in length and had especially long grips (over 2 feet).
Wakizashi	A shorter Japanese sword, often carried as a companion weapon to the katana.
War sword	An early term (fourteenth century) for a larger than average sword. See also 'great sword'.
Waster	A blunt practice sword, often made of wood or whalebone.
Watagami	Shoulder harness of a Japanese armour
Wiffler	Nickname for a member of Henry VIII's bodyguard, so called for carrying a large two-handed sword that 'wiffled' when swung through the air.
Wootz	An early form of crucible steel from India.
Xiphos	A straight-bladed Greek sword.
Xyston	A cavalry lance, around 12 feet in length, with a spear point at either end. Used by both Macedonian and Hellenistic cavalry.
Yabusame	A ritual form of Japanese horse-archery.
Yari	Japanese spear.
Yumi	Japanese bow

Bibliography

Adkin, Mark, *The Waterloo Companion* (London, 2001)

Adkins, Lesley and Adkins, Roy A., *Handbook to Life in Ancient Rome* (New York, 2004)

Angelo, Domenico (Ed. Jared Kirby), *The School of Fencing* (London, 2005)

Anglo, Sydney, *Chivalry in the Renaissance* (Woodbridge, 1990)

Anglo, Sydney, *The Martial Arts of Renaissance Europe* (London, 2000)

Anonymous, *The British Code of Duel* (Surrey, 1971).

Arnold, Thomas F., *The Renaissance at War* (New York, 2006)

Aylward, J.D., *The English Master of Arms* (London, 1956)

Aylward, J.D., *The House of Angelo* (London, 1953)

Aylward, J.D., *The Small-Sword in England* (London, 1945)

Baldick, Robert, *The Duel* (London, 1970)

Barker, Juliet, *Agincourt: The King, the Campaign, the Battle* (London, 2005)

Benecke, Gerhard, *Maximillian I* (London, 1982).

Berry, Herbert, *The Noble Science* (London, 1991)

Bezdek, Richard H., *Swords and Sword Makers of England and Scotland* (Boulder, Colorado, 2003)

Bezdek, Richard H., *Swords of the American Civil War* (Boulder, Colorado, 2007)

Billacois, Francois, *The Duel* (London, 1990)

Bishop, M.C. and Coulston, J.C.N., *Roman Military Equipment* (London, 1993)

Blackmore, David, *Arms & Armour of the English Civil Wars* (London, 1990)

Blair, Claude, *European Armour* (London, 1958)

Bottomley, Ian, *An Introduction to Japanese Swords* (Leeds, 2008)

Buchan, John, *Cromwell* (London, 1970)

Capo Ferro, Ridolfo (Ed. Jared Kirby), *Italian Rapier Combat* (London, 2004)

Capwell, Tobias, *The Real Fighting Stuff* (Glasgow, 2007)

Carcopino, Jerome, *Daily Life in Ancient Rome* (London, 1956)

Carman, John and Harding, Anthony, *Ancient Warfare* (Stroud, 2004)

Castle, Egerton, MA, FSA, *Schools and Masters of Fence* (London, 1969)

Chadwick Hawkes, Sonia, *Weapons and Warfare in Anglo-Saxon England* (Oxford, 1989)

Coe, Michael D., Connolly, Peter, Harding, Anthony, Harris, Victor, Lorocca, Donald J., Richardson, Thom, North, Anthony, Spring, Christopher and Wilkinson, Frederick, *Swords and Hilt Weapons* (London, 1989).

Cohen, Richard, *By the Sword* (Oxford, 2002)

Connolly, Peter, *Greece and Rome at War* (London, 1998)

Cooke, Philip St. Geo., *The 1862 U.S. Cavalry Tactics* (Mechanicsburg, 2004)

Cotton, Edward, *A Voice from Waterloo* (London, 2007)

Cruso, John, *Militarie Instructions for the Cavall'rie* (Kineton, 1972)

Davidson, Hilda Ellis, *The Sword in Anglo-Saxon England* (Woodbridge,1962)

de Lange, William, *Famous Japanese Swordsmen* (Warren, 2006)

Dolinek, Vladimir and Durdik, Jan, *The Encyclopedia of European Historical Weapons* (London, 1993)

Ellis, Joseph J., *His Excellency George Washington* (New York, 2005)

Evangelista, Nick, *The Encyclopedia of the Sword* (London, Greenwood Press, 1995)

Evans, Angela Care, *The Sutton Hoo Ship Burial* (London, 1986)

Ffoulkes, Charles, CB, OBE, and Hopkinson, E.C., MC, *Sword, Lance & Bayonet* (London, 1967)

Firth, C.H., *Cromwell's Army* (London, 1967)

Fletcher, Ian, *Galloping at Everything* (Stroud, 2008)

Forgeng, Jefferey L., *The Medieval Art of Swordsmanship* (Union City, 2003)

Fosten, Bryan, *Wellington's Light Cavalry* (Oxford, 1982)

Garnett, Captain Theodore Stanford, *Riding with Stuart* (Shippensburg, 1994)

Garrisson, Janine, *Henri IV* (Paris, 2000)

Glover, Gareth, *From Corunna to Waterloo* (London, 2007)

Glover, Gareth, *Letters from the Battle of Waterloo* (London, 2004)

Goldsworthy, Adrian, *The Complete Roman Army* (London, 2004)

Hackett, General Sir John, *Warfare in the Ancient World* (London, 1989)

Hare, Christopher, *Maximillain The Dreamer – Holy Roman Emperor 1459–1519* (New York, 2009)

Harvey, Robert, *A Few Bloody Noses: The Realities and Mythologies of the American Revolution* (Woodstock & New York, 2003)

Hatch, Thom, *Clashes of Cavalry* (Mechanicsburg, 2001)

Haythornthwaite, Philip J., *The Armies of Wellington* (London, 1994)

Hibbert, Christopher, *Redcoats and Rebels: The War for America, 1770–1781* (London, 1990)

Hutton, Alfred, FSA, *The Sword and the Centuries* (Rutland, 1973)

James, Simon, *The Atlantic Celts* (London, 1999)

Johnson, Clint, *In the Footsteps of J.E.B. Stuart* (Winston – Salem, 2003)

Kiernan, V.G., *The Duel in European History* (Oxford, 1988)

Le Marchant, Garspard, John, *Rules and Regulations for the Sword Exercise of the Cavalry* (Ontario, 1970)

Lea, Henry Charles, *The Duel and the Oath* (Philadelphia, 1974)

Lendon, J.E., *Soldiers & Ghosts* (London, 2005)

Lindsay, Jack, *The Normans and Their World* (Norwich, 1974)

Longacre, Edward G., *The Cavalry at Gettysburg* (Lincoln, Nebraska, 1986)

McCullough, David, *1776* (New York: Simon & Schuster, 2005)

McDermott, Bridgett, *Warfare in Ancient Egypt* (Stroud, 2004)

Mercer, Malcolm, *Henry V: The rebirth of chivalry* (Richmond, 2004).

Messing, Christine H., Rudder John B., Windham Shaw, Diane, *A Son and his Adoptive Father: The Marquis de Lafayette and George Washington* (Mount Vernon, 2006).

Molloy, Barry, *The Cutting Edge* (Stroud, 2007)

Morrissey, Brendan, *Yorktown 1781* (Oxford, 1997)

Morton, E.D., *A-Z of Fencing* (London, 1992)

Moscati, Sabatino (Ed.), *The Celts* (London, 1991)

Mowbray, Stuart C., *The Ames Sword Company Catalog* (Lincoln, RI, 2003)

Muller, Hans Wolfgang, *Der Waffenfunf von Balata – Sichem und Die Sichelschwerter* (Munich, 1987)

Musashi, Miyamoto (trans. Victor Harris), *A Book Of Five Rings (Go Rin No Sho)* (London, 1974)

Neumann, George G., *Swords & Blades of the American Revolution* (Texakarna, 1991)

Norman, A.V.B and Pottinger, Don, *English Weapons & Warfare 449–1660* (London, 1979)

North, Anthony, *European Swords* (London, 1982)

Oakeshott, Ewart, *European Weapons and Armour* (London, 1980)

Oakeshott, Ewart, *Records of the Medieval Sword* (Woodbridge, 1991)

Oakeshott, Ewart, *Sword in Hand*, Minneapolis, MN: Arms & Armour Inc., 2000.

Oakeshott, R. Ewart, *The Sword in the Age of Chivalry* (London, 1981)

Oakeshott, R. Ewart, *The Archaeology of Weapons* (London, 1960)

Osgood, Richard, Monks, Sarah and Toms, Judith, *Bronze Age Warfare* (Gloucestershire, 2000).

Palmer, Dave R., *George Washington: First In War* (Mount Vernon, 2002)

Partridge, Robert B., *Fighting Pharaohs* (Manchester, 2002)

Peterson, Harold L., *The American Sword 1775–1945* (New York, 2003)

Peterson, Harold L., *Arms and Armor in Colonial America 1526–1783* (New York, 2001)

Pitts, Vincent J., *Henri IV of France* (Baltimore, 2009)

Powell, George H., *Duelling Stories of the Sixteenth Century* (London, 1904)

Pritchard, Shannon, *Collecting the Confederacy* (New York, 2005)

Reilly, Tom, *Cromwell* (London, 1999)

Reverseau, Jean-Pierre, *Musee De L'Armee Paris: Les armes et la vie* (Paris, 1982)

Roberts, Andrew, *Waterloo: Napoleon's Last Gamble* (London, 2005)

Roberts, Keith, *Cromwell's War Machine* (Barnsley, 2005)

Robson, Brian, *Swords of the British Army* (London, 1996)

Royle, Trevor, *Civil War* (London, 2004)

Rush, Philip, *The Book of Duels* (London, 1964)

Satô Kanzan, *The Japanese Sword* (London, 1983)

Seward, Desmond, *The First Bourbon, Henri IV: King of France and Navarre* (London, 1971)

Shaw, Ian, *Egyptian Warfare and Weapons* (Princes Risborough, 1991)

Siborne, Major General H.T., *Waterloo Letters* (London, 1983)

Simpson, Jacqueline, *The Viking World* (London, 1980)

Stead, I.M., *British Iron Age Swords and Scabbards* (London, 2006)

Steinmetz, Andrew, *The Romance of Duelling Volume I* (Richmond, Surrey, 1971)

Steinmetz, Andrew, *The Romance of Duelling Volume II* (Richmond, Surrey, 1971)

Stephenson, I P, *Roman Infantry Equipment* (Stroud, 1999)

Swanton, Michael (Ed.), *The Anglo-Saxon Chronicle* (London, 1996)

Talhoffer, Hans (Ed. Mark Rector), *Medieval Combat* (London, 2000)

Tarassuk, Leonid, and Claude Blair, *The Complete Encyclopaedia of Arms & Weapons* (London, 1982)

Thillmann, John H., *Civil War Cavalry & Artillery Sabers* (Lincoln, RI, 2001)

Thomans, Emory M., *Bold Dragoon* (Norman, 1999)

Thomas, Bruno and Gamber, Ortwin, *Katalog – Kunsthistorisches Museum, Wien* (Wien, 1976)

Turnbull, Stephen, *Battles of the Samurai* (London, 1987)

Turnbull, Stephen, *Kawanakajima 1553–64* (Oxford, 2003)

Turnbull, Stephen, *Samurai: The World of the Warrior* (Oxford, 2006)

Turnbull, Stephen, *The Samurai Sourcebook* (London, 1998)

Turnbull, Stephen, *Warriors of Medieval Japan* (Oxford, 2007)

Turner, Craig and Soper, Tony, *Methods and Practice of Elizabethan Swordplay* (Carbondale, 1990)

Underwood, Richard, *Anglo-Saxon Weapons and Warfare* (Stroud, 1999)

Unger, Harlow Giles, *Lafayette* (Hoboken, NJ, 2002)

Urwin, Gregory J.W., *Custer Victorious* (Lincoln, Nebraska, 1983)

von Clausewitz, Carl, *On War* (London, Penguin Books, 1968)

Wagner, Paul, *Masters of Defence* (Boulder, 2003)

Warry, John, *Warfare in the Classical World* (London, 1980)

Weigley, Russell Frank, *Morristown: Official National Park Handbook* (Washington DC, 1983)

Wert, Jeffry D., *Cavalryman of the Lost Cause* (New York, 2008)

Whitlock, Ralph, *The Warrior Kings of Saxon England* (London, 1977)

Wilkinson-Latham, R.J., *Pictorial History of Swords and Bayonets* (London, 1973)

Wise, Arthur, *The History and Art of Personal Combat* (London, 1971)

Wittenberg, Eric J. and Petruzzi, J. David, *Plenty of Blame to Go Around* (New York, 2006)

Yumoto, John M., *The Samurai Sword* (Rutland, 1958)

Zlatich Marko, *General Washington's Army 1:1775-1778* (Oxford, 1994)

Index